U0885455

微雕大师如是说：

“业精于专，方显卓越”

中国移动通信专注于无线通信事业的发展，

精心打造品质超群的全球通GoTone品牌，赢

得了众多成功人士的信赖。

全球通GoTone采用世界主流技术，依靠遍布

全国**99%**市、县的完善网络覆盖，实现通

达世界**90**个国家和地区的国际漫游，成为

您与世界最可靠的沟通纽带。

全球通GoTone随时随地助您成功。

全球通™ GoTone

专家品质　信赖全球通

PICC

主持工作的党委副书记、副总经理：洪世清

The Vice-Secretary of the Party Committee, vice General Manager(presides works):: Hong Shiqing

中国人民保险公司贵州省分公司是贵州省境内最大的国有商业性财产保险公司，现有分支机构137个，遍及全省各地、州（市）、县；从业人员2000多人，高级管理人员188人。

2001年全系统共实现保费收入65,072万元，较上年同期增加4,860万元，同比增长8.07%。人均保费首次突破50万元，达到51万元，奠定了“十五”发展的良好基础，为安定人民生活、促进全省经济建设继续发挥了重要作用。

The People's Insurance Company of China Guizhou Branch (the PICC Guizhou Branch) is a state-owned and the largest commercial property insurance company in Guizhou province, has 137 subsidiaries which covering all the prefectures, cities and counties of the province. There are more than 2000 employees, 188 senior managers in the company.

In 2001, the PICC Guizhou Branch attained the premiam income of 650.72 million yuan, an increase of 48.60 million yuan and 8.07 percent over the last year,the average premium income by each person first surpassed 500000 yuan,reached 510000 yuan,lade a better foundation on development in the Tenth Five-year Plan,played a leading role in stabilizing the people's living and promoting the economy of Guizhou Province.

中国人民保险公司推出了“金牛”投资保障型家庭财产保险，是集投资、保险保障为一体的新型保险业务，目前，该险种正在贵阳市地区开办。

"Taurus" Insurance, a new business of PICC for family property combining investment and insurance.

全国统一保险服务专线电话95518，受理：保险咨询、报案、预约投保、保险投诉、举报

Unitary national insurance service line 95518 for insurance consulting, subscription, etc.

公司地址：贵阳市遵义路30号

Address of the company: Zunyi Road No.30, Guiyang City.

邮　　编(Post Code):550002

电　　话(Tel):0851-5570272 传真(Fax):0851-5577364

PICC 中国人民保险公司 贵州省分公司

The People's Insurance Company of China, Guizhou Branch

2000年7月19日，中国电信集团贵州省电信公司正式挂牌成立。一年来，贵州电信不断深化改革，强化自身实力，面对国家实施西部大开发战略和十五届五中全会提出加快国民经济信息化进程的历史机遇，积极加快发展步伐，一方面全力提高公司通信能力，保障通信传输；另一方面加强精神文明建设，提高服务水平。

“九五”期间，全省电信共完成固定资产投资78亿元，为同期贵州省社会固定资产总投资的5%；业务收入完成64.9亿元，年均增长率为29.5%，是同期全省国内生产总值增长速度的3.9倍。“九五”末，贵州电信资产总额达到75.9亿元，全省电话用户数是“八五”末的5.45倍。

在抓生产、抓建设的同时公司也非常注意加强精神文明建设，始终把创建文明行业放在重要的位置，全省87个电信企业全部被当地党委、政府评为“文明单位”。今年6月，贵州电信系统荣获全省“1998-2000年度文明行业（系统）”称号。去年，在参加中国电信集团公司组织开展的“中国电信21世纪优秀人才”活动中，有3名同志被评为“中国电信21世纪优秀人才”、15名同志被评为“贵州电信21世纪优秀人才”，极大地鼓舞和鞭策了广大员工。

为了做好服务，树立“用户至上，用心服务”的企业理念，公司在全省范围内推行承诺服务制、首问负责制和值班长制度。2000年底，贵州省电信公司开通了96180总经理热线电话，各分公司开通180投诉电话，建成省、地、县三级客户服务体系，此外，还注意加强对大客户工作的管理，为大客户提供“绿色通道”、“一站式服务”，使用户的满意度不断提高。

贵阳第二长途电信枢纽大楼
The second long-distance telecom pivot building of Guiyang

贵州电信：夯实
Guizhou Telecom Company Build a

宽敞明亮的电信营业厅
Commodious and bright telecom business hall

贵阳卫星通信地球站外景
Satellite communication earth station in Guiyang

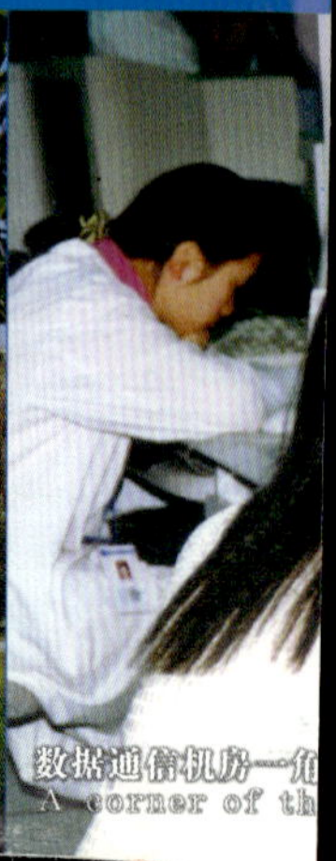
数据通信机房一角
A corner of th

基础　迎接挑战

lid foundation for future ' s challenge

China Telecom Group Guizhou Province Telecom Company was founded in 19th July, 2000. In the year after, Guizhou Telecom kept deepening reform, strengthening management and building itself. Aware of the West Developing Strategy and the historic opportunity of improving an informational National economy, which was proposed in the 5th of 15th session Center Party conference, Guizhou Telecom made efforts to improve its communication on one hand and to strengthen culture and ideological progress on the other hand.

During the period of "Ninth Five-year Plan", telecom industry of the province has invested 7.8 billion yuan to fixed assets, holding 5% of the provincial total social investment on fixed assets. Sales income was up to 6.49 billion yuan. Average annual increase rate was 29.5%, which is 3.9 times of that of provincial output value in the corresponding period. At the end of "Ninth Five-year Plan", Guizhou Telecom owns general assets of 7.59 billion yuan. Users of telephone are 5.45 times those at the end of "Eighth Five-year Plan".

While emphasizing production and construction, Guizhou Telecom also paid attention to culture and ideological progress. All the 87 telecom enterprises of the province were awarded "civilized unit" by local Party Committee or Government. In June of this year, Guizhou Telecom was awarded "Civilized industry (system) for the year of 1998---2000". Last year, in the project of "China Telecom Excellent Talents in 21st Century", organized by China Telecom Group, 3 employees of Guizhou Telecom were awarded "China Telecom Excellent Talents in 21st Century". 15 employees were awarded "Guizhou Telecom Excellent Talents in 21st Century", which encouraged and urged employees greatly.

In order to provide best service and build up the ideal of "users are the God, providing hearty service", the Company conducted Commitment Service, First Receptionist Service and Director on Duty Service. At the end of 2000, Guizhou Telecom built a General Manager Hot Line 96180. Each branch company built protest line of 180. Thus Guizhou Telecom constructed a service system of 3 levels as province, city and county. Besides, it also concentrated on strengthening the management of major clients and provided "Green Access" and "One-stop Service", which made clients feel more satisfied.

lcation motor room

街头业务宣传咨询活动
Promoting and consulting on the street

遍布城乡街头的IC卡公用电话为广大群众提供了便捷的通信服务
IC telephone provides convenience for the public

国酒门

The Gate of Chinese wine

贵州茅台酒股份有限公司

Guizhou Maotai Wine Stock Co., Ltd

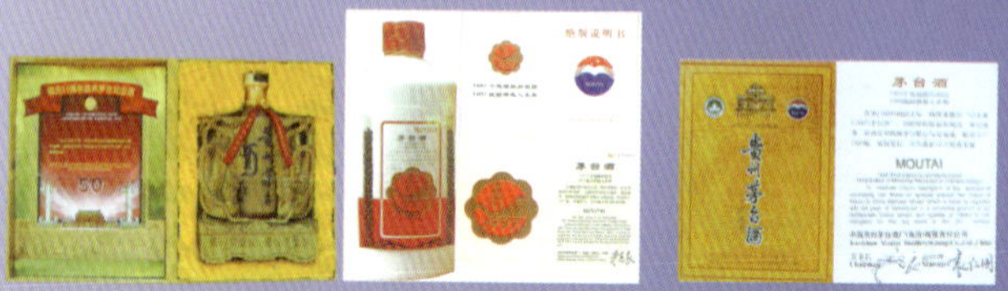

贵州茅台酒股份有限公司位于黔北赤水河畔茅台镇，现有员工3496人，拥有总资产20.8亿元。公司主导产品“贵州茅台酒”是世界三大（蒸馏）名酒之一，是我国大曲酱香型白酒的鼻祖和典型代表。

茅台酒历史悠久、源远流长，因开民族品牌获国际金奖之先河而蜚声世界，因蝉联历次国家名酒评比之冠而誉播九州。先后14次荣获国际金奖。

今天，茅台酒产量已发展到年产6000吨，并形成了一品为主、多品开发、全方位发展的格局。43度、38度、33度茅台酒拓展了茅台酒家族的发展空间；茅台王子酒、茅台迎宾酒满足了大众消费群的需要；15年、30年、50年、80年茅台酒填补了我国极品酒的空白。

Guizhou Maotai Wine Stock Co., Ltd lies in Maotai town by Chi Shui River, north of the province. The Company has 3496 staff at present and 2.08 billion yuan general assets. “Guizhou Maotai Wine”, a main product of the Company is one of the three international famous (distilled) wines, and the earliest ancestor and typical representative of Chinese sauce savor wine.

Maotai wine has a long history. It is famous for being the first Chinese wine awarded international golden prize. It is famous in China for continuos holding the champion of Chinese famous wine evaluation. The wine has successively got 14 international golden prize.

Today, the annual output of Maotai has been developed to be 6000 tons. Meanwhile, the Company has constructed a complete structure led by one brand and developed by several brands. Maotai wines of 43°, 38° and 33° have enlarged the development space of Maotai family. Maotai Prince Wine and Maotai Welcome Wine have met the consuming requirement of mass people. Maotai wines of 15 years, 30 years. 50 years and 80 years have made up for the blank of high standard wine in China.

厂区近景

Recent scene of factory area

业界的精英　　西南的奇葩

Distinguished of the World　　Outstanding in Southwest China

贵州海尔电器有限公司

Guizhou Haier Electrical Appliance Co., Ltd

气势恢弘的贵州海尔

Great and magnificent Guizhou Haier

总经理兼党委书记：顾文海

The General Manager and the secretary of the Party Committee: Gu Wenhai

贵州海尔电器有限公司是青岛对口帮扶贵州，由青岛海尔集团控股与中国江南航天集团风华机器厂于1997年底合资组建成立的。

4年来，贵州海尔通过输入海尔科学的OEC管理和优秀的企业文化，凭借海尔的品牌优势和市场优势，企业保持每年82%的增长速度。成立当年就盘活了沉睡8年之久的风华冰箱生产线，生产冰箱8万多台，创产值1.6亿元，利税560万元，实现当年投产、当年盈利；1999年，贵州海尔生产冰箱17万台，创产值3.2亿元，利税1500万元；2000年，贵州海尔年产50万台海尔冰箱的二期工程在遵义经济技术开发区建成并投产，生产冰箱26万台，创产值5.2亿元；2001年，贵州海尔实现新世纪的开门红，全年生产冰箱达40万台，创产值近10亿元。

整洁明亮的总装生产线

Neat and bright assembly line

Guizhou Haier Electrical Appliance Co., Ltd was founded in 1997, invested by Tsing Tao Haier Group and China Jiangnan Space Group Fenghua Machine Plant and held by Tsing Tao Haier.

In the recent 4 years, Guizhou Haier keep its increase rate at 82% per year through OEC management of Haier Science, enterprise culture, and brand and market preponderance of Haier. In the founding year, it made Fenghua refrigerator production line, which had been stopped for 8 years, to produce over 80 thousand refrigerators and made output value of 160 million yuan, profit and tax of 5.6 million yuan. In 1999, Guizhou Haier produced 170 thousand refrigerators, made output value of 320 million yuan and profit & tax of 15 million yuan. In 2000, the second period of project of Guizhou Haier with its annual output of 500 thousand was finished and put into production. The project produced 260 thousand refrigerators in the years and made output value of 520 million

In 200
succes
centu

遵义铝业股份有限公司

Zunyi Aluminum Industry Co., Ltd

办公大楼
Office building

遵义铝业股份有限公司座落在历史名城遵义南端，紧靠川黔铁路、川黔公路及贵遵高速公路，拥有便利的交通和信息优势。

公司主要产品包括"黔星"牌重熔普通铝锭、电工用铝锭、铸造铝硅合金及磷化铝、碱式氯化铝等。产品合格率保持在100%，一级品以上率达95%以上，质量稳定，是省优质产品。

从1992年至今，公司连续9年盈利，已跻身行业百强、省百强企业之列。1995年名列中国工业企业综合评价最优500家第372位。1999年荣获贵州省"五一"劳动奖状和省文明单位称号。

法人代表：刘撇成
Representative of the corporation: Liu Piecheng
总 经 理：池平刚
General Maneger: Chi Pinggang

联系电话（Contacts）：
办公室（Office）：0852-7227188
重庆供销公司（Sales company in Chongqing）：023-62869601
传　真（Fax）：0852-7252124
遵义供销公司（Sales company in Zunyi）：0852-8838242
经营部（Management Dept）：0852-7227015
三期改扩建指挥部（Command dept for 3rd extension）：0852-7227159

Zunyi Aluminum Industry Co., Ltd is located in the south of the famous historical city---Zunyi. As it is close to Chuan-Qian railway, Chuan-Qian highway and Gui-Zun freeway, It has enjoys convenience traffic and information advantages.

Major products includes: remelted aluminum spindle with "Qian Star", aluminum spindle for electricians, casting aluminum & silicon alloy, aluminum phosphoric, aluminum chlorate, etc. The rate of qualified products is up to 100 percent. The rate of first level products is up to 95 percent. The product has a stable quality and is high quality products in the province.

Since 1992, the Company has continuously makes profits for 9 yeas and is one of the 100 Enterprises of the field and in the province. In 1995, it held 372nd of the 500 Best Chinese Industry Enterprises. In 1999, it was awarded "1st May" Labor testimonial of Guizhou province and civilized unit of the province.

主要产品"黔星"牌重熔普通铝锭
"Qian Star" remelted aluminum spindle.

贵州宏福实业开发有限总公司

Guizhou Hongfu Industry & Commerce Development Co., Ltd

贵州宏福实业开发有限总公司由贵州省瓮福矿肥基地工程建设指挥部改制组建。公司所依托的瓮福矿肥基地，包括瓮福磷矿、瓮福磷肥厂两个项目，是国家“八五”、“九五”期间建设的重点项目，一期投资58.5亿元，已建成年采选能力300万吨的磷矿山和年产60万吨磷铵、80万吨硫酸、30万吨磷酸、1.4万吨氟化铝的磷肥厂。主要技术和设备从国外引进，具有当今国际先进水平。

宏福总公司主要产品有：磷铵、复混肥、氟化铝、磷矿石、磷矿砂、黄磷、饲钙、普钙、工业磷酸、食品磷酸、工业级六偏磷酸钠、食品级六偏磷酸钠、甲酸、过磷酸等。

宏福总公司宗旨是：发挥磷资源优势，服务现代化农业，紧紧围绕国内外市场，坚持“质量第一、用户至上、创一流品牌”的方针，千方百计为用户服务。

宏福总公司竭诚期望与国内外客商友好合作、互惠互利、共同发展。

董事长（法人代表）：涂兴沼
The Chairman of the board (representative of the corporation): Tu Xingzhao

Guizhou Hongfu Industry & Commerce Development Co., Ltd is reorganized by Guizhou Wengfu Mining & Fertilizer Development Group. The company is basing on Wengfu Minging & Fertilizer Group that includes two parts, one is Wengfu Phosphate Mine, the other is Wengfu Phosphate Fertilizer Plant. Both are important construction projects of national “Eighth Five-year Plan” and “Ninth Five-year Plan”. Investment of the first period is 5.85 billion yuan. It has built up annual capacity of 3 million tons of phosphorus mine and beneficiation, and 600 thousand tons of DAP, 800 thousand tons of Sulfuric Acid, 300 thousand tons of P_2O_5, 14 thousand tons of ALF_3 in Wengfu Phosphate Fertilizer Plant. The key technology and equipment are imported which take an international leading place.

Our main products are as follows: DAP, BB fertilizer, ALF_3, Phosphorus Rock/Sand, Yellow Phosphorus, DCP, SSP, Industrial Phosphoric acid, Food Phosphoric acid, Sodium Hexametaphosphate (industrial grade and food grade), Formic acid, Super-phosphate, etc.

The purpose of our company is developing the advantage of phosphate resources, providing service for modern agriculture, insisting on the principle of “Quality is the first, consumer is God, creating a first-class brand” around with the domestic and international market together, by every possible means to work for our customers.

Hongfu Company is sincerely looking forward to co-operate amicably on the mutually beneficial base to be in common quest of development with domestic and overseas business traders.

瓮福磷矿露天采剥现场
Mining in Wengfu Phosphate Mine

[2002]

总第13期 №13

贵州统计年鉴

GUIZHOU STATISTICAL YEARBOOK

贵州省统计局・编
GUIZHOU STATISTICAL BUREAU

中国统计出版社
China Statistics Press

（京）新登字 041 号

图书在版编目（CIP）数据

贵州统计年鉴.2002/贵州省统计局编.–北京：中国统计出版社，2002.7

ISBN 7–5037–3771–9

Ⅰ.贵…Ⅱ.贵…Ⅲ.社会经济统计–统计资料–贵州省–2002–年鉴Ⅳ.C832.73

中国版本图书馆 CIP 数据核字（2002）第 034149 号

贵州统计年鉴——2002

作　　者／贵州省统计局

责任编辑／蔡启新

E–mail／yearbook@stats.gov.cn

出版发行／中国统计出版社

通信地址／北京市西城区三里河月坛南街 75 号　中国统计出版社

电　　话／（010）63262295

印　　刷／北京国彩印刷有限公司

开　　本／850×1168 毫米　1/16

字　　数／1165 千字

印　　张／35

印　　数／1–1400 册

版　　别／2002 年 8 月第 1 版

版　　次／2002 年 8 月第 1 次版

书　　号／ISBN 7–5037–3771–9/F•1373

全　　价／260.00 元

中国统计版图书，版权所有，侵权必究。

中国统计版图书，如有印装错误，本社发行部负责调换。

《贵州统计年鉴——2002》编辑委员会

编委会顾问： 石秀诗（省长）

编委会主任： 陈大卫（副省长）

编委会副主任： 郝嘉伍（省统计局局长）

编 委 委 员：（排名不分先后）

赵家兴（省发展计划委员会主任）
李　平（省经济贸易委员会主任）
苏太恒（省民族宗教事务委员会主任）
王培安（省计划生育委员会主任）
孔令中（省教育厅厅长）
李正辉（省科技厅厅长）
李代胜（省公安厅副厅长）
郭　猛（省民政厅厅长）
方光林（省司法厅厅长）
李隆昌（省财政厅厅长）
李先忱（省人事厅厅长）
李家鑫（省劳动和社会保障厅厅长）
张克湘（省国土资源厅厅长）
江厥中（省建设厅厅长）
彭伯元（省交通厅厅长）
张英峰（省信息产业厅厅长）
郑荣华（省水利厅厅长）
张继增（省文化厅厅长）
陶性潜（省农业厅厅长）
张锦林（省林业厅厅长）
邵祥林（省贸易合作厅厅长）
何崇远（省卫生厅厅长）
周培荣（省农办主任）
李康民（省环保局局长）
蒲明发（省工商局局长）
何国忠（省乡镇企业局局长）
刘毓文（省国税局局长）

刘汉樵（省地税局副局长）
黄世维（省广播电视局局长）
蔡国祥（省体育局局长）
刘援朝（省新闻出版局局长）
杨胜明（省旅游局局长）
高春生（省物价局局长）
石　超（省招商局局长）
董穗生（省药品监督管理局局长）
张梓钟（省质量技术监督局局长）
张建华（省烟草专卖局局长）
兰开锋（成都铁路局贵阳铁路分局局长）
刘雪松（民航贵州省管理局局长）
彭士学（人民银行贵阳中心支行行长）
陈焕祥（工商银行省分行行长）
周清玉（农业银行省分行行长）
龚蜀雄（建设银行省分行行长）
王建授（中国银行省分行副行长）
宋代洪（贵阳市商业银行董事长）
王革凡（国家开发银行贵阳分行行长）
陆辉君（中国农业发展银行贵州省分行行长）
洪世清（中国人民保险省分公司副总经理）
唐　群（中国人寿保险省分公司副总经理）
王久玲（省电力公司总经理）
李德明（省通信管理局局长）
陈本智（中国电信集团贵州省电信公司总经理）
王国昌（贵州移动通信公司总经理）
孙国强（贵阳市政府市长）
卢守祥（遵义市政府市长）
廖少华（六盘水市政府市长）
慕德贵（安顺市政府代市长）
蒙启良（黔南州政府州长）
刘晓凯（黔东南州政府州长）
黄康生（黔西南州政府州长）
张群山（毕节地区行署专员）
杨玉学（铜仁地区行署专员）

Editorial Board

Consultant:	Shi Xiushi (Governor of Gui Zhou Province)
Chairman:	Cheng Dawei (Vice – governor)
Vice – chairman:	Hao Jiawu (Director of the Provincial Statistical Bureau)
Editorial board:	(not in order of priority)
Zhao jiaxing:	Director of the Provincial Committee of Development Planning
Li Ping:	Director of the Provincial Committee of Economy and Trade
SuTaiheng:	Director of the Provincial Committee of Nationality and Religion Affairs
Wang Peian:	Director of the Provincial Committee of Family Pianning
Kong Lingzhong:	Director of the Department of Education
Li Zhenghui:	Director of the Department of Science and Technology
Li Daisheng:	Vice – director of the Department of Public Security
Guo Meng :	Director of the Department of Civil Affairs
Fang Guanglin:	Director of the Department of Justice
Li Longchang:	Director of the Department of Finance
Li Xianyou:	Director of the Department of Personnel
Li Jiaxin:	Director of the Department of Labur and Social Security
Zhang Kexiang:	Director of the Department of Land and Resources
Jiang Juezhong:	Director of the Department of Construction
Peng Boyuan:	Director of the Department of Traffic
Zhang Yingfeng:	Director of the Department of Information Industry
Zheng Ronghua:	Director of the Department of Water Resources
Zhang Jizen:	Director of the Department of Culture
Tao Xingqian:	Director of the Department of Agriculture
Zhang Jinlin:	Director of the Department of Forestry
Shao Xianglin:	Director of the Department of Trade and Coopertion
He Chongyuan:	Director of the Department of Publish Health
Zhou Peirong:	Director of the Provincial Agriculture Office
Li Kangmin:	Director of the Provincial Bureau of Environmental Protection
Pu Mingfa:	Director of the Provincial Administration of Industry and Commerce
He Guozhong:	Director of the Provincial Administration of Township and Village Enterprises

Liu Yuwen: Director of the Provincial Administration of National Taxation

Liu Hanqiao: Vice-director of the Provincial Administration of Local Taxation

Huang Shiwei: Director of the Provincial Bureau of Broadcasting and TV

Cai Guoxiang: Director of the Provincial Bureau of Physical Training

Liu Yuanchao: Director of the Provincial Bureau of Press and Publication

Yang Shengming: Director of the Provincial Bureau of Tourism

Shi Chao: Director of the Provincial Bureau of Merchants

Gao Chunsheng: Director of the provincial Bureall of Price

Dong Huisheng: Director of the Provincial Supervisory Administration of Medicines

Zhang Zizhong: Director of the Provincial Supervisory Administration of Quality and Technology

Zhang Jianhua: Director of the Provincial Administration of Tobacco Monopoly

Lan Kaifeng: Director of the Railway Substation of Chengdu Railway Bureau Guiyang Branch

Liu Xuesong: Director of the Administration of Guizhou Province of Civil Aviation

Peng Shixue: Director of the People' s Bank of China Guiyang Branch

Chen Huanxiang: Director of the Industrial and Commercial Bank of China Guizhou Branch

Zhou Qingyu: Director of the China Agricultural Bank Guizhou Branch

Gong Shuxiong: Director of the China Construction Bank Guizhou Branch

Wang Jianshou: Vice-di rector of the Bank of China Guizhou Branch

Song Daihong: Board chairman the Commercial Bank of Guiyang City

Wang Gefan: National Development Bank of Guiyang Gity Branch

Lu Huijung: Agricultural Development Bank Guizhou Branch

Hong Shiqing: Vice – manager of the People' s Insurance Company of China Guizhou Branch

Tang Qun: Vice – geveral manager of China Life Insurance Company Guizhou Branch

Wang Jiuling: General Manager of the Provincial Electric Power Company

Li Demin: Director of the Provincial Administration of Communication

Chen Benzhi: General Manager of the Provincial Telecommunication Company

Wang Guochang: General Manager of the Provincial Mobile Communication Company

Sun Guoqiang: Mayor of Guiyang City

Lu Shouxiang: Mayor of Zhunyi City

Liao Shaohua: Mayor of Liupanshui City

Mu Degui: Acting Mayor of Anshun City

Meng Qiliang: Chief Executive of Qiannan State

Liu Xiaokai: Chief Executive of Qiandongnan State

Huang Kangsheng: Chief Executive of Qianxinan State

Zhang Qunshan: Chief Executive of Bijie

Yang Yuxue: Chief Executive of Tonren

《贵州统计年鉴——2002》编辑人员

主　　编：郝嘉伍
副 主 编：冯育毅　王正潮　刘带春　张贵平　钟赛梅　李洪刚　贺志权　廖定华
编辑部主任：杨大昆　聂坤琪　刘　晴
分科主编：(姓氏笔画为序)
尤金福　王国静　白文英　李诗刚　汪寿伦　邹陆华
陈景平　张学进　胡　刚　龚　勇　程帮嘉　董安娜
编辑人员：(姓氏笔画为序)
王练练　王　瑛　王冬平　许大陆　冯　露　周　蓉
周玲颖　徐　锋　程大利　谢小清　董建魏
英文翻译：饶晓沐
统计制图：汪　兰
编务人员：雷晓明　韦　博　谭晓英

Editorial Staff

Editor – in – chief：Hao Jiawu
Deputy Editor – in – chief：
Feng Yuyi　Wang Zhengchao　Liu Daichun　Zhang Guiping　Zhong Saimei
Li Honggang　He Zhiquan　Liao Dinhua
Directors of Editorial Department：
Yang Dakun　Nie Kunqi　Liu Qing
Editor – in – chief by Section (in order of strokes of chinese surname)：
You Jinfu　Wang Guojing　Bai Wenying　Li Shigang　Wang Shoulun
Zou Luhua　Chen Jingping　Zhang Xuejin　Hu Gang　Gong Yong
Cheng Bangjia　Dong Anna
Editorial Staff (in order of strokes of chinese surname)：
Wang Lianlian　Wang Ying　Wang Dongping　Xu Dalu　Feng Lu　Zhou Rong
Zhou Lingying　Xu Feng　Cheng Dali　Xie Xiaoqing　Dong Jianwei
English Translators：
Rao Xiaomu
Statistics Drawer：Wang Nan
Staff for Editorial Affairs：
Lei Xiaoming　Wei Bo　Tan Xiaoying

编 者 说 明

一、《贵州统计年鉴——2002》是一部全面反映贵州省国民经济和社会发展的资料性年刊。本书收录了贵州省、各地（州、市）、县2001年经济和社会各方面大量的统计数据，并在保持以往栏目内容不变的前提下，增加了西部各省（区、市）主要统计数据。

二、全书内容分为25个部分，即：1、行政区划和自然资源；2、综合和国民经济核算；3、人口；4就业、职工工资和社会福利；5、固定资产投资；6、能源、原材料消耗；7、农业；8、工业；9、建筑业；10、交通运输、邮电通信；11、国内商业；12、对外贸易；13、旅游；14、价格水平；15、财政、金融、证券、保险；16、人民生活；17、科技、教育、文化；18、体育、卫生、环保及其他；19、民族自治地区；20、城市建设与发展；21、经济强县；22、扶贫与开发；23、地、县社会经济发展概况；24、全国各省主要经济指标；25、西部各省（区、市）主要经济、社会指标。

三、本年鉴资料大部分源自年度统计年报表，一部分来自部门统计资料，全国和西部统计资料来自全国有关统计资料。

四、本年鉴部分数据合计数或相对数由于单位取舍不同而产生的计算误差均未作机械调整。

五、本年鉴表中的符号使用说明："…"表示数据不足最小计量单位数；"空格"表示该项统计指标数据不祥或无该项数据，"#"表示其中的主要项；"*"或"①"表示本表下方有注解。

Preface:

Ⅰ. Guizhou Statistical Yearbook is a large - sized statistics publication to reflect various aspects of Guizhou' s economic and social development. The book contains economic and social indicators of each state, city, prefecture, county and provincial total of Guizhou, newly increases main statistical data on western regions.

Ⅱ. This yearbook contains twenty - five parts. 1. Divisions of Administrative Areas and Natural Resources. 2. General Survey and National Accounting. 3. Population. 4. Employment, Wages of Staff and Workers and Welfare. 5. Investment in Fixed Assets. 6. Consumption of Energy and Raw Material. 7. Agriculture. 8. Industry. 9. Construction. 10. Transportation, Postal and Telecommunications Service. 11. Domestic Trade. 12. Foreign Trade and Economic Cooperation. 13. Tourism. 14. Price Level. 15. Finance, Banking, Securities and Insurance. 16. People' s Livelihood. 17. Science, Education and Culture. 18. Sports, Public Health, Environmental Protection and Others. 19. Minority Nationality Autonomous Areas. 20. General Survey of Cities. 21. Strongly Economic County. 22. Anti - poverty and Development. 23. Prefecture (County) Social and Economic Summary. 24. Information of Each Province of National Total. 25. Information of Each Province (Region, City) of Western Provinces.

Ⅲ. The major data sources of this book are obtained from annual statistical report, a few from sample surveys. The information of national total and western provinces are obtained from related statistical books of national total.

Ⅳ. Statistical Discrepancies due to rounding are not adjusted in this book.

Ⅴ. Notations used in this book: ... indicates the data is not large enough to be measured with the smallest unit in this table; (blank) indicates the figure not available; # indicates the major items of the total; * or ① indicates the notes are under the table.

目　　录
CONTENTS

一　行政区划、自然资源
Divisions of Administrative Areas and Natural Resources

二　综　　合
General Survey

三 人口
Population

四 就业与劳动
Employment and Labor

五 固定资产投资
Investment in Fixed Assets

六 能源、原材料消耗
Consumption of Energy and Raw Material

七　农　业
Agriculture

八 工 业
Industry

九 建 筑 业
Construction

十 交通运输、邮电通信
Transportation, Postal and Telecommunications Services

十一 国内商业
Domestic Trade

十二 对外贸易
Foreign Trade and Economic Cooperation

十三　旅　　游
Tourism

十四　价格水平
Price Level

十五　财政、金融、证券、保险
Finance, Banking, Securities and Insurance

十六　人民生活
People's Livelihood

十七 科技、教育、文化
Science, Education and Culture

十八　体育、卫生、环保及其他
Sports, Public Health, Environmental Protection and Others

十九 民族自治地区
Minority Nationality Autonomous Areas

二十 城市建设与发展
General Survey of Cities

二十一 经济强县
Strongly Economic County

二十二 扶贫与开发
Anti－poverty and Development

二十三 地县社会经济发展概况
Prefecture(County) Social and Economic Summary

二十四　全国各省资料
Information of Each Province of National Total

二十五　西部资料
Western Provinces

行政区划、自然资源

Divisions of Administrative Areas and Natural Resources

One

1-1 各州市地县名称(2001)
Name of Each State, City, Prefecture and County

州(市、地)名称 State(City, Prefecture)	县(市、区、特区)名称 County(City, District, Special Region)
贵阳市 Guiyang	南明区 Nanming　云岩区 Yunyan　小河区 Xiaohe　花溪区 Huaxi　乌当区 Wudang　白云区 Baiyun　清镇市 Qingzhen　开阳县 Kaiyang　息烽县 Xifeng　修文县 Xiuwen
六盘水市 Liupanshui	钟山区 Zhongshan　六枝特区 Liuzhi　盘县 Pan　水城县 Shuicheng
遵义市 Zunyi	红花岗区 Honghuagang　赤水市 Chishui　仁怀市 Renhuai　遵义县 Zunyi　桐梓县 Tongzi　绥阳县 Suiyang　正安县 Zhengan　凤冈县 Fenggang 湄潭县 Meitan　余庆县 Yuqing　习水县 Xishui　道真仡佬族苗族自治县 Daozhen(Gelo & Miao) Autonomous County　务川仡佬族苗族自治县 Wuchuan(Gelo & Miao) Autonomous County
安顺市 Anshun	西秀区 Xixiu　平坝县 Pingba　普定县 Puding　关岭布依族苗族自治县 Guanling(Bouyei & Miao) Autonomous County 镇宁布依族苗族自治县 Zhenning(Bouyei & Miao) Autonomous County　紫云布依族苗族自治县 Ziyun(Miao & Bouyei) Autonomous County
铜仁地区 Tongren	铜仁市 Tongren　江口县 Jiangkou　石阡县 Shiqian　思南县 Sinan　德江县 Dejiang　沿河土家族自治县 Yanhe(Tujia) Autonomous County　松桃苗族自治县 Songtao(Miao) Autonomous County 玉屏侗族自治县 Yuping(Dong) Autonomous County　印江土家族苗族自治县 Yinjiang(Tujia & Miao) Autonomous County　万山特区 Wanshan
黔西南布依族苗族自治州 Qianxinan(Bouyei & Miao) Autonomous State	兴义市 Xingyi　兴仁县 Xingren　普安县 Puan　晴隆县 Qinglong　安龙县 Anlong　望谟县 Wangmo　贞丰县 Zhenfeng　册亨县 Ceheng
毕节地区 Bijie	毕节市 Bijie　大方县 Dafang　黔西县 Qianxi　金沙县 Jinsha　织金县 Zhijin　纳雍县 Nayong　赫章县 Hezhang　威宁彝族回族苗族自治县 Weining(Yi, Hui & Miao) Autonomous County
黔东南苗族侗族自治州 Qiandongnan(Miao & Dong) Autonomous State	凯里市 Kaili　黄平县 Huangping　施秉县 Shibing　三穗县 Sansui　镇远县 Zhenyuan　岑巩县 Cengong　天柱县 Tianzhu　锦屏县 Jinping　剑河县 Jianhe 台江县 Taijiang　黎平县 Liping　榕江县 Rongjiang　从江县 Congjiang　雷山县 Leishan　麻江县 Majiang　丹寨县 Danzhai
黔南布依族苗族自治州 Qiannan(Bouyei & Miao) Autonomous State	都匀市 Duyun　福泉市 Fuquan　荔波县 Libo　贵定县 Guiding　瓮安县 Wengan　平塘县 Pingtang　罗甸县 Luodian　长顺县 Changshun　龙里县 Longli 惠水县 Huishui　独山县 Dushan　三都水族自治县 Sandu(Shui) Autonomous County

1-2 各州(市、地)行政区划(2001)
Administrative Division of Guizhou Province

单位:个
(unit)

州(市、地)名称	State(City, Prefecture)	地级单位 Unit at Pre-fectural Level	#市 Cities	县级单位 Unit at County Level	#县 Counties	#自治县 Autonomous Counties	县级市 Cities at County Level	市区 District under the Jurisdiction of City	特区 Special District	镇 Town	街道办事处 Urban Sub-district Office	乡 Township	#民族乡 Ethnic Community Township	居民委员会 Neighbourhood Committees	村民委员会 Village Committees
全省合计	**Total**	**9**	**4**	**87**	**67**	**11**	**9**	**9**	**2**	**696**	**77**	**764**	**253**	**1980**	**24890**
贵阳市	Guiyang	1	1	10	3	–	1	6	–	28	34	53	19	439	1171
六盘水市	Liupanshui	1	1	4	2	–	–	1	1	30	4	64	50	172	1755
遵义市	Zunyi	1	1	13	10	2	2	1	–	165	13	62	8	351	4604
安顺市	Anshun	1	1	6	5	3	–	1	–	37	6	43	11	106	1814
铜仁地区	Tongren	1	–	10	8	4	1	–	1	69	4	95	56	173	2945
黔西南布依族苗族自治州	Qianxinan (Bouyei & Miao) Autonomous State	1	–	8	7	–	1	–	–	80		49	3	115	2077
毕节地区	Bijie	1	–	8	7	1	1	–	–	98	6	146	77	228	4148
黔东南苗族侗族自治州	Qiandongnan (Miao & Dong) Autonomous State	1	–	16	15	–	1	–	–	90	5	116	17	193	3550
黔南布依族苗族自治州	Qiannan (Bouyei & Miao) Autonomous State	1	–	12	10	1	2	–	–	99	5	136	12	203	2826

注:贵阳市、六盘水市、遵义市、安顺市为省辖市。

Note: Guiyang, Liupanshui, Zunyi, Anshun are cities under the jurisdiction of province.

1-3 自 然 资 源
Natural Resources

指 标	Item	计量单位	Unit	2001 年
土地资源	**Land Resources**			
土地面积	Total Land Area	万平方公里	10000 sq.km	17.61
耕地面积	Area of Cultivated Land	万亩	10000 mu	2748.42
人均耕地面积	Per Capita Cultivated Land	亩	mu	0.73
气候(贵阳市)	**Climate(Guiyang)**			
年均气温	Annual Average Temperature	摄氏度	°C	14.5
相对湿度	Relative Humidity	%	%	81
年降水量	Annual Precipitation	毫米	mm	942.3
年日照时数	Annual Sunshine Hours	小时	hour	921.5
森林资源	**Forest Resources**			
森林面积	Forest Area	万亩	10000 mu	8143
森林覆盖率	Forest - coverage Rate	%	%	30.83
人均森林面积	Per Capita Forest Area	亩	mu	2.14
活立木总蓄积量	Total Standing Stock Volume	亿立方米	100 million cu.m	2.1
水利资源	**Water Resources**			
水资源总量	Surface Water Volume	亿立方米	100 million cu.m	569.8
河川径流量	River Runoff	亿立方米	100 million cu.m	1003
水力资源理论蕴藏量	Theoretical Hydropower Resources	万千瓦	10000 kw	1874.5
#可开发资源	Developable Resources	万千瓦	10000 kw	1683

1-4 部分主要河流(省内部分)主要特征值
Major Feature of Some Part of The Main River

水　　系	Water System	流域面积(平方公里) Area of Valley(sq. km)	河长(千米) Length of River(1000m)	平均坡降(‰) Average Slope Falling
长江流域	**Changjiang River Valley**			
金 沙 江	Jinshajiang	4888	199	1.2
赤 水 河	Chishuihe	11412	299	2.3
乌　　江	Wujiang	66807	889	3.3
清 水 江	Qingshuijiang	17145	459	3.4
洪 州 河	Hongzhouhe	975	81	1.2
㵲 阳 河	Wuyanghe	6474	258	1.1
锦　　江	Jinjiang	4017	168	2.0
松 桃 河	Songtaohe	1536	88	2.3
珠江流域	**Zhujiang River Valley**			
南 盘 江	Nanpanjiang	7651	264	1.6
北 盘 江	Beipanjiang	20982	318	3.1
红 水 河	Hongshuihe	15978	106	2.2
都 柳 江	Duliujiang	11586	330	3.8

1-5 主要矿产资源 Major Mineral Resources

名　　称	Item	计量单位	Unit	2001	居全国的位次 Order in National Total
矿产资源(保有储量)	Mineral Resources(Ensured Reserves)				
煤	Coal	亿吨	100 million tons	492.49	5
磷	Barite	亿吨	100 million tons	27.02	2
汞	Hydrargyrum	万吨	10000 tons	3.31	1
铝土矿	Aluminium Ore	亿吨	100 million tons	4.25	2
锑	Antimony	万吨	10000 tons	24.74	4
镁(炼镁白云岩)	Magnesium	万吨	10000 tons	3213	3
锰	Manganese	万吨	10000 tons	7693	3
稀土	Lanthanon	万吨	10000 tons	149.79	2
镓	Gallium	万吨	10000 tons	1.99	3
重晶石	Barite	亿吨	100 million tons	1.13	1
硫铁矿	Pyrites	亿吨	100 million tons	6.12	4
化肥用砂岩	Gritstone for Fertilizer	亿吨	100 million tons	1.06	1
冶金用砂岩	Gritstone for Metallurgy	万吨	10000 tons	8252	1
熔炼水晶	Fusion Crystal	吨	ton	1110	3
饰面用灰岩	Limestone for Facing	万立方米	10000 cu.m	3701	2
饰面用辉绿岩	Diabase for Facing	万立方米	10000 cu.m	352	1
玻璃用砂岩	Gritstone for Glass	万吨	10000 tons	5128	7
砖瓦用粘土	Clay for Tile	万立方米	10000 cu.m	1672	6
砖瓦用页岩	Shale for Tile	万立方米	10000 cu.m	1242	3
砖瓦用砂岩	Gritstone for Tile	万立方米	10000 cu.m	1760	1
水泥配料用砂岩	Gritstone for the Material of Cement	万吨	10000 tons	9183	5
水泥配料用页岩	Shale for the Material of Cement	万吨	10000 tons	2692	10
水泥配料用粘土	Clay for the Material of Cement	万吨	10000 tons	10714	8

注:1.保有资源储量系指 2001 年底实际拥有的基础储量和资源量总和。

2.全国排列位次按国土资源部信息中心 2001 年 8 月编制的《2000 年保有储量全国排序表》排序。

Note:1.The ensured reserves refers to the sum of basic reserves and resources at the end of 2001.

2.The orders of national tolal are according to the《National Orders Table of Ensured Reserves in 2000》published by the information centre of Ministry of Land Resources.

1-6 城 市 气 象 (2001)
Climate of Major Cities

城市名称	Name of City	年平均气温(℃) Annual Average Temperature(℃)	年降水量(毫米) Annual Precipitation(mm)	年日照时数(小时) Annual Sunshine Hours(hour)	相对湿度(%) Relative Temperature(%)
贵 阳 市	Guiyang	14.5	942.3	921.5	81
水 城 县	Shuicheng	12.8	1256.6	1373.8	81
红花岗区	Honghuagang	16.0	1002.0	1134.2	78
西 秀 区	Xixiu	14.7	1330.0	1192.3	78
铜 仁 市	Tongren	17.4	1257.7	1145.8	77
兴 义 市	Xingyi	16.8	1703.6	1614.2	79
毕 节 市	Bijie	13.3	919.8	1236.1	81
凯 里 市	Kaili	16.1	970.8	1150.9	80
都 匀 市	Duyun	16.7	1066.7	872.7	78
赤 水 市	Chishui	18.3	970.4	1307.9	82
清 镇 市	Qingzhen	14.6	1023.2	1120.4	79
仁 怀 市	Renhuai	16.2	1036.4	1144.0	78
福 泉 市	Fuquan	15.3	932.7	1147.5	81

1－7 主要城市平均气温(2001)
Average Temperature of Major Cities

单位:℃
(℃)

城市名称	Name of City	1月 Jan.	2月 Feb.	3月 Mar.	4月 Apr.	5月 May.	6月 June.	7月 July.	8月 Aug.	9月 Sept.	10月 Oct.	11月 Nov.	12月 Dec.
贵阳市	Guiyang	4.9	6.7	12.1	14.4	17.4	20.2	23.2	21.6	20.6	16.3	11.4	4.7
水城县	Shuicheng	4.9	5.4	10.7	14.1	15.3	18.3	20.5	19.1	17.6	14.3	9.2	4.7
红花岗区	Honghuagang	6.0	7.9	13.5	15.3	19.1	21.8	26.4	24.4	23.0	17.4	12.3	5.4
西秀区	Xixiu	6.1	6.8	12.2	15.5	17.7	20.3	22.7	21.4	20.2	16.2	11.3	5.9
铜仁市	Tongren	6.5	8.2	14.0	16.5	21.6	24.6	28.6	26.7	24.6	18.7	13.4	5.8
兴义市	Xingyi	9.8	9.7	15.4	19.0	19.8	21.6	23.0	22.0	21.3	17.8	12.7	9.1
毕节市	Bijie	4.2	5.7	11.0	13.8	16.0	18.9	22.4	20.3	19.1	14.9	9.8	4.0
凯里市	Kaili	5.4	7.7	13.1	15.8	19.7	23.1	25.7	24.1	22.6	18.0	12.5	4.9
都匀市	Duyun	7.2	8.6	13.9	16.4	20.2	23.2	25.7	24.1	22.9	18.8	13.0	6.3
赤水市	Chishui	8.3	11.0	16.1	17.9	22.2	23.4	28.8	26.1	23.3	19.5	14.9	8.6
清镇市	Qingzhen	5.3	6.9	12.1	14.8	17.5	20.4	23.2	21.7	20.4	16.4	11.3	5.4
仁怀市	Renhuai	6.2	8.2	14.0	15.7	19.1	21.4	26.5	24.3	22.5	17.9	12.9	6.0
福泉市	Fuquan	5.2	7.2	12.3	15.0	18.8	22.0	24.7	22.8	21.5	17.3	11.7	4.7

主要统计指标解释

自然资源 指人类可以直接从自然界获得,并用于生产和生活的物质资源。自然资源一般可以分成可再生资源和非再生资源两大类。可再生资源指在较短时间内可以再生、可以循环利用的资源,包括土地资源、水资源、气候资源、生物资源和海洋资源等。非再生资源指在使用后不能再生的资源,包括矿产资源和地热能源。

耕地面积 指种植各种农作物的土地面积,包括灌溉水田、望天田、水浇地、旱地、菜地等。

活立木总蓄积量 指一定范围内土地上全部树木蓄积的总量,包括森林蓄积、疏林蓄积、散生木蓄积和四旁树蓄积。

森林面积 指由乔木树种构成,郁闭度0.2以上(含0.2)的林地或冠幅宽度10米以上的林带的面积,即有林地面积。森林面积包括天然起源和人工起源的针叶林面积、阔叶林面积、针阔混交林面积和竹林面积,不包括灌木林地面积和疏林地面积。

森林覆盖率 指一个国家或地区森林面积占土地面积的百分比。在计算森林覆盖率时,森林面积包括郁闭度0.2以上的乔木林地面积和竹林地面积,国家特别规定的灌木林地面积、农田林网以及四旁(村旁、路旁、水旁、宅旁)林木的覆盖面积。森林覆盖率是反映森林资源的丰富程度和生态平衡状况的重要指标。计算公式为:

$$森林覆盖率(\%)=\frac{森林面积}{土地总面积}\times 100\%$$

径流 指大气降水扣除损耗外,从地表和地下向流域出口断面汇集的水流。径流可分为地表径流、地下径流和壤中流。地表径流指沿地表向河流、湖泊、沼泽、海洋等汇集的水流;地下径流指沿潜水层或隔水层间的含水层,向河流、湖泊、沼泽、海洋等汇集的地下水水流。

径流量 指在一定时段内通过河流某一过水断面的水量,用以反映一个国家或地区水资源的丰歉程度。计算公式为:

径流量=降水量-蒸发量

矿产保有储量 指探明的矿产储量(包括工业储量和远景储量),扣除已开采部分和地下损失量后的年末实有储量,是反映国家矿产资源现状的重要指标。

气温 指空气的温度,我国一般以摄氏度(℃)为单位表示。气象观测的温度表是放在离地面约1.5米处通风良好的百叶箱里测量的,因此,通常说的气温指的是离地面1.5米处百叶箱中的温度。其统计计算方法为:

月平均气温是将全月各日的平均气温相加,除以该月的天数而得。

年平均气温是将12个月的月平均气温累加后除以12而得。

相对湿度 指空气中实际水气压与当时气温下的饱合水气压之比。其统计方法与气温相同。

降水量 指从天空降落到地面的液态或固态(经融化后)水,未经蒸发、渗透、流失而在地面上积聚的深度。其统计计算方法为:

月降水量是将全月各日的降水量累加而得。

年降水量是将12个月的月降水量累加而得。

日照时数 指太阳实际照射地面的时间。其统计方法与降水量相同。

Explanatory Notes on Main Statistical Indicators

Natural Resources refer to material resources that could be obtained from the nature by human being and used for production and living. Natural resources in general can be classified as renewable resources and non – renewable resources. Renewable resources refer to resources that could be renewed and recycled during a relatively short period of time, including land resource, water resource, climate resource, biology resource and marine resource. Non – renewable resources include resources that could not be renewed, such as minerals and geothermal resource.

Area of Cultivated Land refers to land for the cultivation of various farm crops, including irrigated land, manual – watered land, dry land and vegetable land.

Total Standing Stock Volume refers to the total stock volume of trees growing in land, including trees in forest, trees in sparse forest, scattered trees and trees planted by the side of farm houses and along the roads, rivers and fields.

Forest Area refers to the area of forest land where trees and bamboo grow with canopy density above 0.2, including land of natural woods and planted woods, but excluding bush land and thin forest land. It reflects the total areas of afforestation.

Forest Coverage Rate refers to the ratio of area of afforested land to total land area. This indicator shows the forest resources and afforestation progress of a country or a region. According to regulations of the government, in addition to afforested land, the area of bush forest, the area of forest land inside farm land and the area of trees planted by the side of farm houses and along the roads, rivers and fields should also be included in the area of afforested land in the calculation of the forest coverage – rate. The formula for calculating forest coverage – rate is as follows:

$$\text{Forestry coverage rate}(\%) = \frac{\text{Area of Afforested Land}}{\text{Area of Total Land}} \times 100\%$$

Runoff refers to the water gathered at the way out of the cross section of drainage area either from the surface or underground after deducting the wastage of the precipitation.

Runoff can be divided into surface runoff, underground runoff and within soil runoff. Surface runoff refers to water flow to the rivers, lakes, swamps, and seas on the surface of the earth. Underground runoff refers to water flow to rivers, lakes, swamps, and seas through the water – bearing stratum of confined layer or unconfined layer.

Volume of Runoff refers to the total volume of water running through a certain cross section of a river during a certain period of time, reflecting the water resource condition in a country or a region. The formula for calculating volume or runoff is as follows:

Runoff = Precipitation – Evaporation

Ensured Mineral Reserves refer to the actual mineral reserves, which equal to the proven mineral reserves (including industrial reserves and prospective reserves) minus extracted parts and underground losses. This indicator shows the current condition of the mineral resources of a country.

Temperature refers to the air temperature. China uses centigrade as the unit. The thermometry used for weather observation is put in a breezy shutter, which is 1.5 meters high from the ground. Therefore, the commonly used temperature refers to the temperature in the breezy shutter 1.5 meters away from the ground. The calculation method is as follows:

Monthly average temperature is the summation of average daily temperature of one month divided by the actual days of that particular month.

Annual average temperature is the summation of monthly average of a year divided by 12 months.

Relative Humidity refers to the ratio of actual water vapor pressure to the saturation water vapor pressure under the current temperature. The calculation method is the same as that of temperature.

Volume of Precipitation refers to the deepness of liquid state or solid state (thawed) water falling from the sky to the ground that has not been evaporated, infiltrated or run off. The calculation method is as follows:

Monthly precipitation is the summation of daily precipitation of a month.

Annual precipitation is the summation of 12 months precipitation of a year.

Sunshine Hours refer to the actual hours of sun irradiating the earth. The calculation method is the same as that of the precipitation.

综　合

General Survey

Two

国内生产总值(亿元)
Gross Domestic Product (100 imllion yuan)

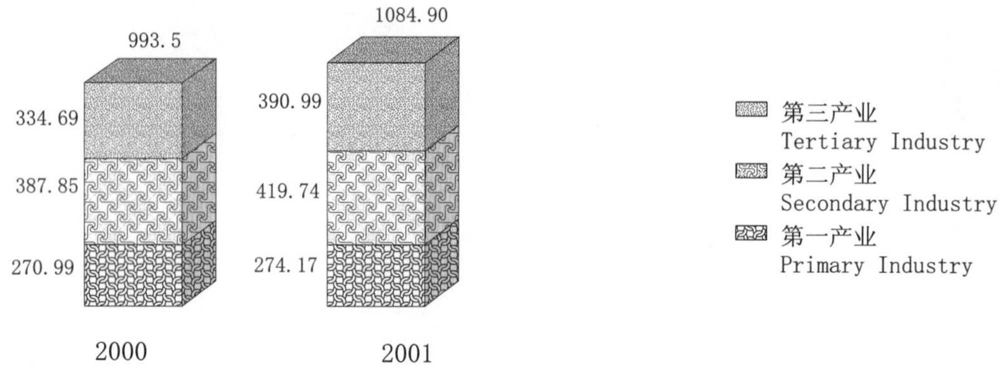

国内生产总值构成 (%)
Composition of Gross Domestic Product %

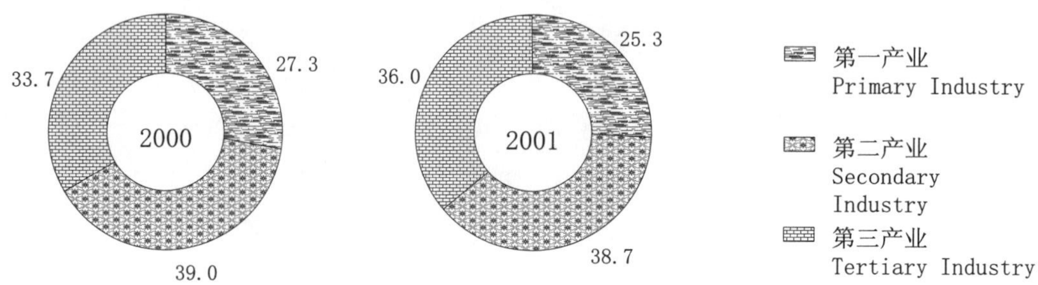

第三产业增加值构成 (%) (第三产业=100) (2001)
Composition of Added Value of Tertiary Industry(Tertiary Industry =100)

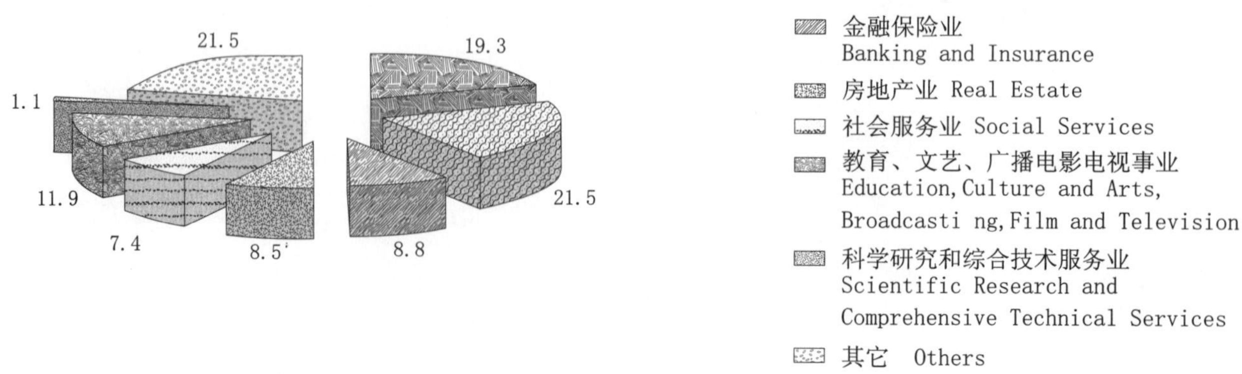

2－1 主要社会经济指标总量
Major Social and Economic Indicators

指　　标	Item	2000	2001	2001年比2000年增长(%) Increase Rate in 2001 over 2000(%)
人口(万人)	**Population(10000 persons)**			
年末总人口	Total Population at the Year－end	3755.72	3798.51	1.1
年平均人口	Annual Average Population	3732.89	3777.12	1.2
农业人口	Agricultural Population	3212.63	3249.24	1.1
非农业人口	Non－agricultural Population	543.09	549.27	1.1
家庭总户数(万户)	Total Family Households(10000 households)	941.43	1018.38	8.2
城镇居民平均每户人口(人)	Average Persons Per Urban Household(person)	3.11	3.11	
农村居民平均每户人口(人)	Average Persons Per Rural Household(person)	4.52	4.52	
准予登记结婚(万对)	Marriage Registration Permitted(10000 households)	28.02	26.81	－4.3
离婚数(万人)	Divorce(10000 persons)	5.17	5.63	8.8
就业(万人)	**Employment(10000 persons)**			
年末就业人员(包括外出人员)	Year－end Employees	2046	2068	1.1
#职工人数	Staff and Workers	193.97	189.17	－2.5
国民经济核算(亿元)	**National Accounting(100 million yuan)**			
国内生产总值	Gross Domestic Product	993.53	1084.90	8.8
第一产业	Primary Industry	270.99	274.17	1.1
第二产业	Secondary Industry	387.85	419.74	11.0
#工业	Industry	314.73	335.00	10.2
建筑业	Construction	73.12	84.74	14.5
第三产业	Tertiary Industry	334.69	390.99	12.6
#交通运输、仓储、邮电通信业	Transportation, Storage, Post and Telecommunications	64.59	75.37	7.5
批发零售贸易餐饮业	Wholesale, Retail & Catering Trade	77.62	84.08	10.1
国内生产总值中	**In GDP**			
#最终消费	Final Consumption	775.25	833.87	7.0
居民消费	Resident Consumption	600.07	611.31	0.6
政府消费	Government Consumption	175.18	222.56	29.0
资本形成总额	Total Investment	495.89	599.95	20.6
固定资本形成	Fixed Assets	458. 84	579.55	25.8

2－1 续表 1(continued)

指 标	Item	2000	2001	2001 年比 2000 年增长(%) Increase Rate in 2001 over 2000(%)
存货增加	Increase in Inventory	37.05	20.40	－43.7
固定资产投资(亿元)	**Investment in Fixed Assets(100 million yuan)**			
全社会固定资产投资	Total Investment in Fixed Assets		533.74	19.3
#国有经济	State－owned Units		357.69	17.3
非国有经济	Non－state－owned Units		176.05	23.5
#公有经济	Public－owned Units		380.14	31.8
非公有经济	Non－public－owned Units		153.60	34.6
#基本建设	Capital Construction		238.81	21.3
更新改造	Innovation		118.55	26.7
房地产开发	Real Estate Development		67.01	43.9
其他投资	Other Investments		109.37	－1.0
农业	**Agriculture**			
耕地面积(万亩)	Cultivated Land(10000 mu)	2765.22	2748.42	－0.6
农林牧渔业增加值(亿元)	Added Value of FFAF(100 million yuan)	270.99	274.17	1.1
农林牧渔业总产值(亿元)	Gross Output Value of FFAF(100 million yuan)	412.97	418.61	1.2
农 业	Farming	279.61	279.95	－0.1
林 业	Forestry	18.04	15.08	－15.9
牧 业	Animal Husbandry	110.67	118.46	6.9
渔 业	Fisheyr	4.65	5.13	10.2
主要农产品产量(万吨)	Output of Major Farm Products(10000 tons)			
粮 食	Grain	1161.30	1100.30	－5.3
油 料	Oil－bearing Crops	74.34	71.32	－4.1
#油菜籽	Rapeseed	66.20	63.48	－4.1
烤 烟	Flue－cured Tobacco	31.09	26.38	－15.1
肉类总产量	Meat	124.06	131.70	6.2
水产品	Aquatic Products	6.24	6.89	10.4
工业	**Industry**			
全部工业增加值(亿元)	Total Added Value of Industry(100 million yuan)	314.73	335.00	10.2

2－1续表2(continued)

指　标	Item	2000	2001	2001年比2000年增长(%) Increase Rate in 2001 over 2000(%)
全部工业总产值(亿元)	Total Gross Industrial Output Value(100 million yuan)	855.51	952.44	13.2
#国有经济	State－owned Units	500.75	535.98	8.2
非国有经济	Non－state－owned Units	354.76	416.46	20.3
#公有经济	Public－owned Units	625.16	676.60	9.6
非公有经济	Non－public－owned Units	230.35	275.83	23.0
#轻工业	Light Industry	300.70	327.55	10.4
重工业	Heavy Industry	554.81	624.89	14.7
主要工业产品产量	Output of Major Industrial Products			
原煤(万吨)	Coal(10000 tons)	3677	3731	1.5
发电量(亿千瓦小时)	Electricity(100 million kwh)	404.70	480.25	18.7
铝(万吨)	Aluminum(10000 tons)	27.19	28.39	4.4
成品钢材	Steel	150.93	138.61	－8.2
轮胎外胎(万条)	Tires(10000 pieces)	255.34	279.74	9.6
磷矿石(万吨)	Phosphorite(10000 tons)	588.70	669.91	13.8
白　酒	Liquor	8.38	12.11	44.5
卷烟(万箱)	Cigarettes(10000 cases)	187.35	180.79	－3.5
建筑业	**Construction**			
建筑业总产值(亿元)	Gross Output Value of Construction(100 million yuan)	109.06	150.20	37.7
房屋建筑施工面积(万平方米)	Floor Space of Buildings under Construction(10000 sq.m)	1792.48	1945.59	8.5
房屋建筑竣工面积(万平方米)	Floor Space of Buildings Completed(10000 sq.m)	824.01	891.93	8.2
交通运输、邮电通信业	**Transportation, Post and Telecommunications**			
运输线路长度(公里)	Length of Transportation Routes(km)			
铁路里程(境内)	Length of Railways	1674	2172	29.7
公路线路里程	Length of Highways in Operation	33948	34617	2.0
内河航道里程	Length of Navigable Inland Waterways in Operation	2132	2132	持平
旅客周转量(亿人公里)	Passenger－Kilometers(100 million passenger－km)	231.28	240.71	4.1
货物周转量(亿吨公里)	Freight Ton－Kilometers(100 million ton－km)	385.28	422.35	9.6
邮电业务总量(亿元)	Business Volume of Post and Telecommunications Service(100 million yuan)	40.92	47.57	

2－1 续表 3(continued)

指　　标	Item	2000	2001	2001年比2000年增长(%) Increase Rate in 2001 over 2000(%)
年末电话用户(万户)	Number of Telephones Subscribers at the Year－end(10000 subscribers)	153.70	277.59	48.1
电话交换机容量(万门)	Capacity of Telephone Exchanges(10000 lines)	260.46	346.51	33.0
国内商业(亿元)	**Domestic Trade(100 million yuan)**			
社会消费品零售总额	Total Retail Sales of Consumer Goods	343.67	378.01	10.0
城　镇	Urban Areas	264.18	292.35	10.7
乡　村	Rural Areas	79.49	85.66	7.8
对外贸易(亿美元)	**Foreign Trade(USD 100 million)**			
进出口贸易总额	Total Exports and Imports	6.60	6.50	－1.6
出口额	Exports	4.21	4.22	0.3
进口额	Imports	2.39	2.28	－4.7
利用外资	**Utilization of Foreign Capital**			
协议合同项目(个)	Projects of Agreements and Contracts(unit)	59	65	10.2
实际利用外资(万美元)	Amount of Foreign Capital Actually Utilized(USD 10000)	19545	14010	－28.3
引进省外项目(个)	Projects Import out of Guizhou Province(unit)	801	910	13.6
引进省外资金(亿元)	Amount Import out of Guizhou Province(100 million yuan)	33.93	48.53	43.0
旅游(万人次)	**Tourism(10000 person－times)**			
来黔旅游人数	Number of Tourists Visiting Guizhou	1998.39	2120.55	6.1
外国人及港澳同胞	Foreigners and Compatriots from Hong Kong and Ma cao	18.39	20.55	11.7
国内旅游人数	Domestic Tourists	1980	2100	6.1
国际旅游收入(亿美元)	International Earnings from Tourism(USD 100 million)	0.61	0.69	12.8
国内旅游收入(亿元)	Domestic Earnings from Tourism(100 million yuan)	57.95	75.81	30.8
价格指数(上年＝100)	**Price Indices(preceding year＝100)**			
商品零售物价总指数	General Retail Price Index	97.3	99.4	1.1(百分点)
居民消费价格指数	General Consumer Price Index	99.5	101.8	2.3(百分点)
农副产品收购价格指数	General Farm and Sideline Products Purchasing Price Index	95.6	97.8	2.2(百分点)
财政(亿元)	**Government Finance(100 million yuan)**			
财政总收入	Total Financial Revenue	153.04	177.04	15.7
地方财政收入	Local Financial Revenue	85.23	99.75	17.0

2－1 续表 4(continued)

指　　标	Item	2000	2001	2001年比2000年增长(%) Increase Rate in 2001 over 2000(%)
省　级	Provincial Level	15.86	21.61	36.3
地　级	Prefectural Level	20.34	21.73	6.8
县　级	County level	25.55	31.69	24.0
乡　级	Township Level	23.49	24.72	5.2
财政支出	Financial Expenditure	201.57	275.20	36.5
金融(亿元)	**Finance(100 million yuan)**			
全部金融机构存款余额	Total Savings Deposit Balance	1106.64	1341.11	21.2
全部金融机构贷款余额	Total Loan Balance	1064.82	1212.23	13.8
城乡居民储蓄存款余额	Urban and Rural Resident Savings Deposit Balance	539.49	641.67	18.9
人均生活水平(元)	**Per Capita Standard of Living(yuan)**			
人均国内生产总值	Per Capita Gross Domestic Product	2662	2895	8.4
城镇居民人均可支配收入	Per Capita Annual Disposable Income of Urban Households	5122.21	5451.91	6.4
城镇居民人均消费性支出	Per Capita Annual Living Expenditures for Consumption of Urban Households	4278.28	4492.25	5.0
农村居民人均纯收入	Annual Per Capita Net Income of Rural Residents	1374.16	1411.73	2.7
农村居民人均生活消费支出	Annual Per Capita Expenditure for Living Cost of Rural Residents	1096.59	1098.39	0.2
城乡居民人均储蓄	Per Capita Urban and Rural Resident Savings	1445	1699	17.6
城镇居民人均居住面积(平方米)	Per Capita Net Floor Space of Urban Rcsidents(sq.m)	9.20	9.15	
农村居民人均居住面积	Per Capita Net Floor Space of Rural Residents	19.75	20.43	3.4
工资	**Wages**			
职工工资总额(亿元)	Total Wages of Staff and Workers(100 million yuan)	144.56	169.65	17.4
职工平均货币工资(元)	Average Wage of Staff and Workers(yuan)	7468	8991	20.4
科技	**Science and Technology**			
科技机构(个)	Number of Scientific Technological Research Institutions(unit)	310	266	－14.2
科技活动人员数(人)	Number of Persons Engaged in Scientific and Technological Activities(person)	34041	33989	－0.2
#科学家、工程师	Scientists and Engineers	18659	19452	4.2
国有经济单位各类专业技术人员(万人)	Scientific and Technical Personnel in State－owned Units(10000 persons)	53.07	54.07	1.9
科技活动经费筹集总额(万元)	Total Income of Scientific and Technological Activities(10000 yuan)	116951	132538	13.3
科技活动经费支出总额	Total Expenditures for Scientific and Technological Activities	108748	133142	22.4

2－1 续表 5(continued)

指　　标	Item	2000	2001	2001 年比 2000 年增长(%) Increase Rate in 2001 over 2000(%)
教育	**Education**			
专任教师数(万人)	Full－time Teachers(10000 persons)			
普通高等学校	Institutions of Higher Education	0.72	0.90	24.4
普通中学	Secondary Schools	8.12	8.81	8.5
小　学	Primary Schools	17.48	17.32	－0.9
在校学生数(万人)	Students Enrollment(10000 persons)			
研究生	Postgraduates	0.10	0.14	41.5
普通高等学校	Institutions of Higher Education	7.98	10.82	35.5
普通中学	Secondary Schools	157.20	184.60	17.4
小　学	Primary Schools	500.21	490.17	－2.0
学龄儿童入学率(%)	Rate of School－age Children Enrollment(%)	98.5	98.2	－0.3 (百分点)
用于教育的财政支出(亿元)	Government Expenditures on EIducation(100 million)	34.74	49.35	42.1
文化	**Culture**			
图书出版量(万册)	Number of Books Pubilshed(10000 copies)	10288	12767	24.1
杂志出版量(万份)	Number of Magazines Issued(10000 copies)	994	1210	21.7
报纸出版量(亿份)	Number of Newspapers Issued(100 million copies)	2.89	3.17	9.7
卫生	**Health Care**			
医院、卫生院数(个)	Number of Hospitals(unit)	1878	1872	－0.3
医院、卫生院医生(万人)	Number of Doctors(10000 persons)	4.57	4.64	－1.5
医院、卫生院床位数(万张)	Number of Hospital Beds(1000 beds)	5.51	5.59	1.5
城市建设	**City Construction**			
自来水供应总量(亿吨)	Volume of Tap Water Supply(100 million tons)	4.59	4.64	1.1
排水管道长度(公里)	Length of Sewer Pipelines(km)	1665	1755	5.4
城镇煤气供应量(万立方米)	Volume of Coal Gas Supply in Urban Areas(10000 cu.m)	8727	9143	4.8
出租车总数(万辆)	Taxis(10000 units)	0.74	0.76	2.7
运营公交汽车数(标台)	Total Number of Operating Public Buses(unit)	4144	4263	2.9
城市道路长度(公里)	Length of Paved Roads(km)	1682	1725	2.6
园林绿地面积(万亩)	Areas of Green Land(10000 mu)	14.91	15.56	4.4
公共绿地面积(万亩)	Public Green Area(10000 mu)	3.76	4.24	12.8
环境	**Environment**			
环保投入资金(亿元)	Devotion of Capital for Environment Protection(100 million yuan)	10.98	14.7	33.6
#老污染源治理资金	Implementation for Industrial Pollution Treatment	2.4	1.6	－33.3
新建项目污染源治理资金	Pollution Prevention for New Projects	1.6	1.2	－33.3

注：表中部分指标增长速度未计算，其原因是两年统计口径不一致，请使用者注意。

Note: The increase rate of some indicators in this table are not calculated, because the statistical coverage of 2001 is inconsistant with 2000.

2-2 主要社会经济指标增长指数
Growth Indices of Major Social and Economic Indicators

单位:%
(%)

指标	Item	2000年比1999年增长 Increase Rate in 2000 over 1999	2001年比2000年增长 Increase Rate in 2001 over 2000	2001年比2000年增长百分点 Up Percentage Points in 2001 over 2000
人口	**Population**			
年末总人口	Total Population at the Year-end	1.2	1.1	-0.1
农业人口	Agricultural Population	1.0	1.1	0.1
非农业人口	Non-agricultural Population	2.7	1.1	-1.7
就业	**Employment**			
年末就业人员	Year-end Employees	3.5	1.1	-2.4
#职工人数	Staff and Workers	-0.1	-2.5	
国民经济核算	**National Accounting**			
国内生产总值	Gross Domestic Product	8.7	8.8	0.1
第一产业	Primary Industry	3.6	1.1	-2.5
第二产业	Secondary Industry	10.3	11.0	0.7
#工业	Industry	10.2	10.2	持平
第三产业	Tertiary Industry	10.5	12.6	2.1
国内生产总值中	**In GDP**			
#最终消费	Final Consumption	5.6	7.0	1.4
居民消费	Resident Consumption	3.3	0.6	-2.7
政府消费	Government Consumption	11.0	29.0	18.0
资本形成总额	Total Investment	12.9	20.6	7.7
固定资本形成	Fixed Assets	12.7	25.8	13.1
存货增加	Increase in Inventory	14.8	-43.7	
固定资产投资	**Investment in Fixed Assets**			
全社会固定资产投资	Total Investment in Fixed Assets	20.5	19.3	-1.2
农业	**Agriculture**			
农林牧渔业总产值	Gross Output Value of FFAF	3.8	1.2	-2.6
工业	**Industry**			
全部工业总产值	Total Gross Industrial Output Value	14.7	13.2	-1.5
轻工业	Light Industry	12.4	10.4	-2.0
重工业	Heavy Industry	15.8	14.7	-1.1
建筑施工企业	**Construction Enterprise**			
施工产值	Gross Output Value of Construction	13.7	37.7	24.0

2－2 续表 1(continued)

单位：%
(%)

指标	Item	2000年比1999年增长 Increase Rate in 2000 over 1999	2001年比2000年增长 Increase Rate in 2001 over 2000	2001年比2000年增长百分点 Up Percentage Points in 2001 over 2000
交通运输、邮电通信业	**Transportation, Post and Telecommunications**			
旅客周转量	Passenger－Kilometers	3.2	4.0	0.8
货物周转量	Freight Ton－Kilometers	7.5	9.6	2.1
年末电话用户	Number of Telephones Subscribers at the Year－end	42.8	48.0	6.3
电话交换机容量	Capacity of Telephone Exchanges	41.7	33.0	－7.0
国内商业	**Domestic Trade**			
社会消费品零售总额	Total Retail Sales of Consumer Goods	9.5	10.0	0.5
实际利用外资	Amount of Foreign Capital Actually Utilized	0.1	－28.3	
对外贸易	**Foreign Trade**			
出口	Exports	17.6	0.3	－17.3
进口	Imports	25.8	－4.7	
旅游	**Tourism**			
来黔旅游人数	Number of Tourists Visiting Guizhou	3.7	6.1	2.4
#外国人及港澳同胞	Foreigners and Compatriots from Hong Kong and Macao	10.1	11.7	1.6
国内旅游人数	Domestic Tourists	3.7	6.1	2.4
国际旅游收入	International Earnings from Tourism	10.7	12.8	2.1
国内旅游收入	Domestic Earnings from Tourism	32.4	30.8	－1.6
财政	**Government Finance**			
财政总收入	Total Financial Revenue	14.4	15.7	1.3
地方财政收入	Local Financial Revenue	14.8	17.0	2.2
省级	Provincial Level	17.9	36.3	18.4
地级	Prefectural Level	21.2	6.8	－14.4
县级	County level	11.2	24.0	12.8
乡级	Township Level	11.6	5.2	－6.4
财政支出	Financial Expenditure	18.1	36.5	18.4
金融	**Finance**			
全部金融机构存款余额	Total Savings Deposit Balance	17.0	21.2	4.2
全部金融机构贷款余额	Total Loan Balance	18.3	13.8	－4.5
城乡居民储蓄存款余额	Urban and Rural Resident Savings Deposit Balance	11.3	18.9	7.6
教育	**Education**			
专任教师数	Full－time Teachers			

单位:%
(%)

2-2 续表 2(continued)

指　　标	Item	2000年比1999年增长 Increase Rate in 2000over 1999	2001年比2000年增长 Increase Rate in 2001 over 2000	2001年比2000年增长百分点 Up Percentage Points in 2001 over 2000
普通高等学校	Institutions of Higher Education	18.0	25.0	7.0
普通中学	Secondary Schools	5.9	8.5	2.6
小　学	Primary Schools	2.4	-0.9	
在校学生数	Students Enrollment			
高等学校	Institutions of Higher Education	33.6	43.3	9.7
普通中学	Secondary Schools	13.4	17.4	4.0
小　学	Primary Schools	-0.1	-2.0	
文化	**Culture**			
图书出版量	Number of Books Pubilshed	-21.2	24.3	
杂志出版量	Number of Magazines Issued	7.5	21.7	14.2
报纸出版量	Number of Newspapers Issued	19.9	9.7	-10.2
人均生活水平	**Per Capita Standard of Living**			
人均国内生产总值	Per Capita Gross Domestic Product	7.2	8.4	1.2
城镇居民人均可支配收入	Per Capita Annual Disposable Income of Urban Households	3.8	6.4	2.6
城镇居民人均消费性支出	Per Capita Annual Living Expenditures for Consumption of Urban Households	7.9	5.0	-2.9
农村居民人均纯收入	Annual Per Capita Net Income of Rural Residents	3.6	2.7	1.9
农村居民人均生活消费支出	Annual Per Capita Expenditure for Living Cost of Rural Residents	2.5	0.2	-2.3
城乡居民人均储蓄	Per Capita Urban and Rural Resident Savings	10.0	17.6	7.6
工资	**Wages**			
职工工资总额	Total Wages of Staff and Workers	11.4	17.4	6.0
职工平均货币工资	Average Wage of Staff and Workers	13.2	20.4	7.2
卫生	**Health Care**			
医院、卫生院床位数	Number of Hospital Beds	0.2	1.5	1.3
医院、卫生院医生	Number of Doctors	0.4	1.5	1.1
城市建设	**City Construction**			
自来水供应总量	Volume of Tap Water Supply	-0.2	1.1	
排水管道长度	Length of Sewer Pipelines	4.5	5.4	0.9
城镇煤气供应量	Volume of Coal Gas Supply in Urban Areas	28.1	4.8	-23.3
出租车运营总数	Operating Taxi	2.8	2.7	-0.1
运营公交汽车数	Total Number of Public Buses	1.7	2.9	1.2
铺装道路长度	Length of Paved Roads	5.1	2.6	-2.5
园林绿地面积	Areas of Green Land	7.1	4.4	-2.7
公共绿地面积	Public Green Area	11.8	12.8	1.0

注:表中"城镇居民人均可支配收入"、"农村居民人均纯收入"指数均未剔除价格因素。

Note:The indices of "Per Capita Annual Disposable Income of Urban Households" and "Annual Per Capita Net Income of Rural Residents" don't get rid of the price factor.

2-3 主要社会经济指标结构
Structure of Major Social and Economic Indicators

单位：%
(%)

指 标	Item	2000	2001	2001年比2000年增长百分点 Up Percentage Points in 2001 over 2000
人口与就业	**Population & Employment**			
人口	Population			
农业非农业结构	Structure of Agricultural and Non - agricultural			
农 业	Agricultural	85.5	85.5	持平
非农业	Non - agricultural	14.5	14.5	持平
※就业	Employment			
从业人员产业结构	Structure of Industry			
第一产业	Primary Industry	69.9	81.8	
第二产业	Secondary Industry	11.9	6.5	
第三产业	Tertiary Industry	18.2	11.7	
宏观经济	**Macroeconomic**			
国民经济核算	National Accounting			
国内生产总值产业结构	Structure of Industry			
第一产业	Primary Industry	27.3	25.3	-2.0
第二产业	Secondary Industry	39.0	38.7	-0.3
第三产业	Tertiary Industry	33.7	36.0	2.3
固定资产投资	**Investment in Fixed Assets**			
全社会固定资产投资结构	Structure of Total Investment in Fixed Assets			
#国有经济	State - owned	64.6	67.0	2.4
非国有经济	Non - state - owned	35.4	33.0	-2.4
#公有经济	Public - owned	71.7	71.2	-0.5
非公有经济	Non - public - owned	28.3	28.8	0.5
#基本建设	Capital Construction	37.7	44.7	7.0
更新改造	Innovation	23.2	22.2	-1.0
房地产开发	Real Estate Development	11.6	12.6	1.0
其他投资	Other Investments	27.4	20.5	-6.9
固定资产投资资金来源结构	Structure of Fixed Assets Investment			
国家预算内资金	State Budgetary Appropriation	8.7	6.5	-2.2
国内贷款	Domestic Loans	26.2	32.5	6.3

2－3 续表 1(continued)

单位：%
(%)

指　　标	Item	2000	2001	2001 年比 2000 年增长百分点 Up Percentage Points in 2001 over 2000
利用外资	Foreign Investment	1.8	1.2	－0.6
自筹资金	Fundraising	46.1	38.9	－7.2
其他投资	Others	10.1	11.4	1.3
农业	**Agriculture**			
农作物播种面积	Sown Areas of Farm Crops			
粮食作物	Grain Crops	67.1	67.1	持平
经济作物	Economic Crops	25.0	24.3	－0.7
其他作物	Other Crops	7.9	8.6	0.7
农林牧渔业总产值结构	Structure of Gross FFAF Output Value			
农　业	Farming	67.7	66.9	－0.8
林　业	Forestry	4.4	3.6	－0.8
牧　业	Animal Husbandry	26.8	28.3	1.5
渔　业	Fishery	1.1	1.2	0.1
工业	**Industry**			
工业总产值结构	Structure of Gross Industrial Output Value			
#国有经济	State－owned	58.5	56.3	－2.2
非国有经济	Non－state－owned	41.5	43.7	2.2
#公有经济	Public－owned	73.1	71.0	－2.1
非公有经济	Non－public－owned	26.9	29.0	2.1
#轻工业	Light Industry	35.1	34.4	－0.7
重工业	Heavy Industry	64.9	65.6	0.7
建筑业	**Construction**			
建筑业总产值结构	Structure of Gross Construction Output Value			
土木工程建筑业	Civil Engineering Construction	84.0	84.8	0.8
线路管理设备安装业	Line and Equipment Installation	15.0	14.1	－0.9
建筑物装修装饰业	Building Decoration	1.0	1.1	0.1
运输业	**Transportation**			
货运量结构	Structure of Freight Traffic			
铁　路	Railways	36.3	37.5	1.2

单位：%
(%)

2-3 续表 2(continued)

指 标	Item	2000	2001	2001年比2000年增长百分点 Up Percentage Points in 2001 over 2000
公 路	Highways	61.8	60.7	-1.1
水 运	Waterways	1.9	1.8	-0.1
客运量结构	Structure of Passenger Traffic			
铁 路	Railways	5.8	5.3	-0.5
公 路	Highways	93.4	93.8	0.4
水 运	Waterways	0.9	0.9	持平
国内商业	**Domestic Trade**			
社会消费品零售总额结构	Structure of Retail Sales of Consumer Goods			
城 镇	Urban	76.9	77.3	0.4
乡 村	Rural	23.1	22.7	-0.4
吸收外资	**Foreign Capital Absorbed**			
实际吸收外资结构	Structure of Foreign Capital Actually Absorbed			
#直接吸引外资	Foreign Capital Directly Absorbed	12.8	20.2	7.4
对外借款	Loans from Abroad	87.2	79.8	-7.4
#合资企业	Joint Ventures	8.3	13.8	5.5
合作企业	Cooperative Ventures	0.6	0.1	-0.5
独资企业	Sole - foreign Enterprises	3.8	6.2	2.4
国际旅游	**International Tourism**			
来黔涉外旅游人数结构	Structure of Tourists Visiting Guizhou			
外国人	Foreigners	38.7	38.2	-0.5
港澳台同胞	Compatriots from Hong Kong, Macao and Taiwan	61.3	61.8	0.5
财政	**Public Finance**			
地方财政收入结构	Structure of Local Financial Revenue			
省 级	Provincial Level	18.6	21.7	3.1
地 级	Prefectural Level	23.9	21.8	-2.1
县 级	County level	30.0	31.8	1.8
乡 级	Township Level	27.6	24.8	-2.8
财政支出结构	Structure of Financial Expenditure			

2－3 续表 3(continued)

单位:%
(%)

指　标	Item	2000	2001	2001 年比 2000 年增长百分点 Up Percentage Points in 2001 over 2000
#基本建设支出	Capital Construction	12.3	15.7	3.4
企业挖潜改造资金	Technical Updates and Transformation of Enterprises	3.2	1.6	－1.6
城市维护费	City Maintenance	3.2	2.9	－0.3
科教文卫事业费	Culture, Education, Science and Health Care	20.4	24.5	4.1
企业税收收入	Taxes			
#国有经济	State－owned	52.9	47.6	－5.3
非国有经济	Non－state－owned	47.1	52.4	5.3
#公有经济	Light Industry	60.1	54.6	－5.5
非公有经济	Heavy Industry	39.9	45.4	5.5
金融	**Finance**			
金融机构存款结构	Structure of Total Savings Deposit Balance			
#企业存款	Enterprise Deposit	38.8	38.0	－0.8
财政存款	Treasury Saving Deposit	3.6	3.6	持平
农业存款	Rural Saving Deposit	2.1	2.1	持平
金融机构贷款结构	Structure of Total Loan Balance			
#短期贷款	Short－term Loan	57.5	48.5	－9.0
中长期贷款	Middle and Long－term Loan	36.8	45.2	8.4
教育	**Education**			
在校学生结构	Structure of Students Enrollment			
大学生	Students Enrollment of Higher Education	1.2	1.6	0.4
中学生	Students Enrollment of Secondary Schools	23.6	26.9	3.3
小学生	Students Enrollment of Primary Schools	75.2	71.5	－3.7
专任教师结构	Structure of Full－time Teachers			
高等教育	Institutions of Higher Education	2.7	3.6	0.9
普通中学	Secondary Schools	30.9	32.5	1.6
小　学	Primary Schools	66.4	63.9	－2.5
人民生活	**People's Livelihood**			
城市居民消费结构	Consumption Structure of Urban Residents			
食品类	Food	42.9	40.5	－2.4

2－3 续表 4(continued)

单位:%
(%)

指　标	Item	2000	2001	2001 年比 2000 年增长百分点 Up Percentage Points in 2001 over 2000
衣着类	Clothing	10.6	11.3	0.7
居住	Residence	7.7	7.6	－0.1
家庭设备、用品及服务	Household Facilities, Articles and Services	9.6	9.0	－0.6
医疗保健	Medicines and Medical Services	5.5	6.0	0.5
交通和通信	Transport and Communications	7.8	8.6	0.8
文教、娱乐、用品及服务	Recreation, Education and Cultural Articles and Services	10.8	12.3	1.5
农村居民消费结构	Consumption Structure of Rural Residents			
食品类	Food	62.7	60.0	－2.7
衣着类	Clothing	4.8	4.6	－0.2
居住	Residence	12.7	13.4	0.7
家庭设备、用品及服务	Household Facilities, Articles and Services	3.5	4.1	0.6
医疗保健	Medicines and Medical Services	2.5	2.8	0.3
交通和通信	Transport and Communications	2.4	3.2	0.8
文教、娱乐、用品及服务	Recreation, Education and Cultural Articles and Services	8.9	9.0	0.1
福利	**Social Welfare**			
离退休职工的离退休费中	In Pensions for Retired or Resigned Persons			
# 医疗卫生费	Medical Care	11.2	13.0	1.8
卫生	**Health Care**			
卫生机构数结构	Structure of Various Health Care Institutions			
# 医院、卫生院	Hospital	20.9	21.3	0.4
卫生机构床位数结构	Structure of Beds of Health Care Institutions			
# 医院、卫生院	Hospital	94.5	94.6	0.1
卫生技术人员结构	Structure of Medical Technical Personnels			
# 医生	Doctors	53.5	45.3	－8.2
# 专业卫生技术人员获得中级以上职称	Titled Technical Intermediate and above	88.1	88.8	0.7
# 主任医、药、护、技师	Director Doctor, Nurse Medicament and Technician	1.6	1.4	－0.2

注:表中"就业"一栏中,2001 年数据为根据人口普查数据整理,与上年不可比,(相关表同)。

Note: Data of employment in 2001 are not comparable with last year, because they base on the national population census. (Same to related tables)

2－4 主要社会经济指标比例、效益
Major Indicators on Proportions and Efficiency in Social Development

指　　标	Item	2000	2001	2001 年比 2000 年增减 Up(Down) Percentage Points in 2001 over 2000
人口与就业	**Population and Employment**			
人口	Population			
人口出生率(‰)	Birth Rate(‰)	20.59	18.56	－2.03 (千分点)
人口死亡率(‰)	Death Rate(‰)	7.53	7.23	－0.30 (千分点)
人口自然增长率(‰)	Natural Growth Rate(‰)	13.06	11.33	－1.73 (千分点)
就业	Employment			
就业者负担人口(城镇)	Dependency Ratio(Urban)	1.92	1.88	－0.04
三次产业从业者比例 (以第一产业为 100)	Employment Ratio by Type of Industry (primary industry = 100)			
第一产业	Primary Industry	100.0	100.0	
第二产业	Secondary Industry	17.0	7.9	
第三产业	Tertiary Industry	26.0	14.3	
城镇登记失业率(%)	Unemployment Rate in Urban Areas(%)	3.8	4.0	0.2
宏观经济	**Macroeconomic**			
国民经济核算	National Accounting			
三次产业增加值比例 (以第一产业为 100)	Valued－added Ratio by Type of Industry (primary industry = 100)			
第一产业	Primary Industry	100.0	100.0	
第二产业	Secondary Industry	143.1	153.1	10.0
第三产业	Tertiary Industry	123.5	142.6	19.1
全社会劳动生产率(元/人)	Overall Labor Productivity(yuan/person)	5324	5246	
第一产业	Primary Industry	2076	1621	
第二产业	Secondary Industry	17487	31352	
第三产业	Tertiary Industry	9868	16170	
固定资产投资	Investment in Fixed Assets			

2－4 续表 1(continued)

指　　标	Item	2000	2001	2001 年比 2000 年增减 Up(Down) Percentage Points in 2001 over 2000
全社会固定资产投资相当于国内生产总值比例(%)	Proportion of Investmetn in Fixed Assets to GDP(%)	40.5	49.2	8.7
全社会房屋建筑面积竣工率(%)	Rate of Total Floor Space of Buildings Completed in Construction(%)	66.5	69.1	2.6
固定资产交付使用率(%)	Rate of Fixed Assets Completed in Capital(%)	84.6	71.7	－12.9
基本建设项目建成投产率(%)	Rate of Projects Completed in Capital Construction and Put into Use(%)	59.8	58.7	－1.1
能源生产与消费	Production and Consumption of Energy			
能源生产弹性系数	Elasticity Ratio of Energy Production	0.88	－1.18	
能源消费弹性系数	Elasticity Ratio of Energy Consumption	0.97	0.33	－0.64
每万元工业总产值综合能耗(吨标准煤)	Energy Consumed Per 10000 yuan Industrial Gross Output Value(ton of SCE)	3.69	3.58	－0.11
每万元国内生产总值综合能耗(吨标准煤)	Energy Consumed Per 10000 yuan Gross Domestic Product(ton of SCE)	3.99	3.67	－0.32
产业	**Industries**			
农业	Agriculture			
农业从业者人均耕地面积(亩)	Cultivated Area Per Rural Employed Person(mu)	2.02	2.01	－0.01
每亩耕地农业机械总动力(千瓦)	Total Power of Agricultural Machinery Per Mu of Cultivated Land(kw)	0.22	0.24	0.02
每亩耕地用电量(千瓦小时)	Electric Power Consumption Per Mu of Cultivated Land(kwh)	51.29	50.65	－0.64
每亩耕地化肥施用量(公斤)	Chemical Fertilizer Consumption Per Mu of Cultivated Land(kg)	25.78	25.45	－0.33
每亩耕地生产的农业产值(元)	Agricultural Output Value Per Mu of Cultivated Land(yuan)	1493.45	1523.09	29.64
农业从业者人均主要农产品产量(公斤)	Output of Farm Products Per Agricultural Laborer(kg)			
粮　食	Grain	846.35	804.15	－42.20
油　料	Oil－bearing Crops	54.18	52.12	－2.06
肉　类	Meat	90.41	96.25	5.84
每亩播种面积农产品产量(公斤)	Output of Farm Crops Per Mu of Sowning Area(kg)			
粮　食	Grain	246	235	－11
油　料	Oil－bearing Crops	97	95	－2

2-4 续表 2(continued)

指　　标	Item	2000	2001	2001 年比 2000 年增减 Up(Down) Percentage Points in 2001 over 2000
工业(规模以上)	Industry			
固定资产利税率(%)	Ratio of Per-tax Profits to Fixed Assets(%)	9.58	9.29	-0.3
资金利税率(%)	Ratio of Per-tax Profits to Capital(%)	6.9	7.0	0.1
产值利税率(%)	Ratio of Per-tax Profits to Gross Output Value(%)	13.8	13.5	-0.3
增加值相当于总产值比例(%)	Value-added as Percentage to Gross Output Value(%)	34.4	34.0	-0.4
全员劳动生产率(元/人,按增加值计算)	Overall Labor Productivity(yuan/person),(account by value-added)	31751	35649	3898
建筑业	Construction			
技术装备率(元/人)	Value of Machinery Per Laborer(yuan/person)	5270	5354	84
产值利税率(%)	Ratio of Per-tax Profits to Gross Output Value(%)	4.3	4.7	0.4
全员劳动生产率(元/人,按增加值计算)	Overall Labor Productivity(yuan/person)(account by value-added)	11243	13013	1770
交通	**Transportation**			
铁路网密度(公里/万平方公里)	Railway Density(km/10000 sq.km)	95.06	123.34	28.28
公路网密度(公里/万平方公里)	Highway Density(km/10000 sq.km)	1927.77	1965.76	37.99
铁路货运密度(万吨公里/公里)	Railway Freight Traffic Density(10000 tons km/km)	2353.13	2608.85	255.72
公路货运密度(万吨公里/公里)	Highway Freight Traffic Density(10000 tons km/km)	19.01	20.33	1.32
每万人拥有公共车辆(辆)	Per 10000 Persons Possession of Buses(unit)	13.62	11.73	
国内商业	**Domestic Trade**			
社会消费品零售总额相当于国内生产总值比例(%)	Retail Sales of Consumer Goods as Percentage to GDP(%)	34.6	34.8	0.2
人均社会消费品零售额(元)	Ratail Sales of Consumer Goods Per Capita(yuan)	920.65	995.15	74.5
对外贸易	**Foreign Trade**			
出口总额相当于国内生产总值比例(%)	Total Value of Exports as Percentage to GDP(%)	3.5	3.2	-0.3
进口总额相当于国内生产总值比例(%)	Total Value of Foreign Imports as Percentage to GDP(%)	2.0	1.7	-0.3
每一来黔外国人及港澳台胞旅游者支出(美元)	Expenditure of Per Tourists Visiting Guizhou(USD)	161.13	161.35	0.22

2－4续表3(continued)

指　标	Item	2000	2001	2001年比2000年增减 Up(Down) Percentage Points in 2001 over 2000
财政	**Government Finance**			
财政总收入相当于国内生产总值比例(％)	Total Financial Revenue as Percentage to GDP(％)	15.4	16.3	0.9
财政支出相当于国内生产总值比例(％)	Financial Expenditure as Percentage to GDP(％)	20.3	25.4	5.1
地方财政收入相当于财政总收入比例(％)	Local Financial Revenue as Percentage to Total Financial Revenue(％)	55.7	56.3	0.6
地方财政收入(以地方财政收入为100)	Local Financial Revenue(local financial revenue＝100)			
#增值税	Valued－added Tax	14.3	14.3	持平
营业税	Sales Tax	23.9	22.1	－1.8
企业所得税	Enterprise Income Tax	8.0	12.4	4.4
个人所得税	Individual Income Tax	5.5	6.7	1.2
金融保险	**Finance and Insurance**			
金融机构存款相当于国内生产总值比例(％)	Bank Deposits as Percentage to GDP(％)	111.38	123.62	12.24
金融机构贷款相当于国内生产总值比例(％)	Bank Loans as Percentage to GDP(％)	107.18	111.74	4.56
国家银行现金支出相当于现金收入比例(％)	Proportion of Cash Outlay to Cash Receipt in State Banking System(％)	101.84	101.24	－0.6
教育、科技、文化	**Education, Science & Technology and Culture**			
教育	Education			
学龄儿童入学率(％)	Rate of School－age Children Enrollment(％)	98.5	98.2	0.3
小学升学率(％)	Rate of Graduates of Primary Schools Entering Junior Secondary Schools(％)	78.7	84.4	6.2
初中升学率(％)	Rate of Graduates of Junior Secondary Schools Entering Senior High Schools(％)	43.7	45.5	1.8
每万人拥有在校学生数(人)	Number of Students Enrollment Per 10000 Persons(person)			
大学生(普通高校)	Students Enrollment of Higher Education	22.4	28.6	6.2

2-4 续表 4(continued)

指 标	Item	2000	2001	2001 年比 2000 年增减 Up(Down) Percentage Points in 2001 over 2000
中学生	Students Enrollment of Secondary Schools	421.1	488.7	67.6
小学生	Students Enrollment of Primary Schools	1340.0	1297.8	-42.2
科技	Science and Technology			
※研究与开发经费支出相当于国内生产总值比例(%)	R&D Expense as Percentage to GDP(%)	0.42	0.49	0.1
科技拨款相当于财政支出比例(%)	S&T Appropriate Fouds as Percentage to Financial Expenditure(%)	1.53	1.29	-0.2
文化	Culture			
每百万人拥有艺术表演团体(个)	Number of Troupes Per Million Persons(unit)	0.75	0.74	-0.01
每百万人拥有公共图书馆(个)	Number of Public Libraries Per Million Persons(unit)	2.38	2.38	持平
家庭、生活、环境	**Family, Livelihood and Environment**			
生活	Livelihood			
城市与农村居民消费水平比例(以农村居民为1)	Ratio of Annual Income of Urban Residents to Rural(rural resident = 1)	1:4.03	1:3.98	
福利	Welfare			
离退休退职人数相当于在职人数比例(%)	Workers Who Have Retired or Resigned as Percentage to Employed Ones(%)	32.18	34.27	2.09
卫生	Health Care			
每万人拥有医生数(人)	Number of Doctors Per 10000 Persons(person)	12.2	12.3	持平
每万人拥有医院床位数(张)	Number of Hospital Beds Per 10000 Persons(bed)	14.8	14.8	持平
城市建设	City Construction			
人均公共绿地面积(平方米)	Per Capita Public Green Areas(sq. m)	8.20	*3.27	
自来水普及率(%)	Percentage of Households with Access to Tap Water(%)	94.17	*38.54	
用气普及率(%)	Percentage of Households with Access to Tap Gas(%)	54.42	*23.53	

注:表中带"*"的数据与上年统计口径不一致,请使用者注意。

Note: The statistical coverage of the data with "*" is inconsistant with last year.

2-5 贵州社会经济主要指标占全国比重
Percentage in the Country of Guizhou Main Social and Economic Indicators

指　标	Item	全　国 National Total		贵　州 Guizhou		贵州占全国比重(%) Percentage of the National Total	
		2000	2001	2000	2001	2000	2001
土地面积(万平方公里)	**Total Land Area(10000 sq.km)**	960	960	17.61	17.61	1.83	1.83
人口	**Population**						
年末总人口(万人)	Total Population at the Year-end(10000 persons)	126743	127627	3756	3777	2.96	2.96
就业	**Employment**						
就业人员	Number of Employed Persons	72085	73025	1866	2068	2.59	2.83
#职工人数	Number of Staff and Workers	11259	10792	194	189	1.72	1.75
国民经济核算	**National Accounting**						
国内生产总值(亿元)	Gross Domestic Product(100 million yuan)	89404	95933	994	1085	1.11	1.13
第一产业	Primary Industry	14212	14610	271	274	1.91	1.88
第二产业	Secondary Industry	45488	49069	388	420	0.85	0.86
#工业	Industry	39570	42607	315	335	0.80	0.79
第三产业	Tertiary Industry	29704	32254	335	391	1.13	1.21
财政和金融	**Government Finance and Banking**						
财政收入(亿元)	Financial Revenue(100 million yuan)	13395	16371	153	177	1.14	1.08
财政支出	Financial Expenditure	15887	18844	202	275	1.27	1.46
金融机构各项存款余额	Total Savings Deposit Balance	123804	143617	1107	1341	0.89	0.93
金融机构各项贷款余额	Total Loan Balance	99371	112315	1065	1212	1.07	1.08
城乡居民储蓄存款余额	Urban and Rural Resident Savings Deposit Balance	64332	73762	539	642	0.84	0.87
交通和邮电	**Transportation, Post and Telecommunications**						
货物周转量(亿吨公里)	Freight Ton-Kilometers(100 million ton-km)	44452	47590	385	422	0.87	0.89
旅客周转量(亿人公里)	Passenger-Kilometers(100 million passenger-km)	12261	13155	231	241	1.88	1.83
邮电业务总量(亿元)	Business Volume of Post and Telecommunications Service(100 million yuan)	4793	4556	41	48	0.86	1.05
固定资产投资	**Investment in Fixed Assets**						
全社会固定资产投资总额(亿元)	Total Investment in Fixed Assets(100 million yuan)	32918	36898		534		1.45
#基本建设	Capital Construction	13427	14567		239		1.64
更新改造	Innovation	5108	5889		119		2.02
房地产开发	Real Estate Development	4984	6246		67		1.07
其他投资	Other Inverstments	9399	10197		109		1.07

2-5 续表(continued)

指　　标	Item	全　国 National Total		贵　州 Guizhou		贵州占全国比重(%) Percentage of the National Total	
		2000	2001	2000	2001	2000	2001
国内商业和对外贸易	**Domestic Trade and Foreign Trade**						
社会消费品零售总额(亿元)	Total Retail Sales of Consumer Goods(100 million yuan)	34153	37595	344	378	1.01	1.01
进出口总额(亿美元)	Total Imports and Exports (USD 100 million)	4743	5098	6.60	6.50	0.14	0.13
出口	Exports	2492	2662	4.21	4.22	0.17	0.16
进口	Imports	2251	2436	2.39	2.28	0.11	0.09
利用外资	**Utitization of Foreign Capital**						
实际利用外资(亿美元)	Amount of Foreign Capital Actually Utilized (USD 100 million)	593.6	496.8	1.95	1.40	0.33	0.28
#外商直接投资	Foreign Direct Investments	407.2	468.8	0.25	0.28	0.06	0.06
旅游	**Tourism**						
入境旅游人数(万人次)	Number of International Tourists(10000 person-times)	8344	8901	18.39	20.55	0.22	0.23
国内旅游人数	Domestic Tourists	74400	78366	1980	2100	2.66	2.68
国际旅游收入(亿美元)	International Earnings from Tourism(USD 100 million)	162.2	177.9	0.61	0.69	0.38	0.39
国内旅游收入(亿元)	Domestic Earnings from Tourism(100 million yuan)	3176	3522	57.95	75.81	1.82	2.15
教育、文化、卫生	**Education, Culture and Health Care**						
专任教师数(万人)	Number of Full-time Teachers(10000 persons)	1091	1105	26	27	2.38	2.44
在校学生数(万人)	Number of Students Enrollment (10000 persons)	21931	22023	665	686	3.03	3.11
图书出版量(亿册)	Number of Books Pubilshed(100 million copies)	62.7	63.4	1.03	1.28	1.64	2.02
杂志出版量(亿册)	Number of Magazines Issued(100 million copies)	29.4	29.0	0.10	0.12	0.34	0.41
报纸出版量(亿份)	Number of Newspapers Issued(100 million copies)	329.3		2.89	3.17	0.88	
职工工资总额(亿元)	Total Wages of Staff and Workers(100 million yuan)	10656	11831	145	170	1.36	1.44
医院、卫生院数(个)	Number of Health Institutions(unit)	66509	65424	1878	1872	2.82	2.86
医院、卫生院床位数(万张)	Number of Hospital Beds(10000 beds)	294.8	297.6	5.51	5.59	1.87	1.88
医生数(万人)	Number of Doctors(10000 persons)	208	210	4.57	4.64	2.20	2.21
人均水平	**Per Capita Standard**						
人均国内生产总值(元)	Per Capita Gross Domestic Product(yuan)	7081	7543	2662	2895	37.59	38.38
城镇居民人均可支配收入(元)	Per Capita Annual Disposable Income of Urban Households(yuan)	6280	6860	5122	5452	81.56	79.48
农村居民人均纯收入(元)	Annual Per Capita Net Income of Rural Residents(yuan)	2253	2366	1374	1412	60.99	59.68
职工平均工资(元)	Average Wage of Staff and Workers(yuan)	9371	10870	7468	8991	79.69	82.71

2-6　按三次产业分国内生产总值
Gross Domestic Product Grouped by Three Industries

单位:亿元
(100 million yuan)

指　　标	Item	2000	2001	2001年比2000年增长(%) Increase Rate in 2001 over 2000(%)
国内生产总值	**Gross Domestic Product**	**993.53**	**1084.90**	**8.8**
第一产业	Primary Industry	270.99	274.17	1.1
第二产业	Secondary Industry	387.85	419.74	11.0
工业	Industry	314.73	335.00	10.2
建筑业	Construction	73.12	84.74	14.5
第三产业	Tertiary Industry	334.69	390.99	12.6
农林牧渔服务业	Farming, Forestry, Animal Husbandry and Fishery	3.44	4.32	23.3
地质勘查业、水利管理业	Geological and Water Conservancy	1.93	2.71	37.8
交通运输、仓储、邮电通信业	Transportation, Storage, Post and Telecommunications	64.59	75.37	7.5
交通运输和仓储业	Transportation and Storage	50.64	58.40	7.5
邮电通信业	Post and Telecommunications	13.95	16.97	7.6
批发和零售贸易、餐饮业	Wholesale Retail & Catering Trade	77.62	84.08	10.1
商业	Trade	65.99	68.65	5.7
餐饮业	Catering Trade	11.63	15.43	34.9
金融保险业	Bank and Insurance	33.12	34.53	4.5
房地产业	Real Estate	27.58	33.19	15.1
社会服务业	Social Services	26.71	28.96	6.5
卫生、体育、社会福利事业	Health, Sports and Social Welfare	17.88	23.39	27.7
教育、文艺、广播电影电视事业	Education, Culture and Arts, Broadcasting, Film and Television	33.71	46.58	20.1
科学研究和综合技术服务业	Scientific Research and Polytechnical Services	4.09	4.14	-0.5
国家政党机关、社会团体	Governments Parties and Social Organizations	38.41	48.13	23.1
其他	Others Sectors	5.61	5.59	-2.1
人均国内生产总值(元)	**Per Capita Gross Domestic Product(yuan)**	**2662**	**2895**	**8.4**

2-7 按三次产业分国内生产总值构成
Composition of Gross Domestic Product Grouped by Three Industries

单位:%
(%)

指　　标	Item	2000	2001	2001年比2000年增长(%) Increase Rate in 2001 over 2000(%)
国内生产总值	Gross Domestic Product	100.0	100.0	
第一产业	Primary Industry	27.3	25.3	-2.0
第二产业	Secondary Industry	39.0	38.7	-0.3
工业	Industry	31.7	30.9	-0.8
建筑业	Construction	7.4	7.8	0.4
第三产业	Tertiary Industry	33.7	36.0	2.3
农林牧渔服务业	Farming, Forestry, Animal Husbandry and Fishery	0.3	0.4	0.1
地质勘查业、水利管理业	Geological Prospecting and Water Conservancy	0.2	0.2	持平
交通运输、仓储、邮电通信业	Transportation, Storage, Post and Telecommunications	6.5	6.9	0.4
交通运输业	Transportation	5.1	5.4	0.3
邮电通信业	Post and Telecommunications	1.4	1.6	0.2
批发和零售贸易、餐饮业	Wholesale and Retail Trade & Catering Services	7.8	7.8	持平
商业	Trade	6.6	6.3	-0.3
餐饮业	Catering Trade	1.2	1.4	0.2
金融保险业	Banking and Insurance	3.3	3.2	-0.1
房地产业	Real Estate	2.8	3.1	0.3
社会服务业	Social Services	2.7	2.7	持平
卫生、体育、社会福利事业	Health, Sports and Social Welfare	1.8	2.2	0.4
教育、文艺、广播电影电视事业	Education, Culture and Arts, Broadcasting, Film and Television	3.4	4.3	0.9
科学研究和综合技术服务业	Scientific Research and Comprehensive Technical Services	0.4	0.4	持平
国家政党机关、社会团体	Governments Parties and Social Organizations	3.9	4.4	0.5
其他	Others Sectors	0.6	0.5	-0.1

2-8 按支出法计算的国内生产总值
Gross Domestic Product Accounted by Expenditure Approach

指　标	Item	2000	2001	2001年比2000年增长(%) Increase Rate in 2001 over 2000(%)
绝对数(亿元)	**Absolute Figure(100 million yuan)**			
国内生产总值	Gross Domestic Product	993.53	1084.90	8.8
最终消费	Final Consumption Expenditure	775.25	833.87	7.0
居民消费	Residont Consumption	600.07	611.31	0.6
农业居民	Agricultural Households	357.99	363.96	1.3
非农业居民	Non-agricultural Households	242.08	247.35	-0.4
人均城乡消费水平对比(农村居民=1)	Urban/Rural Consumption Ratio (rural households=1)	1:4.03	1:3.98	
政府消费	Government Consumption	175.18	222.56	29.0
资本形成总额	Gross Capital Formation	495.89	599.95	20.6
固定资本形成总额	Gross Fixed Capital Formation	458.84	579.55	25.8
库存增加	Changes in Inventories	37.05	20.40	-43.7
货物和服务净出口	Net Export of Goods and Services	-277.61	-348.92	
构成(%)	**Composition(%)**			
以最终消费为100	Final Consumption Expenditure=100			
居民消费	Resident Consumption	77.4	73.3	-4.1
政府消费	Government Consumption	22.6	26.7	4.1
以居民消费为100	Household Consumption=100			
农村居民	Rural Households	59.7	59.5	-0.2
城镇居民	Urban Households	40.3	40.5	0.2
以资本形成总额为100	Gross Capital Formation=100			
固定资本形成总额	Gross Fixed Capital Formation	92.5	96.6	4.1
库存增加	Change in Inventories	7.5	3.5	-4.0
最终消费率(%)	Final Consumption Rate(%)	78.0	76.9	-1.1
资本形成率(%)	Capital Formation Rate(%)	49.9	55.3	-5.4

注:本表绝对数按当年价格计算,增长速度按可比价格计算。

Note: Absolute figures in this table are calculated at current prices, while indices are calculated at comparable prices.

2-9 资金流量表(实物分配)(2000)
Flow of Funds Table(The Part of Income and Distribute)

单位:亿元
(100 million yuan)

机构部门 交易项目	Institutional Sector Transaction	非金融企业部门 Non-financial Enterprises		金融机构部门 Financial Institutions		政府部门 Governments	
		使用 Utilization	来源 Source	使用 Utilization	来源 Source	使用 Utilization	来源 Source
净出口	Net Exports						
增加值	Value-added		417.10		33.12		103.76
劳动者报酬	Compensation of Laborers	205.26		11.42		97.16	
工资和工资性收入	Wages and Related Income	175.57		11.42		97.16	
单位社会保险付款	Employer's Contribution of Social Securities	29.69					
生产税净额	Taxes on Production(Net)	143.68		4.88		1.68	147.05
生产税	Taxes on Production	143.53		4.88		1.68	146.90
生产补贴	Subsidies to Production	-0.15					-0.15
财产收入	Income from Propery	21.03	7.98	13.76	32.18		2.38
利息	Interest	12.88	7.45	13.66	32.18		0.96
红利	Dividend	8.15	0.53				1.42
土地租金	Rent on Land Use						
其他	Others			0.10			
初次分配总收入	Total Income from Primary Distribution		55.11		35.24		154.35
经常转移	Current Transfer	36.15	3.07	14.41	5.57	16.93	167.82
收入税	Taxes on Income	11.90		0.37			14.04
社会保险付款	Payment to Social Security	19.44		10.25			31.64
社会补助	Allowances					15.06	
其他	Others	4.81	3.07	3.79	5.57	1.87	122.14
可支配总收入	Total Disposable Income		22.03		26.40		305.24
最终消费	Final Consumption Expenditure					175.18	
居民消费	Resident Consumption						
政府消费	Government Consumption					175.18	
总储蓄	Total Savings		22.03		26.40		130.06
资本转移	Capital Transfer		39.90		0.17	40.94	20.03
投资性补助	Investment Allowances		27.23		0.17	40.94	16.41
其他	Others		12.67				3.62
资本形成总额	Gross Capital Formation	317.19		2.31		91.37	
固定资本形成总额	Gross fixed Capital Formation	300.14		2.31		91.37	
存货增加	Changes in Inventories	17.05					
其他非金融资产获得减处置	Minus Items from Other Non-financial Capital						
净金融投资	Net Financial Investment	-255.26		24.26		17.78	
统计误差	Statistical Discrepancy	21.05		0.04		-0.66	
金融交易部分的净金融投资	Net Financial Investment of Financial Transaction	-234.21		24.30		17.12	

2－9 续表(continued)

单位:亿元
(100 million yuan)

机构部门 交易项目	Institutional Sector Transaction	住户部门 Households		省内合计 Total of Guizhou Province		省外部门 Outside of Guizhou Province		总　计 Total	
		使用 Utilization	来源 Source	使用 Utilization	来源 Source	使用 Utilization	来源 Source	使用 Utilization	来源 Source
净出口	Net Exports					172.28	449.89	172.28	449.89
增加值	Value Added		439.55		993.53				993.53
劳动者报酬	Compensation of Laborers	290.76	614.42	604.60	614.42	25.07	15.25	629.67	629.67
工资和工资性收入	Wages and Related Income	290.76	584.73	574.91	584.73	25.07	15.25	599.98	599.98
单位社会保险付款	Employer's Contribution of Social Securities		29.69	29.69	29.69			29.69	29.69
生产税净额	Taxes on Production(Net)	33.36		183.60	147.05		36.55	183.6	183.6
生产税	Taxes on Production	33.36		183.45	146.90		36.55	183.45	183.45
生产补贴	Subsidies to Production			－0.15	－0.15			－0.15	－0.15
财产收入	Income from Propery	4.76	10.46	39.55	53.00	15.83	2.38	55.38	55.38
利息	Interest	4.76	6.54	31.30	47.13	15.83		47.13	47.13
红利	Dividend		3.82	8.15	5.77		2.38	8.15	8.15
土地租金	Rent on Land Use								
其他	Others		0.10	0.10	0.10			0.1	0.1
初次分配总收入	Total Income from Primary Distribution		735.55		980.25		290.89		1 271.14
经常转移	Current Transfer	7.64	16.21	75.13	192.67	122.57	5.03	197.7	197.7
收入税	Taxes on Income	4.73		17.00	14.04		2.96	17	17
社会保险付款	Payment to Social Security	1.95		31.64	31.64			31.64	31.64
社会补助	Allowances		15.06	15.06	15.06			15.06	15.06
其他	Others	0.96	1.15	11.43	131.93	122.57	2.07	134.00	134.00
可支配总收入	Total Disposable Income		744.12		1 097.79		173.35		1 271.14
最终消费	Final Consumption Expenditure	600.07		775.25				775.25	
居民消费	Resident Consumption	600.07		600.07				600.07	
政府消费	Government Consumption			175.18				175.18	
总储蓄	Total Savings		144.05		322.54		173.35		495.89
资本转移	Capital Transfer			40.94	60.1	19.16		60.10	60.10
投资性补助	Investment Allowances			40.94	43.81	2.87		43.81	43.81
其他	Others				16.29	16.29		16.29	16.29
资本形成总额	Gross Capital Formation	47.02		457.89		38.00		495.89	
固定资本形成总额	Gross fixed Capital Formation	33.02		426.84		32.00		458.84	
存货增加	Changes in Inventories	14		31.05		6.00		37.05	
其他非金融资产获得减处置	Minus Items from Other Non－financial Capital								
净金融投资	Net Financial Investment	97.03		－116.19		116.19			
统计误差	Statistical Discrepancy	－1.43		19		－19.00			
金融交易部分的净金融投资	Net Financial Investment of Financial Tra nsaction	95.6		－97.19		97.19			

主要统计指标解释

可比价格　指计算各种总量指标所采用的扣除了价格变动因素的价格，可进行不同时期总量指标的对比。按可比价格计算总量指标有两种方法：一种是直接用产品产量乘某一年的不变价格计算；另一种是用价格指数进行缩减。

不变价格　指以同类产品某年的平均价格作为固定价格，用于计算各年的产品价值。按不变价格计算的产品价值消除了价格变动因素，不同时期对比可以反映生产的发展速度。新中国成立后，随着工农业产品价格水平的变化，国家统计局先后五次制定了全国统一的工业产品不变价格和农业产品不变价格。从1952年到1957年使用1952年工(农)业产品不变价格，从1957年到1970年使用1957年不变价格，从1971年到1980年使用1970年不变价格，从1981年到1990年使用1980年不变价格，从1991年开始使用1990年不变价格。

平均增长速度　我国计算平均增长速度有两种方法：一种是习惯上经常使用的"水平法"，又称几何平均法，是以间隔期最后一年的水平同基期水平对比来计算平均每年增长(或下降)速度；另一种是"累计法"，又称代数平均法或方程法，是以间隔期内各年水平的总和同基期水平对比来计算平均每年增长(或下降)速度。在一般正常情况下，两种方法计算的平均每年增长速度比较接近；但在经济发展不平衡、出现大起大落时，两种方法计算的结果差别较大。

本《年鉴》内所列的平均增长速度，除固定资产投资用"累计法"计算外，其余均用"水平法"计算。从某年到某年平均增长速度的年份，均不包括基期年在内。如建国四十三年的平均增长速度是以1949年为基期计算的，则写为1950－1992年平均增长速度，其余类推。

企业(单位)登记注册类型　是以在工商行政管理机关登记注册的各类企业为划分对象，以工商行政管理部门对企业登记注册的类型为依据，将企业登记注册类型分为内资企业、港澳台商投资企业和外商投资企业三大类。内资企业包括国有企业、集体企业、股份合作企业、联营企业、有限责任公司、股份有限公司、私营公司和其他企业；港澳台商投资企业和外商投资企业分别包括合资经营企业、合作经营企业、独资经营企业和股份有限公司。对不在工商行政管理部门进行登记注册的行政机关、事业单位和社会团体，主要按其经费来源和管理方式进行划分。

国有企业　指企业全部资产归国家所有，并按《中华人民共和国企业法人登记管理条例》规定登记注册的非公司制的经济组织。不包括有限责任公司中的国有独资公司。

集体企业　指企业资产归集体所有，并按《中华人民共和国企业法人登记管理条例》规定登记注册的经济组织。

股份合作企业　指以合作制为基础，由企业职工共同出资入股，吸收一定比例的社会资产投资组建，实行自主经营，自负盈亏，共同劳动，民主管理，按劳分配与按股分红相结合的一种集体经济组织。

联营企业　指两个及两个以上相同或不同所有制性质的企业法人或事业单位法人，按自愿、平等、互利的原则，共同投资组成的经济组织。联营企业包括国有联营企业、集体联营企业、国有与集体联营企业和其他联营企业。

有限责任公司　指根据《中华人民共和国公司登记管理条例》规定登记注册，由两个以上、五十个以下的股东共同出资，每个股东以其所认缴的出资额对公司承担有限责任，公司以其全部资产对其债务承担责任的经济组织。有限责任公司包括国有独资公司以及其他有限责任公司。

股份有限公司　指根据《中华人民共和国公司登记管理条例》规定登记注册，其全部注册资本由等额股份构成并通过发行股票筹集资本，股东以其认购的股份对公司承担有限责任，公司以其全部资产对其债务承担责任的经济组织。

私营企业　指由自然人投资设立或由自然人控股，以雇佣劳动为基础的营利性经济组织。包括按照《公司法》、《合伙企业法》、《私营企业暂行条例》规定登记注册的私营有限责任公司、私营股份有限公司、私营合伙企业和私营独资企业。

其他内资企业　指上述企业之外的其他内资经济组织。

与港澳台商合资经营企业　指港澳台地区投资者与内地企业依照《中华人民共和国中外合资经营企业法》及有关法律的规定，按合同规定的比例投资设立、分享利润和分担风险的企业。

与港澳台商合作经营企业　指港澳台地区投资者与内地企业依照《中华人民共和国中外合作经营企业法》及有关法律的规定，依照合作合同的约定进行投资或提供条件设立、分配利润和分担风险的企业。

港澳台商独资经营企业　指依照《中华人民共和国外资企业法》及有关法律的规定，在内地由港澳台地区投资者全额投资设立的企业。

港澳台商投资股份有限公司　指根据国家有关规定，经外经贸部依法批准设立，其中港、澳、台商的股本占公司注册资本的比例达25%以上的股份有限公司。凡其中港、澳、台商的股本占公司注册资本的比例小于25%的，属于内资企业中的股份有限公司。

中外合资经营企业　指外国企业或外国人与中国内地企业依照《中华人民共和国中外合资经营企业法》及有关法律的规

定,按合同规定的比例投资设立、分享利润和分担风险的企业。

中外合作经营企业　指外国企业或外国人与中国内地企业依照《中华人民共和国中外合作经营企业法》及有关法律的规定,依照合作合同的约定进行投资或提供条件设立、分配利润和分担风险的企业。

外资企业　指依照《中华人民共和国外资企业法》及有关法律的规定,在中国内地由外国投资者全额投资设立的企业。

外商投资股份有限公司　指根据国家有关规定,经外经贸部依法批准设立,其中外资的股本占公司注册资本的比例达25% 以上的股份有限公司。凡其中外资股本占公司注册资本的比例小于25%的,属于内资企业中的股份有限公司。

行政机关、事业单位和社会团体　参照企业登记注册类型,主要按其经费来源和管理方式划分。具体规定如下:

(1)行政机关:包括国家机关和政党机关,原则上均列为"国有"。但有特殊规定的,如供销社等,则列为"集体"

(2)事业单位:包括经国家机构编制部门和有关业务主管部门批准成立的各类事业单位,不包括实行企业化管理的事业单位。事业单位的划分办法如下:

①由国家财政预算拨款或列入财政预算外资金管理以及经费主要来源于国有主管部门或国有上级单位的事业单位,列为"国有"。

②经费主要来源于集体单位的事业单位,列为"集体"。

③公民个人(或个人合伙)开办的事业单位,列为"私营"。

④上述以外的其他事业单位,如果其经费来源不明确,按管理方式进行归类。

(3)社会团体:包括经民政部门批准成立以及未纳入社会团体管理条例范围的工会、妇联等各类社会团体。社会团体的划分办法如下:

①未纳入民政部社会团体管理条例范围的工会、妇联、共青团、青联、工商联、科协、侨联等社会团体,国家拨款设立的基金会或基金管理组织以及经费主要来源于国有业务主管部门或国有上级单位的社会团体,列为"国有"。

②经费主要来源于集体单位的社会团体,列为"集体"。

③公民个人(或个人合伙)开办的社会团体,划为"私营"。

④上述以外的其他社会团体,如果其经费来源不明确,改按管理方式进行归类。

国内生产总值(GDP)　指一个国家(或地区)所有常住单位在一定时期内生产活动的最终成果。国内生产总值有三种表现形态,即价值形态、收入形态和产品形态。从价值形态看,它是所有常住单位在一定时期内生产的全部货物和服务价值超过同期中间投入的全部非固定资产货物和服务价值的差额,即所有常住单位的增加值之和;从收入形态看,它是所有常住单位在一定时期内创造并分配给常住单位和非常住单位的初次收入分配之和;从产品形态看,它是所有常住单位在一定时期内最终使用的货物和服务价值与货物和服务净出口价值之和。在实际核算中,国内生产总值有三种计算方法,即生产法、收入法和支出法。三种方法分别从不同的方面反映国内生产总值及其构成。

三次产业　是根据社会生产活动历史发展的顺序对产业结构的划分,产品直接取自自然界的部门称为第一产业,对初级产品进行再加工的部门称为第二产业,为生产和消费提供各种服务的部门称为第三产业。它是世界上较为通用的产业结构分类,但各国的划分不尽一致。我国的三次产业划分是:

第一产业:农业(包括种植业、林业、牧业和渔业)。

第二产业:工业(包括采掘业,制造业,电力、煤气及水的生产和供应业)和建筑业。

第三产业:除第一、第二产业以外的其他各业。由于第三产业包括的行业多、范围广,根据我国的实际情况,第三产业可分为两大部分:一是流通部门,二是服务部门。

最终消费　指常住单位在一定时期内对于货物和服务的全部最终消费支出,也就是常住单位为满足物质、文化和精神生活的需要,从本国经济领土和国外购买的货物和服务的支出;不包括非常住单位在本国经济领土内的消费支出。最终消费分为居民消费和政府消费。

居民消费　指常住住户对货物和服务的全部最终消费支出。居民消费按市场价格计算,即按居民支付的购买者价格计算。购买者价格是购买者取得货物所支付的价格,包括购买者支付的运输和商业费用。居民消费除了直接以货币形式购买货物和服务的消费之外,还包括以其他方式获得的货物和服务的消费支出,即所谓的虚拟消费支出。居民虚拟消费支出包括以下几种类型:单位以实物报酬及实物转移的形式提供给劳动者的货物和服务;住户生产并由本住户消费了的货物和服务,其中的服务仅指住户的自有住房服务;金融机构提供的金融媒介服务;保险公司提供的保险服务。

政府消费　指政府部门为全社会提供公共服务的消费支出和免费或以较低价格向住户提供的货物和服务的净支出。前者等于政府服务的产出价值减去政府单位所获得的经营收入的价值,政府服务的产出价值等于它的经常性业务支出加上固定资产折旧;后者等于政府部门免费或以较低价格向住户提供的货物和服务的市场价值减去向住户收取的价值。

Explanatory Notes on Main Statistical Indicators

Comparable Prices refer to prices that are used to remove the factors of price change in calculating economic aggregates, so as to facilitate comparison of aggregates over time. Two methods are used for calculating economic aggregates at comparable prices: 1. Multiplying the output of products by their constant prices of certain year; 2. Deflation of data at current prices by relevant price index.

Constant Price refers to the average price of a given product in certain year, which is used for comparison of output value over time. As the output value at constant prices removes the factor of price changes, it reflects the trend of production development over time. Since 1949, with the changes in general price level, the State Statistical Bureau has issued nationally unified constant prices five times: the 1952 constant prices for 1952 – 1957; the 1957 constant prices for 1957 – 1970; the 1970 constant prices for 1971 – 1980; the 1980 constant prices for 1981 – 1990; and the 1990 constant prices have been used since 1991.

Average Annual Growth Rate Two methods for calculating average annual growth rate are applied in China, one is often called level approachor the method of calculating geometric average, which is derived by comparing the level of the last year of the interval with that of the beginning year; the other is calledaccumulative approach or algebraic average or equation method, which is derived by the summation of the actual figure of each year in the interval divided by the figure in the base year.

Usually the results calculated by the two methods are fairly close, but they differed sharply when uneven economic development occurred with striking fluctuations in growth.

The average annual growth rates listed in this statistical yearbook are calculated by level approach except for the growth rate of investment in fixed assets. The base years are not listed when the years are listed for average annual growth rates. For instance, the average annual growth rate of 43 years since 1949 is listed as average annual growth rate of 1950 – 1992 without listing the base year 1949. And the analogy of this is also the same for the rest of the years.

Registration Status of Enterprises Enterprises are classified into 3 categories, namely domestic – funded enterprises, enterprises with investment from Hong Kong, Macau and Taiwan, and enterprises with foreign investment, in the light of the registration status of an enterprise in industrial and commercial administration agencies. Domestic – funded enterprises include state – owned enterprises, collective – owned enterprises, cooperative enterprises, joint ownership enterprises, limited liability corporations, share – holding corporations Ltd., private enterprises and other enterprises. Included in the enterprises with investment from Hong Kong, Macau and Taiwan and enterprises with foreign investment are joint – venture enterprises, cooperative enterprises, sole investment enterprises and share – holding corporations Ltd. For government agencies, institutions and social organizations which are not requested to be registered in industrial and commercial administration agencies, they are classified mainly by their sources of funds and way of management.

State – owned Enterprises refer to non – corporation economic units where the entire assets are owned by the state and which have registered in accordance with the Regulation of the Peoples Republic of China on the Management of Registration of Corporate Enterprises. Excluded from this category are sole state – funded corporations in the limited liability corporations.

Collective – owned Enterprises refer to economic units where the assets are owned collectively and which have registered in accordance with the Regulation of the Peoples Republic of China on the Management of Registration of Corporate Enterprises.

Cooperative Enterprises refer to a form of collective economic units (enterprises) where capitals come mainly from employees as their shares, with certain proportion of capital from the outside, where production is organized on the basis of independent operation, independent accounting for profits and losses, joint work, democratic management, and a distribution system that integrates remuneration according to work with dividend according to capital share.

Joint Ownership Enterprises refer to economic units established by two or more corporate enterprises or corporate institutions of the same or different ownership, through joint investment on the basis of equality, voluntary participation and mutual benefits. They include state joint ownership enterprises, collective joint ownership enterprises, joint state – collective enterprises, other joint ownership enterprises.

Limited Liability Corporations refer to economic units established with investment from 2 – 50 investors and registered in accordance with the Regulation of the Peoples Republic of China on the Management of Registration of Corporations, each investor bearing limited liability to the corporation depending on its share of investment, and the corporation bearing liability to its debt to the maximum of its total assets. Limited liability corporations include exclusive state – funded limited liability corporations and other limited liability corporations.

Share – holding Corporations Ltd. refer to economic units registered in accordance with the Regulation of the Peoples Republic of China on the Management of Registration of Corporations, with total registered capitals divided into equal shares and raised through issuing stocks. Each investor bears limited liability to the corporation depending on the holding of shares, and the corporation bears liability to its debt to the maximum of its total assets.

Private Enterprises refer to profit – making economic units invested and established by natural persons, or controlled by natural persons using employed labour.

Included in this category are private limited liability corporations, private share – holding corporations Ltd., private partnership enterprises and private – funded enterprises registered in accordance with the Corporation Law, Partnership Enterprises Law and Interim Regulations on Private Enterprises.

Other Domestic – funded Enterprises refer to domestic – funded economic units other than those mentioned above.

Joint – venture Enterprises with Funds from Hong Kong, Macau and Taiwan refer to enterprises jointly established by investors from Hong Kong, Macau and Taiwan with enterprises in the mainland of China in accordance with the Law of the Peoples Republic of China on Sino – foreign Joint Venture Enterprises and other relevant laws, where the share of investment, profits and risks is stipulated in the contract.

Cooperative Enterprises with Funds from Hong Kong Macau and Taiwan, established by investors from Hong Kong, Macau and Taiwan with enterprises in the mainland of China in accordance with the Law of the Peoples Republic of China on Sino – foreign Cooperative Enterprises and other relevant laws, where the investment or provision of facilities, and the share of profits and risks is stipulated in the cooperative contract.

Enterprises with Sole (exclusive) Investment from Hong Kong, Macau and Taiwan refer to enterprises established in the mainland of China with exclusive investment from investors from Hong Kong, Macau and Taiwan in accordance with the Law of the Peoples Republic of China on Foreign – Funded Enterprises and other relevant laws.

Share – holding Corporations Ltd. with Investment from Hong Kong, Macau and Taiwan refer to share – holding corporations Ltd. established with the approval from the Ministry of Foreign Trade and Economic Relations in line with relevant state regulations, where the share of investment from Hong Kong, Macau or Taiwan businessmen exceeds 25% of the total registered capital of the corporation. In case the share of investment from Hong Kong, Macau or Taiwan is less than 25% of the total registered capital, the enterprise is to be classified as domestic – funded share – holding corporation Ltd.

Joint – venture Enterprises with Foreign Investment refer to enterprises jointly established by foreign enterprises or foreigners with enterprises in the mainland of China in accordance with the Law of the Peoples Republic of China on Sino – foreign Joint Venture Enterprises and other relevant laws, where the share of investment, profits and risks is stipulated in the contract.

Cooperation Enterprises with Foreign Investment refer to enterprises jointly established by foreign enterprises or foreigners with enterprises in the mainland of China in accordance with the Law of the Peoples Republic of China on Sino – foreign Cooperative Enterprises and other relevant laws, where the investment or provision of facilities, and the share of profits and risks is stipulated in the cooperative contract.

Enterprises with Sole (exclusive) Foreign Investment refer to enterprises established in the mainland of China with exclusive investment from foreign investors in accordance with the Law of the Peoples Republic of China on Foreign – Funded Enterprises and other relevant laws.

Share – holding Corporations Ltd. with Foreign Investment refer to share – holding corporations Ltd. established with the approval from the Ministry of Foreign Trade and Economic Relations in line with relevant state regulations, where the share of investment from foreign investors exceeds 25% of the total registered capital of the corporation. In case the share of foreign investment is less than 25% of the total registered capital, the enterprise is to be classified as domestic – funded share – holding corporation Ltd.

Government Agencies, Institutions and Social Organizations are classified into following categories by source of funds and way of management taking reference of the registration status of enterprises:

(1) Government agencies: include state and party agencies, classified in principle as "state – owned". There are exceptions, such as supply and marketing cooperatives which are classified as "collective".

(2) Institutions: include institutions of various types established with the approval by organization and staffing departments of the government, but exclude institutions where enterprise management system is introduced. Institutions are further classified as follows:

(a) Institutions whose main budget is listed in the government budget appropriations or extra – budget funds, or allocated from the budget of their competent government agencies. Such institutions are classified as "state – owned".

(b) Institutions whose budget mainly comes from collective units. Such institutions are classified as "collective".

(c) Social organizations established by individual or a group of citizens, which are classified as "private".

(d) Institutions other than those mentioned above whose source of budget is not clear. Such institutions are classified by way of management.

(3) Social organizations: include social organizations established with the approval from the Ministry of Civil Affairs, and organizations that are not covered by social organization management regulations such as trade unions, women's federations etc. Social organizations are fur-

ther classified as follows:

(a) Social organizations that are not covered by social organization management regulations of the Ministry of Civil Affairs such as trade unions, women's federations, communist youth leagues, youth associations, industrial and commerce associations, scientists associations, overseas Chinese associations, etc., foundations and fund management organizations established with funds from the state, and social organizations whose funds mainly come from the budget of their competent government agencies. Such institutions are classified as "state – owned".

(b) Social organizations whose budget mainly comes from collective units. Such institutions are classified as "collective".

(c) Social organizations established by individual or a group of citizens, which are classified as "private".

(d) Social organizations other than those mentioned above whose source of budget is not clear. Such organizations are classified by way of management.

Gross Domestic Product (GDP) refers to the final products of all resident units in a country(or a region)during a certain period of time. Gross domestic product is expressed in three different forms, i. e. value, income, and products respectively. The form of value refers to the total value of all products and services produced by all resident units during a certain period of time minus total value of intimidate input of materials and services of the nature of non – fixed assets or the summation of the value – added of all resident units; the form of income includes all the income created by all resident units and distributed primarily to all resident and non – resident units; the form of products refers to the value of all final goods and services for final use by all resident units plus the value of net exports of goods and services during a given period of time. In the practice of national accounting, gross domestic product is calculated with three approaches, i. e. production approach, income approach, and expenditure approach, which reflect gross domestic product and its composition from different aspects.

Three Industries Industry structure has been classified according to the historical sequence of development. Primary industry refers to extraction of natural resources; secondary industry involves processing of primary products; and tertiary industry provides services of various kinds for production and consumption. The above classification is universal although it varies to some extent form country to country. Industry in China comprises:

Primary industry: agriculture(including farming, forestry, animal husbandry and fishery).

Secondary industry: industry(including mining and quarrying, manufacturing, production and supply of electricity, water and gas)and construction.

Tertiary industry: all other industries not included in primary or secondary industry. Due to the fact that tertiary industry involves in a large variety of industries in China, it is divided into two sectors: circulation sector and service sector.

Final Consumption refers to the total expenditure of resident units on final consumption of goods and services in a certain period, namely the expenditure of the resident units for purchases of goods and services from domestic economic territory and abroad to meet the requirements of material, cultural and spiritual life. It excludes the expenditure of non – resident units on consumption in the economic territory of the country. The final consumption is classified into household consumption and government consumption.

Households Consumption refers to the total expenditure of resident households on the final consumption of goods and services. The households consumption is calculated at market prices, namely the purchaser's prices which the households pay; the purchasers prices of goods are the prices the households pay when they obtain the goods, including the transport and commercial expenses paid by the households. In addition to the consumption of goods and services bought by the households directly with money, the expenditure on goods and services obtained by the households in other ways, i.e. the so – called imputed expenditure on consumption, is also included in the households consumption. The imputation expenditure of the households on consumption includes the following types: (a) the goods and services provided to the households by the units in the form of payment in kind and transfer in kind; (b) the goods and services produced and consumed by the households themselves, in which the services refer only to the services provided by the residential buildings owned by the households; (c) the services of financial intermediary provided by the financial institutions; (d) the insurance services provided by the insurance companies.

Government Consumption refers to the expenditure on the consumption of the public services provided by the government to the whole society and the net expenditure on the goods and services provided by the government to the households at free charge or lower prices. The former equals to the output value of the government services minus the value of operating income obtained by the government departments. (The output value of the government services equals to its current operating expenditure plus depreciation of fixed assets). The latter equals to the market value of the goods and services provided by the government free of charge or at low prices to the households minus the value received by the government from the households.

3

Three

人口

Population

年末总人口（万人）
（按农业、非农业分）
Total Population at the Year-end （10000 persons）
(By Agriculture and Non-agriculture)

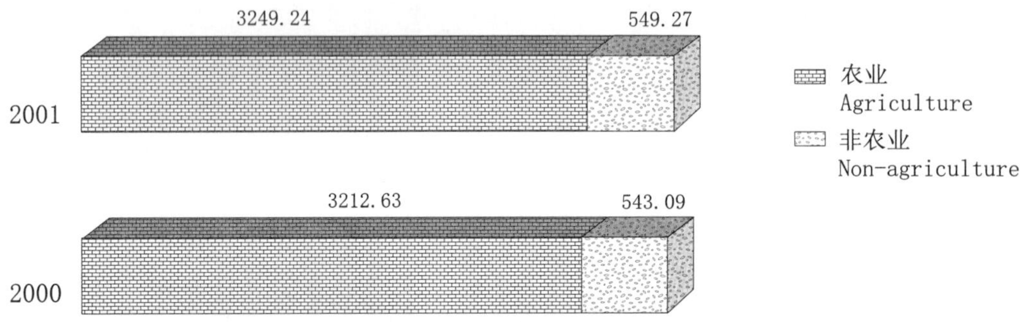

年末总人口（万人）
（按市镇、乡村分）
Total Population at the Year-end（10000 persons）
(By Urban and Rural)

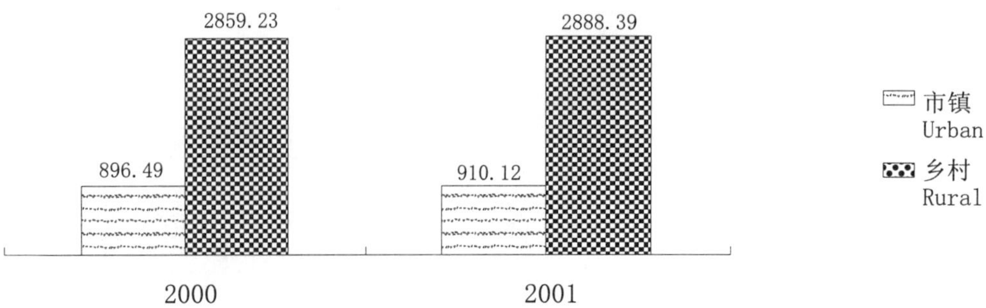

常住人口变动情况（‰）
Changes of Permanent Residents(‰)

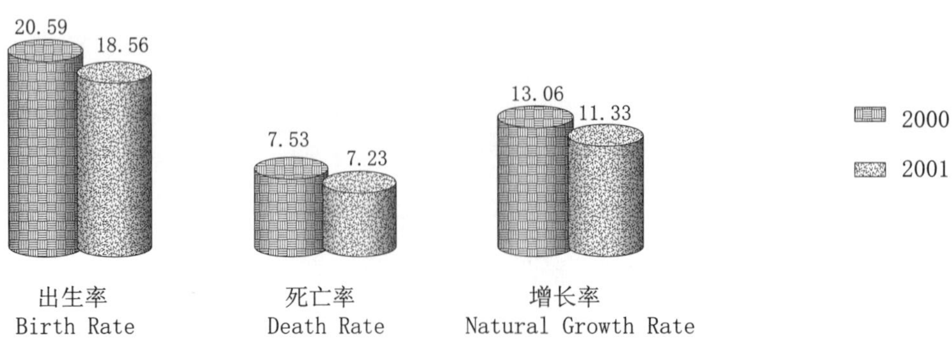

3－1 常住人口变动情况
Changes of Permanent Residents

单位:万人
(10000 persons)

指　　标	Item	2000	2001	2001 年比 2000 年增长(%) Increase Rate in 2001 over 2000(%)
年末总人口	**Total Population at the Year－end**	**3755.72**	**3798.51**	**1.1**
年平均人口	Annual Average Population	3732.89	3777.12	1.2
按农业非农业人口分	**Grouped by Agriculture and Non－agriculture**			
农业	Agriculture	3212.63	3249.24	1.1
非农业	Non－agriculture	543.09	549.27	1.1
按市镇、乡村分	**Grouped by Residence**			
市镇	Urban	896.49	910.12	1.5
乡村	Rural	2859.23	2888.39	1.0
按性别分	**Grouped by Sex**			
男	Male	1968.00	1973.41	0.3
女	Female	1787.72	1825.10	2.1
性别比(以女性为 100)	Sex Ratio(female＝100)	110.10	108.13	－1.97(百分点)
人口自然变动	**Natural Change of Population**			
出生人数	Number of Birth	76.86	70.10	－8.8
出生率(‰)	Birth Rate(‰)	20.59	18.56	－2.03(千分点)
死亡人数	Number of Death	28.11	28.44	1.2
死亡率(‰)	Death Rate(‰)	7.53	7.23	－0.30(千分点)
自然增长人数	Natural Increase of Population	48.75	41.66	－14.5
增长率(‰)	Natural Growth Rate(‰)	13.06	11.33	－1.73(千分点)

3-2 婚姻情况
Marital Status

指　标	Item	2000	2001	2001年比2000年增长(%) Increase Rate in 2001 over 2000(%)
准予登记结婚(对)	Registered Married(couple)	280239	268149	-4.3
初婚(人)	First Married(person)	543331	518046	-4.7
再婚(人)	Re-married(person)	15473	16296	5.3
#女性(人)	Famle(person)	6895	6996	1.5
离婚人数(人)	Divorced(person)	51748	56318	8.8
#民政部门批准(人)	Permitted by Civil Administration Department(person)	15424	17690	14.7
法院调判(人)	Sentenced by Court(person)	36324	38628	6.3
涉外婚姻(对)	Related to Foreign Nationality(couple)	837	978	16.8
#国内公民(人)	Domestic Citizen(person)	837	978	16.8
#女性(人)	famle(person)	816	961	17.8

注:表中2000年部分数据有调整。

Note: Some data in 2000 in this table are adjusted.

3-3 计划生育主要指标
Major Indicators of Family Planning

单位:万人

(10000 persons)

指　标	Item	2000	2001	2001年比2000年增长(%) Increase Rate in 2001 over 2000(%)
符合计划生育人数	Number of Birth within Plan	50.11	48.06	-4.1
计划生育率(%)	Family Planning Rate(%)	88.8	88.9	0.1(百分点)
已婚育龄妇女人数	Number of Married Women of Childbearing Age	659.63	669.74	1.5
领独生子女证人数	Number of Only-child Certificate	44.10	41.70	-2.4
领证率(%)	Acceptance Rate of Only-child Certificate(%)	6.7	6.2	-0.5(百分点)
采取节育措施人数	Number of Contraception User	594.05	622.94	4.9
避孕率(%)	Contraception Rate(%)	90.1	93.0	3.0(百分点)

主要统计指标解释

人口数 指一定时点、一定地区范围内的有生命的个人的总和。年度统计的年末人口数指每年 12 月 31 日 24 时的人口数。

市镇总人口和乡村总人口

其定义有两种口径：

第一种口径(按行政建制)

市人口：市管辖区域内的全部口(含市辖镇，不含市辖区县)；

镇人口：县辖镇的全部人口(不含市辖镇)；

县人口：县辖乡人口。

第二种口径(按常住人口划分)

市人口：设区的市的区人口和不设区的市所辖的街道人口；

镇人口：不设区的市所辖镇的居民委员会人口和县辖镇的居民委员会人口；

县人口：除上述两种人口以外的全部人口。

出生率(又称粗出生率) 指在一定时期内(通常为一年)平均每千人所出生的人数的比率，一般用千分率表示。计算公式为：

$$出生率=\frac{年出生人数}{年平均人数}\times1000‰$$

式中：出生人数指活产婴儿，即胎儿脱离母体时(不管怀孕月数)，有过呼吸或其他生命现象。年平均人数指年初、年底人口数的平均数，也可用年中人口数代替。

死亡率(又称粗死亡率) 指在一定时期内(通常为一年)一定地区的死亡人数与同期平均人数(或期中人数)之比，一般用千分率表示。计算公式为：

$$死亡率=\frac{年死亡人数}{年平均人数}\times1000‰$$

人口自然增长率 指在一定时期内(通常为一年)人口自然增加数(出生人数减死亡人数)与该时期内平均人数(或期中人数)之比，一般用千分率表示。计算公式为：

$$人口自然增长率=\frac{(本年出生人数-本年死亡人数)}{年平均人数}\times1000‰=人口出生率-人口死亡率$$

Explanatory Notes on Main Statistical Indicators

Total Population refers to the total number of people alive at a certain point of time within a given area. The annual statistics on total population is taken at midnight, the 3lst of December.

Urban Population and Rural Population. There are two definitions. The first definition (according to the administrative organizational system):

City population: Total population under the jurisdiction of city (including population of the town under the jurisdiction of city. excluding the population of counties under the jurisdiction of city).

Town population: Total population of town under the jurisdiction of county (excluding the population of town under the jurisdiction of city).

County population: Total population of country under the jurisdiction of county).

The second definition (classified by the permanent population):

City population: Total population of districts under the jurisdiction of city with district establishment and the population of street under the jurisdiction of city without district establishment.

Town population: Total resident – committees population of towns under the jurisdiction of city without district establishment and the resident – committees population of towns under the jurisdiction of county.

County population: Total population except city population and town population.

Birth Rate or (Crude Birth Rate) refers to the ratio of the number of births to the average population during a certain period of time (usually a year) which is often expressed in? The following formula is used:

$$\text{Birth Rate} = \frac{\text{Number of Births}}{\text{Average Number of Population}} \times 1000‰$$

Number of births refers to live births i.e. the births when babies had showed any vital phenomena regardless of the length of pregnancy.

Annual Average Number of Population is the average of the number of population at the beginning of the year and that at the end of the year. Sometimes it is substituted for with the mid year population.

Death Rate(or Crude Death Rate) refers to the ratio of the number of deaths to the average population (or mid year population) during a certain period of time (usually a year) which is often expressed in? The following formula is used:

$$\text{Death Rate umber of Deaths} = \frac{\text{Number of Deaths}}{\text{Annual Average Number of Population}} \times 1000‰$$

Natural Growth Rate of Population refers to the ratio of natural increase in population(number of births minus number of deaths)in a certain period of time(usually a year)to the average population(or mid year population)of the same period which is often expressed in? The following formulas are applied:

$$\text{Natural Growth of Population} = \frac{\text{Number of Births} - \text{Number of Deaths}}{\text{Average Number of Population}} \times 1000‰$$

Natural Growth Rate of Population = Birth Rate – Death Rate

4

就业与劳动

Employment and Labor

Four

城镇新就业人数（万人）

Number of Newly Employed Personnels (10000 persons)

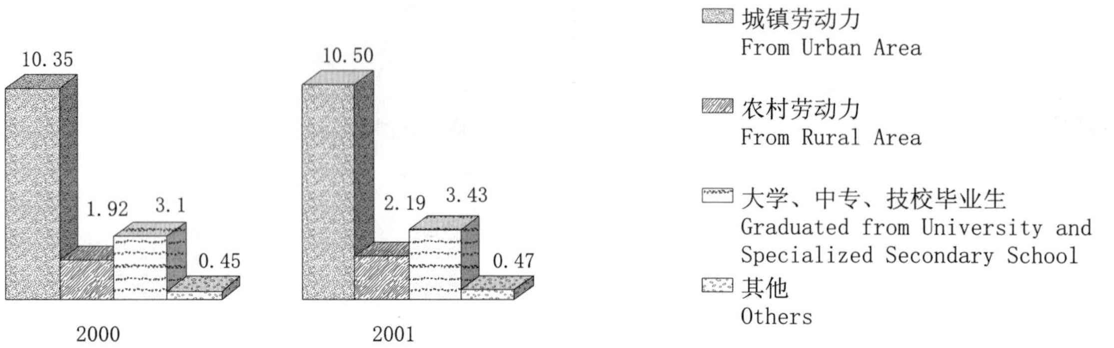

城镇从业人员女职工比重(%)(2001)

Percentage in the Number of Employed Persons in Urban Area of Female Employed Persons (%)

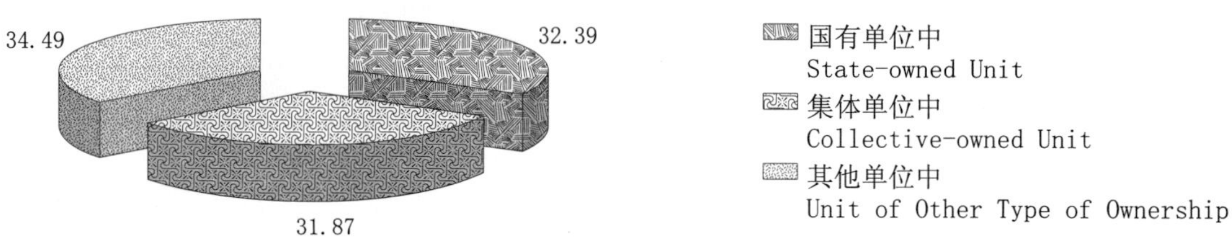

在岗职工人数（万人）

Number of Staff and Workers on Their Posts by Sector(10000 persons)

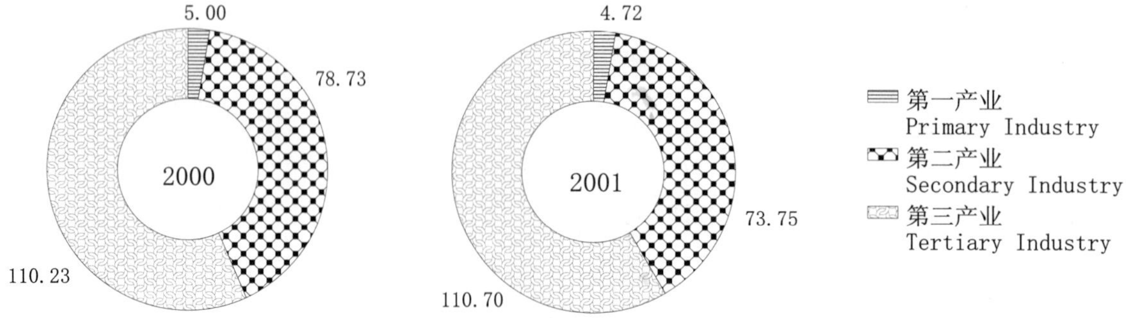

4-1 从业人员及劳动报酬
Number of Employed Personnels and Wages

指　标	Item	2000	2001	2001年比2000年增长(%) Increase Rate in 2001 over 2000(%)
从业人员总计(万人)	**Number of Employed Persons (10000 persons)**	**1866.23**	**2068.01**	
按产业分	Grouped by Type of Industry			
第一产业	Primary Industry	1305.28	1692.33	
第二产业	Secondary Industry	221.79	133.88	
第三产业	Tertiary Industry	339.16	241.80	
职工人数总计(万人)	**Number of Staff and Workers (10000 persons)**	**193.97**	**189.17**	**-2.5**
国有单位	State - owned Unit	153.55	148.87	-3.0
集体单位	Collective - owned Unit	19.01	15.72	-17.3
其他单位	Unit of Other Type of Ownership	21.41	24.58	14.8
职工工资总额(万元)	**Total Wages of Staff and Wokers(10000 yuan)**	**1445619**	**1696490**	**17.4**
国有单位	State - owned Unit	1164147	1381207	18.6
集体单位	Collective - owned Unit	101801	96897	-4.8
其他单位	Unit of Other Type of Ownership	179671	218386	21.5
职工平均工资(元)	**Average Wage of Staff and Workers(yuan)**	**7468**	**8991**	**20.4**
国有单位	State - owned Unit	7594	9308	22.6
集体单位	Collective - owned Unit	5444	6218	14.2
其他单位	Unit of Other Type of Ownership	8325	8831	6.1
城镇登记失业率(%)	**Registered Unemployment Rate in Urban Areas(%)**	**3.8**	**4.0**	**0.2 (百分点)**

注:1.表中职工指“在岗职工”。
2.“2001年从业人员”已根据第五次人口普查结果进行了调整,与往年资料没有可比性。

Note:1.Staff and workers in this table refered to on - post staff and workers figures.
2.Data of employed personnels in 2000 is not comparable with previous year, becuse it was adjusted according to the Fifth National Population Census.

4-2 从业人员及劳动报酬构成
Composition of Employed Personnels and Wages

单位：%
（%）

指 标	Item	2000	2001	2001年比2000年增减百分点 Up(Down) Percentage Points in 2001 over 2000
从业人员总计	Number of Employed Persons	100.0	100.0	
按产业分	Grouped by Type of Industry			
第一产业	Primary Industry	69.9	81.8	
第二产业	Secondary Industry	11.9	6.5	
第三产业	Tertiary Industry	18.2	11.7	
职工人数总计	Number of Staff and Workers			
国有单位	State - owned Unit	79.2	78.7	-0.5
集体单位	Collective - owned Unit	9.8	8.3	-1.5
其他单位	Unit of Other Type of Ownership	11.0	13.0	2.0
职工工资总额	Total Wages of Staff and Wokers			
国有单位	State - owned Unit	80.5	81.4	0.9
集体单位	Collective - owned Unit	7.1	5.7	-1.4
其他单位	Unit of Other Type of Ownership	12.4	12.9	0.5

4-3 城镇新就业人数和失业人数
Number of Incremental Employed and Unemployed

单位:万人
(10000 persons)

指 标	Item	2000	2001	2001年比2000年增长(%) Increase Rate in 2001 over 2000(%)
新就业人数总计	Total of Incremental Employed Personnels	15.82	16.59	4.9
按主要来源分	By Main Source			
城镇劳动力	From Urban Area	10.35	10.50	1.4
农村劳动力	From Rural Area	1.92	2.19	14.1
大学、中专、技校毕业生	Graduated from University and Specialized Secondary School	3.10	3.43	10.6
其他	Others	0.45	0.47	4.4
按安置去向分	By the Direction to Allocate			
国有经济单位	State - owned Unit	6.37	6.12	-3.9
城镇集体经济单位	Collective - owned Unit	2.61	0.85	-67.4
其他经济单位	Unit of Other Type of Ownership	1.69	1.27	-24.9
其他劳动者	Other Labourers	5.15	8.35	62.1
城镇登记失业人数	Number of Registerd Unemployed Persons in Urban Areas	10.24	11.14	8.8
城镇登记失业率(%)	Registerd Unemployment Rate in Urban Areas(%)	3.8	4.0	0.2(百分点)

注:表中资料由省劳动厅提供。

Note: All data of this table offered by Labour Department.

4-4 单位从业人员变动情况(2001)
Changes in the Number of Staff and Workers on Their Posts

单位:人
(person)

指 标	Item	总 计 Total	国有单位 State - owned Unit	集体单位 Collective - owned Unit	其他单位 Unit of Other Type of Ownership
增加人数	Number of Persons Increased	104297	80380	8977	14940
从农村招收	Recruited from Rural Area	29838	21406	4701	3731
从城镇招收	Recruited from Urban Area	9845	6305	1289	2251
录用的复员转业军人	Employment of Demobilized Soldiers	3924	3164	144	616
录用的大、中专、技工学校毕业生	Employment of Gradute from College, Secondary Technical Schools and Workers Training Schools	27408	23025	761	3622
调入人数	Number of Persons Transferred into	21681	19207	459	2015
#省外调入	From Outside Guizhou	1819	1783	11	25
其他	Others	11601	7273	1623	2705
减少人数	Number of Persons Decreased	138957	103119	13055	22783
离休、退休、退职	Retire and Resigned	31105	23769	2336	5000
开除、除名、辞退	Expelled and Discharge	12770	9074	1624	2072
终止、解除合同	Contract Terminated	29980	19052	4136	6792
离开本单位仍保留劳动关系的职工	Remain Labour Ralationship	31176	23405	2987	4784
调出人数	Number of Persons Transferred out	20609	18421	769	1419
#调出省	To Outside Guizhou	864	740	9	115
其他	Others	13317	9398	1203	2716

4-5 城镇单位各行业从业人员数(2001)
Number of Employed in Urban Units by Sector

单位:人
(person)

指　　标	Item	从业人员 Number of Employed	国有单位 State-owned Unit	城镇集体单位 Urban Collective-owned Unit	其他单位 Unit of Other Type of Ownership
总　　计	**Total**	**1994675**	**1579645**	**164336**	**250694**
按企事业、机关分组	**By Enterprises, Institutions and Agencies**				
企业	Enterprises	1155997	747385	158545	250067
事业	Institutions	548133	542035	5471	627
机关	Agencies	290545	290225	320	
按产业分	**By Type of Industry**				
第一产业	Primary Industry	48674	48389	153	132
第二产业	Secondary Industry	776775	454462	108112	214201
第三产业	Tertiary Industry	1169226	1076794	56071	36361
按国民经济行业分组	**By Sector**				
农、林、牧、渔业	Farming, Forestry, Animal Husbandry and Fishery	48674	48389	153	132
采掘业	Mining and Quarrying	89989	56372	623	32994
制造业	Manufacturing	436507	231182	44165	161160
电力、煤气及水的生产和供应业	Production and Supply of Electricity, Gas and Water	54949	51147	704	3098
建筑业	Construction	195330	115761	62620	16949
地质勘探业、水利管理业	Geological Prospecting and Water Conservancy	15542	15508	29	5
交通运输、仓储及邮电通信业	Transportation, Storage, Posts and Telecommunications	97447	90680	2571	4196
批发零售贸易、饮餐业	Wholesale and Retail Trade and Catering Services	149919	105751	28610	15558
#批发业	Wholesale	84860	70240	8958	5662
零售业	Retail	55032	28195	18858	7979
商业经纪与代理业	Commercial Brokerage and Agencies	35	27		8
金融保险业	Banking and Insurance	51073	36169	11020	3884
房地产业	Real Estate	37185	28936	1766	6483
社会服务业	Social Services	50822	38774	6981	5067
#公共服务业	Public Services	24985	22191	2471	323
居民服务业	Residents Services	2771	1146	1107	518
信息、咨询服务业	Information and Consultation Services	1867	1242	88	537
卫生、体育和社会福利业	Health Care, Sports and Social Welfare	87822	86675	1010	137
#卫生	Health Care	85486	84431	963	92
体育	Sports	889	844		45
教育、文化艺术和广播电影电视业	Education, Culture, Art, Radio, Film and Television	359387	357594	1209	584
#教育	Education	341545	340500	510	535
文化艺术业	Culture and Art	10848	10115	699	34
广播电影电视业	Radio, Film and Television	6994	6979		15
科学研究和综合技术服务业	Scientific Research and Polytechnical Services	17911	17335	166	410
国家机关、政党机关和社会团体	Government Agencies, Part Agencies and Social Organizations	285457	285318	139	
其他行业	Others	16661	14054	2570	37

4-6 城镇单位女性从业人员年末人数(2001)
Number of Female Employed in Urban Units at the Year-end by Sector

单位:人
(person)

行业	Sector	女性从业人员数 Number of Female Employed	国有单位 State-owned Unit	集体单位 Collective-owned Unit	其他单位 Unit of Other Type of Ownership
总计	Total	650454	511613	52371	86470
农、林、牧、渔业	Farming, Forestry, Animal Husbandry and Fishery	13886	13786	52	48
采掘业	Mining and Quarrying	19410	12786	161	6463
制造业	Manufacturing	164319	84825	19211	60283
电力、煤气及水的生产和供应业	Production and Supply of Electricity, Gas and Water	17677	16559	236	882
建筑业	Construction	29279	17330	9436	2513
地质勘查业、水利管理业	Geological Prospecting and Water Conservancy	4772	4766	6	
交通运输、仓储及邮电通信业	Transportation, Storage, Posts and Telecommunications	31225	28862	739	1624
批发和零售贸易、餐饮业	Wholesale and Retail Trade and Catering Services	56530	36647	12336	7547
#批发业	Wholesale	29138	23113	3735	2290
零售业	Retail	23890	11689	8122	4079
商业经纪与代理业	Commercial Brokerage and Agencies	17	11		6
金融保险业	Banking and Insurance	21816	15472	4241	2103
房地产业	Real Estate	7447	4807	604	2036
社会服务业	Social Services	24840	19141	3085	2614
#公共服务业	Public Services	11707	10482	1096	129
居民服务业	Residents Services	1261	496	432	333
信息、咨询服务业	Information and Consultation Services	622	419	20	183
卫生、体育和社会福利业	Health Care, Sports and Social Welfare	48269	47590	605	74
#卫生	Health Care	47270	46641	575	54
体育	Sports	309	289		20
教育、文化艺术及广播电影电视业	Education, Culture, Art, Radio, Film and Television	129083	128161	707	215
#教育	Education	121984	121523	267	194
文化艺术业	Culture and Art	4672	4215	440	17
广播电影电视业	Radio, Film and Television	2427	2423		4
科学研究和综合技术服务业	Scientific Research and Polytechnical Services	6186	6107	26	53
国家机关、政党机关和社会团体	Government Agencies, Party Agencies and Social Organizations	72048	72003	45	
其他行业	Others	3667	2771	881	15

4-7 各行业在岗职工人数(2001)
Number of Staff and Workers on Their Posts by Sector

单位:人
(person)

指标	Item	职工人数 Number of Staff and Workers	国有单位 State-owned Unit	集体单位 Collective-owned unit	其他单位 Unit of Other Type of Ownership	#聘用的港澳和外籍人员 Pesonnel of HongKong, Macao and Foreigner
总计	Total	1891671	1488657	157251	245763	112
按企事业、机关分组	**By Enterprises, Institutions and Agencies**					
企业	Enterprises	1083230	686362	151660	245208	86
事业	Institutions	524653	518820	5278	555	26
机关	Agencies	283788	283475	313		
按产业分	**By Type of Industry**					
第一产业	Primary Industry	47185	46900	153	132	
第二产业	Secondary Industry	737453	423982	102247	211224	31
第三产业	Tertiary Industry	1107033	1555844	87690	49344	81
按国民经济行业分组	**By Sector**					
农、林、牧、渔业	Farming, Forestry, Animal Husbandry and Fishery	47185	46900	153	132	
采掘业	Mining and Quarrying	89116	55692	622	32802	
制造业	Manufacturing	427903	226833	42446	158624	31
电力、煤气及水的生产和供应业	Production and Supply of Electricity, Gas and Water	53881	50102	699	3080	
建筑业	Construction	166553	91355	58480	16718	
地质勘探业、水利管理业	Geological Prospecting and Water Conservancy	15208	15174	29	5	
交通运输、仓储及邮电通信业	Transportation, Storage, Posts and Telecommunications	92316	85565	2568	4183	
批发零售贸易、饮餐业	Wholesale and Retail Trade and Catering Services	142230	99214	27999	15017	20
#批发业	Wholesale	78608	64171	8922	5515	
零售业	Retail	53662	27784	18283	7595	20
商业经纪与代理业	Commercial Brokerage and Agencies	35	27		8	
金融保险业	Banking and Insurance	48308	33704	10934	3670	
房地产业	Real Estate	21238	13607	1680	5951	18
社会服务业	Social Services	48578	37193	6617	4768	16
#公共服务业	Public Services	23848	21296	2317	235	
居民服务业	Residents Services	2710	1135	1086	489	15
信息、咨询服务业	Information and Consultation Services	1726	1197	87	442	
卫生、体育和社会福利业	Health Care, Sports and Social Welfare	84166	83035	994	137	
#卫生	Health Care	81858	80819	947	92	
体育	Sports	883	838		45	
教育、文化艺术和广播电影电视业	Education, Culture, Art, Radio, Film and Television	342515	340802	1197	516	26
#教育	Education	324926	323960	499	467	26
文化艺术业	Culture and Art	10697	9965	698	34	
广播电影电视业	Radio, Film and Television	6892	6877		15	
科学研究和综合技术服务业	Scientific Research and Polytechnical Services	17202	16931	144	127	1
国家机关、政党机关和社会团体	Government Agencies, Part Agencies and Social Organizations	278887	278755	132		
其他行业	Others	16385	13795	2557	33	

4－8 各行业职工中专业技术人员数(2001)
Number of Technical Personnel by Sector

单位:人
(person)

指　　标	Item	合计 Total	国有单位 State－owned Unit	集体单位 Collective－owned Unit	其他单位 Unit of Other Type of Ownership
总　　计	**Total**	**585944**	**519478**	**20889**	**45577**
按企事业、机关分组	**By Enterprises, Institutions and Agencies**				
企业	Enterprises	209278	144531	19620	45127
事业	Institutions	341473	339847	1176	450
机关	Agencies	35193	35100	93	
按产业分	**By Type of Industry**				
第一产业	Primary Industry	17152	17100	29	23
第二产业	Secondary Industry	132490	82619	11391	38480
第三产业	Tertiary Industry	436302	419759	9469	7074
按国民经济行业分组	**By Sector**				
农、林、牧、渔业	Farming, Forestry, Animal Husbandry and Fishery	17152	17100	29	23
采掘业	Mining and Quarrying	15493	10734	16	4743
制造业	Manufacturing	78604	43830	3758	31016
电力、煤气及水的生产和供应业	Production and Supply of Electricity, Gas and Water	12055	11296	101	658
建筑业	Construction	26338	16759	7516	2063
地质勘探业、水利管理业	Geological Prospecting and Water Conservancy	4985	4970	15	
交通运输、仓储及邮电通信业	Transportation, Storage, Posts and Telecommunications	13965	12924	296	745
批发零售贸易、饮餐业	Wholesale and Retail Trade and Catering Services	18079	13937	2416	1726
#批发业	Wholesale	12641	10519	1007	1115
零售业	Retail	4657	2763	1376	518
商业经纪与代理业	Commercial Brokerage and Agencies	3	3		
金融保险业	Banking and Insurance	25354	20002	4602	750
房地产业	Real Estate	9076	6622	486	1968
社会服务业	Social Services	5892	4211	375	1306
#公共服务业	Public Services	1888	1598	129	161
居民服务业	Residents Services	314	124	101	89
信息、咨询服务业	Information and Consultation Services	756	455	22	279
卫生、体育和社会福利业	Health Care, Sports and Social Welfare	62095	61373	642	80
#卫生	Health Care	61643	60936	642	65
体育	Sports	227	212		15
教育、文化艺术和广播电影电视业	Education, Culture, Art, Radio, Film and Television	250890	250203	270	417
#教育	Education	243469	242794	260	415
文化艺术业	Culture and Art	5012	5000	10	2
广播电影电视业	Radio, Film and Television	2409	2409		
科学研究和综合技术服务业	Scientific Research and Polytechnical Services	10915	10762	84	69
国家机关、政党机关和社会团体	Government Agencies, Part Agencies and Social Organizations	32009	31986	23	
其他行业	Others	3042	2769	260	13

4-9 在岗职工工资总额(2001)
Total Wages of Staff and Workers on Their Posts

单位:万元
(10000 yuan)

指标	Item	合计 Total	国有单位 State-owned Unit	集体单位 Collective-owned Unit	其他单位 Unit of Other Type of Ownership
总计	**Total**	**1696490**	**1381207**	**96897**	**218386**
按企事业、机关分组	**By Enterprises, Institutions and Agencies**				
企业	Enterprises	957039	645821	93361	217857
事业	Institutions	479892	476088	3275	529
机关	Agencies	259559	259298	261	
按产业分	**By Type of Industry**				
第一产业	Primary Industry	34723	34550	92	81
第二产业	Secondary Industry	654454	406610	62116	185728
第三产业	Tertiary Industry	1007313	940047	34689	32576
按国民经济行业分组	**By Sector**				
农、林、牧、渔业	Farming, Forestry, Animal Husbandry and Fishery	34723	34550	92	81
采掘业	Mining and Quarrying	76577	49673	355	26549
制造业	Manufacturing	369457	201834	26776	140847
电力、煤气及水的生产和供应业	Production and Supply of Electricity, Gas and Water	82398	77824	414	4160
建筑业	Construction	126023	77280	34570	14173
地质勘探业、水利管理业	Geological Prospecting and Water Conservancy	12763	12741	17	5
交通运输、仓储及邮电通信业	Transportation, Storage, Posts and Telecommunications	106811	100191	1558	5062
批发零售贸易、饮餐业	Wholesale and Retail Trade and Catering Services	82200	56811	14030	11359
#批发业	Wholesale	51590	42542	4698	4350
零售业	Retail	27417	12977	8786	5654
商业经纪与代理业	Commercial Brokerage and Agencies	19	14		5
金融保险业	Banking and Insurance	58600	42987	10148	5466
房地产业	Real Estate	17214	11127	1395	4692
社会服务业	Social Services	40575	30952	4374	5250
#公共服务业	Public Services	20427	18446	1457	524
居民服务业	Residents Services	2213	935	909	369
信息、咨询服务业	Information and Consultation Services	1805	1178	63	564
卫生、体育和社会福利业	Health Care, Sports and Social Welfare	83493	82649	724	120
#卫生	Health Care	81181	80402	699	80
体育	Sports	957	957		
教育、文化艺术和广播电影电视业	Education, Culture, Art, Radio, Film and Television	312632	311328	846	459
#教育	Education	296836	295921	504	411
文化艺术业	Culture and Art	9824	9441	342	41
广播电影电视业	Radio, Film and Television	5973	5966		7
科学研究和综合技术服务业	Scientific Research and Polytechnical Services	22406	22176	120	110
国家机关、政党机关和社会团体	Government Agencies, Part Agencies and Social Organizations	256547	256447	100	
其他行业	Others	14072	12639	1377	56

4－10 各行业在岗职工平均工资(2001)
Average Wages of Staff and Workers on Their Posts by Sector

单位:元
(yuan)

指　　标	Item	全省 Total	国有单位 State－owned Unit	集体单位 Collective－owned Unit	其他单位 Unit of Other Type of Ownership
总　　计	Total	8991	9308	6218	8831
按企事业、机关分组	By Enterprises, Institutions and Agencies				
企业	Enterprises	8803	9359	6209	8829
事业	Institutions	9264	9293	6354	9578
机关	Agencies	9212	9212	8649	
按产业分	By Type of Industry				
第一产业	Primary Industry	7530	7539	6013	6152
第二产业	Secondary Industry	8827	9510	6177	8709
第三产业	Tertiary Industry	9162	9304	6295	9606
按国民经济行业分组	By Sector				
农、林、牧、渔业	Farming, Forestry, Animal Husbandry and Fishery	7530	7539	6013	6152
采掘业	Mining and Quarrying	8490	8752	5960	8084
制造业	Manufacturing	8541	8869	6320	8660
电力、煤气及水的生产和供应业	Production and Supply of Electricity, Gas and Water	14385	14529	5978	13760
建筑业	Construction	7811	8617	6075	9610
地质勘探业、水利管理业	Geological Prospecting and Water Conservancy	8345	8347	7208	9000
交通运输、仓储及邮电通信业	Transportation, Storage, Posts and Telecommunications	11581	11708	6135	12295
批发零售贸易、饮餐业	Wholesale and Retail Trade and Catering Services	5782	5741	4960	7612
#批发业	Wholesale	6552	6648	5219	7564
零售业	Retail	5115	4674	4741	7743
商业经纪与代理业	Commercial Brokerage and Agencies	5429	5037		5625
金融保险业	Banking and Insurance	12122	12710	9325	15028
房地产业	Real Estate	7719	7585	7086	8284
社会服务业	Social Services	8556	8594	6582	11029
#公共服务业	Public Services	8835	8966	6295	22380
居民服务业	Residents Services	8091	8051	8346	7608
信息、咨询服务业	Information and Consultation Services	10421	9788	7159	12789
卫生、体育和社会福利业	Health Care, Sports and Social Welfare	9990	10025	7322	8511
#卫生	Health Care	9986	10017	7427	8813
体育	Sports	10826	11470		7960
教育、文化艺术和广播电影电视业	Education, Culture, Art, Radio, Film and Television	9248	9256	7151	8940
#教育	Education	9259	9258	10284	8843
文化艺术业	Culture and Art	9224	9512	4937	12303
广播电影电视业	Radio, Film and Television	8768	8777		4533
科学研究和综合技术服务业	Scientific Research and Polytechnical Services	13100	13153	10118	8855
国家机关、政党机关和社会团体	Government Agencies, Part Agencies and Social Organizations	9261	9262	7299	
其他行业	Others	8825	9304	5909	17968

4-11 城乡私营企业户数和从业人员数(2001)

Number of Enterprises and Employed Persons in Urban and Rural Private Enterprises by Sector

单位:人
(person)

指标	Item	户数(户) Number of Enterprises (unit)	城镇 Urban Areas	乡村 Rural Areas	从业人员 Number of Employed Persons	城镇 Urban Areas	乡村 Rural Areas
总计	Total	22248	14617	7631	283133	169736	113397
按国民经济行业分组	By Sector						
农、林、牧、渔业	Farming, Forestry, Animal Husbandry and Fishery	932	458	474	12167	5542	6625
#农、林、牧、渔服务业	FFAF Services	73	40	33	873	486	387
采掘业	Mining and Quarrying	874	210	664	18279	3003	15276
制造业	Manufacturing	5591	3427	2164	93460	50995	42465
建筑业	Construction	879	564	315	16006	10709	5297
交通运输、仓储业	Transportation, Storage, Post and Telecommunications	289	207	82	5469	3742	1727
#交通运输业	Transportation	158	104	54	3211	1745	1466
批发零售贸易、餐饮业	Wholesale and Retail Trade and Catering Services	9250	6696	2554	90609	62821	27788
#批发零售贸易业	Wholesale and Retail	7503	5297	2206	72041	48330	23711
社会服务业	Social Services	2880	1952	928	29044	19613	9431
#日用品修理业	Repair of Article of Daily Use	49	35	14	427	304	123
旅馆业	Hotels	98	64	34	1359	991	368
娱乐服务业	Recreation	179	135	44	2083	1630	453
其他行业	Others	1553	1103	450	18099	13311	4788
按三次产业分	By Type of Industry						
第一产业	Primary Industry	932	458	474	12167	5542	6625
第二产业	Secondary Industry	7344	4201	3143	127745	64707	63038
第三产业	Tertiary Industry	13972	9958	4014	143221	99487	43734

注:本表资料来源于省工商局。(下表同)

Note: Data in this table are obtained from the Industry and Commerce Department. (same to next)

4-12 城乡个体工商业户数和从业人员数(2001)

Number of Household and Employed of Self-Employed Individuals in Urban and Rural Areas by Sector

单位:人
(person)

指　　标	Item	户数(户) Number of Enterprises (unit)	城镇 Urban Areas	乡村 Rural Areas	从业人员 Number of Employed Persons	城镇 Urban Areas
总　　计	**Total**	**394124**	**191826**	**202298**	**579231**	**303032**
按国民经济行业分组	**By Sector**					
农、林、牧、渔业	Farming, Forestry, Animanl Husbandry and Fishery	4302	435	3867	7686	825
#农、林、牧、渔业服务	FFAF Services	361	113	248	548	169
采掘业	Mining and Quarying	1088	201	887	3899	948
制造业	Manufacturing	41200	17777	23423	68199	30950
建筑业	Construction	648	461	217	1508	979
交通运输、仓储业	Transportation, Storage, Posts and Telecommunications	31389	17216	14173	41724	23710
#交通运输业	Transportation	30773	16700	14073	40783	22787
批发零售贸易、餐饮业	Wholesale and Retail Trade and Catering Services	262837	125040	137797	373621	19016
#批发零售贸易业	Wholesale and Retail	194272	85083	109189	265000	126325
社会服务业	Social Services	49005	28990	20015	76307	47122
#日用品修理业	Repair of Article of Daily Use	11063	4752	6311	15093	7258
旅馆业	Hotels	3566	1960	1606	6680	3660
娱乐服务业	Recreation	3989	2326	1663	6879	4342
其他行业	Others	3655	1736	1919	6287	3282
按三次产业分	**By Type of Industry**					
第一产业	Primary Industry	4302	435	3867	7686	825
第二产业	Secondary Industry	42936	18409	24527	73606	32877
第三产业	Tertiary Industry	346886	172982	173904	497939	269330

4－13 职业介绍机构情况
Basic Conditions of Employment Service

指　　标	Item	2000	2001	2001年比2000年增长(%) Increase Rate in 2001 over 2000(%)
年末职业介绍机构(个)	Number of Labour Exchanges at the Year－end(unit)	1151	735	－36.1
#劳动保障部门办	Run by Labour Department	627	677	8.0
其他组织办	Run by Other Organs	442	15	－96.6
公民个人办	Run by Private	82	43	－47.6
本年末职业介绍机构人数(人)	Number of Staff and Workers of Labour Exchanges at the Year－end(person)	1911	1637	－14.3
#劳动保障部门办	Run by Labour Department	1408	1425	1.2
其他组织办	Run by Other Organs	185	46	－75.1
公民个人办	Run by Private	318	166	－47.8
本年登记招聘人数(人)	Number of Registered Invite Application in 2001(person)	118896	142045	19.5
本年登记求职人次数(人次)	Number of Registered Job Seeking in 2001(person－time)	137762	156795	13.8
#下岗职工	Laid－off Workers	21889	16209	－25.9
失业人员	Former Unemployed	69707	79383	13.9
获得职业资格人员	Person with Certificates	9999	12900	29.0
本年介绍成功人次数(人)	Number of Persons Actually Employed(person)	88971	89065	0.1
#下岗职工	Laid－off Workers	10055	6893	－31.4
失业人员	Former Unemployed	47655	43933	－7.8
获得职业资格人员	Person with Certificates	5491	8225	49.8

资料来源：省劳动厅。

Note: Data in this table are obtained from Labour Department.

4-14 企业下岗职工情况(2001)
Basic Conditions of Laid-off Workers of Enterprises

单位:人
(person)

指标	Item	下岗职工 Number of Laid-off Workers	#当年新增 Newly Increased in 2001	实现再就业 Number of Renew Employed	再就业率(%) Renew Employment Rate(%)
总计	Total	107691	10766	17679	16.4
国有(国有联营)企业、国有独资公司	State-owned(Joint Ownership) Enterprise and State-owned Corporation	91238	9980	17679	19.4
#国有企业	State-owned Enterprises	91228	9980	17526	19.2
#亏损企业	Loss-making Enterprise	74899	5769	15805	21.1
按隶属关系分	Grouped by Administrative Relationship				
中央企业	Central Enterprises	20549	1637	3879	18.9
地方企业	Local Enterprises	70689	8343	13800	19.5
省属企业	Province-owned Enterprises	29671	4093	1970	6.6
地区企业	County-owned Enterprises	19861	1062	6167	31.1
县及县以下	At and Below County	21157	3188	5663	26.8
按国民经济行业分	Grouped by Sector				
采掘业	Mining and Quarrying	6596	28	118	1.8
制造业	Manufacturing	59659	7091	11405	19.1
交通运输、仓储及邮电通讯业	Transportation, Posts and Telecommunications	2868		1048	36.5
电力煤气及水的生产供应业	Production and Supply of Electricity, Gas and Water	382		118	30.9
建筑业	Construction	11042	361	2118	19.2
批发零售贸易餐饮业	Wholesale and Retail Trade and Catering Services	6518	1554	1851	28.4
其他	Others	4173	946	1021	24.5
城镇集体企业	Urban Collective-owned Enterprises	15390	175		
其他企业	Enterprises of Other Type of Ownership	1063	611		

资料来源:省劳动厅。

Note: Data in this table are obtained from labour Department.

4－15 社会服务及设施和民政事业发展主要指标
Major Indicators of Social Work & Establishment and Civil Administration Career Development

指标	Item	2000	2001	2001年比2000年增长(%) Increase Rate in 2001 over 2000(%)
城镇社区服务设施数(个)	Number of Urban Welfare Facilities(unit)	3450	3529	2.3
#社区服务单位数(个)	Number of Community Services(unit)	45	39	－13.3
城镇便民利民服务网点(个)	Number of Urban Service Points for Civilian(unit)	8179	8163	－0.2
农村社会保障网络数(个)	Rural Social Security Network(unit)	20	28	40
农村社会保障网络覆盖率(%)	Coverage Rate of Rural Social Security Network(%)	1.4	1.9	0.5(百分点)
乡镇敬老院覆盖率(%)	Coverage Rate of Villages and Town Elderly Welfare Homes(%)	61.8	56.6	－5.2(百分点)
城乡各类福利院床位数(张)	Number of Beds of Welfare Home in Urban & Rural Area(unit)	16686	15546	－6.8
城乡各类福利院床位利用率(%)	Using Rate of Bed	59.6	60.6	1.0(百分点)
复员军人定补率(%)	Subsidly Rate of Exsevicemen(%)	94.5	98.0	3.5(百分点)
享受城镇低保人数(人)	Number of Persons Receiving Lowest Cost of living in Urban Area(person)	51798	306931	492.6
城镇低保生活保障支出(万元)	Expenditure of Lowest Cost－of living in Urban Area(10000 yuan)	2147.2	7540.1	251.2

4－16 享受国家定期抚恤、补助、救济人员数
Persons Enjoying Regular Subsidy and Commiseration of Country

单位：人
(person)

指标	Item	2000	2001	2001年比2000年增长(%) Increase Rate in 2001 over 2000(%)
合计	**Total**	104666	105012	0.3
伤残抚恤人数	**Number of Persons Receiving Disability Commiseration**	15396	14906	－3.2
在职人员	Persons of Incumbency	9335	9405	0.7
在乡人员	Persons of Rural	6061	5501	－9.2
“三属”抚恤人数	**Number of Persons Comfort and Compensate a Bereaved Family**	6105	5614	－8.0
烈士家属	Family Numbers of Martyr	3952	3536	－10.5
牺牲、病故军人家属	Family Numbers of Immolate & Die of Illness Armyman	2153	2078	－3.5
复退军人定补人数	**Number of Subsidies for Exsevicemen**	83165	84492	1.6

4－17 社会福利单位和工作人员情况
Number of Social Welfare Institutions and Enterprises and Persons Engaged

项　　目	Item	机构数(个) Number of Institutions or Enterprises(unit)		工作人员(人) Number of Persons Engaged(person)	
		2000	2001	2000	2001
总　　计	**Total**	**1310**	**1252**	**9617**	**11092**
收养性福利单位	**Adopting Social Welfare Institutions**	**965**	**887**	**2369**	**2334**
国家办	Run by Government	61	65	1214	1224
集体和民办	Run by Communities and Privates	904	822	1155	1110
社会福利企业	**Social Welfare Enterprises**	**201**	**226**	**4415**	**6156**
国　有	Run by Government	19	22	986	1037
集体和其他	Run by Communities and Others	182	204	3429	5119
优抚事业单位	Administration Agencies for Martyrs	40	40	385	375
收容遣送单位	Collecting and Repatriation Units	20	20	1088	923
殡仪服务单位	Funeral and Interment Institutions	36	37	977	861
彩票发行单位	Collecting Purse Units	3	3	21	38
社区服务单位	Community Service Institutions	45	39	362	405

4－18 社会福利救济主要支出情况
Basic Statistics on Social Welfare Relief Funds

单位：万元
(10000 yuan)

指　　标	Item	2000	2001	2001年比2000年增长(%) Increase Rate in 2001 over 2000(%)
总　　计	**Total**	**25590.9**	**31158.0**	**21.8**
优抚对象补助金额	**Funds for Family Members of Martyrs and Disabled Veterans**	**12089.7**	**12892.4**	**6.6**
国家支出	Government Funds	8103.3	9067.6	11.9
集体供给	Collective Funds	3986.4	3824.8	－4.1
传统救济对象的救济金额	**Funds for Family Members of Traditional Relief**	**6110.5**	**5043.8**	**－17.5**
国家支出	Government Funds	467.9	632.5	35.2
集体供给	Collective Funds	5642.6	4411.3	－21.8
最低生活保障支出	**Expenditure for Persons Receiving Lowest Cost－of－living**	**2808.1**	**8322.7**	**196.4**
城镇	For Urban Area	2147.2	7540.1	251.2
农村	For Rural Area	660.9	782.6	18.4
收养性社会福利单位支出	**Adopting Social Welfare Institution**	**4582.6**	**4899.1**	**6.9**
国家支出	Government Funds	3827.8	4145.6	8.3
集体供给	Collective Funds	754.8	753.5	－0.2

4－19 享受补助、救济人员情况
Persons Receiving Subsidies or Relief Funds

单位：人
(person)

指　　标	Item	2000	2001	2001 年比 2000 年增长(%) Increase Rate in 2001 over 2000(%)
城乡居民最低生活保障人数	Number of Persons Receiving Lowest Cost－of－living in Urban Area and Rural Area	120283	354658	194.9
城镇	Number of Persons Receiving Lowest Cost－of－living in Urban Area	51798	306931	492.6
农村	Number of Persons Receiving Lowest Cost－of－living in Rural Area	68485	47727	－30.3
传统救济情况	Traditional Relief	72956	67831	－7.0
国家定期定量救济人数	Number of Persons Receiving Periodical and Fixed Government Relief Funds	9085	9860	8.9
居家集体供养人数	Number of Persons Receiving Collective Funds	63898	57971	－9.3
收养性福利单位收养三无对象人数	Number of Persons Adopted by Adopting Social Welfare Institutions	9349	8656	－7.4
精减退职老弱残职工得到救济人数	Number of Laid－off, Retired, Elderly and Disabled Staff and Workers Receiving Relief Funds	21969	21760	－1.0
享受原工资 40%救济人数	Persons Receiving 40% of Their Original Wages	8253	8112	－1.7
享受定期定量救济人数	Persons Receiving Periodical and Fixed Government Relief Funds	13716	13648	－0.5

主要统计指标解释

经济活动人口 指在16岁以上,有劳动能力,参加或要求参加社会经济活动的人口;包括从业人员和失业人员。

从业人员 指从事一定社会劳动并取得劳动报酬或经营收入的人员,包括全部职工、再就业的离退休人员、私营业主、个体户主、私营和个体从业人员、乡镇企业从业人员、农村从业人员、其他从业人员(包括民办教师、宗教职业者、现役军人等)。这一指标反映了一定时期内全部劳动力资源的实际利用情况,是研究我国基本国情国力的重要指标。

各单位的从业人员 指在各级国家机关、政党机关、社会团体及企业、事业单位中工作,取得工资或其他形式的劳动报酬的全部人员。包括在岗职工、再就业的离退休人员、民办教师以及在各单位中工作的外方人员和港澳台方人员、兼职人员、借用的外单位人员和第二职业者。不包括离开本单位仍保留劳动关系的职工。各单位的从业人员反映了各单位实际参加生产或工作的全部劳动力。

城镇私营和个体从业人员 城镇私营从业人员指在工商管理部门注册登记,其经营地址设在县城关镇(含城关镇)以上的私营企业从业人员;包括私营企业投资者和雇工。城镇个体从业人员指在工商管理部门注册登记,并持有城镇户口或在城镇长期居住,经批准从事个体工商经营的从业人员;包括个体经营者和在个体工商户劳动的家庭帮工和雇工。

城镇登记失业人员 指有非农业户口,在一定的劳动年龄内,有劳动能力,无业而要求就业,并在当地就业服务机构进行求职登记的人员。

城镇登记失业率 指城镇登记失业人数同城镇从业人数与城镇登记失业人数之和的比。计算公式为:

$$城镇登记失业率=\frac{城镇登记失业人数}{城镇从业人数+城镇登记失业人数}\times 100\%$$

职工 指在国有经济、城镇集体经济、联营经济、股份制经济、外商和港、澳、台投资经济、其他经济单位及其附属机构工作,并由其支付工资的各类人员,不包括返聘的离退休人员、民办教师、在国有经济单位工作的外方人员和港、澳、台人员(1998年以后的数据均为在岗职工数据,其他相关指标如职工工资总额,职工平均工资等指标也从1998年按此口径进行了相应调整)。

国有单位职工 指在国有经济单位及其附属机构工作,并由其支付工资的各类人员。

城镇集体单位职工 指在城镇集体经济单位及其管理部门工作,并由其支付工资的各类人员。

其他单位职工 指在联营经济、股份制经济、外商投资经济、港、澳、台投资经济单位工作,并由其支付工资的各类人员。

在岗职工 指在本单位工作并由单位支付工资的人员,以及有工作岗位,但由于学习、病伤产假等原因暂未工作,仍由单位支付工资的人员。

职工工资总额 指各单位在一定时期内直接支付给本单位全部职工的劳动报酬总额。工资总额的计算原则应以直接支付给职工的全部劳动报酬为根据。各单位支付给职工的劳动报酬以及其他根据有关规定支付的工资,不论是计入成本的还是不计入成本的,不论是按国家规定列入计征奖金税项目的,还是未列入计征奖金税项目的,不论是以货币形式支付的还是以实物形式支付的,均包括在工资总额内。

职工平均工资 指企业、事业、机关单位的职工在一定时期内平均每人所得的货币工资额。

它表明一定时期职工工资收入的高低程度,是反映职工工资水平的主要指标。计算公式为:

$$职工平均工资=\frac{报告期实际支付的全部职工工资总额}{报告期全部职工平均人数}$$

职工平均工资指数 指报告期职工平均工资与基期职工平均工资的比率,是反映不同时期职工货币工资水平变动情况的相对数。计算公式为:

$$职工平均工资指数=\frac{报告期职工平均工资}{基期职工平均工资}$$

职工平均实际工资指数 职工平均实际工资指扣除物价变动因素后的职工平均工资。职工平均实际工资指数是反映实际工资变动情况的相对数,表明职工实际工资水平提高或降低的程度。计算公式为:

$$职工平均实际工资指数=\frac{报告期职工平均工资指数}{报告期城镇居民消费价格指数}\times 100\%$$

Explanatory Notes on Main Statistical Indicators

Economically Active Population refers to the population aged 16 and over who are capable to work, are participating in or willing to participate in economic activities, including employed persons and unemployed persons.

Employed Persons refers to the persons who are engaged in social labour and receive remuneration payment or earn business income, including: total staff and workers, re – employed retirees, employers of private enterprises, employers of individual economy, employed persons in private enterprises and individual economy, employed persons in the enterprises in the urban areas, employed persons in the rural areas, other employed persons (including teachers in the schools run by the local people, people engaged in religious profession and active army, etc.)

This indicator reflects the actual utilization of total labour force during a certain period of time and is often used for the research on China's economic affairs and national power.

Persons Employed in Various Units refer to all the persons working in government agencies of various levels, political and party organizations, social organizations, enterprises and institutions, and receiving wages or other forms of payment. They include fully – employed staff and workers, re – employed retirees, teachers in schools run by the local people, foreigners and Chinese compatriots from Hong Kong, Macao, and Taiwan working in various units, part – time employees, employees of other units working temporarily at current posts, and employees holding the second job, but exclude staff and workers who have left their working units while keeping their labour contract (employment relation) unchanged. This indicator reflects the total number of laborers actually engaged in production or other operations in various units.

Persons Employed in Private Enterprises and Self – Employed Individuals in Urban Areas Persons employed in private enterprises refer to the persons employed in the private enterprises which have been registered at the departments of industrial and commercial administration and are situated at a county town (i.e. a town where the county government is located) for business operation or at urban areas with the level higher than a county town. The self – employed individuals in urban areas refer to persons who hold the certificates of residence in urban areas or have resided in the urban areas for a long time and have been registered at the departments of industrial and commercial administration and approved to be engaged in individual industrial or commercial business, including self – employed persons as well as helpers and hired labourers who work in the individual households engaged in industrial or commercial business.

Registered Urban Unemployed Persons The registered unemployed persons in urban areas refer to the persons who are registered as permanent residents in the urban areas engaged in non – agricultural activities, aged within the range of working age, capable to labour, unemployed but desirous to be employed and have been registered at the local employment service agencies to apply for a job.

Registered Urban Unemployment Rate Registered unemployment rate in urban areas refers to the ratio of the number of the registered unemployed persons to the sum of the number of employed persons and the registered unemployed persons. The formula is as follows:

$$\text{Registered urban unemployment rate} = \frac{\text{number of registered urban unemployed persons}}{\text{number of urban employed persons} + \text{number of registered urban unemployed persons}} \times 100\%$$

Staff and Workers refer to the persons who work in (and receive payment therefrom) enterprises and institutions of state ownership, collective ownership, joint ownership, share holding, foreign ownership, and ownership by entrepreneurs from Hong Kong, Macao, and Taiwan, and other types of ownership and their affiliated units, excluding the retired persons invited to work in the units again, teachers in the schools run by the local people and foreigners and persons coming from Hong Kong, Macao and Taiwan and working in the state – owned economic units.

(Number of staff and workers in this yearbook include only fully employed staff and workers, excluding those who have left their working units while keeping their labour contract/employment relation unchanged).

Staff and Workers in State – owned Economic Units refer to the persons who work in the state – owned economic units or their attached units and are listed in their payrolls.

Staff and Workers of Collective Owned Units in Urban Areas refer to the persons who work in collective owned units in urban areas and their administration departments and receive payment therefrom.

Staff and Workers in Units of Other Types of Ownership refer to those who work in (and receive payment therefrom) enterprises and institutions of joint ownership, share holding, foreign ownership, and ownership by entrepreneurs from Hong Kong, Macao, and Taiwan.

Fully Employed Staff and Workers refer to persons who work in, and receive wages from their working units, as well as persons who have their work posts, but are temporarily absent from work for reasons of study or on sick, injury or maternal leave and still receive wages from their working units.

Total Wages of Staff and Workers refer to the total remuneration payment to staff and workers in various units during a certain period of time. The calculation of total wages is based on the total remuneration payment to the staff and workers. Therefore, all the wages and salaries and other payments to staff and workers are included in the total wages regardless of their sources, category, and forms (in kind or cash).

Average Wage of Staff and Workers refers to the average wage in money terms per person during a certain period of time for staff and workers in enterprises, institutions, and government agencies, which reflects the general level of wage income during a certain period of time and is calculated as follows:

Average Wage of Staff and Workers = Total Wages of Staff and Workers in Reference Period/Average Number of Staff and Workers in Reference Period

Index of Average Wage of Staff and Worker refers to the ratio of average wage of staff and workers at the report time to that at the reference time. It reflects the relative changing degree of average wage in money terms at the various of time, which is calculated as following:

$$\text{Index of Average Wage of Staff and Worker} = \frac{\text{average wage of staff and workers at the report time}}{\text{average wage of staff and workers at the reference time}}$$

Index of Average Real Wage of Staff and Worker refers to the average wage which has removed the factor of price change. Index of average real wage of staff and worker reflects the relative changing degree of average real wage, and indicates the degree of the rising or declining degree of real wage of staff and worker, which is calculated as following:

$$\text{Index of Average Real Wage of Staff and Worker} = \frac{\text{Index of Average Wage of Staff and Worker at the Report Time}}{\text{Urban Consumer Prices Index at the Report Time}} \times 100\%.$$

5

Five

固定资产投资

Investment in Fixed Assets

全社会固定资产投资（亿元）(2001)

Total Investment in Fixed Assets (100 million yuan)

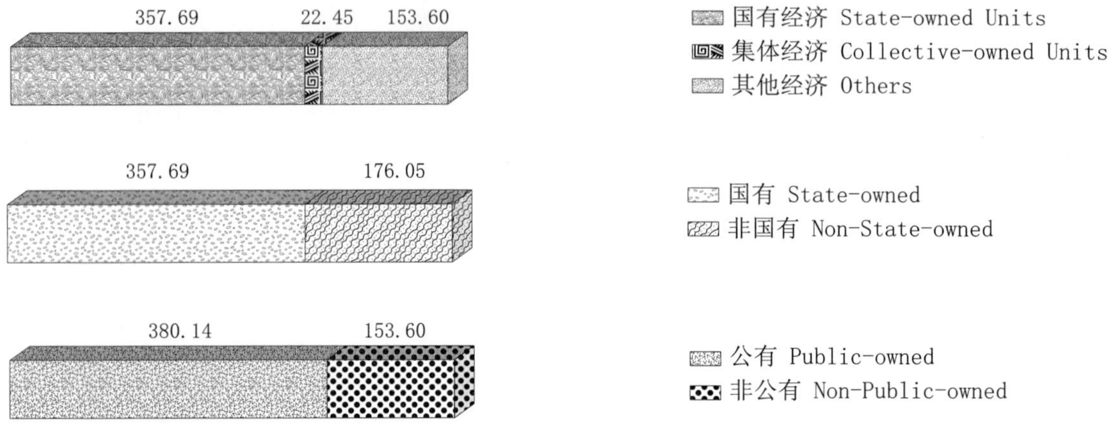

按管理渠道分的全社会固定资产投资（亿元）(2001)

Total Investment in Fixed Assets Grouped by Management (100 million yuan)

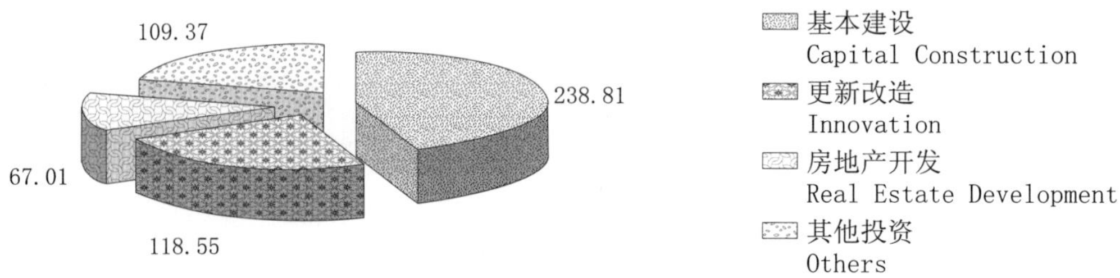

商品房屋竣工、销售面积（万平方米）(2001)

Completed and Sold Space of Commercial Houses (10000 sq.m)

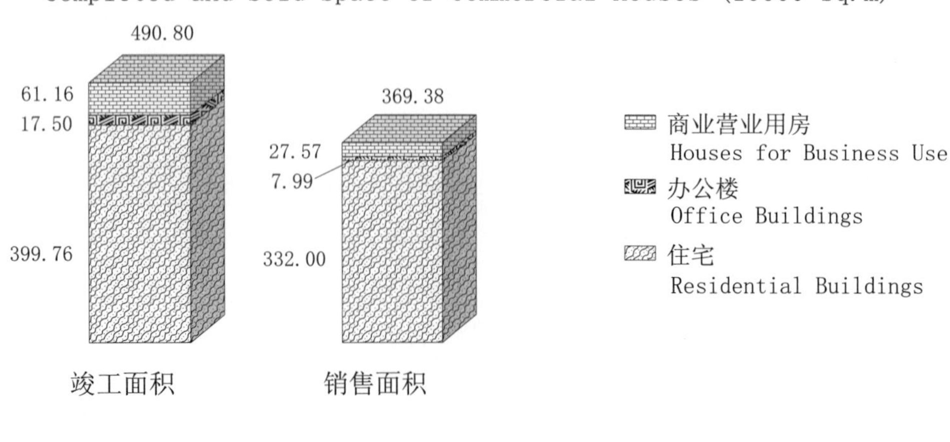

5-1 全社会固定资产投资(2001)
Total Investment in Fixed Assets

单位:亿元
(100 million yuan)

指　　标	Item	绝对数	2001年比2000年增长(%) Increase Rate in 2001 over 2000(%)
全社会固定资产投资	**Total Investment in Fixed Assets**	**533.74**	**19.3**
按隶属关系分:	**Grouped by Administrative Relationship**		
中央	Central	127.54	14.4
地方	Local	406.20	20.9
按经济类型分:	**Grouped by Ownership**		
国有经济	State - owned Units	357.69	17.3
集体经济	Collective - owned Units	22.45	-21.1
其他经济	Others	153.60	34.6
按管理渠道分:	**Grouped by Channel of Management**		
基本建设	Capital Construction	238.81	21.3
更新改造	Innovation	118.55	26.7
房地产开发	Real Estate Development	67.01	43.9
其他投资	Others	109.37	-1.0
1.50万元以上投资额	**Investment over 500000 yuan**	**446.45**	**25.2**
基本建设	Capital Construction	235.53	22.0
更新改造	Innovation	117.37	25.8
房地产投资	Real Estate Development	67.01	43.9
其他投资	Others	26.54	12.0
按经济类型分:	Grouped by Ownership		
国有经济	State - owned Units	352.98	20.6
集体经济	Collective - owned Units	7.61	-4.3
私营经济	Personal Economy Units	27.55	58.2

5-1 续表(continued)

单位:亿元 (100 million yuan)

指　标	Item	绝对数	2001 年比 2000 年增长(%) Increase Rate in 2001 over 2000(%)
个体经济	Individuals	0.31	-81.1
股份制经济	Share Holding Economic Units	38.32	110.3
外商投资	Foreign Funded Economic Units	4.09	25.8
港澳台投资	Economic Units Funded by Entrepreneurs from Hong Kong, Macao and Taiwan	3.47	19.7
其他	Others	12.12	-2.8
按主要行业分:	Grouped by Main Sector		
#农林牧渔业	Farming, Forestry, Animal Husbandry and Fishery	2.46	-33.5
工业	Industry	165.04	34.5
#电力、煤气及水的生产供应业	Production and Supply of Electric Power, Gas and Water	96.64	32.9
邮电通信业	Postal and Telecommunications Services	40.70	82.9
交通运输业	Transportation	94.53	-8.7
按三次产业分:	Grouped by Type of Industry		
第一产业	Primary Industry	1.99	-42.3
第二产业	Secondary Industry	165.96	33.2
第三产业	Tertiary Industry	278.50	21.9
2.5万元以上-50万元以下投资额	**Investment between 50000 yuan and 500000 yuan**	**6.35**	**32.0**
3.农村集体投资	**Investment in Fixed Assets of Collective-owned Units in Rural**	**14.75**	**-27.6**
4.城乡个人投资	**Individual Investment in Fixed Assets in Urban & Rural**	**66.19**	**14.6**
#城镇工矿区私人投资	Individuals Investment in Fixed Assets and Building Construction in Cities, Towns, Industrial and Mining Areas	7.98	1.7
农村私人投资	Individual Investment in Fixed Assets in Rural	58.21	16.7

注:50万元以上是指基本建设.更新改造和其他投资。

Note: The data on investment beyond 500000 yuan and more refer to the data of capital construction, innovation and other investment.

5-2 固定资产投资资金来源(2001)
Total Investment in Fixed Assets by Source of Finance

单位:亿元
(100 million yuan)

指　　标	Item	绝对数	2001年比2000年增长(%) Increase Rate in 2001 over 2000(%)
总　　计	**Total**	**496.84**	**20.4**
#国家预算内资金	State Budgetary Appropriation	32.35	-21.3
国内贷款	Domestic Loans	161.61	14.9
利用外资	Utilization of Foreign Capital	6.11	-34.9
#外商直接投资	Direct Foreign Investments	1.88	-57.9
自筹资金	Fundraising Oneself	193.19	46.3
其他资金	Others	56.46	12.1
基本建设合计	**Capital Construction**	**247.39**	**15.7**
#国家预算内资金	State Budgetary Appropriation	27.48	-23.6
国内贷款	Domestic Loans	92.52	10.2
利用外资	Utilization of Foreign Capital	4.65	-41.6
#外商直接投资	Direct Foreign Investments	0.53	-86.8
自筹资金	Fundraising Oneself	85.43	70.1
其他资金	Others	13.92	-6.1
更新改造合计	**Innovation**	**127.74**	**31.8**
#国家预算内资金	State Budgetary Appropriation	4.55	-10.8
国内贷款	Domestic Loans	46.83	24.0
利用外资	Utilization of Foreign Capital	0.54	-44.3
#外商直接投资	Dired Foreign Investments	0.44	388.9
自筹资金	Fundraising Oneself	67.55	49.0
其他资金	Others	1.62	-26.7

注:表中数据为基本建设、更新改造、其他投资(含城镇集体)、房地产开发投资的资金来源,但基本建设、更新改造、其他投资(含城镇集体)投资额在50万元以上统计口径范围。

Note:In this table,the statistics that have been collected are about projects of capital construction, innovation and other investment each involving 500000 yuan and more.

5-3 按国有、非国有经济分的全社会固定资产投资(2001)
Total Investment in Fixed Assets Grouped by State - owned and Non - state - owned

指　　标	Item	国有经济 State - owned	非国有经济 Non - state - owned
投资总额(万元)	Total Investment(10000 yuan)	3529823	1744088
按投资种类分	Grouped by Type of Investment		
基本建设	Capital Construction	2269988	85337
更新改造	Innovation	1011219	162485
房地产开发	Real Estate Development	95729	574356
其他投资	Other Investment	152887	921910
按资金来源分	Grouped by Source of Funds		
上年末结余资金	Balance Funds at the End of Last Year	269127	127792
国家预算内投资	State Budgetary Appropriation	303273	41800
国内贷款	Domestic Loans	1368622	163883
债券	Bonds	8867	
利用外资	Utilization of Foreign Capital	45572	14832
自筹投资	Fundraising Oneself	1366719	1057812
#发行股票	Issue Stock	27	3800
其他投资	Others	167643	337969
按建设性质分	Grouped by Type of Construction		
#新建	New Construction	1390117	908396
扩建	Expansion	1147225	138212
改建	Reconstruction	783128	57070
按国民经济行业分	Grouped by Sector		
#农林牧渔业	Farming, Forestry, Animal Husbandry and Fishery	22992	115558
工业	Industry	1386801	334958
#电力、煤气及水的生产和供应业	Production and Supply of Electric Power, Gas and Water	964626	11342
运输、仓储及邮电通信业	Transportation, Storage, Postal and Telecommunications Services	1350545	64453
新增固定资产(万元)	Newly Increased Fixed Assets(10000 yuan)	2409216	1372256
房屋建筑面积(万平方米)	Floor Space of Buildings(10000 sq. m)		
施工面积	Floor Space under Construction	1314	3366
#住宅	Residential Buildings	601	2635
竣工面积	Floor Space Completed	504	2166
#住宅	Residential Buildings	292	1755

注:1.表中国有经济的范围为登记注册类型为国有、国有联营和国有独资公司的单位投资 。

2.基本建设、更新改造、其他投资的投资额在50万元以上统计口径范围。(以下各表同)

Note:1. In this table, the bound of state - owned refer to those units registered as state - owned, state joint ownership and sole state - funded corporations.

2. The statistical coverage of capital construction, innovation and other investment is above 500000 yuan. (same to next)

5-4 基本建设(按国民经济行业分)(2001)
Investment in Capital Construction by Sector

行业	Sectors	施工项目(个) Number of Projects under Cons-truction(unit)	全部建成投产项目(个) Number of Projects Completed and Put into Use(unit)	建成投产率(%) Rate of Completed and Put into Use(%)	基本建设投资额(万元) Investment of Capital Construction (10000 yuan)
总计	Total	2553	1499	58.7	2355325
农、林、牧、渔业	Farming, Forestry, Animal Husbandry and Fishery	96	60	62.5	20601
#农业	Farming	18	10	55.6	5150
采掘业	Mining and Quarrying	20	8	40.0	11675
煤炭采选业	Coal Mining and Dressing	7			3493
石油和天然气开采业	Extraction of Petroleum and Natural Gas	2	2	100.0	4612
有色金属矿采选业	Mining and Dressing of Nonferrous Metals	2	1	50.0	189
非金属矿采选业	Mining and Dressing of Nonmetal Minerals	5	3	60.0	2306
制造业	Manufacturing	140	82	58.6	104488
食品加工业	Food Processing	6	4	66.7	1283
食品制造业	Food Production	2	1	50.0	160
饮料制造业	Beverages	12	11	91.7	3956
烟草加工业	Tobacco	4	2	50.0	854
纺织业	Textiles				
服装及其他纤维制品制造业	Garments and Other Fiber Products	1	1	100.0	1200
木材加工及竹、藤、棕、草制品业	Timber Processing, Bamboo, Cane, Palm Fiber and Straw Products				
家具制造业	Furniture Manufacturing	2			77
造纸及纸制品业	Papermaking and Paper Products	1			350
印刷业、记录媒介的复制	Printing and Record Medium Reproduction				
石油加工及炼焦业	Petroleum Processing and Coking	2	1	50.0	800
化学原料及化学制品制造业	Raw Chemical Materials and Chemical Products	10	5	50.0	16725
医药制造业	Medical and Pharmaceutical Products	13	6	46.2	13960
塑料制品业	Plastic Products	4	4	100.0	1364
非金属矿物制品业	Nonmetal Mineral Products	25	18	72.0	7511
黑色金属冶炼及压延加工业	Smelting and Pressing of Ferrous Metals	9	3	33.3	8300

5－4 续表(continued)

行　　业	Sectors	施工项目(个) Number of Projects under Construction(unit)	全部建成投产项目(个) Number of Projects Completed and Put into Use(unit)	建成投产率(%) Rate of Completed and Put into Use(%)	基本建设投资额(万元) Investment of Capital Construction (10000 yuan)
有色金属冶炼及压延加工业	Smelting and Pressing of Nonferrous Metals	9	4	44.4	8150
金属制品业	Metal Products	4	3	75.0	954
普通机械制造业	Ordinary Machinery	2	2	100.0	276
专用设备制造业	Equipment for Special Purposes	7	5	71.4	709
交通运输设备制造业	Transport Equipment	21	9	42.9	27851
电气机械及器材制造业	Electric Equipment and Machinery	1	1	100.0	150
电子及通信设备制造业	Electronic and Telecommunications Equipment	2	1	50.0	9524
仪器仪表及文化、办公用机械制造业	Instruments, Meters, Cultural and Office Machinery Equipment				
电力、煤气及水的生产和供应业	Production and Supply of Electric Power, Gas and Water	157	65	41.4	713269
电力、蒸汽、热水的生产和供应业	Production and Supply of Electric Power, Steam and Hot Water	106	54	50.9	658145
煤气生产和供应业	Production and Supply of Gas	4	2	50.0	867
自来水的生产和供应业	Production and Supply of Tap Water	47	9	19.1	54257
建筑业	Construction	9	4	44.4	6184
地质勘查业、水利管理业	Geological Prospecting and Water Conservancy	157	98	62.4	54413
地质勘查业	Geological Prospecting	5	1	20.0	479
水利管理业	Water Conservancy	152	97	63.8	53934
交通运输、仓储及邮电通信业	Transportation, Storage, Postal and Telecommunication Services	450	271	60.2	815410
#仓储业	Storage	11	6	54.5	7958
邮电通信业	Postal and Telecommunications Services	126	78	61.9	84747
批发和零售贸易、餐饮业	Wholesale & Retail Trade and Catering Services	169	103	60.9	35101
金融、保险业	Banking and Insurance	56	30	53.6	14826
房地产业	Real Estate	22	9	40.9	13711
社会服务业	Social Services	244	107	43.9	345285
卫生、体育和社会福利业	Health Care, Sports and Social Welfare	103	51	49.5	26293
教育、文化艺术及广播电影电视业	Education, Culture and Arts, Radio, Film and Televi sion	426	296	69.5	97907
科学研究和综合技术服务业	Scientific Research and Polytechnical Services	15	8	53.3	4555
国家机关、政党机关和社会团体	Governments, Parties and Social Organizations	478	302	63.2	89443
其他行业	Other Sectors	11	5	45.5	2164

5-5 更新改造主要指标(按国民经济行业分)(2001)
Major Indicators of Innovation by Sector

行业	Sectors	施工项目(个) Number of Projects under Construction(unit)	全部建成投产项目(个) Number of Projects Completed and Put into Use(unit)	建成投产率(%) Rate of Completed and Put into Use(%)	更新改造投资额(万元) Investment of Innovation (10000 yuan)
总计	Total	1404	906	64.5	1173704
农、林、牧、渔业	Farming, Forestry, Animal Husbandry and Fishery	5	4	80.0	495
采掘业	Mining and Quarrying	230	176	76.5	39254
煤炭采选业	Coal Mining and Dressing	225	171	76.0	35951
非金属矿采选业	Mining and Dressing of Nonmetal Minerals	1	1	100.0	1247
制造业	Manufacturing	615	316	51.4	449458
食品加工业	Food Processing	14	10	71.4	2867
食品制造业	Food Production	4	3	75.0	6778
饮料制造业	Beverages	19	6	31.6	35021
烟草加工业	Tobacco	14	3	21.4	14815
纺织业	Textiles	1	1	100.0	120
造纸及纸制品业	Papermaking and Paper Products	4	3	75.0	717
印刷业、记录媒介的复制	Printing and Record Medium Reproduction	1	1	100.0	16
化学原料及化学制品制造业	Raw Chemical Materials and Chemical Products	36	27	75.0	54778
医药制造业	Medical and Pharmaceutical Products	21	11	52.4	34090
化学纤维制造业	Chemical Fiber	1			1515
橡胶制品业	Rubber Products	4	2	50.0	8002
塑料制品业	Plastic Products	3			1290
非金属矿物制品业	Nonmetal Mineral Products	38	19	50.0	23711
黑色金属冶炼及压延加工业	Smelting and Pressing of Ferrous Metals	49	31	63.3	59524
有色金属冶炼及压延加工业	Smelting and Pressing of Nonferrous Metals	281	145	51.6	134094
金属制品业	Metal Products	4	2	50.0	4364
普通机械制造业	Ordinary Machinery	6	3	50.0	1047
专用设备制造业	Equipment for Special Purposes	5	1	20.0	2010

5-5 续表(continued)

行业	Sectors	施工项目(个) Number of Projects under Cons-truction(unit)	全部建成投产项目(个) Number of Projects Completed and Put into Use(unit)	建成投产率(%) Rate of Completed and Put into Use(%)	更新改造投资额(万元) Investment of Innovation (10000 yuan)
交通运输设备制造业	Transport Equipment	85	35	41.2	38873
电气机械及器材制造业	Electric Equipment and Machinery	4	1	25.0	7077
电子及通信设备制造业	Electronic and Telecommunications Equipment	13	7	53.8	16996
仪器仪表及文化、办公用机械制造业	Instruments, Meters, Cultural and Office Machinery	3	1	33.3	489
电力、煤气及水的生产和供应业	Production and Supply of Electric Power, Gas and Water	79	37	46.8	251322
电力、蒸汽、热水的生产和供应业	Production and Supply of Electric Power, Steam and Hot Water	62	32	51.6	244762
煤气生产和供应业	Production and Supply of Gas	3			397
自来水的生产和供应业	Production and Supply of Tap Water	14	5	35.7	6163
建筑业	Construction	2			2513
地质勘查业、水利管理业	Geological Prospecting and Water Conservancy	5	3	60.0	568
水利管理业	Water Conservancy	4	3	75.0	454
交通运输、仓储及邮电通信业	Transportation, Storage, Postal and Telecommunication Services	400	327	81.8	406142
#仓储业	Storage	1	1	100.0	3
邮电通信业	Postal and Telecommunications Services	295	255	86.4	322163
批发和零售贸易、餐饮业	Wholesale & Retail Trade and Catering Services	36	24	66.7	12485
金融、保险业	Banking and Insurance				
社会服务业	Social Services	17	11	64.7	7418
卫生、体育和社会福利业	Health Care, Sports and Social Welfare	1			1214
教育、文化艺术及广播电影电视业	Education, Culture and Arts, Radio, Film and Television	9	4	44.4	1740
科学研究和综合技术服务业	Scientific Research and Polytechnical Services				8
国家机关、政党机关和社会团体	Governments, Parties and Social Organizations	5	4	80.0	1087
其他行业	Other Sectors				

5-6 基本建设、更新改造新增主要生产能力(2001)
Newly Increased Production Capacity through Capital Construction and Innovation

生产能力名称	Productive Capacity	数 量 Amount
原煤开采(万吨/年)	Coal Mining (10000 tons/year)	87
焦炭(万吨/年)	Coke (10000 tons/year)	6
生铁(万吨/年)	Pig Iron(10000 tons/year)	0.8
铁合金(万吨/年)	Iron Alloy(10000 tons/year)	19
钢丝(万吨/年)	Steel Wire(10000 tons/year)	0.6
钢绞线(万吨/年)	Steel Wire(10000 tons/year)	2
锌冶炼(吨/年)	Zinc Smelt(ton/year)	5000
#电解锌(吨/年)	Electroanalysis Zinc(ton/year)	5000
氧化铝(吨/年)	Aluminium Oxide(ton/year)	100000
电解铝(吨/年)	Electrolytic Aluminium (ton/year)	32000
水力发电(万千瓦)	Hydropower(10000 kw)	7.22
火力发电(万千瓦)	Thermal Power(10000 kw)	58.5
输电线路长度(11万伏及以上)(公里)	Transmit Electricity Line (110000 Volt - amper Level and above)(km)	1893.2
变电设备能力(11万伏及以上)(万千伏安)	Transform Electricity Equipment (110000 Volt - amper Level and above)(10000 kv. A)	359.5
水 泥(万吨/年)	Cement(10000 tons/year)	159.2
纤维板(万立方米/年)	Fibre Board(10000 cu. m/year)	1
硫 酸(吨/年)	Sulfuric Acid(ton/year)	600000
合成氨(吨/年)	Compose Ammonia(ton/year)	5400
氮肥(吨/年)	Nitrogenous Fertilizer (ton/year)	75000
磷肥(吨/年)	Phosphorus Fertilizer (ton/year)	738000
钾肥(吨/年)	Potassium Fertilizer (ton/year)	75000
炭 黑(吨/年)	Charcoal(ton/year)	10
塑料树脂及共聚物(吨/年)	Plastic Resin and Polymer(ton/year)	150
轮胎外胎(万条/年)	Tires(10000 bars/year)	30
注射液(万支/年)	Injection Juice(10000 units/year)	13500
片剂(万片/年)	Tablet(10000 tablets/year)	60000
输液(万瓶/年)	Infusion(10000 units/year)	5500

5-6 续表 1(continued)

生产能力名称	Productive Capacity	数 量 Amount
胶囊剂(万粒/年)	Capsule(10000 grain/year)	10000
医药中间体(吨/年)	Intermediate Medicine(ton/year)	20
中成药(吨/年)	Traditional Chinese Medicine and Patent Medicine(ton/year)	200
光纤通讯电缆(芯公里)	Light Communication Cable(fuses.km)	455
原电池(折一号电池)(万只)	Battery(10000 units)	8900
集成电路(万块/年)	Integrated Circuit(10000 units/year)	700
食用植物油(日处理原料:吨)	Edible Vegetable Oil(Dispose material, ton/day)	100
(日精炼油:吨)	Edible Vegetable Oil(Refike Oil, ton/day)	30
啤 酒(万吨/年)	Beer(10000 tons/year)	9
白 酒(万吨/年)	Liquors (10000 tons/year)	0.81
软饮料(吨/年)	Soft Drinks (ton/year)	30400
家用电冰箱(万台/年)	Household Refrigerator(10000 units/year)	30
移动通信基站设备(个/年)	Move Communicate Group Stage Equipment(channel/year)	729
程控交换机(万线/年)	Program - controlled Exchange(10000 lines/year)	38.08
电话单机(万部/年)	Telephone(10000 sets/year)	6.65
新建公路(公里)	Length of New Highways (km)	734.6
#高速公路(公里)	Highways(km)	52
二级公路(公里)	B Road(km)	311.77
改建公路(公里)	Length of Reconstructed Highways (km)	2815.72
#二级公路(公里)	B Road(km)	229
新建独立公路桥梁(延长米)	New Independent Highway Bridge(extending.m)	1093
(座)	New Independent Highway Bridge(bridge)	5
改善内河航道里程(公里)	Ameliorate Freshwater Sea - route Mileage(km)	136
民航机场跑道(条)	Track in Airport(unit)	1
(米)	Track in Airport(m)	2000
候机楼(座)	Waiting Storeies in Airport(unit)	1
(平方米)	Waiting Storeies in Airport(sq.m)	3000

5－6 续表 2(continued)

生产能力名称	Productive Capacity	数 量 Amount
长途电缆线路长度(公里)	Length of Long－distance Cable(km)	2048.68
新建微波电路(路)	Microwave Circuit Newly Built(unit)	101
耕地面积(万亩)	Cultivated Area(10000 mu)	7.9
造林面积(万亩)	Afforestation Area (10000 mu)	37.66
水库容量(总库容)(亿立方米)	The Capacity of Reservior(100 million cu.m)	1.19
有效灌溉面积(万亩)	Effective Irrigated Area(10000 mu)	19.09
除涝面积(万亩)	Area Drought(10000 mu)	1.02
排灌装机(万千瓦)	Drainage and Irrigation(10000 kw)	0.5
商业石油库(万立方米)	Petroleum Storehouses for Business Use(10000 cu.m)	0.1
粮食仓库(万公斤)	Grain Storehouses (10000 kg)	2650
(平方米)	Grain Storehouses (sq.m)	2968
高等院校:学生席位(个)	Number of Students Capacity of Universities and Colleges(unit)	7110
建筑面积(平方米)	Floor Space(sq.m)	27938
中等学校:学生席位(个)	Number of Students Capacity of Middle Schools (unit)	45826
建筑面积(平方米)	Floor Space(sq.m)	114473
小学校:学生席位(个)	Number of Students Capacity of Primary Schools (unit)	72014
建筑面积(平方米)	Floor Space(sq.m)	143541
其他院校:学生席位(个)	Number of Students Capacity of Other Schools (unit)	2602
建筑面积(平方米)	Floor Space(sq.m)	9624
医院病床(张)	Number of Hospital Beds(bed)	963
宾馆、旅馆、招待所客房数(间)	Guest Room of Hotel, Inn and Rest House(unit)	269
(平方米)	Guest Room of Hotel, Inn and Rest House(sq.m)	18231
城市自来水供水能力(万吨/日)	Tap Water Supply Capacity(10000 tons/day)	22.8
城市自来水管道长度(公里)	Length of Tap Water Pipeline Built(km)	28.55
城市道路扩建长度(公里)	Length of Expanded Roads(km)	51.28
城市道路扩建面积(万平方米)	Area of Expanded Roads(10000 sq.m)	122.61
城市排水管道铺设长度(公里)	Length of Drainpipe(km)	32.29
城市污水处理能力(万吨/日)	Disposal Capacity of Sewage(10000 tons/day)	8
城市防洪堤长度(公里)	Length of City's Floodwalls(km)	36.45

5-7 房地产开发投资主要指标(2001)
Major Indicators of Real Estate Development

指标	Item	绝对数 Absolute Figure	2001年比2000年增长(%) Increase Rate in 2001 over 2000(%)
一、企业个数(个)	**Number of Enterprises(unit)**	**610**	**12.8**
内资	Domestic Funded	567	17.4
#国有	State-owned Enterprises	75	-13.8
集体	Collective-owned Enterprises	40	-27.3
港、澳、台投资	Economic Units Funded by Entrepreneurs from Hong Kong, Macao and Taiwan	26	-16.1
外商投资	Foreign Funded Enterprises	17	-37.0
二、平均从业人数(人)	**Average Number of Employed Persons(person)**	**19025**	**35.5**
内资	Domestic Funded	18074	39.9
#国有	State-owned Enterprises	2932	15.1
集体	Collective-owned Enterprises	1262	-15.2
港、澳、台投资	Economic Units Funded by Entrepreneurs from Hong Kong, Macao and Taiwan	511	-1.7
外商投资	Foreign Funded Enterprises	440	-27.3
三、土地开发及购置(万平方米)	**Land Development and Purchase(10000 sq.m)**		
本年土地开发面积	Land Space Developed in 2001	287	41.4
本年土地购置面积	Land Space Purchased in 2001	576	99.3
四、投资总额(万元)	**Total Investment Completed(10000 yuan)**	**670085**	**43.9**
#商品房屋建设投资	Investment of Commercial Houses	486241	54.9
土地开发投资	Investment of Land Development	122893	104.1
投资额中	In Investment		
住宅	Residential Buildings	380647	40.3
#别墅高档公寓	Villas and Good Apartments	950	-88.9
经济适用房屋	Economical Houses	83286	-4.4
写字楼	Office Buildings	33824	16.1
商业营业用房	Houses for Business Use	96688	30.1
其他	Others	158926	74.7
五、资金来源小计(亿元)	**Source of Funds(100 million yuan)**	**94.32**	**28.3**

5－7 续表(continued)

指　　标	Item	绝对数 Absolute Figure	2001 年比 2000 年增长(%) Increase Rate in 2001 over 2000(%)
#国内贷款	Domestic Loans	14.78	6.3
利用外资	Utilization of Foreigns Capital	0.16	-63.6
自筹资金	Fundraising Oneself	24.15	46.2
六、房屋建筑面积(万平方米)	**Floor Space of Buildings(10000 sq.m)**		
施工面积	Floor Space under Construction	1367	34.7
竣工面积	Floor Space Completed	491	40.7
本年新开工面积	Floor Space Started in 2001	518	25.4
#住宅	Residential Buildings	405	26.6
#经济适用房屋	Economical Houses	103	32.1
七、商品房屋销售面积(万平方米)	**Selling Floor Space of Commercial Houses(10000 sq.m)**	**369**	**46.4**
#住宅	Residential Buildings	332	45.0
#经济适用房屋	Economical Houses	90	20.0
商品房屋销售价格(元/平方米)	Selling Price of Commercial Houses(yuan/sq.m)	1164	-8.3
#住宅	Residential Buildings	1026	-6.4
#经济适用房屋	Economical Houses	772	-13.1
八、实收资本合计(亿元)	**Total Capital Hold(100 million yuan)**	**43.83**	**-24.0**
#国家资本金	State Capital	1.1	-79.1
资产负债率(%)	Ratio of Liabilities to Assets(%)	74.3	0.2
九、经营收入(万元)	**Total Revenue(10000 yuan)**	**460126**	**38.7**
土地转让收入	Revenue of Transferring Land	2058	-36.3
商品房屋销售收入	Revenue of Selling Commercial Houses	425256	37.1
#商品住宅销售收入	Revenue of Selling Residential Buildings	344238	35.0
房屋出租收入	Income of Lending Buildings	2045	-43.2
其他收入	Other Revenue	30767	109.6
经营税金及附加	Business Tax and Extra Charges	23316	44.5
利润总额	Total Profits	-5032	-71.0

5-8 商品房竣工、销售(2001)
Completed Space and Sold Space of Commercial Houses

指　　标	Item	绝对数 Absolute Figure	2001年比2000年增长(%) Increase Rate in 2001 over 2000(%)
商品房屋竣工面积(平方米)	**Completed Space of Commercial Houses(sq.m)**	**4908255**	**40.6**
#住宅	Residential Buildings	3997606	38.8
办公楼	Office Buildings	175018	22.9
商业营业用房	Houses for Business Use	611629	46.6
商品房屋销售面积(平方米)	**Sold Space of Commercial Houses(sq.m)**	**3693791**	**46.7**
#住宅	Residential Buildings	3320006	45.1
办公楼	Office Buildings	79917	156.7
商业营业用房	Houses for Business Use	275692	47.5
商品房实际销售额(万元)	**Revenue of Actually Selling Commercial Houses(10000 yuan)**	**429951**	**34.6**
#住宅	Residential Buildings	340724	35.8
办公楼	Office Buildings	14790	101.9
商业营业用房	Houses for Business Use	71386	19.7
商品房空置面积(平方米)	**Empty Space of Commercial Houses(sq.m)**	**663354**	**-7.7**
#住宅	Residential Buildings	436177	9.9
办公楼	Office Buildings	15350	-79.6
商业营业用房	Houses for Business Use	187986	-14.3

主要统计指标解释

全社会固定资产投资 固定资产投资额是以货币表现的建造和购置固定资产活动的工作量，它是反映固定资产投资规模、速度、比例关系和使用方向的综合性指标。

基本建设投资 基本建设指企业、事业、行政单位以扩大生产能力或工程效益为主要目的的新建、扩建工程及有关工作。其综合范围为总投资50万元以上(含50万元，下同)的基本建设项目。

更新改造投资 更新改造指企业、事业单位对原有设施进行固定资产更新和技术改造，以及相应配套的工程和有关工作(不包括大修理和维护工程)。其综合范围为总投资50万元以上的更新改造项目。

房地产开发投资 指房地产开发公司、商品房建设公司及其他房地产开发法人单位和附属于其他法人单位实际从事房地产开发或经营的活动单位统一开发的包括统代建、拆迁还建的住宅、厂房、仓库、饭店、宾馆、度假村、写字楼、办公楼等房屋建筑物和配套的服务设施，土地开发工程(如道路、给水、排水、供电、供热、通讯、平整场地等基础设施工程)的投资;不包括单纯的土地交易活动。

其他固定资产投资 指全社会固定资产投资中未列入基本建设、更新改造和房地产开发投资的建造和购置固定资产的活动。

城镇和工矿区私人建房投资和农村个人投资 城镇和工矿区私人建房包括市、县城、镇、工矿区所辖范围内的全部私人建房，不论其房主是否系本地的常住户口均应包括。农村个人投资包括农村个人建房及购置生产性固定资产的投资。

施工项目 指报告期内曾进行建筑或安装工程施工活动的建设项目，包括报告期内新开工项目、报告期以前开工跨入报告期继续施工的项目以及报告期施过工并在报告期内全部建成投产或停缓建的项目。

新增生产能力 指通过固定资产投资活动而增加的设计能力或工程效益，它是用实物形态表示的固定资产投资的成果。新增生产能力的计算，是以能独立发挥生产能力或工程效益的单项工程(或项目)为对象。当单项工程(或项目)建成，经有关部门鉴定合格，正式移交投入生产，即可计算新增生产能力。

房屋建筑面积 指从房屋外墙线算起的各层平面面积的总和，包括可供使用的有效面积和房屋结构(如柱、墙)占用的面积。多层建筑按各层(包括地下室)面积总和计算。

住宅建筑面积 指施工和竣工房屋建筑面积中供居住用的施工和竣工房屋建筑面积。

施工面积 指报告期内施工的全部房屋建筑面积。包括本期新开工的面积、上期跨入本期继续施工的房屋面积、上期停缓建在本期恢复施工的房屋面积、本期竣工的房屋面积及本期施工后又停缓建的房屋面积。

竣工面积 指在报告期内房屋建筑按照设计要求已全部完工，达到住人和使用条件，经验收鉴定合格，正式移交使用单位的建筑面积。

房屋建筑面积竣工率 指一定时期内房屋竣工面积占同期房屋施工面积的比率。

新增固定资产 指通过投资活动所形成的新的固定资产价值，包括已经建成投入生产或交付使用的工程价值和达到固定资产标准的设备、工具、器具的价值及有关应摊入的费用。它是以价值形式表示的固定资产投资成果的综合性指标，可以综合反映不同时期、不同部门、不同地区的固定资产投资成果。

建设项目投产率 指一定时期内全部建成投入生产项目个数与同期正式施工项目个数的比率。它是从项目建设速度的角度反映投资效果的指标。

固定资产交付使用率 指一定时期新增固定资产与同期完成投资额的比率。它是反映各个时期固定资产动用速度，衡量建设过程中投资效果的一个综合性指标。

Explanatory Notes on Main Statistical Indicators

Total Investment in Fixed Assets in the Whole Country Investment in fixed assets Amount of investment in fixed assets refers to the volume of activities in construction and purchases of fixed assets in monetary terms. It is a comprehensive indicator which shows the size, pace, proportional relations and use orientation of the investment in fixed assets.

Investment in Capital Construction Capital construction refers to the new construction projects or extension projects and the related work of the enterprises, institutions or administrative units mainly for the purpose of expanding production capacity or improving project efficiency covering only projects each with a total investment of 500,000 RMB yuan and over.

Investment in Innovation Innovation refers to the renewal of fixed assets and technological innovation of the original facilities by the enterprises and institutions as well as the corresponding supplementary projects and the related work (excluding major overhaul and maintenance projects) covering only projects each with a total investment of 500,000 RMB yuan and over.

Investment in Real Estate Development It includes the investment by the real estate development companies, commercial buildings construction companies and other real estate development units of various types of ownership in the construction of house buildings, such as residential buildings, factory buildings, warehouses, hotels, guesthouses, holiday villages, office buildings, and the complementary service facilities and land development projects, such as roads, water supply, water drainage, power supply, heating, telecommunications, land leveling and other projects of infrastructure. It excludes the activities in simple land transactions.

Other Investment in Fixed Assets refers to the construcion and purchases of fixed assets not listed in the investment in capital construction, investment in innovation and investment in real estate development.

Private Investment in House Construction in Urban Areas, Industrial and Mining Areas and Individual Investment in Rural Areas The private house construction in the urban areas and industrial and mining areas includes all the private house construction under the jurisdiction of cities, counties, towns and industrial and mining areas, no matter whether the owner of the house is registered as the permanent resident in the locality or not. The individual investment in the rural areas includes the investment in house construction and purchase of productive fixed assets by the individuals in the rural areas.

Projects Under Construction refer to projects having construction and installation activities undertaken in the reference period, including projects started in the reference period, or continued from the previous period, or completed and put into production or suspended in the reference period.

Newly Increased Production Capacity refers to the increase of designed capacity and project efficiency through investment in fixed assets, which reflects the accomplishment of investment in fixed assets in kind. The calculation of newly increased production capacity is based on individual project which operates independently and efficiently. When an individual project is completed and checked and accepted and put into production, it is counted as newly increased production capacity.

Floor Space of Buildings Under Construction and Completed refers to total floor space in each story of buildings calculated from the outside line of building walls, including both usable space and the space occupied by constructions like pillars or walls. The floor space of multi – story buildings includes the total floor space of each story (including basement).

Floor Space of Residential Buildings refers to the floor space of the residential buildings under construction and completed among the total space of buildings under construction and completed.

Floor Space Under Construction refers to total floor space of all buildings under construction during the reference period, including floor space of newly started buildings during the reference period, floor space of construction extended from the previous period to the current period, floor space of construction suspended during the previous period and resumed in the current period, floor space of construction completed in the current period, and floor space of construction started and then suspended in the current period.

Floor Space of Buildings Completed refers to the floor space of buildings completed in the reference period, which have come up to the designed standards and have been put into use.

Completion Rate of Floor Space of Buildings refers to the ratio of the floor space of buildings completed in certain period of time to the floor space of buildings under construction in the same period, which reflects the investment result and economic efficiency of the construction industry from the angle of the speed of project construction.

Newly Increased Fixed Assets refer to the newly increased value of fixed assets through investment, including the value of projects completed and put into production, the value of equipment, tools, and vessels considered as fixed assets, as well as the relevant expenses as investment in fixed assets.

Rate of Construction Projects Completed and Put into Use refers to the ratio of the number of construction projects completed and put into use in certain period of time to the number of projects under construction in the same period. This reflects the investment efficiency from the angle of the speed of projects construction.

Rate of Projects of Fixed Assets Completed and Put into Operation refers to the ratio of the newly increased fixed assets to the total investment made in the same period. This is a comprehensive indicator, reflecting the speed of the employment of fixed assets and the investment efficiency.

6

Six

能源、原材料消耗

Consumption of Energy and Raw Material

一次能源生产总量（万吨标准煤）
Total Production of Primary Energy (10000 tons of SCE)

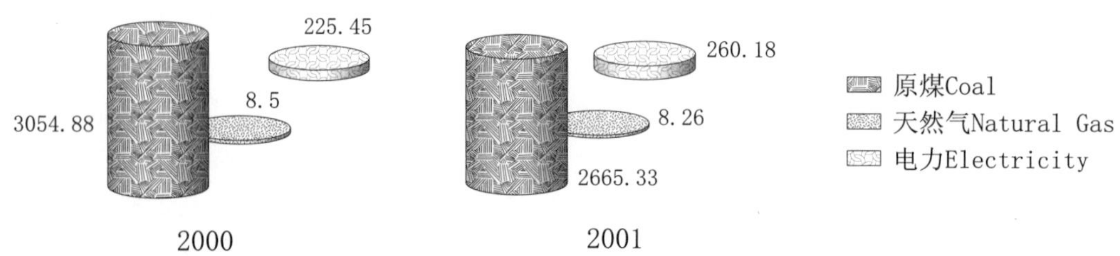

能源终端消费总量（万吨标准煤）(2001)
Total Energy Consumption (10000 tons of SCE)

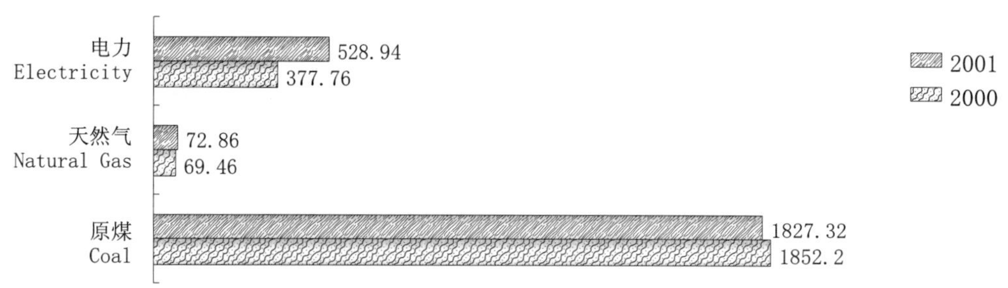

能源生产、消费构成（%）(2001)
Composition of Energy Production and Consumption (%)

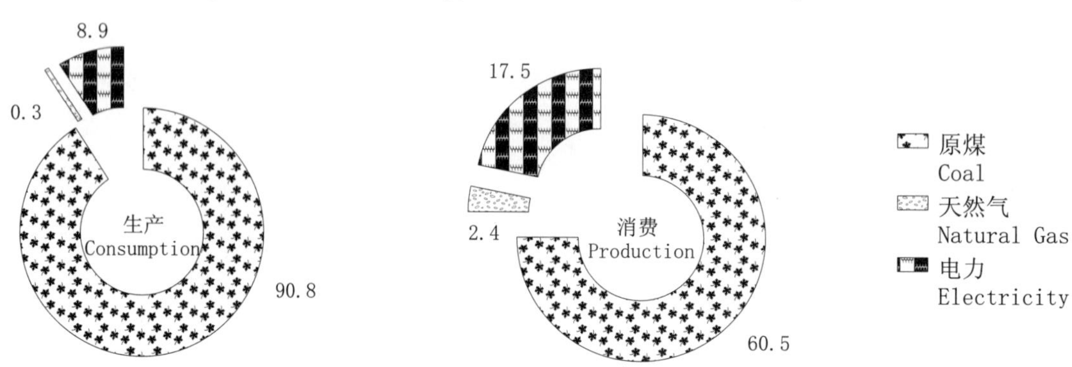

6-1 能源生产、消费总量及构成
Total Production and Consumption of Energy and Its Composition

单位：万吨标准煤
(10000 tons of SCE)

指　　标	Item	2000	2001	2001年比2000年增长(%) Increase Rate in 2001 over 2000(%)
一、绝对数	**Absolute Figure**			
一次能源生产总量	Total Production of Primary Energy	3288.83	2933.77	-10.8
#原煤	Coal	3054.88	2665.33	-12.8
天然气	Natural Gas	8.5	8.26	-2.8
水电	Hydropower	225.45	260.18	15.4
能源终端消费总量	Final Consumption of Energy	2852.97	3021.46	5.9
#原煤	Coal	1852.2	1827.32	-1.3
天然气	Natural Gas	69.46	72.86	4.9
电力	Electricity	377.76	528.94	40.0
二、构成(%)	**Composition(%)**			
一次能源生产总量	Total Production of Primary Energy	100	100	
#原煤	Coal	92.8	90.8	-2.2
天然气	Natural Gas	0.3	0.3	持平
水电	Hydropower	6.9	8.9	29.0
能源终端消费总量	Final Consumption of Energy	100	100	
#原煤	Coal	64.9	60.5	-6.8
天然气	Natural Gas	2.4	2.4	持平
电力	Electricity	13.2	17.5	32.6

注：电、热按当量值计算(以下各表同)。

Note: The conversion of electric power and heat into the SCE are calculated on the basis of heat value equivalent(the same as in the following tables)。

6-2 综合能源平衡表
Overall Energy Balance

单位:万吨标准煤
(10000 tons of SCE)

指　　标	Item	2000	2001	2001年比2000年增长(%) Increase Rate in 2001 over 2000(%)
可供消费的能源总量	**Total Energy Available for Consumption**	**2420.8**	**2327.71**	**-3.9**
一次能源生产量	Primary Energy Output	3288.83	2933.77	-10.8
省外调入	Inflow from Other Provinces	262.14	291.98	11.4
调出省外(-)	Outflow from Guizhou Province(-)	-1152.69	-946.63	-17.9
年初年末库存差额	Stock Changes in the Year	22.52	48.6	115.8
能源消费总量	**Total Energy Consumption**	**3961.34**	**3969.68**	**0.2**
在总量中:	Consumption by Sector			
农、林、牧、渔、水利业	Farming, Forestry, Animal Husbandry, Fishery and Water Conservancy	207.11	206.04	-0.5
工业	Industry	2455.16	2441.1	-0.6
建筑业	Construction	18.66	16.53	-11.4
交通运输和邮电通讯业	Transportation, Post and Telecommunications Services	139.49	143.72	3.0
商业、饮食、物资供销和仓储业	Commerce, Catering Services, Materials Supply and Storage	135.19	126.75	-6.2
其他	Others	152.1	183.91	20.9
生活消费	Residential Consumption	800.75	800.03	-0.1
在总量中:	Consumption by Usage			
终端消费	Final Consumption	2852.97	3021.46	5.9
#工业	Industry	1399.67	1544.47	10.4
加工转换损失量	Losses in Processing and Transformation	1055.49	896.63	-15.1
#炼焦	Coking	159.46	141.11	-11.5
损失量	Other Losses	52.88	51.59	-2.4
平衡差额	Balance	-1540.54	-1641.96	6.6

注:1.物质部门消费量包括二次能源投入量和损失量。2.非物质部门消费量包括生活消费量。3.第二产业消费量未包括二次能源投入量和损失量。

Note: 1. Material sectors consumption include secondary input and loss value of energy.　2. Non-material sectors consumption include residential consumption.　3. Secondary industry consumption exclude secondary input and loss value of energy.

6-3 煤炭平衡表
Coal Balance Sheet

单位:万吨
(10000 tons)

指 标	Item	2000	2001	2001年比2000年增长(%) Increase Rate in 2001 over 2000(%)
可供量	**Total Energy Available for Consumption**	**3376.57**	**2982.79**	**-11.7**
生产量	Output	4276.75	3731.39	-12.8
调出省外(一)	Outflow from Guizhou Province(-)	-934.95	-840.36	-10.1
年初年末库存差额	Stock Changes in the Year	34.77	91.76	163.9
消费量	**Total Energy Consumption**	**5352.00**	**5157.41**	**-3.6**
在消费量中:	Consumption by Sector			
农、林、牧、渔、水利业	Farming, Forestry, Animal Husbandry, Fishery and Water Conservancy	222.00	219.00	-1.4
工业	Industry	3752.00	3588.96	-4.4
建筑业	Construction	4.00	3.80	-5.0
交通运输和邮电通讯业	Transportation, Post and Telecommunications Services	8.03	7.82	-2.6
商业、饮食、物资供销和仓储业	Commerce, Catering Services, Materials Supply and Storage	132.00	129.48	-1.9
其他	Others	173.97	171.00	-1.7
生活消费	Residential Consumption	1015.00	997.41	-1.7
在消费量中:	Consumption by Usage			
终端消费	Final Consumption	2593.00	2558.35	-1.3
#工业	Industry	1038.00	1033.64	-0.4
中间消费(用于加工转换)	Intermediate Consumption (Consumed in Transformation)	2714.00	2559.12	-5.7
发电	Power Generation	1368.00	1413.42	3.3
炼焦	Coking	527.00	438.9	-16.7
洗选损耗	Losses in Coal Washing and Dressing	45.00	40.00	-11.1
平衡差额	Balance	-1975.43	-2174.68	10.1

6-4 电力平衡表
Electricity Balance Sheet

单位：亿千瓦小时
(100 million kwh)

指　　标	Item	2000	2001	2001年比2000年增长(%) Increase Rate in 2001 over 2000(%)
可供量	**Total Energy Available for Consumption**	324.18	449.05	38.5
生产量	Output	408.47	480.25	17.6
水电	Hydropower	183.44	211.70	15.4
火电	Thermal Power	225.03	268.55	19.3
调出省外(-)	Outflow from Guizhou Province(-)	-84.29	-31.20	-63.0
消费量	**Total Energy Consumption**	324.18	449.05	38.5
在消费量中：	Consumption by Sector			
农、林、牧、渔、水利业	Farming, Forestry, Animal Husbandry, Fishery and Water Conservancy	11.13	13.84	24.4
工业	Industry	225.47	340.56	51.0
建筑业	Construction	7.95	8.20	3.1
交通运输和邮电通讯业	Transportation, Post and Telecommunications Services	12.19	12.49	2.5
商业、饮食、物资供销和仓储业	Commerce, Catering Services, Materials Supply and Storage	11.65	12.16	4.4
其他	Others	11.56	11.06	-4.3
生活消费	Residential Consumption	27.42	32.07	17.0
在消费量中：	Consumption by Usage			
终端消费	Final Consumption	307.37	430.38	40.0
#工业	Industry	225.47	340.56	51.0
输配损失量	Losses in Transmission	16.81	18.67	11.1
平衡差额	Balance			

6-5 能源生产消费弹性系数 Elasticity Ratio of Energy Production and Consumption

指　　标	Item	2000	2001
能源生产弹性系数	**Elasticity Ratio of Energy Production**		
能源生产比上年增长	Growth Rate of Energy Production over Preceding Year	7.78	-10.8
电力生产比上年增长	Growth Rate of Electricity Production over Preceding Year	18.25	17.45
国内生产总值比上年增长	Growth Rate of Gross Domestic Product(GDP) over Preceding Year	8.7	8.8
能源生产弹性系数	Elasticity Ratio of Energy Production	0.88	-1.18
电力生产弹性系数	Elasticity Ratio of Electricity Production	1.03	1.61
能源消费弹性系数	**Elasticity Ratio of Energy Consumption**		
能源消费总量比上年增长	Growth Rate of Energy Consumption over Preceding Year	2.77	0.21
电力消费比上年增长	Growth Rate of Electricity Consumption over Preceding Year	18.22	40.02
国内生产总值比上年增长	Growth Rate of Gross Domestic Product(GDP) over Preceding Year	8.7	8.8
能源消费弹性系数	Elasticity Ratio of Energy Consumption	0.97	0.33
电力消费弹性系数	Elasticity Ratio of Electricity Consumption	1.01	1.71

6-6 平均每天各种能源生产、消费量
Average Energy Production and Consumption Per Day by Variety

指　　标	Item	2000	2001	2001年比2000年增长(%) Increase Rate in 2001 over 2000(%)
每天生产量总计(万吨标准煤)	Average Energy Production Per Day(10000 tons of SCE)	8.84	8.04	-9.1
煤炭(万吨)	Coal(10000 tons)	11.72	10.22	-12.8
天然气(万立方米)	Natural Gas(10000 cu.m)	19.17	18.63	-2.8
煤气(万立方米)	Gas(10000 cu.m)	144.93	152.88	5.5
电力(万千瓦时)	Electricity(10000 kwh)	11190.95	13157.53	17.6
每天消费量总计(万吨标准煤)	Average Energy Consumption Per Day (10000 tons of SCE)	10.89	10.87	-0.2
煤炭(万吨)	Coal(10000 tons)	14.66	14.13	-3.6
焦炭(吨)	Coke(ton)	6544.11	6173.7	-5.7
天然气(万立方米)	Natural Gas(10000 cu.m)	156.71	164.38	4.9
液化石油气(吨)	Liquefied Petroleum Gas(ton)	290.68	330.14	13.6
煤气(万立方米)	Gas(10000 cu.m)	144.93	152.88	5.5
汽油(吨)	Gasoline(ton)	1272.88	1310.41	3.0
煤油(吨)	Kerosene(ton)	256.71	64.66	-74.8
柴油(吨)	Diesel Oil (ton)	1583.84	2269.86	43.3
电力(万千瓦时)	Electricity(10000 kwh)	8881.64	11791.23	32.8

6-7 每人年平均生活用能源
Annual Average Per Capita Energy Consumption for Non - Production Purpose

指　　标	Item	2000	2001	2001年比2000年增长(%) Increase Rate in 2001 over 2000(%)
平均每人生活消费能源(千克标准煤/人)	Annual Average Non - productive Consumption Per Capita(kg of SCE/person)	213.21	211.81	-0.7
煤炭(千克)	Coal(kg)	270.25	264.07	-2.3
电力(千瓦小时)	Electricity(kwh)	73.01	84.91	16.3
液化石油气(千克)	Liquefied Petroleum Gas(kg)	1.68	1.88	11.9
煤气(立方米)	Gas(cu.m)	1.36	1.35	-0.7

6-8 能源利用效率
Using Efficiency of Energy

指　　标	Item	2000	2001	2001年比2000年增长(%) Increase Rate in 2001 over 2000(%)
能源消费总量(万吨标准煤)	Total Energy Consumption(10000 tons of SCE)	3961.34	3969.68	0.2
工业能源消费量	Energy Consumption of Industry	2508.04	2492.69	-0.6
每万元工业总产值能源消费量(吨标准煤)	Energy Consumption Per 10000 Yuan Gross Industrial Output Value(ton of SCE)	3.69	3.58	-3.0
每万元工业总产值煤消费量(吨)	Coal Consumption Per 10000 Yuan Gross Industrial Output Value(ton)	5.58	5.21	-6.6
每万元工业总产值电消费量(千瓦小时)	Electricity Consumption Per 10000 Yuan Gross Industrial Output Value(kwh)	3313.79	4888.67	47.5
每万元国内生产总值能源消费量(吨标准煤)	Energy Consumption Per 10000 Yuan GDP(ton of SCE)	3.99	3.67	-8.0
每吨能源生产的国内生产总值(元)	GDP Produced by Per Ton Energy(yuan)	2508.07	2726.14	8.7

注:工业总产值、国内生产总值增长速度均按可比价格计算。

Note:The growth rates of gross industrial output value and GDP are calculated at comparable prices.

6－9 分行业能源消费量和主要能源品种消费量(2001)

Consumption of Total Energy and Its Main Varieties by Sector

行　　业	Sector	能源消费总量(万吨标准煤) Total Energy Consumption (10000 tons of SCE)	万元产值能耗煤(吨标准煤/万元) Coal Consumption Per 10000 yuan Output Value(ton of SCE/10000 yuan)	煤炭消费量(万吨) Goal Consumption (10000 tons)
工业	Industry	2492.69	3.58	3588.96
采掘业	Mining and Quarring	366.57	8.89	1008
煤炭采选业	Coal Mining and Dressing	333.36	14.63	986.44
黑色金属矿采选业	Ferrous Metals Mining and pressing	0.26	0.7	0.34
有色金属矿采选业	Nonferrous Metals Mining and Dressing	3.67	2.29	3.28
非金属矿采选业	Nonmetal Minerals Mining and Dressing	29.22	1.83	17.94
木材及竹材采运业	Logging and Transport of Wood and Bamboo	0.03	0.06	
制造业	Manufacturing	1307.59	2.42	1281.33
食品加工业	Food Processing	7.48	0.46	6.83
食品制造业	Food Production	2.92	0.56	3.52
饮料制造业	Beverage Production	8.82	0.32	10.72
烟草加工业	Tobacco Processing	17.73	0.19	17.67
纺织业	Textile Industry	4.9	1.69	4.41
服装及其他纤维制品制造业	Garments and Other Fiber Products	0.43	0.19	0.34
皮革、毛皮、羽绒及其制品业	Leather, Furs, Down and Related Products	0.03	1	0.02
木材加工及竹、藤、棕、草制品业	Timber Processing, Bamboo, Cane, Palm Fiber and Straw Products	1.55	0.95	1.72
家具制造业	Furniture Manufacturing	0.11	0.52	0.06
造纸及纸制品业	Papermaking and Paper Products	9.64	2.68	11.59
印刷业,记录媒介的复制	Printing and Record Medium Reproduction	1.48	0.24	0.86
文教体育用品制造业	Cultural, Educational and Sports Articles	0.46	1.24	0.59
石油加工及炼焦业	Petroleum Processing and Coking	122.08	642.53	429.22
化学原料及化学制品制造业	Raw Chemical Materials and Chemical Products	304.77	4.85	153.21
医药制造业	Medical and Pharmaceutical Products	5.43	0.16	4.9

6-9 续表 1(continued)

行　　业	Sector	汽油消费量（万吨）Gasoline Consumption (10000 tons)	柴油消费量（万吨）Diesel Oil Consumption (10000 tons)	电力消费量（亿千瓦时）Electricity Consumption (100 million kwh)
工业	Industry	5.82	5.32	340.56
采掘业	Mining and Quarring	0.63	1.26	21.04
煤炭采选业	Coal Mining and Dressing	0.47	0.45	10.66
黑色金属矿采选业	Ferrous Metals Mining and Dressing	0.01		0.01
有色金属矿采选业	Nonferrous Metals Mining and Dressing	0.02	0.07	0.62
非金属矿采选业	Nonmetal Minerals Mining and Dressing	0.12	0.74	9.73
木材及竹材采运业	Logging and Transport of Wood and Bamboo	0.01		0.02
制造业	Manufacturing	4.2	3.17	294.85
食品加工业	Food Processing	0.1	0.02	1.94
食品制造业	Food Production	0.08		0.24
饮料制造业	Beverage Production	0.14	0.03	0.74
烟草加工业	Tobacco Processing	0.24	0.09	3.77
纺织业	Textile Industry	0.03		1.35
服装及其他纤维制品制造业	Garments and Other Fiber Products	0.03		0.12
皮革、毛皮、羽绒及其制品业	Leather, Furs, Down and Related Products			0.02
木材加工及竹、藤、棕、草制品业	Timber Processing, Bamboo, Cane, Palm Fiber and Straw Products			0.26
家具制造业	Furniture Manufacturing			0.06
造纸及纸制品业	Papermaking and Paper Products	0.03	0.02	1.05
印刷业，记录媒介的复制	Printing and Record Medium Reproduction	0.05	0.01	0.64
文教体育用品制造业	Cultural, Educational and Sports Articles			0.03
石油加工及炼焦业	Petroleum Processing and Coking			0.01
化学原料及化学制品制造业	Raw Chemical Materials and Chemical Products	0.46	0.39	64.04
医药制造业	Medical and Pharmaceutical Products	0.09	0.02	1.38

6－9 续表 2(continued)

行业	Sector	能源消费总量(万吨标准煤) Total Energy Consumption (10000 tons of SCE)	万元产值能耗煤(吨标准煤/万元) Coal Consumption Per 10000 yuan Output Value(ton of SCE/10000 yuan)	煤炭消费量(万吨) Goal Consumption (10000 tons)
化学纤维制造业	Chemical Fibers	0.04	0.27	
橡胶制品业	Rubber Products	17.48	0.87	18.63
塑料制品业	Plastic Products	1.57	0.28	1.15
非金属矿物制品业	Nonmetal Mineral Products	270.5	8.88	338.61
黑色金属冶炼及压延加工业	Smelting and Pressing of Ferrous Metals	260.59	4.03	105.84
有色金属冶炼及压延加工业	Smelting and Pressing of Nonferrous Metals	230.62	4.12	102.7
金属制品业	Metal Products	7.89	0.75	2.4
普通机械制造业	Ordinary Machinery Manufacturing	4.61	0.74	3.33
专用设备制造业	Special Purposes Equipment Manufacturing	2.6	0.52	2.2
交通运输设备制造业	Transportation Equipment Manufacturing	23.48	0.45	20.32
武器弹药制造业	Weapon and Munition Manufacturing	0.01		
电气机械及器材制造业	Electric Equipment and Machinery	3.04	0.17	2.81
电子及通信设备制造业	Electronic and Telecommunications Equipment	1.91	0.16	0.42
仪器仪表及文化、办公用机械制造业	Instruments, Meters, Cult ural and Office Machinery	0.74	0.41	0.19
其他制造业	Others	－5.36	－12.76	37.07
电力、煤气及水的生产和供应业	Electric Power, Gas and Tap Water Production and Supply	818.54	7.14	1299.63
电力、蒸汽、热水的生产和供应业	Electric Power、Steam and Hot Water Production and Supply	794.32	7.39	1299.2
煤气生产和供应业	Gas Production and Supply	21.29	6.3	0.2
自来水的生产和供应业	Tap Water Production and Supply	2.92	0.78	0.23
建筑业	Construction	16.53		3.8
交通运输、仓储及邮电通信业	Transportation, Storage, Postal & Telecommunications Services	143.72		7.82
批发和零售贸易餐饮业	Wholesale, Retail Trade and Catering Services	126.75		129.48
其他行业	Others	183.91		171
生活消费	Residential Consumption	800.03		997.41

6-9 续表 3(continued)

行　　业	Sector	汽油消费量（万吨）Gasoline Consumption (10000 tons)	柴油消费量（万吨）Diesel Oil Consumption (10000 tons)	电力消费量（亿千瓦时）Electricity Consumption (100 million kwh)
化学纤维制造业	Chemical Fibers			0.03
橡胶制品业	Rubber Products	0.36	0.01	2.95
塑料制品业	Plastic Products	0.05		0.55
非金属矿物制品业	Nonmetal Mineral Products	0.33	0.43	20.41
黑色金属冶炼及压延加工业	Smelting and Pressing of Ferrous Metals	0.51	0.28	83.86
有色金属冶炼及压延加工业	Smelting and Pressing of Nonferrous Metals	0.31	1.46	97.33
金属制品业	Metal Products	0.28	0.04	4.33
普通机械制造业	Ordinary Machinery Manufacturing	0.01	0.09	1.34
专用设备制造业	Special Purposes Equipment Manufacturing		0.03	0.76
交通运输设备制造业	Transportation Equipment Manufacturing	0.61	0.17	5.72
武器弹药制造业	Weapon and Munition Manufacturing			0.01
电气机械及器材制造业	Electric Equipment and Machinery	0.19	0.05	0.52
电子及通信设备制造业	Electronic and Telecommunications Equipment	0.2	0.03	1.03
仪器仪表及文化、办公用机械制造业	Instruments, Meters, Cultural and Office Machinery	0.1		0.33
其他制造业	Others			0.03
电力、煤气及水的生产和供应业	Electric Power, Gas and Tap Water Production and Supply	0.99	0.89	24.67
电力、蒸汽、热水的生产和供应业	Electric Power、Steam and Hot Water Production and Supply	0.89	0.88	22.14
煤气生产和供应业	Gas Production and Supply	0.02	0.01	0.38
自来水的生产和供应业	Tap Water Production and Supply	0.08		2.15
建筑业	Construction	0.48	1.75	8.2
交通运输、仓储及邮电通信业	Transportation, Storage, Postal & Telecommunications Services	31.31	52.27	12.49
批发和零售贸易餐饮业	Wholesale, Retail Trade and Catering Services	1.1	1.95	12.16
其他行业	Others	7.17	19.18	11.06
生活消费	Residential Consumption			32.07

注：能源消费量包括终端消费和加工转换投入量。

Note: The energy consumption include the final consumption and consumed in transformation.

主要统计指标解释

能源生产总量 指一定时期内全省一次能源生产量的总和。一次能源生产量包括原煤，原油，天然气，水电、核能及其他动力能(如风能、地热能等)发电量，不包括低热值燃料生产量、生物质能、太阳能等的利用和由一次能源加工转换而成的二次能源产量。

能源消费总量 指一定时期内全省物质生产部门、非物质生产部门和生活消费的各种能源的总和。能源消费总量包括原煤和原油及其制品、天然气、电力，不包括低热值燃料、生物质能和太阳能等的利用。能源消费总量分为终端能源消费量、能源加工转换损失量和损失量三部分。

(1)终端能源消费量：指一定时期内全国生产和生活消费的各种能源在扣除了用于加工转换二次能源消费量和损失量以后的数量。

(2)能源加工转换损失量：指一定时期内全国投入加工转换的各种能源数量之和与产出各种能源产品之和的差额，是观察能源在加工转换过程中损失量变化的指标。

(3)能源损失量：指一定时期内能源在输送、分配、储存过程中发生的损失和由客观原因造成的各种损失量，不包括各种气体能源放空、放散量。

能源生产弹性系数 是研究能源生产增长速度与国民经济增长速度之间关系的指标。计算公式为：

能源生产弹性系数 = 能源生产总量年平均增长速度/国民经济年平均增长速度

国民经济年平均增长速度，可根据不同的目的或需要，用国民生产总值、国内生产总值等指标来计算，本年鉴是采用国内生产总值指标计算的。

电力生产弹性系数 是研究电力生产增长速度与国民经济增长速度之间关系的指标。一般来说，电力的发展应当快于国民经济的发展，也就是说电力应超前发展。计算公式为：

电力生产弹性系数 = 电力生产量年平均增长速度/国民经济年平均增长速度

能源消费弹性系数 是反映能源消费增长速度与国民经济增长速度之间比例关系的指标。计算公式为：

$$\text{能源消费弹性系数} = \frac{\text{能源消费量年平均增长速度}}{\text{国民经济年平均增长速度}}$$

电力消费弹性系数 反映电力消费增长速度与国民经济增长速度之间比例关系的指标。计算公式为：

$$\text{电力消费弹性系数} = \frac{\text{电力消费量年平均增长速度}}{\text{国民经济年平均增长速度}}$$

能源加工转换效率 指一定时期内能源经过加工、转换后，产出的各种能源产品的数量与同期内投入加工转换的各种能源数量的比率。它是观察能源加工转换装置和生产工艺先进与落后、管理水平高低等的重要指标。计算公式为：

$$\text{能源加工转换效率} = \frac{\text{能源加工、转换产出量}}{\text{能源加工、转换投入量}} \times 100\%$$

Explanatory Notes on Main Statistical Indicators

Total Energy Production refers to the total production of primary energy by all energy producing enterprises in the country in a given period of time. The production of primary energy includes that of coal, crude oil, natural gas, hydro – power and electricity generated by nuclear energy and other means such as wind power and geothermal power. However, it excludes the production of fuels of low calorific value, bio – energy, solar energy and the secondary energy converted from the primary energy.

Total Domestic Energy Consumption refers to the total consumption of energy of various kinds by material production sectors, non material production sectors and households in the province in a given period of time. It is a comprehensive indicator to show the scale, composition and development of energy consumption. The total energy consumption includes that of coal, crude oil and their products, natural gas and electricity, However, it excludes the consumption of fuel of low calorific value, bio – energy and solar energy. Total domestic energy consumption can be divided into three parts:

(1) Final Energy Consumption: It refers to the total energy consumption by material production sectors, non material production sectors and households in the country(region) in a given period of time, but excludes the consumption in conversion of the primary energy into the secondary energy and the loss in the process of energy conversion.

(2) Loss During the Process of Energy Conversion: It refers to the total input of various kinds of energy for conversion, minus the total output of various kinds of energy in the country in a given period of time. It is an indicator to show the loss that occurs during the process of energy conversion.

(3) Loss: It refers to the total of the loss of energy during the course of energy transport, distribution and storage and the loss caused by any objective reason in a given period of time. The loss of various kinds of gas due to gas discharges and stocktaking is excluded.

Elasticity Ratio of Energy Production is an indicator to show the relationship between the growth rate of energy production and the growth rate of the national economy. The formula is:

$$\text{Elasticity Ratio of Energy Production} = \frac{\text{Average Annual Growth Rate of Energy Production}}{\text{Average Annual Growth Rate of National Economy}}$$

The average annual growth rate of the national economy can be shown by the gross national product, gross domestic product and other indicators, depending upon the purposes or needs. The gross domestic product is used in calculation of the ratio in this chapter.

Elasticity Ratio of Electricity Production is an indicator to show the relationship between the growth rate of electricity production and the growth rate of the national economy. Generally speaking, the growth rate of electricity production should be higher than that of the national economy. Its formula is:

Elasticity Ratio of Electricity Production = Average Annual Growth Rate of Electricity Production/Average Annual Growth Rate of National Economy

Elasticity Ratio of Energy Consumption is an indicator to show the relationship between the growth rate of energy consumption and the growth rate of the national economy. The formula is:

$$\text{Elasticity Ratio of Energy Consumption} = \frac{\text{Average Annual Growth Rate of Energy Consumption}}{\text{Average Annual Growth Rate of National Economy}}$$

Elasticity Ratio of Electricity Consumption is an indicator to show the relationship between the growth rate of electricity consumption and the growth rate of the national economy. The formula is:

$$\text{Elasticity Ratio of Electricity Consumption} = \frac{\text{Average Annual Growth Rate of Electricity}}{\text{Average Annual Growth Rate of National Economy}}$$

Efficiency of Energy Processing and Conversion refers to the ratio of the total output of energy products of various kinds after processing and conversion and the total input of energy of various kinds for processing and conversion in the same reference period. It is an important indicator to show the current conditions of energy processing and conversion equipment, production technique and management. The formula is:

$$\text{Efficiency of Energy Processing \& Conversion} = \frac{\text{Output of Energy After Processing \& Conversion}}{\text{Input of Energy for Processing \& Conversion}} \times 100\%$$

7

Seven

农 业

Agriculture

农村社会基础设施(个)(2001)
Basic Facilities in Rural Areas (unit)

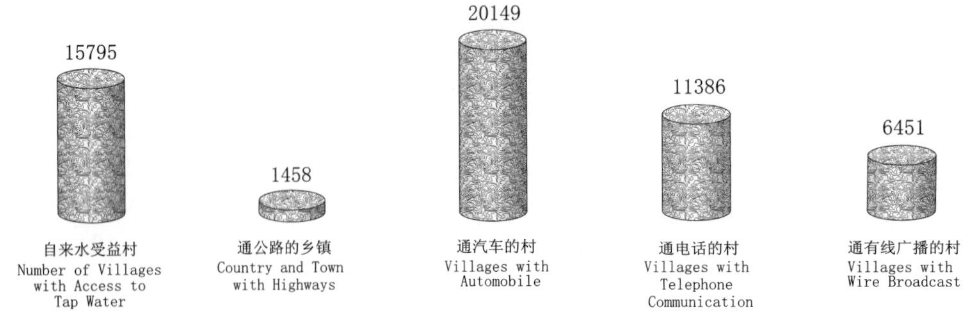

农用机械(万千瓦)
Agricultural Machinery (10000 kw)

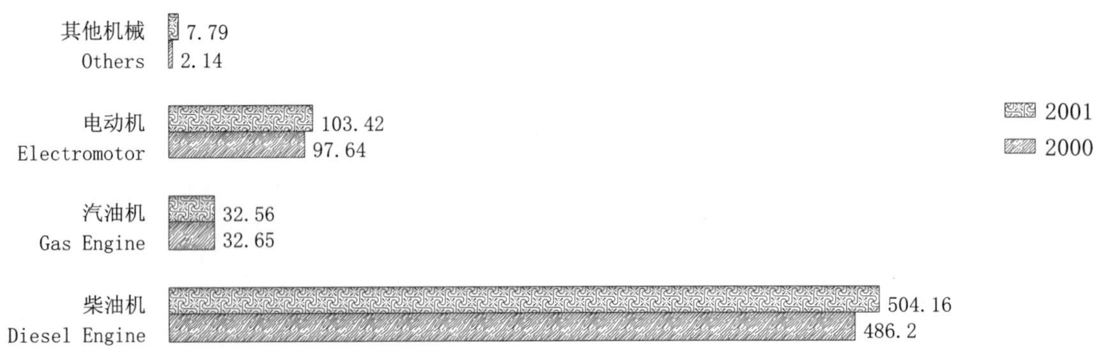

农林牧渔业增加值构成(%)
Composition of Added Value of Farming, Forestry, Animal Husbandry and Fishery(%)

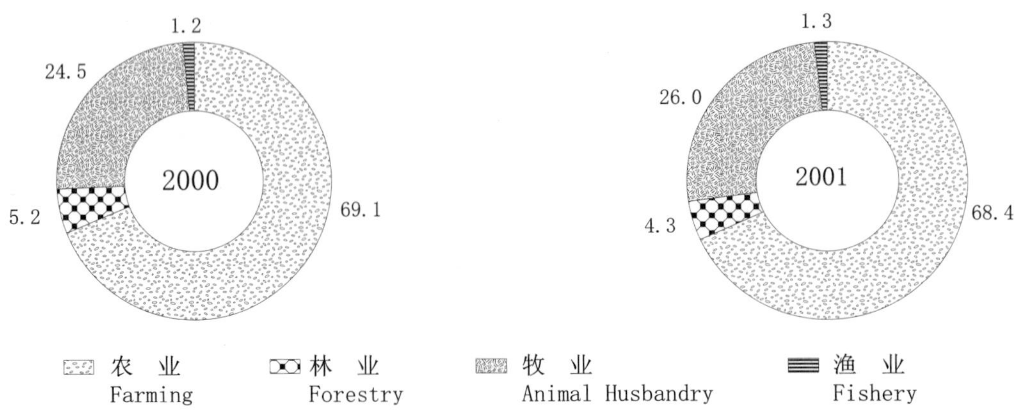

7-1 农村基本情况及农业生产条件
Basic Statistics on Rural Areas and Conditions for Agricultural Production

指　　标	Item	2000	2001	2001年比2000年增长(%) Increase Rate in 2001 over 2000(%)
农村基层组织(个)	Rural Grassroots Units(unit)			
乡镇个数	Township and Village	1463	1460	-0.2
村委会个数	Village Committees	25696	24890	-3.1
农村社会基础设施	Basic Facilities in Rural Areas			
自来水受益村数	Number of Villages with Access to Tap Water	15633	15795	1.0
※通公路的乡镇数	Country and Town with Highways	1463	1458	
※通汽车的村数	Villages with Automobile	20375	20149	
通电话的村数	Villages with Telephone Communication	8218	11386	38.5
通有线广播的村数	Villages with Wire Broadcast	5936	6451	8.7
乡村人口与从业人员	Rural Population and Employment			
乡村户数(万户)	Number of Rural Households(10000 households)	734.65	743.85	1.3
乡村人口数(万人)	Rural Population(10000 persons)	3123.46	3160.64	1.2
乡村从业人员	Rural Employment	1802.63	1821.50	1.0
#农业从业人员	Rural Employment	1372.12	1368.28	-0.3
耕　地	Cultivated Area			
年末实有耕地面积(万亩)	Cultivated Area(year-end)(10000 mu)	2765.22	2748.42	-0.6
水　田	Paddy Fields	1148.07	1144.92	-0.3
旱　地	Dry Fields	1617.15	1603.50	-0.8
当年增加耕地面积	Increased Area of Cultivated Land in 2001	6.86	6.59	-3.9
当年减少耕地面积	Decreased Area of Cultivated Land in 2001	14.1	23.39	65.9
#国家基建占地	Government Capital Construction	5.42	7.38	36.3
乡村集体占地	Village Collective Construction	1.98	2.00	0.8
农民个人建房占地	Peasant Housing Construction	1.46	1.46	持平
农业机械化	Agricultural Mechanization			
农用机械总动力(万千瓦)	Total Power of Agricultural Machinery(10000 kw)	618.63	647.93	4.7
#柴油机	Diesel Engine	486.2	504.16	3.7
汽油机	Gas Engine	32.65	32.56	-0.3
电动机	Electromotor	97.64	103.42	5.9
其他机械	Others	2.14	7.79	264.0
农村主要能源及物资消耗	Main Energy for Agricultural Use and Materials Consumption			
乡村办水电站(个)	Number of Hydropower Stations in Rural Areas(unit)	798	795	-0.4
发电量(万千瓦时)	Electricity(10000 kwh)	35811	39400	10.0
农用化肥施用量(折纯法)(万吨)	Consumption of Chemical Fertilizer(pure)(10000 tons)	71.29	69.95	-1.9
平均每亩耕地化肥施用量(公斤)	Average Per Mu Consumption of Chemical Fertilizer(kg)	25.78	25.45	-1.3
农村用电量(万千瓦时)	Electricity Consumption in Rural Areas(10000 kwh)	141821	139200	-1.8
农药使用量(吨)	Consumption of Chemical Pesticides(ton)	8400	8329	-0.8
地膜使用量	Consumption of Farm Plastic Membrane	12094	12397	2.5
农田水利建设情况(万亩)	Farmland and Irrigation(10000 mu)			
有效灌溉面积	Effective Irrigated Area	980.06	989.72	1.0
旱涝保收面积	Area that Ensure Stable Yields Despite Drought or Excessive Rain	796.08	807.63	1.5
机电排灌面积	Area with Motorized Drainage and Irrigation Facilities	105.11	106.04	0.9

注:带“※”的指标两年数据口径不一致。

Note:The statistical coverage of the data with “※” is inconsistant with last year.

7－2 农林牧渔业总产值、增加值

Gross Output Value and Added Value of Farming, Forestry, Animal Husbandry and Fishery

单位:万元
(10000 yuan)

指 标	Item	2000	2001	2001年比2000年增长(%) Inerease Rate in 2001 over 2000(%)
农林牧渔业总产值(当年价)	**Gross Output Value of Farming, Forestry, Animal Husbandry and Fishery(current price)**	**4129716**	**4186100**	**1.2**
农业产值	Farming	2796153	2799500	－0.1
种植业	Planting	2481355	2473100	－1.4
主产品产值	Main Product	2391050	2386700	－1.3
副产品产值	Sideline Product	90305	86400	－3.9
其他农业	Other Crops	314798	326400	7.6
林业产值	Forestry	180379	150800	－15.9
营 林	Afforestation	91363	64400	－32.4
林产品	Forest Products	56814	57600	0.5
村及村以下竹木采伐	Lumbering at Village level and below	32202	28800	－13.1
牧业产值	Animal Husbandry	1106706	1184600	6.9
牲畜	Animal	953048	1015700	6.5
#大牲畜	Large Animals	132612	144000	7.6
猪	Hogs	794946	843900	6.0
羊	Goats and sheep	25490	27900	7.5
家禽的饲养	Poultry Raising	84924	93100	9.6
其他动物及产品	Others	68734	75800	10.2
渔业产值	Fishery	46478	51300	10.2
农林牧渔业增加值(当年价)	**Added Value of FFAF(current price)**	**2709919**	**2741700**	**1.1**
农 业	Farming	1873055	1874500	－0.2
林 业	Forestry	140341	118500	－16.1
牧 业	Animal Husbandry	664904	713900	6.7
渔 业	Fishery	31619	34800	10.0

7－3 农林牧渔业商品产值及商品率
Commodity Output Value and Commodity Rate of Farming, Forestry, Animal Husbandry and Fishery

指　　标	Item	2000	2001	2001 年比 2000 年增长(%) Increase Rate in 2001 over 2000(%)
商品产值(万元)	**Commodity Output Value(10000 yuan)**	**1728398**	**1919400**	**11.1**
农　业	Farming	1021237	1103100	8.0
种植业	Planting	853093	920000	7.8
主产品	Main Product	848401	914158	7.8
副产品	Sideline Product	4692	5842	24.5
其他农业	Others	168144	183100	8.9
林　业	Forestry	82289	73400	－10.8
牧　业	Animal Husbandry	591895	703500	18.9
牲畜	Animal	494470	546400	10.5
#大牲畜	Large Animals	58647	66200	12.9
猪	Hogs	417620	465000	11.3
羊	Goats & Sheeps	18203	21000	15.4
家禽	Poultry	53486	63900	19.5
活的畜禽产品	Live Animal and Poultry Products	41557	46000	10.7
其它动物及产品	Others	41900	47200	12.6
渔　业	Fishery	33913	39400	16.2
商品率(%)	**Commodity Rate (%)**	**41.9**	**45.9**	**4.0**
农　业	Farming	36.5	39.4	2.9
种植业	Planting	34.4	37.2	2.8
主产品	Main Product	35.5	38.3	2.8
副产品	Sideline Product	5.2	6.8	1.6
其他农业	Others	53.4	56.1	2.7
林　业	Forestry	45.1	48.7	3.6
牧　业	Animal Husbandry	53.5	59.4	5.9
牲畜	Animal	51.9	53.8	1.9
#大牲畜	Large Animals	44.2	46.0	1.8
猪	Hogs	52.5	55.1	2.6
羊	Goats & Sheeps	71.4	75.2	3.8
家禽	Poultry	63.0	68.6	5.6
活的畜禽产品	Live Animal and Poultry Products	64.1	65.0	0.9
其它动物及产品	Others	60.9	62.3	1.4
渔　业	Fishery	73.0	76.8	3.8

注：本表按当年价格计算。

Note: Data in this table are calculated at current prices.

7-4 主要农业机械拥有量
Possession of Agricultural Machinery

指 标	Item	2000	2001	2001年比2000年增长(%) Increase Rate in 2001 over 2000(%)
大中型拖拉机(万台)	Large and Medium Agricultural Tractors(10000 sets)	1.68	1.8	7.1
(万千瓦)	(10000 kw)	45.71	46.19	1.1
大中型拖拉机配套农具(万台)	Suited Farm Tools by Large and Medium Agricultural Tractors(10000 sets)	0.16	0.2	25.0
小型拖拉机(万台)	Mini Agricultural Tractors(10000 sets)	5.5	5.36	-2.5
(万千瓦)	(10000 kw)	55.34	54.18	-2.1
小型拖拉机配套农具(万台)	Suited Farm Tools by Mini Agricultural Tractors (10000 sets)	0.75	0.78	4.0
农用排灌电动机(万台)	Number of Drainage and Irrigation Electromotor Engines (10000 units)	4.45	4.8	7.9
(万千瓦)	(10000 kw)	26.31	27.83	5.8
农用排灌柴油机(万台)	Number of Drainage and Irrigation Diesel Engines(10000 units)	6.74	7.2	6.8
(万千瓦)	(10000 kw)	43.22	49.37	14.2
联合收割机(台)	Combine Harvesters(unit)	53	67	26.4
(万千瓦)	(10000 kw)	0.08	0.08	持平
农用运输车(万辆)	Transport for Agricultural Use(10000 units)	3.75	3.91	4.3
(万千瓦)	(10000 kw)	142.15	128.33	-9.7

注:本表资料由省农机部门提供。

Note: Data in this table are obtained from the agricultural machinery department .

7－5 主要农作物播种面积
Sown Areas of Major Farm Crops

单位:万亩
(10000 mu)

指　　标	Item	2000	2001	2001 年比 2000 年增长(%) Increase Rate in 2001 over 2000(%)
农作物总播种面积	**Total Sown Areas of Farm Crops**	**7044.00**	**6976.05**	**－1.0**
粮食作物	Grain Crops	4726.95	4681.65	－1.0
#稻　谷	Rice	1125.75	1125.00	－0.1
小　麦	Wheat	851.10	780.75	－8.3
玉　米	Corn	1090.95	1082.70	－0.8
大　豆	Soybeans	211.50	208.80	－1.3
薯　类	Tubers	1053.75	1086.00	3.1
#马铃薯	Irish Potato	716.25	742.35	3.6
油　料	Oil－bearing Crops	769.05	747.00	－2.9
#油菜籽	Rapeseeds	691.95	668.24	－3.4
花　生	Peanuts	66.45	68.55	3.2
麻　类	Fiber Crops	4.50	3.90	－13.3
#黄红麻	Jute and Ambary Hemp	0.45	0.20	－56.7
糖　料	Sugar Crops	25.65	27.14	5.8
#甘蔗	Sugarcane	25.50	27.09	6.2
烟　叶	Tobacco	320.55	303.20	－5.4
#烤烟	Flue－cured Tobacco	290.10	273.57	－5.7
药材类	Crude Drugs	20.25	25.82	27.5
蔬　菜	Vegetable	533.10	558.42	4.7

注:"蔬菜"的统计口径与往年不同,它不包含果用瓜。

Note:The statistial coverage of the vegetable is different from the previous years, because it excludes the melon.

7－6　主要农作物产品产量
Yield of Major Farm Crops

单位:万吨
(10000 tons)

指　　标	Item	2000	2001	2001 年比 2000 年增长(%) Increase Rate in 2001 over 2000(%)
粮食作物	**Grain Crops**	**1161.30**	**1100.30**	**－5.3**
稻　谷	Rice	477.40	459.80	－3.7
小　麦	Wheat	103.50	87.70	－15.3
玉　米	Corn	342.20	319.40	－6.7
大　豆	Soybeans	18.10	16.70	－7.7
杂　豆	Incidental Bean	21.40	20.50	－4.2
薯　类	Tubers	186.40	184.90	－0.8
#马铃薯	Irish Potato	124.60	128.10	2.8
其　它	Others	12.30	11.30	－8.1
油料作物	**Oil Plants Crops**	**74.34**	**71.32**	**－4.1**
#油菜籽	Rapeseeds	66.20	63.48	－4.1
花　生	Peanuts	7.45	7.21	－3.2
黄红麻	Jute and Ambary Hemp	0.06	0.02	－66.7
苎　麻	Ramee	0.14	0.12	－14.3
甘　蔗	Sugarcane	66.66	65.11	－2.3
烤　烟	Flue－cured Tobacco	31.09	26.38	－15.1

7－7　主要农作物单产
Yield of Major Farm Crops Per Mu

单位:公斤/亩
(kg/mu)

指　　标	Item	2000	2001	2001 年比 2000 年增长(%) Increase Rate in 2001 over 2000(%)
粮食作物	**Grain Crops**	**246**	**235**	**－4.3**
稻　谷	Rice	424	409	－3.6
小　麦	Wheat	122	112	－7.6
玉　米	Corn	314	295	－6.0
大　豆	Soybeans	86	80	－6.5
杂　豆	Incidental Bean	79	93	18.4
薯　类	Tubers	177	170	－3.8
#马铃薯	Irish Potato	174	173	－0.8
其　它	Others	101	93	－7.9
油料作物	**Oil Plants Crops**	**97**	**95**	**－1.2**
#油菜籽	Rapeseed	96	95	－0.7
花　生	Peanuts	112	105	－6.3
黄红麻	Jute and Ambary Hemp	133	106	－20.4
苎　麻	Ramee	47	42	－10.1
甘　蔗	Sugarcane	2614	2404	－8.1
烤　烟	Flue－cured Tobacco	107	96	－10.0

7-8 茶叶、蚕茧、水果、水产品面积及产量
Toatal Areas and Yield of Tea, Silkworm Cocoon, Fruit and Aquatic Products

指　　标	Item	2000	2001	2001 年比 2000 年增长(%) Increase Rate in 2001 over 2000(%)
面积(万亩)	**Area(10000 mu)**			
茶园面积	Tea Field Area	67.19	70.71	5.2
桑园面积	Mulberry Field Area	13.86	13.73	-0.9
柞坡面积	Breed Tussah Field Area	4.12	3.9	-5.3
果园面积	Orchards Filed Area	135.56	160.58	18.5
产量(万吨)	**Yield (10000 tons)**			
茶　叶	Tea	1.84	1.85	0.5
蚕　茧	Silkworm Cocoon	0.12	0.12	持平
桑蚕茧	Mulberry Silkworm Cocoon	0.12	0.12	持平
柞蚕茧	Tussah Cocoon	…	…	…
水　果	Fruit	58.33	62.93	7.9
#香蕉	Bananas	0.99	1.03	4.0
苹　果	Apples	0.77	0.79	2.6
柑　桔	Citrus	10.13	12.79	26.3
梨	Pears	4.77	6.66	39.6
猕猴桃	Chinese Goosebeerys	0.59	0.99	67.8
柿　子	Persimmons	1.29	1.27	-1.6
杨　梅	Red　Bayberry	0.97	0.89	-8.2
水产品(万吨)	**Aquatic Products(10000 tons)**	**6.24**	**6.89**	**10.4**

注:2001 年水果类统计口径与往年不同,它包含原属于蔬菜类的果用瓜。

Note: The statistial Coverage of the fruit in 2001 is different from the previous years, because it include melon which belonged to the vegetable.

7-9 林产品产量
Yield of Forestery Products

单位:吨
(ton)

指 标	Item	2000	2001	2001年比2000年增长(%) Increase Rate in 2001 over 2000(%)
当年造林面积(万亩)	**Build Forestry Areas(10000 mu)**	440.6	361.04	-18.1
#飞机播种面积	Seeded Areas by Plane	45.24	56.25	24.3
林产品产量	**Yield of Forestry Products**			
生 漆	Lacquer	1006	1047	4.1
油桐籽	Tung - oil Seed	116592	103697	-11.1
油茶籽	Tea - oil Seed	8195	9956	21.5
乌桕籽	Tallow - seeds	4180	4064	-2.8
五倍籽	Nutgall	1495	1469	-1.7
棕 片	Palm - flake	4620	4787	3.6
松 脂	Pine Resin	4392	4118	-6.2
竹 笋	Bamboo Shoot	3593	4115	14.5
核 桃	Walnuts	7492	7010	-6.4
板 栗	Chestnut	7471	7810	4.5

注:表中"造林面积"及相关指标由省林业部门提供。

Note: Build forestry areas and correlative indicators in this table are obtained from forestry department.

7-10 畜牧业生产
Statistics on Livestock

指标	Item	2000	2001	2001年比2000年增长(%) Increase Rate in 2001 over 2000(%)
猪牛羊出栏头数(万头)	Number of Slaughtered Fattened Hogs, Ox, Goats and Sheep(10000 heads)			
当年肉猪出栏头数	Slaughtered Fattened Hogs	1167.51	1229.99	5.4
当年出售和自宰的肉用牛	Ox by Sold and Killed	51.35	55.91	8.9
当年出售和自宰的肉用羊	Goats by Sold and Killed	165.47	179.15	8.3
当年肉类总产量(万吨)	Total Yield of Meat(10000 tons)	124.06	131.70	6.2
#猪　肉	Pork	105.05	110.93	5.6
牛　肉	Beef	6.99	7.58	8.4
羊　肉	Mutton	4.21	4.34	3.1
禽　肉	Poultry	7.32	8.03	9.7
其他畜产品产量(吨)	Others(ton)			
#牛　奶	Cow Milk	16920	20037.28	18.4
蜂　蜜	Honey	1567	1423.00	-9.2
禽　蛋	Poultry Eggs	65259	70049.16	7.3
大牲畜年末头数(万头)	Large Livestock(year-end)(10000 heads)	731.49	746.12	2.0
#役　畜	Draught Animals	518.08	521.05	0.6
牛	Cattle and Buffaloes	658.08	671.40	2.0
#黄　牛	Cattle	430.27	437.47	1.7
水　牛	Buffalo	227.05	232.94	2.6
猪年末数(万头)	Hogs (year-end)(10000 heads)	1687.31	1730.67	2.6
羊年末数(万只)	Sheep and Goats(year-end) (10000 heads)	341.76	350.04	2.4
山　羊	Goats	321.36	329.94	2.7
绵　羊	Sheep	20.4	20.10	-1.5

7－11　乡镇企业主要经济指标
Major Economic Indicators of Township and Village Enterprises

单位：亿元
(100 million yuan)

指　标	Item	2000	2001	2001年比2000年增长(%) Increase Rate in 2001 over 2000(%)
年末固定资产原值	Original Value of Fixed Assets(year－end)	308.8	393.1	27.3
年末营业收入	Operating Revenue(year－end)	1270.9	1499.7	18.0
实交国家税金	Taxes Paid	20.5	23.6	15.1
纯利润	Total Profits	75.5	87.6	16.0
年末职工人数(万人)	Staff and Workers(year－end)(10000 persons)	241.8	253.6	4.9
工资总额	Total Wages	112.4	125.1	11.3

注：1.表中省资料由省乡镇企业局提供(以下各相关表同)。2.本表均含有部分暂不符合四个条件的企业(以下各相关表同)。

Note：1.Data in this table are obtained from Provincial Township and Village Enterprises Bureau(same as in the follwing tables). 2. Some parts of enterprises in this table are don't conform with four conditions(same as in the following tables).

7－12　乡镇企业基本情况(2001)
Basic Statistics on Township and Village Enterprises

项　目	Item	总计 Total	农业 Agriculture	工业 Industry	建筑业 Construction	交通运输业 Transportation	批发零售贸易业 Wholesale and Retail Trade	旅游饮食服务业 Junketing, Catering Trades and Service	其他 Others
企业个数(个)	**Number of Enterprises(unit)**	**679880**	**3949**	**227531**	**17151**	**145638**	**187529**	**78140**	**19942**
集　体	Collective－owned Enterprises	9423	3360	4036	288	133	1345	217	44
私　营	Private Enterprises	27897	24	17704	3711	1786	1905	2156	611
个　体	Individual	642560	565	205791	13152	143719	184279	75767	19287
年末人数(人)	**Staff(year－end)(person)**	**2536289**	**44035**	**1270818**	**282102**	**242890**	**389657**	**241701**	**65086**
集　体	Collective－owned Enterprises	303707	41765	201657	39673	4998	11348	3435	831
私　营	Private Enterprises	423331	752	291114	90306	7876	12522	15197	5564
个　体	Individual	1809251	1518	778047	152123	230016	365787	223069	58691

7－13 乡镇股份制企业及联营企业情况(2001)

Condition of Township and Village Stock－holding Enterprises and Joint－owned Enterprises

项　目	Item	企业个数(个) Number of Enterprises (unit)	职工人数(人) Staff and Workers (person)	营业收入(万元) Operating Revenue (10000 yuan)	利润总额(万元) Total Profits (10000 yuan)	应交税金(万元) Payable Taxes (10000 yuan)
股份制企业	Stock－holding Enterprises	233	13326	120242	5515	6773
股份合作制企业	Stock－holding Cooperation Enterprises	1509	36002	213064	10086	6613
集体企业改制	Collectivity Enterprises Strypped－down	251	25658	162116	6209	4310
#本年改制	Strypped－down at Current Year	8	1226	5225	－974	496
个体、私营企业改制	Individual and Private Enterprises Strypped－down	208	7297	37132	2744	1663
#本年改制	Strypped－down at Current Year	29	629	3199	402	104
新组建	Newly Established Enterprises	1050	3047	13816	1133	640
#本年组建	Established Enterprises at Current Year	11	893	5700	138	256
中外合资企业合计	Sino－Foreign Joint Funded Enterprises	7	1096	13248	1116	298
中外合作企业合计	Sino－Foreign Cooperative Operation Enterprises	1	25	143	1	8
与港澳台合资企业	Joint Enterprises with Investment from Hong Kong, Macao and Taiwan	7	577	1671	－12	149
与港澳台合作企业	Cooperation Enterprises with Investment from Hong Kong, Macao and Taiwan	1	170	2240	112	86

主要统计指标解释

农林牧渔业总产值　指以货币表现的农、林、牧、渔业全部产品的总量，它反映一定时期内农业生产总规模和总成果。农业总产值的计算方法通常是按农林牧渔业产品及其副产品的产量分别乘以各自单位产品价格求得；然后将四业产品产值相加即为农业总产值。

粮食产量　指全社会的产量。包括国有经济经营的、集体统一经营的和农民家庭经营的粮食产量，还包括工矿企业办的农场和其他生产单位的产量。粮食除包括稻谷、小麦、玉米、高粱、谷子及其他杂粮外，还包括薯类和豆类。其产量计算方法，豆类按去豆荚后的干豆计算；薯类（包括甘薯和马铃薯，不包括芋头和木薯）1963年以前按每4公斤鲜薯折1公斤粮食计算，从1964年开始改为按5公斤鲜薯折1公斤粮食计算。城市郊区作为蔬菜的薯类（如马铃薯等）按鲜品计算，并且不作粮食统计。其他粮食一律按脱粒后的原粮计算。

油料产量　指全部油料作物的生产量。包括花生、油菜籽、芝麻、向日葵籽、胡麻籽（亚麻籽）和其他油料。不包括大豆、木本油料和野生油料。花生以带壳干花生计算。

水产品产量　指人工养殖的水产品和天然生长的水产品的捕捞量。包括海水的鱼类、虾蟹类、贝类和藻类以及内陆水域的鱼类、虾蟹类和贝类，不包括淡水生植物。

猪、牛、羊肉产量　指当年出栏并已屠宰、除去头蹄下水后带骨肉（即胴体重）的重量。

期初（末）畜禽存栏头（只）数　指报告期初（末）农村各种合作经济组织和国营农场、农民个人、机关、团体、学校、工矿企业、部队等单位以及城镇居民饲养的大牲畜、猪、羊、家禽等畜禽的存栏数。

耕地面积　指可以用来种植农作物、经常进行耕锄的田地，包括熟地、当年新开荒地、连续撂荒未满三年的耕地和当年的休闲地（轮歇地），还包括以种植农作物为主并附带种植桑树、茶树、果树和其他林木的土地，以及沿海、沿湖地区已围垦利用的“海涂”、“湖田”等面积。不包括属于专业性的桑园、茶园、果园、果木苗圃、林地、芦苇地、天然或人工草地面积。

农作物播种面积　指实际播种或移植有农作物的面积。凡是实际种植有农作物的面积，不论种植在耕地上还是种植在非耕地上，均包括在农作物播种面积中。在播种季节基本结束后，因遭灾而重新改种和补种的农作物面积，也包括在内。

有效灌溉面积　指具有一定的水源，地块比较平整，灌溉工程或设备已经配套，在一般年景下当年能够进行正常灌溉的耕地面积。

农用化肥施用量　指本年内实际用于农业生产的化肥数量，包括氮肥、磷肥、钾肥和复合肥。化肥施用量要求按折纯量计算数量。折纯量是指把氮肥、磷肥、钾肥分别按含氮、含五氧化二磷、含氧化钾的百分之一百成份进行折算后的数量。复合肥按其所含主要成分折算。

农业机械总动力　指主要用于农、林、牧、渔业的各种动力机械的动力总和。包括耕作机械、排灌机械、收获机械、农用运输机械、植物保护机械、牧业机械、林业机械、渔业机械和其他农业机械〔内燃机按引擎马力折成瓦（特）计算、电动机按功率折成瓦（特）计算〕。不包括专门用于乡、镇、村、组办工业、基本建设、非农业运输、科学试验和教学等非农业生产方面用的动力机械与作业机械。

农林牧渔业劳动力　指全社会直接参加农林牧渔业生产活动的劳动力。

Explanatory Notes on Main Statistical Indicators

Gross Output Value of Farming, Forestry, Animal Husbandry and Fishery refers to the total value of products of farming, forestry, animal husbandry and fishery, which reflects the total scale and result of agricultural production during a given period. Gross output value of agriculture is obtained by first multiplying the output of each product or by product by its price, resulting in the output value of each single item.

Grain Yield refers to the yield in the whole country including grains produced by state farms, collective units, industrial enterprises and mines. Grain includes rice, wheat, corn, sorghum, millet and other miscellaneous grains as well as tubers and beans. Output of beans refers to dry beans without pods. The output of tubers (sweet potatoes and potatoes, not including taros and cassava) was converted into that of grain at the ratio 4:1, i.e. 4 kilograms of fresh tubers was equivalent to 1 kilogram of grain up to 1963. Since 1964 the ratio for conversion has been 5:1. Tubers supplied as vegetables (such as potatoes) in cities and suburbs are calculated as fresh vegetables and their output is not included in the output of grain. Output of all other grains refers to husked grain.

Yield of Oil – bearing Crops refers to the total yield of oil bearing crops of various kinds, including peanuts, (dry, in shell) rapeseeds, sesame, sunflower seeds, flax seeds, and other oil bearing crops. Soybeans, oil – bearing woody plants, and wild oil – bearing crops are not included.

Output of Aquatic Products refers to catches of both artificially cultured and naturally grown aquatic products, including fish, shrimps, crabs and shellfish in sea and inland water as well as seaweed. Freshwater plants are not included.

Output of Pork, Beef, and Mutton refers to the meat of slaughtered hogs, cattle, sheep and goats with head, feet, and offal taken away.

Number of Livestock or Poultry in Stock at Beginning (or End) refers to the total number of large animals, pigs, sheep, fowls, etc. raised by rural cooperative organizations, statefarms, ruralindividuals, governmentagencies, schools, industrial and mining enterprises, army, and urban residents at the beginning (or end) of the reference period.

Cultivated Area (Area under cultivation) refers to farmland which is plowed constantly for growing crops, including cultivated land, newly cultivated land in the current year, farmland left without cultivation for less than three years and fallow land in the current year, rotation land, rotation land of grass and crops, farmland with some fruit trees, mulberry trees and other trees and cultivated seashore land, lake land, and etc. The land of mulberry fields, tea plantations, orchards, nurseries of young plants, forest land, reed land, natural and man – made grassland and other land are not included in cultivated land.

Sown Area of Crops refers to area of land sown or transplanted with crops regardless of being in cultivated area or non cultivated area. Area of land re – sown due to natural disasters is also included.

Irrigated Area refers to areas that are effectively irrigated, i.e. level land which has water source and complete sets of irrigation facilities to lift and move adequate water for irrigation purpose under normal conditions.

Consumption of Chemical Fertilizers in Agriculture refers to the quantity of chemical fertilizers applied in agriculture in the year, including nitrogenous fertilizer, phosphate fertilizer, potash fertilizer, and compound fertilizer. The consumption of chemical fertilizers is required in calculation to convert the gross weight into weight containing 100% effective component (e.g. 100% nitrogen content in nitrogenous fertilizer, 100% phosphorous pentoxide contents in phosphate fertilizer, 100% potassium oxide contents in potash fertilizer). Compound fertilizer is converted with its major component.

Total Power of Farm Machinery refers to total mechanical power of machinery used in farming, forestry, animal husbandry, and fishery, including ploughing, irrigation and drainage, harvesting, transport, plant protection, stock breeding, forestry and fishery. The power of internal combustion engines is required to convert horsepower into watts and the power of electric motors is required to be converted into watts. Machinery employed for non agricultural purposes, such as the machines used in township run and village – run industry, construction, non agricultural transport, scientific experiments and teaching, is excluded.

Labour Force Engaged in Farming, Forestry, Animal Husbandry and Fishery refers to the total laborers who are directly engaged in production of farming, forestry, animal husbandry and fishery.

8

工 业

Industry

Eight

全部工业总产值(亿元)(2001)
Gross Output Value of Industry (100 million yuan)

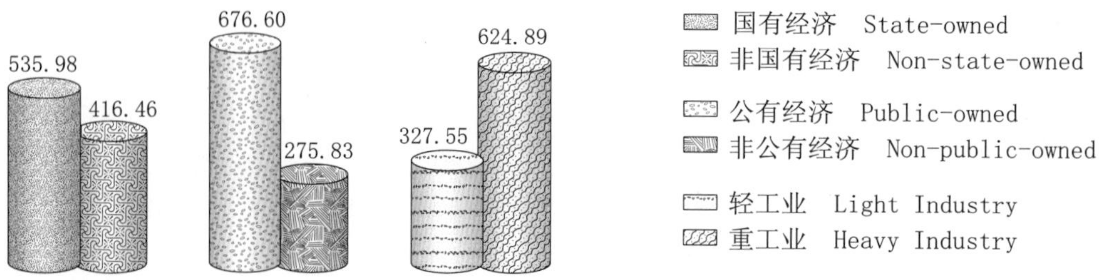

按企业规模分的总产值、增加值(规模以上)(亿元)(2001)
Gross Output Value and Added Value of Industrial Enterprises above Designated Size (100 million yuan)

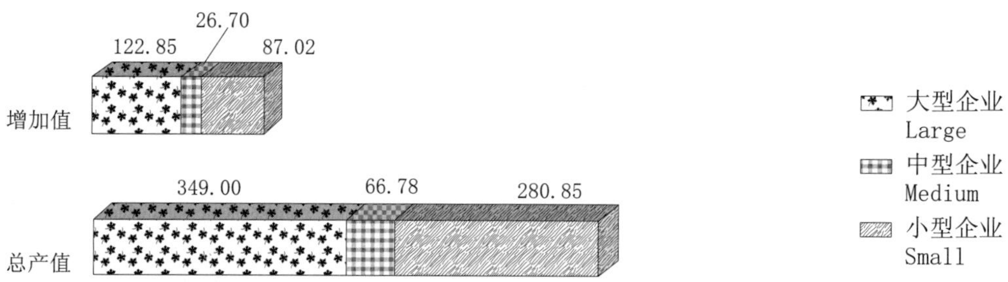

大中型工业企业主要经济指标(亿元)(2001)
Major Economic Indicators of Large-scale and Medium-scale Industrial Enterprises (100 million yuan)

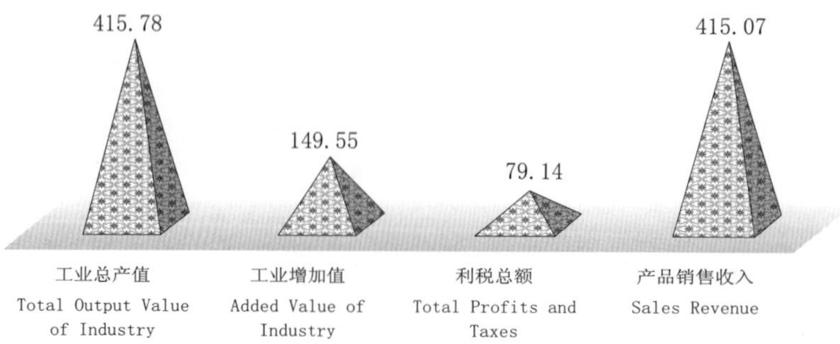

8-1 全部工业总产值
Gross Output Value of Industry

单位:亿元
(100 million yuan)

指标	Item	2000	2001	2001年比2000年增长(%) Increase Rate
总计	Total	855.51	952.44	13.2
按轻重工业分:	Grouped by Type of Light and Heavy Industry			
轻工业	Light Industry	300.70	327.55	10.4
重工业	Heavy Industry	554.81	624.89	14.7
按国有非国有分:	Grouped by Type of State - owned or Non - state - owned			
国有经济	State - owned	500.75	535.98	8.2
非国有经济	Non - state - owned	354.76	416.46	20.3
按公有非公有分:	Grouped by Type of Public - owned or Non - public - owned			
公有经济	Public - owned	625.16	676.61	9.6
非公有经济	Non - public - owned	230.35	275.83	23.0
规模以上工业总产值合计	Gross Output Value of Industry above Designated Size	631.64	696.63	12.6
按登记注册类型分:	Grouped by Registration			
内资企业	Domestic - funded	613.09	675.07	10.9
国有企业	State - owned	319.59	325.89	-2.3
中央	Central	180.52	188.95	1.7
地方	Local	139.07	136.94	-7.3
集体企业	Collective - owned	50.54	32.07	-31.8
股份合作企业	Cooperative Enterprises	7.48	7.65	-0.4
联营企业	Joint Ownership Enterprises	8.51	5.25	-34.9
有限责任公司	Limited Liability Corporations	157.03	204.79	46.7
股份有限公司	Share - holding Corporations Ltd	43.29	46.91	-10.3
私营企业	Private Enterprises	26.62	52.38	96.9
其他企业	Others	0.02	0.13	491.2
港、澳、台商投资企业	Enterprises Funded by Hong kong, Macao and Taiwan	4.75	6.74	42.4
外商投资企业	Foreign Funded Enterprisers	13.80	14.82	9.0
在合计中:	of the Total			
亏损企业	Loss Making Enterprise	92.62	115.59	28.5

8-1 续表(continued)

指 标	Item	2000	2001	2001年比2000年增长(%) Increase Rate
在合计中:	of the Total:			
国有控股企业	Controlling Share Hold by the State Enterprises	500.76	535.98	6.2
在合计中:	of the Total:			
农村工业	Rural Industry	20.33	12.78	-34.1
按轻重工业分:	**Grouped by Type of Light and Heavy Industry**			
轻工业	Light Industry	206.33	220.11	6.4
以农产品为原料	Using Farm Products as Raw Meterials	183.71	194.57	5.2
以非农产品为原料	Using Non-farm Products as Raw Meterials	22.62	25.54	12.8
重工业	Heavy Industry	425.31	476.52	13.6
采掘工业	Mining and Quarring	36.01	41.23	16.5
原料工业	Raw Meterials	247.52	280.85	15.7
加工工业	Manufacturing	141.78	154.44	10.8
按企业规模分:	**Grouped by Scale of Enterprise**			
大型企业	Large	322.56	349.00	8.6
中型企业	Medium	67.64	66.78	6.5
小型企业	Small	241.44	280.85	15.3
规模以下工业总产值合计	**Total Output Value of Industry below Designated Size**	**223.87**	**255.81**	**14.7**
在合计中:	of the Total:			
轻工业	Light Industry	94.37	107.44	14.3
重工业	Heavy Industry	129.50	148.37	15.0
在合计中:	of the Total:			
企业	Enterprises	58.37	67.40	15.9
农村个体	Rural Individual Business	131.99	151.24	15.0
城镇个体	Township Individual Business	33.51	37.17	11.3

注:本表绝对数按当年价格计算,增长速度按可比价格计算。

Note: Absolute figures in this table are calculated at current prices, while the increase rate are calculated at comparable prices.

8－2 规模以上工业企业单位数
Number of Industrial Enterprises

单位:个
(unit)

指　　标	Item	2000	2001	2001年比2000年增长(%) Increase Rate in 2001 over 2000(%)
总　　计	Total	2087	2054	－1.6
按经济类型分:	Grouped by Ownership			
#国有及国有控股企业	State－owned and Controlling Share Hold by the State Enterprises	1397	1269	－9.2
港澳台投资企业	Enterprises Funded by Hong kong, Macao and Taiwan	30	41	36.7
外商投资企业	Enterprises Funded by Foreigners	31	35	12.9
农村工业	Rural Industry	95	72	－24.2
按公有非公有分:	Grouped by Type of Public－owned or Non－public－owned			
公有经济	Public－owned	1798	1598	－11.1
非公有经济	Non－public－owned	289	456	57.8
按国有非国有分:	Grouped by Type of State－owned or Non－state－owned			
国有经济	State－owned	1397	1269	－9.2
非国有经济	Non－state－owned	690	785	13.8
按轻重工业分:	Grouped by Type of Light and Heavy Industry			
轻工业	Light Industry	810	771	－4.8
重工业	Heavy Industry	1277	1283	0.5
按企业规模分:	Grouped by Scale of Enterprise			
#大型企业	Large	103	99	－3.9

8－2续表(continued)

单位:个
(unit)

指　　标	Item	2000	2001	2001年比2000年增长(%) Increase Rate in 2001 over 2000(%)
中型企业	Medium	119	113	－5.0
小型企业	Small	1865	1842	－1.2
按主要行业分	**Grouped by Main Sector**			
采掘业	Mining and Quarring	202	146	－27.7
制造业	Manufacturing	1638	1663	1.5
#食品加工业	Food Processing	181	161	－11.0
食品制造业	Food Production	52	48	－7.7
饮料制造业	Beverage Production	85	98	15.3
烟草加工业	Tobacco Processing	37	35	－5.4
化学原料及化学制品制造业	Raw Chemical Materials and Chemical Products	178	178	0.0
医药制造业	Medical and Pharmaceutical Products	81	82	1.2
橡胶制品业	Rubber Products	14	19	35.7
非金属矿物制品业	Nonmetal Mineral Products	252	259	2.8
黑色金属冶炼及压延加工业	Smelting and Pressing of Ferrous Metals	91	124	36.3
有色金属冶炼及压延加工业	Smelting and Pressing of Nonferrous Metals	99	142	43.4
电气机械及器材制造业	Electric Equipment and Machinery	31	29	－6.5
电力、煤气及水的生产和供应业	Electric Power, Gas and Tap Water Production and Supply	247	245	－0.8

8-3 规模以上工业总产值
Gross Industrial Output Value

单位:亿元
(100 million yuan)

指标	Item	2000	2001	2001 年比 2000 年增长(%) Increase Rate in 2001 over 2000(%)
总计	**Total**	**631.64**	**696.63**	**12.6**
按经济类型分:	**Grouped by Ownership**			
#国有及国有控股企业	State - owned and Controlling Share Hold by the State Enterprises	500.76	535.98	6.2
港澳台投资企业	Enterprises Funded by Hong kong, Macao and Taiwan	4.75	6.74	42.4
外商投资企业	Enterprises Funded by Foreigners	13.80	14.82	9.0
农村工业	Rural Industry	20.33	12.78	-34.1
按公有非公有分:	**Grouped by Type of Public - owned or Non - public - owned**			
公有经济	Public - owned	567.31	581.08	1.7
非公有经济	Non - public - owned	64.33	115.55	84.0
按国有非国有分:	**Grouped by Type of State - owned or Non - state - owned**			
国有经济	State - owned	500.76	535.98	6.2
非国有经济	Non - state - owned	130.88	160.65	27.7
按轻重工业分:	**Grouped by Type of Light and Heavy Industry**			
轻工业	Light Industry	206.33	220.11	6.4
重工业	Heavy Industry	425.31	476.52	13.6
按企业规模分:	**Grouped by Scale of Enterprise**			
#大型企业	Large	322.56	349.00	8.6

8-3 续表(continued)

单位:亿元
(100 million yuan)

指 标	Item	2000	2001	2001 年比 2000 年增长(%) Increase Rate in 2001 over 2000(%)
中型企业	Medium	67.64	66.78	6.5
小型企业	Small	241.44	280.85	15.3
按主要行业分:	Grouped by Main Sector			
采掘业	Mining and Quarring	35.86	41.23	17.1
制造业	Manufacturing	503.67	540.79	10.0
# 食品加工业	Food Processing	13.66	16.16	16.6
食品制造业	Food Production	3.6	5.22	47.2
饮料制造业	Beverage Production	24.92	27.64	22.7
烟草加工业	Tobacco Processing	89.81	94.48	2.2
化学原料及化学制品制造业	Raw Chemical Materials and Chemical Products	57.05	62.87	15.6
医药制造业	Medical and Pharmaceutical Products	31.32	34.23	9.3
橡胶制品业	Rubber Products	17.14	20.04	16.9
非金属矿物制品业	Nonmetal Mineral Products	27.16	30.47	14.1
黑色金属冶炼及压延加工业	Smelting and Pressing of Ferrous Metals	58.45	64.69	13.6
有色金属冶炼及压延加工业	Smelting and Pressing of Nonferrous Metals	55.7	55.92	16.6
电气机械及器材制造业	Electric Equipment and Machinery	16.02	17.43	15.7
电力、煤气及水的生产和供应业	Electric Power, Gas and Tap Water Production and Supply	92.11	114.61	19.5

8－4 规模以上工业企业主要经济指标
Major Economic Indicators of Industrial Enterprises

指　　标	Item	2000	2001	2001 年比 2000 年增长(%) Increase Rate in 2001 over 2000(%)
固定资产原值(亿元)	Original Value of Fixed Assets(100 million yuan)	913.15	1015.1	11.2
固定资产净值平均余额(亿元)	Average Balance Net Value of Fixed Assets(100 million yuan)	608.02	672.36	10.6
流动资产平均余额(亿元)	Average Balance of Circulating Funds(100 million yuan)	650.77	685.41	5.3
产品销售收入(亿元)	Sales Revenue (100 million yuan)	593.8	646.01	8.8
利税总额(亿元)	Total Profits and Taxes(100 million yuan)	87.44	94.3	7.8
#利润(亿元)	Total Profits(100 million yuan)	12.56	18.59	48.0
总资产贡献率(%)	Ratio of Total Assets to Industrial Output Value(%)	7.70	7.08	－0.62(百分点)
资本保值增值率(%)	Ratio of Capital Hold and Rise(%)	114.60	131.93	17.33(百分点)
资产负债率(%)	Asset－debt Ratio(%)	68.60	64.43	－4.17(百分点)
成本费用率(%)	After－tax Profits/Cost(%)	2.30	2.91	0.61(百分点)
产品产销率(%)	Sales Rate of Industrial Products(%)	95.5	95.1	－0.40(百分点)
流动资产周转次数(次/年)	Turnover of Total Circulating Funds(time/year)	0.91	0.89	－0.02(次)
全员劳动生产率(元/人、年)	Overall Labor Productivity(yuan/person, year)	31751	35649	3898(元)

8－5 规模以上工业企业主要财务指标(2001)
Major Financial Indicators of Industrial Enterprises above Designated Size

单位:亿元
(100 million yuan)

指 标	Item	企业单位数(个) Number of Enterprises(unit)	从业人员年平均人数(万人) Annual Average of All Employees (10000 persons)	工业总产值 Total Output Value of Industry	工业增加值 Added Value of Industry	资产合计 Total Property
总 计	Total	2054	66.36	696.63	236.57	1698.58
按登记注册类型分	Grouped by Registration					
内资企业	Domestic－funded Enterprises	1978	64.52	675.07	229.98	1646.54
国有企业	State－owned	1086	33.19	325.89	119.41	929.02
中央企业	Central	92	10.63	188.95	72.21	469.32
地方企业	Local	994	22.56	136.94	47.21	459.70
集体企业	Collective－owned	226	3.69	32.07	8.99	38.46
股份合作企业	Cooperative	68	1.09	7.65	2.16	10.95
联营企业	Joint Ownership	32	0.45	5.25	1.01	8.09
有限责任公司	Limited Liability Corporations	220	19.65	204.79	68.13	527.89
股份有限公司	Share－holding Corporations Ltd	68	2.32	46.91	14.85	79.78
私营企业	Private	275	4.11	52.38	15.40	52.25
其他企业	Others	3	0.02	0.13	0.02	0.10
港、澳、台商投资企业	Enterprises Funded by Hong kong, Macao and Taiwan	41	0.78	6.75	1.95	22.28
外商投资企业	Foreign Funded Enterprises	35	1.06	14.81	4.64	29.76
在总计中:	of the Total:					
国有控股企业	Controlling Share Hold by the State Enterprises	1269	53.14	535.98	188.97	1487.57
在总计中:	of the Total:					
农村工业	Rural Industry	72	0.93	12.78	3.43	10.68
按轻重工业分:	Grouped by Type of Light and Heavy Industry					
轻工业	Light Industry	771	13.75	220.11	87.66	412.57
以农产品为原料	Using Farm Products as Raw Meterials	573	10.96	194.57	81.94	362.71
以非农产品为原料	Using Nonfarm Products as Raw Meterials	198	2.79	25.54	5.72	49.86
重工业	Heavy Industry	1283	52.61	476.52	148.91	1286.01
采掘工业	Mining and Quarring	146	10.79	41.23	10.90	176.39
原料工业	Raw Meterials	659	21.11	280.85	92.47	718.90
加工工业	Manufacturing	478	20.71	154.44	45.54	390.72
按企业规模分:	Grouped by Scale of Enterprise					
大型企业	Large	99	29.48	349.00	122.85	1085.26
中型企业	Medium	113	8.98	66.78	26.70	134.09
小型企业	Small	1842	27.9	280.85	87.02	479.23

8－5 续表(continued)

单位:亿元
(100 million yuan)

指　　标	Item	流动资产合计 Circulating Funds	固定资产原值合计 Original Value of Fixed Assets	产品销售收入 Revenue of Products Sales	利税总额 Total Profits and Taxes	利润总额 Total Profits
总　　计	**Total**	**704.48**	**1015.10**	**646.01**	**94.30**	**18.59**
按登记注册类型分	**Grouped by Funded Enterprises**					
内资企业	Domestic Funded Enterprises	676.96	994.35	625.90	93.73	19.07
国有企业	State－owned	347.69	601.13	318.88	52.59	12.99
中央企业	Central	175.23	321.85	183.34	28.23	6.43
地方企业	Local	172.46	279.28	135.54	24.36	6.56
集体企业	Collective－owned	21.21	18.70	27.89	1.86	－0.15
股份合作企业	Cooperative	4.63	6.436.63	0.31	－0.13	
联营企业	Joint Ownership	2.96	5.14	4.31	0.01	－0.20
有限责任公司	Limited Liability Corporations	236.25	305.71	184.08	30.27	3.21
股份有限公司	Share－holding Corporations Ltd	40.17	32.79	43.68	4.75	1.75
私营企业	Private	23.96	24.42	40.27	3.92	1.59
其他企业	Others	0.08	0.02	0.15	0.02	0.01
港、澳、台商投资企业	Enterprises Funded by Hong kong, Macao and Taiwan	9.80	7.23	6.16	－0.03	－0.34
外商投资企业	Foreign Funded Enterprises	17.72	13.52	13.95	0.61	－0.14
在总计中:	of the Total					
国有控股企业	Controlling Share Hold by the State Enterprises	591.41	925.79	516.05	83.79	15.65
在总计中:	of the Total					
农村工业	Rural Industry	6.19	5.12	11.11	0.59	0.17
按轻重工业分:	**Grouped by Type of Light and Heavy Industry**					
轻工业	Light Industry	229.17	159.04	193.36	51.27	6.98
以农产品为原料	Using Farm Products as Raw Meterials	205.57	133.96	170.35	50.12	6.74
以非农产品为原料	Using Non－farm Products as Raw Meterials	23.60	25.08	23.01	1.15	0.24
重工业	Heavy Industry	475.31	856.06	452.66	43.03	11.61
采掘工业	Mining and Quarring	48.67	139.00	38.75	3.13	0.59
原料工业	Raw Meterials	221.07	530.75	272.74	31.33	9.45
加工工业	Manufacturing	205.56	186.31	141.17	8.57	1.57
按企业规模分:	**Grouped by Scale of Enterprise**					
大型企业	Large	425.87	697.20	364.52	74.22	18.61
中型企业	Medium	62.79	72.80	50.55	4.93	－0.03
小型企业	Small	215.82	245.10	230.94	15.15	0.01

8－6 规模以上工业企业分行业主要经济指标(2001)

Major Economic Indicators of Industrial Enterprises above Designated Size by Branch

单位:亿元
(100 million yuan)

指　　标	Item	企业单位数(个) Number of Enterprises(unit)	从业人员年平均人数(万人) Annual Average of All Employees (10000 persons)	工业总产值 Total Output Value of Industry	工业增加值 Added Value of Industry	资产合计 Total Property
总　　计	Total	2054	66.36	696.63	236.57	1698.58
采掘业	Mining and Quarring	146	10.79	41.23	10.90	176.39
煤炭采选业	Coal Mining and Processing	74	8.03	22.79	7.13	84.17
黑色金属矿采选业	Ferrous Metals Mining and Processing	2	0.09	0.37	0.11	0.44
有色金属矿采选业	Nonferrous Metals Mining and Processing	21	0.79	1.60	0.49	2.60
非金属矿采选业	Nonmetal Minerals Mining and Processing	20	1.57	15.98	3.01	85.92
木材及竹材采运业	Logging and Transport of Timber and Bamboo	29	0.32	0.49	0.16	3.26
制造业	Manufacturing	1663	50.03	540.79	181.95	1073.18
食品加工业	Food Processing	161	1.01	16.17	3.81	19.29
食品制造业	Food Production	48	0.58	5.22	1.87	8.37
饮料制造业	Beverage Production	98	2.48	27.64	14.95	94.10
烟草加工业	Tobacco Processing	35	2.13	94.48	42.88	151.60
纺织业	Textile Industry	32	1.73	2.90	0.81	14.75
服装及其他纤维制品制造业	Garments and Other Fiber Products	9	0.33	2.28	0.70	2.37
皮革、毛皮、羽绒及其制品业	Leather, Furs, Down and Related Products	6	0.03	0.03	0.01	0.55
木材加工及竹、藤、棕、草制品业	Timber Processing, Bamboo, Cane, Palm and Straw Products	19	0.34	1.63	0.38	2.70
家具制造业	Furniture Manufacturing	8	0.06	0.21	0.06	0.43
造纸及纸制品业	Papermaking and Paper Products	28	0.52	3.60	1.08	6.18
印刷业、记录媒介的复制	Printing and Record Pressing	71	0.73	6.07	1.97	12.17
文教体育用品制造业	Stationery, Education and Sports Goods	6	0.05	0.37	0.11	0.49
石油加工及炼焦业	Petroleum Processing and Coking Products	7	0.03	0.19	0.07	0.39

8－6 续表 1(continued)

单位:亿元
(100 million yuan)

指　　标	Item	企业单位数(个) Number of Enterprises(unit)	从业人员年平均人数(万人) Annual Average of All Employees (10000 persons)	工业总产值 Total Output Value of Industry	工业增加值 Added Value of Industry	资产合计 Total Property
化学原料及化学制品制造业	Raw Chemical Materials and Chemical Products	178	5.28	62.87	16.79	126.54
医药制造业	Medical and Pharmaceutical Products	82	1.31	34.23	13.67	51.09
化学纤维制造业	Chemical Fibers	2	0.03	0.15	0.00	0.03
橡胶制品业	Rubber Products	19	1.49	20.04	6.51	38.27
塑料制品业	Plastic Products	33	0.53	5.65	1.57	10.23
非金属矿物制品业	Nonmetal Mineral Products	259	5.78	30.47	9.64	71.89
黑色金属冶炼及压延加工业	Smelting and Pressing of Ferrous Metals	124	6.31	64.69	16.39	107.67
有色金属冶炼及压延加工业	Smelting and Pressing of Nonferrous Metals	142	4.12	55.92	19.19	92.35
金属制品业	Metal Products	36	1.15	10.53	3.11	18.56
普通机械制造业	Ordinary Machinery Manufacturing	58	2.11	6.27	1.82	23.18
专用设备制造业	Special Purposes Equipment Manufacturing	45	1.29	5.03	1.20	15.38
交通运输设备制造业	Transportation Equipment Manufacturing	86	7.00	52.50	16.09	131.06
电气机械及器材制造业	Electric Equipment and Machinery	29	1.50	17.43	3.45	28.43
电子及通信设备制造业	Electronic and Telecommunications Equipment	23	1.32	11.98	3.06	38.69
仪器仪表及文化、办公用机械制造业	Instruments, Meters, Cultural and Official Machinery	10	0.76	1.82	0.63	6.00
其他制造业	Others	9	0.03	0.42	0.13	0.42
电力、煤气及水的生产和供应业	Electric Power, Gas and Tap Water Production and Supply	245	5.54	114.61	43.72	449.01
电力、蒸汽、热水的生产和供应业	Electric Power, Steam and Hot Water Production and Supply	153	4.53	107.50	42.07	415.94
煤气生产和供应业	Gas Production and Supply	4	0.26	3.38	0.40	13.37
自来水的生产和供应业	Tap Water Production and Supply	88	0.75	3.73	1.25	19.70

8－6 续表 2(continued)

单位：亿元
(100 million yuan)

指　标	Item	流动资产合计 Circulating Funds	固定资产原值合计 Original Value of Fixed Assets	产品销售收入 Revenue of Products Sales	利税总额 Total Profits and Taxes	利润总额 Total Profits
总　计	**Total**	**704.48**	**1015.10**	**646.01**	**94.30**	**18.59**
采掘业	Mining and Quarring	48.67	139.00	38.75	3.13	0.59
煤炭采选业	Coal Mining and Processing	31.01	63.24	20.48	2.35	0.54
黑色金属矿采选业	Ferrous Metals Mining and Processing	0.21	0.27	0.34	0.03	0.01
有色金属矿采选业	Nonferrous Metals Mining and Processing	1.17	2.17	1.57	0.04	－0.09
非金属矿采选业	Nonmetal Minerals Mining and Processing	15.29	71.86	15.94	0.71	0.19
木材及竹材采运业	Logging and Transport of Timber and Bamboo	0.99	1.46	0.42	…	－0.06
制造业	Manufacturing	539.51	530.82	489.54	73.87	11.32
食品加工业	Food Processing	8.16	10.37	13.38	0.08	－0.29
食品制造业	Food Production	4.02	3.19	5.10	1.02	0.66
饮料制造业	Beverage Production	47.11	29.75	29.89	14.34	5.90
烟草加工业	Tobacco Processing	102.29	56.21	84.52	30.47	－1.18
纺织业	Textile Industry	5.14	9.57	2.18	－0.33	－0.48
服装及其他纤维制品制造业	Garments and Other Fiber Products	1.52	1.18	2.11	0.08	0.04
皮革、毛皮、羽绒及其制品业	Leather, Furs, Down and Related Products	0.13	0.45	0.02	…	－0.01
木材加工及竹、藤、棕、草制品业	Timber Processing , Bamboo, Cane, Palm Fiber and Straw Products	0.90	1.84	1.21	－0.08	－0.16
家具制造业	Furniture Manufacturing	0.12	0.25	0.19	0.02	0.01
造纸及纸制品业	Papermaking and Paper Products	3.11	3.63	3.21	0.22	－0.08
印刷业、记录媒介的复制	Printing and Record Pressing	5.78	7.21	5.02	0.40	0.09
文教体育用品制造业	Stationery, Education and Sports Goods	0.25	0.16	0.12	…	－0.01
石油加工及炼焦业	Petroleum Processing and Coking Products	0.13	0.25	0.20	0.02	－0.01

8－6 续表 3(continued)

单位:亿元
(100 million yuan)

指　　标	Item	流动资产合计 Circulating Funds	固定资产原值合计 Original Value of Fixed Assets	产品销售收入 Revenue of Products Sales	利税总额 Total Profits and Taxes	利润总额 Total Profits
化学原料及化学制品制造业	Raw Chemical Materials and Chemical Products	58.15	67.60	54.35	5.05	2.10
医药制造业	Medical and Pharmaceutical Products	27.58	10.08	23.00	3.77	2.07
化学纤维制造业	Chemical Fibers	0.03	…	0.02	…	…
橡胶制品业	Rubber Products	20.64	19.10	20.69	2.35	0.52
塑料制品业	Plastic Products	3.87	7.10	4.97	0.19	0.03
非金属矿物制品业	Nonmetal Mineral Products	26.83	45.10	27.18	2.09	－0.11
黑色金属冶炼及压延加工业	Smelting and Pressing of Ferrous Metals	47.52	62.56	60.51	3.16	－0.90
有色金属冶炼及压延加工业	Smelting and Pressing of Non Ferrous Metals	32.55	76.57	52.76	6.72	2.66
金属制品业	Metal Products	9.96	7.32	10.39	0.85	0.34
普通机械制造业	Ordinary Machinery Manufacturing	12.43	12.63	5.19	－0.42	－0.77
专用设备制造业	Special Purposes Equipment Manufacturing	10.39	8.26	4.67	－0.74	－0.98
交通运输设备制造业	Transportation Equipment Manufacturing	67.58	64.58	49.69	2.90	1.33
电气机械及器材制造业	Electric Equipment and Machinery	16.55	9.12	16.48	0.97	0.27
电子及通信设备制造业	Electronic and Telecommunications	24.27	13.59	10.71	0.66	0.30
仪器仪表及文化、办公用机械制造业	Instruments, Meters, Cultural and Official Machinery	2.37	2.93	1.46	0.07	－0.02
其他制造业	Others	0.13	0.22	0.33	0.01	…
电力、煤气及水的生产和供应业	Electric Power, Gas and Tap Water Production and Supply	116.30	345.28	117.72	17.30	6.68
电力、蒸汽、热水的生产和供应业	Electric Power, Steam and Hot Water Production and Supply	104.97	324.03	112.05	16.72	6.54
煤气生产和供应业	Gas Production and Supply	2.99	9.49	2.68	0.14	－0.07
自来水的生产和供应业	Tap Water Production and Supply	8.34	11.76	2.99	0.44	0.21

8-7 规模以上国有工业企业主要经济指标(2001)

Major Economic Indicators of All State-owned above Designated Size Industrial Enterprises

单位:亿元
(100 million yuan)

指　标	Item	企业单位数(个) Number of Enterprises(unit)	从业人员年平均人数(万人) Annual Average of All Employees (10000 persons)	工业总产值 Total Output Value of Industry	工业增加值 Added Value of Industry	资产合计 Total Property
总　计	Total	1269	53.14	535.98	188.97	1487.57
在总计中:	of the Total					
中央企业	Central	109	12.94	241.41	98.20	560.36
地方企业	Local	1160	40.20	294.57	90.77	927.21
按轻重工业分:	Grouped by Type of Light and Heavy Industry					
轻工业	Light Industry	511	9.75	146.63	63.29	332.19
以农产品为原料	Using Farm Products as Raw Meterials	372	7.97	134.63	60.22	293.89
以非农产品为原料	Using Non-farm Products as Raw Meterials	139	1.78	12.00	3.07	38.30
重工业	Heavy Industry	758	43.39	389.35	125.68	1155.38
采掘工业	Mining and Quarring	95	9.91	36.97	9.64	171.49
原料工业	Raw Meterials	362	16.09	227.62	78.50	645.87
加工工业	Manufacturing	301	17.39	124.76	37.54	338.01
按企业规模分:	Grouped by Scale of Enterprise					
大型企业	Large	95	28.98	346.72	122.40	1063.33
中型企业	Medium	106	8.67	58.23	24.43	126.69
小型企业	Small	1068	15.49	131.03	42.14	297.55
按工业行业分	Grouped by Industrial Sector	1269	53.14	535.98	188.97	1487.57
采掘业	Mining and Quarring	95	9.91	36.97	9.64	171.49
煤炭采选业	Coal Mining and Processing	45	7.72	21.36	6.73	81.61
黑色金属矿采选业	Ferrous Metals Mining and Processing	1	0.02	0.14	0.04	0.42
有色金属矿采选业	Nonferrous Metals Mining and Processing	11	0.56	0.88	0.27	1.98
非金属矿采选业	Nonmetal Minerals Mining and Processing	10	1.31	14.12	2.45	84.23
木材及竹材采运业	Logging and Transport of Timber and Bamboo	28	0.30	0.48	0.15	3.25
制造业	Manufacturing	935	37.78	385.95	136.16	885.19
食品加工业	Food Processing	119	0.74	9.95	2.35	14.09
食品制造业	Food Production	35	0.40	1.56	0.53	4.40
饮料制造业	Beverage Production	65	1.86	19.52	11.93	85.79
烟草加工业	Tobacco Processing	34	2.13	94.32	42.86	151.46

8－7 续表 1(continued)

单位:亿元
(100 million yuan)

指　　标	Item	流动资产合计 Circulating Funds	固定资产原值合计 Original Value of Fixed Assets	产品销售收入 Revenue of Products Sales	利税总额 Total Profits and Taxes	利润总额 Total Profits
总　　　计	**Total**	**591.41**	**925.79**	**516.05**	**83.79**	**15.65**
在总计中：	of the Total：					
中央企业	Central	230.70	361.40	232.38	46.62	6.52
地方企业	Local	360.71	564.39	283.67	37.17	9.13
按轻重工业分：	**Grouped by Type of Light and Heavy Industry**					
轻工业	Light Industry	181.06	132.17	137.11	44.90	3.91
以农产品为原料	Using Farm Products as Raw Meterials	163.91	111.80	126.24	44.43	3.92
以非农产品为原料	Using Non－farm Products as Raw Meterials	17.15	20.37	10.87	0.47	－0.01
重工业	Heavy Industry	410.35	793.62	378.94	38.89	11.74
采掘工业	Mining and Quarring	47.09	136.13	35.10	2.68	0.46
原料工业	Raw Meterials	183.26	494.30	227.26	28.95	9.94
加工工业	Manufacturing	180.00	163.19	116.58	7.26	1.34
按企业规模分：	**Grouped by Scale of Enterprise**					
大型企业	Large	413.61	691.12	359.95	74.27	18.98
中型企业	Medium	58.92	69.90	42.95	3.74	－0.80
小型企业	Small	118.88	164.77	113.15	5.78	－2.53
按工业行业分	**Grouped by Industrial Sector**	**591.41**	**925.79**	**516.05**	**83.79**	**15.65**
采掘业	Mining and Quarring	47.09	136.13	35.10	2.69	0.46
煤炭采选业	Coal Mining and Processing	30.57	61.83	19.20	2.12	0.43
黑色金属矿采选业	Ferrous Metals Mining and Processing	0.20	0.25	0.11	…	…
有色金属矿采选业	Nonferrous Metals Mining and Processing	0.78	1.86	0.88	…	－0.09
非金属矿采选业	Nonmetal Minerals Mining and Processing	14.56	70.74	14.50	0.57	0.18
木材及竹材采运业	Logging and Transport of Timber and Bamboo	0.98	1.45	0.41	…	－0.06
制造业	Manufacturing	442.57	448.14	364.65	64.61	9.09
食品加工业	Food Processing	5.46	8.03	7.50	0.03	－0.21
食品制造业	Food Production	1.64	2.17	1.64	0.14	0.01
饮料制造业	Beverage Production	43.28	26.75	24.73	13.73	5.81
烟草加工业	Tobacco Processing	102.16	56.20	84.36	30.46	－1.18

8-7 续表 2(continued)

单位:亿元
(100 million yuan)

指标	Item	企业单位数(个) Number of Enterprises(unit)	从业人员年平均人数(万人) Annual Average of All Employees (10000 persons)	工业总产值 Total Output Value of Industry	工业增加值 Added Value of Industry	资产合计 Total Property
纺织业	Textile Industry	27	1.62	2.45	0.67	14.21
服装及其他纤维制品制造业	Garments and Other Fiber Products	3	0.17	1.50	0.49	1.46
皮革、毛皮、羽绒及其制品业	Leather, Furs, Down and Related Products	6	0.03	0.03	0.01	0.55
木材加工及竹、藤、棕、草制品业	Timber Processing, Bamboo, Cane, Palm and Straw Products	12	0.17	0.36	0.11	1.20
家具制造业	Furniture Manufacturing	5	0.03	0.03	0.01	0.15
造纸及纸制品业	Papermaking and Paper Products	13	0.31	1.51	0.47	3.49
印刷业,记录媒介的复制	Printing and Record Pressing	50	0.39	1.32	0.45	4.39
文教体育用品制造业	Stationery, Education and Sports Goods	4	0.02	0.07	0.01	0.18
石油加工及炼焦业	Petroleum Processing and Coking Products	5	0.02	0.13	0.04	0.22
化学原料及化学制品制造业	Raw Chemical Materials and Chemical Products	84	3.87	42.86	11.57	92.75
医药制造业	Medical and Pharmaceutical Products	20	0.26	1.27	0.35	13.15
橡胶制品业	Rubber Products	10	1.20	17.89	5.87	37.07
塑料制品业	Plastic Products	15	0.18	1.43	0.38	5.44
非金属矿物制品业	Nonmetal Mineral Products	117	3.20	16.68	5.41	50.99
黑色金属冶炼及压延加工业	Smelting and Pressing of Ferrous Metals	26	4.62	45.92	11.46	91.97
有色金属冶炼及压延加工业	Smelting and Pressing of Nonferrous Metals	73	3.15	40.74	15.79	79.99
金属制品业	Metal Products	15	0.88	7.09	2.14	14.79
普通机械制造业	Ordinary Machinery Manufacturing	41	1.90	4.24	1.22	20.53
专用设备制造业	Special Purposes Equipment Manufacturing	38	0.93	3.51	0.97	11.11
交通运输设备制造业	Transportation Equipment Manufacturing	70	6.52	49.35	15.25	118.36
电气机械及器材制造业	Electric Equipment and Machinery	14	1.22	8.85	2.22	23.18
电子及通信设备制造业	Electronic and Telecommunications Equipment	21	1.31	11.89	3.04	38.54
仪器仪表及文化、办公用机械制造业	Instruments, Meters, Cultural and Official Machinery	6	0.63	1.40	0.53	5.56
其他制造业	Others	6	0.02	0.08	0.03	0.17
电力、煤气及水的生产和供应业	Electric Power, Gas and Tap Water Production and Supply	239	5.45	113.05	43.17	430.89
电力、蒸汽、热水的生产和供应业	Electric Power, Steam and Hot Water Production and Supply	147	4.44	105.95	41.52	397.82
煤气生产和供应业	Gas Production and Supply	4	0.26	3.38	0.40	13.37
自来水的生产和供应业	Tap Water Production and Supply	88	0.75	3.72	1.25	19.70

8－7 续表 3(continued)

单位:亿元
(100 million yuan)

指 标	Item	流动资产合计 Circulating Funds	固定资产原值合计 Original Value of Fixed Assets	产品销售收入 Revenue of Products Sales	利税总额 Total Profits and Taxes	利润总额 Total Profits
纺织业	Textile Industry	4.80	9.32	1.82	－0.37	－0.48
服装及其他纤维制品制造业	Garments and Other Fiber Products	1.00	0.79	1.40	0.04	0.03
皮革、毛皮、羽绒及其制品业	Leather, Furs, Down and Related Products	0.13	0.45	0.02	…	－0.01
木材加工及竹、藤、棕、草制品业	Timber Processing, Bamboo, Cane, Palm and Straw Products	0.38	0.71	0.41	0.01	－0.02
家具制造业	Furniture Manufacturing	0.04	0.14	0.03	…	…
造纸及纸制品业	Papermaking and Paper Products	1.57	2.40	1.48	0.11	－0.08
印刷业,记录媒介的复制	Printing and Record Pressing	1.90	3.24	1.18	0.10	－0.01
文教体育用品制造业	Stationery, Education and Sports Goods	0.08	0.09	0.06	…	…
石油加工及炼焦业	Petroleum Processing and Coking Products	0.08	0.14	0.11	…	－0.01
化学原料及化学制品制造业	Raw Chemical Materials and Chemical Products	43.76	49.65	37.53	3.94	1.70
医药制造业	Medical and Pharmaceutical Products	1.36	1.67	0.74	…	－0.06
橡胶制品业	Rubber Products	20.05	18.26	18.97	2.27	0.54
塑料制品业	Plastic Products	1.52	3.11	1.30	0.07	…
非金属矿物制品业	Nonmetal Mineral Products	18.68	31.31	15.08	0.95	－0.25
黑色金属冶炼及压延加工业	Smelting and Pressing of Ferrous Metals	38.78	55.33	44.22	2.80	－0.49
有色金属冶炼及压延加工业	Smelting and Pressing of Nonferrous Metals	27.43	69.80	40.62	6.54	3.12
金属制品业	Metal Products	7.72	5.59	7.37	0.81	0.39
普通机械制造业	Ordinary Machinery Manufacturing	11.34	10.75	3.64	－0.49	－0.76
专用设备制造业	Special Purposes Equipment Manufacturing	7.50	5.28	3.15	－0.43	－0.56
交通运输设备制造业	Transportation Equipment Manufacturing	62.72	62.44	46.83	2.81	1.42
电气机械及器材制造业	Electric Equipment and Machinery	12.84	8.07	8.53	0.35	－0.09
电子及通信设备制造业	Electronic and Telecommunications Equipment	24.17	13.53	10.65	0.65	0.30
仪器仪表及文化、办公用机械制造业	Instruments, Meters, Cultural and Official Machinery	2.11	2.81	1.21	0.07	－0.02
其他制造业	Others	0.07	0.11	0.07	…	…
电力、煤气及水的生产和供应业	Electric Power, Gas and Tap Water Production and Supply	101.75	341.52	116.30	16.49	6.10
电力、蒸汽、热水的生产和供应业	Electric Power, Steam and Hot Water Production and Supply	90.42	320.27	110.62	15.91	5.96
煤气生产和供应业	Gas Production and Supply	2.99	9.49	2.68	0.14	－0.07
自来水的生产和供应业	Tap Water Production and Supply	8.34	11.76	2.99	0.44	0.21

8－8 规模以上集体工业企业主要经济指标(2001)

Major Economic Indicators of All Collective－owned above Designated Size Industrial Enterprises

单位：亿元
(100 million yuan)

指 标	Item	企业单位数(个) Number of Enterprises(unit)	从业人员年平均人数(万人) Annual Average of All Employees (10000 persons)	工业总产值 Total Output Value of Industry	工业增加值 Added Value of Industry	资产合计 Total Property
总 计	**Total**	**226**	**3.69**	**32.07**	**8.99**	**38.46**
在总计中：	of the Total:					
亏损企业	Loss Making Enterprise	83	1.30	10.73	2.95	14.72
在总计中：	of the Total:					
农村工业	Rural Industry	35	0.46	4.90	1.26	3.59
按轻、重工业分：	**Grouped by Type of Light and Heavy Industry**					
轻工业	Light Industry	54	0.86	9.95	2.91	15.42
以农产品为原料	Using Farm Products as Raw Meterials	36	0.52	7.21	2.21	12.91
以非农产品为原料	Using Non－farm Products as Raw Meterials	18	0.34	2.74	0.70	2.51
重工业	Heavy Industry	172	2.83	22.12	6.08	23.04
采掘工业	Mining and Quarring	13	0.24	1.44	0.43	1.09
原料工业	Raw Meterials	92	1.57	13.67	3.72	15.06
加工工业	Manufacturing	67	1.02	7.01	1.93	6.89
按企业规模分：	**Grouped by Scale of Enterprise**					
小型企业	Small	226	3.69	32.07	8.99	38.46
按工业行业分：	**Grouped by Industrial Sector**					
采掘业	Mining and Quarring	13	0.24	1.44	0.43	1.09
煤炭采选业	Coal Mining and Processing	5	0.06	0.26	0.08	0.30
黑色金属矿采选业	Ferrous Metals Mining and processing	1	0.07	0.23	0.07	0.03
有色金属矿采选业	Nonferrous Metals Mining and Processing	1	…	0.07	0.03	0.05
非金属矿采选业	Nonmetal Minerals Mining and Processing	5	0.10	0.86	0.25	0.70
木材及竹材采运业	Logging and Transport of Timber and Bamboo	1	0.01	0.02	…	0.01
制造业	Manufacturing	210	3.43	30.43	8.49	36.68
食品加工业	Food Processing	9	0.05	0.99	0.28	1.63
食品制造业	Food Production	3	0.02	0.19	0.04	0.50
饮料制造业	Beverage Production	1	0.02	0.32	0.11	0.27

8－8 续表 1(continued)

单位:亿元
(100 million yuan)

指　　标	Item	流动资产合　计 Circulating Funds	固定资产原值合计 Original Value of Fixed Assets	产品销售收　入 Revenue of Products Sales	利税总额 Total Profits and Taxes	利润总额 Total Profits
总　　计	**Total**	**21.21**	**18.70**	**27.89**	**1.86**	**－0.15**
在总计中:	of the Total:					
亏损企业	Loss Making Enterprise	7.91	7.27	8.79	－0.24	－0.74
在总计中:	of the Total:					
农村工业	Rural Industry	2.05	1.73	4.26	0.21	0.01
按轻、重工业分:	**Grouped by Type of Light and Heavy Industry**					
轻工业	Light Industry	9.08	6.25	7.97	0.74	－0.03
以农产品为原料	Using Farm Products as Raw Meterials	7.83	4.90	5.84	0.64	－0.05
以非农产品为原料	Using Non－farm Products as Raw Meterials	1.25	1.35	2.13	0.10	0.02
重工业	Heavy Industry	12.13	12.45	19.93	1.12	－0.12
采掘工业	Mining and Quarring	0.36	0.69	1.18	0.15	0.03
原料工业	Raw Meterials	6.95	9.02	12.46	0.50	－0.28
加工工业	Manufacturing	4.82	2.74	6.29	0.47	0.13
按企业规模分:	**Grouped by Scale of Enterprise**					
小型企业	Small	21.21	18.70	27.89	1.86	－0.15
按工业行业分:	**Grouped by Industrial Sector**					
采掘业	Mining and Quarring	0.36	0.69	1.18	0.15	0.03
煤炭采选业	Coal Mining and Processing	0.08	0.11	0.16	0.02	0.01
黑色金属矿采选业	Ferrous Metals Mining and processing	0.01	0.02	0.23	0.03	0.01
有色金属矿采选业	Nonferrous Metals Mining and Processing	0.03	0.03	0.05	…	…
非金属矿采选业	Nonmetal Minerals Mining and Processing	0.23	0.53	0.73	0.09	0.01
木材及竹材采运业	Logging and Transport of Timber and Bamboo	0.01	…	0.01	0.01	…
制造业	Manufacturing	20.74	17.39	26.55	1.70	－0.18
食品加工业	Food Processing	0.72	0.85	1.04	…	－0.02
食品制造业	Food Production	0.08	0.29	0.11	…	…
饮料制造业	Beverage Production	0.11	0.12	0.31	0.02	0.01

8－8 续表 2(continued)

单位:亿元
(100 million yuan)

指 标	Item	企业单位数(个) Number of Enterprises(unit)	从业人员年平均人数(万人) Annual Average of All Employees (10000 persons)	工业总产值 Total Output Value of Industry	工业增加值 Added Value of Industry	资产合计 Total Property
烟草加工业	Tobacco Processing	1	0.07	0.88	0.37	2.86
服装及其他纤维制品制造业	Garments and Other Fiber Products	2	0.08	0.25	0.09	0.30
木材加工及竹、藤、棕、草制品业	Timber Processing, Bamboo, Cane, Palm and Straw Products	1	…	0.04	0.01	0.19
家具制造业	Furniture Manufacturing	1	0.01	0.05	0.02	0.03
造纸及纸制品业	Papermaking and Paper Products	4	0.08	0.28	0.07	0.54
印刷业、记录媒介的复制	Printing and Record Pressing	8	0.10	0.92	0.30	1.83
文教体育用品制造业	Stationery, Education and Sports Goods	2	0.03	0.31	0.09	0.31
化学原料及化学制品制造业	Raw Chemical Materials and Chemical Products	32	0.28	3.45	0.73	4.47
医药制造业	Medical and Pharmaceutical Products	8	0.12	3.41	0.96	4.84
橡胶制品业	Rubber Products	3	0.09	0.54	0.15	0.42
塑料制品业	Plastic Products	6	0.14	1.26	0.29	1.40
非金属矿物制品业	Nonmetal Mineral Products	46	0.95	3.85	1.18	5.21
黑色金属冶炼及压延加工业	Smelting and Pressing of Ferrous Metals	32	0.71	5.62	1.70	6.12
有色金属冶炼及压延加工业	Smelting and Pressing of Nonferrous Metals	19	0.18	3.26	0.69	2.31
金属制品业	Metal Products	8	0.10	1.07	0.29	0.49
普通机械制造业	Ordinary Machinery Manufacturing	9	0.13	0.74	0.22	0.93
专用设备制造业	Special Purposes Equipment Manufacturing	4	0.08	0.35	0.12	0.46
交通运输设备制造业	Transportation Equipment Manufacturing	3	0.10	0.57	0.18	0.48
电气机械及器材制造业	Electric Equipment and Machinery	6	0.09	1.79	0.52	0.92
其他制造业	Others	2	0.01	0.29	0.09	0.18
电力、煤气及水的生产和供应业	Electric Power, Gas and Tap Water Production and Supply	3	0.02	0.20	0.07	0.68
电力、蒸汽、热水的生产和供应业	Electric Power, Steam and Hot Water Production and Supply	3	0.02	0.20	0.07	0.68

8－8 续表 3(continued)

单位:亿元
(100 million yuan)

指　　标	Item	流动资产合计 Circulating Funds	固定资产原值合计 Original Value of Fixed Assets	产品销售收入 Revenue of Products Sales	利税总额 Total Profits and Taxes	利润总额 Total Profits
烟草加工业	Tobacco Processing	1.79	1.37	1.17	0.45	…
服装及其他纤维制品制造业	Garments and Other Fiber Products	0.11	0.23	0.25	0.02	…
木材加工及竹、藤、棕、草制品业	Timber Processing, Bamboo, Cane, Palm Fiber and Straw Products	0.09	0.06	0.03	…	…
家具制造业	Furniture Manufacturing	0.02	0.01	0.04	…	…
造纸及纸制品业	Papermaking and Paper Products	0.29	0.26	0.22	…	－0.01
印刷业、记录媒介的复制	Printing and Record Pressing	0.92	1.02	0.84	0.03	－0.01
文教体育用品制造业	Stationery, Education and Sports Goods	0.18	0.08	0.06	…	…
化学原料及化学制品制造业	Raw Chemical Materials and Chemical Products	2.37	2.24	3.02	0.02	－0.08
医药制造业	Medical and Pharmaceutical Products	3.76	0.73	1.95	0.12	…
橡胶制品业	Rubber Products	0.20	0.20	0.38	－0.02	－0.02
塑料制品业	Plastic Products	0.69	0.92	1.13	0.04	0.01
非金属矿物制品业	Nonmetal Mineral Products	2.24	3.82	3.57	0.34	0.07
黑色金属冶炼及压延加工业	Smelting and Pressing of Ferrous Metals	3.68	2.63	5.26	0.17	－0.11
有色金属冶炼及压延加工业	Smelting and Pressing of Non Ferrous Metals	1.14	1.26	2.99	0.11	－0.12
金属制品业	Metal Products	0.33	0.20	1.01	0.02	－0.01
普通机械制造业	Ordinary Machinery Manufacturing	0.49	0.47	0.55	0.04	…
专用设备制造业	Special Purposes Equipment Manufacturing	0.33	0.21	0.24	0.03	0.01
交通运输设备制造业	Transportation Equipment Manufacturing	0.40	0.09	0.44	0.07	0.02
电气机械及器材制造业	Electric Equipment and Machinery	0.74	0.26	0.70	0.21	0.11
其他制造业	Others	0.06	0.07	0.27	0.01	…
电力、煤气及水的生产和供应业	Electric Power, Gas and Tap Water Production and Supply	0.11	0.62	0.16	0.01	…
电力、蒸汽、热水的生产和供应业	Electric Power, Steam and Hot Water Production and Supply	0.11	0.62	0.16	0.01	…

8-9　规模以上外商投资和港澳台投资工业企业主要经济指标(2001)
Major Economic Indicators of all above Designated Size Industrial Enterprises Funded by Foreigners and Hong kong, Macao and Taiwan

单位:万元
(10000 yuan)

指　标	Item	企业单位数(个) Number of Enterprises(unit)	从业人员年平均人数(万人) Annual Average of All Employees (10000 persons)	工业总产值 Total Output Value of Industry	工业增加值 Added Value of Industry	资产合计 Total Property
总　计	Total	76	18456	215639	65904	520473
在总计中:	of the Total:					
亏损企业	Loss Making Enterprises	41	10611	76787	12048	282631
在总计中:	of the Total:					
港、澳、台商投资企业	Enterprises with Investment from Hong kong, Macao and Taiwan	41	7861	67453	19505	222808
合资经营企业(港或澳、台资)	Joint Venture Enterprises (with Funds from Hong Kong, Macao and Taiwan)	31	5494	44418	11540	186125
港澳台商独资企业	Enterprises with Sole Investment from Hong Kong, Macao and Taiwan	9	1367	13810	5094	18878
港澳台商投资股份有限公司	Share Holding Co. Ltd with Investment from Hong kong, Macao and Taiwan	1	1000	9226	2871	17804
外商投资企业	Enterprises with Foreign Investment	35	10595	148186	46399	297666
中外合资经营企业	Joint-venture Enterprises	29	9961	141055	44615	282415
中外合作经营企业	Cooperation Enterprises	1	98	1635	491	4899
外资企业	Enterprises with Sole Foreign Investment	5	536	5496	1293	10351
在总计中:	of the Total:					
国有控股企业	Controlling Share Hold by the State Enterprises	21	4683	46397	6861	112308
在总计中:	of the Total:					
乡村企业	Rural Industry	1	250	800	104	1086
按轻重工业分:	Grouped by Type of Light and Heavy Industry					
轻工业	Light Industry	27	5266	116341	45621	196855
以农产品为原料	Using Farm Products as Raw Meterials	21	4410	109221	43282	186903
以非农产品为原料	Using Non-farm Products as Raw Meterials	6	856	7119	2339	9952
重工业	Heavy Industry	49	13190	99298	20283	323618
采掘工业	Mining and Quarring	2	77	1088	326	910
原料工业	Raw Meterials	16	4083	32314	8376	71174
加工工业	Manufacturing	31	9030	65897	11581	251534
按企业规模分:	Grouped by Scale of Enterprise					
大型企业	Large	5	5536	28618	1784	252562
中型企业	Medium	4	1835	21098	3397	32772
小型企业	Small	67	11085	165922	60723	235139

8-9 续表 1(continued)

单位:万元
(10000 yuan)

指　　标	Item	流动资产合计 Circulating Funds	固定资产原值合计 Original Value of Fixed Assets	产品销售收入 Revenue of Products Sales	利税总额 Total Profits and Taxes	利润总额 Total Profits
总　　计	Total	275180	207501	201200	5725	-4851
在总计中:	of the Total:					
亏损企业	Loss Making Enterprises	115698	134113	72724	-14822	-17653
在总计中:	of the Total:					
港、澳、台商投资企业	Enterprises with Investment from Hong kong, Macao and Taiwan	98042	72285	61614	-331	-3422
合资经营企业(港或澳、台资)	Joint Venture Enterprises(with Funds from Hong Kong, Macao and Taiwan)	79408	50188	41978	-1013	-3464
港澳台商独资企业	Enterprises with Sole Investment from Hong Kong, Macao and Taiwan	10269	3270	11627	574	37
港澳台商投资股份有限公司	Share Holding Co. Ltd with Investment from Hong kong, Macao and Taiwan	8366	18827	8009	108	5
外商投资企业	Enterprises with Foreign Investment	177138	135215	139586	6056	-1429
中外合资经营企业	Joint-venture Enterprises	169409	123513	133368	6337	-543
中外合作经营企业	Cooperation Enterprises	3165	4229	1325	-224	-325
外资企业	Enterprises with Sole Foreign Investment	4564	7474	4893	-57	-561
在总计中:	of the Total:					
国有控股企业	Controlling Share Hold by the State Enterprises	46711	69497	44389	-2124	-4312
在总计中:	of the Total:					
乡村企业	Rural Industry	812	295	835	-61	-93
按轻重工业分:	Grouped by Type of Light and Heavy Industry					
轻工业	Light Industry	136604	55659	107335	13821	8314
以农产品为原料	Using Farm Products as Raw Meterials	130591	51738	100282	13377	8204
以非农产品为原料	Using Non-farm Products as Raw Meterials	6013	3920	7053	444	110
重工业	Heavy Industry	138576	151842	93865	-8096	-13165
采掘工业	Mining and Quarring	433	614	958	187	95
原料工业	Raw Meterials	31156	30232	29544	1373	-262
加工工业	Manufacturing	106988	120997	63363	-9655	-12998
按企业规模分:	Grouped by Scale of Enterprise					
大型企业	Large	131331	87546	52005	-6447	-9206
中型企业	Medium	16707	20318	19024	1149	190
小型企业	Small	127143	99636	130171	11023	4166

8－9续表2(continued)

单位:万元
(10000 yuan)

指　　标	Item	企业单位数(个) Number of Enterprises(unit)	从业人员年平均人数(万人) Annual Average of All Employees (10000 persons)	工业总产值 Total Output Value of Industry	工业增加值 Added Value of Industry	资产合计 Total Property
按工业行业分	**Grouped by Industrial Sector**	**76**	**18456**	**215639**	**65904**	**520473**
采掘业	Mining and Quarring	2	77	1088	326	910
煤炭采选业	Coal Mining and Processing	2	77	1088	326	910
制造业	Manufacturing	74	18379	214551	65578	519563
食品制造业	Food Production	2	431	7142	2896	5978
饮料制造业	Beverage Production	1	90	1271	440	1758
木材加工及竹、藤、棕、草制品业	Timber Processing, Bamboo, Cane, Palm and Straw Products	1	252	1211	413	1023
造纸及纸制品业	Papermaking and Paper Products	2	132	4179	1373	6322
印刷业、记录媒介的复制	Printing and Record Pressing	2	296	3746	1152	5999
化学原料及化学制品制造业	Raw Chemical Materials and Chemical Products	9	2041	35110	5919	56526
医药制造业	Medical and Pharmaceutical Products	11	1806	65948	33213	133982
橡胶制品业	Rubber Products	1	111	213	49	676
塑料制品业	Plastic Products	7	1719	17557	5535	26220
非金属矿物制品业	Nonmetal Mineral Products	11	2959	21810	7050	50144
黑色金属冶炼及压延加工业	Smelting and Pressing of Ferrous Metals	3	623	5865	1383	6267
有色金属冶炼及压延加工业	Smelting and Pressing of Nonferrous Metals	5	1092	9073	1830	15038
金属制品业	Metal Products	2	497	3401	1059	7895
普通机械制造业	Ordinary Machinery Manufacturing	3	732	3321	706	11821
专用设备制造业	Special Purposes Equipment Manufacturing	3	2855	11745	1031	36829
交通运输设备制造业	Transportation Equipment Manufacturing	5	1838	17168	－89	137307
电气机械及器材制造业	Electric Equipment and Machinery	2	94	881	203	4552
电子及通信设备制造业	Electronic and Telecommunications Equipment	2	542	2742	672	9086
仪器仪表及文化、办公用机械制造业	Instruments, Meters, Cultural and Official Machinery	2	269	2169	743	2340

8－9 续表 3(continued)

单位：万元
(10000 yuan)

指　　标	Item	流动资产合计 Circulating Funds	固定资产原值合计 Original Value of Fixed Assets	产品销售收入 Revenue of Products Sales	利税总额 Total Profits and Taxes	利润总额 Total Profits
按工业行业分	**Grouped by Industrial Sector**	**275180**	**207501**	**201200**	**5725**	**－4851**
采掘业	Mining and Quarring	433	614	958	187	95
煤炭采选业	Coal Mining and Processing	433	614	958	187	95
制造业	Manufacturing	274748	206887	200242	5538	－4946
食品制造业	Food Production	1469	1513	6640	－173	－230
饮料制造业	Beverage Production	766	1173	964	65	－82
木材加工及竹、藤、棕、草制品业	Timber Processing, Bamboo, Cane, Palm and Straw Products	621	633	726	1	－49
造纸及纸制品业	Papermaking and Paper Products	4513	2766	3699	565	311
印刷业、记录媒介的复制	Printing and Record Pressing	2289	5038	3746	205	102
化学原料及化学制品制造业	Raw Chemical Materials and Chemical Products	24983	36890	34090	791	－352
医药制造业	Medical and Pharmaceutical Products	109070	16828	59861	11499	7764
橡胶制品业	Rubber Products	656	72	186	－73	－91
塑料制品业	Plastic Products	13539	23426	15366	636	220
非金属矿物制品业	Nonmetal Mineral Products	20546	20179	19783	3600	1569
黑色金属冶炼及压延加工业	Smelting and Pressing of Ferrous Metals	3760	2209	5829	－133	－335
有色金属冶炼及压延加工业	Smelting and Pressing of Nonferrous Metals	7495	7863	7331	－863	－1065
金属制品业	Metal Products	5103	5750	3165	－350	－525
普通机械制造业	Ordinary Machinery Manufacturing	5245	8716	3115	－624	－812
专用设备制造业	Special Purposes Equipment Manufacturing	24549	27674	12558	－3303	－4138
交通运输设备制造业	Transportation Equipment Manufacturing	42578	37770	18474	－6223	－6835
电气机械及器材制造业	Electric Equipment and Machinery	1817	1764	679	－267	－250
电子及通信设备制造业	Electronic and Telecommunications Equipment	4581	5997	1836	－92	－299
仪器仪表及文化、办公用机械制造业	Instruments, Meters, Cultural and Official Machinery	1169	627	2194	279	149

8－10 规模以上工业企业主要经济效益指标(2001)

Major Economic Results Indicators of all above Designated Size Industrial Enterp rises

指　　标	Item	每百元固定资产原值实现利税(元) Pre－Tax Profit Per 100 yuan Fixed Assets(yuan)	产值利税率(%) Rate Between Pre－Tax Profit and Output Value(%)	资金利税率(%) Rate Between Pre－Tax Profit and Assets(%)	销售利税率(%) Rate Between Pre－Tax Profit and Sales(%)	全员劳动生产率(元/人)(按增加值计算) Total Labor Productivity (yuan/person)(caculated at added value)
总　　计	**Total**	**9.29**	**13.54**	**6.95**	**14.60**	**35648.82**
内资企业	Domestic Enterprise	9.43	13.88	7.10	14.97	35647.12
国有企业	State－owned Enterprise	8.75	16.14	7.16	16.49	35980.86
中央企业	Central	8.77	14.94	7.52	15.40	67956.74
地方企业	Local	8.72	17.79	6.77	17.97	20922.41
集体企业	Collective－owned Enterprise	9.92	5.79	5.59	6.65	24393.82
股份合作企业	Cooperation Enterprises	4.81	4.04	3.42	4.67	19876.36
联营企业	Joint－owned Enterprises	0.24	0.23	0.18	0.29	22191.80
有限责任公司	Limited Liability Corporations	9.90	14.78	6.91	16.44	34668.74
股份有限公司	Share Holding Co.Ltd	14.50	10.13	8.50	10.88	63933.59
私营企业	Private Enterprises	16.05	7.48	9.41	9.73	37486.98
其他企业	Others	96.39	15.44	28.07	13.48	11685.19
港、澳、台商投资企业	Enterprises Funded by Hong kong,Macao and Taiwan	－0.46	－0.49	－0.23	－0.54	24812.11
外商投资企业	Foreign Funded Enterprises	4.48	4.09	2.47	4.34	43793.02
在总计中：	of the Total：					
国有控股企业	Controlling Share Hold by the State Enterprises	9.05	15.63	7.04	16.24	35560.29
在总计中：	of the Total：					
农村工业	Rural Industry	11.56	4.63	6.39	5.33	36976.62

8－10 续表 1(continued)

指　　标	Item	每百元固定资产原值实现利税(元) Pre－Tax Profit Per 100 yuan Fixed Assets(yuan)	产值利税率(%) Rate Between Pre－Tax Profit and Output Value(%)	资金利税率(%) Rate Between Pre－Tax Profit and Assets(%)	销售利税率(%) Rate Between Pre－Tax Profit and Sales(%)	全员劳动生产率(元/人)(按增加值计算) Total Labor Productivity (yuan/person)(caculated at added value)
按轻重工业分:	**Grouped by Type of Light and Heavy Industry**					
轻工业	Light Industry	32.24	23.29	15.29	26.51	63740.55
以农产品为原料	Using Farm Products as Raw Meterials	37.41	25.76	16.87	29.42	74739.39
以非农产品为原料	Using Non－farm Products as Raw Meterials	4.58	4.50	3.01	4.99	20519.43
重工业	Heavy Industry	5.03	9.03	4.21	9.51	28304.65
采掘工业	Mining and Quarring	2.25	7.60	2.03	8.09	10102.85
原料工业	Raw Meterials	5.90	11.16	5.63	11.49	43802.77
加工工业	Manufacturing	4.60	5.55	2.75	6.07	21989.66
在总计中:	of the Total					
大型企业	Large	10.64	21.27	8.64	20.36	41676.33
中型企业	Medium	6.77	7.38	4.58	9.75	29733.28
小型企业	Small	6.18	5.40	3.88	6.56	31184.59
按工业行业分	**Grouped by Industrial Sector**	**9.29**	**13.54**	**6.95**	**14.60**	**35648.82**
采掘业	Mining and Quarring	2.25	7.60	2.03	8.09	10102.85
煤炭采选业	Coal Mining and Processing	3.73	10.34	3.15	11.51	8888.35
黑色金属矿采选业	Ferrous Metals Mining and Processing	10.18	7.43	6.73	8.20	12611.56
有色金属矿采选业	Nonferrous Metals Mining and Processing	1.83	2.48	1.69	2.53	6135.84
非金属矿采选业	Nonmetal Minerals Mining and Processing	0.98	4.43	0.95	4.43	19175.21

8－10 续表 2(continued)

指　　标	Item	每百元固定资产原值实现利税(元) Pre－Tax Profit Per 100 yuan Fixed Assets(yuan)	产值利税率(%) Rate Between Pre－Tax Profit and Output Value(%)	资金利税率(%) Rate Between Pre－Tax Profit and Assets(%)	销售利税率(%) Rate Between Pre－Tax Profit and Sales(%)	全员劳动生产率(元/人)(按增加值计算) Total Labor Productivity (yuan/person)(caculated at added value)
木材及竹材采运业	Logging and Transport of Timber and Bamboo	0.19	0.57	0.14	0.67	5057.72
制造业	Manufacturing	13.92	13.66	8.51	15.09	36368.36
食品加工业	Food Processing	0.73	0.47	0.40	0.56	37794.70
食品制造业	Food Production	32.12	19.61	17.50	20.09	31969.33
饮料制造业	Beverage Production	48.19	51.88	22.41	47.96	60307.43
烟草加工业	Tobacco Processing	54.20	32.24	20.79	36.04	201012.33
纺织业	Textile Industry	－3.49	－11.53	－3.18	－15.34	4667.50
服装及其他纤维制品制造业	Garments and Other Fiber Products	6.65	3.45	3.95	3.74	21017.50
皮革、毛皮、羽绒及其制品业	Leather, Furs, Down and Related Products	－1.08	－14.41	－1.02	－21.18	2029.24
木材加工及竹、藤、棕、草制品业	Timber Processing, Bamboo, Cane, Palm and Straw Products	－4.13	－4.67	－2.87	－6.31	11250.44
家具制造业	Furniture Manufacturing	6.61	7.94	5.26	8.64	10760.26
造纸及纸制品业	Papermaking and Paper Products	6.17	6.21	4.37	6.97	20684.92
印刷业、记录媒介的复制	Printing and Record Pressing	5.57	6.62	3.87	8.00	27175.41
文教体育用品制造业	Stationery, Education and Sports Goods	1.97	0.87	0.85	2.79	20088.68
石油加工及炼焦业	Petroleum Processing and Coking Products	6.17	7.98	4.83	7.61	22024.02
化学原料及化学制品制造业	Raw Chemical Materials and Chemical Products	7.47	8.03	5.20	9.29	31813.70
医药制造业	Medical and Pharmaceutical Products	37.42	11.02	12.32	16.41	104701.33
化学纤维制造业	Chemical Fibers		－1.00	－4.63	－7.65	510.27

8-10 续表 3(continued)

指标	Item	每百元固定资产原值实现利税(元) Pre-Tax Profit Per 100 yuan Fixed Assets(yuan)	产值利税率(%) Rate Between Pre-Tax Profit and Output Value(%)	资金利税率(%) Rate Between Pre-Tax Profit and Assets(%)	销售利税率(%) Rate Between Pre-Tax Profit and Sales(%)	全员劳动生产率(元/人)(按增加值计算) Total Labor Productivity (yuan/person)(caculated at added value)
橡胶制品业	Rubber Products	12.30	11.73	7.02	11.36	43677.85
塑料制品业	Plastic Products	2.66	3.34	2.50	3.80	29541.79
非金属矿物制品业	Nonmetal Mineral Products	4.63	6.85	3.64	7.68	16707.33
黑色金属冶炼及压延加工业	Smelting and Pressing of Ferrous Metals	5.06	4.89	3.40	5.23	25967.94
有色金属冶炼及压延加工业	Smelting and Pressing of Nonferrous Metals	8.78	12.02	9.31	12.74	46581.72
金属制品业	Metal Products	11.59	8.05	5.37	8.16	27074.60
普通机械制造业	Ordinary Machinery Manufacturing	-3.34	-6.73	-1.99	-8.13	8606.69
专用设备制造业	Special Purposes Equipment Manufacturing	-8.90	-14.64	-5.10	-15.77	9253.21
交通运输设备制造业	Transportation Equipment Manufacturing	4.49	5.52	2.87	5.83	22975.41
电气机械及器材制造业	Electric Equipment and Machinery	10.65	5.57	4.43	5.89	23045.03
电子及通信设备制造业	Electronic and Telecommunications Equipment	4.86	5.52	2.15	6.17	23260.07
仪器仪表及文化、办公用机械制造业	Instruments, Meters, Cultural and Official Machinery	2.53	4.07	1.75	5.07	8271.22
其他制造业	Others	6.35	3.32	5.92	4.15	46710.62
电力、煤气及水的生产和供应业	Electric Power, Gas and Tap Water Production and Supply	5.01	15.09	5.15	14.69	78874.61
电力、蒸汽、热水的生产和供应业	Electric Power, Steam and Hot Water Production and Supply	5.16	15.56	5.37	14.93	92905.09
煤气生产和供应业	Gas Production and Supply	1.46	4.11	1.36	5.18	15293.27
自来水的生产和供应业	Tap Water Production and Supply	3.70	11.69	3.10	14.54	16660.94

8－11 规模以上国有及国有控股工业企业主要经济效益指标(2001)

Major Economic Results Indicators of State－owned or Controlling Share Hold above Designated Size Industrial Enterprises

指　　标	Item	每百元固定资产原值实现利税(元) Pre－Tax Profit Per 100 yuan Fixed Assets(yuan)	产值利税率(%) Rate Between Pre－Tax Profit and Output Value(%)	资金利税率(%) Rate Between Pre－Tax Profit and Assets(%)	销售利税率(%) Rate Between Pre－Tax Profit and Sales(%)	全员劳动生产率(元/人)(按增加值计算) Total Labor Productivity (yuan/person)(caculated at added value)
总　　计	**Total**	**9.05**	**15.63**	**7.04**	**16.24**	**35560.29**
在总计中：	of the Total：					
中央企业	Central	12.90	19.31	10.23	20.06	75906.49
地方企业	Local	6.59	12.62	5.07	13.10	22576.84
按轻、重工业分：	**Grouped by Type of Light and Heavy Industry**					
轻工业	Light Industry	33.97	30.62	16.35	32.75	64932.19
以农产品为原料	Using Farm Products as Raw Meterials	39.74	33.00	18.12	35.20	75612.90
以非农产品为原料	Using Non－farm Products as Raw Meterials	2.29	3.89	1.59	4.29	17215.30
重工业	Heavy Industry	4.90	9.99	4.25	10.26	28963.28
采掘工业	Mining and Quarring	1.97	7.26	1.78	7.64	9723.53
原料工业	Raw Meterials	5.86	12.72	5.87	12.74	48779.87
加工工业	Manufacturing	4.45	5.82	2.67	6.22	21590.03
按企业规模分：	**Grouped by Scale of Enterprise**					
大型企业	Large	10.75	21.42	8.77	20.63	42235.36
中型企业	Medium	5.35	6.42	3.67	8.71	28190.24
小型企业	Small	3.50	4.40	2.39	5.10	27197.37
按工业行业分：	**Grouped by Industrial Sector**	**9.05**	**15.63**	**7.04**	**16.24**	**35560.29**
采掘业	Mining and Quarring	1.97	7.26	1.78	7.64	9723.53
煤炭采选业	Coal Mining and Processing	3.43	9.92	2.89	11.03	8717.76
黑色金属矿采选业	Ferrous Metals Mining and Processing	－0.28	－0.49	－0.18	－0.65	23075.68
有色金属矿采选业	Nonferrous Metals Mining and Processing	－0.24	－0.51	－0.25	－0.50	4905.62
非金属矿采选业	Nonmetal Minerals Mining and Processing	0.81	4.05	0.78	3.95	18513.46
木材及竹材采运业	Logging and Transport of Timber and Bamboo	－0.19	－0.58	－0.14	－0.68	5097.26
制造业	Manufacturing	14.42	16.74	8.98	17.72	36039.80
食品加工业	Food Processing	0.54	0.43	0.30	0.57	31535.96
食品制造业	Food Production	6.68	9.31	4.24	8.83	13267.59
饮料制造业	Beverage Production	51.32	70.33	23.62	55.51	64078.75
烟草加工业	Tobacco Processing	54.20	32.29	20.80	36.11	201573.68

8－11 续表(continued)

指　　标	Item	每百元固定资产原值实现利税(元) Pre－Tax Profit Per 100 yuan Fixed Assets(yuan)	产值利税率(%) Rate Between Pre－Tax Profit and Output Value(%)	资金利税率(%) Rate Between Pre－Tax Profit and Assets(%)	销售利税率(%) Rate Between Pre－Tax Profit and Sales(%)	全员劳动生产率(元/人)(按增加值计算) Total Labor Productivity (yuan/person)(caculated at added value)
纺织业	Textile Industry	－3.93	－14.93	－3.65	－20.09	4137.48
服装及其他纤维制品制造业	Garments and Other Fiber Products	5.21	2.74	3.27	2.95	28680.68
皮革、毛皮、羽绒及其制品业	Leather, Furs, Down and Related Products	－1.08	－14.41	－1.02	－21.18	2029.24
木材加工及竹、藤、棕、草制品业	Timber Processing, Bamboo, Cane, Palm and Straw Products	1.69	3.35	1.33	2.90	6507.21
家具制造业	Furniture Manufacturing	1.58	7.20	1.62	7.42	3768.92
造纸及纸制品业	Papermaking and Paper Products	4.75	7.57	3.74	7.74	14914.24
印刷业,记录媒介的复制	Printing and Record Pressing	3.08	7.58	2.43	8.51	11560.82
文教体育用品制造业	Stationery, Education and Sports Goods	－1.63	－2.13	－0.92	－2.42	5957.35
石油加工及炼焦业	Petroleum Processing and Coking Products	3.05	3.27	2.54	3.79	17900.86
化学原料及化学制品制造业	Raw Chemical Materials and Chemical Products	7.93	9.18	5.72	10.49	29894.74
医药制造业	Medical and Pharmaceutical Products	－0.02	－0.03	－0.01	－0.05	13605.25
橡胶制品业	Rubber Products	12.41	12.67	6.98	11.95	48768.53
塑料制品业	Plastic Products	2.35	5.12	1.86	5.65	21414.08
非金属矿物制品业	Nonmetal Mineral Products	3.04	5.71	2.37	6.31	16892.15
黑色金属冶炼及压延加工业	Smelting and Pressing of Ferrous Metals	5.07	6.10	3.55	6.34	24883.66
有色金属冶炼及压延加工业	Smelting and Pressing of Nonferrous Metals	9.36	16.04	10.63	16.09	50165.30
金属制品业	Metal Products	14.43	11.37	6.55	10.94	24194.12
普通机械制造业	Ordinary Machinery Manufacturing	－4.57	－11.60	－2.72	－13.50	6398.64
专用设备制造业	Special Purposes Equipment Manufacturing	－8.13	－12.23	－4.28	－13.60	10462.03
交通运输设备制造业	Transportation Equipment Manufacturing	4.50	5.69	2.96	6.00	23383.38
电气机械及器材制造业	Electric Equipment and Machinery	4.34	3.96	1.91	4.11	18199.48
电子及通信设备制造业	Electronic and Telecommunications Equipment	4.82	5.48	2.14	6.12	23226.53
仪器仪表及文化、办公用机械制造业	Instruments, Meters, Cultural and Official Machinery	2.41	4.85	1.70	5.60	8344.15
其他制造业	Others	3.84	5.15	3.29	6.31	19194.81
电力、煤气及水的生产和供应业	Electric Power, Gas and Tap Water Production and Supply	4.83	14.59	5.16	14.18	79222.42
电力、蒸汽、热水的生产和供应业	Electric Power, Steam and Hot Water Production and Supply	4.97	15.03	5.39	14.39	93630.27
煤气生产和供应业	Gas Production and Supply	1.46	4.11	1.36	5.18	15293.27
自来水的生产和供应业	Tap Water Production and Supply	3.70	11.69	3.10	14.54	16660.94

8－12　规模以上集体工业企业主要经济效益指标(2001)

Major Economic Results Indicators of Collective－owned above Designated Size Industrial Enterprises

指　　标	Item	每百元固定资产原值实现利税(元) Pre－Tax Profit Per 100 yuan Fixed Assets(yuan)	产值利税率(%) Rate Between Pre－Tax Profit and Output Value(%)	资金利税率(%) Rate Between Pre－Tax Profit and Assets(%)	销售利税率(%) Rate Between Pre－Tax Profit and Sales(%)	全员劳动生产率(元/人)(按增加值计算) Total Labor Productivity (yuan/person)(caculated at added value)
总　　计	Total	9.92	5.79	5.59	6.65	24393.82
在总计中：	of the Total:					
亏损企业	Loss Making Enterprise	－3.26	－2.21	－1.74	－2.69	22732.67
在总计中：	of the Total:					
农村工业	Rural Industry	12.05	4.25	7.14	4.88	27137.66
按轻、重工业分：	Grouped by Type of Light and Heavy Industry					
轻工业	Light Industry	11.83	7.44	6.14	9.29	33944.15
以农产品为原料	Using Farm Products as Raw Meterials	13.03	8.86	6.21	10.94	42608.75
以非农产品为原料	Using Non－farm Products as Raw Meterials	7.51	3.71	5.71	4.77	20693.01
重工业	Heavy Industry	8.96	5.04	5.28	5.60	21498.85
采掘工业	Mining and Quarring	21.20	10.20	14.96	12.42	18360.63
原料工业	Raw Meterials	5.58	3.68	3.75	4.04	23712.85
加工工业	Manufacturing	17.01	6.64	6.89	7.41	18829.98
按企业规模分：	Grouped by Scale of Enterprise					
小型企业	Small	9.92	5.79	5.59	6.65	24393.82
按工业行业分：	Grouped by Industrial Sector	9.92	5.79	5.59	6.65	24393.82
采掘业	Mining and Quarring	21.20	10.20	14.96	12.42	18360.63
煤炭采选业	Coal Mining and Processing	18.39	8.21	15.79	12.97	14660.14
黑色金属矿采选业	Ferrous Metals Mining and Dressing	176.06	12.34	118.36	12.34	9764.71
有色金属矿采选业	Nonferrous Metals Mining and Processing	8.61	2.80	4.47	4.48	253000.00
非金属矿采选业	Nonmetal Minerals Mining and Processing	16.80	10.45	11.70	12.28	25766.50
木材及竹材采运业	Logging and Transport of Timber and Bamboo	253.64	35.45	72.19	50.64	4058.33
制造业	Manufacturing	9.79	5.60	5.39	6.41	24791.85
食品加工业	Food Processing	0.26	0.22	0.17	0.21	59004.14

8－12 续表(continued)

指　　标	Item	每百元固定资产原值实现利税(元) Pre－Tax Profit Per 100 yuan Fixed Assets(yuan)	产值利税率(%) Rate Between Pre－Tax Profit and Output Value(%)	资金利税率(%) Rate Between Pre－Tax Profit and Assets(%)	销售利税率(%) Rate Between Pre－Tax Profit and Sales(%)	全员劳动生产率(元/人)(按增加值计算) Total Labor Productivity (yuan/person)(caculated at added value)
食品制造业	Food Production	0.28	0.43	0.24	0.75	17055.81
饮料制造业	Beverage Production	16.05	6.01	8.43	6.25	53459.60
烟草加工业	Tobacco Processing	32.59	50.51	17.46	38.24	56081.04
服装及其他纤维制品制造业	Garments and Other Fiber Products	6.67	6.32	6.84	6.19	10394.71
木材加工及竹、藤、棕、草制品业	Timber Processing, Bamboo, Cane, Palm Fiber and Straw Products	1.06	1.76	0.55	2.26	43916.67
家具制造业	Furniture Manufacturing	35.47	9.57	17.97	10.46	16551.02
造纸及纸制品业	Papermaking and Paper Products	1.83	1.69	1.09	2.15	8422.88
印刷业、记录媒介的复制	Printing and Record Pressing	3.33	3.69	2.33	4.05	29970.33
文教体育用品制造业	Stationery, Education and Sports Goods	6.10	1.52	2.05	8.12	29435.74
化学原料及化学制品制造业	Raw Chemical Materials and Chemical Products	0.74	0.48	0.37	0.55	26799.93
医药制造业	Medical and Pharmaceutical Products	16.91	3.60	3.35	6.33	83496.10
橡胶制品业	Rubber Products	－9.19	－3.37	－7.55	－4.75	16186.50
塑料制品业	Plastic Products	3.89	2.84	3.19	3.19	20412.94
非金属矿物制品业	Nonmetal Mineral Products	9.07	8.99	7.61	9.72	12492.80
黑色金属冶炼及压延加工业	Smelting and Pressing of Ferrous Metals	6.57	3.07	3.06	3.28	24378.61
有色金属冶炼及压延加工业	Smelting and Pressing of Nonferrous Metals	8.67	3.34	5.42	3.64	37623.57
金属制品业	Metal Products	10.58	1.97	5.15	2.11	28231.29
普通机械制造业	Ordinary Machinery Manufacturing	8.67	5.47	5.17	7.33	16707.63
专用设备制造业	Special Purposes Equipment Manufacturing	14.37	8.73	6.73	12.92	14895.86
交通运输设备制造业	Transportation Equipment Manufacturing	81.45	12.91	17.81	16.55	17991.94
电气机械及器材制造业	Electric Equipment and Machinery	79.91	11.74	25.82	12.31	55529.47
其他制造业	Others	13.96	3.27	14.69	3.59	123710.14
电力、煤气及水的生产和供应业	Electric Power, Gas and Tap Water Production and Supply	0.98	3.04	0.99	3.79	26752.03
电力、蒸汽、热水的生产和供应业	Electric Power, Steam and Hot Water Production and Supply	0.98	3.04	0.99	3.79	26752.03

8－13　大中型工业企业主要经济指标(2001)

Major Economic Indicators of Large－scale and Medium－scale Industrial Enterprises

单位:亿元
(100 million yuan)

指　　标	Item	企业单位数(个) Number of Enterprises(unit)	从业人员年平均人数(万人) Annual Average of All Employees (10000 persons)	工业总产值 Total Output Value of Industry	工业增加值 Added Value of Industry	资产合计 Total Property
总　　计	Total	212	38.46	415.78	149.55	1219.35
采掘业	Mining and Quarring	11	7.90	32.80	8.24	160.90
煤炭采选业	Coal Mining and Processing	5	6.49	18.40	5.68	76.27
黑色金属矿采选业	Ferrous Metals Mining and Processing	1	0.11	0.20	0.05	0.37
非金属矿采选业	Nonmetal Minerals Mining and Processing	5	1.30	14.20	2.51	84.27
制造业	Manufacturing	177	28.34	300.73	112.12	719.36
食品加工业	Food Processing	2	0.06	1.42	0.18	1.56
饮料制造业	Beverage Production	12	1.56	17.49	11.27	80.16
烟草加工业	Tobacco Processing	5	1.06	53.59	30.30	91.94
纺织业	Textile Industry	9	0.67	1.10	0.33	6.45
服装及其他纤维制品制造业	Garments and Other Fiber Products	1	0.15	1.43	0.47	1.28
木材加工及竹、藤、棕、草制品业	Timber Processing, Bamboo, Cane, Palm Fiber and Straw Products	1	0.07	0.05	0.02	0.50
造纸及纸制品业	Papermaking and Paper Products	2	0.22	1.08	0.28	1.96
印刷业、记录媒介的复制	Printing and Record Pressing	2	0.13	0.46	0.16	1.85
化学原料及化学制品制造业	Raw Chemical Materials and Chemical Products	19	2.54	32.54	8.95	70.31
医药制造业	Medical and Pharmaceutical Products	3	0.16	2.22	1.53	9.53

8－13 续表 1(continued)

单位:亿元
(100 million yuan)

指　　标	Item	企业单位数(个) Number of Enterprises(unit)	从业人员年平均人数(万人) Annual Average of All Employees (10000 persons)	工业总产值 Total Output Value of Industry	工业增加值 Added Value of Industry	资产合计 Total Property
橡胶制品业	Rubber Products	3	0.99	17.59	5.78	33.87
塑料制品业	Plastic Products	3	0.20	1.60	0.50	6.09
非金属矿物制品业	Nonmetal Mineral Products	9	1.29	7.74	2.59	25.07
黑色金属冶炼及压延加工业	Smelting and Pressing of Ferrous Metals	4	4.26	43.08	10.63	87.05
有色金属冶炼及压延加工业	Smelting and Pressing of Nonferrous Metals	7	2.76	38.30	15.81	75.56
金属制品业	Metal Products	3	0.74	5.79	2.04	13.32
普通机械制造业	Ordinary Machinery Manufacturing	13	1.48	3.12	0.90	15.85
专用设备制造业	Special Purposes Equipment Manufacturing	11	0.95	4.17	0.95	11.96
交通运输设备制造业	Transportation Equipment Manufacturing	42	6.19	46.50	14.25	124.04
电气机械及器材制造业	Electric Equipment and Machinery	9	1.17	11.91	2.08	22.04
电子及通信设备制造业	Electronic and Telecommunications Equipment	13	1.14	8.42	2.68	34.09
仪器仪表及文化、办公用机械制造业	Instruments, Meters, Cultural and Official Machinery	2	0.55	1.13	0.44	4.91
电力、煤气及水的生产和供应业	Electric Power, Gas and Tap Water Production and Supply	24	2.22	82.25	29.19	339.09
电力、蒸汽、热水的生产和供应业	Electric Power, Steam and Hot Water Production and Supply	22	2.02	80.62	28.63	329.13
自来水的生产和供应业	Tap Water Production and Supply	2	0.20	1.63	0.56	9.96

8－13 续表 2(continued)

单位:亿元
(100 million yuan)

指　　标	Item	流动资产合计 Circulating Funds	固定资产原值合计 Original Value of Fixed Assets	产品销售收入 Revenue of Products Sales	利税总额 Total Profits and Taxes	利润总额 Total Profits
总　　计	Total	488.66	770.00	415.07	79.14	18.59
采掘业	Mining and Quarring	43.55	128.74	31.38	2.39	0.56
煤炭采选业	Coal Mining and Processing	28.75	57.67	16.56	1.82	0.39
黑色金属矿采选业	Ferrous Metals Mining and Processing	0.16	0.34	0.22	－0.01	－0.02
非金属矿采选业	Nonmetal Minerals Mining and Processing	14.64	70.73	14.60	0.58	0.19
制造业	Manufacturing	370.19	364.57	296.74	62.00	11.87
食品加工业	Food Processing	0.72	0.92	1.05	－0.01	－0.02
饮料制造业	Beverage Production	41.67	24.25	23.34	13.52	5.85
烟草加工业	Tobacco Processing	61.56	34.44	54.21	28.90	0.32
纺织业	Textile Industry	1.70	4.50	0.71	－0.29	－0.36
服装及其他纤维制品制造业	Garments and Other Fiber Products	0.91	0.72	1.36	0.03	0.03
木材加工及竹、藤、棕、草制品业	Timber Processing, Bamboo, Cane, Palm Fiber and Straw Products	0.17	0.18	0.05	－0.02	－0.02
造纸及纸制品业	Papermaking and Paper Products	1.01	1.39	1.08	0.04	－0.05
印刷业、记录媒介的复制	Printing and Record Pressing	0.65	1.58	0.38	0.05	…
化学原料及化学制品制造业	Raw Chemical Materials and Chemical Products	35.35	35.92	28.16	3.87	2.12
医药制造业	Medical and Pharmaceutical Products	6.80	2.00	3.58	0.68	0.37

8－13 续表 3(continued)

单位:亿元 (100 million yuan)

指 标	Item	流动资产合计 Circulating Funds	固定资产原值合计 Original Value of Fixed Assets	产品销售收入 Revenue of Products Sales	利税总额 Total Profits and Taxes	利润总额 Total Profits
橡胶制品业	Rubber Products	19.06	17.08	17.76	2.04	0.37
塑料制品业	Plastic Products	1.84	4.46	1.36	0.05	0.01
非金属矿物制品业	Nonmetal Mineral Products	12.85	15.34	7.36	0.32	－0.32
黑色金属冶炼及压延加工业	Smelting and Pressing of Ferrous Metals	37.06	52.56	41.85	3.06	－0.06
有色金属冶炼及压延加工业	Smelting and Pressing of Nonferrous Metals	25.29	66.91	38.76	6.46	3.21
金属制品业	Metal Products	7.01	5.02	5.65	0.56	0.19
普通机械制造业	Ordinary Machinery Manufacturing	9.48	8.17	2.76	－0.42	－0.65
专用设备制造业	Special Purposes Equipment Manufacturing	8.46	5.94	3.98	－0.64	－0.83
交通运输设备制造业	Transportation Equipment Manufacturing	64.03	60.86	43.87	2.38	1.13
电气机械及器材制造业	Electric Equipment and Machinery	11.97	7.54	11.19	0.57	0.13
电子及通信设备制造业	Electronic and Telecommunications Equipment	20.81	12.27	7.36	0.79	0.46
仪器仪表及文化、办公用机械制造业	Instruments, Meters, Cultural and Official Machinery	1.79	2.52	0.92	0.06	－0.01
电力、煤气及水的生产和供应业	Electric Power, Gas and Tap Water Production and Supply	74.92	276.69	86.95	14.75	6.16
电力、蒸汽、热水的生产和供应业	Electric Power, Steam and Hot Water Production and Supply	69.59	271.41	85.81	14.53	6.01
自来水的生产和供应业	Tap Water Production and Supply	5.33	5.28	1.14	0.22	0.15

8-14 大中型工业企业主要经济指标及占全省比重(2001)

Major Economic Indicators and Its Proportion in Provincial Total of Large - scale and Medium - scale Industrial Enterprises

单位:亿元
(100 million yuan)

指　标	Item	全省工业 Total Provincial Industry	#大中型 Large - scale and Medium - scale Industrial Enterprises		#国有大中型 State - owned Large - scale and Medium - scale Industrial Enterprises	
			绝对数 Absolute Figure	占全省(%) As Percentage to Provincial Total(%)	绝对数 Absolute Figure	占全省(%) As Percentage to Provincial Total(%)
企业单位数(个)	Number of Industrial Enterprises(unit)	2054	212	10.3	201	9.8
亏损企业个数(个)	Number of Loss Making Industrial Enterprises(unit)	804	74	9.2	72	9.0
工业总产值	Total Output Value of Industry	696.63	415.78	59.7	404.95	58.1
工业增加值	Added Value of Industry	236.57	149.55	63.2	146.83	62.1
资产总计	Total Property	1698.58	1219.35	71.8	1190.02	70.1
#流动资产年平均余额	Average Balance of Circulating Funds	685.41	475.47	69.4	461.58	67.3
固定资产净值年平均余额	Annual Average Balance Net Value of Fixed Assets	672.36	491.28	73.1	486.89	72.4
负债总计	Total Liabilities	1066.76	729.22	68.4	710.15	66.6
所有者权益	Creditors' Equity	631.83	490.13	77.6	270.29	42.8
#实收资本	Total Capital Hold	427.58	315.53	73.8	305.71	71.5
产品销售收入	Sales Revenue	646.01	415.07	64.3	402.9	62.4
#产品销售成本	Cost of Sales	494.03	302.61	61.3	293.58	59.4
产品销售税金及附加	Sales Tax and Extra Charges	33.91	30.11	88.8	30.02	88.5
亏损企业亏损额	Total Deficit of Loss Making Industrial Enterprises	14.53	6.15	42.3	5.54	38.1
利税总额	Total Profits and Taxes	94.3	79.15	83.9	78.02	82.7
从业人员年平均人数(万人)	Annual Average Number of All Employees(10000 persons)	66.86	38.46	57.5	37.65	56.3
资金利税率(%)	Rate between Pre - Tax Profit and Assets(%)	6.95	8.19	117.8	8.23	118.4
全员劳动生产率(元/人、年)	Total Labor Productivity(yuan/person, year)	35649.49	38884.56	109.1	38998.67	109.4

8－15 工业产品销售产值(2001)
Total Sales Value of Industrial Products

单位:万元
(10000 yuan)

类别	Item	销售产值 Sales Value	#出口交货值 Delivery Value of Industry	新产品产值 New Products Value
总计	Total	6668686	278704	370959
按登记注册类型分:	Grouped by Registration			
内资企业	Domestic－funded	6456211	266761	348511
国有企业	State－owned	3156238	42330	124041
中央企业	Central	1836454	26577	110837
地方企业	Local	1319784	15753	13204
集体企业	Collective－owned	295032	9056	258
股份合作企业	Cooperative	71572	2649	41
联营企业	Joint Ownership	44265	3249	
有限责任公司	Limited Liability Corporations	1975491	99915	181792
股份有限公司	Share－holding Corporations Ltd	443228	79275	31863
私营企业	Private	469053	30287	10411
其他企业	Others	1332		105
港、澳、台商投资企业	Enterprises Funded by Hong kong, Macao and Taiwan	65680	6849	3620
外商投资企业	Foreign Funded Enterprises	146795	5094	18828
在总计中:	of the Total			
国有控股企业	Controlling Share Hold by the State Enterprises	5223875	219118	252587
按轻重工业分:	Grouped by Type of Light and Heavy Industry			
轻工业	Light Industry	2008543	13005	172502
重工业	Heavy Industry	4660143	265699	198457
按企业规模分:	Grouped by Scale of Enterprise			
大型企业	Large	3454440	172137	204544
中型企业	Medium	646766	32290	76784
小型企业	Small	2567480	74277	89631

8-16 主要工业产品销售量和产销率(2001)
Sales Volume of Major Industrial Products and Its Proportion of Products Sold

产品名称	Item	产量 Output	销售量 Sales Volume	产销率(%) Proportion of Products Sold(%)	2001年比2000年增长(%) Increase Rate(%)	
					产量 Output	销售量 Sales Volume
原煤(万吨)	Coal(10000 tons)	3731.39	3172.28	85.02	1.5	1.0
洗煤(万吨)	Washing Coal(10000 tons)	666.58	579.11	86.88	-6.8	-20.6
天然气(万立方米)	Naturalgas(10000 cu.m)	6826	6826	100.00	-3.1	-3.1
煤气生产量(万立方米)	Volume of Coal Gas Production (10000 cu.m)	23197.93	23197.93	100.00	16.8	16.8
发电量(亿千瓦小时)	Electricity(100 million kwh)	480.25	480.25	100.00	18.7	18.7
#水电(亿千瓦小时)	Hydro-Power(100 million kwh)	211.7	211.7	100.00	15.4	15.4
铁矿石成品矿(万吨)	Iron Mineral(Finished Product)(10000 tons)	22.28	0.08	0.34	-19.6	-3.1
硫铁矿(生产量含S35%)(万吨)	Sulfur Iron Mineral(10000 tons)	176.77	174.98	98.99	27.9	25.0
磷矿石(生产量含$P_2O_5$30%)(万吨)	Phosphorite Mineral(10000 tons)	669.91	546.85	81.63	13.8	1.7
木材(万立方米)	Timber(10000 cu.m)	8.28	7.59	91.60	-58.5	-66.5
配混合饲料(万吨)	Forage(10000 tons)	19.80	18.53	93.56	15.1	10.2
机制糖(万吨)	Sugar(10000 tons)	1.18	1.18	100.00	2.8	2.8
乳制品(万吨)	Dairy Products(10000 tons)	2.03	1.70	83.80	1733.8	1804.5
罐头(吨)	Canned Food(tons)	1471.92	1420	96.47	24.1	15.2
白酒(万吨)	Liquor(10000 tons)	12.11	11.57	95.60	44.4	43.7
啤酒(万吨)	Beer(10000 tons)	9.47	9.20	97.17	1.7	-0.5
软饮料(万吨)	Soft Drink(10000 tons)	3.18	3.06	96.25	20.5	16.0
卷烟(万吨)	Cigarettes(10000 tons)	180.79	176.78	97.78	-3.5	-5.8
纱(万吨)	Yarn(10000 tons)	1.62	0.77	47.75	-18.2	-11.3
布(万米)	Cloth(10000 m)	4720.35	3441.62	72.91	-31.6	-44.2
棉布(万米)	Pure Cotton Cloth(10000 m)	1024.74	1012.48	98.80	-29.8	-37.9
混纺交织布(万米)	Cotton/Chemical Fiber Blend Cloth(10000 m)	3695.61	2416.14	65.38	-32.1	-46.7
绒线(毛线)(吨)	Knitting Wool(ton)	133	177	133.08	-65.3	227.8
丝(吨)	Silk(ton)	47.1	41.3	87.69	-27.1	-35.1
服装(万件)	Garment(10000 pieces)	311.8	300.9	96.50	18.1	20.8
锯材(万立方米)	Wood Sawn(10000 cu.m)	2.75	1.47	53.27	-22.7	-61.7
人造板(万立方米)	Artificial Board(10000 cu.m)	8.99	8.38	93.18	12.6	8.9
机制纸(万吨)	Machine-made Paper(10000 tons)	4.09	3.97	97.15	-15.8	-22.7

8－16 续表 1(continued)

产品名称	Item	产量 Output	销售量 Sales Volume	产销率(%) Proportion of Products Sold(%)	2001年比2000年增长(%) Increase Rate (%) 产量 Output	销售量 Sales Volume
凸版纸(吨)	Protruding Edition Paper(ton)	1432	1537	107.33	－6.2	6.0
机制纸板(万吨)	Machine－made Paperboard(10000 tons)	14564.4	11638	79.91	69.5	71.6
焦炭(万吨)	Coke(10000 tons)	148.46	80.93	54.51	11.0	4.8
硫酸(折100%)(万吨)	Sulfuric Acid(10000 tons)	46.06	23.61	51.26	36.1	82.4
氢氧化钠(烧碱折100%)(万吨)	Caustic Soda(10000 tons)	4.50	4.32	96.02	22.9	26.4
碳化钙(电石折300升/千克)(万吨)	Calcium Carbide(10000 tons)	16.39	8.85	54.01	19.6	38.5
合成氨(万吨)	Synthetic Ammonia(10000 tons)	64.64	43.40	67.14	－3.4	－10.3
农用化学肥料总计(折纯)(万吨)	Chemical Fertilizer(10000 tons)	86.75	92.82	107.00	3.2	16.2
氮肥(折含N100%)(万吨)	Nitrogen Fertilizer(10000 tons)	47.60	54.22	113.90	－5.4	16.2
尿素(万吨)	Carbamide(10000 tons)	41.78	48.25	115.49	－7.8	16.1
磷肥(折合$P_2O_5$100%)(万吨)	Phosphate Fertilizer(10000 tons)	38.61	38.06	98.60	17.0	15.8
化学农药(吨)	Chemical Pesticide(ton)	307.18	261.73	85.20	－14.9	－32.2
纯苯(吨)	Pure Benzene(ton)	7484	7221	96.49	7.5	1.8
油漆(吨)	Oil Paint(ton)	5608	5625	100.30	－9.3	－9.9
合成洗涤剂(万吨)	Synthetic Detergents(10000 tons)	5.51	5.40	97.98	－16.8	－18.5
化学原料药(吨)	Chemical Medicine(ton)	2336	2148	91.95	－16.2	－17.3
化学纤维(吨)	Chemical Fiber(ton)	1580.96	1273	80.52	－65.0	－70.9
合成纤维(吨)	Synthetic Fiber(ton)	1580.96	1278.28	80.85	－65.0	－70.8
轮胎外胎(万条)	Tires(bar)	279.74	280.76	100.36	9.6	7.9
塑料制品(万吨)	Plastic Products(10000 tons)	3.52	3.42	97.13	7.7	2.8
农用薄膜(吨)	Rural Use Membrane(ton)	4369.84	4414.79	101.03	10.7	10.4
水泥(万吨)	Cement(10000 tons)	920.01	906.87	98.57	17.4	17.7
生铁(万吨)	Pig Iron(10000 tons)	149.52	27.94	18.68	－0.5	12.0
钢(万吨)	Steel(10000 tons)	146.99	4.62	3.14	－11.9	－68.0
成品钢材(万吨)	Steel Products(10000 tons)	138.61	138.75	100.10	－8.2	－7.6
普通中型钢材(吨)	Ordinary Rolled－steel Medium(ton)	353	353	100.00	－12.4	－12.4
普通小型钢材(万吨)	Ordinary Rolled－steel Small(10000 tons)	62.00	62.27	100.43	－23.1	－21.8
优质型钢材(万吨)	High Quality Section Steel(10000 tons)	12.51	12.35	98.73	－13.2	－15.9

8－16 续表 2(continued)

产品名称	Item	产量 Output	销售量 Sales Volume	产销率(%) Proportion of Products Sold(%)	2001年比2000年增长(%) Increase Rate (%) 产量 Output	销售量 Sales Volume
线材(万吨)	Wire Rod(10000 tons)	63.63	63.66	100.05	15.1	15.3
无缝钢管(吨)	Seamless Steel Pipe(ton)	4398	4385	99.70	－19.3	－18.9
铁合金(万吨)	Iron Alloy(10000 tons)	76.12	68.18	89.56	23.9	22.4
十种有色金属(万吨)	10Nonferrous Metal(10000 tons)	36.76	35.26	95.92	1.9	－1.3
铅(吨)	Lead(ton)	4465	4465	100.00	12.6	3.5
锌(万吨)	Zinc(10000 tons)	7.31	6.89	94.20	－7.2	－12.1
铝(万吨)	Aluminium(10000 tons)	28.39	27.44	96.66	4.4	2.5
氧化铝(万吨)	Alumina(10000 tons)	51.95	6.40	12.32	7.9	56.4
铝材(万吨)	Aluminium Material(10000 tons)	0.96	0.96	99.99	－8.6	－6.1
日用精铝制品(吨)	Fine Aluminium Products for Daily－use(ton)	804	797	99.13	－4.4	－6.8
工业锅炉(蒸发量吨)	Boiler Industry Use(vaporize－ton)	16.9	21.9	129.59	－51.7	－5.6
内燃机(生产量)(万千瓦时)	Internal Combustion Engines(10000 kwh)	10.17	7.78	76.50	9.4	－11.6
金属切削机床(台)	Metal－cutting Machine Tools(set)	399	354	88.72	31.7	18.0
大型机床(台)	Large Machine Tools(set)	8	8	100.00	100.0	100.0
小型拖拉机(辆)	Mini－tractors(set)	295	599	203.05	2.1	103.1
汽车(辆)	Motor Vehicles(set)	1285	1692	131.67	－5.2	－15.9
载货汽车(辆)	Trucks(set)	4	48	1200.00	－97.9	－80.7
公路客车(辆)	Buses(set)	28	49	175.00	－91.1	－83.3
轿车(辆)	Cars(set)	1253	1595	127.29	46.5	8.5
摩托车(辆)	Motorcycles(set)	1176	1100	93.54	－32.6	－53.2
民用钢质船舶(综合吨)	Civil Steel Ships(syn－ton)	346.2	346.2	100.00	34.3	60.0
交流电动机(万千瓦)	Alternating Current Motor(10000 kw)	8.28	7.86	94.94	19.5	12.6
家用电冰箱(万台)	Household Refrigerators(10000 sets)	37.21	38.43	103.28	43.4	54.8
程控交换机(万线)	Program－controlled Exchange(10000 lines)	3.16	3.05	96.53	29.6	23.7
数字程控交换机(万线)	Digital Program－controlled Exchange(10000 lines)	3.16	3.05	96.53	29.6	23.7
微型电子计算机(万部)	Microcomputers(10000 sets)	0.28	0.27	95.27	－90.7	－91.3
半导体集成电路(万块)	Semiconductor Integrated Circui(10000 pcs)	1636.84	1516.93	92.67	30.1	25.0
彩色电视机(万部)	Color TV Sets(10000 sets)	23.11	21.76	94.16	4.9	12.9
黑白电视机(部)	Non－color TV Sets(set)	0.10	0.15	150.00	－92.9	－95.8

8－17 重点企业建立现代企业制度主要经济指标
Main Economic Indicators on Major Enterprises Set up Modern Enterprises System

单位:万元
(10000 yuan)

分类	Item	单位数(个) Number of Units(unit)	从业人员年末人数(人) Employment Personnel (year－nd) (person)	年末资产总计 Total Assets (year－end)	主营业务收入 Revenue of Main Business	利润总额 Total Profits
总计	**Total**	59	293749	10342218	3646452	197677
按重点企业类型分	**By Type of Major Enterprises**					
520户国家重点企业	520 Major Enterprises of State	7	91122	2885518	1237540	84288
重组为集团公司的原512户国家重点企业	Company Group Rebuilded by 512 Major Enterprises of State	3	48546	3097105	988293	59105
省级重点企业	Major Enterprises at Province Level	54	256532	9803855	3244588	194672
现企原国家百户试点企业	100 Enterprises Been Made Experiments by State in Modern Enterprises System	2	12272	363227	126466	8605
现企原省级试点企业	Enterprises Been Made Experiments in Modern Enterprises System at Province Level	27	167650	6897083	2348923	142057
试点集团母公司	Parent Company of Enterprises Groups Been Made Experiments	1	10790	399410	89846	6746
按登记注册类型划分	**By Registration**					
国有企业	State－owned Enterprise	20	80505	4245103	1362944	59496
国有独资公司	State－owned Corporation	17	113459	3278213	1149798	24132
其他有限责任公司	Other Limited Liability Corporations	14	83802	2261431	829171	91343
股份有限公司	Share－holding Corporations Ltd	7	13274	523549	292317	26668
中外合资企业	Enterprises of China and Foreign Countries Joint Venture	1	2709	33922	12222	－3962
按控股情况划分	**By Controlling Share**					
国有绝对控股	State－owned Absolute Holding	56	289082	10295085	3433491	201599

8－17 续表(continued)

单位:万元
(10000 yuan)

分 类	Item	单位数(个) Number of Units(unit)	从业人员年末人数(人) Employment Personnel (year－nd)(person)	年末资产总计 Total Assets (year－end)	主营业务收入 Revenue of Main Business	利润总额 Total Profits
国有相对控股	State－owned Relatively Holding	1	290	5184	4572	10
其 他	Other	2	4377	41949	15235	－3932
按企业规模划分	**By Size of Enterprises**					
特大型	Oversize	4	66221	3742346	1223388	12290
大 型	Large－size	42	211359	6107347	2298156	75971
中 型	Medium－size	11	15574	485798	119716	－596
小 型	Small－size	2	595	6727	5192	12
按主营行业划分	**By Main Business Sector**					
采掘业	Mining and Quarrying	4	66813	893245	221623	1673
制造业	Manufacturing	48	161807	6077157	2301029	143024
电气水的生产和供应业	Production and Supply of Electric Power, Gas and Water	2	28382	2624184	708058	50363
建筑业	Construction	1	32551	505756	388833	4589
运输邮电业	Transportation, Postal and Telecommunication	1	1561	9570	2557	9
批发零售贸易餐饮业	Wholesale & Retail Trade and Catering Services	2	2093	68201	20664	－1189
其 他	Others	1	543	164105	3688	426

8－18 企业集团主要经济指标
Main Economic Indicators of Enterprises Groups

单位：亿元
(100 million yuan)

分类	Item	集团个数(个) Number of Enterprises Group(unit)	从业人员年末人数(人) Employment Personnel (year－end) (person)	资产总计 Total Assets	年末负债合计 Total Liabilities (year－end)	主营业务收入 Revenue of Main Business	利润总额 Total Profits
总计	Total	33	287368	601.59	360.84	234.92	7.53
按审批部门划分	By Department of Approving Enterprise Groups						
国务院主管部门	Departments Managed by the State Council	4	118726	228.32	145.48	84.69	1.12
省级人民政府	Government at Province Level	8	50954	108.77	74.10	55.53	－0.37
省级政府主管部门	Departments Managed by Government at Province Level	19	113081	255.43	135.13	89.12	6.72
其他	Others	2	4607	9.06	6.13	5.58	0.07
按母公司登记注册类型划分	By Main Business Sector of Parent Company						
国有企业	State－owned Enterprise	5	45723	74.03	55.56	26.36	0.38
国有独资公司	State－owned Corporation	10	144539	288.31	181.06	97.33	1.01
其他有限责任公司	Other Limited Liability Corporations	11	80103	150.93	85.90	79.10	0.48
股份有限公司	Share－holding Corporations Ltd	5	14577	79.12	32.58	26.32	5.36
中外合资企业	Enterprises of China and Foreign Countries Joint Venture	1	918	1.45	0.57	0.31	0.03
其他	Others	1	1508	7.75	5.16	5.10	0.28
按控投情况划分	By Controlling Share						
国有绝对控股	State－owned Absolute Holding	29	283265	586.95	352.53	227.18	7.04
其他	Other	4	4103	14.64	8.31	7.74	0.49
按企业规模划分	By Size of Enterprises						
特大型	Oversize	3	37392	143.36	77.87	37.69	6.08
大型	Large－size	22	219375	418.42	257.57	173.54	1.29
中型	Medium－size	5	28006	32.92	22.45	21.04	－0.06
小型	Small－size	2	1930	3.70	2.13	1.26	0.10
其他	Others	1	665	3.19	1.01	1.38	0.11
按主营行业划分	By Main Business Sector						
采掘业	Mining and Quarrying	4	66813	89.32	41.33	22.16	0.52
制造业	Manufacturing	22	158325	424.05	253.97	151.42	6.89
建筑业	Construction	2	56244	66.71	50.18	48.29	0.35
批发零售贸易餐饮业	Wholesale & Retail Trade and Catering Services	4	4111	13.46	10.92	8.84	－0.26
电气水的生产和供应业	Production and Supply of Electric Power, Gas and Water	1	1875	8.05	4.45	4.20	0.04
按母公司是否为国家重点企业划分	By Parent Company is or is not Major Enterprises of State						
是国家重点企业	Major Enterprises of State	7	143518	348.93	192.78	118.23	7.52
其他	Others	26	156301	289.97	185.47	123.56	0.50

主要统计指标解释

工业　指从事自然资源的开采，对采掘品和农产品进行加工和再加工的物质生产部门。具体包括：(1)对自然资源的开采，如采矿、晒盐、森林采伐等(但不包括禽兽捕猎和水产捕捞)；(2)对农副产品的加工、再加工，如粮油加工、食品加工、轧花、缫丝、纺织、制革等；(3)对采掘品的加工、再加工，如炼铁、炼钢、化工生产、石油加工、机器制造、木材加工等，以及电力、自来水、煤气的生产和供应等；(4)对工业品的修理、翻新，如机器设备的修理、交通运输工具(包括小卧车)的修理等。

本年鉴中涉及的企业登记注册类型：

(1)国有及国有控股企业　指国有企业加上国有控股企业。国有企业(即过去的全民所有制工业或国营工业)是指企业全部资产归国家所有，并按《中华人民共和国企业法人登记管理条例》规定登记注册的非公司制的经济组织。包括国有企业、国有独资公司和国有联营企业。

(2)集体企业　指企业资产归集体所有，并按《中华人民共和国企业法人登记管理条例》规定登记注册的经济组织。是社会主义公有制经济的组成部分。包括城乡所有使用集体投资举办的企业，以及部分个人通过集资自愿放弃所有权并依法经工商行政管理机关认定为集体所有制的企业。

(3)股份有限公司　指根据《中华人民共和国企业法人登记管理条例》规定登记注册，其全部注册资本由等额股份构成并通过发行股票筹集资本，股东以其认购的股份对公司承担有限责任，公司以其全部资产对其债务承担责任的经济组织。

(4)港、澳、台商投资企业　指企业注册登记类型中的港、澳、台资合资、合作、独资经营企业和股份有限公司之和。

(5)外商投资企业　指企业注册登记类型中的中外合资、合作经营企业、外资企业和外商投资股份有限公司之和。

(6)本年鉴中涉及的名为“其他”的企业　均指除国有企业、集体企业、个体经营以外的其他类型工业企业(单位)。包括联营企业、私营企业、股份有限公司，有限责任公司；外商投资企业(中外合资经营、中外合作经营、外资企业)；港、澳、台投资企业(与大陆合资经营、与大陆合作经营、港、澳、台独资企业)及其他企业。

轻工业　指主要提供生活消费品和制作手工工具的工业。按其所使用的原料不同，可分为两大类：(1)以农产品为原料的轻工业，是指直接或间接以农产品为基本原料的轻工业。主要包括食品制造、饮料制造、烟草加工、纺织、缝纫、皮革和毛皮制作、造纸以及印刷等工业；(2)以非农产品为原料的轻工业，是指以工业品为原料的轻工业。主要包括文教体育用品、化学药品制造、合成纤维制造、日用化学制品、日用玻璃制品、日用金属制品、手工工具制造、医疗器械制造、文化和办公用机械制造等工业。

重工业　是指为国民经济各部门提供物质技术基础的主要生产资料的工业。按其生产性质和产品用途，可以分为下列三类：(1)采掘(伐)工业，是指对自然资源的开采，包括石油开采、煤炭开采、金属矿开采、非金属矿开采和木材采伐等工业；(2)原材料工业，指向国民经济各部门提供基本材料、动力和燃料的工业。包括金属冶炼及加工、炼焦及焦炭、化学、化工原料、水泥、人造板以及电力、石油和煤炭加工等工业；(3)加工工业，是指对工业原材料进行再加工制造的工业。包括装备国民经济各部门的机械设备制造工业、金属结构、水泥制品等工业，以及为农业提供的生产资料如化肥、农药等工业。

根据上述划分原则，修理业中以重工业产品为修理作业对象的划为重工业，反之划为轻工业。

工业总产值　是以货币表现的工业企业在一定时期内生产的已出售或可供出售工业产品总量，它反映一定时间内工业生产的总规模和总水平。它包括：在本企业内不再进行加工，经检验、包装入库(规定不需包装的产品除外)的成品价值，对外加工费收入，自制半成品、在产品期末初差额价值。工业总产值采用“工厂法”计算，即以工业企业作为一个整体，按企业工业生产活动的最终成果来计算，企业内部不允许重复计算，不能把企业内部各个车间(分厂)生产的成果相加。但在企业之间、行业之间、地区之间存在着重复计算。

轻重工业总产值的划分也是按“工厂法”计算的，即一个工业企业在正常情况下生产的主要产品的性质属于轻工业，产的主要产品的性质属于重工业，则该企业的全部总产值作为重工业总产值。

工业增加值　是指工业行业在报告期内以货币表现的工业生产活动的最终成果。

实收资本　指企业实际收到的投资人投入的资本。按投资主体可分为国家资本、集体资本、法人资本、个人资本、港澳台资本和外商资本等。

资产合计　指企业拥有或控制的能以货币计量的经济资源。包括各种财产、债权和其他权利。资产按其流动性划分为流动资产、长期投资、固定资产、无形及递延资产和其他资产。

负债合计　指企业承担的能以货币计量，将以资产或劳务偿付的债务。负债一般按偿还期长短分为流动负债和长期负债、递延税项等。

所有者权益　指企业投资人对企业净资产的所有权。企业净资产等于企业全部资产减去全部负债后的余额，其中包括投资者对企业的最初投入,以及资本公积金、盈余公积金和未分配利润,对股份制企业即为股东权益。

固定资产原价 指企业在建造、购置、安装、改建、扩建、技术改造某项固定资产时所支出的全部货币总额。它一般包括买价、包装费、运杂费和安装费等。

固定资产净值 是指固定资产原价减去历年已提折旧额后的净额。

流动资产 是指可以在一年或者超过一年的一个营业周期内变现或者耗用的资产,包括现金及各种存款、短期投资、应收及预付货款、存货等。

产品销售收入 指企业销售产品和提供劳务等主要经营业务取得的业务总额。

产品销售成本 指企业销售产品和提供劳务等主要经营业务的实际成本。

产品销售税金及附加 指企业销售产品和提供工业性劳务等主要经营业务应负担的城市维护建设税、消费税、资源税和教育费附加。

产品销售利润 指企业销售产品和提供工业性劳务等主要经营业务收入扣除其成本、费用、税金后的利润。

利润总额 指企业实现的利润。

应交增值税 指企业在报告期内应交纳的增值税额。

总资产贡献率 反映企业全部资产的获利能力,是企业经营业绩和管理水平的集中体现,是评价和考核企业盈利能力的核心指标。计算公式为:

$$总资产贡献率(\%)=\frac{(利润总额+税金总额+利息支出)}{平均资产总额}\times 100\%$$

资产负债率 该指标既反映企业经营风险的大小,也反映企业利用债权人提供的资金从事经营活动的能力。计算公式为:

$$资产负债率(\%)=\frac{负债总额}{资产总额}\times 100\%$$

工业成本费用利润率 指在一定时期内实现的利润与成本费用之比,是反映工业生产成本及费用投入的经济效益指标,同时也是反映降低成本的经济效益的指标。计算公式为:

$$工业成本费用利润率(\%)=\frac{利润总额}{成本费用总额}\times 100\%$$

工业增加值率 指在一定时期内工业增加值占同期工业总产值的比重,反映降低中间消耗的经济效益。计算公式为:

$$工业增加值率(\%)=\frac{工业增加值(现价)}{工业总产值(现价)}\times 100\%$$

流动资产周转次数 指在一定时期内流动资产完成的周转次数,反映流动资产的周转速度。计算公式为:

$$流动资金周次数=\frac{产品销售收入}{全部流动资产平均余额}$$

产品销售率 指报告期工业销售产值与同期全部工业总产值之比,是反映工业产品已实现销售的程度,分析工业产销衔接情况,研究工业产品满足社会需求程度的指标。计算公式为:

$$产品销售率(\%)=\frac{工业销售产值}{工业总产值(现价)}\times 100\%$$

全员劳动生产率 指根据产品的价值量指标计算的平均每一个从业人员在单位时间内的产品生产量。是考核企业经济活动的重要指标,是企业生产技术水平、经营管理水平、职工技术熟练程度和劳动积极性的综合表现。目前我国的全员劳动生产率是将工业企业的工业增加值除以同一时期全部从业人员的平均人数来计算的。计算公式为:

$$全员劳动生产率=\frac{工业增加值}{全部从业人员平均人数}$$

Explanatory Notes on Main Statistical Indicators

Industry refers to the material production sector which is engaged in extraction of natural resources and processing and reprocessing of minerals and agricultural products, including (1) extraction of natural resources, such as mining, salt production, logging (but not including hunting and fishing); (2) processing and reprocessing of farm and sideline produces, such as rice husking, flour milling, wine making, oil pressing, cotton ginning, silk reeling, spinning and weaving, and leather making; (3) manufacture of industrial products, such as steel making, iron smelting, chemicals manufacturing, petroleum processing, machine building, timber processing; water and gas production and electricity generation and supply; (4)repairing of industrial products such as the repairing of machinery and means of transport (including cars).

(1)State – owned and state holding majority shares enterprises refer to state – owned enterprises and the enterprises which state holds majority shares. State – owned enterprises (industry ownership by the whole people or state – run industry) refers to non – corporation economic units, where the entire assets are owned by the state and which have registered in accordance with the Regulation of the Peoples Republic of China on the Management of Registration of Corporate Enterprises, including the state – owned enterprise, sole state – funded corporation and state – owned joint ownership enterprise.

(2)Collective – owned Enterprises refers to industrial enterprises where the means of production are owned collectively, including urban and rural enterprises invested by collectives and some enterprises which were formerly owned privately but have been registered in industrial and commercial administration agency as collective units through raising fund from the public.

(3)Share – holding Corporations Ltd. Refer to economic units registered in accordance with the Regulation of the People Republic of China on the Management of Registration of Corporate Enterprises, with total registered capitals divided into equal shares and raised throught issuing stocks. Each investor hears limited liability to the corporation depending on the holding of shares, and the corporation bears liability to its debt to the maximum of its total assets.

Light Industry refers to the industry that produces consumer goods and hand tools. It consists of two categories, depending on the materials used:

(1)Industries using farm products as raw materials. These are branches of light industry which directly or indirectly use farm products as basic raw materials, including the manufacture of food and beverages, tobacco processing, textile, clothing, fur and leather manufacturing, paper making, printing, etc.

(2)Industries using non farm products as raw materials. These are branches of light industry which use manufactured goods as raw materials, including the manufacture of cultural, educational articles and sports goods, chemicals, synthetic fiber, chemical products for daily use, glass products for daily use, metal products for daily use, hand tools, medical apparatus and instruments, and the manufacture of cultural and clerical machinery.

Heavy Industry refers to the industry which produces capital goods, and provides various sectors of the national economy with necessary material and technical basis. It consists of the following three branches according to the purpose of production or the use of products:

(1)Mining, quarrying and logging industry refers to the industry that extracts natural resources, including extraction of petroleum, coal, metal and non – metal ores and logging.

(2)Raw materials industry refers to the industry that proides various sectors of the national economy with raw materials, fuels and power. It includes smelting and processing of metals, coking and coke chemistry, chemical materials and building materials such as cement, plywood, and power, petroleum refining and coal dressing.

(3)Manufacturing industry refers to the industry that processes raw materials. It includes machine building industry which equips sectors of the national economy, industries of metal structure and cement products, industries producing means of agricultural production, such as chemical fertilizers and pesticides. According to the above principle of classification, the repairing trades which are engaged primarily in repairing products of heavy industry are classified into heavy industry while these engaged in repairing products of light industry are classified into light industry.

Gross Industrial Output Value is the total volume of industrial products sold or available for sale in value terms which reflects the total achievements and overall scale of industrial production during a given period. It includes the value of the finished products, which are not to be further processed in the enterprises and have been inspected, packed and put in storage, the value of industrial services rendered to other units, and the changes in the value of the semi – finished products and products in process between the beginning and closing of the period. The gross industrial output value is calculated with factory method. No double calculations are to be made within the same enterprise. However, double counting does occur among different enterprises.

Output value of light and heavy industries is also classified with the factory method. Under normal conditions, if the major products of an industrial enterprise belong to light industry products, the gross output value of that enterprise is classified wholly into light industry; the same principle applies to heavy industry.

Value – added of Industry refers to the final results of industrial production of the industrial trade in money terms during the reference period.

Capital Obtained refers to capital actually received by the enterprise from investors. It can be further classified by investors as state capital, collective capital, corporate capital, individual capital, capital from Hong Kong, Macau and Taiwan and foreign capital.

Total Assets refer to all economic resources, owned or controlled by enterprises, that could be measured in monetary terms, including properties, creditors equity and other economic rights of all forms. Classified by the degree of equitability, total assets include circulating assets, long term investment, fixed assets, intangible assets and deferred assets, and other assets.

Total Liabilities refer to the debts, measured in monetary terms, that enterprises are responsible for repayment in the form of cash, assets or labour. Classified by terms of repayment, liability include liquid liabilities and long – term liabilities.

Creditors Equity refers to investors ownership of net assets of the enterprise. It is equal to the total assets of the enterprise minus its total liabilities, including the primary input from investors, capital accumulation fund, surplus accumulation fund and undistributed profit. It is the shareholders equity in share – holding companies.

Original Value of Fixed Assets refers to the original value of all fixed assets owned by industrial enterprises, calculated at the cost paid at the time of purchase, installation, reconstruction, expansion, and technical innovation and transformation of the said assets, which includes expenses on purchase, package, transportation, and installation, etc.

Net Value of Fixed Assets is obtained by deducting depreciation over years from the original value of fixed assets.

Working Capital (Circulating Assets) refers to assets which can be cashed in or spent or consumed in an operating cycle of one year or over one year, which includes cash, various deposits, short term investment, and receivable payments, and advance payments, stock, etc.

Sales Revenue of Industrial Products refers to the revenue from the sales of products by industrial enterprises and the revenue from services provided and etc.

Sales Cost of Industrial Products refers to the actual cost of products of industrial enterprises and industrial services provided, etc.

Tax and Extra Charges on Sales of Products refer to the tax on city maintenance and construction, consumption tax, resources tax and extra charges for education, which should be borne by the enterprises in selling products and providing industrial services.

Sales Profit of Products refers to the profit gained by the enterprises by deducting cost, charges and taxes from the business income of the enterprises obtained in selling products and providing industrial services.

Total Profits refer to the profits gained by the enterprises.

Value – added Tax Payable refers to the amount of the value added tax which should be paid by the enterprises in the reporting period.

Ratio of Profits, Taxes and Interests to Average Assets reflects the profit – making capability of all assets of the enterprise and is a key indicator manifesting the performance and management and evaluating the profit – making potential of the enterprise. It is calculated as follows:

Ratio of profits, taxes and interests to average assets (%) = [(Total profits + total taxes + interest payment) ÷ average assets] × 100%

Ratio of Debts to Assets reflect both the operation risk and the capability of the enterprise in making use of the capital from the creditors. It is calculated as follows:

Ratio of debts to assets (%) = (Total debts ? total assets) × 100%

Ratio of Profits to Total Industrial Costs refers to the ratio of profits realized in a given period to the total costs in the same period, which reflects the economic efficiency of input cost and is calculated as follows:

Ratio of Profits to Total Industrial Cost(%) = (Total Profits? Total Costs) × 100%

Value – added Rate of Industry refers to the ratio of value added of industry in a given period to the gross output value in the same period, which reflects the economic efficiency of cutting down the intermediate input and is calculated as follows:

Value – added Rate of Industry(%) = [Value – added of Industry (at current prices)] ÷ [Gross Output Value (at Current Prices)] × 100%

Turnover of Working Capital refers to the number of times of turnover of working capital in a given period of time, which reflects the speed of the turnover of working capital and is calculated as follows:

Turnover of Working Capital(%) = (Sales Revenue of Products) ? (Average Balance of Total Working Capital) × 100%

Ratio of Sales to Gross Output Value refers to the sales of industrial products to the gross industrial output value during the reference period, and is important in reflecting the linkage between production and sales and the extent of the needs of the society that has been met by the supply of industrial products. It is calculated as follows:

Ratio of Sales to Gross Output Value = Industrial sales? Gross industrial output value (at current prices) × 100%

Overall Labour Productivity of Industrial Enterprises refers to the average output per employed person in industrial enterprises in value terms. At present, the value added and the average number of staff and workers of an industrial enterprises in a given period are used to calculate the overall labour productivity. The formula used is:

Overall Labour Productivity = (Value Added of Industry) ? (Average Number of Staff and Workers)

9

Nine

建筑业

Construction

贵州统计年鉴 2002

GUIZHOU STATISTICAL YEARBOOK

建筑企业增加值（万元）(2001)

Added Value of Construction(10000 yuan)

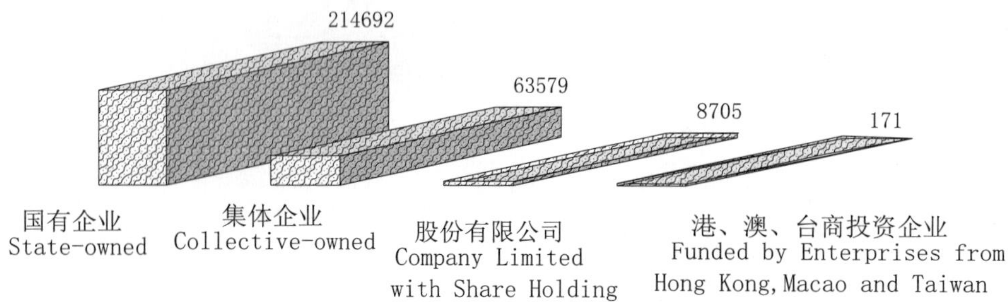

建筑业增加值构成（%）(2001)

Added Value of Construction(%)

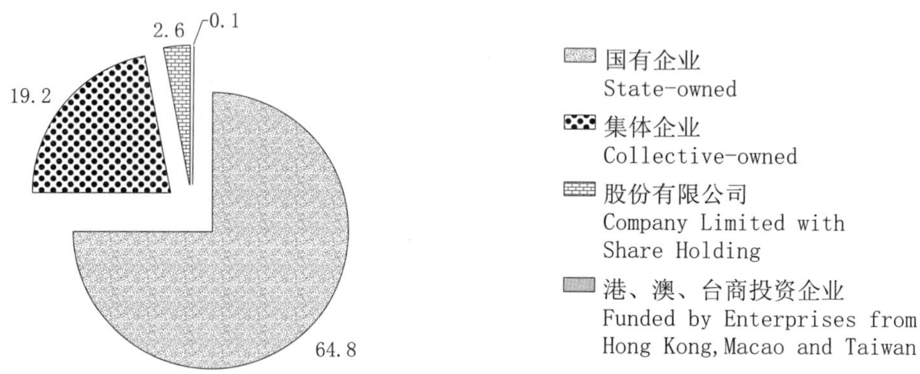

建筑业施工、竣工面积（万平方米）(2001)

Floor Space of Buildings under Contruction and Completed of Construction Enterprises (10000 sq. m)

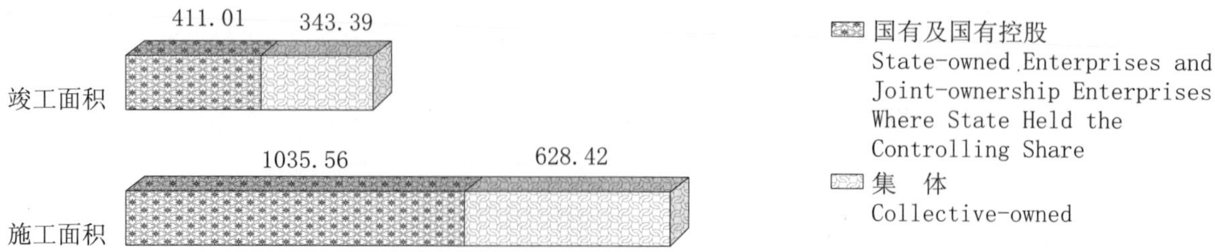

9-1 建筑业主要指标
Main Indicators on Construction Enterprises

指标	Item	2000	2001	2001年比2000年增长(%) Increase Rate in 2001 over 2000(%)
企业单位数(个)	Number of Construction Enterprises(unit)	620	633	2.1
#国有及国有控股	State - owned Enterprises and Joint - ownership Enterprises Where State Held The Controlling Share	157	156	-0.6
集体	Collective - owned	359	340	-5.3
从业人员(万人)	Number of Persons Engaged (10000 persons)	22.3	25.91	16.2
#国有及国有控股	State - owned Enterprises and Joint - ownership Enterprises Where State Held The Controlling Share	12.84	15.88	23.7
集体	Collective - owned	7.74	7.06	-8.8
建筑业总产值(亿元)	Gross Output Value of Construction (100 million yuan)	109.06	150.2	37.7
#国有及国有控股	State - owned Enterprises and Joint - ownership Enterprises Where State Held The Controlling Share	77.04	110.4	43.3
集体	Collective - owned	24.82	26.18	5.5
建筑业增加值(亿元)	Value Added of Construction (100 million yuan)	24.67	33.16	34.4
#国有及国有控股	State - owned Enterprises and Joint - ownership Enterprises Where State Held The Controlling Share	16.75	23.38	39.6
集体	Collective - owned	5.91	6.36	7.6
建筑业企业利税总额(亿元)	Profits and Taxes of Construction Enterprises(100 million yuan)	4.7	7.11	51.3
#国有及国有控股	State - owned Enterprises and Joint - ownership Enterprises Where State Held The Controlling Share	2.67	4.48	67.8
集体	Collective - owned	1.19	1.67	40.3
建筑业利润总额(亿元)	Total Profits(100 million yuan)	0.99	1.73	74.7
#国有及国有控股	State - owned Enterprises and Joint - ownership Enterprises Where State Held The Controlling Share	0.19	0.82	331.6
集体	Collective - owned	0.26	0.56	115.4
建筑业劳动生产率(元/人)	Overall Labor Productivity (yuan/person)	49713	58942	18.6
施工面积(万平方米)	Floor Space of Buildings under Construction (10000 sq.m)	1792.48	1945.59	8.5
#国有及国有控股	State - owned Enterprises and Joint - ownership Enterprises Where State Held The Controlling Share	1017.57	1035.56	1.8
集体	Collective - owned	626.32	628.42	0.3
竣工面积(万平方米)	Floor Space of Buildings Completed (10000 sq.m)	824.01	891.93	8.2
#国有及国有控股	State - owned Enterprises and Joint - ownership Enterprises Where State Held The Controlling Share	404.72	411.01	1.6
集体	Collective - owned	345.38	343.39	-0.6

9－2 建筑业企业主要经济指标
Main Economic Indicators on Construction Enterprises

指　　标	Item	2000	2001	2001年比2000年增长(%) Increase Rate in 2001 over 2000(%)
建筑业企业个数(个)	Number of Construction Enterprises(unit)	620	633	2.1
从业人员(万人)	Number of Persons Engaged (10000 persons)	22.3	25.91	16.2
自有固定资产原价(亿元)	Fixed Assets Owned(original value) (100 million yuan)	42.44	52.97	24.8
自有固定资产净价(亿元)	Fixed Assets Owned(net value) (100 million yuan)	29.73	38.53	29.6
自有机械设备台数(万台)	Number of Machinery and Equipment Owned (10000 sets)	5.42	5.79	6.8
自有机械设备净值(亿元)	Net Value of Machinery and Equipment Owned(100 million yuan)	11.56	13.64	18
自有机械设备总功率(万千瓦)	Total Power of Machinery and Equipment Owned(10000 kw)	88.01	98.08	11.4
建筑业总产值(亿元)	Gross Output Value of Construction (100 million yuan)	109.06	150.2	37.7
建筑业增加值(亿元)	Value Added of Construction (100 million yuan)	24.67	33.16	34.4
#本年固定资产折旧(亿元)	Depreciation of Fixed Assets in 2001(100 million yuan)	2.18	3.08	41.3
主营业务应付工资(亿元)	Main Business Wages Payable(100 million yuan)	14.31	18.81	31.4
主营业务应付福利费(亿元)	Main Business Welfare Expenses Payable(100 milloin yuan)	1.61	2.03	26.1
工程结算税金及附加(亿元)	Taxes and Extra Charges on Project Settle Accounts(100 million yuan)	3.46	4.85	40.2
管理费用中的税金(亿元)	Taxes in Management Expenses(100 million yuan)	0.26	0.53	103.8
营业利润(亿元)	Operating Profits (100 million yuan)	1.7	2.5	47.1
施工面积(万平方米)	Floor Space of Buildings under Construction(10000 sq.m)	1792.48	1945.59	8.5
竣工面积(万平方米)	Floor Space of Buildings Completed(10000 sq.m)	824.01	891.93	8.2
利润总额(亿元)	Total Profits(100 million yuan)	0.99	1.73	74.7
税金总额(亿元)	Total Taxes(100 million yuan)	3.71	5.38	45
劳动生产率	Overall Labor Productivity			
按总产值计算(元/人)	In Terms of Gross Output Value(yuan/person)	49713	58942	18.6
按增加值计算(元/人)	In Terms of Value－added(yuan/person)	11243	13013	15.7
技术装备率(元/人)	Value of Machines Per Laborer(yuan/person)	5270	5354	1.6
动力装备率(千瓦/人)	Power of Machines Per Laborer(kw/person)	4.01	3.85	－4
房屋建筑面积竣工率(%)	Ratio of Floor Space of Buildings Completed(%)	46	45.8	－0.2(百分点)
工程质量优良品率(%)	Ratio of High Quality Projects(%)	22.4	23.5	1.1(百分点)
产值利润率(%)	Ratio of Profit to Gross Output Value(%)	0.9	1.2	0.3(百分点)
产值利税率(%)	Ratio of Pre－tax Profit to Gross Output Value(%)	4.3	4.7	0.4(百分点)

9-3 建筑企业生产主要指标(2001)
Main Indicators on Construction Enterprises

指标	Item	企业个数(个) Number of Construstion Enterprises (unit)	建筑业总产值(万元) Total Output Value of C onstruction (10000 yuan)				
			合计 Total Output Value	建筑工程 Output Value of Construction	安装工程 Output Value of Installation	房屋构筑物修理 Output Value of Building Repair and Maintenance	非标准设备制造 Output Value of Non-Standard Equipment Manufactured
总计	**Total**	**633**	**1502008**	**1328482**	**163395**	**6147**	**3984**
#一、二级企业	The First and Second Level Construction Enterprises	119	1145625	1014903	125213	2062	3447
#国有及国有控股	State - owned Enterprises and Joint - ownership Enterprises Where State Held The Controlling Share	156	1104015	1010246	88377	2006	3386
按登记注册类型分组	**By Registration**						
内资企业	Domestic Funded	630	1501134	1327609	163395	6147	3984
#国有企业	State - owned	133	1038204	946430	86958	1511	3305
集体企业	Collective - owned	340	261817	217838	40018	3584	376
股份有限公司	Company Limited with Share Holding	18	30760	29107	1445	146	63
港、澳、台商投资企业	Funded by Enterprises from Hong Kong, Macao and Taiwan	2	831	831			
按经济组织类型分组	**By the Type of Economy Organise**						
独资企业	Solely Owned	480	1302297	1166544	126977	5095	3681
合作、合伙企业	Cooperate and Partnership	22	37644	17527	20099	18	
股份有限公司	Stock - holding Companies Liabilities	34	37386	35024	2154	146	63
有限责任公司	Companies with Limited Liability	97	124681	109388	14166	888	240
按国民经济行业分组	**By Sector**						
土木工程建筑业	Civil Engineering	543	1274127	1188693	75505	6055	3874
房屋	Building	459	783137	731007	43783	5022	3326
矿山	Mines	4	4426	4149	278		
铁路公路隧道桥梁	Railways, Tunnels, Highways and Bridges	45	340955	339403	1500	50	2
堤坝电站码头	Dyke, Electricity Stage and Dock	11	125386	95185	29470	731	
其他土木工程	Other Civil Engineering	24	20222	18950	474	252	547
线路管道设备安装业	Pipes, Lines and Equipment Installation	49	211383	123363	87818	92	110
线路管道安装业	Pipes and Lines Installation	21	32697	10218	22447	32	
设备安装业	Equipment Installation	28	178686	113145	65371	60	110
装修装饰业	Building Decoration	41	16499	16426	73		

9－3 续表(continued)

指　　标	Item	房屋建筑施工面积(万平方米) Floor Space of Buildings under Construction (10000 sq.m)	房屋建筑竣工面积(万平方米) Floor Space of Buildings Completed (10000 sq.m)	自有机械设备年末总台数(台) Number of Machinery and Equipment Owned (year－end) (unit)	自有机械设备年末总功率(万千瓦) Total Power of Machinery and Equipment Owned (year－end) (10000 kw)	施工机械功率 Power of Construction Machinery (10000 kw)
总　　计	Total	1945.59	891.93	57944	98.08	64.27
#一、二级企业	The First and Second Level Construction Enterprises	1103.9	432.97	31781	67.82	41.4
#国有及国有控股	State－owned Enterprises and Joint－ownership Enterprises Where State Held The Controlling Share	1035.56	411.01	30844	66.74	40.23
按登记注册类型分组	**By Registration**					
内资企业	Domestic Funded	1940.4	886.75	57924	98.07	64.26
#国有企业	State－owned	1004.9	393.18	26901	59.96	37.07
集体企业	Collective－owned	628.42	343.39	19247	18.05	14.82
股份有限公司	Company Limited with Share Holding	84.53	35.95	2232	3.33	2.57
港、澳、台商投资企业	Funded by Enterprises from Hong Kong, Macao and Taiwan	5.18	5.18	6	0.01	0.01
按经济组织类型分组	**By the Type of Economy Organise**					
独资企业	Solely Owned	1640.09	741.56	46358	78.47	52.3
合作、合伙企业	Cooperate and Partnership	50.11	25.84	1107	1.04	0.81
股份有限公司	Stock－holding Companies Liabilities	104.49	47.02	2986	3.81	3.01
有限责任公司	Companies with Limited Liability	150.9	77.52	7493	14.76	8.15
按国民经济行业分组	**By Sector**					
土木工程建筑业	Civil Engineering	1902.91	885.65	52198	88.06	59.03
房屋	Building	1813.23	838.16	38125	51.28	35.31
矿山	Mines	2.27	0.4	959	0.86	0.65
铁路公路隧道桥梁	Railways, Tunnels, Highways and Bridges	22.95	9.22	8329	27.1	17.15
堤坝电站码头	Dyke, Electricity Stage and Dock	3.53	2.25	3002	6.28	3.93
其他土木工程	Other Civil Engineering	60.93	35.62	1783	2.54	1.99
线路管道设备安装业	Pipes, Lines and Equipment Installation	24.91	3.55	5273	7.6	3.88
线路管道安装业	Pipes and Lines Installation	1.32	1.28	796	1.4	1.2
设备安装业	Equipment Installation	23.59	2.28	4477	6.2	2.69
装修装饰业	Building Decoration	17.76	2.73	473	2.42	1.35

9-4 建筑企业主要财务指标(2001)
Main Financial Indicators of Construction Enterprises

单位:万元
(10000 yuan)

指标	Item	年末资产负债 Assets and Liabilities(year-end) 资产合计 Total Assets	流动资产小计 Liquid Assets	固定资产小计 Fixed Assets	负债合计 Total liabilities	流动负债小计 Liquid Liabilities
总计	**Total**	**1815631**	**1323637**	**385267**	**1328836**	**1260112**
#一、二级企业	The First and Second Level Construction Enterprises	1400777	1027965	289311	1064141	1005246
#国有及国有控股	State-owned Enterprises and Joint-ownership Enterprises Where State Held The Controlling Share	1382755	1023450	281920	1069661	1009994
按登记注册类型分组	**By Registration**					
内资企业	Domestic Funded	1813460	1321525	385210	1328499	1259776
#国有企业	State-owned	1298291	957339	266374	1009426	959040
集体企业	Collective-owned	262248	181466	65480	168483	162453
股份有限公司	Company Limited with Share Holding	48911	38868	6691	33925	33680
港、澳、台商投资企业	Funded by Enterprises from Hong Kong, Macao and Taiwan	2084	2037	47	261	261
按经济组织类型分组	**By the Type of Economy Organise**					
独资企业	Solely Owned	1564413	1141525	332833	1179943	1123527
合作、合伙企业	Cooperate and Partnership	44056	32256	8395	32030	31943
股份有限公司	Stock-holding Companies Liabilities	57631	44596	9204	38044	37741
有限责任公司	Companies with Limited Liability	149532	105260	34836	78819	66900
按国民经济行业分组	**By Sector**					
土木工程建筑业	Civil Engineering	1572047	1137550	348582	1146787	1079489
房屋	Building	1010677	723742	218903	733508	706428
矿山	Mines	12282	10809	1336	10220	6181
铁路公路隧道桥梁	Railways, Tunnels, Highways and Bridges	444380	332627	101907	333448	299436
堤坝电站码头	Dyke, Electricity Stage and Dock	82685	59343	16350	58812	57977
其他土木工程	Other Civil Engineering	22025	11029	10086	10800	9466
线路管道设备安装业	Pipes, Lines and Equipment Installation	221364	167046	34805	168861	167791
线路管道安装业	Pipes and Lines Installation	60975	51405	5070	50002	49946
设备安装业	Equipment Installation	160389	115641	29736	118859	117845
装修装饰业	Building Decoration	22220	19042	1880	13187	12833

9－4 续表(continued)

单位:万元
(10000 yuan)

指 标	Item	所有者权益合计 Creditors Equity	损益及分配 Loss－profit and Allocation 工程结算税金及附加 Taxes and Extra Charges on Project Settlement Accounts	工程结算利润 Profits of Project Settlement Accounts	营业利润 Operating Profits	利润总额 Total Profits	增加值 Value－added of Construction
总 计	Total	486796	48509	105264	25029	17334	331610
#一、二级企业	The First and Second Level Construction Enterprises	336636	35180	78144	15185	6321	239577
#国有及国有控股	State－owned Enterprises and Joint－ownership Enterprises Where State Held The Controlling Share	313094	33858	78659	17119	8204	233769
按登记注册类型分组	**By Registration**						
内资企业	Domestic Funded	484961	48470	105067	25003	17308	331429
#国有企业	State－owned	288865	32205	68420	13289	3877	214692
集体企业	Collective－owned	93766	9525	16391	4354	5615	63579
股份有限公司	Company Limited with Share Holding	14987	1466	5352	3301	3263	8705
港、澳、台商投资企业	Funded by Enterprises from Hong Kong, Macao and Taiwan	1823	38	184	27	27	171
按经济组织类型分组	**By the Type of Economy Organise**						
独资企业	Solely Owned	384470	41849	85040	17686	9540	278963
合作、合伙企业	Cooperate and Partnership	12026	1151	2487	2010	1918	7968
股份有限公司	Stock－holding Companies Liabilities	19587	1635	5881	3396	3382	10541
有限责任公司	Companies with Limited Liability	70713	3874	11856	1937	2494	34138
按国民经济行业分组	**By Sector**						
土木工程建筑业	Civil Engineering	425261	41073	76815	8929	7942	271334
房屋	Building	277169	26316	43856	4265	3496	175912
矿山	Mines	2062	159	338	－80	－45	847
铁路公路隧道桥梁	Railways, Tunnels, Highways and Bridges	110932	10111	22830	1303	2689	66632
堤坝电站码头	Dyke, Electricity Stage and Dock	23872	3787	8318	3813	947	22769
其他土木工程	Other Civil Engineering	11225	699	1473	－373	856	5174
线路管道设备安装业	Pipes, Lines and Equipment Installation	52503	6890	27365	16609	9875	57811
线路管道安装业	Pipes and Lines Installation	10973	1192	6140	4955	5233	10566
设备安装业	Equipment Installation	41530	5698	21225	11654	4642	47245
装修装饰业	Building Decoration	9033	545	1084	－509	－483	2465

9-5 建筑业增加值及构成(2001)
Value Added of Construction and Its Composition

单位:万元
(10000 yuan)

指标	Item	合计 Total	中央 Central Enterprises	地方 Local Enterprises	国有及国有控股 State-owned Enterprises and Joint-ownership Enterprises Where State Held The Controlling Share	集体 Collective-owned
建筑业增加值	Value-added of Construction	331610	98436	233174	233769	63579
本年提取的固定资产折旧	Depreciation of Fixed Assets in 2001	30754	12174	18580	25893	3276
主营业务应付工资	Wages Payable in Major Business	188141	46928	141213	127193	40900
主营业务应付福利费	Welfare Expenses Payable in Major Business	20266	5002	15264	14748	2994
管理费用中的劳动待业保险费	Labor and Unemployment Insurance in Management Expenses	13657	7073	6584	12174	972
工程结算税金及附加	Taxes and Extra Charges on Project Settlement Accounts	48509	14875	33634	33858	9525
管理费用中的税金	Taxes in Management Expenes	5254	1484	3770	2785	1558
营业利润	Operating Profits	25029	10900	14129	17119	4354
建筑业劳动生产率(元/人,按增加值计算)	Overall Labor Productivity in Term of Value-added(yuan/person)	13013	23393	10960	15285	8961
建筑业增加值构成(%)	Composing of Value-added of Construction(%)					
本年提取的固定资产折旧	Depreciation of Fixed Assets in 2001	9.3	12.4	8	11.1	5.2
主营业务应付工资	Wages Payable in Major Business	56.8	47.6	60.6	54.4	64.3
主营业务应付福利费	Welfare Expenses Payable in Major Business	6.1	5.1	6.5	6.3	4.7
管理费用中的劳动待业保险费	Labor and Unemployment Insurance in Management Expenses	4.1	7.2	2.8	5.2	1.5
工程结算税金及附加	Taxes and Extra Charges on Project Settlement Accounts	14.6	15.1	14.4	14.5	15
管理费用中的税金	Taxes in Management Expenses	1.6	1.5	1.6	1.2	2.5
营业利润	Operating Profits	7.5	11.1	6.1	7.3	6.8

主要统计指标解释

建筑业统计单位 指从事房屋、构筑物建造和设备安装活动的法人企业。建筑业法人企业应同时具备的条件是:①依法成立,有自己的名称、组织机构和场所,能够承担民事责任;②独立拥有和使用资产,承担负债,有权与其他单位签订合同;③独立核算盈亏,能够编制资产负债表。

建筑业总产值(即自行完成施工产值) 是以货币表现的建筑安装企业在一定时期内生产的建筑业产品的总和。建筑业总产值包括:

(1)建筑工程产值:指列入建筑工程预算内的各种工程价值。

(2)设备安装工程产值:指设备安装工程价值,不包括被安装设备本身价值。

(3)房屋、构筑物修理产值:指房屋、构筑物修理所完成的价值,但不包括被修理房屋、构筑物本身的价值和生产设备的修理价值。

(4)非标准设备制造产值:指加工制造没有定型的、非标准的生产设备的加工费和原材料价值,以及附属加工厂为本企业承建工程制作的非标准设备的价值。

建筑业增加值 指建筑业企业在报告期内以货币表现的建筑业生产经营活动的最终成果。目前建筑业增加值采用分配法(收入法)计算,即从收入的角度出发,根据生产要素在生产过程中应得的收入份额计算。具体计算公式为:

建筑业增加值 = 本年提取的固定资产折旧 + 应付工资 + 应付福利费 + 管理费用中的劳动待业保险金、税金 + 工程结算税金及附加 + 工程结算利润

房屋建筑施工面积 指在报告期内施工的全部房屋建筑面积,包括本期新开工的房屋面积、上期施工跨入本期继续施工的房屋面积、上期停缓建在本期恢复施工的房屋面积、本期竣工的房屋面积及本期施工后又停缓建的房屋面积。

房屋建筑竣工面积 指在报告期内房屋建筑按照设计要求全部完工,达到了住人和使用条件,经验收鉴定合格,正式移交使用单位的房屋建筑面积。

工程结算收入 指企业承包工程实现的工程价款结算收入,以及向发包单位收取的除工程价款以外的按规定列作营业收入的各种款项,如临时设施费、劳动保险费、施工机械调迁费等以及向发包单位收取的各种索赔款。

工程结算利润 指已结算工程实现的利润,如亏损以"－"号表示。计算公式为:

工程结算利润 = 工程结算收入 － 工程结算成本 － 工程结算税金及附加

企业总收入 指与企业生产经营直接有关的各项收入,包括工程结算收入和其他业务收入。计算公式为:

企业总收入 = 工程结算收入 + 其他业务收入

Explanatory Notes on Main Statistical Indicators

Statistical Unit in Construction refers to corporate enterprise engaged in the construction of buildings and structures and in the installation of equipment. Acorporate construction enterprise should meet the following 3 requirements: ①being set up in line with relevant legal basis, having its full name, organization and location, and capable of taking civil liabilities; ②independently possessing and using its assets and assuming its liabilities, and entitled to sign contracts with other institutions; and ③ making independent accounts of its profits and losses, and capable of compiling its own balance sheet.

Gross Output Value of Construction (Output Value of Projects Under Construction) refers to total of construction products, expressed in money terms, completed by construction and installation enterprises during a given period of time. It includes:

(1) Output value of construction projects, that is the value of projects covered by the project budgets;

(2) Output value of installation projects, that is the value of the installation of equipment, (excluding the value of the equipment to be installed);

(3) Output value of repair of buildings and structures, that is the value created through the repairs of buildings or structures, but does not include the value of buildings or structures being repaired and the value of the repair of production equipment;

(4) Output value of manufactured non – standard equipment, that is the value of non – standard production equipment (including raw materials and manufacturing cost) made for the construction project, and the equipment manufactured by subsidiary workshops.

Value – added of Construction refers to the final result of the activities of production and management of construction in monetary terms in the reference period. At present, the value – added of construction is calculated with the income approach. In other words, it is the sum of income of various production factors in the production process. The formula is as follows:

Value – added of construction = depreciation of fixed assets in the year + wages payable + welfare expenses payable + insurance premium and tax for waiting for employment in the administrative expenses + taxes and surcharges on project settlement + profit gained from project settlement.

Floor Space of Buildings Under Construction refers to floor space of buildings under construction during the reference period, including newly started buildings, buildings started earlier and continued during the reference period, and buildings suspended earlier but restarted during the reference period, buildings completed during the reference period, and buildings under construction and then suspended during the reference period.

Floor Space of Buildings Completed refers to the floor space of buildings that are completed in the reference period in accordance with the requirements of the design, up to the standard for putting them into use, and have been checked and accepted by concerned departments as qualified ones.

Income from Settlement of Projects refers to the income received by the construction enterprise from the contracted project through settlement procedures, and other charges to the contractoree as operational costs in addition to the value of the project, such as temporary facility fee, labour insurance premium, moving cost of construction equipment, as well as various types of claims to the contractee.

Profit from Settlement of Projects refers to profit realized through settled projects. It is calculated with the following formula:

Profit from Settlement of Projects = Income from Settlement of Projects – Settled Cost – Settled Taxes and Other Cost

Total Revenue of Enterprises refers to the sum of income from production and operation of enterprises, including income from settlement of projects and other operational income, namely:

Total Revenue of Enterprises = Income from Settlement of Projects + Other Operational Income.

10

Ten

交通运输、邮电通信

Transportation, Postal and Telecommunications Services

公路线路里程（公里）
Total Length of Highways (km)

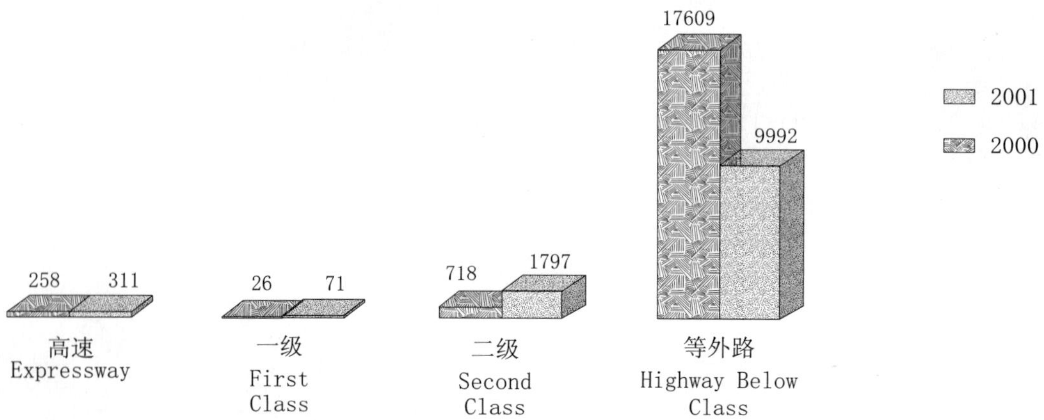

货物运输量(万吨)(2001)
Freight Traffic (10000 tons)

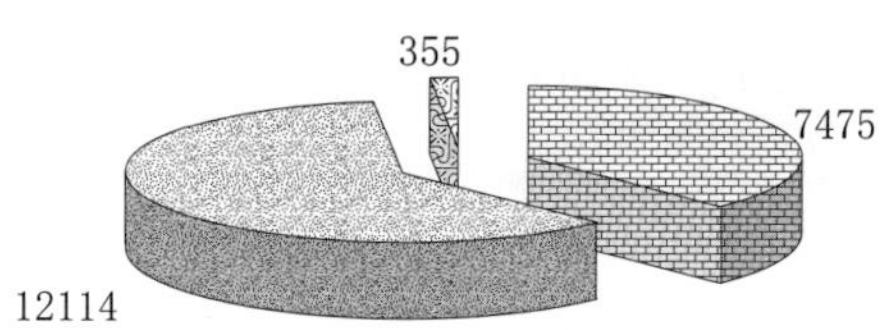

旅客运量(万人)(2001)
Passenger Traffic (10000 persons)

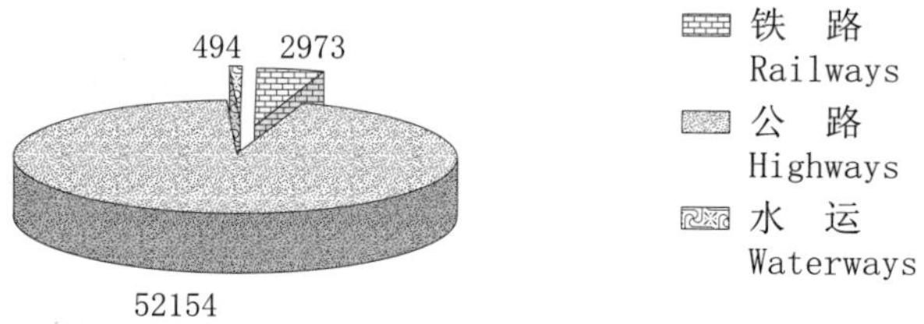

货物、旅客周转量（2001）
Ton-kilometers and Passenger-kilometers

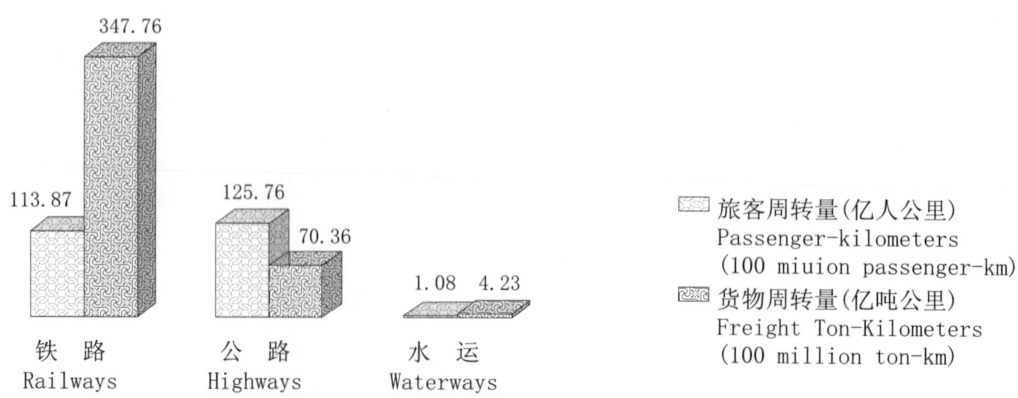

10-1 境内运输线路长度
Length of Transportation Routes

单位:公里
(km)

指　标	Item	2000	2001	2001年比2000年增长(%) Increase Rate in 2001 over 2000(%)
***铁路里程**	**Length of Railways**	**1674**	**2172**	**29.8**
铁路营业里程	Length of Railways in Operation	1340	1333	-0.5
#复线里程	Double - tracking Length	68	551	710.3
公路线路里程	**Total Length of Highways**	**(33948)**	**34617**	**2.0**
#等级路	Expressway and Class I to IV Highways	17034	24625	44.6
#高速	Expressway	258	311	20.5
一级	First Class	26	71	173.1
二级	Second Class	718	1797	150.3
等外路	Highway Below Class IV	17609	9992	-43.3
内河航道里程	**Length of Navigable Inland Waterways**	**2132**	**2132**	**持平**

注:1.数据与以往年鉴不一致的,以本年鉴为准。2.*数据为境内铁路里程。3.带“()”数据为2000年公路普查数。

Note:1.These are the standard data while the data in other books are out of accord with this table. 2.Data with * refer to the length of railways in Guizhou. 3.Data with () refer to the data obtained from general survey of highways in 2000.

10－2 民用汽车拥有量
Number of Civil Motor Vehicles Owned

指　　标	Item	2000	2001	2001年比2000年增长(%) Increase Rate in 2001 over 2000(%)
民用汽车总计(辆)	**Total Number(unit)**	**262627**	**283291**	**7.8**
载客汽车(辆)	Buses and Cars(unit)	111214	125763	13.1
#客位(客位)	Number of Seats(seat)	1245597	1340013	7.6
普通载货汽车(辆)	Ordinary Trucks(unit)	144340	150391	4.2
#载重量(万吨)	Trucks Capacity(10000 tons)	43.16	42.86	－0.7
专用载货汽车(辆)	Special Trucks(unit)	3074	2822	－8.2
#载重量(万吨)	Trucks Capacity(10000 tons)	1.46	1.32	－9.6
其他专用汽车(辆)	Other Special Vehicles(unit)	490	536	9.4
特种汽车(辆)	Special Motor Vehicles(unit)	3509	3779	7.7
私人汽车合计(辆)	**Number of Motor Vechicles Owned by Individuals(unit)**	**104874**	**122479**	**16.8**
载客汽车(辆)	Passenger Vehicles(unit)	45412	53377	17.5
#客位(客位)	Number of Seats(seat)	502892	581916	15.7
普通载货汽车(辆)	Ordinary Trucks(unit)	59007	68619	16.3
#载重量(万吨)	Trucks Capacity(10000 tons)	17.43	18.78	7.6

10－3 旅客运量及周转量
Passenger Traffic and Passenger－Kilometers

指　　标	Item	2000	2001	2001 年比 2000 年增长(%) Increase Rate in 2001 over 2000(%)
旅客运量总计(万人)	**Total Passenger Traffic(10000 persons)**	**53978**	**55621**	**3.0**
铁　路	Railways	3113	2973	－4.5
公　路	Highways	50397	52154	3.5
水　运	Waterways	468	494	5.6
旅客周转量总计(亿人公里)	**Passenger－Kilometers(100 million passenger－km)**	**231.28**	**240.71**	**4.1**
铁　路	Railways	113.71	113.87	0.1
公　路	Highways	116.54	125.76	7.9
水　运	Waterways	1.03	1.08	4.9
民航旅客吞吐量(万人)	Civil Aviation(10000 persons)	138.95	152.99	10.1

注：本表民航资料均按全社会口径统计。(下表同)

Note：The statistial coverage of the civil aviation transport in this table are collected the all social sectors.(same as in the following tables)

10－4 货物运输量及周转量
Freight Traffic and Ton－Kilometers

指　　标	Item	2000	2001	2001 年比 2000 年增长(%) Increase Rate in 2001 over 2000(%)
货物运输量总计(万吨)	**Total Freight Traffic(10000 tons)**	**18891**	**19944**	**5.6**
铁　路	Railways	6853	7475	9.1
公　路	Highways	11684	12114	3.7
水　运	Waterways	354	355	0.3
货物周转量总计(亿吨公里)	**Total Freight Ton－Kilometers(100 million ton－km)**	**385.28**	**422.35**	**9.6**
铁　路	Railways	315.32	347.76	10.3
公　路	Highways	65.86	70.36	6.8
水　运	Waterways	4.1	4.23	3.2
民航货邮吞吐量(万吨)	Civil Aviation(10000 tons)	2.02	2.33	15.4

注：铁路按发送量计算。

Note：Data of the railways are calculated at departing.

10－5 铁路、公路、水运主要经济技术指标
Principal Economic and Technical Indicators of Railways, Highways and Waterways Transportation

指 标	Item	2000	2001	2001年比2000年增长(%) Increase Rate in 2001 over 2000(%)
铁路运输	Railways			
货车平均周转时间(天)	Average Turning around Time of Freight Cars(day)	2.1	2.19	4.3
货车净载重(吨)	Static Load of Freight Cars(ton)	58.4	58.6	0.3
逐年下降货车列车旅行速度(公里/小时)	Running Speed of Freight Trains(km/hr)	22.9	23	0.4
货物机车平均日产量(万吨公里)	Average Daily Ton－kilometers of Freight Locomotives (10000 tons－km)	61.5	62.8	2.1
平均每日运用货车(车)	Density of Freight Trains (coach)	7544	8351	10.7
内燃机车每万吨公里耗油(公斤)	Oil Consumption of Diesel Locomotives (kg)	68.2	69.3	1.6
电机车每万吨公里耗电(千瓦小时)	Electricity Consumption of Electric Locomotives (kwh)	148.4	138.8	－6.5
公路运输	Highways			
载货汽车每百车公里耗汽油(升)	Gasoline Consumption of Trucks(litre)	30.9	29.8	－3.6
载货汽车每百车公里耗柴油(升)	Diesel Oil Consumption of Trucks (litre)	31	29.9	－3.6

注：本表所列指标均为交通系统内的数据。

Note: Data in this table are obtained from the traffic department.

10－6 邮电线路及通信工具拥有量
Number of Postal Routes and Telecommunications Facilities

指　　标	Item	2000	2001	2001年比2000年增长(%) Increase Rate in 2001 over 2000(%)
邮电局所总数(处)	Number of Post & Telecommunications Offices(unit)	2515	3407	35.5
#设在农村的	Rural	1109	1023	-7.8
邮路总长度(公里)	Length of Postal Routes(km)	63538	67387	6.1
#汽车邮路	Highways Routes	25546	27642	8.2
铁路邮路	Railways Routes	6768	6426	-5.1
电话交换机容量(门)	Capacity of Telephone Exchanges(line)	2604566	3465060	33.0
#农村	Rural	261656	705699	169.7
邮电业务总量(亿元)	Business Volume of Post and Telecommunications Service(100 million yuan)	40.92	*47.57	
函件(万件)	Number of Letters(10000 pcs)	6942.6	6221	-10.4
报刊、杂志、累计订销数(万份)	Number of Newspapers and Magazines Circulation(10000 copies)	25936.9	23702.2	-8.6
年末电话用户数(万户)	Number of Telephone Subscribers (year-end)(10000 subscribers)	153.7	227.59	48.1
#农话用户数	Number of Rural Telephone Subscribers	26.62	46.7	75.4
年末市内电话(万户)	Number of Local(urban) Telephone Subscribers(year-end)(10000 subscribers)	127.1	180.89	42.3
#公用	Number of Public Telephone Subscribers	4.45	5.32	19.6
住宅电话(万户)	Residential Telephone Subscribers(10000 subscribers)	124.77	168.46	35.0
国内长途电话(万次)	Number of Internal Long-distance Telephone Calls (10000 times)	25238.9	22623.9	-10.4
国际及港澳长途电话(万次)	Number of Long-distance Telegraph Calls of International and Hongkong, Macao(10000 times)	36.0	38.9	8.1

注："*"数据为按现价计算。

Note: Data with * are calculated at current prices.

10－7 电信主要指标
Major Indicators of Telecommunications

指标	Item	2000	2001	2001年比2000年增长(%) Increase Rate in 2001 over 2000(%)
国内特快专递(万件)	Pieces of Internal Express Mail Services(10000 pcs)	151.4	115.5	－23.7
国际特快专递	Pieces of International Express Mail Services	0.6	0.5	－16.7
邮政储蓄期末余额(亿元)	Postal Saving Deposit Balance(100 million yuan)	45.2	59.4	31.4
集邮业务(万枚)	Philately(10000 units)	5994.3	3665.7	－38.9
长话业务电路(路)	Long－distance Telephone Lines(line)	28895	75438	161.1
电话主线普及率(%)	Rate of Popularization of Telephones (%)	6.20	11.11	4.9(百分点)
住宅电话普及率(%)	Rate of Popularization of Residential Telephones(%)	13.40	16.54	3.1(百分点)
净增电话用户	Telephone Users Added(10000 subscribers)	96.0	73.88	－23.0
移动电话用户	Number of Mobile Telephone Subscribers	78.50	168.96	115.2
无线寻呼用户	Number of Subscribers of Pageing Service	130.0	45.3	－65.2
分组交换用户(户)	Packet Switching Users(subscriber)	1211	918	－24.2
数字数据用户	Digital and Data Users	3438	5558	61.7
国际互联网用户	Number of Subscribers of Internet Service	59593	176929	196.9

10－8 邮电企业主要财务指标
Major Financial Indicators of Post and Telecommunication Enterprises

单位：万元
(10000 yuan)

指标	Item	2000	2001	2001年比2000年增长(%) Increase Rate in 2001 over 2000(%)
全部邮电企业	Total Post and Telecommunication Enterprises			
业务收入	Revenue	351033	406638	15.8
业务支出	Business Expenditure	360113	342202	－5.0
营业税金及附加费	Pre－tax and Related Payment	12041	13428	11.5
收支差额	Net Revenue or Expenditure	－70780	－14895	－79.0

主要统计指标解释

铁路营业里程 又称营业长度(包括正式营业和临时营业里程),指办理客货运输业务的铁路正线总长度。凡是全线或部分建成双线及以上的线路,以第一线的实际长度计算;复线、站线、段管线、岔线和特殊用途线以及不计算运费的联络线都不计算营业里程。铁路营业里程是反映铁路运输业基础设施发展水平的重要指标,也是计算客货周转量、运输密度和机车车辆运用效率等指标的基础资料。

公路里程 指在一定时期内实际达到《公路工程技术标准 JTJ01-88》规定的等级公路,并经公路主管部门正式验收交付使用的公路里程数。包括大中城市的郊区公路以及通过小城镇街道部分的公路里程和桥梁、渡口的长度,不包括大中城市的街道、厂矿、林区生产用道和农业生产用道的里程。两条或多条公路共同经由同一路段,只计算一次,不得重复计算里程长度。

内河航道里程 也称内河通航里程,指在一定时期内,能通航运输船舶及排筏的天然河流、湖泊水库、运河及通航渠道的长度。包括全年季节性通航累计三个月以上的航道,不包括仅供零散流放竹、木排的河道。

民用航空航线里程 指民航运输定期班机飞行的航线长度的总和。航线长度按机场之间的距离计算,通常有两种计算方法:一是将每条航线长度相加称为重复计算航线里程;一是将两线或两条以上航线经过同一区段里程,只计算一次航线长度称为不重复计算航线里程,一般常用的是后者。

货(客)运量 指在一定时期内,各种运输工具实际运送的货物(旅客)数量。货运按吨计算,客运按人计算。货物不论运输距离长短、货物类别,均按实际重量统计。旅客不论行程远近或票价多少,均按一人一次客运量统计;半价票、小孩票也按一人统计。

货物(旅客)周转量 指在一定时期内,由各种运输工具运送的货物(旅客)数量与其相应运输距离的乘积之总和。计算货物周转量通常按发出站与到达站之间的最短距离,也就是计费距离计算。计算公式为:

货物(旅客)周转量 = ∑货物(旅客)运输量 × 运输距离

邮电业务总量 指以价值量形式表现的邮电通信企业为社会提供各类邮电通信服务的总数量。邮电业务量按专业分类包括函件、包件、汇票、报刊发行、邮政快件、特快专递、邮政储蓄、集邮、公众电报、用户电报、传真、长途电话、出租电路、市话无线寻呼、移动电话、分组交换数据通信、出租代维等。计算方法为各类产品乘以相应的平均单价(不变价)之和,再加上出租电路和设备、代用户维护电话交换机和线路等的服务收入。其计算公式为:

邮电业务总量 = ∑(各类邮电业务量 × 不变单价) + 出租代维及其他业务收入

无线寻呼电话用户 指携带小型寻呼机,接收市话用户通过无线寻呼中心,在规定范围内向其发出声音、数字或文字显示信息的用户。在寻呼台办理登记手续的无线寻呼用户,每一部寻呼机按一户计算。

移动电话用户 指在移动电话营业部门登记,通过移动电话交换机进入移动电话网、占有移动电话号码的电话用户。用户数量以实际办理登记手续进入邮电部门移动电话网的户数进行计算,一部或一台移动电话统计为一户。

电话用户 指接入国家公众固定电话网,并按固定电话业务进行经营管理的电话用户。

Explanatory Notes on Main Statistical Indicators

Length of Railways in Operation refers to the total length of the trunk line under passenger and freight transportation(including both full operation and temporary operation). The calculation is based on the actual length of the first line even if this line has a full or partial double track or more tracks, excluding double tracks, station sidings, tracks under the charge of stations, branch lines, special-purpose lines and the non-payable connecting lines. The length of railways in operation is an important indicator to show the development of the infrastructure for the railway transport, and also the essential data to calculate volume of passenger freight transport, traffic density and utilization efficiency of the locomotives and carriages.

Length of Highways refers to the length of highways which are built in conformity with the grades specified by the highway engineering standard formulated by the Ministry of Communications, and have been formally checked and accepted by the departments of highways and put into use. The length of highways includes that of the suburb highways at large and medium – sized cities, highways passing through streets at small cities and towns, and also the length of bridges and ferries. It does not include the length of streets in big and medium – sized cities and highways built for the production purpose at factories, mines, forest areas and agricultural areas. If two or more highways go the same section of the way, the length of the section is only calculated for once and no duplication is allowed.

Length of Navigable Inland Waterways an indicator reflecting the size and development of inland water network, it refers to the length of the natural rivers, lakes, reservoirs, canals, and ditches open to navigation during a given period, which enables the transport by ships and rafts. It includes the channels open to navigation for over an accumulative 3 months in a year, yet this does not include the river courses which are only used to float odd logs and bamboo rafts.

Length of Civil Aviation Routes refers to the length of all routes for regular civil aviation flights. There are usually two ways to calculate the distance between airports connected by the route length: One is to put the length of all air routes together, called duplicated calculation of the length of the routes; the other is not to allow the duplication in calculation when two or more routes passing the same section of aviation routes. The latter is usually used, as it can precisely show the size of the civil aviation network and indicate the extent of civil aviation serving the national economy and the people.

Freight(Passenger)Traffic refers to the volume of freight(passenger) transported with various means. Freight transport is calculated in tons and passenger traffic is calculated in the number of persons. Despite the type of freight and travelling distance, the freight transport is calculated in the actual weight of the goods; and despite the travelling distance and ticket price, the passenger traffic is calculated by the principle that one person can be counted only once in one travel. The passenger who travel with a half price ticket or a child ticket is also calculated as one person.

Freight Ton – kilometers (Passenger – kilometers) refer to the sum of the products of the volume of transported cargo (passengers) multiplying by the transport distance, usually using ton – kilometer and passenger – kilometer as units for measurement. Normally, the shortest distance between the departure station and the destination station (i.e., the payable distance) is the basis to calculate the freight ton – kilometers. The formula is as follows:

Freight Ton – kilometers (Passenger – kilometers) = $\sum$ {Freight (Passenger) Traffic x Distance of Transportation}

Measuring unit: ton – kilometer (person – kilometer)

Business Volume of Post and Telecommunications refers to the total amount of post and telecommunications services, expressed in value terms, provided by the post and telecommunications departments for the society. Post and telecommunication services can be classified as letters, parcels, remittance, issue of newspapers and magazines, fast mail service, express mail service, savings deposits, stamps for collection, public and individual telegraph service, facsimiles, long – distance telephone service, leasing of telephone lines, urban paging service, mobile telephone service, data transfer and transmission, etc. The accounting approach is to multiply the service products of all types with their average unit price (constant price) to get sum of business value, plus income from other services such as leasing of telephone lines and equipment, maintenance of telephone switchboards and lines on behalf of customers.

The formula is as follows:

Business Volume of Post and Telecommunications

= $\sum$(Transaction of Post and Telecommunication Service × Constant Price) + Income from Leasing, Maintenance and other Services

Subscribers of Paging Services refer to subscribers who carry small – size pagers and receive audio signals, digital signals or character signals sent out by city telephone through wireless paging center within assigned area. Each pager is counted as a subscriber.

Mobile Telephone Subscribers refer to the persons who own mobile telephone number connected with the mobile telephone communication network and have registered in mobile communication enterprises. The number of subscribers is calculated only when the subscribers who have gone through all the register formalities and entered into the mobile telephone network. One mobile telephone is treated as a subscriber.

Telephone Subscribers refer to subscribers that are connected to the public line telephone network provided with telephone services.

11

Eleven

国内商业

Domestic Trade

社会消费品零售总额(亿元)
Total Retail Sales of Consumer Goods (100 million yuan)

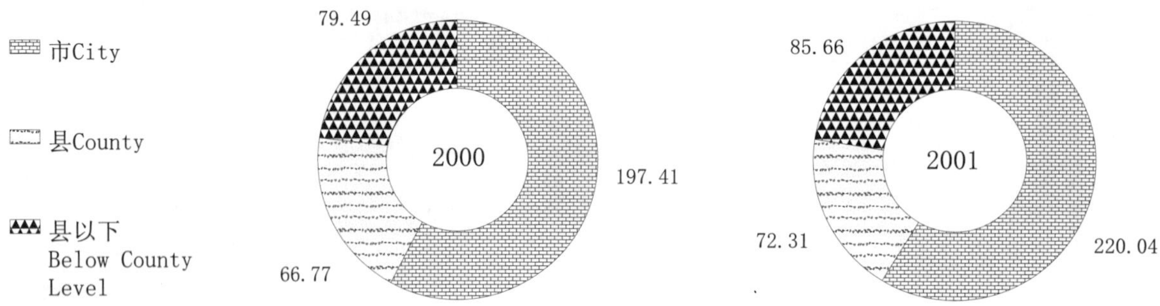

消费品市场数（个）(2001)
Number of Consumable Markets (unit)

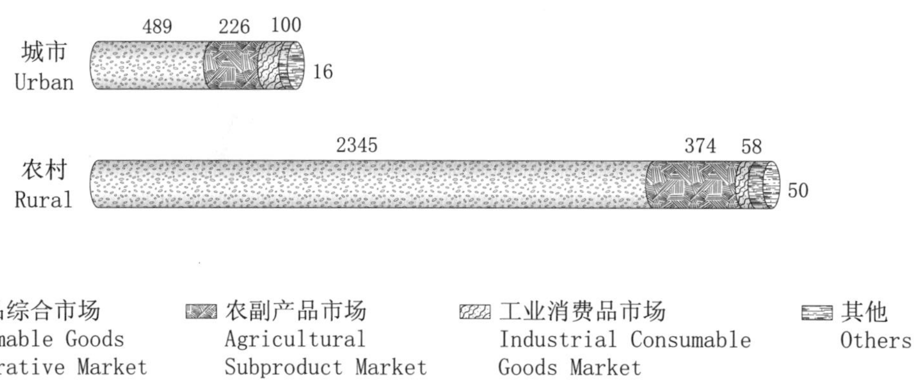

交易市场成交额 (万元) (2001)
Transaction of Markets(10000 yuan)

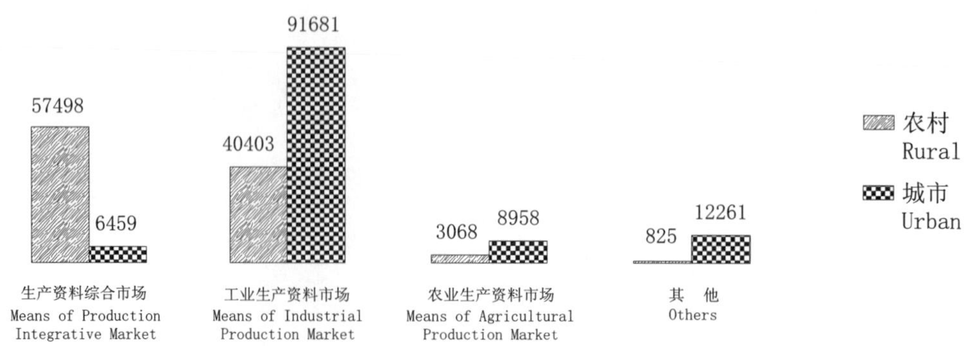

11－1 商品交易市场情况
Number of Commodity Exchange Markets

单位：个
(unit)

指标	Item	2000 合计 Total	2000 城市 Urban	2000 农村 Rural	2001 合计 Total	2001 城市 Urban	2001 农村 Rural
消费品市场数	Number of Consumable Markets	2696	463	2233	2834	489	2345
消费品综合市场	Consumable Goods Integrative Market	2144	185	1959	2010	147	1863
农副产品市场	Agricultural Subproduct Integrative Market	413	165	248	600	226	374
农副产品综合市场	Agricultural Subproduct Integrative Market	327	122	205	517	180	337
农副产品专业市场	Agricultural Subproduct Special Market	86	43	43	83	46	37
工业消费品市场	Industrial Consumable Goods Market	111	97	14	158	100	58
工业消费品综合市场	Industrial Consumable Goods Integrative Market	55	46	9	101	47	54
工业消费品专业市场	Industrial Consumer Goods Special Market	56	51	5	57	53	4
其他	Others	28	16	12	66	16	50
生产资料市场数	Means of Production Market	72	11	61	104	15	89
生产资料综合市场	Means of Production Integrative Market	5		5	25	3	22
工业生产资料市场	Means of Industrial Production Market	47	11	36	56	10	46
工业生产资料综合市场	Means of Industrial Production Integrative Market						
工业生产资料专业市场	Means of Industrial Production Special Market						
农业生产资料市场	Means of Agricultural Production Market	19		19	22	2	20
农业生产资料综合市场	Means of Agricultural Production Integrative Market	2		2	4	2	2
农业生产资料专业市场	Means of Agricultural Production Special Market	17		17	18		18
其他	Others	1		1	1		1

11－2 社会消费品零售总额
Total Retail Sales of Consumer Goods

单位:万元
(10000 yuan)

指标	Item	2000	2001	2001年比2000年增长(%) Increase Rate in 2001 over 2000(%)
总计	Total	3436657	3780105	10.0
按销售单位所在地分	Grouped by Location of Establishments			
市	City	1974072	2200417	11.5
县	County	667674	723086	8.3
县以下	Below County Level	794911	856602	7.8
按行业分	Grouped by Sector			
批发零售贸易业	Wholesales and Retail Sales Trade	2324167	2534837	9.1
餐饮业	Catering Trade	422919	524288	24.0
其他行业	Others	689571	720980	4.6
制造业	Manufacturing	180080	189421	5.2
农业生产者	Farm Producers	430813	453539	5.3

11－3 生产资料交易市场成交额情况
Basic Statistics of Means of Production Exchange Market

单位:万元
(10000 yuan)

指标	Item	2000			2001		
		合计 Total	城市 Urban	农村 Rural	合计 Total	城市 Urban	农村 Rural
总计	Total	144018	42364	101654	221153	102033	119120
生产资料综合市场	Means of Production Integrative Market	14167	85	14082	63957	6459	57498
工业生产资料市场	Means of Industrial Production Market	113199	41769	71430	132084	91681	40403
农业生产资料市场	Means of Agricultural Production Market	5919		5919	12026	3068	8958
其他	Others	10733	510	10223	13086	825	12261

11－4 消费品交易市场成交额情况
Transaction of Consumable Markets

单位：万元
(10000 yuan)

指　　标	Item	2000 合计 Total	2000 城市 Urban	2000 农村 Rural	2001 合计 Total	2001 城市 Urban	2001 农村 Rural
消费品市场	**Consumable Transaction Markets**	**1965695**	**981601**	**984094**	**2138910**	**908617**	**1230293**
消费品综合市场	Consumable Goods Integrative Market	1055470	327101	728369	1184700	289577	895123
农副产品市场	Agricultural Subproduct Market	599835	395707	204128	603086	376228	226858
工业消费品市场	Industrial Consumable Goods Market	276483	239417	37066	238565	208038	30527
其他	Others	33907	19376	14531	112559	34774	77785
按商品类别分	**Grouped by Category of Commodities**						
粮食类	Grain	233446	115395	118051	334394	124445	209949
油脂油料类	Axunge and Oil Plants	69317	25818	43499	79053	24426	54627
棉烟麻类	Cotton, Hemp and Tobacco	20316	6231	14085	136344	7431	128913
肉食禽蛋类	Meat, Poultry and Eggs	587941	278963	308978	556512	238953	317559
水产品类	Aquatic Products	76213	46915	29298	81893	48698	33195
蔬菜类	Fresh Vegetable	211053	82051	129002	228685	85470	143215
干鲜果类	Dried and Fresh Fruits	89082	49660	39422	101445	54012	47433
大牲畜类	Large Domestic Animals	67766	3851	63915	83051	4086	78965
家畜幼禽类	Livestock and Poult	89760	17545	72215	82202	26551	55651
工业品类	Industrial Products	346117	243990	102127	313143	206543	106600
其他	Others	174684	111182	63502	142188	88002	54186

11-5 限额以上批发零售贸易企业基本情况(2001)

Basic Conditions of Enterprises above Designated Size in Wholesale and Retail Sales, Catering Trades

单位:个/人
(unit/person)

指　　标	Item	法人企业 Number of Corporation Unit	产业活动单位数 Number of Active Unit	从业人数 Persons Engaged
总　　计	Total	231	233	42545
批发业	Wholesale Trade	155	157	26407
#国有及国有控股	of which: State-owned and Controlling Share Hold by The State	142	144	24563
按登记注册类型分组	Grouped by Registration			
内资企业	Domestic-funded Enterprise	153	155	26258
国有企业	State-owned Enterprise	121	123	21301
集体企业	Collective-owned Enterprise	12	12	1812
股份合作企业	Copperative Enterprise	2	2	50
联营企业	Joint Ownership	2	2	48
国有联营企业	State-owned Joint Ownership	1	1	28
国有与集体联营企业	State and Collective-owned Joint Ownership	1	1	20
有限责任公司	Limited Liability Corporations	5	5	1290
国有独资企业	State-owned Corporation	2	2	945
其他有限责任公司	Other Limited Liability Corporations	3	3	345
股份有限公司	Share Holding Co. Ltd	9	9	1474
私营企业	Private Enterprise	2	2	283
私营有限责任公司	Private Limited Liability Corporations	2	2	283
港、澳、台商投资企业	Enterprises Funded by Hong kong, Macao and Taiwan	2	2	149
合资经营企业	Joint Venture Enterprises	1	1	76
独资经营企业	Enterprise with Sole Investment	1	1	73
按国民经济行业分组	Grouped by National Economic Sector			
食品、饮料、烟草和家庭用品批发业	Wholesale of Food, Beverages, Tobaccos and Household Articles	92	93	19414
食品、饮料、烟草批发业	Wholesale of Food, Beverages and Tobaccos	81	82	18043
粮食、食用油批发业	Wholesale of Grains and Edible Oil	6	6	718
烟草及其制品批发业	Wholesale of Tobaccos and Related Products	65	66	16228
纺织品、服装和鞋帽批发业	Wholesale of Textiles, Garments, Shoes and Hats	2	2	131
日用百货批发业	Wholesale of Daily Consumer Goods	2	2	51
五金、交电、化工批发业	Wholesale of Hardware, Transport, Electric and Chemical Products	3	3	617
药品及医疗器械批发业	Wholesale of Medicines and Medical Appliances	4	4	572
能源、材料和机械电子设备批发业	Wholesale of Energy, Material, Mechanic and Electronic Equipment	51	52	5297
能源批发业	Wholesale of Energy Products	23	23	2874
石油及制品批发业	Wholesale of Petroleum and Related Products	21	21	2508
煤炭及制品批发业	Wholesale of Coal and Related Products	2	2	366
化工材料批发业	Wholesale of Chemical Materials	3	3	264
矿产品批发业	Wholesale of Mineral Products	2	3	405
金属材料批发业	Wholesale of Metal Materials	3	3	256
机械、电子设备批发业	Wholesale of Machinery and Electronic Equipment	13	13	1147
汽车、摩托车及零配件批发业	Wholesale of Motor Vehicles, Motorcycles and Parts	5	5	239

11－5 续表(continued)

单位:个/人
(unit/person)

指　　标	Item	法人企业 Number of Corporation Unit	产业活动单位数 Number of Active Unit	从业人数 Persons Engaged
汽车批发业	Wholesale of Motor Vehicles	3	3	138
再生物资回收批发业	Wholesale of Recycled Materials	2	2	112
其他批发业	Other Wholesale Trade	12	12	1696
图书报刊批发业	Wholesale of Books, Newspaper and Magazines	3	3	356
农业生产资料批发业	Wholesale of Means of Agricultural Production	7	7	603
其他类未包括的批发业	Other Wholesale Not Classified Elsewhere	2	2	737
零售业	**Retail Trade**	**76**	**76**	**16138**
#国有及国有控股	of which: State－owned and Controlling Share Hold by the State	54	54	10783
按登记注册类型分组	**Grouped by Registration**			
内资企业	Domestic－funded Enterprise	76	76	16138
国有企业	State－owned Enterprise	36	36	7610
集体企业	Collective－owned Enterprise	4	4	433
股份合作企业	Copperative Enterprise	2	2	213
联营企业	Joint Ownership	1	1	218
国有与集体联营企业	State and Collective－owned Joint Ownership	1	1	218
有限责任公司	Limited Liability Corporations	10	10	2349
国有独资企业	State－owned Corporation	1	1	216
其他有限责任公司	Other Limited Liability Corporations	9	9	2133
股份有限公司	Share Holding Co. Ltd	11	11	2748
私营企业	Private Enterprise	12	12	2567
私营独资企业	Private Enterprise with Sole Investment	2	2	771
私营合伙企业	Private Enterprise with Partnership	1	1	60
私营有限责任公司	Private Limited Liability Corporations	7	7	1568
私营股份有限公司	Private Share Holding Co. Ltd	2	2	168
按国民经济行业分组	**Grouped by National Economic Sector**			
食品、饮料和烟草零售业	Retail of Food, Beverages and Tobaccos	10	10	2134
粮油食品零售业	Retail of Grains and Edible Oil	1	1	867
副食品零售业	Retail of Non－staple Food	3	3	370
日用百货零售业	Retail of Daily Consumer Goods	19	19	7424
百货零售业	Retail of Consumer Goods	17	17	7187
文化体育用品零售业	Retail of Stationery and Sports Goods	1	1	60
纺织品、服装和鞋帽零售业	Retail of Textiles, Garments, Shoes and Hats	3	3	802
日用杂品零售业	Retail of Daily Consumer Goods	1	1	110
五金、交电、化工零售业	Retail of Hardware, Transport, Electric and Chemical Products	8	8	2412
药品及医疗器械零售业	Retail of Medicines and Medical Appliances	6	6	1045
图书报刊零售业	Retail of Books, Newspaper and Magazines	9	9	505
其他零售业	Other Retail Trade	20	20	1706
汽车、摩托车及其零配件零售业	Retail of Motor Vehicles, Motorcycles and Parts	5	5	448
计算机及软件、办公设备零售业	Retail of Computers, Software and Office Appliances	1	1	60

11－6 限额以上批发零售贸易业商品购进、销售、库存总额(2001)
Total Purchases, Sales and Inventory of Enterprises above Designated Size in Wholesale and Retail Trade

单位:万元
(10000 yuan)

指　　标	Item	购进总额 Total Purchases	销售总额 Total Sales	批　发 wholesale Trade	零　售 Retail Trade	年末库存额 Inventory (year－end)
总　　计	Total	2431242.0	2733150.9	2310862.9	422288.0	352897.2
批发业	Wholesale Trade	2092303.6	2389933.3	2238265.8	151667.5	295911.7
#国有及国有控股	of which: State－owned and Controlling Share Hold by the State	2029451.4	2320896.7	2187948.1	132948.6	290546.2
按登记注册类型分组	Grouped by Registration					
内资企业	Domestic－funded Enterprise	2084071.6	2381369.1	2235004.8	146364.3	295162.2
国有企业	State－owned Enterprise	1807701.2	2071615.4	1987053.6	84561.8	248162.6
集体企业	Collective－owned Enterprise	66045.7	69448.3	57713.7	11734.6	6449.3
股份合作企业	Cooperative Enterprise	7599.3	6600.2	6600.2		2107.3
联营企业	Joint Ownership	7423.4	9541.4	9541.4		618.4
国有联营企业	State－owned Joint Ownership	4609.5	4821.1	4821.1		209.1
国有与集体联营企业	State and Collective－owned Joint Ownership	2813.9	4720.3	4720.3		409.3
有限责任公司	Limited Liability Corporations	70774.6	83689.4	78531.4	5158.0	26489.9
国有独资企业	State－owned Corporation	45088.4	51911.9	51911.9		25017.0
其他有限责任公司	Other Limited Liability Corporations	25686.2	31777.5	26619.5	5158.0	1472.9
股份有限公司	Share Holding Co. Ltd	118309.0	134390.1	92254.6	42135.5	10305.4
私营企业	Private Enterprise	6218.4	6084.3	3309.9	2774.4	1029.3
私营有限责任公司	Private Limited Liability Corporations	6218.4	6084.3	3309.9	2774.4	1029.3
港、澳、台商投资企业	Enterprises Funded by Hong kong, Macao and Taiwan	8232.0	8564.2	3261.0	5303.2	749.5
合资经营企业	Joint Venture Enterprises	2921.0	3261.0	3261.0		613.4
独资经营企业	Enterprise with Sole Investment	5311.0	5303.2		5303.2	136.1
按国民经济行业分组	Grouped by National Economic Sector					
食品、饮料、烟草和家庭用品批发业	Wholesale of Food, Beverages, Tobaccos and Household Articles	1414460.6	1658213.8	1624249.6	33964.2	234814.0
食品、饮料、烟草批发业	Wholesale of Food, Beverages and Tobaccos	1331019.3	1563882.4	1554510.1	9372.3	223322.6
粮食、食用油批发业	Wholesalel of Grain and Edible Oil	95305.1	92254.0	90170.1	2083.9	7914.3
烟草及其制品批发业	Wholesale of Tobaccos and Related Products	1186416.4	1405842.6	1399147.8	6694.8	204703.0
纺织品、服装和鞋帽批发业	Wholesale of Textiles, Gaments, Shoes and Hats	9543.9	10285.6	10285.6		975.8
日用百货批发业	Wholesale of Daily Consumer Goods	6114.0	8169.8	7660.3	509.5	927.3

11－6 续表 1(continued)

单位:万元
(10000 yuan)

指　　标	Item	购进总额 Total Purchases	销售总额 Total Sales	批　发 wholesale Trade	零　售 Retail Trade	年末库存额 Inventory (year－end)
五金、交电、化工批发业	Wholesale of Hardware, Transport, Electric and Chemical Products	40159.3	45867.7	44486.2	1381.5	3405.5
药品及医疗器械批发业	Wholesale of Medicines and Medical Appliances	27624.1	30008.3	7307.4	22700.9	6182.8
能源、材料和机械电子设备批发业	Wholesale of Energy Products, Materials, Machinery and Electronic Equipment	574452.8	624278.2	510691.7	113586.5	52237.0
能源批发业	Wholesale of Energy Products	282651.9	303320.6	212893.0	90427.6	21823.8
石油及制品批发业	Wholesale of Petroleum and Related Products	273829.3	292884.0	202961.7	89922.3	21823.8
煤炭及制品批发业	Wholesale of Coal and Related Products	8822.6	10436.6	9931.3	505.3	
化工材料批发业	Wholesale of Chemical Materials	26787.1	30876.2	30876.2		2118.0
矿产品批发业	Wholesale of Mineral Products	86704.8	102753.4	102753.4		4695.4
金属材料批发业	Wholesale of Metal Materials	14190.4	15951.1	15701.0	250.1	1511.5
机械、电子设备批发业	Wholesale of Machinery and Electronic Equipment	138941.6	145948.9	135247.2	10701.7	20689.2
汽车、摩托车及零配件批发业	Wholesale of Motor Vehicles, Motorcycles and Parts	22079.4	21103.6	8896.5	12207.1	644.6
汽车批发业	Wholesale of Motor Vehicles	12311.0	12600.1	393.0	12207.1	362.6
再生物资回收批发业	Wholesale of Recycled Materials	3097.6	4324.4	4324.4		754.5
其他批发业	Other Wholesale Trade	103390.2	107441.3	103324.5	4116.8	8860.7
图书报刊批发业	Wholesale of Books, Newspaper and Magazines	52437.8	51707.3	50896.1	811.2	2257.8
农业生产资料批发业	Wholesale of Means of Agricultural Production	42725.1	47780.0	47780.0		5982.4
其他类未包括的批发业	Other Wholesale Not Classified Elsewhere	8227.3	7954.0	4648.4	3305.6	620.5
零售业	**Retail Trade**	**338938.4**	**343217.6**	**72597.1**	**270620.5**	**56985.5**
#国有及国有控股	of which: State－owned and Controlling Share Hold by the State	178213.1	200611.1	66984.9	133626.2	25726.9
按登记注册类型分组	**Grouped by Registration**					
内资企业	Domestic－funded Enterprise	338938.4	343217.6	72597.1	270620.5	56985.5
国有企业	State－owned Enterprise	103065.9	119197.1	58434.5	60762.6	15234.6
集体企业	Collective－owned Enterprise	3512.1	5491.2	1722.3	3768.9	1775.2
股份合作企业	Copperative Enterprise	292.7	1000.1	430.3	569.8	100.2
联营企业	Joint Ownership	2213.4	1104.4		1104.4	682.3
国有与集体联营企业	State and Collective－owned Joint Ownership	2213.4	1104.4		1104.4	682.3
有限责任公司	Limited Liability Corporations	60403.2	50898.6	3338.3	47560.3	17020.6

11－6续表 2(continued)

单位:万元
(10000 yuan)

指　　标	Item	购进总额 Total Purchases	销售总额 Total Sales	批　发 wholesale Trade	零　售 Retail Trade	年末库存额 Inventory (year－end)
国有独资企业	State－owned Corporation	1984.7	2327.2		2327.2	551.2
其他有限责任公司	Other Limited Liability Corporations	58418.5	48571.4	3338.3	45233.1	16469.4
股份有限公司	Share Holding Co. Ltd	64923.2	70916.7	6689.2	64227.5	9202.3
私营企业	Private Enterprise	104527.9	94609.5	1982.5	92627.0	12970.3
私营独资企业	Private Enterprise with Sole Investment	37797.9	21540.4	1755.4	19785.0	3523.0
私营合伙企业	Private Enterprise with Partnership	1845.0	3773.1	129.0	3644.1	372.2
私营有限责任公司	Private Limited Liability Corporations	63324.0	67804.8	98.1	67706.7	8909.0
私营股份有限公司	Private Share Holding Co. Ltd	1561.0	1491.2		1491.2	166.1
按国民经济行业分组	**Grouped by National Economic Sector**					
食品、饮料和烟草零售业	Retail of Food, Beverages and Tobaccos	28916.6	35600.0	27323.5	8276.5	3328.9
粮油食品零售业	Retail of Grains and Edible Oil	2055.0	2389.6		2389.6	76.0
副食品零售业	Retail of Non－staple Food	3069.8	2680.0	837.5	1842.5	528.3
日用百货零售业	Retail of Daily Consumer Goods	98914.7	97428.7	17805.0	79623.7	24407.9
百货零售业	Retail of Consumer Goods	95465.9	93025.1	15718.3	77306.8	23669.6
文化体育用品零售业	Retail of Stationery and Sports Goods	1779.0	1849.9	503.6	1346.3	50.5
纺织品、服装和鞋帽零售业	Retail of Textiles, Garments, Shoes and Hats	9473.1	9009.7		9009.7	1230.6
日用杂品零售业	Retail of Daily Consumer Goods	357.2	500.0	80.3	419.7	524.3
五金、交电、化工零售业	Retail of Hardware, Transport, Electric and Chemical Products	105635.8	101822.6	8615.7	93206.9	14988.7
药品及医疗器械零售业	Retail of Medicines and Medical Appliances	7393.2	7747.9	1425.5	6322.4	2849.9
图书报刊零售业	Retail of Books, Newspaper and Magazines	16171.1	14990.5	4002.4	10988.1	2267.7
其他零售业	Other Retail Trade	72076.7	76118.2	13344.7	62773.5	7387.5
汽车、摩托车及其零配件零售业	Retail of Motor Vehicles, Motorcycles and Parts	30305.5	31507.0	5498.5	26008.5	3219.7
计算机及软件、办公设备零售业	Retail of Computers, Software and Office Appliances	3981.2	2726.5		2726.5	1056.1

11－7 限额以上批发零售贸易业主要财务指标(2001)

Main Financial Indicators of Enterprises above Designated Size in Wholesale and Retail Trade

单位：万元
(10000 yuan)

指　　标	Item	商品销售收入 Sales Revenue	商品销售成本 Cost of Sales	经营费用 Management Cost	商品销售税金及附加 Sales Tax and Extra Changes	营业利润 Total Profits
总　　计	**Total**	**2066369.9**	**1788155.9**	**98795.2**	**6734.4**	**821.6**
批发业合计	**Wholesale Trade**	**1735384.9**	**1500223.9**	**78127.1**	**5398.2**	**954.7**
内资企业	Domestic－funded Enterprise	1727371.4	1492474.9	77753.7	5397.4	1027.5
国有企业	State－owned Enterprise	1438462.3	1222406.6	64972.3	5119.9	4469.3
集体企业	Collective－owned Enterprise	69352.5	62782.1	4104.2	84.2	－1236.2
股份合作企业	Cooperative Enterprises	6694.5	6312.0	125.6	10.5	133.1
联营企业	Joint Ownership	8840.9	8293.0	157.0	13.6	22.5
有限责任公司	Limited Liability Corporations	77388.9	72691.7	4220.8	96.1	－2246.3
股份有限公司	Share Holding Co.Ltd	120547.9	114412.5	3874.7	57.0	－140.6
私营企业	Private Enterprises	6084.4	5577.0	299.1	16.1	25.7
港、澳、台商投资企业	Enterprises Funded by Hong kong, Macao and Taiwan	8013.5	7749.0	373.4	0.8	－72.8
零售业合计	**Retail Trade**	**330985.0**	**287932.0**	**20668.1**	**1336.2**	**－133.1**
内资企业	Domestic－funded Enterprise	330985.0	287932.0	20668.1	1336.2	－133.1
国有企业	State－owned Enterprise	108851.3	91992.4	8030.1	459.4	－2750.9
集体企业	Collective－owned Enterprise	4805.9	4048.4	605.1	23.2	－262.2
股份合作企业	Cooperative Enterprises	203.8	144.9	65.1		－58.2
联营企业	Joint Ownership	963.3	809.5	116.3	0.5	－244.4
有限责任公司	Limited Liability Corporations	44337.8	38065.5	3149.8	184.3	－524.6
股份有限公司	Share Holding Co.Ltd	72178.2	62025.1	3594.7	498.6	4391.8
私营企业	Private Enterprises	99644.7	90846.2	5107.0	170.2	－684.6

11－8 限额以上批发零售贸易业商品分类销售额(2001)

Total Sales of Enterprises above Designated Size in Wholesale and Retail Trade by Category of Main Commodities

单位:万元
(10000 yuan)

项目	Item	销售合计 Total Sales	批发 Wholesales Trade	零售 Retail Trade
总计	Total	2562202	2204547	357655
食品、饮料、烟酒类	Food, Beverage and Tobacco and Liquor	1260978	1221029	39950
肉禽蛋类	Meat, Poultry and Eggs	4124	2340	1784
其他食品类	Others Food	43593	24141	19453
饮料类	Beverage	4912	178	4734
烟酒类	Tobacco and Liquor	1208349	1194370	13979
服装鞋帽、针、纺织品类	Garments, Footwear and Hats, Kintwear and Textiles	51383	4653	46730
服装类	Garments	37485	3758	33727
鞋帽类	Footwear and Hats	10255	2	10253
针、纺织品类	Kintwear and Textiles	3643	893	2750
化妆品类	Cosmetics	9386	2530	6856
金银珠宝类	Gold, Silver and Jewelry	6151	16	6134
日用品类	Articles for Daily Use	20740	8753	11986
洗涤用品类	Washing Articles	8029	4892	3137
儿童玩具类	Children's Toy	1263	16	1247
五金、电料类	Hardware and Electrical Materials	1241	707	534
体育、娱乐用品类	Sports and Recreation Articles	4045	1346	2699
书报杂志类	Newspaper and Magazines	58131	47563	10569
电子出版物及音像制品类	Electric Publication and Sound－video Materials	42		42
家用电器和音像器材类	Household Appliances and Video Appliances	46814	8410	38405
中西药品类	Traditional Chinese and Western Medicines	37144	8902	28242
西药	Western Medicines	29017	7021	21996
中草药及中成药	Traditional Chinese Medicines	7282	1824	5458
文化办公用品类	Culture and Office Articles	9533	2783	6750
家具类	Furniture	636	185	451
通讯器材类	Communication Appliances	2734	2257	477
煤炭及制品类	Coal and Related Products	4214	4214	
木材及制品类	Timber and Related Products	94	94	
石油及制品类	Petroleum and Related Products	310010	204740	105270
化工材料及制品类	Raw Chemical Materials and Related Products	152659	152322	337
化肥类	Chemical Fertilizers	40313	40313	
金属材料类	Metal Materials	59761	58516	1245
建筑及装潢材料类	Building and Decoration Materials	16076	16076	
机电产品及设备类	Mechanical and Electrical Instruments	190793	150895	39899
农机类	Agricultural Machinery	4106	3656	450
汽车类	Automobile	54887	20370	34517
种子饲料类	Seed and Feed	1554	1554	
棉麻类	Cotton and Jute Products	3	3	
其他类	Others	318082	307000	11082

11－9 限额以上批发零售贸易业商品销售数量

Total Sales Number of Enterprises above Designated Size in Wholesale and Retail Sales Trade by Commodities

项　目	Item	合计 Total		批发 Wholesale		零售 Retail Sales	
		2000	2001	2000	2001	2000	2001
粮食(吨)	Grain(ton)	4020	36723	1282	28833	2738	7890
食用植物油(吨)	Edible Vegetable Oil (ton)	2855	5326	1573	1685	1282	3641
食糖(吨)	Sugar (ton)	25971	14062	25431	7434	540	6628
电视机(台)	TV Sets (unit)	58574	53346	5411	3472	53163	49874
组合音响(台)	Hi－Fi Stereo Component (unit)	4782	12541	196	1820	4586	10721
摄像机(台)	Pickup Camera (unit)	228	364			228	364
录像机(台)	Video－recorder (unit)	122	6			122	6
影碟机(台)	Video Disc Player (unit)	17093	20914	1427	3385	15666	17529
家用电冰箱(台)	Household Refrigerator (unit)	35951	27357	3921	4292	32030	23065
家用洗衣机(台)	Household Washing Machines (unit)	44021	37257	6349	4804	37672	32453
房间空调器(台)	Room Air Conditioner (unit)	6701	4764	133	88	6568	4676
微波炉(台)	Microwave Oven (unit)	49846	37759	8804	12443	41042	25316
微型计算机(台)	Personal Computer (unit)	10751	6628	6153	1940	4598	4688
普通电话机(台)	Telephone (unit)	4905	3370	6		4899	3370
化学肥料(吨)	Chemical Fertilizer (ton)	433386	186242	433386	186242		
化学农药(吨)	Chemical Pesticide (ton)	607	552	607	552		
农用薄膜(吨)	Farming Pellicle (ton)	55	4	55	4		
煤炭(吨)	Coal (ton)	581405	445012	581405	445012		
汽油(吨)	Gasoline (ton)	259853	272999	204509	177923	55344	95076
柴油(吨)	Diesel Oil (ton)	492817	564306	388923	366995	103894	197311
钢材(吨)	Steel (ton)	38648	115269	27125	114304	1523	965
铜(吨)	Copper (ton)	192	429	192	429		
铝(吨)	Aluminium (ton)	22857	28196	22857	28196		
水泥(吨)	Cement (ton)	270594	316784	270404	316784	190	
汽车(辆)	Motor Vehicles(unit)	5686	4738	3396	2134	2290	2604
#轿车(辆)	Car (unit)	2801	3216	1597	1355	1204	1861
摩托车(辆)	Motor(unit)	13672	10525	6744	5623	6928	4902
拖拉机(台)	Tractors (unit)	138	111	138	111		

11－10 限额以上餐饮企业主要财务指标(按注册类型分)(2001)
Main Financial Indicators of Enterprises above Designated Size in Catering Trade by Registration

单位:万元
(10000 yuan)

指 标	Item	营业收入 Sales Revenue	营业成本 Cost of Sales	营业费用 Management Cost	营业税金及附加 Sales Tax and Extra Changes	经营利润 Total Profits
总 计	Total	27178.5	14792.1	6618.2	1483.4	4284.8
内资企业	Domestic－funded Enterprise	27178.5	14792.1	6618.2	1483.4	4284.8
国有企业	State－owned Enterprise	2018.0	468.2	1256.6	118.5	174.7
集体企业	Collective－owned Enterprise	879.8	462.2	318.7	50.3	48.6
有限责任公司	Limited Liabilty Corporations	8003.9	4055.4	1075.5	285.7	2587.3
股份有限公司	Share Holding Co.ltd	1239.4	846.1	349.3	69.3	－25.3
私营企业	Private Enterprises	14278.8	8631.1	3397.3	902.7	1347.7
私营独资企业	Privare－funded Enterprises	4201.1	2319.7	732.2	270.8	878.4
私营有限责任公司	Private Limited Liabilty Corporations	8912.6	5579.2	2464.9	505.0	363.5
私营股份有限公司	Private Share－holding Corporations Ltd.	1165.1	732.2	200.2	126.9	105.8
其他企业	Other Enterprises	758.6	329.1	220.8	56.9	151.8
按国民经济行业分	Grouped by National Economic Sector					
正 餐	Dinner	26961.7	14725.0	6541.7	1477.9	4217.1
其它餐饮业	Others	216.8	67.1	76.5	5.5	67.7

主要统计指标解释

社会消费品零售总额 指国民经济各行业直接售给城乡居民和社会集团的消费品总额。它是反映各行业通过多种商品流通渠道向居民和社会集团供应的生活消费品总量，是研究国内零售市场变动情况、反映经济景气程度的重要指标。

社会消费品零售总额包括：⑴售给城乡居民作为生活用的商品和修建房屋用的建筑材料；⑵售给社会集团的各种办公用品和公用消费品；⑶售给机关、团体、学校、部队、企业、事业单位的职工食堂和旅店（招待所）附设专门供本店旅客食用，不对外营业的食堂的各种食品、燃料；企业、单位和国营农场直接售给本单位职工和职工食堂的自己生产的产品；⑷售给部队干部、战士生活用的粮食、副食品、衣着品、日用品、燃料；⑸售给来华的外国人、华侨、港澳台同胞的消费品；⑹居民自费购买的中、西药品、中药材及医疗用品；⑺报社、出版社直接售给居民和社会集团的报纸、图书、杂志，集邮公司出售的新、旧纪念邮票、特种邮票、首日封、集邮册、集邮工具等；⑻旧货寄售商店自购、自销部分的商品；⑼煤气公司、液化石油气站售给居民和社会集团的煤气灶具和罐装液化石油气；⑽农民售给非农业居民和社会集团的商品。不包括售给国民经济各部门企业、事业单位（包括国有经济的农场）生产经营用的各种原材料、燃料、设备、工具等和售给批发零售贸易业、餐饮业作为转卖用的商品，旧货寄售商店受托寄售卖出的商品，服务业的营业收入，邮局出售邮票的收入，自来水、电力、煤气生产（供应）单位的产品供应收入，也不包括农民之间的商品销售。

批发零售贸易业商品购、销、存总额 指各种登记注册类型的批发、零售贸易业（不包括个体）企业（单位）以本企业（单位）为总体的商品购进、销售、库存总额。

商品购进总额 指从本企业（单位）以外的单位和个人购进（包括从境外直接进口）作为转卖或加工后转卖的商品总额。它反映批发零售贸易业从国内、国外市场上购进商品的总量。商品购进总额包括：(1)从工农业生产者购进的商品；(2)从出版社、报社的出版发行部门购进的图书、杂志和报纸；(3)从各种登记注册类型的批发零售贸易企业（单位）购进的商品；(4)从其他单位购进的商品，如从机关、团体、企业等单位购进的剩余物资，从餐饮业、服务业购进的商品，从海关、市场管理部门购进的缉私和没收的商品，从居民手中收购的废旧商品等；(5)从国（境）外直接进口的商品。不包括企业（单位）为自身经营用和未通过买卖行为而收入的商品以及销售退回、商品升溢等。

商品销售总额 指对本企业（单位）以外的单位和个人出售（包括对境外直接出口）的商品总额。它反映批发零售贸易业在国内市场上销售商品以及出口商品的总量。商品销售总额包括：⑴售给城乡居民和社会集团消费用的商品；⑵售给工业、农业、建筑业、运输邮电业、批发零售贸易业、餐饮业、服务业等作为生产、经营使用的商品；⑶售给批发零售贸易业作为转卖或加工后转卖的商品；⑷对国（境）外直接出口的商品。不包括出售本企业（单位）自用的废旧包装用品；未通过买卖行为付出的商品；经本单位介绍，由买卖双方直接结算，本单位只收取手续费的业务；购货退出的商品以及商品损耗和损失等。

批发零售贸易业库存 指报告期末各种登记注册类型的批发零售贸易企业（单位）已取得所有权的商品。它反映批发零售贸易企业（单位）的商品库存情况和对市场商品供应的保证程度。

消费品市场成交额 指从事消费品交易的商品市场的全部商品成交金额。消费品市场包括农副产品市场和工业消费品市场。

Explanatory Notes on Main Statistical Indicators

Total Retail Sales of Consumer Goods refer to the sum of retail sales of consumer goods sold by all sectors of the national economy to urban and rural residents and social groups. This indicator is used to show the supply of consumers goods through various channels to households and institutions, and is very important for the study on changes at the domestic retail market, and on economic cycles.

The retail sales of consumer goods include: (1) commodities sold to urban and rural residents for their daily use and building materials sold to them for the construction or repair of houses; (2) office appliances and supplies sold to institutions; (3) food and fuels sold to canteens of institutions, enterprises, schools, military units and to canteens of hotels and hostels that only serve their guests, and commodities produced by enterprises, institutions or state farms and sold directly to their employees or their canteens; (4) grain and non-staple food, clothing, daily articles and fuels sold to military personnel; (5) consumer goods sold to foreigners, overseas Chinese, and Chinese compatriots from Taiwan, Hong Kong and Macao during their stay in the mainland of China; (6) Chinese and western medicines, herbs and medical facilities purchased by residents; (7) newspapers, books and magazines directly sold to residents and social groups by publishers, new and old commemorative stamps, special stamps, first-day covers, stamp albums and other stamp-collection articles sold by stamp companies; (8) consumer goods purchased and then sold by second-hand shops; (9) stoves and other heating facilities and liquefied gas sold by gas companies to households and institutions; and (10) commodities sold by farmers to non-agricultural residents and social groups. Excluded under this heading are: raw materials, fuels, equipment, tools sold to enterprises, institutions and state farms for production purpose; commodities sold to trade establishments for re-selling; commissioned sales at second-hand shops; operational income of urban public utilities; stamps sold at post offices; income of water, power, gas production and supply establishments from the supply of their products; and sales of commodities among farmers.

Purchase, Sales and Stock of Commodities by Wholesale and Retail Trade refer to the purchase, sales and stock of commodities by wholesale and retail establishments of different status of registration (excluding individual sellers).

Total Purchases of Commodities refer to the total value of purchases of commodities by the establishments from other establishments or individuals (including direct import from abroad) for the purpose of re-selling, either with or without further processing of the commodities purchased. This indicator is used to show the total value of purchases of commodities by wholesale and retail establishments from domestic and overseas markets. The total purchases include: (1) agricultural and industrial products purchased from producers; (2) books, magazines and newspapers purchased from distribution departments of the publishers; (3) commodities purchased from wholesale and retail establishments of different status of registration; (4) commodities purchased from other units, such as surplus materials purchased from government agencies, enterprises or institutions, commodities purchased from catering and service establishments, confiscated goods purchased from customs authorities or market management agencies, second-hand goods and wastes purchased from residents; and (5) commodities directly imported from abroad. Excluded are commodities purchased by establishments (units) for use in their own business operation, commodities obtained without buying or selling procedures, rejected commodities, etc.

Total Sales of Commodities refer to value of commodities sold by the establishments to other establishments and individuals (including direct export). This indicator is used to show the total value of sales of commodities at domestic markets and export. The total sales include: (1) commodities sold to urban and rural residents and social groups for their consumption; (2) commodities sold to establishments in industry, agriculture, construction, transportation, post and telecommunications, wholesale and retail trades, catering trade and public utility for their production and operation; (3) commodities sold to wholesale and retail establishments for re selling, with or without further processing; and(4) commodities for direct export to other countries. Excluded are selling of waste packaging materials used by the establishments (units) themselves, commodities transferred without buying or selling procedures, commission income from brokerage in transactions whose settlement is directly handled by buyers and sellers, rejected commodities in the purchase, loss in commodities, etc.

Commodity Stock of Wholesale and Retail Enterprises refers to total commodities possessed by wholesale and retail enterprises(units) of various types of registration status at the end of the reference period, which reflects the commodity stock level of various wholesale and retail enterprises and the potential for market supply.

Volume of Transaction at Free Markets for Consumer Goods refers to the value of transaction of all goods at the free trade markets for consumer goods, where markets include both free markets for farm and sideline products and for manufactured consumer goods.

12

对外贸易

Foreign Trade and Economic Cooperation

Twelve

按地区分的外贸进、出口商品总额(万美元)(2001)

Import and Export Value by Territories (USD 10000)

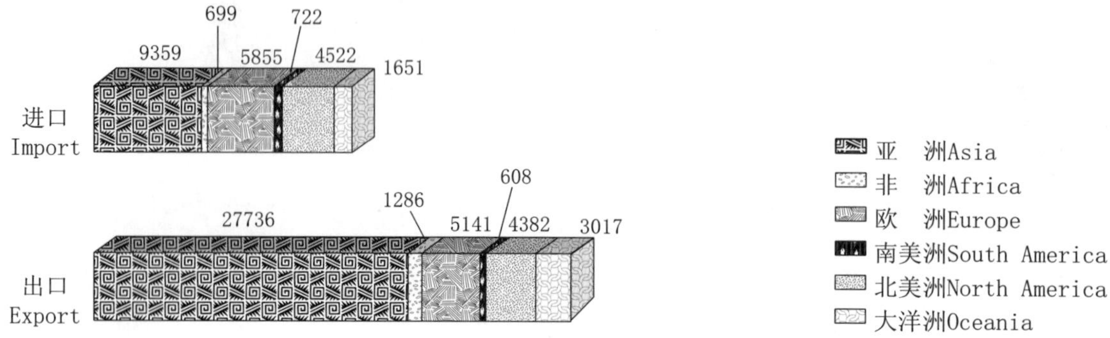

利用外资额(万美元)(2001)

Amount of Utilization of Foreign Capital and Foreign Investment (USD 10000)

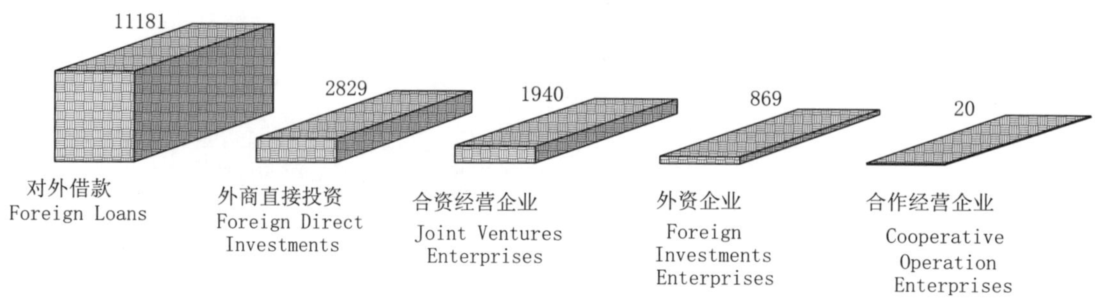

按行业分的外商实际直接投资额(万美元)(2001)

Actually Used Amount of Foreign Direct Investment by Sector(USD 10000)

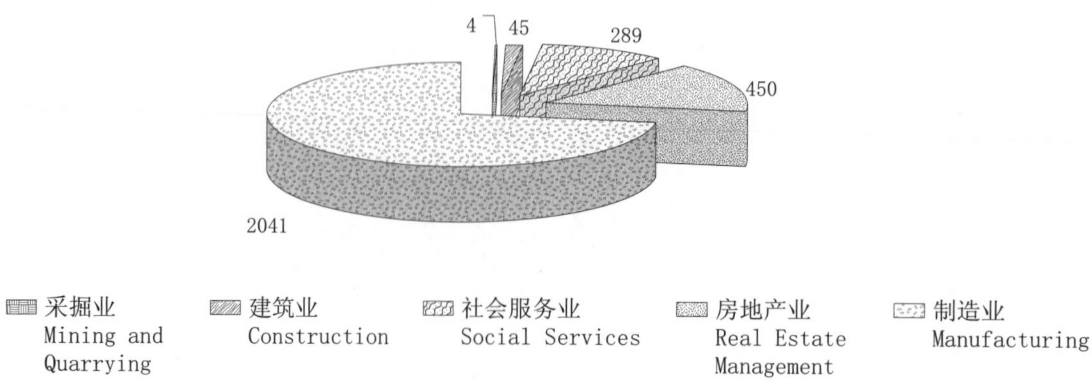

12－1 对外经济贸易
Foreign Trade and Economic Cooperation

指 标	Item	2000	2001	2001年比2000年增长(%) Increase Rate in 2001 over 2000(%)
进出口总额(万元)	**Total Imports and Exports(RMB 10000 yuan)**	**546374**	**537816**	**-1.6**
出口总额	Total Exports	348179	349037	0.2
进口总额	Total Imports	198195	188779	-4.8
进出口差额	Balance	149984	160258	6.9
进出口总额(万美元)	**Total Imports and Exports(USD 10000)**	**66002**	**64978**	**-1.6**
出口总额	Total Exports	42060	42170	0.3
进口总额	Total Imports	23942	22808	-4.7
进出口差额	Balance	18118	19362	6.9

12－2 按国别(地区)分的进出口商品总额
Import and Export Value by Country and Regions

单位:万美元
(USD 10000)

指 标	Item	进出口总额 Total		出口总额 Exports		进口总额 Imports	
		2000	2001	2000	2001	2000	2001
总 计	**Total**	**66002**	**64978**	**42060**	**42170**	**23942**	**22808**
亚 洲	Asia	41100	37095	28181	27736	12919	9359
非 洲	Africa	1450	1985	850	1286	600	699
欧 洲	Europe	9875	10996	5376	5141	4499	5855
南美洲	South America	1698	1330	999	608	699	722
北美洲	North America	7403	8904	4726	4382	2677	4522
大洋洲	Oceania	4476	4668	1928	3017	2548	1651

12－3 按地区分的出口商品总额
Foreign Export Trade with Related Countries(Territories)

单位:万美元
(USD 10000)

地区名	Country(Territory)	2000	2001	2001年比2000年增长(%) Increase Rate in 2001 over 2000(%)
总　计	Total	42060	42170	0.3
亚　洲	Asia	28181	27736	－1.6
非　洲	Africa	850	1286	51.3
欧　洲	Europe	5376	5141	－4.4
南美洲	South America	999	608	－39.1
北美洲	North America	4726	4382	－7.3
大洋洲	Oceania	1928	3017	56.5

12－4 按地区分的进口商品总额
Foreign Import Trade with Related Countries(Territories)

单位:万美元
(USD 10000)

地区名	Country(Territory)	2000	2001	2001年比2000年增长(%) Increase Rate in 2001 over 2000(%)
总　计	Total	23942	22808	－4.7
亚　洲	Asia	12919	9359	－27.6
非　洲	Africa	600	699	16.5
欧　洲	Europe	4499	5855	30.1
南美洲	South America	699	722	3.3
北美洲	North America	2677	4522	68.9
大洋洲	Oceania	2548	1651	－35.2

12－5 海关出口商品分类情况
Export Commodities in Volume and Value by Category (Customs Statistics)

单位:数量:吨 (Volume:ton)
金额:万美元(Value:USD 10000)

指标	Item	2000		2001		2001年比2000年增长(%) Increase Rate(%)	
		数量 Volume	金额 Value	数量 Volume	金额 Value	数量 Volume	金额 Value
总计	Total	2564011	42060	2920444	42170	13.9	0.3
活动物;动物产品	Live Animals & Animal Products	2195	293	3507	352	59.8	20.1
植物产品	Vegetables, Fruits and Cereals	4974	42	11355	453	128.3	978.6
动、植物油、脂及其分解产品;精制的食用油脂;动、植物蜡	Animal and Vegetable Oils, Fats and Wax, Refined Edible Oils and Fats	2647	201	1619	102	－38.8	－49.3
食品;饮料、酒及醋;烟草及烟草代用品的制品	Food, Beverages, Liquor and Vinegar, Tobacco and Tobacco Substitutes	49304	1956	55598	3300	12.8	68.7
矿产品	Minerals	1862655	7765	2217863	8774	19.1	13.0
化学工业及其相关工业的产品	Chemicals and Related Products	302864	8731	398363	10076	31.5	15.4
塑料及其产品;橡胶及其产品	Plastics and Related Products, Rubber and Related Pr oducts	3397	5754	1930	5122	－43.2	－11.0
生皮、皮革、毛皮及其制品;鞍具及挽具;旅行用品、手提包及类似物品;动物肠线(蚕胶 丝除外)制品	Raw Hides, Leather, Furs and Related Products, Saddle, Travel Articles, Handbags and Similar Containers	2017	102	536	33	－73.4	－67.6
木及木制品;木炭;软木及软木制品;稻草、秸秆、针茅或其他编结材料制品;篮筐及柳条编织品	Wood and Wooden Products, Charcoal, Cork and Related Products, Straws, Plaited Products, Baskets and Wickerwork	801	157	530	52	－33.8	－66.9
木浆及其他纤维状纤维素浆;回收(废碎)纸或纸板;纸、纸板及其制品	Paper Pulp and Cellulose Pulp, Paper and Waste Paper, Paperboard and Related Products	80	11	29	7	－63.8	－36.4
纺织原料及纺织制品	Textile Materials and Products	12984	1939	15932	877	22.7	－54.8

12－5 续表(continued)

单位:数量:吨 (Volume:ton)
金额:万美元(Value:USD 10000)

指　　标	Item	2000		2001		2001年比2000年增长(%) Increase Rate(%)	
		数量 Volume	金额 Value	数量 Volume	金额 Value	数量 Volume	金额 Value
鞋、帽、伞、杖、鞭及其零件;已加工的羽毛及其制品;人造花;人发制品	Footwear, Headgear, Umbrellas, Canes, Whips Processed Feather, Artificial, Flowers, Wigs	1379	320	382	34	－72.3	－89.4
石料、石膏、水泥、石棉、云母及类似材料的制品;陶瓷产品;玻璃及其制品	Gypsum, Cement, Asbestos, Mica, Ceramic Glass	3979	105	3882	63	－2.4	－40.0
天然或养殖珍珠、宝石或半宝石、贵金属、包贵金属及其制品;仿首饰;硬币	Natural or Cultivated Pearls, Precious or Semi－Precious Stones, Jewelery of Precious Metal or Rolled Precious Metal, Artificial Jewelery, Coins	46	11	51	11	10.9	持平
贱金属及其制品	Base Metals and Related Products	205372	9682	154326	8808	－24.9	－9.0
机器、机械器具、电气设备机器零件、录音机及放声机、电视图象、声音的录制和重放设备及其零件、附件	Machinery, Electric Equipment and Accessories, Recorders, Videor ecorder and Accessories	65642	3374	38511	2950	－41.3	－12.6
车辆、航空器、船舶及有关运输设备	Locomotives, Vehicles, Aircraft, Ship and Related Transportation Equipment	2550	692	1969	510	－22.8	－26.3
光学、照相、电影、计量、检验、医疗或外科用仪器及设备、精密仪品及设备,钟表,乐器 及其零附件	Optical, Photographic, Film, Measuring and Checking and Medical Instruments and Equipment, Precision Instr uments and Equipment, Clocks, Musical Instruments, Related Parts and Accessories	6020	321	6319	363	5.0	13.1
杂项制品	Miscellaneous Products	35105	604	7742	282	－77.9	－53.3
艺术品、收藏品及古物	Art, Collection and Antique			0.3	1		

12－6 海关进口商品分类情况
Import Commodities in Volume and Value by Category (Customs Statistics)

单位:数量:吨 (Volume: ton)
金额:万美元(Value: USD 10000)

指 标	Item	2000 数量 Volume	2000 金额 Value	2001 数量 Volume	2001 金额 Value	2001年比2000年增长(%) Increase Rate(%) 数量 Volume	2001年比2000年增长(%) Increase Rate(%) 金额 Value
总 计	Total	1501642	23942	1681160	22808	12.0	－4.7
活动物;动物产品	Live Animals & Animal Products						
植物产品	Vegetables, Fruits and Cereals	83497	1642	115	18	－99.9	－98.9
动、植物油、脂及其分解产品;精制的食用油脂;动、植物蜡	Animal and Vegetable Oils, Fats and Wax, Refined Edible Oils and Fats						
食品;饮料、酒及醋;烟草及烟草代用品的制品	Food, Beverages, Liquor and Vinegar, Tobacco and Tobacco Substitutes	15880	653	13800	660	－13.1	1.1
矿产品	Minerals	1 194691	4072	1443130	5048	20.8	24.0
化学工业及其相关工业的产品	Chemicals and Related Products	37306	1730	4299	966	－88.5	－44.2
塑料及其产品;橡胶及其产品	Plastics and Related Products, Rubber and Related, Products	47997	2979	48436	2557	0.9	－14.2
生皮、皮革、毛皮及其制品;鞍具及挽具;旅行用品、手提包及类似物品;动物肠线(蚕胶 丝除外)制品	Raw Hides, Leather, Furs and Related Products, Saddle, Travel, Articles, Handbags and Similar Containers			27	2		
木及木制品;木炭;软木及软木制品;稻草、秸秆、针茅或其他编结材料制品;篮筐及柳条 编织品	Wood and Wooden Products, Charcoal, Cork and Related Products, Straws, Plaited Products, Baskets and Wickerwork	20	21	5	6	－75.0	－71.4
木浆及其他纤维状纤维素浆;回收(废碎)纸或纸板;纸、板及其制品纸	Paper Pulp and Cellulose Pulp, Paper and Waste Paper, Paperboard and Related Products	11715	1130	3462	302	－70.4	－73.3
纺织原料及纺织制品	Textile Materials and Products	2485	799	3555	1105	43.1	38.3

12－6 续表(continued)

单位:数量:吨 (Volume: ton)
金额:万美元(Value: USD 10000)

指　　标	Item	2000		2001		2001年比2000年增长(%) Increase Rate(%)	
		数量 Volume	金额 Value	数量 Volume	金额 Value	数量 Volume	金额 Value
鞋、帽、伞、杖、鞭及其零件;已加工的羽毛及其制品;人造花;人发制品	Footwear, Headgear, Umbrellas, Canes, Whips, Processed Feather, Artificial Flowers, Wigs				1		
石料、石膏、水泥、石棉、云母及类似材料的制品;陶瓷产品;玻璃及其制品	Gypsum, Cement, Asbestos, Mica, Ceramic Glass	39	79	43	77	10.3	－2.5
天然或养殖珍珠、宝石或半宝石、贵金属、包贵金属及其制品;仿首饰;硬币	Natural or Cultivated Pearls, Precious or Semi－Precious Stones, Jewelery of Precious Metal or Rolled Precious Metal, Artificial Jewelery, Coins	250	10	41	2	－83.6	－80.0
贱金属及其制品	Base Metals and Related Products	97422	4932	155796	4115	59.9	－16.6
机器、机械器具、电气设备机器零件、录音机及放声机、电视图象、声音的录制和重放设备 及其零件、附件	Machinery, Electric Equipment and Accessories, Recorders, Videor ecorder and Accessories	10327	4917	8358	6992	－19.1	42.2
车辆、航空器、船舶及有关运输设备	Locomotives, Vehicles, Aircraft, Ship and Related Transportation Equipment	11	66	71	168	545.5	154.5
光学、照相、电影、计量、检验、医疗或外科用仪器及设备、精密仪器及设备;钟表;乐器;上述物品的零件、附件	Optical, Photographic, Film, Measuring and Checking and Medical Instruments and Equipment, Precision Instruments and Equipment, Clocks, Musical Instruments, Related Parts and Accessories	1	906	2	782	100.0	－13.7
杂项制品	Miscellaneous Products	1	6	20	7	1900.0	16.7
艺术品、收藏品及古物							

12－7 吸收外资情况
Foreign Capital Absorbed

指　　标	Item	2000	2001	2001年比2000年增长(%) Increase Rate in 2001 over 2000(%)
签订合同项目(个)	**Number of Signed Contracts**	**59**	**65**	**10.2**
#直接吸收外资	Direct Foreign Investment	55	59	7.3
合资企业	Joint Ventures	26	30	15.4
合作经营企业	Cooprative Ventures	9	8	－11.1
独资企业	Sole－Foreign Enterprises	20	21	5.0
签订合同金额(万美元)	**Contracted Foreign Capital(USD 10000)**	**8098**	**33979**	**319.6**
#直接吸收外资	Direct Foreign Investment	6738	9111	35.2
合资企业	Joint Ventures	3058	3689	20.6
合作经营企业	Cooprative Ventures	1490	3732	150.5
独资企业	Sole－Foreign Enterprises	2190	1690	－22.8
实际吸收外资金额(万美元)	**Foreign Capital Actually Absorbed(USD 10000)**	**19545**	**14010**	**－28.3**
#直接吸收外资	Direct Foreign Investment	2501	2829	13.1
合资企业	Joint Ventures	1630	1940	19.0
合作经营企业	Cooprative Ventures	121	20	－83.5
独资企业	Sole－Foreign Enterprises	750	869	15.9
外商投资企业基本情况	**Registered Foreign－funded Enterprises**			
年末实有外商投资企业(个)	Number of Foreign－funded Enterprises(year－end)(unit)	715	714	－0.1
年底登记户数(户)	Number of Registered Enterprises(unit)	45	57	26.7
投资总额(万美元)	Total Investment(USD 10000)	149349	159936	7.1
注册资本(万美元)	Registered Capital(USD 10000)	116635	119663	2.6
#外　方	Capital from Foreign Partners	75936	78864	3.9
对外经济合作	**Economic Cooperation with Foreign Countries & Territories(USD 10000)**			
引进省外项目(个)	Number of Contracted Projects(unit)	801	910	13.6
引进省外资金(亿元)	Contracted Value(100 million yuan)	33.93	48.53	43.0

12-8 外商直接投资按行业分吸收外资情况(协议金额)
Agreement of Foreign Direct Investment by Sector

行业	Sector	2000	2001	2001年比2000年增长(%) Increase Rate in 2001 over 2000(%)
总计	Total	6738	9111	35.2
农、林、牧、渔业	Farming, Forestry, Animal Husbandry and Fishery	150	1189	692.7
采掘业	Mining and Quarrying	83	46	-44.6
制造业	Manufacturing	4069	7006	72.2
电力、煤气及水的生产和供应业	Electric Power, Gas and Water Production and Supply	943	641	-32.0
建筑业	Construction	648	368	-43.2
批发和零售贸易餐饮业	Wholesale & Retail Trade and Catering Services			
房地产业	Real Estate Management	461	-203	-144.0
社会服务业	Social Services	384	63	-83.6
其他	Other Sectors		1	

12-9 按行业分对外签订外商直接投资协议额
Agreement of Foreign Direct Investment by Sector

指标	Item	项目(个) Number of Projects(unit)		金额(万美元) Amount of Capital(USD 10000)		2001年比2000年增长(%) Increase Rate in 2001 over 2000(%)	
		2000	2001	2000	2001	项目	金额
总计	Total	55	59	6738	9111	7.3	35.2
农、林、牧、渔业	Farming, Forestry, Animal Husbandry and Fishery	5	3	150	1189	-40.0	692.7
采掘业	Mining and Quarrying	3	2	83	46	-33.3	-44.6
制造业	Manufacturing	36	41	4069	7006	13.9	72.2
电力、煤气及水的生产和供应业	Electric Power, Gas and Water Production and Supply	1	2	943	641	100.0	-32.0
建筑业	Construction	2	2	648	368	持平	-43.2
批发和零售贸易餐饮业	Wholesale & Retail Trade and Catering Services						
房地产业	Real Estate Management	3	3	461	-203	持平	-144.0
社会服务业	Social Services	5	5	384	63	持平	-83.6
其他行业	Other Sectors		1		1		

12－10 利用外资额(按方式分)
Amount of Utilization of Foreign Capital and Foreign Investment

单位:项目:个 (Project:unit)
金额:万美元(Value: USD 10000)

指 标	Item	2000 项目 Number of Projects	2000 合同金额 Contract Value	2000 实际使用 Used Value
总 计	**Total**	**59**	**8098**	**19545**
对外借款	Foreign Loans	4	1360	17044
外商直接投资	Foreign Direct Investments	55	6738	2501
合资经营企业	Joint Ventures Enterprises	26	3058	1630
合作经营企业	Cooperative Operation Enterprises	9	1490	121
外资企业	Foreign Investments Enterprises	20	2190	750

12－10 续表(continued)

指 标	Item	2001 项目 Number of Projects	2001 合同金额 Contract Value	2001 实际使用 Used Value
总 计	**Total**	**65**	**43090**	**14010**
对外借款	Foreign Loans	6	33979	11181
外商直接投资	Foreign Direct Investments	59	9111	2829
合资经营企业	Joint Ventures Enterprises	30	3689	1940
合作经营企业	Cooperative Operation Enterprises	8	3732	20
外资企业	Foreign Investments Enterprises	21	1690	869

12－11 按行业分外商实际直接投资额

Actually Used Amount of Foreign Direct Investment by Sector

指　　标	Item	项目(个) Number of Projects(unit)	
		2000	2001
总　　计	**Total**	**55**	**59**
农、林、牧、渔业	Farming, Forestry, Animal Husbandry and Fishery	5	3
采掘业	Mining and Quarrying	3	2
制造业	Manufacturing	36	41
电力、煤气及水的生产和供应业	Electric Power, Gas and Water Production and Supply	1	2
建筑业	Construction	2	2
房地产业	Real Estate Management	3	3
社会服务业	Social Services	5	5
其他行业	Other Sectors		1

12－11 续表(continued)

指　　标	Item	金额(万美元) Amount of Capital (USD 10000)		2001年比2000年增长(%) Increase Rate(%)	
		2000	2001	项　目 Number of Projects	金　额 Amount of Capital
总　　计	**Total**	**2501**	**2829**	**7.3**	**13.1**
农、林、牧、渔业	Farming, Forestry, Animal Husbandry and Fishery	23		－40.0	
采掘业	Mining and Quarrying		4	－33.3	
制造业	Manufacturing	793	2041	13.9	157.4
电力、煤气及水的生产和供应业	Electric Power, Gas and Water Production and Supply			100.0	
建筑业	Construction	20	45	持平	125.0
交通运输、仓储及邮电通信业	Transportation, Storage, Postal and Telecommunications Services	24			
批发和零售贸易餐饮业	Wholesale & Retail Trade and Catering Services	191			
房地产业	Real Estate Management	1373	450	持平	－67.2
社会服务业	Social Services	77	289	持平	275.3

12－12 对外承包工程和劳务合作
Contracted Projects and Labour Cooperation with Foreign Countries or Territories

指标	Item	2000	2001	2001年比2000年增长(%) Increase Rate in 2001 over 2000(%)
签订合同项目(个)	**Number of Contracted Projects(unit)**	**40**	**38**	**-5.0**
# 对外承包工程	Contracted Projects	4	3	-25.0
劳务合作	Labour Cooperation	36	35	-2.8
签订合同金额(万美元)	**Value of Contract(USD 10000)**	**3357**	**8558**	**154.9**
# 对外承包工程	Contracted Projects	3151	8512	170.1
劳务合作	Labour Cooperation	206	46	-77.5
实际营业额(万美元)	**Actual Turnover(USD 10000)**	**1948**	**7461**	**283.0**
# 对外承包工程	Contracted Projects	1810	7145	294.8
劳务合作	Labour Cooperation	138	316	129.0
年末在外人员(人)	**Persons in Abroad(year-end)(person)**	**345**	**356**	**3.2**
# 对外承包工程	Contracted Projects	14		
劳务合作	Labour Cooperation	331	356	7.6

主要统计指标解释

进出口总额 海关进出口总额指实际进出我国国境的货物总金额。包括对外贸易实际进出口货物,来料加工装配进出口货物,国家间、联合国及国际组织无偿援助物资和赠送品,华侨、港澳台同胞和外籍华人捐赠品,租赁期满归承租人所有的租赁货物,进料加工进出口货物,边境地方贸易及边境地区小额贸易进出口货物(边民互市贸易除外),中外合资企业、中外合作经营企业、外商独资经营企业进出口货物和公用物品,到、离岸价格在规定限额以上的进出口货样和广告品(无商业价值、无使用价值和免费提供出口的除外),从保税仓库提取在中国境内销售的进口货物,以及其他进出口货物。进出口总额用以观察一个国家在对外贸易方面的总规模。我国规定出口货物按离岸价格统计,进口货物按到岸价格统计。

利用外资 指我国各级政府、部门、企业和其他经济组织通过对外借款、吸收外商直接投资以及用其他方式筹措的境外现汇、设备、技术等。

对外借款 是我国利用外资的重要部分。指通过对外正式签订借款协议,从境外筹措的资金,包括外国政府贷款、国际金融组织贷款、外国银行商业贷款、出口信贷以及对外发行债券等。1996 年及以前还包括对外发行股票。

外商直接投资 指外国企业和经济组织或个人(包括华侨、港澳台胞以及我国在境外注册的企业)按我国有关政策、法规,用现汇、实物、技术等在我国境内开办外商独资企业、与我国境内的企业或经济组织共同举办中外合资经营企业、合作经营企业或合作开发资源的投资(包括外商投资收益的再投资),以及经政府有关部门批准的项目投资总额内企业从境外借入的资金。

外商其他投资 指除对外借款和外商直接投资以外的各种利用外资的形式。包括企业在境内外股票市场公开发行的以外币计价的股票(目前主要是在香港证券市场发行的 H 股和在境内证券市场发行的 B 股)发行价总额,国际租赁进口设备的应付款,补偿贸易中外商提供的进口设备、技术、物料的价款,加工装配贸易中外商提供的进口设备、物料的价款。

对外承包工程 指各对外承包公司以招标议标承包方式承揽的下列业务:(1)承包国外工程建设项目,(2)承包我国对外经援项目,(3)承包我国驻外机构的工程建设项目,(4)承包我国境内利用外资进行建设的工程项目,(5)与外国承包公司合营或联合承包工程项目时我国公司分包部分,(6)对外承包兼营的房屋开发业务。对外承包工程的营业额是以货币表现的本期内完成的对外承包工程的工作量,包括以前年度签订的合同和本年度新签订的合同在报告期内完成的工作量。

对外劳务合作 指以收取工资的形式向业主或承包商提供技术和劳动服务的活动。我国对外承包公司在境外开办的合营企业,中国公司同时又提供劳务的,其劳务部分也纳入劳务合作统计。劳务合作营业额按报告期内向雇主提交的结算数(包括工资、加班费和奖金等)统计。

对外设计咨询 指以服务成果向业主收费的技术服务项目。包括承担地形地貌测绘,地质资源勘探与普查,建设区域规划,提供设计文件、图纸、生产工艺技术资料和工程技术经济咨询,工程项目的可行性考察、研究和评估,进行技术指导和培训人员等;也包括承担国(境)内利用外资进行建设的工程项目的上述规定的设计咨询项目的收取外币部分。

Explanatory Notes on Main Statistical Indicators

Total Imports and Exports at Customs refer to the value of commodities imported into and exported from the boundary of China. They include the actual imports and exports through foreign trade, imported and exported goods under the processing and assembling trades and materials, supplies and gifts as aid given gratis between governments and by the United Nations and other international organizations, and contributions donated by overseas Chinese, compatriots in Hong Kong and Macao and Chinese with foreign citizenship, leasing commodities owned by tenant at the expiration of leasing period, the imported and exported commodities processed with imported materials, commodities trading in border areas(excluding mutual exchange goods), the imported and exported commodities and articles for public use of the Sino – foreign joint ventures, cooperative enterprises and ventures exclusively with foreign own investment . Also included are import or export of samples and advertising goods for whose CIF or FOB value are beyond the permitted ceiling (excluding goods of no trading or use value and free commodities for export), imported goods sold in China from bonded warehouses and other imported or exported goods. The indicator of the total imports and exports at customs can be used to observe the total size of external trade in a country. In accordance with the stipulation of the Chinese government, imports are calculated at CIF, while exports are calculated at FOB.

Utilization of Foreign Capital refers to remittance, equipment and technology financed from abroad, by loans, foreign direct investment and other forms undertaken by the Chinese governments at all levels, by various departments, enterprises and other economic units.

Foreign Borrowings an important part of China utilization of foreign capital, it refer to funds borrowed from abroad through formal signing of borrowing agreements with foreign institutions, including loans of foreign governments, loans of international financial institutions, commercial loans of foreign banks, export credit, and funds raised by Chinese bonds (and shares before 1996) issued abroad.

Direct Investment by Foreign Entrepreneurs refers to the investments inside China by foreign enterprises and economic organizations or individuals(including overseas Chinese, compatriots from Hong Kong and Macao, and Chinese enterprises registered abroad), following the relevant policies and laws of China, for the establishment of ventures exclusively with foreign own investment, Sino – foreign joint ventures and cooperative enterprises or for co – operative exploration of resources with enterprises or economic organizations in China. It includes the re investment of the foreign entrepreneurs with the profits gained from the investment and the funds that enterprises borrow from abroad in the total investment of projects which are approved by the relevant department of the government.

Other Investment by Foreign Entrepreneurs refers to all forms of utilization of foreign capitals other than foreign borrowings and foreign direct investment. It includes the total value of stock shares in foreign currencies issued by enterprises at domestic or foreign stock exchanges (now mainly consisting of H shares issued at Hong Kong Security Market and B shares issued at domestic security markets), rent payable for the imported equipment through international leasing arrangement, cost of imported equipment, technology and materials provided by foreign counterparts in compensation trade and processing and assembly trade.

Contracted Projects with Foreign Countries refer to projects undertaken by Chinese contractors (project contracting companies) through bidding process. They include: (1) overseas civil engineering construction projects financed by foreign investors; (2) overseas projects financed by the Chinese government through its foreign aid programs; (3) construction projects of Chinese diplomatic missions, trade offices and other institutions stationed abroad; (4) construction projects in China financed by foreign investment; (5) sub – contracted projects to be taken by Chinese contractors through a joint umbrella project with foreign contractor(s); (6) housing development projects. The business income from international contracted projects is the work volume of contracted projects completed during the reference period, expressed in monetary terms, including completed work on projects signed in previous years.

Service Cooperation with Foreign Countries refers to the activities of providing technology and labour services to employers or contractors in the forms of receiving salaries and wages. Labour services providing by contractual joint ventures of Chihe statistics of service cooperation with foreign countries. The business income of labour service cooperation is the income in the form of wages and salaries, overtime pay, bonuses and other remuneration received from the employers during the reference period.

Overseas Design and Consultation Service refers to projects with charges for technical services from overseas operators. It includes geographic and topographic mapping, geological resource prospecting and survey, planning of construction areas, provision of design documents, blueprints, materials on production process and techniques, as well as engineering, technical and economic consultation, and feasibility study, research and evaluation of projects. Also included under this category are the above – mentioned services of foreign – financed projects in China that are paid in foreign currencies.

13

Thirteen

旅游

Tourism

入境旅游人数(万人次)

Total Number of International Tourists Inbound (10000 person-times)

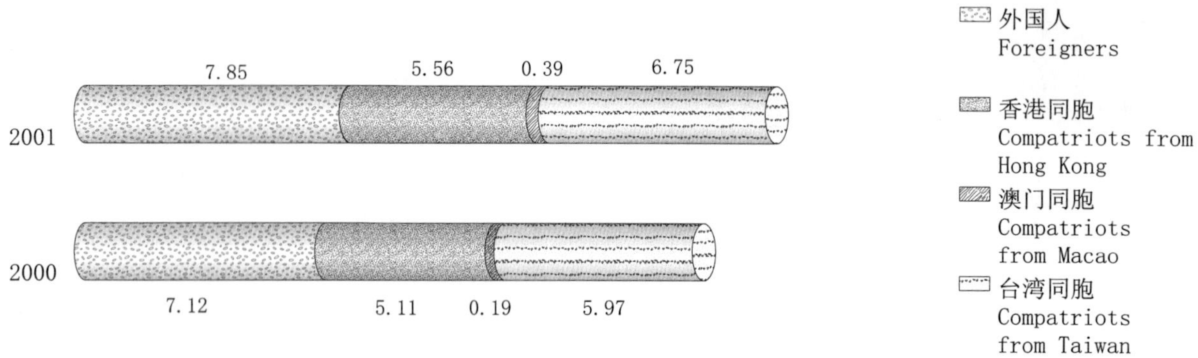

接待外国旅游人数(按地区分)(人)(2001)

Number of Overseas Tourists Visiting Guizhou by Country (Territory)(person)

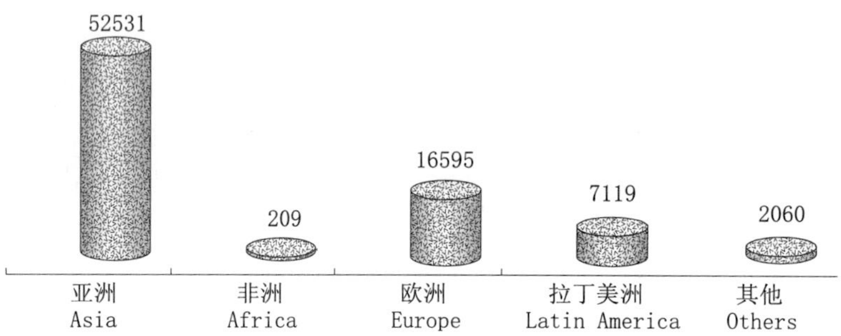

旅游外汇收入(万美元)(2001)

Foreign Exchange Earnings (USD 10000)

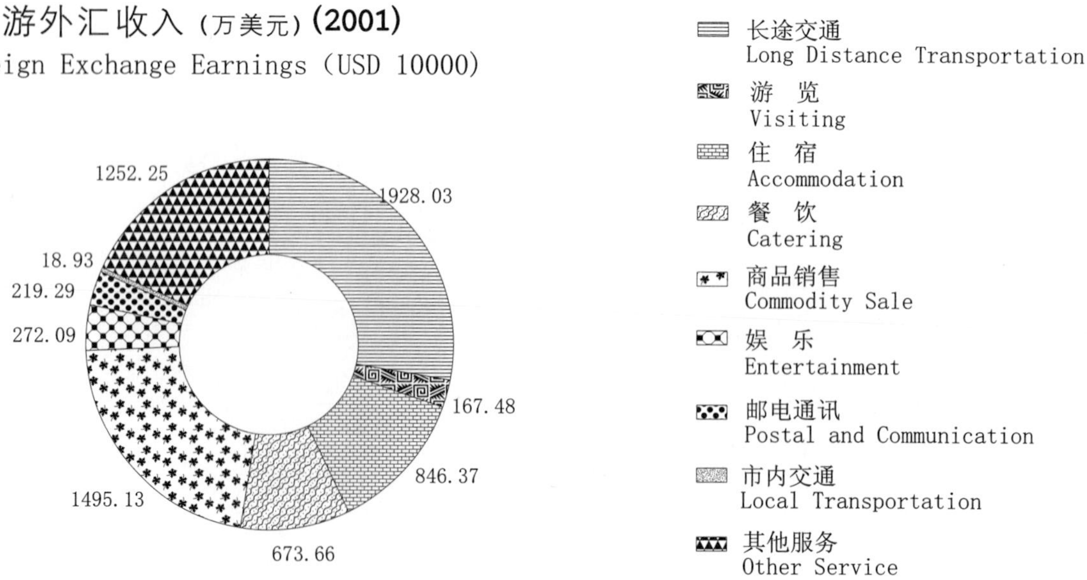

13－1 旅游业发展主要指标
Development of Tourism

指　　标	Item	2000	2001	2001年比2000年增长(%) Increase Rate in 2001 over 2000(%)
旅行社总数(个)	**Total Number of Travel Agencies(unit)**	**107**	**135**	**26.2**
国际旅行社	International Travel Agencies	13	13	持平
国内旅行社	Domestic Travel Agencies	94	122	29.8
旅行社职工人数(人)	**Number of Staff and Workers of Travel Agencies(person)**	**875**	**1154**	**31.9**
国际旅行社	International Travel Agencies	464	510	9.9
国内旅行社	Domestic Travel Agencies	411	644	56.7
旅行社经营和财务状况(万元)	**Management and Financial Status of Travel Agencies(10000 yuan)**			
营业收入	Operational Income	21231.74	29040.97	36.8
利润总额	Total Profit	－100.69	－163.98	62.9
涉外饭店总数(个)	Total Number of Tourist Hotel(unit)	113	225	99.1
入境旅游人数(万人次)	**Total Number of International Tourists Inbound(10000 person－times)**	**18.39**	**20.55**	**11.7**
外国人	Foreigners	7.12	7.85	10.3
香港同胞	Compatriots from Hong Kong	5.11	5.56	8.8
澳门同胞	Compatriots from Macao	0.19	0.39	105.3
台湾同胞	Compatriots from Taiwan	5.97	6.75	13.1
三大旅行社接待入境旅游人数(万人)	Number of International Tourists Received by Three Major Travel Service(10000 persons)	4.44	5.76	29.7
中国国际旅行社	China International Travel Service	1.6	2.01	25.6
贵州海外旅游总公司	Giuzhou Overseas Tourism Corporation	1.63	2.24	37.4
中国青年旅行社	China Youth Travel Service	1.21	1.51	24.8
国内旅游人数(万人次)	**Total Number of Domestic Tourists(10000 person－times)**	**1980**	**2100**	**6.1**
国际旅游收入(万美元)	**Earnings from International Tourism(USD 10000)**	**6092.23**	**6873.23**	**12.8**
国内旅游收入(万元)	**Earnings from Domestic Tourism(10000 yuan)**	**579500**	**758100**	**30.8**

13－2　接待外国旅游人数(按地区分)
Number of Overseas Tourists Visiting Guizhou by Country (Territory)

单位:人
(person)

国　别(地区)	Country(Territory)	2000	2001	2001年比2000年增长(%) Increase Rate in 2001 over 2000(%)
总　计	**Total**	**71183**	**78514**	**10.3**
亚　洲	Asia	45921	52531	14.4
非　洲	Africa		209	
欧　洲	Europe	15849	16595	4.7
拉丁美洲	Latin America	8915	7119	－20.1
其　他	Others	498	2060	313.7

13－3　来黔海外旅游人数及人均消费支出
Number of Overseas Tourists Visiting Guizhou and Average Per Capita Spending

指　标	Item	2000	2001	2001年比2000年增长(%) Increase Rate in 2001 over 2000(%)
来黔海外旅游者人数(人次)	**Number of Overseas Tourists Visiting Guizhou(person－times)**	**183898**	**205466**	**11.7**
外国人	Foreigner	71183	78514	10.3
香港同胞	Hong kong Chinese	51054	55613	8.9
台湾同胞	Taiwanese	59718	67491	13.0
澳门同胞	Macao Chinese	1943	3848	98.0
平均每人逗留天数(天/人)	Average Time Tourists Staying in Guizhou Per Capita(day/person)	2.13	2.08	－2.3
平均每人天消费支出(美元/人天)	Average Per Capita Daily Spending(USD/persen－day)	161.13	161.35	0.1

13－4 旅馆业接待经营情况
Operation of Hotels

指　　标	Item	2000	2001	2001 年比 2000 年增长（%） Increase Rate in 2001 over 2000（%）
接待能力	**Capacity**			
年末客房数（万间）	Year－end Guest Rooms（10000 units）	6082	8658	42.4
年末客房床位数（万张）	Year－end Guest Beds（10000 beds）	13073	16957	29.7
客房开房率（%）	Room Occupancy Rate（%）	56.1	59.8	3.7（百分点）
#星级宾馆	Star－rated Hotels	56.1	59.8	3.7（百分点）
实际住宿人次数（万人次）	Actual Number of Guests（10000 person－times）	173.62	217.02	25.0
#海外来黔	Overseas Visitors	18.39	20.55	11.7
实际住宿人天数（万人天）	Actual Number of Guests and Days of Stay（10000 person－day）	238.41	290.41	21.8
#海外来黔	Overseas Visitors	39.25	42.65	8.7
经营和财务	**Management and Financial**			
营业收入（万元）	Operational Income（10000 yuan）	39355.59	46039.52	17.0

13－5 涉外饭店情况
Number of Tourist Hotels

单位：个
(unit)

指 标	Item	2000	2001	2001 年比 2000 年增长(%) Increase Rate in 2001 over 2000(%)
总 计	Total	62	80	29.0
按经济类型分	Grouped by Ownership			
国有经济	State－owned	57	75	31.6
集体经济	Collective－owned	1	1	持平
外商投资经济	Foreign Funded	4	4	持平
按规模分	Grouped by Capacity			
客房总数 500 间以上	With 500 Rooms and Over	2	2	持平
客房总数 300－499 间	With 300－499 Rooms	3	3	持平
客房总数 200－299 间	With 200－299 Rooms	7	19	171.4
客房总数 100－199 间	With 100－199 Rooms	21	25	19.0
客房总数 99 间以下	With Less than 100 Rooms	29	31	6.9

13－6 旅游外汇收入
Foreign Exchange Earnings

单位：万美元
(USD 10000)

类 别	Item	2000	2001	2001 年比 2000 年增长(%) Increase Rate in 2001 over 2000(%)
总 计	Total	6092.23	6873.23	12.8
长途交通	Long Distance Transportation	1858.13	1928.03	3.8
游 览	Visiting	158.39	167.48	5.7
住 宿	Accommodation	816.36	846.37	3.7
餐 饮	Catering	584.85	673.66	15.2
商品销售	Commodity Sale	1504.78	1495.13	－0.6
娱 乐	Entertainment	85.29	272.09	219.0
邮电通讯	Postal and Communication	286.33	219.29	－23.4
市内交通	Local Transportation	42.65	18.93	－55.6
其他服务	Other Service	755.45	1252.25	65.8

主要统计指标解释

旅游者人数

(1)入境国际旅游者人数:指来中国参观、访问、旅行、探亲、访友、休养、考察、参加会议和从事经济、科技、文化、教育、宗教等活动的外国人、华侨、港澳同胞和台湾同胞的人数。不包括外国在我国的常驻机构,如使领馆、通讯社、企业办事处的工作人员;来我国常住的外国专家、留学生以及在岸逗留不过夜人员。

(2)出境居民人数:指大陆居民因公务活动或私人事务短期出境的人数。公务活动出境居民人数包括在国际交通工具上的中国服务员工,因私出境居民人数不包括在国际交通工具上的中国服务员工。

(3)国内旅游者人数:指我国大陆居民和在我国常住 1 年以上的外国人、华侨、港澳台同胞离开常住地在境内其他地方的旅游设施内至少停留一夜,最长不超过 6 个月的人数。

国际旅游(外汇)收入 指入境旅游的外国人、华侨、港澳同胞和台湾同胞在中国大陆旅游过程中发生的一切旅游支出,对于国家来说就是国际旅游(外汇)收入。

国际旅行社 指经营对外招徕并接待外国人、华侨、港澳同胞和台湾同胞来中国、归国或回内地旅游业务的旅行社。

国内旅行社 指负责经营招徕、组团、接待国内旅客的旅游业务,以及不对外招徕,负责经营接待国际旅行社或其它涉外部门组织的外国人、华侨、港澳同胞和台湾同胞来中国、归国或回内地的旅游业务的旅行社。

涉外饭店 指经有关部门批准,允许接待外国人、华侨、港澳同胞和台湾同胞的饭店。

Explanatory Notes on Main Statistical Indicators

Number of Tourists:

(1) International tourists refer to foreigners, overseas Chinese, Chinese compatriots from Hong Kong, Macao and Taiwan coming to China for sightseeing, visits, tours, family reunions, vacations, study tours, conferences and other activities of a business, scientific and technological, cultural, educational and religious nature. It does not include representatives and employees of resident institutions of foreign countries in China such as embassies, consulates, news agencies and offices of foreign companies and organizations, nor does it include long – term foreign experts or students residing in China, or persons in transition without spending a night in China.

(2) Chinese residents going abroad refer to Chinese residents going abroad for short terms for either public business or private purposes. Chinese employees working on international transport carriers are included in those going abroad for public business purpose, not in those for private purpose.

(3) Domestic tourists refer to residents of the mainland of China who stay for one night at least but no more than 6 months at tourist facilities in other places than their permanent residence within the territory of the mainland China, including foreigners, overseas Chinese and Chinese compatriots from Hong Kong, Macao and Taiwan who have resided in China for over one year.

Foreign Exchange Earnings from International Tourism refer to the total expenditures of foreigners, overseas Chinese, Chinese compatriots from Hong Kong, Macao and Taiwan during their stay in the mainland of China, which are earnings of foreign exchange from international tourism from the point of view from China.

International Travel Agencies refer to travel agencies engaged in the promotion, solicitation, organization and reception of tours to the mainland of China by foreigners, overseas Chinese, Chinese compatriots from Hong Kong, Macao and Taiwan.

Domestic Travel Agencies refer to travel agencies engaged in the promotion, solicitation, organization and reception of domestic tourists, and in the reception of foreigners, overseas Chinese, Chinese compatriots from Hong Kong, Macao and Taiwan organized by international travel agencies or other departments concerned, without their own promotion and solicitation programmes.

Tourist Hotels refer to hotels that are able, with the approval of departments concerned, to accommodate foreigners, overseas Chinese, Chinese compatriots from Hong Kong, Macao and Taiwan Province.

14

价格水平

Price Level

Fourteen

居民消费价格分类指数（2001）
（上年=100）
Residents Consumer Price Indices by Category (preceding year=100)

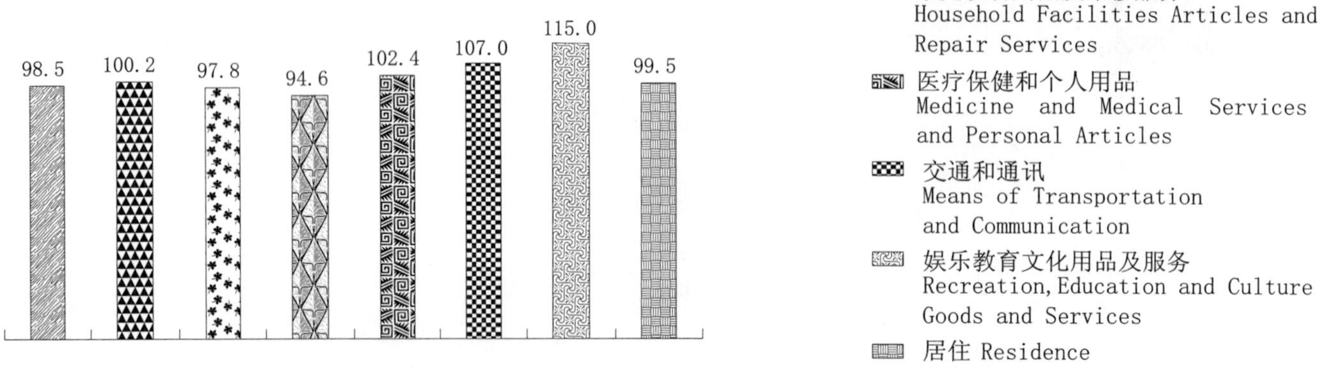

工业品出厂价格分类指数
（上年=100）
Ex-Factory Price Indices of Industrial Products (preceding year=100)

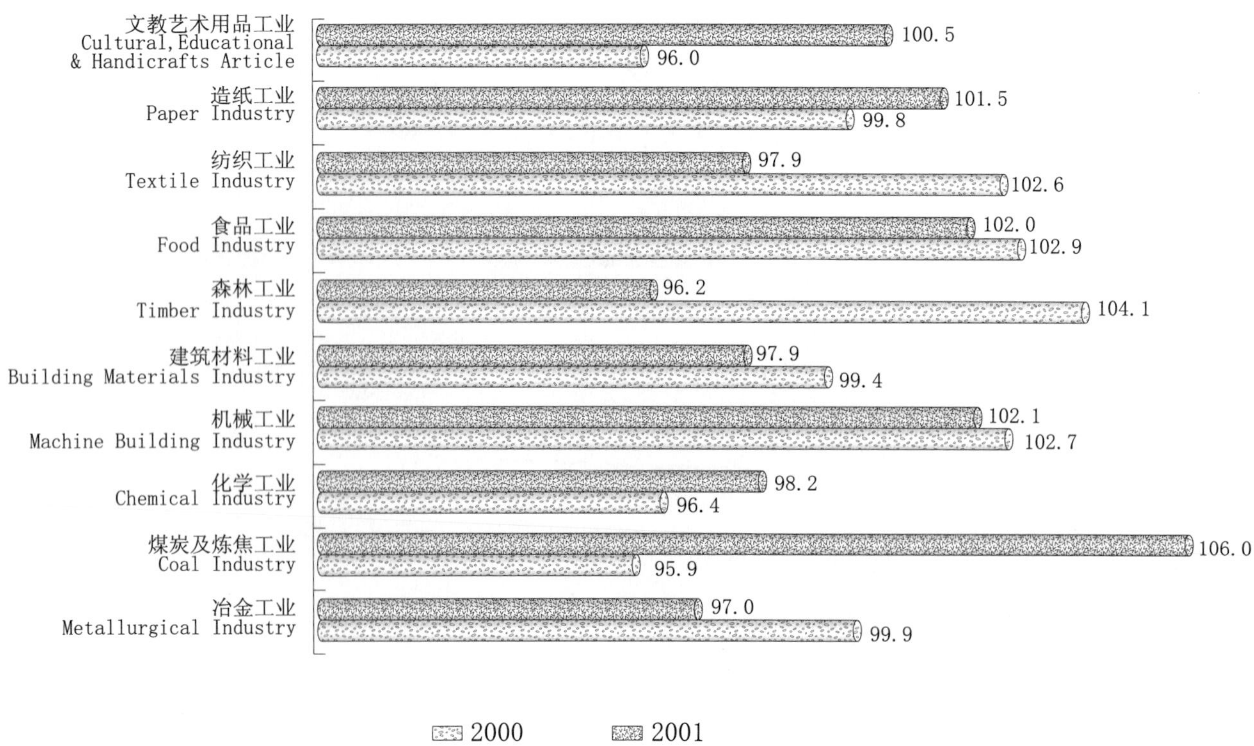

14－1 居民消费价格分类指数(上年＝100)
Residents Consumer Price Indices by Category (preceding year＝100)

指　　标	Item	2000	2001	2001年比2000年增减百分点 Up(Down) Percentage Points in 2001 over 2000
居民消费价格总指数	General Consumer Price Index	99.5	101.8	2.3
非食品价格指数	Non－ Food Price Index	－	103.7	－
服务项目价格指数	Services Price Index	117.2	114.0	－3.2
扣除鲜菜鲜果总指数	Non－Vegetables and Fresh Fruits Price Index		102.1	－
消费品价格总指数	Consumer Price Index		98.1	－
食品	Food	95.3	98.5	3.2
粮食	Grain	92.7	95.6	2.9
淀粉及薯类	Starches and Tubers	95.6	83.4	－12.2
干豆类及豆制品	Beans and Its Products	96.1	100.4	4.3
干豆	Beans		113.3	
豆制品	Beans Products		96.9	
油脂	Oil or Fat	82.1	86.6	4.5
肉禽及其制品	Meat, Poultry and Their Products	94.8	97.8	3.0
食用畜肉及副产品	Livestock for Slaughtering and Sideline Products		98.3	
禽	Poultry		97.2	
肉禽加工制品	Meat, Poultry and Their Products		96.5	
蛋	Eggs	91.7	107.8	16.1
水产品	Aquatic Products	94.2	95.8	1.6
鱼	Fish		96.5	
其他水产品	Other Aquatic Products		92.6	
菜	Vegetables	100.1	99.6	－0.5
鲜菜	Fresh Vegetables	102.4	100.3	－2.1
调味品	Flavoring	99.8	113.9	14.1
糖	Sugars	103.2	104.9	1.7
茶及饮料	Tea and Beverages		98.9	
茶叶	Tea		99.2	
饮料	Beverages		98.8	
干鲜瓜果	Dried and Fresh Fruits	91.4	99.2	7.8
鲜果	Fresh Fruits	88.3	99.1	10.8
干(坚)果及瓜果制品	Dried and Melons Fruits and Their Products	99.8	99.4	－0.4
糕点饼干面包	Pastry, Cake and Bread		100.8	
奶及奶制品	Milk and Its Products	101.6	100.4	－1.2

14－1 续表 1(continued)

指 标	Item	2000	2001	2001 年比 2000 年增减百分点 Up(Down) Percentage Points in 2001 over 2000
鲜奶	Fresh Milk		101.0	
奶粉	Powdered Milk		99.8	
在外用膳食品	Food for Dining Out		100.2	
其他食品及食品加工服务	Other Food and Food Processing Services		96.9	
烟酒及用品	**Tobacco, Liquor and Articles**		**100.2**	
烟草	Tobacco	94.3	100.2	5.9
国产卷烟	Cigarette Made in China		100.3	
进口卷烟	Cigarette Imported		101.2	
酒	Liquor	97.8	99.8	2.0
白酒	White Spirit		101.6	
啤酒	Beer		98.5	
吸烟饮酒用品	Smoke and Beverages Liquor Articles		101.3	
衣着	**Clothing**	**99.6**	**97.8**	**-1.8**
服装	Dress	98.9	95.8	-3.1
男式服装	Dress for Men		86.1	
女式服装	Dress for Women		99.1	
儿童服装	Dress for Children		98.0	
衣着材料	Clothing Materials	96.1	99.2	3.1
鞋袜帽	Shoes, Socks and Hats	102.8	101.3	-1.5
鞋	Shoes	104.0	102.0	-2.0
袜子	Socks and Stockings	95.3	96.4	1.1
帽子	Hats	99.2	99.0	-0.2
家庭设备用品及维修服务	**Household Facilities Articles and Repair Services**	**95.9**	**94.6**	**-1.3**
耐用消费品	Durable Consumer Goods	94.4	90.4	-4.0
家具	Furniture	93.0	93.7	0.7
家庭设备	Household Facilities	95.4	87.4	-8.0
室内装饰品	Interior Decorations	97.8	92.8	-5.0
床上用品	Bed Articles	99.6	95.8	-3.8
家庭日用杂品	Daily Used Household Articles	96.7	98.7	2.0
家庭服务及加工维修服务	Daily Services and Processing, Repair Services	97.3	100.2	2.9
医疗保健和个人用品	**Medical Treatment and Health Care and Personal Articles**		**102.4**	
医疗保健	Medical Treatment and Health Care	98.5	99.0	0.5

14-1 续表 2(continued)

指　标	Item	2000	2001	2001年比2000年增减百分点 Up(Down) Percentage Points in 2001 over 2000
医疗器具及用品	Medical Appliance and Articles	100.6	100.0	-0.6
中药材及中成药	Traditional Chinese Medicine and Patent Medicine	98.7	101.1	2.4
西药	Western Medicine	98.2	94.2	-4.0
保健器具及用品	Health Care Appliance and Articles		92.3	
医疗保健服务	Medical Treatment and Health Care Services		107.5	
个人用品及服务	Personal Articles and Services		107.7	
化妆美容用品	Cosmetics		99.4	
卫生用品	Health Articles		98.1	
个人饰品	Articles for Personal Adornment		107.1	
个人服务	Personal Services		115.4	
交通和通讯	**Means of Transportation and Communication**	**94.4**	**107.0**	**12.6**
交通	Traffic	98.2	107.0	8.8
交通工具	Traffic Facilities		98.9	
车用燃料及零配件	Fuel and Spares for Vehicles		99.0	
车辆使用及维修	Usage and Maintenance of Vehicles		103.4	
市区公共交通	Public Traffic		124.6	
城市间交通	Traffic between Two Cities		96.7	
通信	Communication	91.6	107.0	15.4
通信工具	Communication Facilities		81.4	
通信服务	Communication Services		113.1	
娱乐教育文化用品及服务	**Recreation, Education and Culture Goods and Services**	**97.2**	**115.0**	**17.8**
文娱用耐用消费品及服务	Durable Consumer Goods for Recreational Use	92.3	91.1	-1.2
教育	Education		124.9	
教材及参考资料	Teaching Materials and Reference Books	106.1	96.8	-9.3
学杂托幼费	Tuition Fee and Child-care Fee	141.7	126.4	-15.3
文化娱乐用品	Recreational and Cultural Articles	99.5	106.3	6.8
文化娱乐	Recreational and Cultural Articles	98.7	106.9	8.2
书报杂志	Books, Newspapers and Magazines	100.7	104.7	4.0
文娱费	Recreation Fee		107.4	
旅游及外出	Tourism and Out		107.1	
居住	**Residence**	**104.8**	**99.5**	**-5.3**
建房及装修材料	Construction and Decoration	98.7	99.0	0.3
租房	Rent house	102.3	105.9	3.6
自有住房	Personal House		100.0	
水、电、燃料	Water, Electricity and Fuels	108.1	99.3	-8.8

14－2 商品零售价格分类指数(上年＝100)
Retail Price Indices by Category of Commodities (preceding year＝100)

指　　标	Item	2000	2001	2001年比2000年增减百分点 Up(Down) Percentage Points in 2001 over 2000
商品零售价格总指数	**General Retail Price Index of Commodities**	**97.3**	**98.4**	**1.1**
食品类	Food	94.4	99.4	5.0
粮食	Grain	93.2	96.9	3.7
油脂类	Oil or Fat	81.6	87.6	6.0
肉禽蛋	Meat, Poultry & Eggs	94.6	98.8	4.2
水产品	Aquatic Products	95.2	93.4	－1.8
鲜菜	Vegetables	99.4	107.4	8.0
干菜	Dried Vegetables	92.7	91.8	－0.9
鲜果	Fresh Fruits	89.3	99.3	10.0
干果	Dried Fruits	99.3	96.9	－2.4
饮食业	Catering Trade	98.3	100.0	1.7
饮料烟酒类	Beverages, Tobacco and Liquor	96.2	100.1	3.9
服装鞋帽类	Clothing, Shoes and Hats	100.6	98.2	－2.4
纺织品类	Textiles	98.4	98.7	0.3
中西医药类	Traditional Chinese & Western Medicines	98.6	98.6	持平
化妆品类	Cosmetics	97.6	97.3	－0.3
报纸杂志类	Newspapers and Magazines	103.4	100.0	－3.4
文化体育用品类	Cultural and Sports Goods	98.5	96.6	－1.9
日用品类	Articles for Daily Use	97.2	97.5	0.3
家用电器类	Household Appliances	93.8	95.6	1.8
首饰类	Jewelry	95.1	95.2	0.1
燃料类	Fuels	113.4	103.2	－10.4
建筑装潢材料类	Building Decoration Materials	95.8	99.9	4.1
机电产品类	Mechanical and Electrical Products	95.2	92.9	－2.3

14-3 农副产品收购价格分类指数(上年=100)

Farm and Sideline Procucts Purchasing Price Indices by Category of Commodities(preceding year=100)

指标	Item	2000	2001	2001年比2000年增减百分点 Up(Down) Percentage Points in 2001 over 2000
农副产品收购价格总指数	**General Purchasing Price Index**	**95.6**	**97.8**	**2.2**
粮食类	Grain	97.1	95.8	-1.3
稻谷	Rice	95.6	88.1	-7.5
玉米	Corn	97.9	97.7	-0.2
小麦	Wheat	97.5	88.0	-9.5
黄豆	Soybeans	91.8	92.0	0.2
经济作物类	Industrial Crops	93.6	101.0	7.4
食用植物油及油料	Edible Vegetable Oil and Oil-bearing Crops	89.9	96.0	6.1
烟叶	Tobacco	106.4	115.6	9.2
糖类	Sugars	89.4	99.1	9.7
茶叶	Tea	98.1	83.1	-15.0
竹木材类	Bamboo and Timber	86.7	92.8	6.1
工业用油漆类	Oil and Lacquer for Industrial Use	131.5	83.2	-48.3
禽畜产品类	Livestock Products, Poultry and Eggs	95.8	97.9	2.1
肉畜	Livestock for Slaughtering	95.4	97.9	2.5
#肥猪	Fattened Hogs	93.6	97.6	4.0
禽蛋	Poultry Eggs	96.9	96.8	-0.1
#鸡蛋	Chicken Eggs	100.0	94.5	-5.5
皮张	Hides and Skins	119.7	133.7	14.0
蚕茧蚕丝类	Silkworn Cocoons and Silk	103.0	94.5	-8.5
干鲜果类	Dried and Fresh Fruits	85.2	96.2	11.0
干鲜菜及调味品类	Dried and Fresh Vegetables, Condiments	90.8	96.6	5.8
#鲜菜	Fresh Vegetables	96.9	97.5	0.6
药材类	Raw Drugs	102.3	111.2	8.9
土副产品类	Native Products	114.3	106.7	-7.6

14-4 农业生产资料价格分类指数(上年=100)
Price Indices of Agricultural Means of Production by Category(preceding year=100)

指　　标	Item	2000	2001	2001年比2000年增减百分点 Up(Down) Percentage Points in 2001 over 2000
农业生产资料价格总指数	General Price Index of Agricultural Means of Production	100.6	99.4	-1.2
小农具	Small Farm Tools	94.6	101.0	6.4
饲料	Forage	106.7	101.3	5.4
幼禽家畜	Young Livestock & Fowls	102.5	100.0	-2.5
大牲畜	Large Animals	107.3	107.1	-0.2
半机械化农具	Semi-mechanized Farm Tools	99.9	100.0	0.1
机械化农具	Mechanized Farm Machinery	96.3	100.6	4.3
化学肥料	Chemical Fertilizer	104.7	96.8	-7.9
农药及农药械	Pesticide & Its Appliances	98.0	99.0	1.0
化学农药	Pesticide	95.1	98.6	3.5
农药械	The Appliances for Pesticide	107.8	100.4	-7.4
农机用油	Oil for Farm Machinery	116.2	101.2	-15.0
其他	Others	94.1	99.5	5.4

14－5 工业品出厂价格分类指数(上年＝100)
Ex－Factory Price Indices of Industrial Products(preceding year＝100)

指标	Item	2000	2001	2001年比2000年增减百分点 Up(Down) Percentage Points in 2001 over 2000
全部工业品出厂价格指数	Total Ex－Factory Price Index of Industrial Products	100.4	102.2	1.8
按轻、重工业分	Grouped by Industries			
轻工业	Light Industry	102.6	101.4	－1.2
重工业	Heavy Industry	99.3	102.5	3.2
按用途分	Grouped by Use			
生产资料	Means of Production	99.2	102.5	3.3
采掘工业	Mining & Quarrying Industry	96.7	105.5	8.8
原材料工业	Raw Materials Industry	99.8	102.8	3.0
加工工业	Manufacturing Industry	98.5	100.5	2.0
生活资料	Consumer Goods	102.9	101.5	－1.4
食品类	Food	102.9	102.0	－0.9
衣着类	Clothing	96.5	97.6	1.1
一般日用品	Articles for Daily Use	106.2	96.3	－9.9
耐用消费品	Durable Consumer Goods	106.3	100.5	－5.8
按工业部门分	Grouped by Sector			
冶金工业	Metallurgical Industry	99.9	97.0	－2.9
煤炭及炼焦工业	Coal Industry	95.9	106.0	10.1
化学工业	Chemical Industry	96.4	98.2	1.8
机械工业	Machine Building Industry	102.7	102.1	－0.6
建筑材料工业	Building Materials Industry	99.4	97.9	－1.5
森林工业	Timber Industry	104.1	96.2	－7.9
食品工业	Food Industry	102.9	102.0	－0.9
纺织工业	Textile Industry	102.6	97.9	－4.7
造纸工业	Paper Industry	99.8	101.5	1.7
文教艺术用品工业	Cultural, Educational & Handicrafts Article	96.0	100.5	4.5

14－6 原材料、燃料、动力购进价格指数(上年＝100)
Purchasing Price Indices of Raw Materials, Fuels and Power(preceding year＝100)

指　　标	Item	2000	2001	2001年比2000年增减百分点 Up(Down) Percentage Points in 2001 over 2000
全部原材料、燃料、动力	**Total Raw Materials, Fuels and Power**	**102.9**	**100.2**	**－2.7**
燃料、动力类	Fuels and Power	105.7	103.5	－2.2
黑色金属材料类	Ferrous Metals	99.0	102.6	3.6
#钢材	Rolled－steel			
有色金属材料类	Nonferrous Metals	109.4	88.1	－21.3
化工原料类	Chemical Raw Materials	102.3	101.0	－1.3
木材及纸浆类	Wood and Paper Pulps	108.6	96.8	－11.8
建筑材料及非金属矿类	Building Materials and Nonmetal Minerals Processing	105.0	99.1	－5.9
其他工业原材料及半成品类	Other Industrial Raw Materials and Semi－products	95.1	96.2	1.1
农副产品类	Farm and Sideline Products	100.6	99.6	－1.0
纺织原料类	Textile Raw Material	110.8	96.1	－14.7

14－7 固定资产投资和房地产销售价格指数(上年＝100)
Fixed Asset and Real Estate Price Indices(preceding year＝100)

指　　标	Item	2000	2001	2001年比2000年增减百分点 Up(Down) Percentage Points in 2001 over 2000
固定资产投资价格指数	**Price Index of Fixed Asset Investment**	**102.2**	**100.4**	**－1.8**
建筑安装工程	Construction and Installation	102.5	101.2	－1.3
设备工、器具	Purchase of Equipment, Tools and Instrument	102.7	98.6	－4.1
其他费用	Others	100.0	100.0	持平
贵阳市房屋销售价格指数	Price Index of Real Estate Sales of Guiyang City	103.9	100.8	－3.1
#商品房销售	Sales of Commodity Housing	103.8	100.8	－3.0
#住宅	Residence	104.2	100.9	－3.3

14－8 建筑业产值价格指数(上年＝100)
Price Indices of Construction Output Value(preceding year＝100)

指　　标	Item	2000	2001	2001年比2000年增减百分点 Up(Down) Percentage Points in 2001 over 2000
施工产值价格指数	Price Indices of Output Value of Buildings under Construction	102.5	101.2	－1.3
直接费	Direct Costs	102.0	101.3	－0.7
人工费	Manpower	101.6	102.7	1.1
材料费	Materials	102.2	101.2	－1.0
钢材	Steel Products	102.3	100.5	－1.8
木材	Timber	100.2	100.2	持平
水泥	Cement	100.8	101.6	0.8
地方材料	Local Materials	103.4	102.3	－1.1
其他材料	Others	100.1	104.2	4.1
机械使用费	Costs for Using Machine	101.6	100.5	－1.1
间接费用	Indirect Costs	104.6	100.8	－3.8

主要统计指标解释

商品零售价格指数　是反映城乡商品零售价格变动趋势的一种经济指数。零售物价的变动直接反映城乡居民的生活支出和国家的财政收入,反映居民购买力和市场供需平衡,反映消费与积累的比例。

居民消费价格指数　是反映一定时期内城乡居民所购买的生活消费品价格和服务项目价格变动趋势和程度的相对数,是对城市居民消费价格指数和农村居民消费价格指数进行综合汇总计算的结果。

农产品收购价格指数　是反映国有商业、集体商业、个体商业、外贸部门、国家机关、社会团体等各种经济类型的商业企业和有关部门收购农产品价格的变动趋势和程度的相对数。

工业品出厂价格指数　是反映全部工业产品出厂价格总水平的变动趋势和程度的相对数,包括工业企业售给本企业以外所有单位的各种产品和直接售给居民用于生活消费的产品。

固定资产投资价格指数　是反映固定资产投资额价格变动趋势和程度的相对数。固定资产投资额是由建筑安装工程投资完成额、设备、工器具购置投资完成额和其他费用投资完成额三部分组成的。编制固定资产投资价格指数应首先分别编制上述三部分投资的价格指数,然后采用加权算术平均法求出固定资产投资价格总指数。

Explanatory Notes on Main Statistical Indicators

Retail Price Index　reflects the general change in retail prices of commodities. The change and adjustment in retail prices directly affect the living expenditure of urban and rural residents, government revenue, purchasing power of residents and the equilibrium of market supply and demand, and the ratio of consumption to accumulation.

Consumer Price Index　reflects the trend and degree of changes in prices of consumer goods and services purchased by urban and rural residents, and is a composite index derived from the urban consumer price index and the rural consumer price index.

Index of Purchasing Prices of Farm Products　reflects the trend and degree of changes in purchasing prices of farm products purchased by state – owned, collective – owned, and individual commercial enterprises, foreign trade sectors, government agencies, social organizations and other units of various types of ownership. It is used to observe the impact of change in purchasing prices of farm products on the cash income of peasants, and serves as basis for the formulation and supervision of pricing policies for farm products.

Ex – factory Price Index of Industrial Products　reflects the trend and degree of changes in general ex – factory prices of all industrial products, including sales of industrial products by an industrial enterprise to all units outside the enterprise, as well as sales of consumer goods to residents.

Price Index of Investment in Fixed Assets　reflects the trend and degree of changes in prices of investment in fixed assets. The investment in fixed assets consists of three components, namely the investment in construction and installation, the investment in purchases of equipment and instrument, and the investment in other items. Price index of investment in fixed assets is calculated as the weighted arithmetic mean of the price indices of the three components of investment in fixed assets.

15 财政、金融、证券、保险

Finance, Banking, Securities and Insurance

Fifteen

地方财政收入(亿元) (2001)

Total Revenue(100 million yuan)

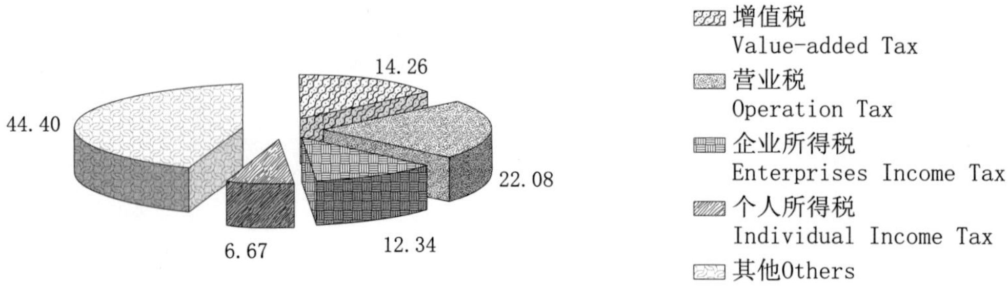

地方财政收入、支出(亿元) (2001)

Local Government Revenue and Expenditure(100 million yuan)

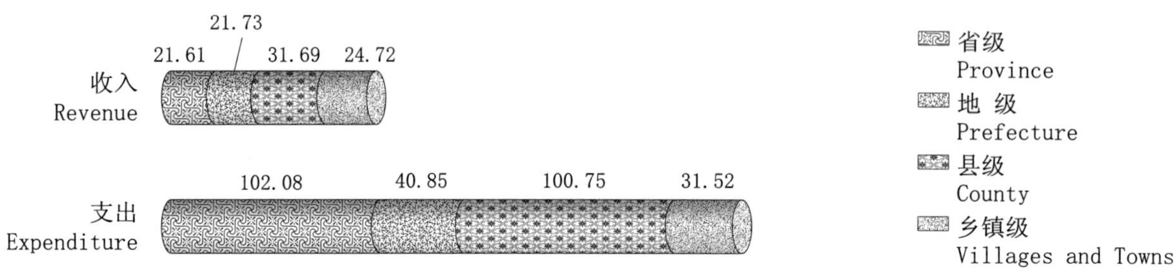

金融机构存款余额(亿元)

Saving Deposits and Loans of Financial Institutions (100 million yuan)

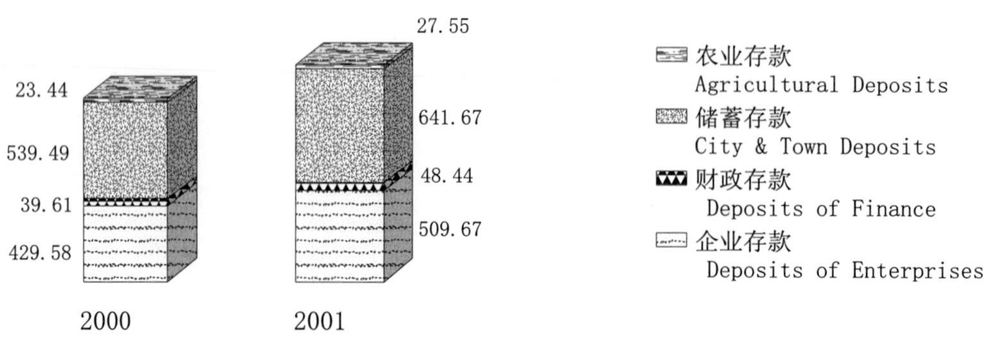

15－1 财政收入基本情况
Government Revenue

单位:亿元
(100 million yuan)

指　　标	Item	2000	2001	2001年比2000年增长(%) Increase Rate in 2001 over 2000(%)
财政总收入	**Total Revenue**	**153.04**	**177.04**	**15.7**
#地方	Local	85.23	99.75	17.0
#增值税	Value－added Tax	12.18	14.26	17.1
营业税	Operation Tax	20.34	22.08	8.6
企业所得税	Enterprises' Income Tax	6.78	12.34	82.0
个人所得税	Individual Income Tax	4.73	6.67	41.0
财政收入按项目分	**Government Revenue by Source**			
工商税收	Industrial and Commercial Tax	111.51	123.41	10.7
农业四税	Agricultural and Related	10.06	9.33	－7.3
企业收入	Revenue from Enterprises	9.14	14.06	53.8
企业亏损补贴	Subsidies to Loss－making Enterprises	－0.63	－0.52	
教育费附加收入	Revenue from Extra Charges for Education	2.4	2.52	5.0
排污费收入	Revenue from Drainage	0.68	0.95	39.7
罚没、行政性收费收入	Penalty and Confiscatory Revenue	8.44	12.55	48.7
其他收入	Other Revenue	5.58	5.70	2.2

15－2 财政支出基本情况
Financial Expenditure

单位：亿元
(100 million yuan)

指 标	Item	2000	2001	2001 年比 2000 年增长(%) Increase Rate in 2001 over 2000(%)
财政总支出	**Total Expenditure for Finance**	**201.57**	**275.2**	**36.5**
经济建设费	Expense of Economic Construction	56.99	79.76	40.0
#基本建设费	Expenditure for Capital Construction	24.82	43.13	73.8
企业挖潜改资金	Innovation Funds	6.41	4.45	－30.6
工业交通部门事业费	Operating Expenses of Indusrtial and Transportation Departments	1.88	2.73	45.2
城市维护费	City Maintenance Expenditure	6.49	7.97	22.8
社会文教费	Expenditure for Social Cultural and Educational Development	41.07	56.72	38.1
#通信广播	Communicate Broadcast	1.33	1.51	13.5
国防费	Expenditure for National Defense	0.17	0.20	17.6
行政管理费	Expenditure for Government Administration	24.31	32.19	32.4
抚恤、社会福利费及社会保障支出	Pensions, Social Welfare and Relief Funds	15.06	21.02	39.6
财政补贴支出	Expense for Finance Subsidies	3.84	5.10	32.8
其他	Others	60.12	80.21	33.4
国家财政用于教育支出	**Government Expenditure for Education**	**34.74**	**49.35**	**42.1**
教育事业费	Operating Expenses for Education	31.78	44.42	39.8
#高等学校	Higher Education	3.25	3.51	8.0
中等学校	Secondary Schools	9	13.84	53.8
小学	Primary Schools	15.97	23.08	44.5
广播电视教育	Broadcast, TV and Education	0.1	0.11	10.0
教育基建投资	Investment for Education Capital Construction	0.94	2.36	151.1
各部门事业费中用于教育的支出	Expenditure for Education in Expense of Cause of Departments	0.05	0.05	持平
城市教育费附加支出	Expenditure from Extracharges for Education of Cities	1.97	2.52	27.9

15－2 续表(continued)

单位:亿元
(100 million yuan)

指　标	Item	2000	2001	2001年比2000年增长(%) Increase Rate in 2001 over 2000(%)
国家财政用于农业的支出	**Government Expenditure for Agriculture**	**31.9**	**42.5**	**33.2**
支援农村生产支出和各项农业事业费	Expenditure for Supporting Agriculture Production and Agriculture Operating Expenses	14.39	18.12	25.9
基本建设支出	Expenditure for Capital Construction	6.78	12.54	85.0
科技三项费用	Expense on S&T Promotion	0.08	0.13	62.5
农村救济费	Rural Relief Funds	0.12	0.20	66.7
其他	Others	10.53	11.51	9.3
国家财政用于抚恤和社会福利支出	**Government Expenditure for Pensions and Social Welfare**	**3.19**	**4.78**	**49.8**
抚恤支出	Pension for Handicapped and Bereaved Families	0.97	1.10	13.4
离退休费	Pension for Retires	0.23	0.31	34.8
社会福利救济费	Social Welfare and Relief Funds	0.84	1.51	79.8
自然灾害救济费	Expenses on Disaster Relief	0.67	1.21	80.6
其他	Others	0.48	0.65	35.4
国家财政用于科学研究的支出	**Government Expenditure for Scientific Research**	**3.07**	**3.54**	**15.3**
科技三项费	Expense on S&T Promotion	1.34	1.49	11.2
科学事业费	Operating Expenses for Sciences	1.54	1.74	13.0
自然科学	Natural Science	1.35	1.48	9.6
#技术开发研究经费	Expense for Technique Exploitation Investigate	0.25	0.25	持平
社会科学	Social Science	0.10	0.15	50.0
其他科研事业费	Other S&T Operating Expenses	0.09		
科研基建费	Expenses for Capital Construction of S&T Institutes	0.19	0.31	63.2
国家财政用于卫生支出	**Government Expenditure for Sanitation**	**11.06**	**13.55**	**22.5**
卫生事业费	Expense for Sanitation Cause	5.44	7.07	30.0
公费医疗	Free Medical Service	5.11	5.75	12.5

15－3 各级地方财政分类别收入(2001)
Each Level Local Government Revenue

单位:万元
(10000 yuan)

指标	Item	全省合计 Provincial Total	省级 Province	地级 Prefecture	县级 County	乡镇级 Villages and Towns	2001年比2000年增长(%) Increase Rate in 2001 over 2000(%)
总计	**Total**	**997494**	**216069**	**217284**	**316943**	**247198**	**17.0**
工商税收类	Industry and Commercial Tax	557529	107229	153040	150961	146299	11.1
农业四税	Agricultural and Related	93340		3731	16368	73241	－7.2
企业所得税类	Income Tax of Enterprises	123437	47542	25061	36050	14784	81.9
国有资产经营收益	State－owned Assets Profit	19896	542	8645	10286	423	－16.3
国有企业计划亏损补贴类	Planning Subsidies to Loss－making of Suffering State－owned Enterprises	－5242	－1430	－3572	－240		
所得税退税类	Drawback for Income Tax	－2775	－2740		－35		
罚没收入行政性收费收入	Penalty and Confiscatory Income	125547	55645	13190	53131	3581	48.7
其他收入类	Other Income	85762	9281	17189	50422	8870	6.5

注:本表数据不含基金数。

Note: Figures in the table do not include the funds.

15－4 分部门财政收入(2001)
Local Financial Revenue by Department

单位:万元
(10000 yuan)

指标	Item	合计 Total	#企业所得税 Income Tax of Enterprises	#国有资产经营收益 State－owned Assets Profit	#国有企业计划亏损补贴 Planning Subsidies to Loss－making State－owned Enterprises	#企业所得税退税 Return for Enterprises' Income Tax	2001年比2000年增长(%) Increase Rate in 2001 over 2000(%)
总计	Total	135316	123437	19896	－5242	－2775	59.1
工业部门	Industry Department	31008	37981	201	－4434	－2740	67.5
#冶金工业	Metallurgy Industry	29	27	2			－12.1
煤炭工业	Coal Industry	－1597	398	33	－1308	－720	
电力工业	Electric Power Industry	4858	6780	98		－2020	53.8
建筑材料工业	Construction Materials Industry	1363	1336	68	－41		80.3
轻工业	Light Industry	25991	26217		－226		112.1
建筑工程企业	Construction Project Enterprises	279	339		－60		－34.2
交通邮电部门	Transportation, Postal and Telecommunications Departments	175	181		－6		－46.6
商业企业	Commerce Enterprises	1021	965	224	－168		－10.0
粮食企业	Food Supplies Enterprises	100	208	27	－135		
外贸企业	Foreign Trade Enterprises	－7	71		－78		
文教企业	Culture and Education Enterprises	4038	4038				11.5
农林水等部门	Agriculture, Forestry and Water Departments	－143	105	11	－259		
罚款和滞纳金收入	Income of Forfeit and Late Fee	1003	1003				132.7
其他部门	Others Departments	97842	78546	19433	－102	－35	54.4

15－5 地方财政分类别支出(2001)
Local Financial Expenditure by Category

单位:万元
(10000 yuan)

指 标	Item	全省合计 Provincial Total	省级 Province	地级 Prefecture	县级 County	乡镇级 Villages and Towns	2001年比2000年增长(%) Increase Rate in 2001 over 2000(%)
总 计	Total	2751975	1020774	408501	1007489	315211	36.5
基本建设支出	Expenditure for Capital Construction	431347	389460	26631	14886	370	73.8
企业挖掘改造资金	Enterprises' Innovation Funds	44494	13820	19557	10507	610	－30.6
地质勘探费	Geological Prospecting Expenses	26865	26860		5		43.1
科技三项费用	Expense on Science and Technology Promotion	14869	6714	4517	3486	152	10.8
支援农村生产支出	Expenditure for Supporting Agricultural Production	49582	6311	11182	28660	3429	4.5
农林水利气象等事业费	Expenditure for Operating Expenses of Departments of Agriculture, Forestry, Water Conservancy and Meteorology	131595	19942	14824	69200	27629	36.4
工业交通部门事业费	Operating Expenses of Industial and Commercial Departments	27334	12964	2917	10929	524	45.1
流通部门事业费	Operating Expenses of Circulate Department	6515	161	2610	3744		22.1
城市维护费	Expenditure for City Maintenance	79706	627	32403	42552	4124	22.8
文教卫生事业费	Operating Expenses for Culture, Education & Health Care	657837	101203	86923	336189	133522	35.3
科学事业费	Operating Expenses for Science	17406	12285	3353	1742	26	12.7
抚恤和社会福利救济费	Pensions, Social Welfare and Relief Funds	47842	1866	8913	33742	3321	49.9
国防支出	Expenditure for National Defense	2006	950	315	721	20	20.9
行政管理费	Expenditure for Government Administration	321894	30443	55047	136694	99710	32.4
武装警察部队支出	Expenditure for Armed Police Troops	1852	1085	419	348		48.4
公检法司支出	Expenditure for Public Security Agency, Procuratorial Agency and Court of Justice	182523	77296	34387	69356	1484	25.6
政策性补贴支出	Expenditure for Price Subsidies	50967	45521	2424	3015	7	32.6
支援不发达地区支出	Expenditure for Support Underdeveloped Areas	96380	2259	13562	76694	3865	8.5
行政事业单位离退休经费	Pension of Administration Branch	22398	2526	659	16114	3099	73.7
农业综合开发支出	Expenditure for Synthetical Agricultural Development	18684	454	4419	13798	13	13.6
其他支出	Other Expenses	519879	268027	83439	135107	33306	45.7

15－6 用于农村生产及其事业费支出

Expenditure for Supporting Agricultural Production and Agricultural Operating Expenses

单位：万元
(10000 yuan)

指　　标	Item	2000	2001	2001年比2000年增长(％) Increase Rate in 2001 over 2000(％)
支援农村生产支出	Expenditure for Supporting Agricultural Production	47462	49582	4.5
小型农田水利和水土保持补助	Minitype Cropland Water Conservancy and Natural Environment Preserve Subsidy	13767	14978	8.8
支援农村合作生产组织资金	Capital for Support Country Cooperate Product Organise	15320	16508	7.8
农村农技推广和植保补助	Subsidy for Country Skill Extend and Plant Protect	7667	7837	2.2
农村草场和畜禽保护补助	Subsidy for Protect Grass and Domestic Animal & Birds	2846	4137	45.4
农村造林和林木保护补助	Subsidy for Forestation and Protect Forest	4682	5063	8.1
农村水产补助	Subsidy for Country Aquatic Product	808	946	17.1
粮食自给工程资金	Funds for Commissariat Self－support Project	2372	113	－95.2
农林水利气象部门事业费	Expenditure for Operating Expenses of Departments of Agriculture, Forestry, Water Conservancy and Meteorology	96471	131595	36.4
#农业事业费	Operating Expenses of Agriculture	17584	25048	42.4
畜业事业费	Operating Expenses of Domestic Animal	9437	12415	31.6
林业事业费	Operating Expenses of Forestry	14602	19159	31.2
水利事业费	Operating Expenses of Water Conservancy	15341	18208	18.7
气象事业费	Operating Expenses of Weather	1781	2190	23.0

15－7 用于科学、教育的事业费支出
Government Expenditure on Scientific Research and Education

单位：万元
(10000 yuan)

指标	Item	2000	2001	2001年比2000年增长(%) Increase Rate in 2001 over 2000(%)
科学事业费	**Operating Expenses for Sciences**	**15448**	**17406**	**12.7**
自然科学事业费	Operating Expenses for Natural Science	13524	14834	9.7
#技术开发研究经费	Operating Expenses for Technigue Development	2485	2542	2.3
社会公益和农业研究经费	Operating Expenses of Society Commonweal and Agriculture Investigation	7262	7274	0.2
行业技术开发基金	Funds for Industry Technique Empolder	70	70	持平
科研管理机构经费	Operating Expenses for Institution of Science Investigation	2189	2603	18.9
科协事业费	Operating Expenses for Science Assist	924	1046	13.2
社会科学事业费	Operating Expenses for Social Science	1000	1526	52.6
教育事业费	**Operating Expenses for Education**	**317809**	**444172**	**39.8**
#高等学校	Higher Education	32537	35131	8.0
中等专业学校	Specialized Secondary Schools	23077	26370	14.3
中学	Secondary Schools	66939	101642	51.8
小学	Primary Schools	159696	230780	44.5
广播电视教育经费	Expenses for Broadcast, TV & Education	1039	1111	6.9
特殊教育经费	Expenses for Special Education	704	942	33.8

15－8 金融机构存贷款余额
Saving Deposits and Loans of Financial Institutions

单位:亿元
(100 million yuan)

指　　标	Item	2000	2001	2001年比2000年增长(%) Increase Rate in 2001 over 2000(%)
资金来源合计	**All Sources**	**1109.73**	**1278.73**	**15.2**
各项存款	Deposits	1106.64	1341.11	21.2
#企业存款	Deposits of Enterprise	429.58	509.67	18.6
财政存款	Deposits of Finance	39.61	48.44	22.3
储蓄存款	City & Town Deposits	539.49	641.67	18.9
农业存款	Agricultural Deposits	23.44	27.55	17.5
资金运用合计	**All Uses**	**1109.73**	**1278.73**	**15.2**
各项贷款	Loans	1064.82	1212.23	13.8
#短期贷款	Short－term Loans	612.49	587.74	－4.0
#工业	Industrial Loans	179.62	186.54	3.9
商业	Commercial Loans	226.17	211.06	－6.7
建筑业	Construction Loans	15.75	23.76	50.9
农业	Agricultural Loans	52.29	65.32	24.9
乡镇企业	Loans to Township and Village Enterprises	14.46	15.8	9.3
私营企业及个体	Loans to Private Enterprises	12.02	8.85	－26.4
中长期贷款	Medium－term & Long－term Loans	391.84	548.08	39.9

15－9　金融机构现金收入
Cash Income of Financial Institutions

单位：亿元
(100 million yuan)

指　　标	Item	2000	2001	2001年比2000年增长(%) Increase Rate in 2001 over 2000(%)
收入总计	**Total Income**	**2283.63**	**2712.1**	**18.8**
商品销售收入	Income from Commodity Sales	269.10	289.00	7.4
服务业收入	Income from Service Trade	138.26	171.99	24.4
税款收入	Income from Taxes	19.23	23.18	20.5
城乡个体经营收入	Income from Urban and Rural Individual Business	123.46	125.50	1.7
储蓄存款收入	Income from Savings Deposit	1435.71	1803.57	25.6
其他金融机构收入	Income from Other Financial Institutions	38.04	15.15	－60.2
居民归还贷款收入	Income from Repayment of Loans by Residents	44.49	57.89	30.1
汇兑收入	Income from Remittances	45.81	48.83	6.6
有价证券收入	Income from Securities	13.11	12.26	－6.5
其他收入	Others	156.43	164.72	5.3
# 兑换外币收入	Income from Exchange of Foreign Currencies	1.89	0.52	－72.5

15－10　金融机构现金支出
Cash Expenditures of Financial Institutions

单位：亿元
(100 million yuan)

指　　标	Item	2000	2001	2001年比2000年增长(%) Increase Rate in 2001 over 2000(%)
支出总计	**Total**	**2325.68**	**2745.70**	**18.1**
工资性支出	Expenditure for Wages	245.57	278.35	13.3
农副产品采购支出	Expenditure for Purchases of Agricultural and Sideline Products	56.16	54.44	－3.1
工矿及其他产品采购支出	Expenditure for Purchases of Industrial and Mineral Products	53.71	56.33	4.9
行政企业事业管理费支出	Expenditure for Government and Enterprises Overhead	132.04	155.61	17.9
城乡个体经营支出	Expenditure for Individual Business	141.29	158.29	12.0
储蓄存款支出	Expenditure for Savings Deposits	1404.27	1750.13	24.6
其他金融机构支出	Expenditure for Other Financial Institutions	28.57	11.47	－59.9
居民提取贷款支出	Expenditure for Loans by Residents	49.59	57.7	16.4
汇兑支出	Expenditure for Remittances	29.4	43.17	46.8
有价证券支出	Expenditure for Securities	6.74	7.97	18.2
其他支出	Other Expenditure	178.34	172.26	－3.4

15－11 贵州企业公开发行股票(A股)一览表(一)
Summary List of Stocks Publicly Issued by Guizhou Enterprises(A Shares)(1)

单位:万股
(10000 share)

年份 Year	上市公司名称	Listed Companies	股票价格(元)Price(yuan) 面值 Face Value	发行价 Issued Price	总股本 Total Capital Stock
1993	世纪中天	Century Zhoutian	1	3.10	5400
1995	黔轮胎	Qian Tyre	1	4.50	11855
1996	力源液压	Liyuan Hydraulic Pressure	1	5.80	5110
1997	天创置业	Tianchuang	1	4.02	6000
1997	振华科技	Zhenhua Science & Technology	1	7.81	17500
1997	长征电器	Changzheng Electricity	1	4.31	16000
1998	中国七砂	China No.7 Grinding Wheel	1	3.63	17300
1999	南方汇通	Southern Huitong	1	5.55	19000
1999	赤天化	Chitianhua	1	7.20	17000
2001	红星发展	Hongxing Development	1	12.66	10000
2001	盘江精煤	Panjiang Coal	1	6.00	37130
2001	贵州茅台	Guizhou Maotai	1	31.39	25000
2001	贵航股份	Guihang share	1	4.93	22000

15－11 续表(continued)

单位:万股
(10000 share)

年份 Year	上市公司名称	Listed Companies	股本构成 Face Value 国家股 Government Share	社会法人股 Cooperation Share	流通股 Circulating Share	募集总额 Total Amount Issued
1993	世纪中天	Century Zhoutian	3000	400	2000	6200
1995	黔轮胎	Qian Tyre	7855		4000	18000
1996	力源液压	Liyuan Hydraulic Pressure	3610		1500	8700
1997	天创置业	Tianchuang	1880	2120	2000	8040
1997	振华科技	Zhenhua Science & Technology		10500	7000	54670
1997	长征电器	Changzheng Electricity	12000		4000	17240
1998	中国七砂	China No.7 Grinding Wheel	6300	6500	4500	16335
1999	南方汇通	Southern Huitong		12000	7000	38850
1999	赤天化	Chitianhua	9778	222	7000	50400
2001	红星发展	Hongxing Development	6860	140	3000	37980
2001	盘江精煤	Panjiang Coal	25130		12000	72000
2001	贵州茅台	Guizhou Maotai	17700	150	7150	224439
2001	贵航股份	Guihang share	2157	12843	7000	34510

注:原“贵华旅业”经改组后更名为“天创置业”。

Note:“Guihua Travel”was renamed“Tianchuang”.

15－12 贵州企业公开发行股票(A股)一览表(二)

Summary for Stocks Publicly Issued by Guizhou Enterprises(A Shares)(2)

单位:万股
(10000 share)

年份 Year	上市公司名称	Listed Companies	年末总股本 Total Issued Capital	国家股 Government Share	社会法人股 Cooperation Share	个人股 Personal Share	上市至今增扩股 Shares Increased or Expanded	本年增扩股 Shares Increased in 2001
1993	世纪中天	Century Zhoutian	32681	3624	17769	11288	27281	13457
1995	黔轮胎	Qian Tyre	25433	12971		12462	13578	
1996	力源液压	Liyuan Hydraulic Pressure	11103		7653	3450	5993	
1997	天创置业	Tianchuang	9900	1603	4997	3300	3900	
1997	振华科技	Zhenhua Science & Technology	35812		18012	17800	18312	4500
1997	长征电器	Changzheng Electricity	17200	12000		5200	1200	
1998	中国七砂	China No.7 Grinding Wheel	22490	8203	6539	7748	5190	
1999	南方汇通	Southern Huitong	19000		12000	7000		
1999	赤天化	Chitianhua	17000		10000	7000		
2001	红星发展	Hongxing Development	10000	6860	140	3000		
2001	盘江精煤	Panjiang Coal	37130	25130		12000		
2001	贵州茅台	Guizhou Maotai	25000	17700	150	7150		
2001	贵航股份	Guihang share	22000	2157	12843	7000		

注:原"贵华旅业"经改组后更名为"天创置业"。

Note:Note:"Guihua Travel"was renamed"Tianchuang".

15－13 保险系统机构、人员数(2001) Number of Institutios and Persons Engaged in Insurance System

项目	Item	机构数(个) Number of Insisution(unit)		职工人数(人) Employees(person)		# 女性(Female)	
		人保 People's Insurance Companies	寿保 Life Insurance Companies	人保 People's Insurance Companies	寿保 Life Insurance Companies	人保 People's Insurance Companies	寿保 Life Insurance Companies
总计	Total	131	99	1297	891	434	343
机构部门按行政区划	By Administrative Areas						
# 省级分公司	Provincial Branches	1	1	82	80	28	29
地市级分公司	Prefecture/City Branches	9	9	289	352	108	165
地市营业部	Prefecture/City Business Departments		9				
县级支公司	County Branches	52	52	599	237	172	68
县级营业部	County Business Departments	38		243		88	
办事处或营业部	Business Offices and Departments	31	32	84	222	38	81
机构分布按经济区划	By Economic Level						
# 一级分公司	First Level Filiales	1	1	82	80	28	29
二级分公司	Second Level Filiales	9	18	289	352	108	165
支公司	Branches	90	52	842	237	260	68
办事处或营业部	Offices or Business Dempartments	31	32	84	222	38	81

注：本表资料仅含中国人民保险公司及中国人寿保险公司数据。(以下相关表同)

Note: Data in this table only include data from PICC and China Life Insurance Company. (same to related tables)

15－14　人民保险主要指标(2001)
Major Indicators of People's Insurence Company

指　　标	Item	合计 Total	财产险 Property Insurance	# 企财险 Enterprise Property Insurance	# 家财险 Family Property Insurance	# 工程险 Engineering Insurance	# 责任险 Responsibility Insurance
承保额(万元)	Amount Insured(10000 yuan)	11161745	4439135	3310309	405911	83299	598895
保险金额(万元)	Insurance Value(10000 yuan)	7636543	3781697	3310309	405482	25218	
期末有效数	Virtual Value at The End of Period	308256	307537		305939		
责任限额(万元)	Liability Limit(10000 yuan)	3525202	657438		429	58081	598895
保费收入(万元)	Premium Income(10000 yuan)	65074	13071	9590	1126	280	1812
储金(万元)	Deposits(10000 yuan)	47	47		44		
期末有效数	Virtual Value at The End of Period	5568	5480		5452		
已决赔案件数(件)	Cases of Settled Claims(case)	81293	5500	1027	2788	8	1378
已决赔案金额	Indemnity Expenditure	33463	4503	3023	452	50	951
满期返还数量(件)	Amount of Expiration Return(case)	230274	32074		30230		
满期返还金额	Value of Expiration Return	795	695		685		

15－14 续表(continued)

指　　标	Item	其　他 Others	机动车辆险 Transportation Equipment Insurance	货物运输险 Freight Transport Insurance	农业险 Agricultural Insurance	其他 Others
承保额(万元)	Amount Insured(10000 yuan)	40721	5275643	1437967	3076	5923
保险金额(万元)	Insurance Value(10000 yuan)	40688	2408731	1437167	3076	5872
期末有效数	Virtual Value at The End of Period	1598				719
责任限额(万元)	Liability Limit(10000 yuan)	33	2866903	800		61
保费收入(万元)	Premium Income (10000 yuan)	263	48261	3621	38	83
储金(万元)	Deposits(10000 yuan)	3				
期末有效数	Virtual Value at The End of Period	28			88	
已决赔案件数(件)	Cases of Settled Claims(case)	299	75183	450	148	12
已决赔案金额	Indemnity Expenditure	27	27448	1071	53	388
满期返还数量(件)	Amount of Expiration Return(case)	44			200000	
满期返还金额	Value of Expiration Return	10			100	

15－15 人寿保险主要指标(2001)
Major Indicators of Life Insurance Company

指　　标	Item	合计 Total	团体业务 Group Business	寿险业务 Normal Life Insurance	意外险业务 Unforeseen Human Injury Insurance	健康险业务 Health Insurance	个人保险 Personal Business	寿险业务 Normal Life Insurance	健康险业务 Health Insurance
保费收入(万元)	Premium(10000 yuan)	81059	25182	15761	8687	734	55877	55442	435
寿险业务(万元)	Normal Life Insurance(10000 yuan)	71203	15761	15761			55442	55442	
短期业务(万元)	Short－term Business(10000 yuan)	9856	9421		8687	734	435		435
承保金额(亿元)	Amount Insured(100 million yuan)	2393	2343	1	2178	163	50	33	17
#长险(亿元)	Insurance Value of Guarantee Slip Newly Increased(100 million yuan)	35	2	2			33	33	
承保人数(万人)	Number of Accepted Insurance Person(10000 persons)	269	246	10	216	20	23	17	6
#长险(万人)	Number of Persons of Guarantee Slip Newly Increased (10000 persons)	27	10	10			17	17	
承保件数(万件)	Number of Accepted Insurance (10000 cases)	42	19		19		23	18	5
#长险(万件)	Number of Guarantee Slip Newly Increased(10000 cases)	18					18	18	
赔付及给付金额(万元)	Amount of Claim and Payment (10000 yuan)	11132	6743	325	4397	2021	4389	3268	1121
伤残给付(万元)	Payment for Injured Person and Invalid(10000 yuan)	4142	3125	21	2716	388	1017	389	628
医疗给付(万元)	Payment for Medical Treatment (10000 yuan)	3585	2810	58	1159	1593	775	309	466
死亡给付(万元)	Payment for Death(10000 yuan)	3405	808	246	522	40	2597	2570	27
赔付及给付人数(人/次)	Number of Claim and Payment Person(person/time)	74306	54932	1496	34067	19369	19374		
伤残给付(人/次)	Payment for Injured Person and Invalid(person/time)	26757	22152	84	18742	3326	4605	1768	2837
医疗给付(人/次)	Payment for Medical Treatment (person/time)	38759	30079	366	13844	15869	8680	3777	4903
死亡给付(人/次)	Payment for Death(person/time)	8790	2701	1046	1481	174	6089	6022	67
生存金给付(万元)	Payment for Survival(10000 yuan)	14456	6066	6066			8390	8390	
年金给付(万元)	Payment for Annuity(10000 yuan)	5637	883	883			4754	4754	
满期给付(万元)	Payment for Expiration(10000 yuan)	8819	5183	5183			3636	3636	
退保金额(万元)	Insurance Withdrawed(10000 yuan)	8987	2735	2735			6252	6252	

主要统计指标解释

财政收入 包括地方财政收入和上划中央增值税、消费税两部分。地方财政收入包括营业税、地方企业所得税、个人所得税、城镇土地使用税、固定资产投资方向调节税、城镇维护建设税、房产税、车船使用税、印花税、屠宰税、农牧业税、农业特产税、耕地占用税、契税、增值税25%部分、证券交易税(印花税)的50%部分和除海洋石油资源税以外的其他资源税。

财政支出 国家财政将筹集起来的资金进行分配使用,以满足经济建设和各项事业的需要,主要包括:

基本建设支出,企业挖潜改造资金,地质勘探费用,科技三项费用,支援农村生产支出,农林水利气象等部门的事业费用,工业交通商业等部门的事业费,文教科学卫生事业费,抚恤和社会福利救济费,国防支出,行政管理费,价格补贴支出。

预算外资金收支 预算外资金指国家机关、事业单位和社会团体为履行或代行政府职能,依据国家法律、法规和具有法律效力的规章而收取、提取和安排使用的未纳入国家预算管理的各种财政性资金。

信贷资金 指金融机构以信用方式积聚和分配的货币资金。金融机构信贷资金的来源有各项存款、对国际金融机构负债、流通中货币、银行自有资金及当年结益等;信贷资金的运用有各项贷款、黄金占款、外汇占款、财政借款及在国际金融机构中的资产等。

存款 指企业、机关、团体或居民根据资金必须收回的原则,把货币资金存入银行或其他信用机构保管并取得一定利息的一种信用活动形式。根据存款对象的不同可划分为企业存款、财政存款、机关团体存款、基本建设存款、城镇储蓄存款、农村存款等科目。它是银行信贷资金的主要来源。

贷款 指银行或其他信用机构根据资金必须归还的原则,按一定利率,为企业、个人等提供资金的一种信用活动形式。我国银行贷款分为流动资金贷款、固定资产贷款、城乡个体工商户贷款以及农业贷款等科目。

保险金额 指保险人承担赔偿或者给付保险金责任的最高限额。

保费 指投保人为取得保险人在约定范围内所承担赔偿责任而支付给保险人的费用。

赔款 指保险人根据保险合同的规定,向被保险人支付的赔偿保险责任损失的金额。

给付 包括死伤医疗给付和满期给付。死伤医疗给付是指保险人根据人寿保险及长期健康保险合同的规定,因被保险人在保险期内发生保险责任范围内的保险事故支付给被保险人(或受益人)的金额。满期给付是指被保险人生存期满,保险人按人寿保险合同规定支付给被保险人的满期保险金额。

城乡居民储蓄存款余额 指某一时点城乡居民存入银行及农村信用社的储蓄金额,包括城镇居民储蓄存款和农民个人储蓄存款,不包括居民的手存现金和工矿企业、部队、机关、团体等单位存款。

Explanatory Notes on Main Statistical Indicators

Government Revenue includes the local government revenue and the consumption tax and value added tax transfered to central government. The revenue of the local government includes business tax, income tax of the enterprises subordinated to the local government, personal income tax, tax on the use of urban land, tax on the adjustment of the investment in fixed assets, tax on town maintenance and construction, tax on real estates, tax on the use of vehicles and ships, stamp tax, slaughter tax, tax on agriculture and animal husbandry, tax on special agricultural products, tax on the occupancy of cultivated land, contract tax, 25% of the value added tax, 50% of the tax on stock dealing (stamp tax) and tax on resources other than the ocean petroleum resources.

Government Expenditure refers to the distribution and use of the funds the government finance has raised, so as to meet the needs of economic construction and various causes. It includes the following main items:

Expenditure for capital construction, Innovation funds of the enterprises, Geological prospecting expenses, Expenditures for science and technology promotion, Expenditure for supporting rural production, Operating expenses of the departments of farming, forestry, water conservancy and meteorology etc, Operating expenses of the departments of industry, transport and commerce, Operating expenses of the departments of culture, eduation, science and public health, Pension for the disabled or for the families of the bereaved and relief funds for social welfare, Expenditures for national defence, Administrative expenses, Expenditure for price subsidies.

Extra – budgetary Revenue and Expenditure Extra – budgetary fund refers to financial fund of various types not covered by the regular government budgetary management, which is collected, allocated or arranged by government agencies, institutions and social organizations while performing duties delegated to them or on behalf of the government in accordance with laws, rules and regulations.

Credit Funds refer to the funds issued as loans by banking institutions. The sources of credit funds of the banking institutions included deposits, liabilities to international financial institutions, currency in circulation, self – owned funds and current retained profits, etc. The credit funds can be used in forms of loans, gold, foreign exchange, government debt and assets in the international financial institutions.

Deposit is a form of credit by which enterprises, institutions, organizations or households can put money into banks and other credit institutions for safekeeping and interest earning under the principle of free withdrawal. According to different depositors, deposits are divided into enterprise deposits, treasury deposits, deposits of government agencies and organizations, capital construction deposits, urban savings deposits, rural deposits and other deposits. Deposits are major sources of the credit funds of banks.

Loan is a form of credit by which banks and other credit institutions provide funds at certain interest rate to enterprises and individuals in the light of the principle of unconditional repayment. Loans from Chinese banks include circulating capital loans, fixed assets loans, loans to urban and rural individuals engaged in industrial and commercial business and agricultural loans.

Amount Insured refers to the maximum that the insurant will get for the claim of the case insured.

Premium is the fee paid by the insurant to the insurer to obtain the obligation of compensation from the insurance within the agreed terms.

Settled Claim is the compensation paid by the insurer to the insurant in accordance with the insurance contract.

Payment includes payment for death, injury or medical treatment and mature payment. Payment for death, injury or medical treatment refers to the money paid to the insurant (or the beneficiary) in accordance with the life or health insurance contract when the insurant encounters accidents within the insured period covered in the contract. Mature payment refers to the mature payment to the insurant in accordance with the life insurance contract at the end of the insured period.

The Savings Deposits of Urban and Rural Residents refers to the total value of savings deposits of urban and rural households in banks and rural credit cooperatives at a given point of time, including the savings deposit of urban residents and the savings deposit of rural residents. The cash in hand by residents and the deposits of organizations such as enterprises, military units, government agencies, institutions, etc. are not included.

16

人民生活

People's Livelihood

Sixteen

城镇居民家庭人均可支配收入(元)(2001)

Urban Household Per Capita Annual Actural Income and Disposable Income (yuan)

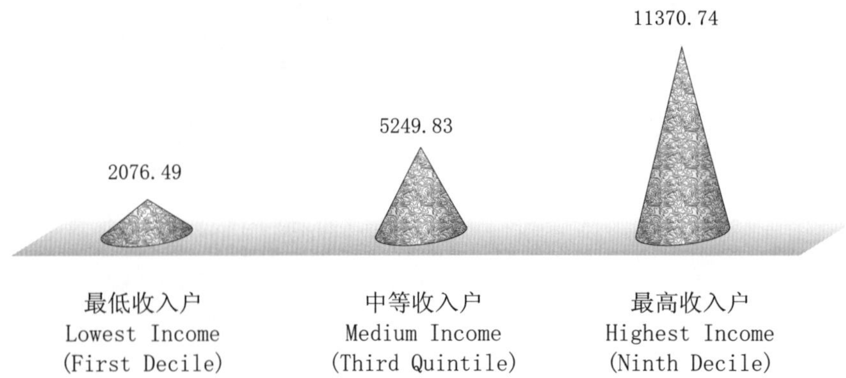

农民家庭人均纯收入(元)(2001)

Per Capita Annual Net Income and Its Composition of Rural Households (yuan)

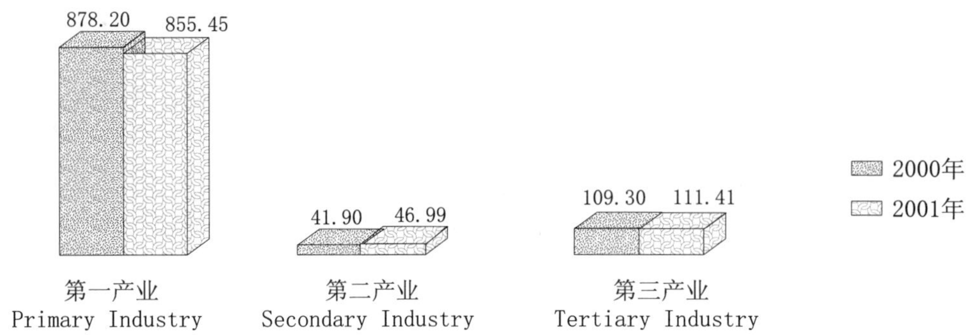

农民生活消费支出(元)(2001)

Consumption Expenditure(yuan)

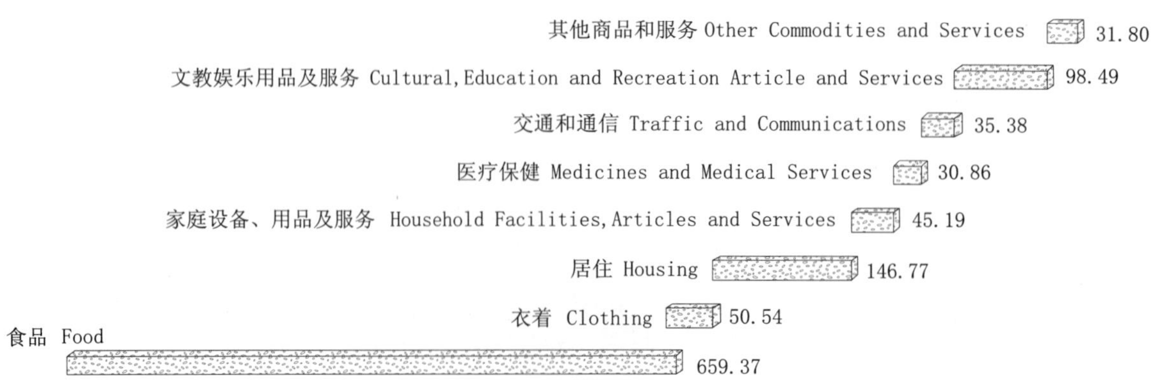

16－1 城镇居民家庭生活基本情况(2001)
Basic Conditions of Urban Households

指 标	Item	2000	总平均 Total Average	最低收入户 Lowest Income	低收入户 Low Income	中等偏下户 Medium Low
调查户数(户)	**Number of Households Surveyed(household)**	850	980	98	98	196
平均每户常住家庭人口(人)	Average Number of Permanent Persons Per Household(person)	3.11	3.12	3.54	3.52	3.33
平均每户就业人员(人)	Average Number of Employees Per Household(person)	1.62	1.66	1.43	1.62	1.66
平均每户就业面(%)	Percentage of Employees Per Household(%)	52.09	53.21	40.4	46.02	49.84
国有经济单位职工人数(人/户)	Staff and Workers in State－owned Units(person/household)	1.32	1.29	0.73	1.05	1.18
集体经济单位职工人数(人/户)	Staff and Workers in Collective－owned Units(person/household)	0.13	0.14	0.23	0.22	0.23
其他经济单位职工人数(人/户)	Staff and Workers in Other Ownership Units(person/household)	0.01	0.02			0.04
平均每个就业者赡养人口(人)	Pesons Supported by Each Employee(person)	1.92	1.88	2.48	2.17	2.01
平均每人年可支配收入(元)	**Average Annual Disposable Income Per Capita(yuan)**	5122.21	5451.91	2076.49	2983.41	3990.24
平均每人年实际收入(元)	**Annual Actural Income Per Capita(yuan)**	5137.19	5467.18	2085.87	3006.4	4001.68
国有单位职工收入	Income of Staff & Workers in State－owned Units	3243.42	3508.89	812.43	1589.57	2442.51
集体单位职工收入	Income of Staff & Workers in Collective－owned Units	183.18	202.84	216.26	181.8	271.76
其他经济单位职工收入	Income of Staff & Workers in Units of Other Type of Ownership	25.32	35.86	1.41	0.42	83.13
个体经营者净收入	Net Income of Self－employed Laborers	224.13	285.13	328.87	231.2	271.54
个体被雇劳动者收入	Income of Privately－hired Laborers	38.59	31.70	26.9	98.33	34.46
离退休人员再就业收入	Reemployment Income of Retirees	25.83	27.03	5.12	55.38	1.36
其他就业者收入	Income of Other Employees	4.9	7.48	23.39	12.68	
其他劳动收入	Other Income	157.46	191.97	193.23	143.58	181.96
平均每人年财产性收入	Property Income	40.04	18.71	3.24	2.79	12.06
平均每人年转移性收入	Transfer Income	1192.66	1154.4	474.54	677.6	698.1
#离退休金	Pension	985.36	955.03	375.15	591.32	608.64
平均每人年储蓄借贷收入(元)	**Savings and Lending Annual Income Per Capita(yuan)**	1049.3	896.39	248.9	387.58	440.27
平均每人年实际支出(元)	**Annual Actural Expenditure Per Capita(yuan)**	5075.81	5331.41	2091.23	2898.93	3981.19
消费性支出	Consumption Expenditure	4278.28	4492.25	1898.3	2597.9	3535.28
非消费性支出	Nonconsumption Expenditure	794.84	836.5	191.39	286.23	443.95
平均每人年储蓄借贷支出(元)	**Savings and Lending Expenditure Per Capita(yuan)**	912.39	1143.93	259.32	432.57	519.12

16－1 续表(continued)

指　　标	Item	中等收入户 Medium Income	中等偏上户 Medium high	高收入户 High Income	最高收入户 Highest Income	2001年比2000年增长(%) Increase Rate in 2001 over 2000(%)
调查户数(户)	**Number of Households Surveyed(household)**	**196**	**196**	**98**	**98**	
平均每户常住家庭人口(人)	Average Number of Permanent Persons Per Household(person)	3.12	2.95	2.73	2.66	0.3
平均每户就业人员(人)	Average Number of Employees Per Household(person)	1.79	1.69	1.65	1.63	2.5
平均每户就业面(%)	Percentage of Employees Per Household(%)	57.37	57.88	60.44	61.28	2.2
国有经济单位职工人数(人/户)	Staff and Workers in State－owned Units(person/household)	1.42	1.56	1.38	1.46	－2.3
集体经济单位职工人数(人/户)	Staff and Workers in Collective－owned Units(person/household)	0.1	0.7	0.1	0.04	7.7
其他经济单位职工人数(人/户)	Staff and Workers in Other Ownership Units(person/household)	0.02		0.02	0.01	100.0
平均每个就业者赡养人口(人)	Pesons Supported by Each Employee(person)	1.74	1.75	1.69	1.63	2.1
平均每人年可支配收入(元)	**Average Annual Disposable Income Per Capita(yuan)**	**5249.83**	**6778.67**	**8407.75**	**11370.74**	**6.4**
平均每人年实际收入(元)	**Annual Actural Income Per Capita(yuan)**	**5263.84**	**6794.94**	**8426.03**	**11390.85**	**6.4**
国有单位职工收入	Income of Staff & Workers in State－owned Units	3684.47	4888.24	5405.22	6892.09	8.2
集体单位职工收入	Income of Staff & Workers in Collective－owned Units	165.91	195.63	278.48	56.05	10.7
其他经济单位职工收入	Income of Staff & Workers in Units of Other Type of Ownership	44.72	19.36	37.34	24.68	41.6
个体经营者净收入	Net Income of Self－employed Laborers	449.44	125.57	158.98	430.53	27.2
个体被雇劳动者收入	Income of Privately－hired Laborers	28.97	2.11	0.61	46.87	－17.9
离退休人员再就业收入	Reemployment Income of Retirees	7.42	11.96	137.07	49.31	4.7
其他就业者收入	Income of Other Employees	5.3	12.39			52.7
其他劳动收入	Other Income	159.4	120.31	230.39	475.45	21.9
平均每人年财产性收入	Property Income	14.61	18.31	57.99	47.13	－53.3
平均每人年转移性收入	Transfer Income	703.36	1398.26	2110.36	3368.75	－3.2
#离退休金	Pension	545.94	1134.95	1848.9	2718.48	－3.1
平均每人年储蓄借贷收入(元)	**Savings and Lending Annual Income Per Capita(yuan)**	**674**	**1156.82**	**1860.15**	**2528.52**	**－14.6**
平均每人年实际支出(元)	**Annual Actural Expenditure Per Capita(yuan)**	**4977.22**	**6744.24**	**8506.8**	**10757.67**	**5.0**
消费性支出	Consumption Expenditure	4354.17	5666.54	6708.72	8358.3	5.0
非消费性支出	Nonconsumption Expenditure	622.27	1077.47	1797.78	2397.41	5.2
平均每人年储蓄借贷支出(元)	**Savings and Lending Expenditure Per Capita(yuan)**	**940.28**	**1432**	**1817.98**	**4009.25**	**25.4**

16－2 城镇居民家庭人均实际收入和可支配收入

Urban Household Per Capita Annual Actural Income and Disposable Income

单位：元
(yuan)

指　　标	Item	2000	2001	2001年比2000年增长(%) Increase Rate in 2001 over 2000(%)
平均每人年实际收入	Annual Actual Income Per Capita	5137.19	5467.18	6.4
最低收入户	Lowest Income(First Decile)	2102.28	2085.87	－0.8
低收入户	Low Income(Second Decile)	2971.89	3006.4	1.2
中等偏下户	Medium－low Income(Second Quintile)	3964.23	4001.68	0.9
中等收入户	Medium Income(Third Quintile)	5066.62	5263.84	3.9
中等偏上户	Medium－high Income(Fourth Quintile)	6252.53	6794.94	8.7
高收入户	High Income(Tenth Decile)	7477.6	8426.03	12.7
最高收入户	Highest Income(Ninth Decile)	10295.36	11390.85	10.6
平均每人年可支配收入	Annual Disposable Income Per Capita	5122.21	5451.91	6.4
最低收入户	Lowest Income(First Decile)	2094.47	2076.49	－0.9
低收入户	Low Income(Second Decile)	2957.48	2983.41	0.9
中等偏下户	Medium－low Income(Second Quintile)	3952.22	3990.24	1
中等收入户	Medium Income(Third Quintile)	5049.42	5249.83	4
中等偏上户	Medium－high Income(Fourth Quintile)	6236.86	6778.67	8.7
高收入户	High Income(Tenth Decile)	7452.75	8407.75	12.8
最高收入户	Highest Income(Ninth Decile)	10279.98	11370.74	10.6

16－3 城镇居民家庭人均消费性支出(2001)
Urban Household Per Capita Annual Consumer Expenditures

单位:元
(yuan)

指　　标	Item	2000	总平均 Total Average	最低收入户 Lowest Income	低收入户 Low Income	中等偏下户 Medium Low
恩格尔系数(%)	Engel Quotiety(%)	43	41			
消费性支出	Total Consumer Expenditures	4278.28	4492.25	1898.3	2597.9	3535.28
食　品	Food	1837.49	1821.15	1053.96	1311.26	1649.31
#粮　食	Grain	185.68	171.89	156.56	159.43	181.06
烟、酒、茶、饮料	Cigarette, Liquor and Tea	265.39	260.89	133.76	187.8	245.36
在外饮食	Dining Out	251.92	268.24	87.77	126.44	165.16
衣　着	Clothing	453.1	506.17	163.02	235.06	398.48
家庭设备、用品及服务	Household Facilities, Articles and Services	408.93	402.94	61.84	153.79	175.95
#家庭设备耐用品	Durable Goods of Household Facilities	239.24	213.31	8.81	69.42	54.32
医疗保健	Medicines and Medical Services	233.28	268.42	86.71	96.71	224.94
交通和通信	Traffic and Communications	335.28	384.76	162.35	191.3	261.85
交　通	Transportation	135.62	138.73	53.49	72.5	94.79
通　信	Telecommunications	199.66	246.03	108.86	118.79	167.06
娱乐、教育、文化服务	Recreation, Education and Cultural Services	460.44	551.27	145.41	329.45	446.49
#耐用消费品	Durable Consumer Goods for Recreational Use	110.57	105.46	2.95	22.55	65.97
学杂费	Tuition Fee	161.7	244.72	77.84	216.79	255.6
托幼费	Child－care Fee	22.46	24.33	14.25	7.68	25.03
文娱用品	Cultural and Recreational Articles	20.09	24.23	6.53	8.16	15.24
书报杂志	Books, Newspaper and Magazines	21.99	22.26	4.19	7.45	12.45
文化娱乐费	Funds for Cultural and Recreational Activities	55.28	60.45	19.26	35.03	33.49
居　住	Residence	331.41	342.55	168.05	202.66	257.36
#房　租	Rent	15.76	11.33	10.11	6.19	15.58
水　费	Water	30.9	32.91	25.55	27.52	28.46
电　费	Electricity	115.89	127.92	73.3	97.14	114.35
燃料费	Fuels	72.1	69.79	49.57	59.83	69.97
杂项商品和服务	Miscellaneous Commodities and Services	218.35	214.99	56.96	77.68	120.89

16－3 续表(continued)

指　　标	Item	中等收入户 Medium Income	中等偏上户 Medium high	高收入户 High Income	最高收入户 Highest Income	2001年比2000年增长(%) Increase Rate in 2001 over 2000(%)
恩格尔系数(%)	**Engel Quotiety(%)**					
消费性支出	Total Consumer Expenditures	4354.17	5666.54	6708.72	8358.3	5.0
食　品	Food	1847.61	2074.34	2430.66	2722.65	－1.4
#粮　食	Grain	168.96	158.34	197.91	197.51	－7.4
烟、酒、茶、饮料	Cigarette, Liquor and Tea	268.21	275.45	371.03	402.61	－1.9
在外饮食	Dining Out	278.59	396.07	429.94	480.97	6.5
衣　着	Clothing	576.2	601.79	856.3	863.63	11.7
家庭设备、用品及服务	Household Facilities, Articles and Services	284.84	625.72	751.67	1183.97	－1.5
#家庭设备耐用品	Durable Goods of Household Facilities	125.43	360.27	459.89	701.21	－10.8
医疗保健	Medicines and Medical Services	246.34	342.05	417.8	589.41	15.1
交通和通信	Traffic and Communications	351.61	535.51	663.31	702.47	14.8
交　通	Transportation	124.87	221.42	181.35	256.19	2.3
通　信	Telecommunications	226.73	314.09	481.96	446.27	23.2
娱乐、教育、文化服务	Recreation, Education and Cultural Services	578	775.83	701.53	944.28	19.7
#耐用消费品	Durable Consumer Goods for Recreational Use	110	138.74	152.06	323.2	－4.6
学杂费	Tuition Fee	243.47	337.85	274.05	247.81	51.3
托幼费	Child－care Fee	36.05	23.17	27.17	31.01	8.3
文娱用品	Cultural and Recreational Articles	20.23	34.46	47.93	54.16	20.6
书报杂志	Books, Newspaper and Magazines	23.57	27.9	36.94	60.36	1.2
文化娱乐费	Funds for Cultural and Recreational Activities	66.48	83.78	77.45	133.91	9.4
居　住	Residence	268.11	431.27	444.71	854.44	3.4
#房　租	Rent	7.99	7.32	19.58	17.78	－28.1
水　费	Water	35.42	34.22	41.36	43.65	6.5
电　费	Electricity	129.6	147.86	191.19	170.32	10.4
燃料费	Fuels	72.64	69.51	81.69	92.27	－3.2
杂项商品和服务	Miscellaneous Commodities and Services	201.47	280.03	442.74	497.45	－1.5

16－4 城镇居民家庭人均现金收支情况
Per Capita Annual Cash Income and Expenditure of Urban Households

单位:元
(yuan)

指标	Item	2000	2001	2001年比2000年增长(%) Increase Rate in 2001 over 2000(%)
可支配收入	**Per Capita Disposable Income**	**5122.21**	**5451.91**	**6.4**
现金收入	**Cash Income**	**6186.5**	**6363.57**	**2.9**
实际收入	Actual Income	5137.19	5467.18	6.4
国有单位职工收入	Income of Staff & Workers in State－Owned Units	3243.42	3508.89	8.2
集体单位职工收入	Income of Staff & Workers in Collective－Owned Units	183.18	202.84	10.7
其他所有制职工全部收入	Income of Staff & Workers in Other Ownership	25.32	35.86	41.6
个体劳动者收入	Income of Individual Employer	262.72	316.83	20.6
离退休再就业人员收入	Income of Taking up Occupation Again of Retirees	25.83	27.03	4.7
转移收入	Transfer Income	1192.66	1154.4	3.2
财产性收入	Property Income	40.04	18.71	－53.3
家庭副业生产收入	Income of Household Sideline Production	1.66	3.17	91.0
其它就业者收入	Income of Other Employed Persons	4.9	7.48	52.7
其它劳动收入	Income of Other Labour	157.46	191.97	21.9
借贷收入	Income of Borrow Money and Loan	1049.3	896.39	－14.6
提取储蓄存款	Drawing Money from Banks	913.45	781.85	－14.4
兑售有价证券	Exchanging or Saling Securities	3		
其他借贷收入	Others	12.41	32.33	160.5
现金支出	**Cash Expenditure**	**5988.2**	**6475.34**	**8.1**
实际支出	Actual Expenditure	5075.81	5331.41	5.0
消费性支出	Expenditure for Consumption	4278.28	4492.25	5.0
非消费性支出	Expenditure for Non－Consumption	794.84	836.5	5.2
家庭副业生产支出	Expenditure of Household Sideline Production	2.69	2.66	－1.1
借贷支出	Expenditure for Lend Money and Saving	912.39	1143.93	25.4
存入储蓄款	Savings Deposits	647.26	850.08	31.3
购置有价证券	Purchasing Securities	4.3	12.76	196.7
其他借贷支出	Others	48.06	46.16	－4.0
期末手存现金	Cash Now Available(year－end)	375.11	424.7	13.2

16－5 城镇居民家庭人均购买主要商品数量
Urban Household Per Capita Purchase of Principal Goods

单位:公斤
(kg)

指　　标	Item	2000	2001	2001年比2000年增长(%) Increase Rate in 2001 over 2000(%)
粮　食	Grain	85.4	81.8	－4.2
食用植物油	Edible Vegetable Oil	8.2	5.9	－28.1
猪　肉	Pork	25.2	24	－4.8
牛、羊肉	Beef and Mutton	1.5	1.3	－13.3
家禽类	Poultry	6	6	持平
蛋　类	Eggs	6.9	6.5	－5.8
水产品类	Aquatic Products	3.5	3.6	2.9
鲜　菜	Fresh Vegetables	105.5	101.9	－3.4
食　糖	Sugar	2	1.8	－10
卷烟(盒)	Cigarettes(pack)	44.1	42.7	－3.2
酒　类	Liquor	8	7.7	－3.8
糖果、糕点类	Sugar, Fruits and Pastry	4.1	3.9	－4.9
水果类	Fruits	42.8	45.9	7.2
奶类及制品	Milk and Its Products	7.4	9	21.6

16－6 每百户城镇居民家庭耐用消费品拥有量
Per 100 Urban Households Possession of Durable Consumer Goods

指　　标	Item	2000	2001	2001 年比 2000 年增长(%) Increase Rate in 2001 over 2000(%)
自行车(辆)	Bicycle	24.82	25.79	3.9
摩托车(辆)	Motorcycle	8.92	9.21	3.3
收录音机(台)	Recorder	29.06	26.54	－8.7
彩色电视机(台)	Color TV Set	113.78	117.42	3.1
录放像机(台)	Video－recorder	16.22	14.3	－11.8
影碟机(台)	Video Disc Player	50.44	60.93	20.8
组合音响(台)	Hi－Fi Stereo Component System	31.29	34.8	11.2
家用空调器(台)	Household Air Conditioner	3.3	3.41	3.3
热水淋浴器(台)	Water Heater	34.84	36.3	4.2
微波炉(台)	Microwave Oven	13.16	15.39	17.0
家用电脑(台)	Personal Computer	5.74	7.86	36.9
电风扇(台)	Electric Fan	98.17	99.13	1.0
电冰箱(台)	Refrigerator	82.82	84.42	1.9
洗衣机(台)	Washing Machine	96.09	98.62	2.6
照相机(架)	Camera	30.19	27.79	－8.0
摄像机(架)	Video Camera	0.28	0.7	150.0
钢琴(架)	Piano	0.66	1.13	71.2
移动电话(台)	Mobile Telephone	6.26	29.37	369.2

16－7 农村居民家庭生活基本情况
Basic Conditions of Rural Households

指　　标	Item	2000	2001	2001年比2000年增长(%) Increase Rate in 2001 over 2000(%)
调查户数(户)	**Households Surveyed(household)**	**2240**	**2240**	
平均每户人口(人)	Average Number of Persons Per Household(person)	4.52	4.47	－1.1
平均每户劳动力(人)	Average Number of Laborers Per Household(person)	2.77	2.74	－1.1
平均每一劳动力赡养人口(人)	Persons Supported by Each Laborer(person)	1.63	1.63	
平均每百个劳动力中(人)	In Per 100 Laborers(person)			
文盲或半文盲	Illiterate or Semi－Illiterate	21.42	20.17	－5.8
小学程度	Elementary School	39.77	39.84	0.2
初中程度	Junior High School	33.95	34.48	1.6
高中程度	Senior High School	3.27	3.62	10.7
中专程度	Technical Secondary School	1.37	1.58	15.3
大专以上	Junior College	0.21	0.31	47.6
劳动力平均受教育年限(年)	Average Fixed Number of Year of Receiving Education of the Laborers(year)	6.03	6.17	2.3
平均每人年总收入(元)	Annual Average Income Per Capita(yuan)	1947.47	1987.53	2.1
平均每人年纯收入	**Annual Average Net Income Per Capita(yuan)**	**1374.16**	**1411.73**	**2.7**
劳动者的报酬收入	Payment for Labour	274.90	317.54	15.5
家庭经营纯收入	Household Business Income	1029.45	1013.91	－1.5
转移性和财产性收入	Property and Transfer Income	69.81	80.27	15.0
平均每人年总支出(元)	**Annual Average Expenditure Per Capita(yuan)**	**1717.47**	**1709.92**	**－0.4**

16－7 续表(continued)

指　　标	Item	2000	2001	2001年比2000年增长(%) Increase Rate in 2001 over 2000(%)
恩格尔系数(%)	**Engel Quotiety(%)**	**62.68**	**60.03**	**－2.65百分点**
生活消费支出(元)	**Consumption Expenditure(yuan)**	**1096.59**	**1098.39**	**0.2**
食品	Food	687.32	659.37	－4.1
衣着	Clothing	53.03	50.54	－4.7
居住	Housing	138.90	146.77	5.7
家庭设备、用品及服务	Household Facilities, Articles and Services	38.23	45.19	18.2
医疗保健	Medicines and Medical Services	27.68	30.86	11.5
交通和通信	Traffic and Communications	26.92	35.38	31.4
文教娱乐用品及服务	Cultural, Education and Recreation Article and Services	97.26	98.49	1.3
其他商品和服务	Other Commodities and Services	27.25	31.80	16.7
家庭经营支出(元)	**Household Business Expenditure(yuan)**	**447.10**	**442.15**	**－1.1**
#种植业生产支出	Farming Production Costs	169.23	157.97	－6.7
牧业生产支出	Animal Husbandry Costs	232.64	241.47	3.8
购置生产性固定资产支出(元)	Buying Fixed Assets of Production(yuan)	45.07	42.09	－6.6
纳税、上交集体、集体提留和摊派支出(元)	Tax Payment, Payment for the Collective Contract, the Collective Retainment and Apportioned Charges(yuan)	36.09	34.78	－3.6
转移性支出(元)	Transfer Expenditures(yuan)	89.03	86.81	－2.5
平均每人年底居住房屋面积(平方米)	Average Per Capita Living Space at The Year－end(sq.m)	19.75	20.43	3.4

16－8 农村住户家庭经营情况 Indicators of Household Business in Rural Households

指　　标	Item	2000	2001	2001年比2000年增长(%) Increase Rate in 2001 over 2000(%)
经营耕地面积(亩/人)	Management Cultivated Area(mu/person)	1.06	1.08	1.9
自留地面积(亩/人)	Family Plots(mu/person)	0.11	0.10	-9.1
经营山地面积(亩/人)	Management Hilly Country(mu/person)	0.36	0.35	-2.8
年内出售肥猪头数(头/户)	Number of Sold Fattened Hogs in The Year(head/household)	1.21	1.34	10.7
年内自宰肥猪头数(头/户)	Number of Fattened Hogs Slaughtered by Peasants Themselves(head/household)	0.86	0.89	3.5
出售、自宰肥猪肉产量(公斤/户)	Output of Pork Slaughtered by Peasants Themselves and Sold(kg/household)	219.65	227.59	3.6
每头猪肉产量(公斤/头)	Output of Per Slaughtered Hog(kg/head)	106.11	102.06	-3.8
年内出售菜羊只数(只/户)	Number of Sold Mutton Sheep and Goat in The Year (head/household)	0.15	0.07	-53.3
出售、自宰羊的肉产量(公斤/户)	Output of Mutton Slaughtered by Peasants Them selves and Sold(kg/household)	3.71	1.77	-52.3
年内出售肉牛数(头/百户)	Number of Sold Fattened Cattle in The Year(head/100 household)	5.54	7.05	27.3

16－9 按劳动力文化程度分组的农村住户家庭基本情况(2001)
Basic Conditions of Rural Households Grouped by Education Level of Laborers

指　标	Item	文盲 Illiterate	小学 Elementary School	初中 Junior High School	高中 Senior High School	中专 Technical Secondary School	大学 College
调查户数(户)	**Number of Households Surveyed (Household)**	**68**	**622**	**1256**	**190**	**78**	**16**
常住人口(人)	Number of Permanent Residents (person)	250	2649	5737	917	361	67
整半劳动力(个)	Number of Able－bodied and Semi－able－bodied Laborers Per Household(person)	126	1578	3592	566	220	47
平均每一劳动力负担人口(人)	Average Number of Persons Supported by a Laborer(person)	1.98	1.68	1.60	1.62	1.64	1.43
人均家庭经营耕地面积(亩)	Per Capita Management Cultivated Areas(mu)	1.16	1.13	1.06	1.03	1.05	0.89
人均家庭经营山地面积	Per Capita Runned Hilly Areas	0.50	0.42	0.32	0.36	0.22	0.37
人均生产性固定资产原值(元)	Per Capita Original Value of Productive Fixed Assets(yuan)	427.77	560.62	716.45	846.76	757.88	1304.93
人均使用房屋面积(平方米)	Per Capita Floor Space(sq.m)	15.34	18.71	20.64	23.32	22.93	36.22
人均使用房屋价值(元)	Per Capita Houses Value(yuan)	1521.32	1606.50	2306.10	2899.75	2581.80	9000.00
人均总收入	**Per Capita Annual Income**	**1753.40**	**1777.72**	**2033.24**	**2090.17**	**2505.94**	**2942.57**
现金收入	Cash Income	1014.43	1004.85	1259.47	1369.75	1689.07	1936.78
非收入所得	Income Not from Earning	98.24	158.28	225.83	224.15	186.16	46.57
人均纯收入	**Per Capita Net Income**	**1265.96**	**1260.28**	**1442.90**	**1498.27**	**1751.34**	**2213.94**
人均生活费支出	Per Capita Living Expenditures	1061.13	948.55	1126.77	1219.65	1409.72	1400.19
常住人口外出劳动人数(人)	Laborers Outside between Permanent Residents(person)	3	161	481	81	22	1

16－10 农民家庭人均经营费用和生产性固定资产购置
Per Capita Expenditure for Household Business Operation and Expenditure for Purchasing Productive Fixed Assets of Rural Households

单位:元
(yuan)

指　　标	Item	2000	2001	2001年比2000年增长(%) Increase Rate in 2001 over 2000(%)
家庭经营费用支出	**Expenditure for Household Business Operation**	**447.10**	**442.15**	**－1.1**
农业生产支出	Expenditure for Agricultural Production	172.40	160.28	－7.0
#种植业生产支出	Farming	169.23	157.87	－6.7
林业生产支出	Forestry	3.77	1.37	－63.7
牧业生产支出	Animal Husbandry	232.64	241.47	3.8
渔业生产支出	Fishery	0.86	0.35	－59.3
工业生产支出	Industry	6.24	9.41	50.8
建筑业支出	Construction	5.28	4.84	－8.3
交通运输邮电业支出	Transport & Post	11.82	8.72	－26.2
批发和零售贸易、餐饮业支出	Wholesale and Retail, Trade & Catering Services	6.17	9.66	56.6
社会服务业支出	Social Services	1.86	1.63	－12.4
文教卫生业支出	Culture, Education and Health Care	0.37	0.27	－27.0
其他经营支出	Others	5.69	4.14	－27.2
购置生产用固定资产支出	**Expenditure for Purchasing Productive Fixed Assets**	**45.07**	**42.09**	**－6.6**
#大中型铁木农具	Large and Medium, Wood and Iron Farm Tools	0.53	0.39	－26.4
农林牧渔业机械	Machinery of Farming, Forestry, Animal Husbandry and Fishery	2.24	4.26	90.2
工业机械	Industrial Machinery	3.77	2.83	－24.9
运输机械	Transportation Machinery	13.18	11.34	－14.0
役畜、产品畜	Draught Animals and Commodity Animals	23.29	22.08	－5.2

16－11 农村住户人均主要产品产量及商品率(2001)
Per Capita Output of Major Agricultural Products and Commodity Rate of Rural Household

单位:公斤 (kg)

指　　标	Item	产品产量 Output of Products	出售量 Sales of Commodity	商品率(%) Commodity Rate(%)
粮食	Grain	403.80	74.92	18.6
油料	Oil－bearing Crops	20.06	11.63	58.0
糖料	Sugar Crops	11.79	6.87	58.3
烟叶	Tobacco	13.23	10.87	82.2
蔬菜	Vagetable	281.76	57.14	20.3
果用瓜	Melon	4.14	3.58	86.5
水果	Fruits	8.62	4.90	56.8
茶叶	Tea	1.92	0.51	26.6
油桐籽	Tung－oil Seeds	3.02	2.44	80.8
油茶籽	Tea－oil Seeds	0.15	0.03	20.0
核桃	Walnuts	0.25	0.10	40.0
出售、自宰猪肉	Pork Slaughtered by Peasants Themselves & Sold	50.94	30.17	59.2
出售、自宰羊肉	Mutton Slaughtered by Peasants Themselves & Sold	0.50	0.40	80.0
出售、自宰家禽	Poultry Slaughtered by Peasants Themselves & Sold	3.02	1.89	62.6
禽蛋	Poultry and Eggs	1.71	0.81	47.4
蚕茧	Silkworm Cocoons	…	…	…

16－12 农民人均粮食收支存

Per Capita Grain Income, Expense and Stock of Rural Households

单位:公斤
(kg)

指　　标	Item	2000	2001	2001 年比 2000 年增长(%) Increase Rate in 2001 over 2000(%)
年内粮食收入合计	**Grain Income within Current Year**	**495.36**	**461.78**	**－6.8**
家庭经营生产的	From Household Operation	423.19	403.80	－4.6
购入	Bought Grain	70.65	55.53	－21.4
借入	Borrowed Grain	0.89	0.78	－12.4
收回借出粮	Recall of Loaned Grain	0.25	1.25	400.0
其它粮食收入	Other Grain Income	0.38	0.42	10.5
年内粮食支出合计	**Grain Expense within Current Year**	**459.39**	**423.28**	**－7.9**
主食用粮	Staple Food Grain	227.44	212.66	－6.5
其它生活用粮	Other Living Expense of Grain	3.64	2.15	－40.9
出售	Sold Grain	77.12	74.92	－2.9
种籽	Seed	13.58	12.41	－8.6
饲料	Forage	133.69	116.77	－12.7
借出	Loaned Grain	0.30	0.39	30.0
归还借粮	Return of Borrowed Grain	0.50	0.30	－40.0
其它粮食支出	Other Grain Expenses	3.12	3.68	17.9
年末结存	**Stock of Grain at the Year－end**	**296.14**	**327.11**	**10.5**
# 口粮	Grain Ration	210.26	215.40	2.4
种籽	Seed	13.10	9.80	－25.2
饲料	Forage	67.67	76.88	13.6

16－13 农民家庭人均纯收入及构成
Per Capita Annual Net Income and Its Composition of Rural Households

指标	Item	2000	2001	2001年比2000年增长(%)或百分点 Increase Rate in 2001 over 2000
绝对数(元)	**Absolute Figure(yuan)**			
全年纯收入	**Annual Net Income**	1374.16	1411.73	2.7
基本收入	Basic Income	1304.35	1331.45	2.1
劳动者报酬	Laborers Remuneration	274.90	317.54	15.5
#乡村企业劳动报酬	From Township Enterprises	21.93	21.19	－3.4
家庭经营收入	Income from Household Business Operation	1029.45	1013.91	－1.5
第一产业	Primary Industry	878.20	855.45	－2.6
农业收入	Agriculture	674.30	648.49	－3.8
#种植业收入	Farming	597.50	577.91	－3.3
林业收入	Forestry	14.36	18.67	30.0
牧业收入	Animal Husbandry	187.82	186.93	－0.5
渔业收入	Fishery	1.72	1.36	－20.9
第二产业	Secondary Industry	41.92	46.99	12.1
工业收入	Industry	22.20	21.55	－2.9
建筑业收入	Construction	19.72	25.44	29.0
第三产业	Tertiary Industry	109.33	111.41	2.0
交通运输邮电业收入	Transport & Post	26.83	24.08	－10.2
批发贸易餐饮业收入	Wholesale and Retail Trade & Catering Services	35.33	46.29	31.0
社会服务业收入	Social Services	8.76	9.46	8.0
其他家庭经营收入	Others	38.41	31.64	－17.6
转移性收入	Transfer Income	62.84	67.72	7.8
财产性收入	Property Income	6.97	12.55	80.1

16－13 续表(continued)

指　　标	Item	2000	2001	2001年比2000年增长(%)或百分点 Increase Rate in 2001 over 2000
构成(%)	**Composition(%)**			
全年纯收入	Annual Net Income	100.0	100.0	
基本收入	Basic Income	94.9	94.3	-0.6
劳动者报酬	Laborers Remuneration	20.0	22.5	2.5
#乡村企业劳动报酬	From Township Enterprises	1.6	1.5	-0.1
家庭经营收入	Income from Household Business Operation	74.9	71.8	-3.1
第一产业	Primary Industry	63.9	60.6	-3.3
农业收入	Agriculture	49.1	45.9	-3.2
#种植业收入	Farming	43.5	40.9	-2.6
林业收入	Forestry	1.0	1.3	0.3
牧业收入	Animal Husbandry	13.7	13.2	-0.5
渔业收入	Fishery	0.1	0.1	持平
第二产业	Secondary Industry	3.1	3.3	0.2
工业收入	Industry	1.6	1.5	-0.1
建筑业收入	Construction	1.4	1.8	0.4
第三产业	Tertiary Industry	8.0	7.9	-0.1
交通运输邮电业收入	Transport & Post	2.0	1.7	-0.3
批发贸易餐饮业收入	Wholesal and Retail, Trade & Catering Services	2.6	3.3	0.7
社会服务业收入	Social Service	0.6	0.7	0.1
其他家庭经营收入	Others	2.8	2.2	-0.6
转移性收入	Transfer Income	4.6	4.8	0.2
财产性收入	Property Income	0.5	0.9	0.4

16－14 农民家庭人均总支出及构成
Per Capita Annual Gross Expenditures and Its Composition of Rural Households

指　　标	Item	2000	2001	2001年比2000年增长(%) Increase Rate in 2001 over 2000(%)
绝对数(元)	**Absolute Figure(yuan)**			
全年总支出	**Gross Expenditure**	1717.47	1709.92	－0.4
家庭经营费用支出	Expenditure for Household Business	447.10	442.15	－1.1
购置生产用固定资产支出	Expenditure for Purchasing Productive Fixed Assets	45.07	42.09	－6.7
税费支出	Taxes	22.00	22.07	0.3
村提留、乡统筹	Expenses for the Collective Apportion	11.13	10.84	－2.6
其他各项收费	Others	2.95	1.87	－36.8
生活消费支出	Living Expenditure for Consumption	1096.59	1098.39	0.2
转移性支出	Transfer Expenditures	89.03	86.81	－2.5
寄给和带给在外人口	Posting or Taking to Outside City	6.91	9.22	33.4
赠送农村外部亲友	Presenting to Relatives and Friends	6.84	5.45	－20.3
支付保险费支出	Payment of Insurance	0.15	0.69	360.0
财产性支出	Property Expenditures	3.59	5.71	59.1
非生产性贷款利息支出	Expenditure for Interest of Nonproductive Loan	0.53	1.41	166.0
其他支出	Other Payment	3.06	4.30	40.5
构成(%)	**Composition(%)**			
全年总支出	Gross Expenditure	100.0	100.0	
家庭经营费用支出	Expenditure for Household Business	26.0	25.9	－0.1
购置生产用固定资产支出	Expenditure for Purchasing Productive Fixed Assets	2.6	2.5	－0.1
税费支出	Taxes	1.3	1.3	持平
村提留、乡统筹	Expenses for the Collective Apportion	0.6	0.6	持平
其他各项收费	Othersx	0.2	0.1	－0.1
生活消费支出	Living Expenditure for Consumption	63.8	64.2	0.4
转移性支出	Transfer Expenditures	5.2	5.1	－0.1
寄给和带给在外人口	Posting or Taking to Outside City	0.4	0.5	0.1
赠送农村外部亲友	Presenting to Relatives and Friends	0.4	0.3	－0.1
支付保险费支出	Payment of Insurance	…	…	－
财产性支出	Property Expenditures	0.2	0.3	0.1
非生产性贷款利息支出	Expenditure for Interest of Nonproductive Loan	…	0.1	－
其他支出	Other Payment	0.2	0.3	0.1

16－15 农民人均现金收入
Per Capita Annual Cash Income of Rural Households

单位:元
(yuan)

指　　标	Item	2000	2001	2001年比2000年增长(%) Increase Rate in 2001 over 2000(%)
年内现金收入合计	**Total Annual Cash Income**	**1382.06**	**1421.19**	**2.8**
基本现金收入	Basic Cash Income	1022.06	1084.46	6.1
劳动者报酬	Laborers Remuneration	273.55	317.07	15.9
#乡镇企业报酬	From Township and Village Enterprises	21.89	22.51	2.8
家庭经营现金收入	Income from Household Business Operation	748.51	767.39	2.5
出售产品收入	Income from Saling Product	568.41	578.25	1.7
工业加工费收入	Industry Processing Fee	19.83	21.86	10.2
建筑业收入	Construction	25.74	30.99	20.4
交通运输邮电业收入	Transport & Post	40.62	34.09	－16.1
批发和零售贸易餐饮业收入	Wholesale and Retail, Trade & Catering Services	42.53	57.38	34.9
社会服务业收入	Social Service	10.93	11.33	3.7
文教卫生业收入	Culture, Education and Health Care	3.58	4.38	22.3
其他家庭经营现金收入	Others	34.27	27.27	－20.4
转移性现金收入	Transfer Cash Income	107.35	119.26	11.1
#在外人口寄回和带回	Income from Outside City	27.91	27.72	－0.7
亲友赠送	Income from Friends and Relatives as Presents	45.39	49.76	9.6
抚恤金	Pension	…	1.66	…
财产性现金收入	Property Cash Income	6.97	12.73	82.6
#租金收入	Rental Income	2.51	2.89	15.1
股息收入	Dividend	0.01	…	…
借贷性现金收入	Cash Income of Borrow Money and Loan	245.68	204.74	－16.7
银行、信用社贷款	Loans of Bank and Credit Union	63.25	41.74	－34.0
借入款	Borrowed Money	107.40	90.90	－15.4
收回借出款	Drawing Back Loan	23.18	17.99	－22.4
从银行、信用社取回存款	Drawing Money from Banks and Credit Union	27.64	25.45	－7.9
收回投资款	Disinvestment	0.07	0.18	157.1

16－16 农民人均现金支出及构成
Per Capita Annual Cash Expenditures of Rural Households

指　　标	Item	2000	2001	2001年比2000年增长(%) Increase Rate in 2001 over 2000(%)
绝对数(元)	Absolute Figure(yuan)			
支出合计	Total Expenditure	1063.25	1096.59	3.1
生产费用支出	Expenditure for Operating Costs	317.36	316.99	-0.1
缴纳税金	Taxes	18.50	20.30	9.7
村提留、乡统筹及其他	Expenses for the Collective Apportion and Other	12.83	12.36	-3.7
生活消费支出	Living Expenditure for Consumption	622.51	656.26	5.4
转移性支出	Transfer Expenditures	88.45	84.94	-4.0
#寄给在外人口	Posting to Outside City	6.89	9.06	31.5
赠送亲友	Present to Relatives and Friends	76.61	69.42	-9.4
非消费性现金支出	Nonconsurnptive Expenditure	129.08	140.48	8.8
归还银行、信用社存款	Deposits of Bank and Credit Union Recession	23.23	24.10	3.7
借出款	Loan	13.71	13.22	-3.6
归还借款	Loan Recession	71.26	74.18	4.1
存入银行、信用社	Deposit	18.74	27.97	49.3
购买股票及投资	Expenditure for Purchasing Stock and Investment	…	…	…
构成(%)	Composition(%)			
支出合计	Total Expenditure	100.0	100.0	
生产费用支出	Expenditure for Operating Costs	29.8	28.9	-0.9
缴纳税金	Taxes	1.7	1.9	0.2
村提留、乡统筹及其他	Expenses for the Collective Apportion and Other	1.2	1.1	-0.1
生活消费支出	Living Expenditure for Consumption	58.5	59.8	1.3
转移性支出	Transfer Expenditures	8.3	7.7	-0.6
非消费性现金支出	Nonconsurnptive Expenditure	12.1	12.8	0.7

16－17　农村居民家庭平均每人全年主要消费品消费量
Per Capita Consumption of Major Consumer Goods in Rural Households

单位:公斤
(kg)

指　　标	Item	2000	2001	2001 年比 2000 年增长(%) Increase Rate in 2001 over 2000(%)
粮　食	Grain	227.15	211.54	－6.9
#大　米	Rice	153.55	148.36	－3.4
食　油	Edible Oil	4.97	4.64	－6.6
肉禽及其制品	Meat, Poultry and Related Product	25.44	26.55	4.4
#猪　肉	Pork	23.83	24.80	4.1
家　禽	Poultry	1.00	1.16	16.0
蛋类及蛋制品	Eggs and Their Products	1.25	1.27	1.6
水产品	Aquatic Products	0.34	0.32	－5.9
#鱼　类	Fish	0.25	0.22	－12.0
虾　类	Shrimp	…	…	…
蔬　菜	Vegetables	139.14	131.18	－5.7
瓜　果	Melon and Fruits	5.41	6.18	14.2
食　糖	Sugar	0.91	0.92	1.1
卷烟(盒)	Cigarette(pack)	25.62	24.93	－2.7
酒	Liquor	5.77	6.03	4.5
棉布(米)	Cotton Cloth(m)	0.19	0.13	－31.6
化纤布	Chemical Fibre Cloth	0.14	0.13	－7.1
毛　料	Wollens	0.04	0.02	－50.0

16－18 每百户农村居民家庭年末耐用消费品拥有量

Annual Average Possession of Durable Consumer Goods Per 100 Rural Households

单位:台

(unit)

指　　标	Item	2000	2001	2001年比2000年增长(%) Increase Rate in 2001 over 2000(%)
自行车(辆)	Bicycle(unit)	8.2	7.2	-12.2
黑白电视机	Black/White TV Set	40.3	37.4	-7.2
彩色电视机	Color TV Set	21.2	25.9	22.2
电风扇	Electric Fan	22.0	26.2	19.1
电冰箱	Refrigerator	2.4	3.0	25.0
洗衣机	Washing Machine	12.1	12.7	5.0
收录机	Recorder	12.2	12.6	3.3
录像机	Video－recorder	1.0	1.3	30.0
照相机(架)	Camera	0.8	0.9	12.5
影碟机	Video Disc Player	7.7	10.6	37.7
无线寻呼机	Pager	0.8	1.1	37.5
大型家具	Large Furniture	392.6	400.5	2.0

主要统计指标解释

城镇居民家庭全部收入 指被调查城镇居民家庭全部的实际收入，包括经常或固定得到的收入和一次性收入。不包括周转性收入，如提取银行存款、向亲友借款、收回借出款以及其他各种暂收款。

城镇居民家庭可支配收入 指被调查的城镇居民家庭在支付个人所得税、财产税及其他经常性转移支出后所余下的实际收入。

城镇居民家庭消费性支出 指被调查的城镇居民家庭用于日常生活的全部支出，包括购买商品支出和文化生活、服务等非商品性支出。不包括罚没、丢失款和缴纳的各种税款（如个人所得税、牌照税、房产税等），也不包括个体劳动者生产经营过程中发生的各项费用。

城镇居民家庭购买商品支出 指被调查的城镇居民家庭为自用或赠送亲友而购买商品的全部支出，包括从商店、工厂、饮食业、工作单位食堂、集市以及直接从农民手中购买各种商品的开支。商品支出分为以下八类：食品；衣着；家庭设备用品及服务；医疗保健；交通与通信；娱乐、教育、文化服务；居住；杂项商品和服务。

农村居民家庭纯收入 指农村常住居民家庭总收入中，扣除从事生产和非生产经营费用支出、缴纳税款和上交承包集体任务金额以后剩余的，可直接用于进行生产性、非生产性建设投资、生活消费和积蓄的那一部分收入。农村居民家庭纯收入包括从事生产性和非生产性的经营收入，取自在外人口寄回带回和国家财政救济、各种补贴等非经营性收入；既包括货币收入，又包括自产自用的实物收入。但不包括向银行、信用社和向亲友借款等属于借贷性的收入。

农村居民家庭生活消费支出 指农村常住居民家庭用于日常生活的全部开支，是反映和研究农民家庭实际生活消费水平高低的重要指标。

Explanatory Notes on Main Statistical Indicators

Total Income of Urban Households refers to the total actual income of the sample households, including regular or fixed income and occasional income. The income of a circulating nature such as withdrawal from bank deposits, loans borrowed from relatives or friends, repayment of loans received and various temporary collection of money is excluded.

Disposable Income of Urban Households refers to the income of the sample households which can be used for daily expenses, i.e.. total income minus income tax, property tax and other current transfers.

Expenditure for Consumption of Urban Households refers to total expenditure of the sample households for consumption in daily life, including expenditure for various commodities and expenses for non – commodity items such as culture and service, etc., but excluding fines and confiscation, loss, tax payments (such as income tax, license tax, real estates tax, etc.) and various expenses by individual laborers for business purposes.

Expenditure for Purchases of Commodities of Urban Households refers to total expenses of the sample households for the purchases of commodities, for their own use or as gifts to relatives and friends, from shops, factories, catering trade, canteens, markets and from the peasants. Such expenditure is classified into eight categories: food, clothing, household appliances and services, health care and medical services, transport and communications, recreation, education and cultural services, housing, miscellaneous goods and services.

Net Income of Rural Households refers to the total income of the permanent residents of the rural households during a year after the deduction of the expenses for productive and non – productive business operation, the payment for taxes and the payment for collective units for their contracted tasks, which can then be spent for investments in productive and non – productive construction, for consumption in daily life and for savings deposit. It is a comprehensive indicator to show the actual level of the income of the peasants household. The net income of the rural households includes not only the income from the productive and non – productive business operation, but also the income from the non – business operation, such as the money remitted or brought back by the members of the household who are in other places, the government relief payment and various subsidies. It includes not only the money income, but also the income in kind. Butthe income from borrowing from banks, friends and relatives is excluded.

Expenditure of Rural Households for Consumption refers to total expenses of rural households on daily life, including expenses on food, clothing, housing, fuel, articles for daily use, and expenses on cultural life and services. This indicator is used to show the actual consumption level of peasants.

17

Seventeen

科技、教育、文化

Science, Education and Culture

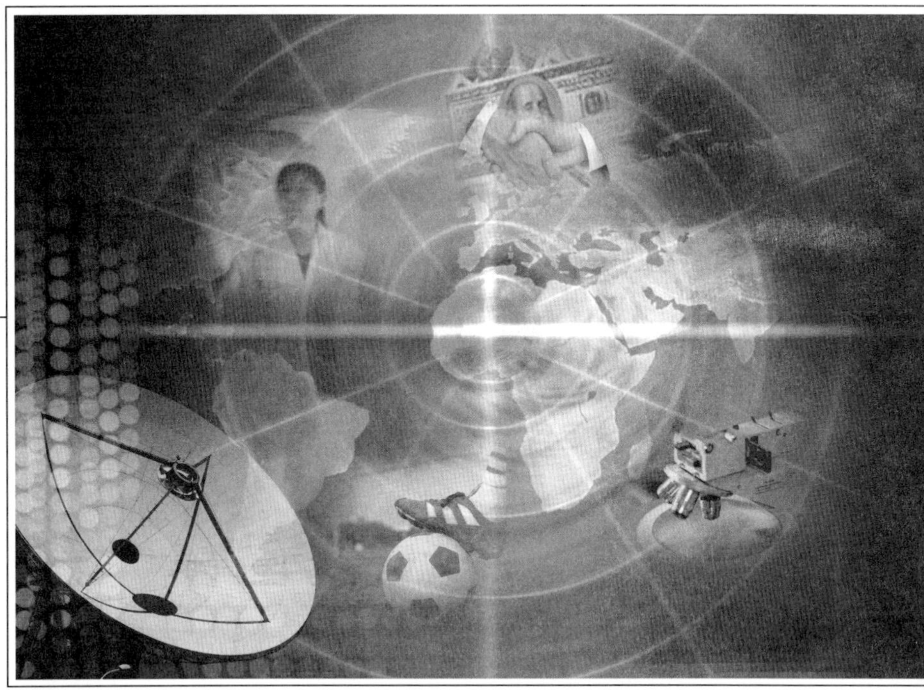

科技、事业、企业单位专业技术人员（人）（2001）
Number of Scientific and Technological Personnel of National Economy Units by Category (person)

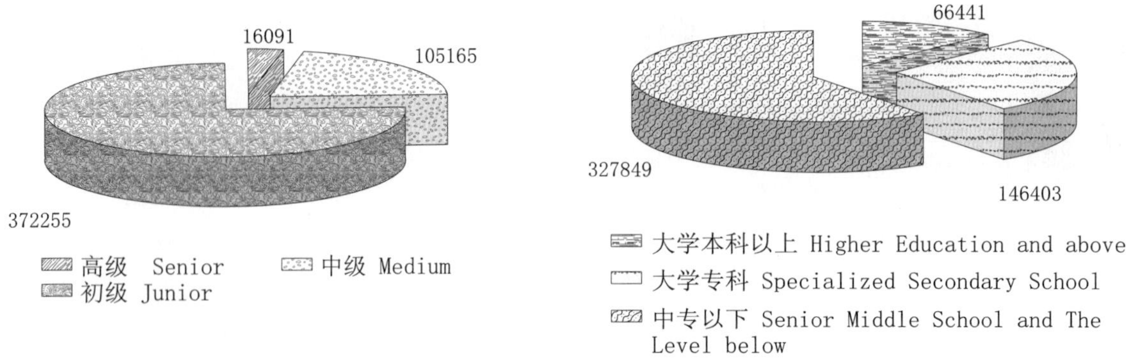

在校学生数（万人）
Student Enrollment(10000 persons)

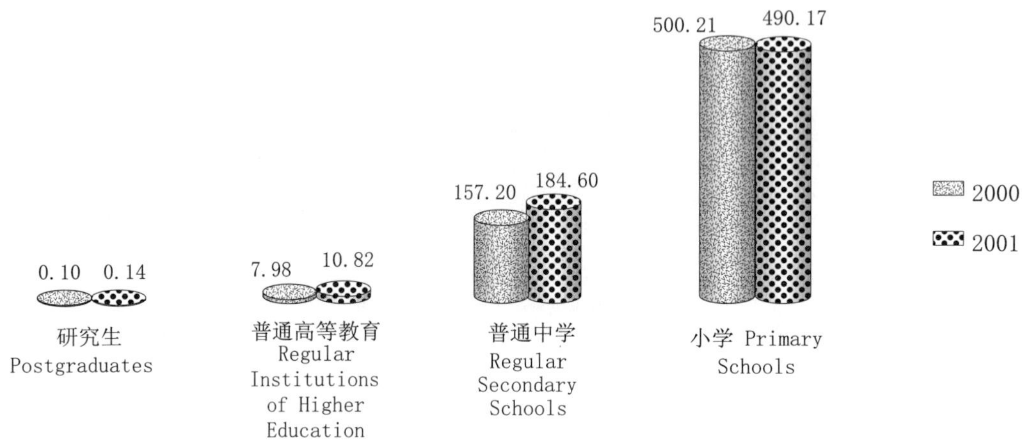

申请、授权专利情况（项）（2001）
Patent Applications and Certified(item)

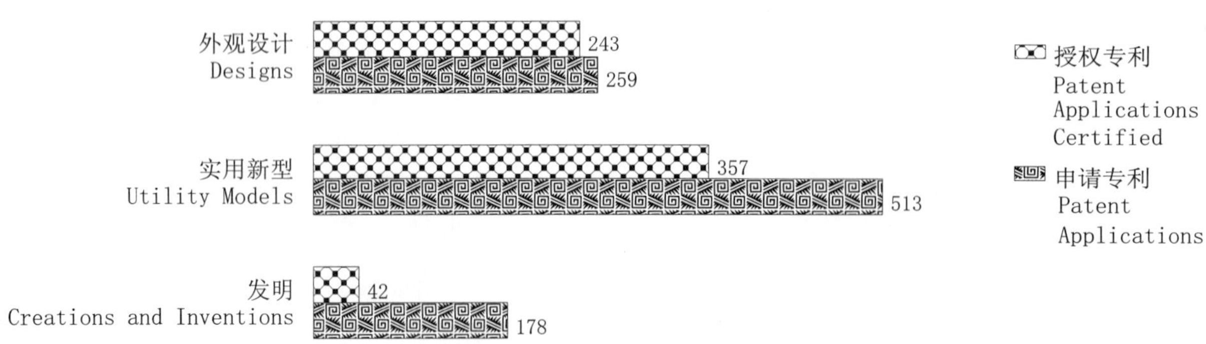

17-1 科 技 活 动 情 况
Basic Statistics on Scientific and Techno6logical Activities

指　　标	Item	2000	2001	2001年比2000年增长(%) Increase Rate in 2001 over 2000(%)
科技机构数(个)	**Number of Scientific Technological Research Institutions(unit)**	**310**	**266**	**-14.2**
科研单位	Scientific Reseach Unit	135	116	-14.1
大中型工业企业	In Large and Medium Industrial Enterprises	98	87	-11.2
高等院校	Institutions of Higher Education	33	25	-24.2
其他	Others	44	38	-13.6
科技活动人员数(人)	**Number of Persons Engaged in Scientific and Technological Activities(person)**	**34041**	**33989**	**-0.2**
科研单位	Scientific Reseach Unit	5089	4768	-6.3
大中型工业企业	In Large and Medium Industrial Enterprises	19554	19390	-0.8
高等院校	Institutions of Higher Education	2356	3023	28.3
其他	Others	7042	6808	-3.3
#科学家、工程师	Scientists and Engineers	18659	19452	4.2
#研究与试验发展人员(人年)	Personnel Engaged in Activities of Research and Experiment(person.year)	8131	9488	16.7
科技活动经费筹集总额(万元)	**Sum of Funds for Scientific and Technological Activities(10000 yuan)**	**116951**	**132538**	**13.3**
政府资金	From Government	33803	37123	9.8
企业资金	From Corporation	64772	72825	12.4
事业单位资金	From Institution	9265	6949	-25.0
金融机构贷款	Loans of Financial Institutions	6580	7055	7.2
国外资金	From Abroad	60	93	55.0
其他	Others	2471	8493	243.7
科技活动经费支出总额(万元)	**Expenditures for Scientific and Technological Activities(10000 yuan)**	**108748**	**133142**	**22.4**
#内部支出	Inner Expenditure	101052	124165	22.9
#劳务费	Service Fee	29805	112200	276.4
固定资产购建支出	Purchases for Fixed Assets	31915	35430	11.0
财政对科技拨款(万元)	Government Expenditure for Scientific Research(10000 yuan)	30774	35393	15.0
科技拨款占财政支出的比重(%)	Expenditure for Scientific Research as Percentage in Financial Expenditure(%)	1.53	1.29	-0.2 (个百分点)
研究与发展经费(R&D)支出(万元)	Expenditures for Research and Development(10000 yuan)	41774	53486	28.0
R&D经费支出占国内生产总值的比重(%)	R&D Expenditure as Percentage in GDP(%)	0.42	0.49	0.1 (个百分点)

注:本表数据采用R&D清查数据口径。

Note:Data in this table were obtained from statistics of R&D investgation.

17－2 事业、企业单位各类专业人员情况

Number of Scientific and Technological Personnel of National Economy Units by Category

单位：人
(person)

指　　标	Item	2000	2001	2001年比2000年增长(%) Increase Rate in 2001 over 2000(%)
总　　计	**Total**	**530704**	**540693**	**1.9**
#女性	Female	198127	203603	2.8
按专业分	**By Specialized Subject**			
#工程技术人员	Engineering Technical Personnel	67299	66473	-1.2
农业技术人员	Agricultural Technical Personnel	25833	26491	2.5
卫生技术人员	Medical Technical Personnel	70667	71203	0.8
科学研究人员	Scientific Research Personnel	1724	1682	-2.4
教学人员	Teaching Personnel	294295	307008	4.3
经济人员	Economic Personnel	23490	21706	-7.6
财会人员	Financial Accounting Personnel	22342	21460	-3.9
统计人员	Statistical Personnel	3430	3213	-6.3
新闻出版、播音人员	Media and Publishing Personnel	3693	3688	-0.1
翻译人员	Translator	240	233	-2.9
艺术人员	Art Personnel	2112	2096	-0.8
按专业技术职务分	**By Professional Titles**			
高　级	Senior	15205	16091	5.8
中　级	Midium	101897	105165	3.2
初　级	Junior	413602	372255	-10.0
按学历分	**By Education Background**			
大学本科以上	Higher Education and above	63726	66441	4.3
大学专科	Specialized Secondary School	136548	146403	7.2
中专以下	Senior Middle School and the Level below	330430	327849	-0.8

17-3 县及县以上政府属独立研究与开发机构科技活动基本情况
Main Statistics of Scientific and Technological Activities of Research and Development Institutions Managed by Government at and above County Level

指标	Item	2000	2001	2001年比2000年增长(%) Increase Rate in 2001 over 2000(%)
科技机构数(个)	**Number of Institutions (unit)**	**135**	**116**	**-14.1**
#县级以上研究与开发机构	Research and Development Institutions above County Level	103	84	-22.6
县级以上部门属科技情报与文献机构	Scientifical and Technological Information and Document Institutions Managed by Department above County Level	10	10	持平
县级政府部门属研究与开发机构	Research and Development Institutions Managed by Government at County Level	21	20	-5.0
社会、人文科学研究机构	Social Sciences and Humanities Institutions	1	2	50.0
科技活动人员数(人)	**Science and Technology Personnel(person)**	**5127**	**4768**	**-7.0**
#县级以上研究与开发机构	Research and Development Institutions above County Level	4661	4255	-8.7
县级以上部门属科技情报与文献机构	Scientifical and Technological Information and Document Institutions Managed by Department above County Level	138	139	0.7
县级政府部门属研究与开发机构	Research and Development Institutions Managed by Government at County Level	203	202	-0.5
社会、人文科学研究机构	Social Sciences and Humanities Institutions	125	172	27.3
#科学家、工程师	**Scientists and Engineers**	**3278**	**2820**	**-14.0**
#县级以上研究与开发机构	Research and Development Institutions above County Level	3051	2557	-19.3
县级以上部门属科技情报与文献机构	Scientifical and Technological Information and Document Institutions Managed by Department above County Level	84	84	持平
县级政府部门属研究与开发机构	Research and Development Institutions Managed by Government at County Level	36	34	-5.9
社会、人文科学研究机构	Social Sciences and Humanities Institutions	107	145	26.2

17－3 续表(continued)

指　　标	Item	2000	2001	2001 年比 2000 年增长(%) Increase Rate in 2001 over 2000(%)
科技活动经费收入总额(万元)	**Funding for Scientific and Technological Activities(10000 yuan)**	**35024.6**	**39581.4**	**13.0**
#县级以上研究与开发机构	Research and Development Institutions above County Level	33547.7	37738.8	11.1
县级以上部门属科技情报与文献机构	Scientifical and Technological Information and Document Institutions Managed by Department above County Level	639.4	668.2	4.3
县级政府部门属研究与开发机构	Research and Development Institutions Managed by Government at County Level	342.4	446.9	23.4
社会、人文科学研究机构	Social Sciences and Humanities Institutions	495.1	727.5	32.0
科技活动经费支出总额(万元)	**Expenditures for Scientific and Technological Activities(10000 yuan)**	**30559.5**	**36994.0**	**21.1**
#县级以上研究与开发机构	Research and Development Institutions above County Level	29204.6	35149.6	16.9
县级以上部门属科技情报与文献机构	Scientifical and Technological Information and Document Institutions Managed by Department above County Level	528.9	649.6	18.6
县级政府部门属研究与开发机构	Research and Development Institutions Managed by Government at County Level	316	449.3	29.7
社会、人文科学研究机构	Social Sciences and Humanities Institutions	510	745.5	31.6
#研究与试验发展经费支出	**Expenditures for Activities of Research and Experiment**	**4728.5**	**4767.9**	**0.8**
#县级以上研究与开发机构	Research and Development Institutions above County Level	4702	4755.3	36.9
县级政府部门属研究与开发机构	Research and Development Institutions Managed by Government at County Level	26.5	12.6	－110.3

注：县级以上研究与开发机构减少主要是科研机构体制改革

Note: There has been a decrease in research and development institutions above county level because of the structural reform of scientific research.

17－4 高等学校科技活动基本情况
Basic Statistics on Scientific and Technological Activities of Higher Education

指　　标	Item	2000	2001	2001 年比 2000 年增长(%) Increase Rate in 2001 over 2000(%)
从事科技活动人数(人)	**S&T Personnel(person)**	**2356**	**3030**	**28.6**
#教师	Teacher	2100	2393	14.0
其他技术人员	Other Technical Personnel	240	577	140.4
辅助人员	Assistant	16	60	275.0
从事研究与发展活动人员(人年)(1)	**Personnel Engaged in Activities of Research and Development(person. year)**	**752**	**1069**	**42.2**
#正教授	Professor	151	124	－17.9
副教授	Associate Professor	257	353	37.4
讲师	Lecturer	258	134	－48.1
助教	Assistant	86	458	432.6
研究与发展机构(个)	Research and Development Institutions (unit)	33	33	持平
机构中研究与发展人员(人)	Research and Development Personnel in the Institutions(person)	336	197	－41.4
当年科技经费收入(万元)	**Income of Scientific and Technological Activities(10000 yuan)**	**3252**	**4604**	**41.6**
#科研事业费	Expenses for Scientific Research	706	1235	74.9
研究与发展课题(项)	**Project on Research and Development(unit)**	**555**	**912**	**64.3**
#基础研究	Basic Research	169	332	96.5
应用研究	Applied Research	274	291	6.2
试验发展	Activities of Experiment	112	289	158.0
研究与发展成果	Achievement of Research and Development			
出版科学专著(部)	Scientific Work Published(unit)	100	94	－6.0
发表学术论文(篇)	Research Paper Issued(unit)	4499	4503	0.1
科技成果获奖(项)	Scientific Achievement Rewarded(unit)	92	42	－54.4

注:(1)指折合全时数。

Note:The (1) Refers to the full－time persons.

17－5 大中型工业企业科技活动人员情况
Basic Statistics on Persons Engaged in Scientific and Technological Activities in Large and Medium Industrial Enterprises

单位:人
(person)

指　　标	Item	科技活动员 Persons Engaged in Scientific and Technological Activities	全时人员 Full－time Personnel	非全时人员 Part－time Personnel	#科学家和工程师 Scientists and Engineers	#研究与试验人员 Research and Experiment Personnel
总　　计	**Total**	**19390**	**6980**	**12410**	**9754**	**9287**
按企业规模分组	**Grouped by Scale of Enterprises**					
大型企业	Large	15027	4775	10252	7517	7511
特大型企业	Oversize	1297	992	305	917	1017
大一型企业	Size－one	5450	1796	3654	2919	2079
大二型企业	Size－two	8280	1987	6293	3681	4415
中型企业	Medium	4363	2205	2158	2237	1776
中一型企业	Size－one	1497	565	932	654	694
中二型企业	Size－two	2866	1640	1226	1583	1082
按登记注册类型分组	**Grouped by Registration**					
内资企业	Domestic－funded	19147	6824	12323	9626	9044
国有	State－owned Enterprise	11573	4343	7230	5835	4986
#大型企业	of which:Large	7847	2455	5392	3921	3596
国有独资公司	State－owned Corporation	6130	1679	4451	2964	3207
#大型企业	of which:Large	5881	1578	4303	2878	3061
其他有限责任公司	Other Limited Liability Corporations	523	343	180	305	358
股份有限公司	Share－holding Corporations Ltd	921	459	462	522	493
港澳台商投资	Enterprises Funded by Hong kong,Macao and Taiwan	10	10		10	10
#大型企业	of which:Large	10	10		10	10
港澳台商投资股份有限公司	Share－holding Corporations Ltd Funded by Hong kong,Macao and Taiwan	10	10		10	10
外商投资	Foreign Funded Enterprises	233	146	87	118	233
#大型企业	of which:Large	233	146	87	118	233
中外合资经营	Enterprises of China and Foreign Countries Joint Venture	233	146	87	118	233
煤炭采选业	Coal Mining and Processing	350	122	228	319	197

17－5 续表(continued)

指　　标	Item	科技活动员 Persons Engaged in Scientific and Technological Activities	全时人员 Full－time Personnel	非全时人员 Part－time Personnel	# 科学家和工程师 Scientists and Engineers	# 研究与试验人员 Research and Experiment Personnel
非金属矿采选业	Nonmetal Minerals Mining and Processing	160	75	85	160	59
饮料制造业	Beverage Production	302	165	137	184	68
烟草加工业	Tobacco Processing	95	53	42	66	46
化学原料及化学制品制造业	Raw Chemical Materials and Chemical Products	804	337	467	348	432
医药制造业	Medical and Pharmaceutical Products	18	15	3	18	18
橡胶制品业	Rubber Products	393	225	168	208	152
塑料制品业	Plastic Products	20	18	2	18	10
非金属矿物制品业	Nonmetal Mineral Products	283	95	188	132	127
黑色金属冶炼及压延加工业	Smelting and Pressing of Ferrous Metals	1021	365	656	476	312
有色金属冶炼及压延加工业	Smelting and Pressing of Nonferrous Metals	1649	886	763	929	1014
金属制品业	Metal Products	312	95	217	187	12
普通机械制造业	Ordinary Machinery Manufacturing	654	366	288	392	299
专用设备制造业	Special Purposes Equipment Manufacturing	852	650	202	521	536
交通运输设备制造业	Transportation Equipment Manufacturing	9571	2319	7252	4302	4948
武器弹药制造业	Weapon and Munition Equipment Manufacturing	34	10	24	3	34
电气机械及器材制造业	Electric Equipment and Machinery	728	349	379	336	452
电子及通信设备制造业	Electronic and Telecommunications Equipment	1333	560	773	598	440
仪器仪表及文化办公用机械制造业	Instruments, Meters, Cultural and Official Machinery	123	97	26	69	61
电力、蒸汽、热水的生产和供应业	Electric Power, Steam and Hot Water Production and Supply	688	178	510	488	70
中央属	At Centre Level	12764	4232	8532	6209	6552
省(直辖市)属	At Province (Municipality Directly under The Central Government) Level	4676	1702	2974	2502	1743
地区属	At District Level	1701	884	817	861	832
县属	At County Level	93	59	34	51	24
其他属	At Other Level	156	103	53	131	136

17－6 大中型工业企业科技活动经费筹集情况
Basic Statistics on Sum of Funds for Scientific and Technological Activities in Large and Medium Industrial Enterprises

单位：万元
(10000 yuan)

指　　标	Item	科技活动经费筹集总额 Sum of Funds for Scientific and Technological Activities	企业资金 From Corporation	金融机构贷款 Loans of Financial Institutions	政府资金 From Government	事业单位资金 From Institution	其他 Others
总　　计	Total	75692.4	59130.2	3859.6	11039.5	61	1602.1
按企业规模分组	Grouped by Scale of Enterprises						
大型企业	Large	63737.4	51448.6	2294.6	8940.9		1053.3
特大型企业	Oversize	16926.8	16651.8		275		
大一型企业	Size－one	30191.9	26922.9	2000	1083.5		185.5
大二型企业	Size－two	16618.7	7873.9	294.6	7582.4		867.8
中型企业	Medium	11955	7681.6	1565	2098.6	61	548.8
中一型企业	Size－one	4138.8	2511.8	852	335	51	389
中二型企业	Size－two	7816.2	5169.8	713	1763.6	10	159.8
按登记注册类型分组	Grouped by Registration						
内资企业	Domestic－funded	75110.2	58548	3859.6	11039.5	61	1602.1
国有	State－owned Enterprise	45600.2	35103.1	3574.6	6266.5		656
#大型企业	of which: Large	35171.3	28142.6	2009.6	4508.4		510.7
国有独资公司	State－owned Corporation	21747.5	16612.9	285	4039	10	800.6
#大型企业	of which: Large	21161.1	16440	285	4039		397.1
其他有限责任公司	Other Limited Liability Corporations	1304.7	848.2		405.5	51	
股份有限公司	Share－holding Corporations Ltd	6457.8	5983.8		328.5		145.5
港澳台商投资	Enterprises Funded by Hong kong, Macao and Taiwan	22	22				
#大型企业	of which: Large	22	22				
港澳台商投资股份有限公司	Share－holding Corporations Ltd Funded by Hong kong, Macao and Taiwan	22	22				
外商投资	Foreign Funded Enterprises	560.2	560.2				
#大型企业	of which: Large	560.2	560.2				
中外合资经营	Enterprises of China and Foreign Countries Joint Venture	560.2	560.2				
煤炭采选业	Coal Mining and Processing	1536	1526		10		

17－6 续表(continued)

单位:万元
(10000 yuan)

指　　标	Item	科技活动经费筹集总额 Sum of Funds for Scientific and Technological Activities	企业资金 From Corporation	金融机构贷款 Loans of Financial Institutions	政府资金 From Government	事业单位资金 From Institution	其他 Others
非金属矿采选业	Nonmetal Minerals Mining and Processing	241.3	241.3				
饮料制造业	Beverage Production	2439.2	2414.4		24.8		
烟草加工业	Tobacco Processing	426.6	426.6				
化学原料及化学制品制造业	Raw Chemical Materials and Chemical Products	2359.5	1447.5	840	72		
医药制造业	Medical and Pharmaceutical Products	250	250				
橡胶制品业	Rubber Products	3918.5	3883.5		35		
塑料制品业	Plastic Products	42.4	42.4				
非金属矿物制品业	Nonmetal Mineral Products	1099.3	165.8	285	624		24.5
黑色金属冶炼及压延加工业	Smelting and Pressing of Ferrous Metals	10617.3	10617.3				
有色金属冶炼及压延加工业	Smelting and Pressing of Nonferrous Metals	17079.8	14744.8	2000	335		
金属制品业	Metal Products	1238.6	1138.6		100		
普通机械制造业	Ordinary Machinery Manufacturing	1995.8	1611.8		384		
专用设备制造业	Special Purposes Equipment Manufacturing	3197.4	2138.4	563	496		
交通运输设备制造业	Transportation Equipment Manufacturing	19457.2	10182.8	159.6	7661.7	61	1392.1
武器弹药制造业	Weapon and Munition Equipment Manufacturing	20	20				
电气机械及器材制造业	Electric Equipment and Machinery	1960.7	1701.2		219.5		40
电子及通信设备制造业	Electronic and Telecommunications Equipment	3475.1	2297.1		1032.5		145.5
仪器仪表及文化办公用机械制造业	Instruments, Meters, Cultural and Official Machinery	156.3	126.3		30		
电力、蒸汽、热水的生产和供应业	Electric Power, Steam and Hot Water Production and Supply	4181.4	4154.4	12	15		
中央属	At Centre Level	50253.5	39454.1	734.6	8611.7	61	1392.1
省(直辖市)属	At Province (Municipality Directly under The Central Government) Level	17319.4	12772.6	2840	1521.3		185.5
地区属	At District Level	7191	6032.5	285	849		24.5
县属	At County Level	282.4	282.4				
其他属	At Other Level	646.1	588.6		57.5		

17－7 大中型工业企业科技活动经费支出情况
Expenditures for Scientific and Technological Activities in Large and Medium Industrial Enterprises

单位：万元
(10000 yuan)

指标	Item	科技活动经费支出总额 Expenditures for Scientific and Technological Activities	内部支出 Inner Expenditure	#劳务费 Service Fee	#原材料费 Raw Material Fee	#非基建项目购买和自制责备支出 Expenditure for Purchasing Non－Capital Construction Project and Equipment Made by Oneself
总计	Total	72628.0	65702.2	16089.5	15742.0	18776.5
按企业规模分组	Grouped by Scale of Enterprises					
大型企业	Large	61531.7	55343.7	12735.5	10881.9	17730.7
特大型企业	Oversize	16800.4	15567.5	2509.7	1429.5	5099.8
大一型企业	Size－one	30310.1	27642.3	5345.8	6512.6	10998.6
大二型企业	Size－two	14421.2	12133.9	4880	2939.8	1632.3
中型企业	Medium	11096.3	10358.5	3354	4860.1	1045.8
中一型企业	Size－one	3570.2	3480.2	1093.0	1654.0	181.0
中二型企业	Size－two	7526.1	6878.3	2261.0	3206.1	864.8
按登记注册类型分组	Grouped by Registration					
内资企业	Domestic－funded	72061.1	65172.7	15839.2	15638.0	18761.2
国有	State－owned Enterprise	44316.2	40461.5	11163.3	10534.9	8157.6
#大型企业	of which: Large	34772.8	31655.9	8290.5	6257.7	7209.6
国有独资公司	State－owned Corporation	19915.0	17266.8	3042.5	2878.8	8788.1
#大型企业	of which: Large	19391.7	16743.5	2889.4	2827.9	8776.1
其他有限责任公司	Other Limited Liability Corporations	1373.1	1373.1	433.1	742.5	106.8
股份有限公司	Share－holding Corporations Ltd	6456.8	6071.3	1200.3	1481.8	1708.7
港澳台商投资	Enterprises Funded by Hong kong, Macao and Taiwan	22.0	22.0	14.0	8.0	
#大型企业	of which: Large	22.0	22.0	14.0	8.0	
港澳台商投资股份有限公司	Share－holding Corporations Ltd Funded by Hong kong, Macao and Taiwan	22.0	22.0	14.0	8.0	
外商投资	Foreign Funded Enterprises	544.9	507.5	236.3	96.0	15.3
#大型企业	of which: Large	544.9	507.5	236.3	96.0	15.3
中外合资经营	Enterprises of China and Foreign Countries Joint Venture	544.9	507.5	236.3	96.0	15.3
按工业行业大类分组	Grouped by Industrial Sector					
煤炭采选业	Coal Mining and Processing	1536.0	1064.5	377.3	331.0	167.0

17－7 续表 1(continued)

单位:万元
(10000 yuan)

指　　标	Item	科技活动经费支出总额 Expenditures for Scientific and Technological Activities	内部支出 Inner Expenditure	#劳务费 Service Fee	#原材料费 Raw Material Fee	#非基建项目购买和自制责备支出 Expenditure for Purchasing Non－Capital Construction Project and Equipment Made by Oneself
非金属矿采选业	Nonmetal Minerals Mining and Processing	241.3	241.3	166.5	20.2	54.6
饮料制造业	Beverage Production	2339.0	2141.0	574.3	1024.1	298.0
烟草加工业	Tobacco Processing	427.6	427.6	147.3	176.6	5.9
化学原料及化学制品制造业	Raw Chemical Materials and Chemical Products	1971.0	1863.0	490.1	910.6	184.0
医药制造业	Medical and Pharmaceutical Products	234.7	197.3	43.2	16.4	15.3
橡胶制品业	Rubber Products	3918.5	3898.5	546.0	826.0	1200.0
塑料制品业	Plastic Products	42.4	37.8	20.4	8.0	
非金属矿物制品业	Nonmetal Mineral Products	862.3	806.3	80.0	118.0	594.5
黑色金属冶炼及压延加工业	Smelting and Pressing of Ferrous Metals	10433.1	10420.3	426.8	1397.0	7575.2
有色金属冶炼及压延加工业	Smelting and Pressing of Nonferrous Metals	17031.7	15278.8	2474.9	1262.0	5151.4
金属制品业	Metal Products	1238.6	1238.6	434.0	3.9	114.0
普通机械制造业	Ordinary Machinery Manufacturing	2016.6	1765.6	440.9	787.6	400.7
专用设备制造业	Special Purposes Equipment Manufacturing	2802.0	2453.0	972.9	1248.9	163.2
交通运输设备制造业	Transportation Equipment Manufacturing	17475.3	17236.3	6543.9	5103.5	1854.8
武器弹药制造业	Weapon and Munition Equipment Manufacturing	20.0	20.0	16.0		
电气机械及器材制造业	Electric Equipment and Machinery	2013.2	1897.2	516.4	928.9	174.5
电子及通信设备制造业	Electronic and Telecommunications Equipment	3460.1	3064.4	1071	1051.3	540.9
仪器仪表及文化办公用机械制造业	Instruments, Meters, Cultural and Official Machinery	156.3	152.3	103.3	16.3	15.8
电力、蒸汽、热水的生产和供应业	Electric Power, Steam and Hot Water Production and Supply	4408.3	1498.4	644.3	511.7	266.7
按隶属关系分组	**Grouped by Subordination**					
中央属	At Centre Level	48109.3	45223.4	10422.9	8696.5	14828.8
省(直辖市)属	At Province(Municipality Directly under The Central Government) Level	16562.2	12693.3	4082.8	4684.1	1857.8
地区属	At District Level	6950.0	6787.0	1383.7	1817.7	1952.9
县属	At County Level	191.9	183.9	55.3	101.3	17.2
其他属	At Other Level	814.6	814.6	144.8	442.4	119.8

17－7 续表 2(continued)

单位:万元
(10000 yuan)

指　　标	Item	# 其他 Other	# 内部支出中研究与试验发展支出 Expenditure for Development of Research and Experiment in Inner Expenditure	外部支出中研究与试验发展支出 Expenditure for Development of Research and Experiment in Outer Expenditure
总　　计	**Total**	15094.2	36156.8	6925.8
按企业规模分组	**Grouped by Scale of Enterprises**			
大型企业	Large	13995.6	29091.8	6188.0
特大型企业	Oversize	6528.5	6565.0	1232.9
大一型企业	Size－one	4785.3	13016.5	2667.8
大二型企业	Size－two	2681.8	9510.3	2287.3
中型企业	Medium	1098.6	7065.0	737.8
中一型企业	Size－one	552.2	2775.8	90.0
中二型企业	Size－two	546.4	4289.2	647.8
按登记注册类型分组	**Grouped by Registration**			
内资企业	Domestic－funded	14934.3	35764.9	6888.4
国有	State－owned Enterprise	10605.7	24274.0	3854.7
# 大型企业	of which: Large	9898.1	18293.8	3116.9
国有独资公司	State－owned Corporation	2557.4	5956.3	2648.2
# 大型企业	of which: Large	2250.1	5433.0	2648.2
其他有限责任公司	Other Limited Liability Corporations	90.7	617.0	
股份有限公司	Share－holding Corporations Ltd	1680.5	4917.6	385.5
港澳台商投资	Enterprises Funded by Hong kong, Macao and Taiwan		22.0	
# 大型企业	of which: Large		22.0	
港澳台商投资股份有限公司	Share－holding Corporations Ltd Funded by Hong kong, Macao and Taiwan		22.0	
外商投资	Foreign Funded Enterprises	159.9	369.9	37.4
# 大型企业	of which: Large	159.9	369.9	37.4
中外合资经营	Enterprises of China and Foreign Countries Joint Venture	159.9	369.9	37.4
按工业行业大类分组	**Grouped by Industrial Sector**			
煤炭采选业	Coal Mining and Processing	189.2	950.2	471.5

17－7 续表 3(continued)

单位:万元
(10000 yuan)

指标	Item	# 其他 Other	# 内部支出中研究与试验发展支出 Expenditure for Development of Research and Experiment in Inner Expenditure	外部支出中研究与试验发展支出 Expenditure for Development of Research and Experiment in Outer Expenditure
非金属矿采选业	Nonmetal Minerals Mining and Processing		121.0	
饮料制造业	Beverage Production	244.6	1617.6	198.0
烟草加工业	Tobacco Processing	97.8	197.6	
化学原料及化学制品制造业	Raw Chemical Materials and Chemical Products	278.3	1280.0	108.0
医药制造业	Medical and Pharmaceutical Products	122.4	59.7	37.4
橡胶制品业	Rubber Products	1326.5	3492.0	20.0
塑料制品业	Plastic Products	9.4	22.0	4.6
非金属矿物制品业	Nonmetal Mineral Products	13.8	659.9	56.0
黑色金属冶炼及压延加工业	Smelting and Pressing of Ferrous Metals	1021.3	342.0	12.8
有色金属冶炼及压延加工业	Smelting and Pressing of Nonferrous Metals	6390.5	6296.8	1752.9
金属制品业	Metal Products	686.7	7.7	
普通机械制造业	Ordinary Machinery Manufacturing	136.4	1228.2	251.0
专用设备制造业	Special Purposes Equipment Manufacturing	68.0	1866.3	349.0
交通运输设备制造业	Transportation Equipment Manufacturing	3734.1	15287.6	239.0
武器弹药制造业	Weapon and Munition Equipment Manufacturing	4.0	20.0	
电气机械及器材制造业	Electric Equipment and Machinery	277.4	964.9	116.0
电子及通信设备制造业	Electronic and Telecommunications Equipment	401.2	1576.4	395.7
仪器仪表及文化办公用机械制造业	Instruments, Meters, Cultural and Official Machinery	16.9	49.0	4.0
电力、蒸汽、热水的生产和供应业	Electric Power, Steam and Hot Water Production and Supply	75.7	117.9	2909.9
按隶属关系分组	**Grouped by Subordination**			
中央属	At Centre Level	11275.2	22232.1	2885.9
省(直辖市)属	At Province (Municipality Directly Under the Central Government) Level	2068.6	7807.4	3868.9
地区属	At District Level	1632.7	5566.2	163.0
县属	At County Level	10.1	47.0	8.0
其他属	At Other Level	107.6	504.1	

17－8 民营科技企业情况
Scientific and Technological Research Institutions Running by Local People

指　　标	Item	2000	2001
机构数(个)	Number of Institutions(unit)	353	328
#集体经济单位	Collective－owned Units	74	64
从业人员(人)	Employment(person)	21821	24409
#从事科技活动的中高级职称人数	Personnels with Senior or Midium Titles Engaged in Scientific and Technological Activities	3632	3290
技工贸收入(万元)	Income(10000 yuan)	280000	299448
研究开发支出(万元)	Expenditures(10000 yuan)	10000	10008

注:本资料由省科委提供。两年数据口径不一致,不可比。

Note:Data in this table are obtained from Science Commission. Data in 2001 are inconsistant with 2000.

17－9 专 利 授 权 情 况
Status of Patent Applications Certified

单位:件
(item)

指　　标	Item	2000	2001	2001年比2000年增长(%) Increase Rate in 2001 over 2000(%)
申请专利总计	Patent Applications	986	950	－3.7
按种类分	Grouped by Sort			
发明	Creations and Inventions	173	178	2.9
实用新型	Utility Models	503	513	2.0
外观设计	Designs	310	259	－16.5
按对象分	Grouped by Applicant			
非职务发明创造	Non－service Creations and Inventions	708	684	－3.4
职务发明创造	Service Creations and Inventions	278	266	－4.3

17－9 续表(continued)

单位:件
(item)

指　　标	Item	2000	2001	2001 年比 2000 年增长(%) Increase Rate in 2001 over 2000(%)
大专院校	Universities and Colleges	3	2	－33.3
科研单位	Research Institutions	20	26	30.0
工矿企业	Industrial and Mineral Enterprises	250	234	－6.4
机关团体	Government Agencies and Organizations	5	4	－20.0
授权专利总计	**Patent Applications Certified**	**710**	**642**	**－9.6**
按种类分	**Grouped by Sort**			
发明	Creations and Inventions	65	42	－35.4
实用新型	Utility Models	377	357	－5.3
外观设计	Designs	268	243	－9.3
按对象分	**Grouped by Applicant**			
非职务发明创造	Non－service Creations and Inventions	449	443	－1.3
职务发明创造	Service Creations and Inventions	261	199	－23.8
大专院校	Universities and Colleges	2	4	100.0
科研单位	Research Institutions	11	16	45.5
工矿企业	Industrial and Mineral Enterprises	244	177	－27.5
机关团体	Government Agencies and Organizations	4	2	－50.0

17－10　教育事业基本情况
Basic Statistics on Education

指　　标	Item	2000	2001	2001年比2000年增长(%) Increase Rate in 2001 over 2000(%)
学校数(所)	**Number of Schools**			
研究生	Postgraduates	7	7	持平
普通高等学校	Regular Institutions of Higher Education	24	30	25.0
成人高等教育	Adult Higher Education			
#成人高等学校	Adult Higher Education Schools	10	7	-30.0
普通中等专业学校	Specialized Secondary Schools	104	89	-14.4
中等技术学校	Technical Secondary Schools	79	66	-16.5
中等师范学校	Teacher Secondary Schools	25	23	-8.0
成人中等专业教育	Adult Secondary Education			
#成人中等专业学校	Adult Specialized Secondary Schools	34	33	-2.9
普通中学	Regular Secondary Schools	1953	2222	13.8
高中	Senior Secondary Schools	305	328	7.5
初中	Junior Secondary Schools	1648	1523	-7.6
九年一贯制学校	Schools of Nine－year Consistent System	…	371	
职业中学	Vocational Secondary Schools	258	217	-15.9
小学	Primary Schools	17985	15339	-14.7
幼儿园	Kindergartens	1435	1006	-29.9
特殊教育	Special Education	28	35	25.0
工读学校	Missed Children Schools	3	3	持平
成人中学	Adult Secondary Schools	27	7	-74.1
成人技术培训学校	Adult Technical Training Schools	15235	14153	-7.1
成人初等学校	Adult Primary Schools	4387	6586	50.1
专任教师(人)	**Number of Full－time Teachers(person)**			
研究生	Postgraduates	614	694	13.0
普通高等学校	Regular Institutions of Higher Education	7240	9007	24.4
成人高等教育	Adult Higher Education	1109	856	-22.8
普通中等专业学校	Specialized Secondary Schools	6628	5748	-13.3
中等技术学校	Technical Secondary Schools	4808	3937	-18.1
中等师范学校	Teacher Secondary Schools	1820	1811	-0.5
成人中等专业教育	Adult Secondary Education	1484	1480	-0.3
普通中学	Regular Secondary Schools	81156	88079	8.5
高中	Senior Secondary Schools	11658	13613	16.8
初中	Junior Secondary Schools	69498	74466	7.1
职业中学	Vocational Secondary Schools	5368	5001	-6.8
小学	Primary Schools	174822	173238	-0.9
幼儿园	Kindergartens	14204	6991	-50.8

17－10 续表 1(continued)

指　　标	Item	2000	2001	2001 年比 2000 年增长(%) Increase Rate in 2001 over 2000(%)
特殊教育	Special Education	1482	485	－67.3
工读学校	Missed Children Schools	35	34	－2.9
成人中学	Adult Secondary Schools	61	67	9.8
成人技术培训学校	Adult Technical Training Schools	3530	1514	－57.1
成人初等学校	Adult Primary Schools	2177	2985	37.1
招生数(人)	**New Student Enrollment(person)**			
研究生	Postgraduates	458	659	43.9
普通高等教育	Regular Institutions of Higher Education	33718	44597	32.3
成人高等教育	Adult Higher Education	35109	38298	9.1
＃成人高等学校	Adult Higher Education Schools	16403	13735	－16.3
普通中等专业学校	Specialized Secondary Schools	38447	31159	－19.0
中等技术学校	Technical Secondary Schools	29188	22744	－22.1
中等师范学校	Teacher Secondary Schools	9259	8415	－9.1
成人中等专业教育	Adult Secondary Education	14171	10083	－28.8
＃成人中等专业学校	Adult Specialized Secondary Schools	8256	7077	－14.3
普通中学	Regular Secondary Schools	641859	747907	16.5
高中	Senior Secondary Schools	84393	109691	30.0
初中	Junior Secondary Schools	557466	638216	14.5
职业中学	Vocational Secondary Schools	31824	30896	－2.9
小学	Primary Schools	810492	830232	2.4
幼儿园	Kindergartens	444311	429725	－3.3
特殊教育	Special Education	2225	2690	20.9
工读学校	Missed Children Schools	901	813	－9.8
成人中学	Adult Secondary Schools	1458	926	－36.5
成人技术培训学校	Adult Technical Training Schools	3165266	3364734	6.3
成人初等学校	Adult Primary Schools	316615	311600	－1.6
在校学生(人)	**Student Enrollment(person)**			
研究生	Postgraduates	1002	1418	41.5
普通高等教育	Regular Institutions of Higher Education	79833	108159	35.5
成人高等教育	Adult Highe Education	57627	82648	43.4
＃成人高等学校	Adult Higher Education Schools	26569	31337	17.9
普通中等专业学校	Specialized Secondary Schools	119991	114765	－4.4
中等技术学校	Technical Secondary Schools	91187	87673	－3.9
中等师范学校	Teacher Secondary Schools	28804	27092	－5.9
成人中等专业教育	Adult Secondary Education	40270	36650	－9.0
＃成人中等专业学校	Adult Specialized Secondary Schools	26219	23061	－12.0

17－10 续表 2(continued)

指　　标	Item	2000	2001	2001 年比 2000 年增长(%) Increase Rate in 2001 over 2000(%)
普通中学	Regular Secondary Schools	1572025	1846015	17.4
高中	Senior Secondary Schools	191059	244571	28.0
初中	Junior Secondary Schools	1380966	1601444	16.0
职业中学	Vocational Secondary Schools	79937	74427	－6.9
小学	Primary Schools	5002082	4901665	－2.0
幼儿园	Kindergartens	496044	493770	－0.5
特殊教育	Special Education	15845	16007	1.0
工读学校	Missed Children Schools	918	837	－8.8
成人中学	Adult Secondary Schools	3699	3316	－10.4
成人技术培训学校	Adult Technical Training Schools	3158125	3425939	8.5
成人初等学校	Adult Primary Schools	319027	342411	7.3
毕业生数(人)	**Graduates(person)**			
研究生	Postgraduates	218	231	6.0
普通高等教育	Regular Institutions of Higher Education	13737	15092	9.9
成人高等教育	Adult Higher Education	12977	14507	11.8
#成人高等学校	Adult Higher Education Schools	6886	6208	－9.8
普通中等专业学校	Specialized Secondary Schools	35003	34361	－1.8
中等技术学校	Technical Secondary Schools	25468	24727	－2.9
中等师范学校	Teacher Secondary Schools	9535	9634	1.0
成人中等专业教育	Adult Secondary Education	12115	13217	9.1
#成人中等专业学校	Adult Specialized Secondary Schools	9329	7550	－19.1
普通中学	Regular Secondary Schools	377175	409768	8.6
高中	Senior Secondary Schools	45846	47121	2.8
初中	Junior Secondary Schools	331329	362647	9.5
职业中学	Vocational Secondary Schools	24438	21530	－11.9
小学	Primary Schools	732301	778446	6.3
幼儿园	Kindergartens		277319	
特殊教育	Special Education	960	1414	47.3
工读学校	Missed Children Schools	854	616	－27.9
成人中学	Adult Secondary Schools	1081	281	－74.0
成人技术培训学校	Adult Technical Training Schools	3144644	3378679	7.4
成人初等学校	Adult Primary Schools	285360	298330	4.5

注：1.研究生学校数指培养研究生单位数。2.教育厅对上年数据有所调整。

Note: 1.Schools for postgraduates refer to the number of organizations for cultivating postgraduates. 2.Data in 2000 are adjusted by Education Department.

17－11 各级各类学校基本情况(2001)
Basic Statistics in Various Schools

单位:人
(person)

指　　标	Item	学校数(所) Number of School(unit)	专任教师数 Full－time Teachers	在校生数 Students Enrollment	毕业生数 Graduates	招生数 New Students Enrollments
总　　计	Total	39687	293149	11348027	5243791	5844319
研究生	Postgraduates	(7)	(694)	1418	231	659
普通高等学校	Regular Institutions of Higher Education	30	9007	108159	15092	44597
成人高等教育	Adult Higher Education			82648	14507	38298
#成人高等学校	Adult Higher Education Schools	7	856	31337	6208	13735
普通中等专业学校	Specialized Secondary Schools	89	5748	114765	34361	31159
成人中等专业教育	Adult Secondary Education			36650	13217	10083
#成人中等专业学校	Adult Specialized Secondary Schools	33	1480	23061	7550	7077
普通中学	Regular Secondary Schools	2222	88079	1846015	409768	747907
职业中学	Vocational Secondary Schools	217	5001	74427	21530	30896
小学	Primary Schools	15339	173238	4901665	778446	830232
幼儿园	Kindergartens	1006	6991	493770	277319	429725
特殊教育学校	Special Education	35	485	16007	1414	2690
工读学校	Missed Children Schools	3	34	837	616	813
成人中学	Adult Secondary Schools	7	67	3316	281	926
成人技术培训学校	Adult Technical Training Schools	14153	1514	3425939	3378679	3364734
成人初等学校	Adult Primary Schools	6586	2985	242411	298330	311600

17－12 各级学校女学生和女教师情况
Statistics on Female Students and Teachers

单位：人
(person)

类别	Sort	2000	2001	2001年比2000年增长(%) Increase Rate in 2001 over 2000(%)
女学生数	Number of Female Students			
高等学校	Institutions of Higher Education	54128	81913	51.3
中等专业学校	Specialized Secondary Schools	65040	65962	1.4
普通中学	Regular Secondary Schools	663294	792994	19.6
职业中学	Vocational Secondary Schools	34900	32010	－8.3
小学	Primary Schools	2319257	2276008	－1.9
女教师数	Number of Female Teachers			
高等学校	Institutions of Higher Education	3404	4172	22.6
中等专业学校	Specialized Secondary Schools	3528	3262	－7.5
普通中学	Regular Secondary Schools	24631	27324	10.9
职业中学	Vocational Secondary Schools	1657	1603	－3.3
小学	Primary Schools	66103	68944	4.3

17－13 研究生和留学生情况
Number of Postgraduates and Students Studying Abroad

单位：人
(person)

类别	Sort	2000	2001	2001年比2000年增长(%) Increase Rate in 2001 over 2000(%)
招研究生数	Number of New Students Enrollment of Postgraduate	458	659	43.9
#女性	Female	165	219	32.7
在校研究生数	Number of Students Enrollment of Postgraduate	1002	1418	41.5
#女性	Female	356	497	39.6
毕业研究生数	Number of Graduates of Postgraduate	218	231	6.0
#女性	Female	75	85	13.3

17－14 高等学校基本情况(2001)
Basic Statistics for Institution of Higher Education

单位:人
(person)

类别	Sort	学校数(所) Number of Schools(unit)	毕业生数 Graduates	招生数 New Students Enrollments	在校学生人数 Students Enrollment	教职员工 Teachers, Staff and Workers	#专任教师 Full－time Teachers	#正、副教授 Professors and Asso. Prof.
总计	Total	30	15092	44597	108159	17959	9007	2724
综合大学	Comprehensive Universities	1	4144	7412	19835	2832	1251	507
理工院校	Science and Engineering	1	1600	3838	10149	2139	977	391
医药院校	Medicine	4	1644	5761	17166	2686	1436	523
师范院校	Teacher Training	10	5427	16770	36837	4485	2323	612
财经院校	Economics and Finance	2	1106	4447	10880	1210	732	223
民族院校	Nationality Academy	1	650	2304	6073	898	469	154
职业技术学院	Vocational Technical Universities	11	521	4065	7219	3709	1819	314

17－15 高等学校分科专任教师数和学生数(2001)
Number of Full－time Teachers and Students in Institutions of Higher Education by Field of Study

单位:人
(person)

类别	Sort	专任教师数 Full－time Teachers	教授 Professors	副教授 Asso. Prof.	讲师 Lecturers	助教 Assistants	教员 Instructors	毕业生人数 Graduates	招生人数 New Student Enrollment	在校学生人数 Student Enrollment
总计	Total	9007	505	2219	3377	2181	725	15092	44597	108159
哲学	Philosophy	326	10	74	168	62	12	43	62	204
经济学	Economics	686	25	146	278	176	61	324	1131	3158
法学	Law	402	11	100	179	92	20	1164	3993	9337
教育学	Education	683	10	132	288	183	70	1202	3075	6499
文学	Literature	1730	66	345	650	469	200	3169	9311	19825
历史学	History	201	11	52	85	43	10	316	374	1419
理学	Science	1752	108	490	667	343	144	2864	6956	16971
工学	Engineering	1214	90	349	374	320	81	2440	7449	17840
农学	Agriculture	538	39	118	198	165	18	394	731	2933
医学	Medicine	1182	124	351	368	263	76	1688	5741	16995
管理学	Administrators	293	11	62	122	65	33	1488	5774	12978

17－16 中等专业学校基本情况(2001)
Basic Statistics on Specialized Secondary Schools

单位:人
(person)

类别	Sort	学校数(所) Number of Schools(unit)	毕业生数 Graduates	招生数 New Student Enrollment	在校学生 Student Enrollment	教职员工 Teachers, Staff and Workers	#专任教师 Full－time Teachers
总计	Total	89	34361	31159	114765	9736	5748
中等技术学校	Secondary Technical School	66	24727	22744	87673	7060	3937
工业学校	Industry	18	6490	6868	29936	2062	1190
农业学校	Agriculture	10	7347	3328	16939	1075	562
林业学校	Forestry	1	403	243	1284	143	71
医药学校	Medicine	12	2698	5273	14479	1185	585
财经学校	Economics and Finance	15	4346	4035	13553	1398	806
政法学校	Politics and Law	4	205	664	1962	373	157
体育学校	Physical Culture	2	642	823	2760	324	215
艺术学校	Art	2	435	153	781	25	24
其他学校	Others	2	2161	1357	5979	475	327
中等师范学校	Teacher Training	23	9634	8415	27092	2676	1811
#幼儿师范	Preschool Teacher Training	1	176	357	762	77	54

17－17 初中毕业生和小学毕业生升学率及小学学龄儿童入学率
Percentage of Graduates of Junior Secondary Schools and Primary Schools Entering Higher Level Schools and Percentage of School－Age Children Enrolled

类别	Sort	2000	2001	2001年比2000年增长(%) Increase Rate in 2001 over 2000(%)
初中毕业生	Graduates of Junior Secondary Schools			
初中毕业生数(万人)	Graduates of Junior Secondary Schools(10000 persons)	34.2	37.26	8.95
高级中等学校招生数(万人)	Students Entering Senior Secondary Schools(10000 persons)	14.94	16.94	13.39
升学率(%)	Percentage of Graduates of Junior Secondary Schools Entering Senior Secondary Schools(%)	43.7	45.5	1.8(百分点)
小学毕业生	Graduates of Primary Schools			
小学毕业生数(万人)	Graduates of Primary Schools(10000 persons)	73.23	77.84	6.30
初级中等学校招生数(万人)	Students Entering Junior Secondary Schools(10000 persons)	57.65	65.70	13.96
升学率(%)	Percentage of Graduates of Primary Schools Entering Junior Secondary Schools(%)	78.7	84.4	5.7(百分点)
小学学龄儿童	School－Age Children			
学龄儿童数(万人)	School－Age Children(10000 persons)	434.37	433.27	－0.25
已入学学龄儿童数(万人)	School－Age Children Enrolled in Schools(10000 persons)	427.65	425.27	－0.56
入学率(%)	Enrollment Rate (%)	98.5	98.2	－0.3(百分点)

17－18 各级各类成人教育基本情况(2001)

Student Enrollment in Adult Schools by Level and Type

单位:人
(person)

类别	Sort	学校(所) Number of Schools (unit)	毕业生数 Graduates	招生数 New Student Enrollment	在校学生 Student Enrollment	教职员工 Tea chers, Staff and Workers	#专任教师 Full－time Teachers
总计	**Total**	6633	326335	360907	465025	19957	5388
成人高等教育	**Higher Education Institutions for Adults**	7	14507	38298	82648	1732	856
广播电视大学	Radio and TV Universities	1	3404	5757	12545	929	389
职工高等学校	Worker's Colleges	3	598	1622	3517	289	208
教育学院	Educational Colleges	3	2206	6356	15275	514	259
普通高校举办	Run by Regular HEIs		8299	24563	51311		
函授	Divisions of Correspondence		2076	9682	20293		
夜大学	Evening Schools		115	471	1128		
成人脱产	Short－cycle Courses for Adults		6108	14410	29890		
成人中等教育	**Secondary Education for Adult**	33	13217	10083	36650	2629	1480
广播电视中专	Radio and TV Specialized Secondary Schools	3	4434	3626	13081	726	333
职工中专	Specialized Secondary Schools for Staff	18	1678	2565	7257	855	548
干部中专	Specialized Seeondary Schools for Cadres	7	668	607	1389	378	198
函授中专	Corrspondence Specialized Secondary Schools	2	719	185	1120	595	350
教师进修学校	In－service Teachers Training Schools	3	51	94	214	75	51
其他类学校举办	Run by Regular Secondary School		5667	3006	13589		
成人中学	**General Secondary Schools for Adults**	7	281	926	3316	86	67
初中	Junior	7	281	926	3316	86	67
成人初等学校	**Adult Primary Schools**	6586	298330	311600	342411	15510	2985
职工初等学校	Worker Primary Schools	2	600	142	142	41	34
农民初等学校	Peasant Primary Schools	6584	297730	311458	342269	15469	2951
#扫盲班	Literacy Courses	6540	295837	308401	334282	15264	2798

17－19 文化事业机构和人员
Number of Institutions and Personnel in Culture

指　　标	Item	2000	2001	2001 年比 2000 年增长(%) Increase Rate in 2001 over 2000(%)
机构数总计(个)	**Number of Institutions(unit)**	**1295**	**1364**	**5.3**
#艺术事业	Art	63	61	－3.2
文物事业	Cultural Relics	95	97	2.1
图书馆事业	Libraries	89	90	1.1
群众文化事业	Mass Culture	1030	1097	6.5
其他文化事业	Other Culture Units	14	10	－28.6
人员数总计(人)	**Number of Persons Engaged(person)**	**6824**	**6754**	**－1.0**
#艺术事业	Art	2688	2636	－1.9
文物事业	Cultural Relics	606	589	－2.8
图书馆事业	Libraries	876	887	1.3
群众文化事业	Mass Culture	2142	2229	4.1
其他文化事业	Other Culture Units	484	309	－36.2

注:2000 年数字有变动。

Note:Datas in 2000 were changed.

17－20　文化部门艺术剧团情况(2001)
Basic Statistics on Art Troupes of Culture Department

指　标	Item	剧团数(个) Number of Troupes (unit)	从业人员(人) Number of Staff and Workers (person)	国内演出(场) Times of Domestic Performance (show)	#在农村演出 Shows in Rural Areas	国内观众人数(万人次) Number of Domestic Spectators (10000 person－times)	国外出访演出(场) Number of Performances Outbound (show)
总　计	**Total**	**28**	**2116**	**3144**	**750**	**349.3**	**1696**
按隶属关系分	**Grouped by Administrative Relationship**						
国有剧团	State－owned	28	2116	3144	750	349.3	1696
按剧种分	**Grouped by Art Troupes**						
话剧、儿童剧、滑稽剧团	Drama, Children's play and Comedy Troupes	1	65	90		3.6	
歌剧、舞剧、歌舞剧团	Song and Dance Troupes	2	252	109	60	36.9	
乐团、歌舞团、轻音乐团	Philharmonic Troupes, Song and Dance and Light Music Troups	4	361	558	140	41	161
戏曲剧团	Local Opera Troupes	14	954	978	368	98.2	
曲艺、杂技、木偶、皮影团	Recitation and Ballad Troupe, Acrobatics and Circus Troupes, Puppet Show Troupes and Shadow Play Troupe	3	268	1177	43	69.5	1535
文工团	Cultural Troupes	4	216	232	139	100.1	

17－21　文化娱乐业基本情况(2001)
Culture and Entertainment Undertakings

类　别	Sort	机构数(个) Institution (unit)	从业人员(人) Employment (person)	主营营业收入(万元) Primary Business Income(10000 yuan)	主营业务利润(万元) Primary Business Profit(10000 yuan)
总　计	**Total**	**2995**	**8870**	**19753.7**	**7612**
歌舞厅、舞厅、夜总会、卡拉OK厅	Singing and Dancing Room, Dancing Room, Karoke Room	942	4500	12044.7	3783.7
电子游艺厅	Video Games Room	595	1146	2106.5	1090.5
台球厅	Billiards Room	251	462	690.5	411.3
保龄球馆	Bowling Alley	6	92	99.9	23.3
高尔夫球场	Golf Course	1	57		

17－22 艺术表演场所情况(2001)
Basic Statistics on Art Preformances Places

类别	Sort	机构数(个) Number of Institutions (unit)	从业人员(人) Number of Staff and Workers (person)	座席数(个) Seats (unit)	演(映)出场次(场) Number of Performances (show)	#艺术演出场次 Art Performance	观众人次(万人次) Number of Spectators (10000 person－times)	#艺术演出场次 Art Performances
总计	Toatl	13	313	9106	10829	482	59.6	18.6
按隶属关系分	Grouped by Administrative Relationship							
省级	Province Level	4	155	3146	276	134	11.5	10.5
地级	Prefectural Level	7	110	3947	10176	220	41.7	6.2
县级	County Level	2	48	2013	327	128	6.4	1.9
按系统分	Grouped by Administration Relationship							
文化系统	Cultural Organizations and Institutions	13	313	9106	10829	482	59.6	18.6

17－23 群众艺术馆和文化馆(站)情况(2001)
Basic Statistics on Mass Art Centers and Culture Centers(Stations)

指标	Item	合计 Total	群众艺术馆 Mass Art Centers	文化馆 Culture Centers	文化站 Culture Stations
馆(站)个数(个)	Number of Centers(unit)	1097	11	83	1003
录像放映场次(场次)	Number of Videotape Shows(shows)	9366		1921	7445
观众人次(万人次)	Number of Spectators(10000 person－times)	78.9		12.2	66.7
组织文艺活动次数(次)	Organizing Art Performances (time)	3753	188	1349	2216
举办业余文艺训练班(班次)	Conducting Amateur Art Training Courses(class)	961	55	389	517
结业人数(万人次)	Number of Persons Completed(10000 person－times)	3.2	0.2	10	20
举办展览个数(个)	Number of Conducting Exhibitions(unit)	847	16	202	629

17－24 公共图书馆情况(2001)
Basic Statistics on Public Libraries

指标	Item	合计 Total	省级 Province Level	地级 Prefectural Level	县级 County Level
机构数(个)	Number of Public Libraries (unit)	90	1	8	81
从业人员(人)	Number of Staff and Workers (person)	887	129	242	516
总藏量(万册)	Total Collections(10000 volumes)	686	218.6	150.3	317.1
#图书	Books	567.8	181.9	127	258.9
建筑面积(万平方米)	Floor Space of Buildings(10000 sq.m)	14.2	0.1	7.5	6.6
#书库	Stack Rooms	2.6		1.1	1.5
阅览室	Reading Rooms	3		1.5	1.5
阅览座位(万个)	Seats in Reading Rooms(10000 seats)	1		0.3	0.7
总流通人次(万人次)	Total Number of Circulation (10000 persen－tims)	193.9	7.8	67	119.1
书刊外借人次	Number of Person－times of Lending	102.6	5.9	29	67.7
书刊外借册次(万册次)	Number of Books Borrowed by the Readers(10000 Volume－times)	159.6	6.3	47.4	105.9

17－25 图书分类出版数量(2001)
Number of Books Published by Category

类别	Sort	种数(种) Number of Publications (kind)	#新出版 New－Published	总印数(万册、张) Total Printed (10000 copies)	总印张数(千印张) Total Printed Sheets (1000 sheets)
总计	Total	961	486	12767	567538
#书籍	Books	869	457	3947	119309
#哲学、社会科学	Philosophy and Social Sciences	54	42	13	1537
文化教育	Culture and Education	536	180	12601	551101
文学艺术	Literature and Arts	178	83	41	4227
少年儿童读物	Juvenile and Children's books	79	24	278	4202
#课本	Textbooks	92	29	8820	448229
#大专课本	For Colleges and Universities	4	4	1	132
中学课本	For Secondary Schools	27	11	2822	237989
小学课本	For Primary Schools	36	13	5888	201151
教学用书	For Teaching References	24		75	6584

17－26 杂志分类出版数量(2001)
Number of Magazines Published by Category

类　别	Sort	种数(种) Number of Publications(kind)	每期平均印数(万册) Average Publication Per Issue(10000 copies)	总印数(万册、份) Total Printed (10000 copies)	总印张数(千印张) Total Printed Sheets (1000 sheets)
总　计	**Total**	**97**	**95**	**1210**	**40394**
综　合	Comprehensive	6	5	54	1970
哲学、社会科学	Philosophy and Social Sciences	38	48	597	19193
自然科学技术	Natural Sciences and Technology	34	12	106	3981
文化教育	Culture and Education	7	10	109	3429
文学艺术	Literature and Arts	9	16	293	9738
少年儿童读物	Juvenile and Children's books	2	4	49	2024

17－27 报纸分类出版数量(2001)
Number of Newspaper Published by Category

类　别	Sort	种数(种) Number of Publications (kind)	每期平均印数(万份) Average Publication Per Issue (10000 copies)	总印数(万份) Total Printed (10000 copies)	总印张数(千印张) Total Printed Sheets (1000 sheets)
总　计	**Total**	**39**	**136**	**31677**	**734231**
综合报	Comprehensive	31	111	28511	677857
专业报	Specialized	8	25	3166	56374
在总计中	of the Total				
贵州日报	Guizhou Daily	1	12	4195	167820
贵州都市报	Guizhou Urban Newspaper	1	15	5475	164250
贵阳晚报	Guiyang Evening Newspaper	1	20	7280	218400
文摘	Press Digest	1	17	1598	7990
每周广播电视报	Broadcasting and Television Newspaper Every Week	1	11	571	11731

17－28 电视台、广播电台情况(一)
Basic Statistics on Broadcasting and Television Stations(1)

指　标	Item	2000	2001	2001年比2000年增长(%) Increase Rate in 2001 over 2000(%)
电视台	Television Stations			
无线电视台(座)	No－wire Television Stations(unit)	10	10	
自办节目(套)	Self－Produced Programs(set)	16	31	93.8
平均每周播出时间(小时)	Program Hours Per Week(hour)	1485	2359	58.9
电视人口覆盖率(%)	Viewer Rating(%)	85.3	87.2	1.9(百分点)
广播电台	Broadcasting Stations			
无线电台(座)	No－wire Broadcasting Stations(unit)	4	4	
自办节目(套)	Self－produced Programs (set)	14	14	
平均每周播出时间(小时)	Program Hours Per Week(hour)	189	189	
广播人口覆盖率(%)	Listener Rating(%)	76.2	78.3	2.1(百分点)
乡镇广播电视站(座)	Number of Broadcasting and TV Stations in Township and Town(unit)	1281	1289	0.6
通广播的乡镇(个)	Number of Towship and Town with Broadcasting(unit)	1434	1402	－2.2
通电视的乡镇(个)	Number of Towship and Town with TV(unit)	1463	1453	－0.7
通广播的村(个)	Number of Village with Broadcating(unit)	20055	22140	10.4
通电视的村(个)	Number of Village with TV (unit)	23643	24494	3.6

注:1.表中个别指标数据起伏过大的,为年度统计口径变动所致。2.电视台自办节目套数增加的原因是有线电视台和电视台合并增加的有线节目套数。

Note: 1. Statistical coverage of this table was adjusted, therefore figures of some indicators occurred with striking fluctuations in growth. 2. The self－produced programs increase because the wire TV stations and TV stations merged.

17－29 电视台、广播电台情况(二)(2001)
Basic Statistics on Broadcasting and Television Stations(2)

类　别	Sort	自办节目(套) Self－Produced Programs(set)	平均每周(日)播出时间(小时) Program Hours Per Week(Day)(hour)	#自办节目 Self－Produced Programs	#新闻 News	#教育 Education	#文艺 Entertainment	全年制作节目时间(小时) Annual Production of Programs(hour)
无线电视台	No－wire Television Stations							
省　级	Province Level	6	546	542	42	12	307	4 979
地　级	Prefectural Level	20	1 565	1 471	66	58	964	10 798
县　级	Connty Level	5	249	104	21	19	22	4 519
无线广播电台	No－wire Broadcasting Stations							
省　级	Province Level	4	83	78	4	1	41	28 561
地　级	Prefectural Level	4	61	56	7		23	19 751
县　级	Connty Level	6	44	27	6	1	8	8 601

注:有线电视台已与电视台合并、所以无有线电视台数据。

Note: There are not data of wire television stations because the wire TV stations and TV stations merged.

主要统计指标解释

普通高等学校 指按照国家规定的设置标准和审批程序批准举办，通过国家统一招生考试，招收高中毕业生为主要培养对象，实施高等教育的全日制大学、独立设置的学院和高等专科学校、短期职业大学。

成人高等学校 指按照国家有关规定审批，招收通过全国成人高教统一招生考试的具有高中毕业或同等学历的在职从业人员，利用脱产、半脱产、业余或函授等多种形式对其实施高等学历教育，培养高等教育专科或本科毕业水平的专门人才，修业年限、课程设置和总学时数均按高等学历教育要求付诸实施的学校。包括广播电视大学、职工高等学校、农民高等学校、管理干部学院、教育学院、独立设置的函授学院等。

小学学龄儿童入学率 指调查范围内已入小学学习的学龄儿童占校内外学龄儿童总数（包括弱智儿童，不包括盲聋哑儿童）的比重。计算公式为：

$$小学学龄儿童入学率 = \frac{已入学的小学学龄儿童数}{校内外小学学龄儿童总数} \times 100\%$$

独立研究与开发机构 指有明确的任务和研究方向，有一定学术水平的业务骨干和一定数量的研究人员，具有研究、开发、开展学术工作的基本条件，主要进行科学研究与技术开发活动，并且在行政上有独立的组织形式，财务上独立核算盈亏，有权与其他单位签订合同，在银行有单独户头的单位。包括国务院各部门、中国科学院、中国社会科学院和各省、自治区、直辖市以及地（市）以上〔含地（市）〕各部门所属的国有科学研究与技术开发机构。

独立研究与开发机构职工 指在独立研究与开发机构工作，并由其支付工资的人员。包括长期职工、临时职工和招聘人员，不包括编制以外的离休、退休人员和停薪留职人员。

研究与发展经费支出 指用于研究与发展课题活动（基础研究、应用研究、实验发展）的全部实际支出，包括用于研究与发展课题活动的直接支出和间接用于研究与发展活动的支出（如研究院、所管理费，维持研究院、所正常运转的必需费用和与研究发展有关的基本建设支出）。

科学家和工程师 指具有大学本科及以上学历和不具备上述学历但有高、中级职称的人员。

其他科技人员 指大专、中专毕业和具有初级职称的从事科技活动人员。

专业技术人员 指已取得科学技术职称，或大学、中专的理、工、农、医科系毕业，以及国民经济各部门从工作实践中提拔，从事理、工、农、医等自然科学技术的研究、教学、生产的专业人员和在机关、企业、事业中从事科学技术业务管理工作的专业人员。

工程技术人员 指在国民经济各行业中从事工程技术工作的自然科学技术专业人员，包括高级工程师、工程师、助理工程师、技术员和未评定职称的技术人员。

农业技术人员 指在国民经济各行业中从事农业技术工作的自然科学技术专业人员，包括高级农艺师、农艺师、助理农艺师、技术员和未评定职称的技术人员。

卫生技术人员 指在国民经济各行业中从事卫生医务工作的自然科学技术专业人员，包括正副主任医师、主治医师、医师、医（护）士和未评定职称的技术人员。

科学研究人员 指在国民经济各行业中从事科学技术活动的自然科学技术专业人员，包括正副研究员、助理研究员、研究实习员、技术员和未评定职称的技术人员。

自然科学教学人员 指在国民经济各行业中从事自然科学技术教学活动的专业人员，包括正副教授、讲师、助教、教师和在中学从事自然科学技术教学活动的人员。

发明 是专利法及其实施细则所称的发明，指对有关产品、方法或其改进所提出的新的技术方案。

实用新型 是专利法及其实施细则所称的实用新型，指对产品的形状、构造或者其结合所提出的适于实用的新的技术方案。

外观设计 专利法及其实施细则所称的外观设计,指对产品的形状、图案、色彩或者其结合所作出的富有美感并适于工业上应用的新设计。

文化事业机构 指从事专业文化工作和为专业文化工作服务的独立建制的单位。不包括这些单位另外举办独立核算的其他机构和各部门的业余文化组织。

艺术表演团体 指从事戏曲、音乐、舞蹈、杂技等专业艺术表演,有独立帐户的单位,不包括半工半艺、半农半艺和民间职业剧团。

电影放映单位 指具有放映机器设备、固定或不固定的放映场所与专职或兼职的放映技术人员,经有关部门登记批准,经常为一定的观众对象放映电影的机构。包括经批准对外开放进行营业,并与电影发行放映管理机构分帐的专用放映单位和军委系统租片单位。

艺术表演观众人数(人次) 指售票、包场演出或民族地区免费演出的艺术表演观众人次数,不包括彩排审查和内部观摩演出的观看人次数。

Explanatory Notes on Main Statistical Indicators

Regular Institutions of Higher Learning refer to educational establishments set up according to the government evaluation and approval procedures, enrolling graduates from senior secondary schools and providing higher education courses and training for senior professionals. They include full – time universities, colleges, high professional schools and short – term professional universities.

Institutions of Higher Learning for Adults refer to educational establishments, set up in line with relevant rules approved by the government, enrolling staff and workers with senior secondary school or equivalent education , and providing higher education courses in many forms of full time, part time, spare time, or correspondence for adults. Professionals thus trained receive a qualification equivalent to graduates studying regular courses at regular universities, colleges and professional colleges. Institutions of higher learning for adults include Radio and TV universities, schools of high education for staff and workers and peasants, colleges for management cadres, pedagogical colleges, independent correspondence colleges.

Enrollment Rate of Primary School Age Children refers to the proportion of school age children enrolled at schools to the total number of school age children both in and outside schools (including retarded children , but excluding blind, deaf and mute children). The formula is:

Enrollment Rate of Primary School age Children = (Total Primary School age Children at Schools)? (Total Primary School age Children Both at and Outside Schools) ? 00%

Independent Research and Development Institutions refer to the state owned institutions which have direct mission and research purpose, a certain number of core member with higher research level and a certain number of research personnel, necessary conditions for R & D activities and engaging in scientific research and technological development. The institutions also have their own independent organization and finance, authority to sign contracts with other units, with their own accounts in banks. Independent research and development institutions include the institutions attached to central government agencies, Chinese Academy of Sciences. Chinese Academy of Social Sciences and the institutions attached to local governments.

Personnel of Independent Research and Development Institutions refers to the persons working in and receiving payment from research and development institutions. It includes regular full – time and temporary staff and workers and employees working on contracts, but excludes retirees and persons leaving their work without payment but still retaining their posts, who are not on the employee list.

Total Expenditure on Research and Development refers to all actual expenditure made for R&D (basic research, applied research and experimental development) in reference period. It includes direct expenditure on R&D and indirect expenditure on R&D (including management and necessary administrative expenses of research institutes, investment in capital construction relating to R&D).

Scientists and Engineers refer to persons who have completed university or higher education or obtained titles of senior and middle level professional positions.

Other Technical Personnel refers to persons involved in science and technology with secondary specialized education or three – year college education and persons with junior professional titles.

Natural Scientific and Technical Personnel refers to those professionals holding scientific and technical titles or taking such positions, or being graduated from departments of science, engineering, agriculture and medicine, and/or having been promoted in practice in different sectors of the national economy and working on research, teaching and production technique in the scientific and technological fields such as science, engineering, agriculture and medicine, etc. and the professionals doing administrative work related to science and technology in government agencies, enterprises and institutions.

Engineering Professionals refer to the persons who are engaged in engineering science and technology in different sectors of the national economy, including senior engineers, engineers, assistant engineers, technicians and technical personnel without professional titles.

Agricultural Professionals refer to the persons who are working on the science of agriculture in different sectors of the national economy, including senior agronomists, agronomists, assistant argonomists, technicians and technical personnel without professional titles.

Public Health Professionals refer to the persons who are engaged in medical and health work in different sectors of the national economy, including director doctors and their deputies, doctors in charge, doctors, paramedics, nurses and technical personnel without professional titles.

Scientific Research Personnel refers to those personnel engaged in scientific and technical activities in different sectors of the national economy, including research fellows and their deputies, assistant research fellows, research trainees, technicians and technical personnel without professional titles.

Teaching personnel of Natural Sciences refers to those professionals engaged in the teaching of natural science and technology in different sectors of the national economy, including professors, associate professors, lecturers, teaching assistants, teachers and teaching personnel in science and technology in middle schools.

Inventions refer to the inventions as specified by the patent law and its detailed rules and regulations for implementation. They refer to the new technical proposals to the products or methods or their modifications.

Utility Models refer to the utility models as specified by the patent law and its detailed rules and regulations for implementation. They refer to the practical and new technical proposals on the shape and structure of the product or the combination of both.

Designs refer to the designs as specified by the patent law and its detailed rules and regulation for implementation. They refer to the aesthetics and industry applicable new designs for the shape, pattern and color of the product, or their combinations.

Cultural Institutions refer to units which have their own organizational system and independent accounting system and specialize in or serve cultural development. They exclude other establishments run by these cultural institutions and amateur cultural groups established by various departments.

Art Troupe refers to the troupe which is engaged in drama, opera, music, dance, acrobatics or other art performance, opens independent accounts with banks and has self – supporting accounting system; excluding the troupes which are engaged partly in industrial or agricultural activities, partly in art performance and the professional troupes organized by the people.

Film Projection Units refer to units with film projection equipment, full or part time projectionists, permanent or non permanent places, approved by related administrative departments to show films regularly for certain groups of audience, including those film projection units which have been approved to give commercial shows and run business with independent accounting system as well as those filmrenting units of the military system.

Number of Spectators at Art Performance refers to the number of attendants at commercial shows, completely booked shows or free shows given in minority national areas, and does not include the number of spectators at rehearsals for examination and internal shows for study.

18

Eighteen

体育、卫生、环保及其他

Sports, Public Health, Environmental Protection and Others

体育运动员情况（人）（2001）
Sports Athletes (peron)

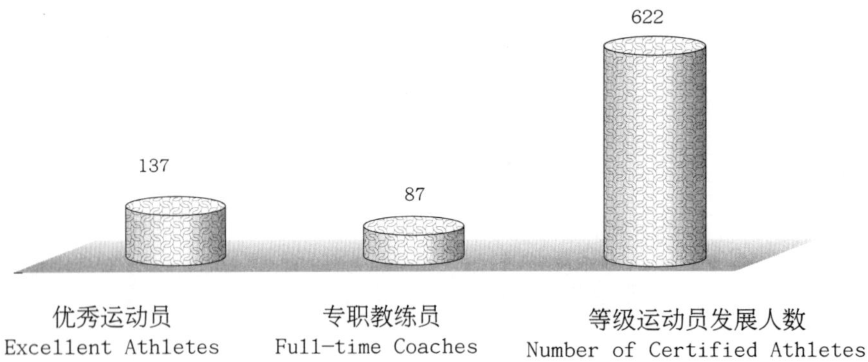

平均每千人拥有卫生人员、床位数（2001）
Number of Medical Technical Personnel and Hospital Beds Per 1000 Person

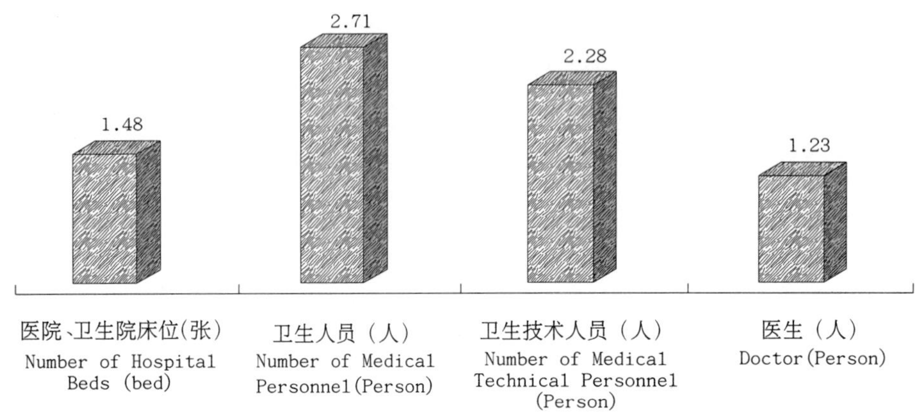

交通事故情况(2001)
Basic Statistics on Traffic Accidents

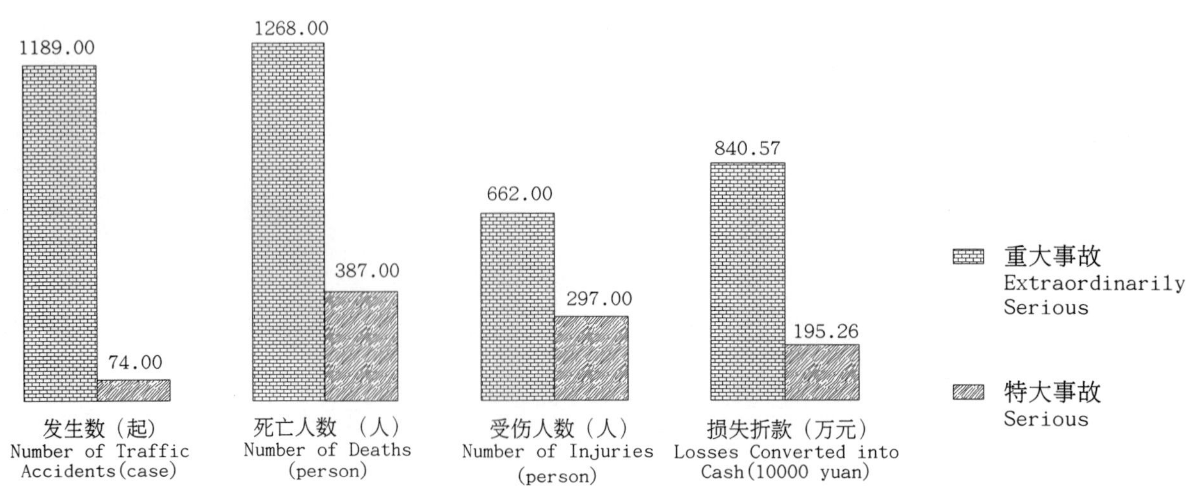

18－1 体育运动员情况
Sports Athletes

单位:人
(person)

指 标	Item	2000	2001	2001年比2000年增长(%) Increase Rate in 2001 over 2000(%)
优秀运动员	Excellent Athletes	142	137	-3.5
#女运动员	Female	54	50	-7.4
专职教练员	Full-time Coaches	85	87	2.3
#女专职教练员	Female	20	20	持平
等级运动员发展人数	Number of Certified Athletes	597	622	4.2
#国际运动健将	International Master Athletes			
运动健将	Master Athletes	10	2	-80
等级裁判员发展人数	Number of Certified Referees	808	1905	135.8
#国际级	International Referees	3		
国家级	National Referees	2	5	150

18－2 公共体育场地
Number of Public Stadiums and Gymnasiums

单位:个
(unit)

指 标	Item	2000	2001	2001年比2000年增长(%) Increase Rate in 2001 over 2000(%)
总 计	Total	11965	11987	0.2
#体育场	Stadiums	33	42	27.3
体育馆	Gymnasiums	14	16	14.3
游泳池	Swimming Pools	84	84	持平
有固定看台的灯光球场	Illuminated Fields with Fixed Seating	164	168	2.4

18－3 群众体育活动情况
Mass Sport Activities

单位:万人
(10000 persons)

指 标	Item	2000	2001	2001年比2000年增长(%) Increase Rate in 2001 over 2000(%)
举办县级以上运动会(万次)	Number of Sports Meeting above County Level(10000 times)	0.11	0.1	-9.1
参加运动会的运动员(万人次)	Number of Athletes Attending Sports Meets	52.35	48.2	-7.9
青少年体育俱乐部(个)	Athletic Club for Youngsters(unit)	11	8	-27.3
全民健身工程(条)	Body-building Activities of The Whole Nation(unit)	54	69	27.8

18－4 卫生事业基本情况
Basic Statistics on Health Care

类　　别	Sort	2000	2001	2001年比2000年增长(%) Increase Rate in 2001 over 2000(%)
卫生机构(个)	**Total Number of Health Care Institution(unit)**	**8992**	**8791**	**－2.2**
#医院、卫生院	Hospitals	1878	1872	－0.3
床位数(万张)	**Number of Beds(bed)**	**5.86**	**5.91**	**0.9**
#医院、卫生院床位	Number of Hospital Beds	5.51	5.59	1.5
卫生人员合计(万人)	**Number of Medical Technical Personnel(person)**	**10.16**	**10.24**	**0.8**
#卫生技术人员	Medical Technical Personnels	8.54	8.61	0.8
#医生	Doctor	4.57	4.64	1.5
平均每千人拥有:	**Per 1000 Person**			
#医院、卫生院床位(张)	Number of Hospital Beds(bed)	1.48	1.48	持平
卫生人员(人)	Number of Medical Technical Personnel(person)	2.72	2.71	－0.4
#卫生技术人员	Medical Technical Personnels	2.29	2.28	－0.4
#医生	Doctor	1.22	1.23	0.8

18－5 卫生部门县及县以上医院机构、床位、人员数(2001)
Number of Health Institutions, Beds and Personnels of Hospitals at and above County Level

类别	Sort	机构数(个) Institutions (unit)	床位数(张) Hospital Beds(bed)	人员数(人) Number of Personnels (person)	平均每院 Per Hospital Average 床位数(张) Hospital Beds(bed)	人员数(人) Number of Personnels (person)
总计	**Total**	**196**	**27018**	**33526**	**137.85**	**171.05**
省属	Governed by Province	7	3816	5309	545.14	758.43
省辖市、地、州属	Governed by Cities under The Jurisdiction of Province, Prefecture and State	25	7540	9502	301.60	380.08
省辖市区、地(州)辖市属	Governed by Cities under The Jurisdiction of Province and Cities under The Jurisdiction of Prefecture(State)	36	4102	5239	113.94	145.53
县(区、特区)属	Governed by County(District, Special District)	128	11560	13476	90.31	105.28
综合医院计	**Comprehensive Hospitals**	**108**	**18675**	**22878**	**172.92**	**211.83**
省属	Governed by Province	1	851	1335	851.00	1335.00
省辖市、地、州属	Governed by Cities under The Jurisdiction of Province, Prefecture and State	14	5967	7323	426.21	523.07
省辖市区、地(州)辖市属	Governed by Cities under The Jurisdiction of Province and Cities under The Jurisdiction of Prefecture(State)	24	3125	3910	130.21	162.92
县(区、特区)属	Governed by County(District, Special District)	69	8732	10310	126.55	149.42
中医医院计	**Hospital of Chinese Medicine**	**63**	**4001**	**4850**	**63.51**	**76.98**
省属	Governed by Province	1	135	194	135.00	194.00
省辖市、地、州属	Governed by Cities under The Jurisdiction of Province, Prefecture and State	4	667	980	166.75	245.00
省辖市区、地(州)辖市属	Governed by Cities under The Jurisdiction of Province and Cities under The Jurisdiction of Prefecture(State)	7	630	809	90.00	115.57
县(区、特区)属	Governed by County(District, Special District)	51	2569	2867	50.37	56.22
其他各类医院计	**Other Kind of Hospitals**	**25**	**4342**	**5798**	**173.68**	**231.92**
省属	Governed by Province	5	2830	3780	566.00	756.00
省辖市、地、州属	Governed by Cities under The Jurisdiction of Province, Prefecture and State	7	906	1199	129.43	171.29
省辖市区、地(州)辖市属	Governed by Cities under The Jurisdiction of Province and Cities under The Jurisdiction of Prefecture(State)	5	347	520	69.40	104.00
县(区、特区)属	Governed by County(District, Special District)	8	259	299	32.38	37.38

18-6 县及县以上医院、卫生院医疗工作情况(2001)
Status of Hospitals and Rural Township Hospitals at and above County Level

类　别	Sort	机构合计(个) Institutions (unit)	诊疗人次数(人次) Total Patients Treated (person-times)	#门诊人次数 Out-Patients	入院人数(人次) Hospital Admissions (person-times)	出院人数(人次) Leave Hospital (person-times)	出院病人治愈率% Recovering Rate
县及县以上医院合计	Hospitals at and above County Level	397	14922332	13540705	722639	720805	66.8
#卫生部门计	Health Department	195	10076559	8990161	539709	539455	64.5
#综合医院	Comprehensive Hospitals	108	6258447	5529440	389309	389045	63.6
#县医院	Hospitals at County Level	69	2901494	2552476	199013	198420	65.2
中医医院	Hospital of Chinese Medicine	62	1890706	1774880	64296	64184	67.3
医学院校附院	Hospitals Attached to Medical Colleges	4	1203758	1019624	55170	54995	61.6
妇幼保健院	Maternity and Child Care Hospital	10	515970	465754	23058	22960	83.2
工业及其他部门计	Industrial and Other Department	192	4573177	4297916	172110	171103	74.1
集体所有制计	Collective - Owned	9	245671	235302	8750	8257	70.0
卫生院合计	Township Hospitals	1469	12537259	11874572	366604	364994	81.9
#农村乡镇卫生院	Rural Township Hospitals	1456	12460418	11801595	365174	363186	81.8
#中心乡镇卫生院	Central Township Hospitals	456	5890266	5431727	193587	192827	82.1
一般乡镇卫生院	Ecumenic Township Hospitals	1000	6570152	6369868	171587	170737	81.6

18－6 续表(continued)

类别	Sort	平均开放病床数(张) Sickbeds Setup (bed)	病床周转次数(次) Turnover of Beds (time)	病床工作日(日) Number of Days Per Bed in Use (day)	病床使用率(%) Utilization Rate of Beds(%)	出院者平均住院日(天) Average Hospitalization Period(day)	每百门急诊次入院人数(人) Hospital Admissions Per 100 Out－Patient Times and Emergency Patient－Times(person)
县及县以上医院合计	Hospitals at and above County Level	38219	18.9	214.5	58.8	10.5	5.0
#卫生部门计	Health Department	26008	20.7	238.6	65.4	10.5	5.5
#综合医院	Comprehensive Hospitals	17962	21.7	235.5	64.5	9.7	6.4
#县医院	Hospitals at County Level	8564	23.2	194.9	53.4	7.4	7.1
中医医院	Hospital of Chinese Medicine	3518	17.9	194.8	53.4	9.8	3.5
医学院校附院	Hospitals Attached to Medical Colleges	2624	21.0	346.2	94.8	16.1	4.7
妇幼保健院	Maternity and Child Care Hospital	691	33.2	248.9	68.2	7.4	4.6
工业及其他部门计	Industrial and Other Department	11798	14.5	161.6	44.3	10.7	3.9
集体所有制计	Collective－Owned	330	25.0	192.0	52.7	7.0	3.6
卫生院合计	Township Hospitals	11371	32.1	129.2	35.4	4.0	3.1
#农村乡镇卫生院	Rural Township Hospitals	11315	32.1	129.2	35.4	4.0	3.1
中心乡镇卫生院	Central Township Hospitals	5848	33.0	128.6	35.2	3.9	3.5
一般乡镇卫生院	Ecumenic Township Hospitals	5467	31.2	129.8	35.6	4.1	2.7

18－7 卫生防疫防治和妇幼卫生事业情况
Statistics of Sanitation and Epidemic Prevention, Maternity and Child Care

类　　别	Sort	2000	2001	2001 年比 2000 年增长(%) Increase Rate in 2001 over 2000(%)
防治所、站机构数(个)	**Prevention and Treatment Centers or Stations(unit)**	**62**	**61**	**-1.6**
人员总数(人)	Number of Personnels(person)	848	802	-5.4
卫生技术人员数(人)	Medical Technical Personnels(person)	649	603	-7.1
床位数(张)	Hospital Beds(bed)	113	120	6.2
卫生防疫机构数(个)	**Institutions of Sanitation and Antiepidemic Agencies(unit)**	**113**	**113**	**持平**
人员总数(人)	Number of Personnels(person)	4909	4946	0.8
卫生技术人员数(人)	Medical Technical Personnels(person)	3984	3986	0.1
妇幼保健机构合计(个)	**Maternity and Child Care Centers(unit)**	**98**	**99**	**1.0**
人员总数(人)	Number of Personnels(person)	3073	3166	3.0
卫生技术人员数(人)	Medical Technical Personnels(person)	2585	2648	2.4
床位数(张)	Hospital Beds(bed)	1613	1691	4.8

18－8 卫生机构、床位、人员数(2001)
Number of Health Institutions, Beds and Personnels

类　　别	Sort	总　计 Total	卫生部门 Health Department	工业及其他部门 Industrial and Other Department	集体所有制 Collective－owned	私人办 Private Practice
机构数(个)	Number of Institutions(unit)	8791	2178	1204	321	5088
构　成	Composition	100.00	24.78	13.70	3.65	57.87
床位数(张)	Number of Beds(bed)	59120	42607	15646	636	231
构　成	Composition	100.00	72.07	26.46	1.08	0.39
人员数(人)	Number of Personnels(person)	102436	68348	23694	1845	8549
构　成	Composition	100.00	66.72	23.13	1.80	8.35
卫生技术人员数(人)	Medical Technical Personnels(person)	86103	57241	18654	1724	8484
构　成	Composition	100.00	66.48	21.66	2.00	9.86

18－9 农村三级卫生服务网情况
Health Organization at County, Town and Village Level

指　　标	Item	2000	2001	增减 Increase or Decrease
县医院个数(个)	**Number of Hospitals at County Level(unit)**	**69**	**69**	**持平**
平均每院病床数(张)	Number of Beds Per Hospital(bed)	126.87	126.55	－0.3
平均每院人员数(人)	Personnels Per Hospital(person)	147.04	149.42	2.4
#平均每院卫生技术人员数(人)	Medical Technical Personnels Per Hospital(person)	121.41	123.97	2.6
#平均每院医生数(人)	Number of Doctors Per Hospital(person)	47.14	49.39	2.3
平均每院护师、士	Number of Senior and Junior Nurses Per Hospital	50.64	52.20	1.6
县妇幼保健所、站机构数(个)	**Maternity and Child Care Centers at County Level(unit)**	**62**	**62**	**持平**
平均每所站床位数(张)	Number of Beds Per Station(bed)	12.44	12.50	0.1
平均每所站人员数(人)	Personnels Per Station(person)	21.40	21.52	0.1
#每所站卫生技术人员数(人)	Medical Technical Personnels Per Station(person)	18.65	18.52	－0.1
县卫生防疫站机构数(个)	**Institutions of Epidemic Prevention Station at County Level(unit)**	**67**	**67**	**持平**
平均每所站人员数(人)	Personnels Per Station(person)	35.88	36.06	0.2
#平均每站卫生技术人员数(人)	Medical Technical Personnels Per Station(person)	30.54	30.34	－0.2
农村乡镇卫生院机构数(个)	Institutions of Rural Township Hospitals(unit)	1457	1456	－1.0
农村乡镇卫生院床位数(张)	Number of Beds of Rural Township Hospitals(bed)	14307	14427	120.0
平均每院床位数(张)	Average Number of Beds Per Hospital(bed)	9.82	9.91	0.1
平均每千农业人口乡镇卫生院床位数(张)	Average Number of Beds of Rural Township Hospitals Per 1000 Rural Personnels(bed)	0.45	0.44	…
农村乡镇卫生院人员数(人)	**Personnels of Rural Township Hospitals(person)**	**23008**	**22874**	**－134.0**
平均每院人员数(人)	Personnels Per Hospital(person)	15.79	15.71	－0.1
平均每院卫生技术人员数(人)	Medical Technical Personnels Per Hospital(person)	14.5	14.43	－0.1

18－9续表(continued)

指　　标	Item	2000	2001	增减 Increase or Decrease
平均每千农业人口乡镇卫生院人员数(人)	Average Number of Personnels of Rural Township Hospitals Per 1000 Rural Personnels(person)	0.72	0.70	持平
设置医疗点的村数(个)	**Villages Set up Medical Treatment Sations(unit)**	**21374**	**21258**	**－116.0**
无医疗点的的村数(个)	Villages without Medical Treatment Sations(unit)	4481	4234	－247.0
村卫生室覆盖率(%)	Coverage Rate of Township Hospitals(%)	82.67	83.39	0.7
开展合作医疗的村数(个)	Villages of Pushing Cooperative Medical Treatment(unit)	2034	2321	287.0
开展合作医疗的村覆盖率(%)	Coverage Rate of Villages Pushed Cooperative Medical Treatment(%)	7.87	9.10	1.2
村设置的医疗点数(个)	Medical Treatment Stations Run by Village(unit)	21925	22069	144.0
#村或群众集体办	Run by Village or Collectivity	5232	4813	－419.0
乡村医生或卫生员合办	Run by Doctors and Health Workers	2189	2192	3.0
乡镇卫生院设点	Township Hospitals Founded	1580	1365	－215.0
个体办	Private Practice	12924	13699	775.0
平均每村设置的医疗点数(个)	Average Number of Medical Treatment Stations Run by Village Per Village(unit)	0.85	0.87	…
乡村医生和卫生员数(人)	Doctors and Health Workers(person)	38567	37976	－591.0
#乡村医生占%	Proportion of Rural Doctors(%)	55.93	53.90	－2.0
平均每村乡村医生和卫生员数(人)	Average Number of Doctors and Health Workers Per Village(person)	1.49	1.49	持平
平均每千农业人口乡村医生和卫生员数(人)	Average Number of Doctors and Health Workers Per 1000 Rural Personnels(person)	1.20	1.17	…
农村接生员总数(人)	Midwife of Rural Area(person)	18527	18111	－416.0

注：县医院个数不含县级市，省辖市区和特区。

Note: Number of hospitals at county level excluded cities at county level, distri cts and cities under the jurisdiction of province and special districts.

18－10 各类卫生人员情况
Persons Engaged in Health Care Institutions by Type of Occupation

类别	Sort	绝对数(人) Absolute Figure(person)		增减 Increase or Decrease	构成(%) Composition(%)	
		2000年	2001年		2000年	2001年
卫生人员总数	Total Number of Persons Engaged in Health Care Institutions	101614	102436	822	100.00	100.00
卫生技术人员数	Medical Technical Personnels	85397	86103	706	84.04	84.06
#医生	Doctors	45673	46412	739	44.95	45.31
#医师	Senior Doctors	32764	34053	1289	32.24	33.24
医士	Junior Doctors	12616	12077	－539	12.42	11.79
护师、士	Senior and Junior Nurses	21755	22053	298	21.41	21.53
#护师	Senior Nurses	14255	14690	435	14.03	14.34
护士	Junior Nurses	7500	7363	－137	7.38	7.19
助产士	Midwives	1069	956	－113	1.05	0.93
药剂师、士	Pharmacists and Junior Pharmacists of Chinese Medicine	5120	5068	－52	5.04	4.95
#药剂师	Pharmacists of Chinese Medicine	3954	3964	10	3.89	3.87
药剂士	Junior Pharmacists of Chinese Medicine	1166	1104	－62	1.15	1.08
检验师、士	Laboratory and Junior Laboratory Technicians	3098	3109	11	3.05	3.04
#检验师	Laboratory Technicians	2306	2331	25	2.27	2.28
检验士	Junior Laboratory Technicians	792	778	－14	0.78	0.76
其他技师、士	Other Technicians and Junior Technicians	2079	2057	－22	2.05	2.01
#其他技师	Other Technicians	1602	1552	－50	1.58	1.52
其他技士	Other Junior Technicians	477	505	28	0.47	0.49
其他初级卫生技术人员	Other Junior Medical Technical Personnel	6603	6448	－155	6.5	6.29
其他技术人员	Other Technical Personnel	2260	2803	543	2.22	2.74
管理人员	Managerial Personnel	7849	7391	－458	7.72	7.22
工勤人员	Logistics Workers	6108	6139	31	6.01	5.99

18－11 获得中级及以上卫生技术职称的人数
Number of Titled Medical Technical Intermediate and above Personnels

单位:人
(person)

指　　标	Item	2000	2001	2001 年比 2000 年增长(%) Increase Rate in 2001 over 2000(%)
总　　计	Total	18486	19575	5.9
卫生技术人员中获得中级及以上职称人数	Titled Technical Intermediate and above Personnels in Medical Technical Personnel	16278	17385	6.8
主任医、药、护、技师数	Director Doctor, Medicament, Nurse and Technician	256	282	10.2
#主任医师	Director Doctor	248	264	6.5
主任护师	Director Nurse		6	-
主任药师	Director Medicament	1	4	300.0
主任技师	Director Technician	7	8	14.3
副主任医、药、护、技师数	Assistant Director Doctor, Medicament, Nurse and Technician	2120	2264	6.8
#副主任医师	Assistant Director Doctor	1885	2011	6.7
副主任护师	Assistant Director Nurse	70	83	18.6
副主任药师	Assistant Director Medicament	97	109	12.4
副主任技师	Assistant Director Technician	68	61	-10.3
主治医、药、护、技师数	Doctor, Medicament, Nurse and Technician in Charge	13902	14839	6.7
#主治(主管)医师	Doctor in Charge	8835	9240	4.6
主管护师	Nurse in Charge	3208	3566	11.2
主管药师	Medicament in Charge	1026	1064	3.7
主管技师	Technician in Charge	833	969	16.3
其他技术和管理人员中获得中级及以上职称人数	Titled Technical Intermediate and above Personnels in Other	2208	2190	-0.8
#主任医、药、护、技师数	Director Doctor, Medicament, Nurse and Technician	56	79	41.1
副主任医、药、护、技师数	Assistant Director Doctor, Medicament, Nurse and Technician	316	333	5.4
主治医、药、护、技师数	Doctor, Medicament, Nurse and Technician in Charge	965	933	-3.3
高级会计、统计、经济师及其他	Senior Accountant, Statistician and Others	100	221	121.0
会计、统计、经济师及其他	Accountant, Statistician and Others	771	624	-19.1

注:本表数字均不包括诊所、卫生保健所、医务室等机构的卫生人员中获得中级及以上技术职称的卫生技术人员数。

Note: Data in this table excluded the medical technical personnels in clinique, hygiene centre and infirmary.

18－12 卫生部门城市医院住院病人前十位疾病构成(2001)
Composition of 10 Major Diseases of Impatient in Urban Areas Compared with National Total

疾病种类 Kind of Disease	贵州省 Guizhou Province	疾病构成(%) Composition (%)	位次 Order
消化系病	Digestive Disease	17.95	1
损伤及中毒	Trauma and Toxicosis	14.42	2
呼吸系病	Respiratory Disease	14.25	3
妊娠系病.分娩病及产褥期迸发症	Gravid System Disease, Puerperal Disease and Ebullition in The Period of Childbed	6.17	6
传染病和寄生虫	Infectious and Parasitic Diseases	11.58	4
泌尿和生殖系病	Genitourinary Disease	6.97	5
心脏病	Heart Trouble	3.42	8
恶性肿瘤	Malignant Tumour	3.36	9
脑血管病	Cerebrovascular Disease	3.11	10
神经系统和感觉器官疾病	Nervous System Disease and Sensorium Disease	3.68	7
十种疾病构成比合计	Total of the Composition Ratio	84.91	

18－13 卫生部门县医院住院病人前十位疾病构成(2001)
Composition of 10 Major Diseases of Impatient in Hospitals at County Level Compared with National Total

疾病种类 Kind of Disease	贵州省 Guizhou Province	疾病构成(%) Composition (%)	位次 Order
消化系病	Digestive Disease	18.04	2
损伤及中毒	Trauma and Toxicosis	20.79	1
呼吸系病	Respiratory Disease	15.33	3
妊娠系病.分娩病及产褥期迸发症	Gravid System Disease, Puerperal Disease and Ebul lition in the Period of Childbed	7.59	5
传染病和寄生虫	Infectious and Parasitic Diseases	15.02	4
泌尿和生殖系病	Genitourinary Disease	5.45	6
心脏病	Heart Trouble	2.29	7
神经系统和感觉器官疾病	Nervous System Disease and Sensorium Disease	1.90	8
脑血管病	Cerebrovascular Disease	1.90	9
内分泌、营养和代谢及免疫疾病	Endocrine and Immunity Disease	1.05	10
十种疾病构成比合计	Total of the Composition Ratio	71.32	

18－14 环保系统机构、人员数
Enviornmental Protection Agencies and Persons Engaged

指　　标	Item	2000	2001	2001年比2000年增长(%) Increase Rate in 2001 over 2000(%)
机构总数(个)	Number of Agencies(unit)	248	261	5.2
省	Province	12	12	0.0
地	Prefecture	29	31	6.9
县	County	207	215	3.9
年末人员总数(人)	Number of Staff and Workers(person)	1707	1930	13.1
#省	Province	298	309	3.7
地	Prefecture	497	523	5.2
县	County	912	1089	19.4
#科研人员(人)	Scientific and Technical Personnel (person)	86	91	5.8
监测人员(人)	Monitoring Personal (person)	418	585	40.0
监理人员(人)	Supervising and Administrative Personnel(person)	438	496	13.2

18－15 环境综合整治情况
Comprehensive Treatment of Environment

指　　标	Item	2000	2001	2001年比2000年增长(%) Increase Rate in 2001 over 2000(%)
环境质量	Environment Quality			
大气总量浮微粒年平均值(毫克/立方米)	The Average Yearly Indicators of Airborne Dust (mg/cu.m)	0.23	0.19	…
二氧化硫年平均值(毫克/立方米)	The Average Yearly Indicators of Sulfur Dioxide (mg/cu.m)	0.11	0.08	…
氮氧化物年平均值(毫克/立方米)	The Average Yearly Indicators of Nitrogen Oxide (mg/cu.m)	0.03	0.02	…
区域环境噪声平均值(分贝)	The Average Indicator of Urban Noise(decibel)	59.2	58.6	－0.6
交通干线噪声平均值(分贝)	The Average Indicator of Traffic Main Line Noise (decible)	72.8	70.4	－2.4
污染控制	Pollution Control			
工业废水排放达标率(%)	Up－to－standard Rate of Industrial Waste Water Discharge(%)	47.4	58.2	10.8(百分点)
工业固体废物综合利用率(%)	Rate of Comprehensive Utilization of Solid Industrial Waste(%)	30.3	36.3	6.0(百分点)
环境建设	Environment Improvement			
城市污水处理率(%)	Rate of Traetment of City Waste Water(%)	3.1	3.7	0.6(百分点)
城市气化率(%)	Rate of Gas Utilization in The City(%)	54.4	23.5	－
建成区绿化覆盖率(%)	Green Coverage Rate in Constructed Areas(%)	24.8	25.5	0.7(百分点)
环境处理	Environment Treatment			
"三同时"合格执行率(%)	Up－to－standard Rate of The "Three－Simultaneous" Implementation(%)	85.7	87.1	1.4(百分点)
环境影响评价制度执行率(%)	Up－to－standard Rate of The Envionment Evaluating System(%)	96.4	97.5	1.1(百分点)

18－16 工业"三废"排放情况
Discharge of Waste Water, Waste Gas and Solid Wastes by Industry

指　　标	Item	2000	2001	2001年比2000年增长(%) Increase Rate in 2001 over 2000(%)
工业废水量	Waste Water			
工业废水排放量(万吨/日)	Total Volume of Industrial Waste Water Disch arged(10000 tons/day)	56.43	57.02	1.0
#符合排放标准的	Up to the Standards	26.76	33.19	24.0
工业废水排放的污染物(公斤/日)	Pollution of Industrial Waste Water Discharge(kg/day)			
#镉及其无机化合物	Cadmium and Inorganic Compound	0.38	0.52	36.8
六价铬化合物	6－valence Chromium Compound	1.18	1.07	－9.3
砷及其无机化合物	Arsenic and Inorganic Compound	5.37	3.70	－31.1
铅及其无机化合物	Plumbum and Inorganic Compound	22.38	20.49	－8.4
氰化物	Cyanide	66.19	82.77	25.0
石油类	Petroleum Type	1657.56	1124.16	－32.2
汞	Mercury	1.12	0.03	－97.3
化学需氧量	Chemical Oxygen Demand	141095.89	82465.75	－41.6
氨氮	Ammonia and Nitrogen		3835.62	
废气中排放的污染物	Pollution of Industrial Waste Gas Emission			
#二氧化硫(万吨/年)	Sulphur of Dioxide(10000 tons/year)	64.25	57.14	－11.1
烟尘(万吨/年)	Soot(10000 tons/year)	34.24	28.17	－17.7
工业粉尘	Industrial Dust			
工业粉尘排放量(万吨/年)	Industrial Dust Produced(10000 tons/year)	40.62	24.99	－38.5
工业粉尘去除率(%)	Dismissed Rate of Industrial Dust(%)	54.20	74.39	20.2(百分点)
工业固体废物产生量(万吨/年)	Solid Waste Residue Produced(10000 tons/year)	2272	2367	4.2
工业蒸气锅炉数(台/万蒸吨)	Steam Boiler(set/10000 steam tons)	1331/1.80	1255/1.78	
工业炉窑数(座)	Industrial Stove(unit)	5384	6394	18.8
其他	Others			
"三废"综合利用产品产值(万元)	Output Value Products Made from Waste Gas, Waste Water and Waste Residue(10000 yuan)	46457	46612	0.3
"三废"综合利用产品利润	Profits of Products Made from Waste Gas, Waste Water and Waste Residue	8920	8950	0.3

18－17 环境保护治理与成效 Treatment and Effect of Environment Protection

指　　标	Item	2000	2001	2001年比2000年增长(%) Increase Rate in 2001 over 2000(%)
污染源限期治理	Pollution Headstream Treatment within Limit Time			
当年完成限期治理项目数(个)	Number of Environment Treatment Item in This Year(unit)	613	286	－53.3
当年完成限期治理投资额(亿元)	Investment of Environment Treatment in This Year (100 million yuan)	1.8	1.6	－11.1
关停并转企业数(个)	Number of Shut, Stopped, Amalgamated, and Transferred Enterpeises(unit)	513	671	30.8
城市环境综合整治	Comprehensive Treatment of Urban Environment			
已建成工业废水集中处理厂(座)	Number of Built Factories for Treatment Industrial Waste Water(unit)	1	2	100.0
建成区土地面积(平方公里)	Areas of Buildings(Sq.km)	291.7	304.1	4.3
建成烟尘控制区个数(个)	Number of Soot Control District(unit)	59	57	－3.4
建成烟尘控制区面积(平方公里)	Areas of Soot Control District(sq.km)	201.5	203.39	0.9
建成环境噪声达标区数(个)	Number of Dictrict Up－to－standard of Noise(unit)	36	37	2.8
建成环境噪声达标面积(平方公里)	Areas of Dictrict Up－to－standard of Noise(sq.km)	170.3	152.51	－10.4
环境保护投资总额(亿元)	Throw into Funds(100 million yuan)	11	14.7	33.6
#老污染源治理资金	Founds for Old Pollution Headstream Treatment	2.4	1.6	－33.3
新建项目污染源治理资金	Funds for New Treatment Item	1.6	1.2	－25.0
环保科研成果(项)	Achievements of Environment Protection Research(item)			
获省(部)级科技成果奖数	Prized by Province(Ministry) Level	3	2	－33.3
#一等	First Class			
二等	Secondary Class	1		
三等	Third Class	2	2	

18－18 人民法院刑事一审案件收结案情况(2001)
First Trail Criminal Cases Accepted and Settled by Courts

单位:件
(case)

类　别	Sort	收　案 Cases Accepted	结　案 Cases Settled
总　　计	Total	22361	21992
危害国家安全罪	Offences Against National Security	3	3
危害公共安全罪	Offences Against Public Security	1450	1437
破坏社会主义市场经济秩序罪	Offences Against Socialist Economic Order	242	235
侵犯公民人身权利民主权利罪	Offences Against Citizens' Personal and Democratic Rights	6954	6758
侵犯财产罪	Offences Against Properties	8718	8627
妨害社会管理秩序罪	Offences Against Social Management of Order	4318	4273
危害国防利益罪	Offences Against National Defense	2	2
贪污贿赂罪	Offences on Corruption and Bribery	614	598
渎职罪	Offences on Dereliction of Duty	60	59

18－19 人民法院刑事案件中青少年犯罪情况(2001)
Juvenile Delinquency Among Criminal Cases

单位:人
(person)

类　别	Sort	2000	2001
刑事罪犯总数	Offenders	19915	24081
#青少年罪犯	Young Offenders	6476	7395
#不满 18 岁	Less Than 18	1226	1587
18－25 岁	Between 18 to 25	5250	5808
青少年罪犯占刑事罪犯(%)	Proportion to Total(%)	32.5	24.12

18-20 律师、公证、调解及其他
Basic Statistics on Lawyers, Notarization, Mediation and Judicature

指标	Item	2000	2001	2001年比2000年增长(%) Increase Rate in 2001 over 2000(%)
律师工作	Lawyers			
法律律师事务所(个)	Number of Law Offices(unit)	153	169	10.5
辅助工作人员(人)	Assistant(person)	358	310	-13.4
#专职律师	Full-time Lawyers	790	865	9.5
聘请常年法律顾问(个)	Number of Permanent Legal Advisors(person)	1728	1941	12.3
全年办理(件)	Number of Cases in Whole Year(case)	110471	85337	-22.8
民事诉讼代理	Agent of Civil Cases	9746	10630	9.1
刑事案件	Defender of Criminal Cases	6388	7032	10.1
经济案件诉讼代理	Agent of Economic Cases	3254	2921	-10.2
非诉讼法律事务	Agent of Non-litigious Legal Affairs	2571	4104	59.6
解答法律询问	Agent of Legal Advisory Services	67505	46231	-31.5
代写法律事务文书	Agent of Legal Document Written on Behalf of Clients	20152	13571	-32.7
行政诉讼代理	Agent of Administrative Action	855	848	-0.8
公证工作	Notarization			
公证处(个)	Number of Notarial Offices(unit)	96	96	持平
公证辅助人员(人)	Notarial Assistant(person)	117	117	持平
#公证员	Notaries	229	222	-3.1
办理公证文书(件)	Number of Notarized Documents(case)	215518	111223	-48.4
#经济合同公证	Notarized Documents on Economic Affairs	122251	54278	-55.6
办理公证文书中	In Notarized Documents			
涉外公证(件)	Notarization of Foreign-related(case)	5738	6939	20.9
国内公证(件)	Domestic Notarization(case)	208662	102988	-50.6

18－20 续表(continued)

指　　标	Item	2000	2001	2001 年比 2000 年增长(%) Increase Rate in 2001 over 2000(%)
公证费收入(万元)	Income of Notarization	703.81	663.49	－5.7
人民调解工作	**People's Mediation**			
人民调解委员会(个)	Number of People's Mediation Committees(unit)	21636	30678	41.8
人民调解人员(人)	Number of Mediators(person)	149746	160220	7.0
调解民间纠纷(件)	Number of Civil Disputes Mediated(case)	159245	168293	5.7
调解成功率(%)	The Rate of Success of Mediation(%)	95	94	－1.0(百分点)
司法调解工作	**Judicature**			
司法调解中心(个)	Judicature Mediation Centre(unit)	847	1431	68.9
司法调解人员(人)	Judicature Mediators(person)	7904	8626	9.1
调解一般纠纷(件)	Number of Common Disputes Mediated(case)	3740	27001	622.0
调解成功率(%)	The Rate of Success of Mediation(%)	95.2	75.4	－19.8(百分点)
基层法律服务工作	**Law Service at Basic Level(unit)**			
法律服务所(个)	Bureau for Law Service(unit)	652	617	－5.4
法律工作者(人)	Law Staffs(person)	2167	2074	－4.3
代理案件(件)	Cases Deputed(case)	36968	37940	2.6
避免经济损失(万元)	Number of Avoided Economical Loss(10000 yuan)	10973	8000	－27.1
刑释解教人员安置帮教工作	**Settling and Assisting and Teaching Work for People That Been Released After Serving a Sentence**			
设立工作机构(个)	Institutions Established(unit)	97	98	1.0
工作人员(人)	Staffs(person)	522	1376	163.6
安置人数(人)	Number of Persons Been Helped Settle Down(person)	7985	10850	35.9
帮教人数(人)	Number of Persons Been Assisted and Teached(person)	6414	10208	59.2

18-21 国内公证文书分类情况
Domestic Notarial Documents by Type

单位:件
(unit)

指标	Item	2000	2001	2001年比2000年增长(%) Increase Rate in 2001 over 2000(%)
总计	Total	215518	111223	-48.4
经济合同公证合计	Notarized Documents on Economic Affairs	122251	54278	-55.6
#购销	Purchases and Sales of Products	372	402	8.1
联营	Joint Business	113	60	-46.9
贷款	Loans	16491	16913	2.6
招标、投标	Bidding and Invite Public Bjdding	346	217	-37.3
劳务合同	Labor Contracts	643	521	-19.0
建筑工程承包	Construction Project Countracts	201	130	-35.3
农、林、牧、副、渔业承包	Farming, Forestry, Animal Husbandry, Sideline Production and Fishery Contracts	125	614	391.2
财产租赁	Property Leases	89	137	53.9
法人(代表)资格	Legal Person(Agent)Identification	9	40	344.4
委托书	Trust Deeds	46	97	110.9
民事法律关系公证合计	Notarized Documents on Civil Legal Relations	86411	48710	-43.6
#收养	Child Adoption	617	188	-69.5
解除收养	Adoption Renouncement	17	10	-41.2
继承权	Right of Inheritance	845	1009	19.4
遗嘱	Testaments	656	705	7.5
产权	Property Right	165	128	-22.4
亲属关系	Relatives	805	481	-40.2
房屋买卖	Purchases and Sales of Houses	2613	3445	31.8
房屋租赁	House Leases	150	152	1.3
留学协议	Foreign Study Contracts	172	114	-33.7
遗赠抚养协议	Donations and Family Fostering	917	155	-83.1
其他民事协议	Other Civil Agreements	5491	3688	-32.8
委托书	Trust Deeds	620	816	31.6
赠与书	Presentation Documents	2599	2566	-1.3
声明书	Declarations	776	1006	29.6
建房宅基使用协议	Right to Housing Site	101	245	142.6

18－22 消费者协会受理投诉情况

Basic Statistics on Cases Accepted and Heard by Consumer Association

单位：件
(piece)

指　　标	Item	2000	2001	2001年比2000年增长(%) Increase Rate in 2001 over 2000(%)
总　　计	Total	8511	7876	－7.5
家用电器类	Household Appliances	1238	1361	9.9
#电视机	Televison	489	575	17.6
电冰箱	Refrigerators	114	107	－6.1
洗衣机	Washing Machines	79	109	38.0
收录音机(音响)	Radio－Recorder(acoustics)	101	93	－7.9
空调器	Air－Conditioner	17	37	117.6
家用机械类	Household Machinery	611	514	－15.9
#照相机	Cameras	42	19	－54.8
自行车	Bicycles	59	27	－54.2
摩托车	Motorcycles	134	132	－1.5
钟表	Clocks and Watches	141	115	－18.4
燃气热水器	Gas－fired Water Heater	70	64	－8.6
日用百货类	Daily Use Goods	1709	1631	－4.6
#家具	Furniture	138	146	5.8
针纺织品(服装)	Textile Fabric(Dress)	461	371	－19.5
鞋	Shoes	740	728	－1.6
化妆品	Cosmetic	156	112	－28.2
食品类	Foods	1914	1511	－21.1
药和医疗用品类	Drug and Midical Appliances	256	212	－17.2
服务类	Services	1620	1535	－5.2
#邮电	Telecommunications	647	343	－47.0
修理、装修业	Repairing and Ornament	257	204	－20.6
农用生产资料类	Agricultural Production Materials	378	414	9.5
其他类	Others	785	698	－11.1

18－23 火灾情况(2001)
Basic Statistics on Fires

指标	Item	合计 Total	特大 Extraordinarily Serious	重大 Serious	一般 Ordinary
发生数(起)	Number of Fires(case)	720	2	14	704
死亡人数(人)	Number of Deaths(person)	95		32	63
伤残人数(人)	Number of Injuries(person)	92		7	85
损失折款(万元)	Losses Converted into Cash(10000 yuan)	1977	280	244	1454
按火灾原因分(起)	Grouped by Cause(unit)				
#放火	Setting on Fire	68			68
违反电器安装规定	Violate Install Regulation of Electric Equipment	201		2	199
违反安全制度	Violate Safety Regulation	41		3	38
吸烟	Smoking	24			24
生活用火不慎	Not Careful with Cooking Fire	211	2	6	203
玩火	Playing with Fire	61			61
自燃	Natural Five	11			11
其他	Others	38			38
不明	Uncertain	65		3	62
平均每起事故损失(万元)	Average Loss Per Fire(10000 yuan)	3	139	17	2

18－24 交通事故情况(2001)
Basic Statistics on Traffic Accidents

指标	Item	发生数(起) Number of Traffic Accidents(case)	死亡人数(人) Number of Deaths(person)	受伤人数(人) Number of Injuries(person)	损失折款(万元) Losses Converted into Cash(10000 yuan)
总计	**Total**	**4064**	**1655**	**2704**	**2067.81**
#重大事故	Extraordinarily Serious	1189	1268	662	840.57
特大事故	Serious	74	387	297	195.26
机动车	Motor Vehicles	3877	1516	2634	2003.3
#汽车	Automobiles	3241	1066	2077	1785.41
摩托车	Motorcycles	315	199	295	105.14
拖拉机	Tractors	110	94	106	25.23
非机动车	Non－Motor Vehicles	19	13	17	3
#自行车	Bicycle	14	10	8	2.03
行人乘车人	Pedestrians and Passengers	168	126	53	61.52

主要统计指标解释

等级运动员人数 指经考核正式批准授予等级运动员称号的人数。运动员等级分为国际级运动健将、运动健将、一级运动员、二级运动员、三级运动员、少年级运动员。

等级裁判员人数 指经考核正式批准授予等级裁判员称号的人数。裁判员等级分为国际裁判、国家级裁判、一级裁判、二级裁判、三级裁判。

体育场 指有400米跑道(中心含足球场),有固定道牙,跑道6条以上,并有固定看台的室外田径场地。体育场按看台容纳观众人数分为:甲级25000人以上,乙级15000-25000人,丙级5000~15000人,丁级5000人以下。

体育馆 指有固定看台,可供篮球、排球、羽毛球、乒乓球、体操等项目训练比赛活动用的室内运动场地。体育馆按看台容纳观众人数分为:甲级6000人以上,乙级4000-6000人,丙级2000-4000人,丁级2000人以下。

医院 指设有固定床位,能收容病人住院并能为病人提供医疗、护理服务的医疗机构,包括县及县以上医院、农村乡卫生院和其他医院三部分。医院按所属性质不同分为卫生部门、工业及其他部门和集体经济单位三类。县及县以上医院按业务性质不同分为综合医院和专科医院。

卫生技术人员 指卫生事业机构支付工资的全部职工中现任职务为卫生技术工作的专业人员,包括中医师、西医师、中西医结合高级医师、护师、中药师、西药师、检验师、其他技师、中医士、西医士、护士、助产士、中药剂士、西药剂士、检验士、其他技士、其他中医、护理员、中药剂员、西药剂员、检验员和其他初级卫生技术人员。

医生 指经卫生部门审查合格,从事医疗工作的专业人员。分为中医医生和西医医生。包括卫生技术人员中的中医师、西医师、中西医结合高级医师、中医士、西医士和其他中医。

公证人员 指在国家公证机关依法办理公证事务的司法人员,包括公证员、助理公证员和在公证处工作的其他人员。

办理公证文书 指公证处在一定时期内办结的公证文书件数。公证文书按司法部规定或批准的格式制作,包括国内公证和涉外公证两部分。国内公证分为经济合同公证和民事法律关系公证两大类。

调解人员 指在人民调解委员会担负调解民间一般民事纠纷和轻微违法行为引起纠纷的工作人员,包括调解委员会的委员和调解小组的调解员。

调解民间纠纷 指调解委员会依照法律规定,根据自愿原则,用说服教育的方法调解民间发生的有关民事权利和义务的争执,促成当事双方达到协议和谅解,解决纠纷。包括婚姻家庭纠纷,财产权益纠纷等,不包括法院受理调解的民事案件数。

离休、退休、退职人员 指正式办理了离休、退休、退职手续,并享受相应的离休、退休、退职待遇的人员。

保险福利费用 指企业、事业、机关单位在工资以外实际支付给职工和离休、退休、退职人员个人以及用于集体的

(1)职工保险福利费用包括:医疗卫生费;文体宣传费;集体福利事业补贴费;集体福利设施费;其他。

(2)离休、退休、退职人员保险福利费用包括:离休金;退休金;退职生活费;其他。

工业废水排放量 指经过企业厂区所有排放口排到企业外部的工业废水量。包括生产废水、外排的直接冷却水、超标排放的矿井地下水和与工业废水混排的厂区生活污水,不包括外排的间接冷却水(清污不分流的间接冷却水应计算在内)。

Explanatory Notes on Main Statistical Indicators

Number of Athletes in Grades refers to the number of athletes who have been given titles through examination. The titles of athletes include international masters of sports, masters of sports, first – grade, second – grade and third – grade sportsmen and young athletes.

Number of Referees in Grades refers to the number of referees who have been given titles after examination. They are classified as international referees, national referees and referees of the first, second and third grades.

Stadiums refer to stadiums for track and field events with six lane 400 – meter tracks around soccer fields, permanent track marks and permanent bleachers. Stadiums are classified according to seating capacity. They include: Class A stadiums seating 25000 people each. Class B stadiums seating 15000 to 25000 people each. Class C stadiums seating 5000 to 15000 people each, and Class D stadiums seating fewer than 5000 people.

Gymnasiums refer to indoor sports grounds with permanent seats in which basketball, volleyball. badminton, table tennis and gymnastics competitions can be held. Gymnasiums are classified according to seating capacity. They include Class A gymnasiums seating over 6000 people. Class B gymnasiums seating 4000 to 6000 people. Class C gymnasiums seating 2000 to 4000 people, and Class D gymnasiums seating fewer than 2000 people.

Hospitals refer to medical institutions with permanent hospital beds, which are able to take in patients and provide them with medical and nursing services. Hospitals are classified into three categories: hospitals at or above the county level, hospitals of rural townships, and other hospitals. According to their ownership, hospitals can be classified into three categories: hospitals under the public health departments, hospitals under industrial and other departments and collective – owned hospitals. Hospitals at or above county level are divided into comprehensive and specialized hospitals.

Medical Technical Personnel refers to all medical staff and workers employed by medical institutions, including doctors of Chinese and Western medicine, senior doctors who integrate traditional Chinese therapeutics with Western therapeutics in practice, senior nurses, pharmacists of Chinese and Western medicine, laboratory specialists, other specialists, paramedics of Chinese and Western medicine, nurses, midwives, druggists in Chinese and Western medicine, laboratory technicians, other technicians, other practitioners of Chinese medicine, nursing attendants, pharmacological workers of Chinese and Western medicine, laboratory workers, and other primary medical personnel.

Doctors refer to qualified professional medical workers approved to practice by public health departments. They are classified into doctors of Chinese medicine, doctors of Western medicine, senior doctors who integrate traditional Chinese therapeutics with Western therapeutics in practice, paramedics of Chinese medicine and Western medicine, and other specialists of Chinese medicine.

Notary Personnel refers to judicial workers of the state notary offices handling notarization work according to law. They include notaries, assistant notaries, and other people working for notary offices.

Notarized Documents refer to the documents settled by notary offices in a year. The notary documents are drawn up in accordance with the regulations of the Ministry of Justice, including domestic documents and foreign – related documents. Domestic documents are divided into two major categories, documents on economic contracts and documents on civil legal relations.

Mediators refer to workers on peoples mediation committees responsible for mediating in civil disputes and cases of slight infraction of the law. They include members of the mediation committees and mediators of mediation groups.

Mediation of Civil Disputes refers to mediation committeeswork in mediating in civil disputes concerning civil rights and duties through persuasion and education in accordance with the provisions of law on a voluntary basis, so as to solve disputes by helping the parties involved come to an agreement and understanding. These disputes include divorce cases and disputes over property ownership, but exclude the civil cases to be handled by the court.

Retired or Resigned Personnel refers to the persons who have formally gone through the formalities for their retirement or quitting work and enjoy the corresponding treatments.

Insurance and Welfare Funds refers to labour insurance and welfare fund paid by enterprises, organizations and institutions to their staff and workers as well as retired and resigned persons in addition to their wages and salaries.

(1) Insurance and Welfare Funds for Staff and Workers include: Medical Care Allowance; Expenses for Recreational, Sports and Publicity Activities; Subsidies to Collective Welfare Undertakings: Expenses for Collective Welfare Facilities, Others

(2)Insurance and Welfare Funds for Retired and Resigned Staff and Workers: Pensions for retired veteran cadres, Pensions for Retirement, Resignation Allowances for Living Expenses, Others.

Volume of Industrial Waste Water Discharged refers to the volume of industrial waste water discharged, through all outlets, to the outside of industrial enterprises, including waste water produced, direct – cooling water, underground water from mines that does not meet the standard of discharge, and the domestic sewage mixed up with industrial waste water when discharged, but excluding discharged indirect – cooling water.

19

Nineteen

民族自治地区

Minority Nationality Autonomous Areas

19-1 少数民族自治地方行政区划(2001)
Administrative Division of Minority Nationality Autonomous Areas

单位:个
(unit)

民族自治州(县)名称	Autonomous State(County)	地级 Prefectural Level	县级 County Level	#县级市 City at County Level
黔东南苗族侗族自治州	Qiandongnan(Miao & Dong)Autonomous State	1	16	1
黔南州布依族苗族自治州	Qiannan(Bouyei & Miao)Autonomous State	1	12	2
黔西南布依族苗族自治州	Qianxinan(Bouyei & Miao)Autonomous State	1	8	1
道真仡佬族、苗族自治县	Daozhen(Gelo & Miao)Autonomous County		1	
务川仡佬族、苗族自治县	Wuchuan(Gelo & Miao)Autonomous County		1	
玉屏侗族自治县	Yuping(Dong)Autonomous County		1	
印江土家族、苗族自治县	Yinjiang(Tujia & Miao)Autonomous County		1	
沿河土家族自治县	Yanhe(Tujia)Autonomous County		1	
松桃苗族自治县	Songtao(Miao)Autonomous County		1	
关岭布依族苗族自治县	Guanling(Bouyei & Miao)Autonomous County		1	
镇宁布依族苗族自治县	Zhenning(Bouyei & Miao)Autonomous County		1	
紫云苗族布依族自治县	Ziyun(Miao & Bouyei)Autonomous County		1	
威宁彝族、回族、苗族自治县	Weining(Yi,Hui & Miao)Autonomous County		1	
三都水族自治县	Sandu(Shui)Autonomous County		1	

19－2 少数民族分布情况
Geographic Distribution of Minority Nationalities

民 族	Nationality	分布的主要地区	Main Geographic Distribution
苗 族	Miao	黔东南州、松桃县、威宁县	Qiandongnan, Songtao, Weining
布依族	Bouyei	黔南州、黔西南州	Qiannan, Qianxinan
侗 族	Dong	黔东南州、玉屏县	Qiandongnan, Yuping
土家族	Tujia	铜仁地区	Tongren
彝 族	Yi	毕节地区、六盘水市	Bijie, Liupanshui
仡佬族	Gelo	遵义市、安顺市	Zunyi, Anshun
水 族	Shui	三都县	Sandu
回 族	Hui	威宁县、兴仁县、平坝县	Weining, Xingren, Pingba
白 族	Bai	毕节地区	Bijie
瑶 族	Yao	黔东南州、三都县	Qiandongnan, Sandu
壮 族	Zhuang	从江县、黎平县、独山县、荔波县	Congjiang, Liping, Dushan, Nibo
畲 族	She	凯里市、麻江县、都匀市、福泉市	Kaili, Majiang, Duyun, Fuquan
毛南族	Maonan	平塘县、独山县、惠水县	Pingtang, Dushan, Huishui
蒙古族	Mongolian	毕节地区、石阡县	Bijie, Shiqian
仫佬族	Mulam	凯里市、麻江县、黄平县	Kaili, Majiang, Huangping
满 族	Man	黔西县、大方县、金沙县	Qianxi, Dafang, Jinsha
羌 族	Qiang	石阡县、江口县	Shiqian, Jiangkou

19-3 少数民族自治地方基本情况(2001)
Basic Conditions of Minority Nationality Autonomous Areas

民族自治州(县)名称	Autonomous State(County)	成立时间 Time of Come into Existence	土地面积(平方公里) Total Land Area(sq.km)	年末人口(万人) Total Population at The Year-end (10000 persons)	#少数民族 Minority Nationalities
黔东南苗族侗族自治州	Qiandongnan(Miao & Dong) Autonomous State	1956.07.23	30302	427.30	315.14
黔南州布依族苗族自治州	Qiannan(Bouyei & Miao) Autonomous State	1956.08.08	26197	384.11	205.29
黔西南布依族苗族自治州	Qianxinan(Bouyei & Miao) Autonomous State	1982.05.01	16796	299.91	125.66
道真仡佬族、苗族自治县	Daozhen(Gelo & Miao) Autonomous County	1987.11.29	2156	33.27	26.18
务川仡佬族、苗族自治县	Wuchuan(Gelo & Miao) Autonomous County	1987.11.26	2766	41.42	33.69
玉屏侗族自治县	Yuping(Dong) Autonomous County	1984.11.07	517	13.94	2.27
印江土家族、苗族自治县	Yinjiang(Tujia & Miao) Autonomous County	1987.11.20	1969	40.75	13.68
沿河土家族自治县	Yanhe(Tujia) Autonomous County	1987.11.23	2476	54.89	25.40
松桃苗族自治县	Songtao(Miao) Autonomous County	1956.12.31	2688	62.92	36.04
关岭布依族苗族自治县	Guanling(Bouyei & Miao) Autonomous County	1981.12.31	1466	31.98	18.60
镇宁布依族苗族自治县	Zhenning(Bouyei & Miao) Autonomous County	1963.09.11	1718	34.10	19.07
紫云苗族布依族自治县	Ziyun(Miao & Bouyei) Autonomous County	1966.02.11	2280	33.25	22.00
威宁彝族、回族、苗族自治县	Weining(Yi, Hui & Miao) Autonomous County	1954.11.11	6295	107.29	26.06
三都水族自治县	Sandu(Shui) Autonomous County	1957.01.02	2380	31.88	29.89

19-3 续表(continued)

民族自治州(县)名称	Autonomous State(County)	公路线路里程(公里) Length of Highways(km)	国内生产总值(万元) Gross Domestic Product(10000 yuan)	地方财政收入(万元) Local Financial Revenue(10000 yuan)
黔东南苗族侗族自治州	Qiandongnan(Miao & Dong) Autonomous State	5874	859138	51659
黔南州布依族苗族自治州	Qiannan(Bouyei & Miao) Autonomous State	7696	1062412	60304
黔西南布依族苗族自治州	Qianxinan(Bouyei & Miao) Autonomous State	5349	672053	45903
道真仡佬族、苗族自治县	Daozhen(Gelo & Miao) Autonomous County	1292	63638	4278
务川仡佬族、苗族自治县	Wuchuan(Gelo & Miao) Autonomous County	1338	60039	3688
玉屏侗族自治县	Yuping(Dong) Autonomous County	145	57463	3408
印江土家族、苗族自治县	Yinjiang(Tujia & Miao) Autonomous County	465	63783	2931
沿河土家族自治县	Yanhe(Tujia) Autonomous County	496	70660	3608
松桃苗族自治县	Songtao(Miao) Autonomous County	583	92843	3603
关岭布依族苗族自治县	Guanling(Bouyei & Miao) Autonomous County	547	50088	2841
镇宁布依族苗族自治县	Zhenning(Bouyei & Miao) Autonomous County	868	70238	5708
紫云苗族布依族自治县	Ziyun(Miao & Bouyei) Autonomous County	399	40290	2243
威宁彝族、回族、苗族自治县	Weining(Yi, Hui & Miao) Autonomous County	1501	175629	7123
三都水族自治县	Sandu(Shui) Autonomous County	571	43385	1722

19－4 民族自治地方经济社会主要指标
Major Social and Economic Indicators of Minority Nationality Autonomous Areas

指　　标	Item	2000	2001	2001年比2000年增长(%) Increase Rate in 2001 over 2000(%)
年末常住人口(万人)	Number of Permanent Population at The Year－end(10000 persons)	1547.5	1565.13	1.1
#少数民族人口	Minority Population	882.44	869.08	－1.5
国内生产总值(亿元)	Gross Domestic Product(100 million yuan)	309.30	333.83	7.9
第一产业	Primary Industry	130.13	135.04	3.8
第二产业	Secondary Industry	98.50	103.89	5.5
第三产业	Tertiary Industry	80.67	94.90	17.6
固定资产投资(亿元)	Investment in Fixed Assets(100 million yuan)			
固定资产投资总额	Total Investment in Fixed Assets	57.99	77.90	34.0
#基本建设	Capital Construction	29.56	38.70	30.9
更新改造	Innovation	20.89	24.81	18.8
房地产	Real Estate Development	2.59	7.07	173.0
财政、金融(亿元)	Government Finance and Banking(100 million yuan)			
地方财政收入	Local Financial Revenue	18.27	19.73	8.0
财政支出	Financial Expenditure	46.47	63.11	35.8
金融机构年末存款余额	Total Savins Deposit Balance at The Year－end	214.14	257.45	20.2
金融机构年末贷款余额	Total Loan Balance at The Year－end	231.39	243.52	5.2
城乡居民储蓄余额	Urban and Rural Resident Savings Deposit Balance	137.33	161.08	17.3
农业	Agriculture			
耕地面积(万亩)	Cultivated Area(10000 mu)	1199.58	1192.46	－0.6
农业总产值(亿元)	Gross Agricultural Output Value(100 million yuan)	205.38	212.33	3.4
粮食产量(万吨)	Output of Grain(10000 tons)	512.47	506.46	－1.2
油料产量	Output of Oil－bearing Crops	26.10	25.29	－3.1
烟叶产量	Output of Flue－cured Tobacco	11.17	10.91	－2.3
大牲畜年底头数(万头)	Large Animals(year－end)(10000 heads)	458.89	469.73	2.4
猪年底头数(万头)	Hogs(year－end)(10000 heads)	826.21	851.34	3.0
羊年底头数(万只)	Sheep and Goats(year－end)(10000 heads)	200.95	206.30	2.7
工业	Industry			

19－4 续表(continued)

指　　标	Item	2000	2001	2001年比2000年增长(%) Increase Rate in 2001 over 2000(%)
工业总产值(亿元)	Total Gross Industrial Output Value(100 million yuan)	116.29	133.95	15.2
原煤产量(万吨)	Output of Coal(10000 tons)	694.24	959.49	38.2
发电量(亿千瓦小时)	Output of Electricity(100 million kwh)	146.17	181.79	24.4
木材产量(万立方米)	Output of Timber(10000 cu.m)	20.02	10.14	-49.4
运输邮电	**Transportation and Post**			
公路里程(公里)	Length of Highways(km)	25848	26553	2.7
邮路总长度(公里)	Length of Postal Routes(km)	10273	10538	2.6
邮电业务总量(万元)	Business Volume of Post and Telecommunications Service(10000 yuan)	85601	110668	29.3
商业	**Trade**			
社会消费品零售总额(亿元)	Total Retail Sales of Consumer Goods(100 million yuan)	80.58	87.13	8.1
教育	**Education**			
在校学生数(万人)	Students Enrollment(10000 persons)			
高等学校	Institutions of Higher Education	0.86	1.05	22.1
中等学校	Secondary Schools	63.53	72.22	13.7
小学校	Primary Schools	210.05	197.97	-5.8
专任教师(万人)	Full-time Teachers(10000 persons)			
高等学校	Institutions of Higher Education	0.07	0.15	114.3
中等学校	Secondary Schools	3.28	3.39	3.4
小学校	Primary Schools	7.39	7.51	1.6
卫生	**Health**			
卫生机构(个)	Number of Health Institutions(units)	1157	1164	0.6
卫生机构床位(万张)	Number of Beds in Health Institutions(10000 beds)	1.98	1.98	…
卫生技术人员(万人)	Number of Medical Professionals(10000 persons)	2.19	2.19	…
人均水平	**Per Capita Standard of Living**			
人均国内生产总值(元)	Per Capita Gross Domestic Product(yuan)	2039	2145	5.2
人均地方财政收入(元)	Per Capita Local Financial Revenue(yuan)	119	127	6.7
城乡居民人均储蓄(元)	Per Capita Urban and Rural Resident Savings(yuan)	902	1035	14.7

19－5 少数民族自治地方经济发展主要指标(2001)
Major Economic Indicators of Minority Nationality Autonomous Areas

指标名称	Item	民族自治地方 Minority Nationality Autonomous Areas	民族自治州 Minority Nationality Autonomous State	民族自治县 Minority Nationality Autonomous County
国内生产总值(万元)	**Gross Domestic Product(10000 yuan)**	**3338274**	**2593603**	**788056**
第一产业	Primary Industry	1350389	943271	432441
第二产业	Secondary Industry	1038881	878150	165152
第三产业	Tertiary Industry	949004	772182	190463
农业	**Agriculture**			
乡村人口(万人)	Rural Population(10000 persons)	1387.97	969.81	447.43
年末实有耕地面积(万亩)	Cultivated Areas(year－end)(10000 mu)	1192.46	810.00	400.86
农用机械总动力(万千瓦)	Total Agricultural Machinery Power(10000 kw)	256.91	198.00	63.39
农村用电量(万千瓦小时)	Electricity Consumed in Rural Areas(10000 kwh)	44218	34252	10499
化肥使用量(折纯量)(万吨)	Consumption of Chemical Fertilizers(10000 ton)	33.76	17.01	16.94
有效灌溉面积(万亩)	Effective Irrigated Areas(10000 mu)	457.25	355.50	111.63
农作物播种面积	Sown Areas of Farm Crops	2902.50	1962.00	984.44
#粮食	Grain Crops	1897.70	1279.50	650.21
油料	Oil－bearing Crops	317.09	216.00	107.18
粮食总产量(吨)	Total Grain Yield(ton)	5064636	3529973	1618360
油料产量	Oil－bearing Crops Yield	252910	168532	89245
烟叶产量	Tobacco Yield	109074	56377	52817
茶叶产量	Tea Yield	7659	5798	1866
水果产量	Fruits Yield	201241	164095	41565
当年造林面积(万亩)	Afforested Areas in 2001(10000 mu)	206.25	141.00	68.85
牲畜当年出栏数	Number of Slaughtered Animals			
大牲畜(万头)	Large Animals(10000 heads)	64.45	47.84	18.15
猪	Hogs	634.52	453.59	193.17
羊(万只)	Sheep and Goats(10000 heads)	120.15	51.14	69.36
牲畜当年存栏数	Animals in Hand			
大牲畜(万头)	Large Animals(10000 heads)	469.73	347.47	134.33
猪	Hogs	851.34	585.59	279.86
羊(万只)	Sheep and Goats(10000 heads)	206.30	96.72	110.27
肉类总产量(万吨)	Output of Meat(10000 tons)	64.50	44.64	20.80
水产品产量	Aquatic Products	2.95	2.41	0.62
农林牧渔业总产值(万元)	Gross Output Value of Farming, Forestry, Animal Husbandry and Fishery(10000 yuan)	2123292	1499843	663008
农业	Farming	1352295	944379	432992

19－5 续表(continued)

指标名称	Item	民族自治地方 Minority Nationality Autonomous Areas	民族自治州 Minority Nationality Autonomous State	民族自治县 Minority Nationality Autonomous County
林　业	Forestry	101270	79404	23605
牧　业	Animal Husbandry	640883	452442	200529
渔　业	Fishery	28844	23618	5882
农林牧渔业增加值	Value－added of Farming, Forestry, Animal Husbandry and Fishery	1359881	954288	430916
工业(规模以上)	**Industry(above designated size)**			
企业单位数(个)	Number of Industrial Enterprises(unit)	772	653	130
规模以上工业总产值(万元)	Total Gross Industrial Output Value above Designated Size(10000 yuan)	1339536	1214125	129639
工业销售产值(万元)	Sales Output Value of Industry(10000 yuan)	1289916	1170789	120820
工业增加值	Value－added of Industry	451119	405942	46832
利税总额	Total Profits and Taxes	93656	78519	15257
主要工业产品产量	Output of Major Industrial Products			
原煤(万吨)	Coal(10000 tons)	959.49	849.28	110.21
木材(万立方米)	Timber(10000 cu.m)	10.14	8.98	3.62
卷烟(万箱)	Cigarettes(10000 cases)	21.74	21.74	
水泥(万吨)	Cement(10000 tons)	269.10	230.19	38.91
发电量(万千瓦小时)	Electricity(10000 kwh)	1817855	1735497	82358
固定资产投资	**Investment in Fixed Assets**			
固定资产投资完成额(万元)	Total Investment in Fixed Assets (10000 yuan)	778959	667436	116055
基本建设	Capital Construction	387022	313085	78469
更新改造	Innovation	248116	235362	12754
其他投资	Other Investment	73075	53260	19815
房地产开发	Real Estate Development	70746	65729	5017
商　业	**Trade**			
限额以上批发、零售贸易业商品购销存总额(万元)	Total Purchases, Sales and Inventory of Enterprise above Designated Size in Wholesale and Retail Sale Trades(10000 yuan)	779353	523770	255583
社会消费品零售总额	Total Retail Sales of Consumer Goods	871338	703568	182757
财政、金融	**Government Finance and Banking**			
地方财政收入(万元)	Local Financial Revenue(10000 yuan)	197297	157866	41153
财政支出	Financial Expenditure	631128	497294	146243
存款余额	Deposits	2574453	2175603	425084
贷款余额	Loans	2435180	2018289	442361
城乡居民储蓄余额	Urban and Rural Resident Savings Deposit Balance	1610821	1337547	290772

19－6　少数民族自治地方社会发展主要指标(2001)
Major Indicators on Social Development of Minority Nationality Autonomous Areas

指标名称	Item	民族自治地方 Minority Nationality Autonomous Areas	民族自治州 Minority Nationality Autonomous State	民族自治县 Minority Nationality Autonomous County
人口	**Population**			
年末人口(万人)	Number of Population at The Year－end(10000 persons)	1565.13	1111.32	485.69
#少数民族人口	Minority Population	869.08	646.09	252.88
按农业非农业分	Grouped by Agricultural and Non－agricultural Population			
农业人口	Agricultural Population	1417.00	991.98	455.22
非农业人口	Non－agricultural Population	148.13	119.34	30.47
人口密度(人/平方公里)	Population Density(person/sq.km)	160.32	151.62	181.83
运输条件	**Traffic Condition**			
民用汽车拥有量(辆)	Number of Civil Motor Vehicles Owned(unit)	75773	61528	14537
公路线路里程(公里)	Length of Highways(km)	26553	18919	8205
内河航道里程	Length of Navigable Inland Waterways	1145	884	306
邮电、通讯	**Post and Telecommunications**			
邮电所总数(处)	Number of Post and Telecommunications Offices(unit)	700	493	242
#农村局所	Postal Offices of Rural Areas	574	389	217
邮路总长度(公里)	Length of Postal Routes(km)	10538	7304	3339
农村投递线路总长度	Length of Rural Delivery Routes	33442	24104	10796
本地电话年末用户(万户)	Number of Telephone Sets of Urban Areas(10000 unit)	63.23	53.00	11.14
#城市电话用户	Number of Telephone Sets of Urban Areas	45.11	38.00	7.65
邮电业务总量(万元)	Business Volume of Post and Telecommunications Service(10000 yuan)	110668	101916	9302
教育	**Education**			
普通高等学校	Regular Institutions of Higher Education			
学校数(所)	Number of Schools(unit)	7	7	
在校学生数(人)	Students Enrollment(person)	10527	10527	

19－6 续表(continued)

指 标 名 称	Item	民族自治地方 Minority Nationality Autonomous Areas	民族自治州 Minority Nationality Autonomous State	民族自治县 Minority Nationality Autonomous County
招生数	New Student Enrollment	5464	5464	
毕业生数	Graduates	1319	1319	
专任教师数	Full－time Teachers	1477	1477	
中等专业学校	Specialized Secondary Schools			
学校数(所)	Number of Schools(unit)	21	19	3
在校学生数(人)	Students Enrollment(person)	25907	23938	2787
招生数	New Student Enrollment	6434	5790	1034
毕业生数	Graduates	9271	8424	1097
专任教师数	Full－time Teachers	1228	1079	215
普通中学	Regular Secondary Schools			
学校数(所)	Number of Schools(unit)	882	665	233
在校学生数(人)	Students Enrollment(person)	722155	559814	173454
招生数	New Student Enrollment	297741	228207	73958
毕业生数	Graduates	161374	124974	38581
专任教师数	Full－time Teachers	33852	25604	8725
小学校	Primary Schools			
学校数(所)	Number of Schools(unit)	6690	4942	1889
在校学生数(万人)	Students Enrollment(10000 persons)	197.97	140.41	61.99
招生数	New Student Enrollment	33.64	21.80	12.71
毕业生数	Graduates	32.75	23.66	9.70
专任教师数	Full－time Teachers	7.51	5.57	2.09

19－7 少数民族自治地方财政收入(2001)
Total Financial Revenue of Minority Nationality Autonomous Areas

单位:万元
(10000 yuan)

指　标	Item	民族自治地方合计 Miniority Nationality Autonomous Area	民族自治州合计 Minority Nationality Autonomous State	民族自治县合计 Minority Nationality Autonomous County
总　计	**Total**	**197043**	**152545**	**44498**
工商税收类	Industrial and Commercial Tax	91871	75547	16324
农业四税	Agricultural Taxes and Related	36214	24528	11686
企业所得税类	Income Tax of Enterprises	18868	14225	4643
国有资产经营收益	Business Revenue of State－owned Properties	2840	1710	1130
国有企业计划亏损补贴类	Subsidies to Loss－making State－owned Enterprises	－58	－35	－23
其他收入类	Other Revenue	14172	10772	3400
专项收入类	Revenue of Special Item	4995	4306	689
罚没收入行政性收费收入类	Fine, Administrative Collecting Fees	28141	21492	6649

注:本表中民族自治县部分未含三都水族自治县。(下表同)

Note: Minority nationality autonomous counties in this table exclude Sandu(shui) autonomous county. (same to next)

19－8 少数民族自治地方财政支出(2001)
Total Financial Expenditure of Minority Nationality Autonomous Areas

单位:万元
(10000 yuan)

指　标	Item	民族自治地方合计 Miniority Nationality Autonomous Area	民族自治州合计 Minority Nationality Autonomous State	民族自治县合计 Minority Nationality Autonomous County
总　计	**Total**	**631128**	**474293**	**156835**
基本建设支出	Capital Construction	4444	3543	901
企业挖掘改造资金	Innovation Funds of Enterprises	8184	6556	1628
科技三项费用	Science and Technology Promotion	787	707	80
支援农村生产支出	Supporting Agriculture Production	14724	12189	2535
农业综合开发支出	Comprehensive Development of Agriculture	5456	4566	890
农林水利气象等事业费	Operating Expenses of Department of Agriculture, Forestry, Water	49627	36653	12974
工业交通部门事业费	Operating Expenses of Department of Industry Transportation	4463	3567	896
城市维护费	City Maintenance Expenditure	17903	15206	2697
文教卫生事业费	Operating Expenses for Culture, Education Science & Health Care	229212	168140	61072
科学事业费	Operating Expenses of Department of Science	1351	1108	243
其他部门事业费	Operating Expenses of Other Department	27207	22377	4830
抚恤和社会福利救济费	Pensions and Relief Funds for Social Welfare	15317	11142	4175
行政管理费	Government Administration	116134	86424	29710
公检法支出	Agencies of Public Security, Procuratorial and Court of Justice	34334	26498	7836
支援不发达地区支出	Supporting Underdeveloped Areas	49791	36065	13726
其他支出	Others	52194	39552	12642

19－9 少数民族教育基本情况(2001)
Basic Statistics on Minority Nationality Education

单位:人
(person)

类别	Sort	毕业生 Graduates	招生 New Students Enrollment	在校生 Students Enrollment	毕业班学生 Students in Graduated Class	专任教师 Full－time Teachers	独立设置的少数民族学校 Minority Nationality Schools 学校数 Number of Schools	独立设置的少数民族学校 Minority Nationality Schools 在校学生 Students Enrollment
普通中学	Regular Secondary Schools	145059	279877	675415	175810	41813	82	83821
高　中	Senior	16804	43387	96097	22032	4502		35366
初　中	Junior	128255	236490	579318	153778	37311		48455
职业中学	Vocational Secondary Schools	7383	10721	26287	7604	1609	18	6204
高　中	Senior	3565	3454	8553	2956	750		2958
初　中	Junior	3818	7267	17734	4648	859		3246
小　学	Primary Schools	284719	325766	1896676	302424	70188	150	
特殊教育学校	Special Schools			5024		177		
幼儿园	Kindergartens	85271	137243	154340		1987		

19－10 少数民族出版物(2001)
Publications of Monority Nationality

类别	Sort	种数(种) Number of Publications (kind)	新出 Newly Published	总印数(万册) Total Printed (10000 copies)	总印张(千印张) Total Printed Signatures (1000 sheets)
总　计	Total	6	6	1	71.00
使用《中国标准书号》合计	Publications with China Standard Book Number				
#文　学	Literature	3	3	0.3	37.72
历史、地理	History and Geography	1	1	0.1	10.68
语　言	Language	1	1	0.1	3.25
艺　术	Art	1	1	0.1	19.64

19－11 民族自治地方卫生事业发展情况
Basic Statistics of Health Care of Minority Nationality Autonomous Areas

类　别	Item	2000	2001	2001 年比 2000 年增长(%) Increase Rate in 2001 over 2000(%)
卫生机构数合计(个)	**Total Number of Health Care Institution(unit)**	**1368**	**1369**	**0.1**
#医院和卫生院计	Hospitals	1083	1081	-0.2
#专科防治所	Specialized Prevention and Treatment Centers or Station	29	29	持平
卫生防疫站	Sanitation and Antiepidemic Agencies	49	49	持平
妇幼保健站	Maternity and Child Care Centers	42	42	持平
其他卫生事业机构	Other Health Care Institutions	153	152	-0.7
床位数合计(张)	**Number of Beds(bed)**	**22178**	**21540**	**-2.9**
#医院和卫生院床位数	Number of Hospital Beds	20819	20309	-2.4
专业卫生人员数合计(人)	**Number of Medical Technical Personnel(person)**	**34313**	**33883**	**-1.3**
#卫生技术人员数	Medical Technical Personnels	29289	28893	-1.4
#医　生	Doctor	16905	16729	-1.0
村卫生室覆盖率(%)	**Coverage Rate of Village Hospitals(%)**	**78.94**	**79.85**	**0.9(百分点)**
平均每村设置医疗点数(个)	Average Number of Medical Treatment Stations Run by Village Per Village(unit)	0.81	0.83	2.5
平均每村乡村医生和卫生员数(人)	Average Number of Doctors and Health Workers Per Village (person)	1.36	1.35	-0.7

注:表中数据均不包括诊所、卫生保健所和医务室的机构和人员数

Note: Datas in this table excluded the number of institutions and personnels of clinique, hygiene centre and infirmary.

19－12 各少数民族自治州经济发展主要指标(2001)
Major Indicators on Economic Development of Minority Nationality Autonomous States

指标名称	Item	黔西南州 Qianxinan	黔东南州 Qiandongnan	黔南州 Qiannan
国内生产总值(万元)	**Gross Domestic Product(10000 yuan)**	**672053**	**859138**	**1062412**
第一产业	Primary Industry	228981	356926	357364
第二产业	Secondary Industry	228436	249542	400172
第三产业	Tertiary Industry	214636	252670	304876
农业	**Agriculture**			
乡村人口(万人)	Rural Population(10000 persons)	269.57	372.52	327.72
年末实有耕地面积(万亩)	Cultivated Areas(year－end)(10000 mu)	253.50	277.50	279.00
农用机械总动力(万千瓦)	Total Agricultural Machinery Power(10000 kw)	56	72	70
农村用电量(万千瓦小时)	Electricity Consumed in Rural Areas(10000 kwh)	8634	16061	9557
化肥使用量(折纯量)(万吨)	Consumption of Chemical Fertilizers(10000 ton)	6.00	4.93	6.08
有效灌溉面积(万亩)	Effective Irrigated Areas(10000 mu)	72.00	160.50	123.00
农作物播种面积	Sown Areas of Farm Crops	570.00	756.00	636.00
#粮食	Grain Crops	388.50	457.50	433.50
油料	Oil－bearing Crops	39.00	85.50	91.50
粮食总产量(吨)	Total Grain Yield(ton)	1002065	1342420	1185488
油料产量	Oil－bearing Crops Yield	25455	70297	72780
烟叶产量	Tobacco Yield	18357	12057	25963
茶叶产量	Tea Yield	1987	1930	1881
水果产量	Fruits Yield	42402	82764	38929
当年造林面积(万亩)	Afforested Areas in 2001(10000 mu)	40.50	43.50	57.00
牲畜当年出栏数	Number of Slaughtered Animals			
大牲畜(万头)	Large Animals(10000 heads)	14.39	20.37	13.08
猪	Hogs	139.72	169.88	143.99
羊(万只)	Sheep and Goats(10000 heads)	12.10	27.56	11.48
牲畜当年存栏数	Animals in Hand			
大牲畜(万头)	Large Animals(10000 heads)	102.74	124.42	120.31
猪	Hogs	158.00	239.87	187.72
羊(万只)	Sheep and Goats(10000 heads)	22.98	54.24	19.50
肉类总产量(万吨)	Output of Meat(10000 tons)	14.59	15.83	14.22
禽蛋产量(吨)	Output of Poultry and Eggs(ton)	12369	4931	5225
水产品产量	Aquatic Products	4215	15923	3976
农林牧渔业总产值(万元)	Gross Output Value of Farming, Forestry, Animal Husbandry and Fishery(10000 yuan)	393934	560466	545443
农业	Farming	233639	364865	345875

19－12 续表(continued)

指 标 名 称	Item	黔西南州 Qianxinan	黔东南州 Qiandongnan	黔南州 Qiannan
林 业	Forestry	19061	25753	34590
牧 业	Animal Husbandry	137913	153247	161282
渔 业	Fishery	3321	16601	3696
农林牧渔业增加值	Value－added of Farming, Forestry, Animal Husbandry and Fishery	239998	356926	357364
工业(规模以上)	**Industry(above designated size)**			
企业单位数(个)	Number of Industrial Enterprises(unit)	195	214	244
规模以上工业总产值(万元)	Total Gross Industrial Output Value above Designated Size(10000 yuan)	435640	275044	503441
工业销售产值(万元)	Sales Output Value of Industry(10000 yuan)	432814	264157	473818
工业增加值	Value－added of Industry	155068	98321	152553
利税总额	Total Profits and Taxes	26476	9981	42062
主要工业产品产量	Output of Major Industrial Products			
原煤(万吨)	Coal(10000 tons)	381.10	173.74	294.44
木材(万立方米)	Timber(10000 cu.m)	1.38	5.14	2.46
卷烟(万箱)	Cigarettes(10000 cases)	4.74	－	17.00
水泥(万吨)	Cement(10000 tons)	75.06	46.74	108.39
发电量(万千瓦小时)	Electricity(10000 kwh)	1286435	401985	47077
固定资产投资	**Investment in Fixed Assets**			
固定资产投资完成额(万元)	Total Investment in Fixed Assets(10000 yuan)	141593	337314	188529
基本建设	Capital Construction	62318	178398	72369
更新改造	Innovation	62667	98673	74022
其他投资	Other Investment	9597	31974	11689
房地产开发	Real Estate Development	7011	28269	30449
商 业	**Trade**			
限额以上批发、零售贸易业商品购销存总额(万元)	Total Purchases, Sales and Inventory of Enterprise above Designated Size in Wholesale and Retail Trade(10000 yuan)	111151	201440	211179
社会消费品零售总额	Total Retail Sales of Consumer Goods	188881	225069	289618
财政、金融	**Government Finance and Banking**			
地方财政收入(万元)	Local Financial Revenue (10000 yuan)	45903	51659	60304
财政支出	Financial Expenditure	122484	194754	180056
存款余额	Deposits	602395	789755	783453
贷款余额	Loans	478609	785643	754037
城乡居民储蓄余额	Urban and Rural Resident Savings Deposit Balance	307194	517651	512702

19－13 各少数民族自治州社会发展主要指标(2001)
Major Indicators on Social Development of Minority Nationality Autonomous State

指标名称	Item	黔西南州 Qianxinan	黔东南州 Qiandongnan	黔南州 Qiannan
人口	Population			
年末人口(万人)	Number of Population at The Year－end(10000 persons)	299.91	427.30	384.11
#少数民族人口	Minority Population	125.66	315.14	205.29
按农业非农业分	Grouped by Agricultural and Non－agricultural Population			
农业人口	Agricultural Population	272.88	382.79	336.31
非农业人口	Non－agricultural Population	27.03	44.51	47.80
人口密度(人/平方公里)	Population Density(persons/sq.km)	178.56	141.01	146.62
运输条件	Traffic Condition			
民用汽车拥有量(辆)	Number of Civil Motor Vehicles Owned(unit)	16075	33998	11455
公路线路里程(公里)	Length of Highways(km)	5349	5874	7696
内河航道里程	Length of Navigable Inland Waterways	515	369	
邮电、通讯	Post and Telecommunications			
邮电所总数(处)	Number of Post and Telecommunications Offices(unit)	106	241	146
#农村局所	Postal Offices of Rural Areas	87	196	106
邮路总长度(公里)	Length of Postal Routes(km)	1520	3851	1933
农村投递线路总长度	Length of Rural Delivery Routes	5729	8588	9787
本地电话年末用户(万户)	Number of Telephone Sets of Urban Areas(10000 units)	12	20	21
#城市电话用户	Number of Telephone Sets of Urban Areas	9	14	15
邮电业务总量(万元)	Business Volume of Post and Telecommunications Service(10000 yuan)	19880	45989	36047
教育	Education			
普通高等学校	Regular Institutions of Higher Education			
学校数(所)	Number of Schools(unit)	1	3	3
在校学生数(人)	Students Enrollment(person)	3094	3463	3970

19－13 续表(continued)

指 标 名 称	Item	黔西南州 Qianxinan	黔东南州 Qiandongnan	黔南州 Qiannan
招生数	New Student Enrollment	1766	1913	1785
毕业生数	Graduates	360	457	502
专任教师数	Full－time Teachers	137	631	709
普通中等学校	Secondary Schools			
中等专业学校	Specialized Secondary Schools			
学校数(所)	Number of Schools(unit)	8	6	5
在校学生数(人)	Students Enrollment(person)	5536	11153	7249
招生数	New Student Enrollment	1281	2780	1729
毕业生数	Graduates	1911	2812	3701
专任教师数	Full－time Teachers	433	338	308
普通中学	Regular Secondary Schools			
学校数(所)	Number of Schools(unit)	202	254	209
在校学生数(人)	Students Enrollment(person)	160498	214228	185088
招生数	New Student Enrollment	66250	88135	73822
毕业生数	Graduates	32242	48270	44462
专任教师数	Full－time Teachers	6591	9772	9241
小学校	Primary Schools			
学校数(所)	Number of Schools(unit)	1132	2102	1708
在校学生数(人)	Students Enrollment(person)	443624	508781	451726
招生数	New Student Enrollment	63848	79448	74734
毕业生数	Graduates	71120	92987	72470
专任教师数	Full－time Teachers	14768	21313	19666

19－14 各少数民族自治县经济发展主要指标(2001)
Major Indicators on Economic Development of Minority Nationality Autonomous Countys

指 标 名 称	Item	道真县 Daozhen	务川县 Wuchuan	玉屏县 Yuping	印江县 Yinjiang	沿河县 Yanhe	松桃县 Songtao
国内生产总值(万元)	**Gross Domestic Product(10000 yuan)**	**63638**	**60039**	**57463**	**63783**	**70660**	**92843**
第一产业	Primary Industry	37495	32451	20076	43817	46413	58764
第二产业	Secondary Industry	11170	14275	18260	8818	7670	14523
第三产业	Tertiary Industry	14973	13313	19127	11148	16577	19556
农业	**Agriculture**						
乡村人口(万人)	Rural Population(10000 persons)	29.81	38.18	11.22	37.62	51.65	59.73
年末实有耕地面积(万亩)	Cultivated Areas(year－end)(10000 mu)	34.50	42.00	9.00	28.50	40.50	40.50
农用机械总动力(万千瓦)	Total Agricultural Machinery Power(10000 kw)	6	5	3	6	7	7
农村用电量(万千瓦小时)	Electricity Consumed in Rural Areas(10000 kwh)	1010	879	272	1631	612	1153
化肥使用量(折纯量)(万吨)	Consumption of Chemical Fertilizers(10000 tons)	0.99	0.76	1.00	2.00	4.00	4.00
有效灌溉面积(万亩)	Effective Irrigated Areas(10000 mu)	10.50	12.00	6.00	10.50	10.50	18.00
农作物播种面积	Sown Areas of Farm Crops	99.63	126.69	27.00	79.50	102.00	106.50
#粮食	Grain Crops	64.77	87.05	16.50	54.00	76.50	78.00
油料	Oil－bearing Crops	12.15	16.94	6.00	10.50	10.50	15.00
粮食总产量(吨)	Total Grain Yield(ton)	130576	146144	51291	129306	146709	257701
油料产量	Oil－bearing Crops Yield	9959	14739	5774	10556	8518	15340
烟叶产量	Tobacco Yield	11188	11261	55	4481	4799	2310
茶叶产量	Tea Yield	369	140	24	333	79	782
水果产量	Fruits Yield	2923	1378	1122	6628	3035	1863
当年造林面积(万亩)	Afforested Areas in 2001(10000 mu)	4.80	3.75	4.50	6.00	6.00	6.00
牲畜当年出栏数	Number of Slaughtered Animals						
大牲畜(万头)	Large Animals(10000 heads)	1.77	1.90	0.96	1.85	1.17	2.06
猪	Hogs	23.84	16.51	9.06	23.90	21.69	26.29
羊(万只)	Sheep and Goats(10000 heads)	3.98	10.49	1.11	7.07	24.43	9.23
牲畜当年存栏数	Animals in Hand						
大牲畜(万头)	Large Animals(10000 heads)	7.97	12.65	3.47	9.99	12.69	12.33
猪	Hogs	30.81	24.67	8.38	25.88	29.98	34.59
羊(万只)	Sheep and Goats(10000 heads)	8.68	16.05	2.06	9.97	29.56	10.16
肉类总产量(万吨)	Output of Meat(10000 tons)	2.43	1.93	0.83	2.57	2.48	2.65
禽蛋产量(吨)	Output of Poultry and Eggs(ton)						
水产品产量	Aquatic Products	213	131	617	962	900	1373
农林牧渔业总产值(万元)	Gross Output Value of Farming, Forestry, Animal Husbandry and Fishery(10000 yuan)	57897	51347	31130	70802	72726	94742
农 业	Farming	34072	34094	20751	44354	44523	66410

19－14 续表 1(continued)

指 标 名 称	Item	道真县 Daozhen	务川县 Wuchuan	玉屏县 Yuping	印江县 Yinjiang	沿河县 Yanhe	松桃县 Songtao
林 业	Forestry	2281	1686	1771	2126	2457	2093
牧 业	Animal Husbandry	21331	15460	7929	23311	24666	24993
渔 业	Fishery	213	107	679	1011	1080	1246
农林牧渔业增加值(万元)	Value－added of Farming, Forestry, Animal Husbandry and Fishery	36406	32453	20278	43814	46551	58766
工业(规模以上)	**Industry(above designated size)**						
企业单位数(个)	Number of Industrial Enterprises(unit)	9	7	16	7	14	17
规模以上工业总产值(万元)	Total Gross Industrial Output Value above Designated Size(10000 yuan)	5458	3736	20335	4411	4871	12432
工业销售产值(万元)	Sales Output Value of Industry(10000 yuan)	4878	3592	18964	3608	4590	11535
工业增加值	Value－added of Industry	1673	1078	7121	1763	1482	3536
利税总额	Total Profits and Taxes	204	244	934	153	272	429
主要工业产品产量	Output of Major Industrial Products						
原煤(万吨)	Coal(10000 tons)	7.37	12.00		6.07	22.40	
木材(万立方米)	Timber(10000 cu.m)	0.14					
卷烟(万箱)	Cigarettes(10000 cases)						
水泥(万吨)	Cement(10000 tons)	8.10	0.21	3.66	3.84	9.12	3.96
发电量(万千瓦小时)	Electricity(10000 kwh)	5441	2423	25987	2769	1543	2860
固定资产投资	**Investment in Fixed Assets**						
固定资产投资完成额(万元)	Total Investment in Fixed Assets(10000 yuan)	11594	4751	27263	8979	8889	18255
基本建设	Capital Construction	8859	4214	16213	5568	5767	13868
更新改造	Innovation	2400	500	580	1170	74	1353
其他投资	Other Investment	335	37	9950	2241	538	1534
房地产开发	Real Estate Development			520		2510	1500
商业	**Trade**						
限额以上批发、零售贸易业商品购销存总额(万元)	Total Purchases, Sales and Inventory of Enterprise above Designated Size in Wholesale and Retail Sale Trades(10000 yuan)	42859	40588		14817	11825	10907
社会消费品零售总额	Total Retail Sales of Consumer Goods	13973	18543	11886	13164	15711	24267
财政、金融	**Government Finance and Banking**						
地方财政收入(万元)	Local Financial Revenue(10000 yuan)	4278	3688	3408	2931	3608	3603
财政支出	Financial Expenditure	11552	12788	8177	13315	15947	15441
存款余额	Deposits	48462	33921	35415	41918	43471	45422
贷款余额	Loans	36830	40580	37827	45629	44416	50047
城乡居民储蓄余额	Urban and Rural Resident Savings Deposit Balance	34892	23767	26920	33148	30180	33088

19－14 续表 2(continued)

指 标 名 称	Item	关岭县 Guanling	镇宁县 Zhenning	紫云县 Ziyun	威宁县 Weining	三都县 Sandu
国内生产总值(万元)	**Gross Domestic Product(10000 yuan)**	**50088**	**70238**	**40290**	**175629**	**43385**
第一产业	Primary Industry	27140	24478	27623	88861	25323
第二产业	Secondary Industry	11656	31100	5144	38115	4421
第三产业	Tertiary Industry	11292	14660	7523	48653	13641
农业	**Agriculture**					
乡村人口(万人)	Rural Population(10000 persons)	30.30	31.23	31.35	97.08	29.27
年末实有耕地面积(万亩)	Cultivated Areas(year－end)(10000 mu)	22.50	24.00	29.96	111.00	18.41
农用机械总动力(万千瓦)	Total Agricultural Machinery Power(10000 kw)	5.00	5.00	3.00	11.91	4.48
农村用电量(万千瓦小时)	Electricity Consumed in Rural Areas(10000 kwh)	742.00	588.00	476.00	2602.87	533.13
化肥使用量(折纯量)(万吨)	Consumption of Chemical Fertilizers(10000 tons)	…	1.00	1.00	2.00	0.19
有效灌溉面积(万亩)	Effective Irrigated Areas(10000 mu)	7.50	12.00	9.00	5.75	9.89
农作物播种面积	Sown Areas of Farm Crops	48.69	49.50	72.99	228.00	43.94
＃粮食	Grain Crops	36.00	37.50	50.88	117.00	32.01
油料	Oil－bearing Crops	6.75	9.00	12.75	1.50	6.09
粮食总产量(吨)	Total Grain Yield(ton)	104306	114434	114571	339625	83697
油料产量	Oil－bearing Crops Yield	4459	9126	4532	1375	4867
烟叶产量	Tobacco Yield	1096	63	1035	16409	120
茶叶产量	Tea Yield	17	37	21	59	5
水果产量	Fruits Yield	4192	2657	2747	10601	4419
当年造林面积(万亩)	Afforested Areas in 2001(10000 mu)	3.00	1.50	10.50	19.20	3.60
牲畜当年出栏数	Number of Slaughtered Animals					
大牲畜(万头)	Large Animals(10000 heads)	1.41	1.53	0.96	3.00	1.54
猪	Hogs	8.36	7.83	10.45	33.00	12.24
羊(万只)	Sheep and Goats(10000 heads)	0.93	…	0.77	11.00	0.35
牲畜当年存栏数	Animals in Hand					
大牲畜(万头)	Large Animals(10000 heads)	13.22	11.73	12.46	25.75	12.07
猪	Hogs	11.22	11.91	20.75	67.56	14.11
羊(万只)	Sheep and Goats(10000 heads)	2.02	0.56	2.52	28.00	0.69
肉类总产量(万吨)	Output of Meat(10000 tons)	0.92	0.85	1.25	3.95	0.94
禽蛋产量(吨)	Output of Poultry and Eggs(ton)					
水产品产量	Aquatic Products	223	674	265	56	784
农林牧渔业总产值(万元)	Gross Output Value of Farming, Forestry, Animal Husbandry and Fishery(10000 yuan)	43101	33515	37892	130297	39559
农 业	**Farming**	**26983**	**22247**	**21176**	**93306**	**25076**

19－14 续表 3(continued)

指 标 名 称	Item	关岭县 Guanling	镇宁县 Zhenning	紫云县 Ziyun	威宁县 Weining	三都县 Sandu
林 业	Forestry	2248	1766	3597	1841	1739
牧 业	Animal Husbandry	13643	9011	13006	35091	12088
渔 业	Fishery	227	491	113	59	656
农林牧渔业增加值(万元)	Value－added of Farming, Forestry, Animal Husbandry and Fishery(10000 yuan)	27140	23701	27623	88861	25323
工业(规模以上)	**Industry(above designated size)**					
企业单位数(个)	Number of Industrial Enterprises(unit)	15	13	6	15	11
规模以上工业总产值(万元)	Total Gross Industrial Output Value above Designated Size(10000 yuan)	13359	30951	2171	27687	4227
工业销售产值(万元)	Sales Output Value of Industry(10000 yuan)	14044	29604	1917	26395	1693
工业增加值	Value－added ofIndustry	6843	15923	1014	4744	1655
利税总额	Total Profits and Taxes	1081	9891	179	1750	120
主要工业产品产量	Output of Major Industrial Products					
原煤(万吨)	Coal(10000 tons)		0.16		62.22	
木材(万立方米)	Timber(10000 cu. m)		0.20	0.82		2.46
卷烟(万箱)	Cigarettes(10000 cases)					
水泥(万吨)	Cement(10000 tons)	2.70	0.71	2.40	4.21	
发电量(万千瓦小时)	Electricity(10000 kwh)	20727	12230	5247	3131	
固定资产投资	**Investment in Fixed Assets**					
固定资产投资完成额(万元)	Total Investment in Fixed Assets(10000 yuan)	7406	18858	3670	1858	4532
基本建设	Capital Construction	4922	10450	2921	1155	4532
更新改造	Innovation	2100	4109	12	456	
其他投资	Other Investment	144	4299	737		
房地产开发	Real Estate Development	240			247	
商业	**Trade**					
限额以上批发、零售贸易业商品购销存总额(万元)	Total Purchases, Sales and Inventory of Enterprise above Designated Size in Wholesale and Retail Sale Trades(10000 yuan)		11884	7419	115284	
社会消费品零售总额	Total Retail Sales of Consumer Goods	15653	17106	14965	22502	14987
财政、金融	**Government Finance and Banking**					
地方财政收入(万元)	Local Financial Revenue(10000 yuan)	2841	5708	2243	7123	1722
财政支出	Financial Expenditure	11499	14485	10260	20370	12409
存款余额	Deposits	33806	42910	23590	49935	26234
贷款余额	Loans	29695	47242	32253	52372	25470
城乡居民储蓄余额	Urban and Rural Resident Savings Deposit Balance	21575	25552	12507	31645	17498

19－15 各少数民族自治县社会发展主要指标(2001)
Major Indicators on Social Development of Minority Nationality Autonomous Countys

指标名称	Item	道真县 Daozhen	务川县 Wuchuan	玉屏县 Yuping	印江县 Yinjiang	沿河县 Yanhe	松桃县 Songtao
人口	**Population**						
年末人口(万人)	Number of Population at The Year－end(10000 persons)	33.27	41.42	13.94	40.75	54.89	62.92
#少数民族人口	Minority Population	26.18	33.69	2.27	13.68	25.40	36.04
按农业非农业分	Grouped by Agricultural and Non－agricultural Population						
农业人口	Agricultural Population	30.61	38.52	11.48	38.28	51.64	59.72
非农业人口	Non－agricultural Population	2.66	2.90	2.46	2.47	3.25	3.20
人口密度(人/平方公里)	Population Density(persons/sq.km)	154.31	149.75	269.63	206.96	221.69	234.08
运输条件	**Traffic Condition**						
民用汽车拥有量(辆)	Number of Civil Motor Vehicles Owned(unit)	1595	1756	471	529	640	868
公路线路里程(公里)	Length of Highways(km)	1292	1338	145	465	496	583
内河航道里程	Length of Navigable Inland Waterways			11		132	48
邮电、通讯	**Post and Telecommunications**						
邮电所总数(处)	Number of Post and Telecommunications Offices(unit)	39	26	4	14	24	15
#农村局所	Postal Offices of Rural Areas	36	24	2	12	21	13
邮路总长度(公里)	Length of Postal Routes(km)	347	256	2	228	442	1283
农村投递线路总长度	Length of Rural Delivery Routes	535	996	583	848	1277	547
本地电话年末用户(万户)	Number of Telephone Sets of Urban Areas(10000 units)	1.16	1.27	1.00	1.20	1.00	1.20
#城市电话用户	Number of Telephone Sets of Rural Areas	0.73	0.75	0.70	0.80	0.60	0.70
邮电业务总量(万元)	Business Volume of Post and Telecommunications Service(10000 yuan)	1294	1340	189	258	201	319
教育	**Education**						
普通中学	Regular Secondary Schools						
学校数(所)	Number of Schools(unit)	24	20	12	21	26	34
在校学生数(人)	Students Enrollment(person)	16952	16238	7873	20275	21057	25720
招生数	New Student Enrollment	6735	6783	3219	8655	9289	11503
毕业生数	Graduates	3596	3411	2138	4773	4339	5483
专任教师数	Full－time Teachers	934	820	414	976	1029	1221
小学校	Primary Schools						
学校数(所)	Number of Schools(unit)	158	170	81	142	216	308
在校学生数(人)	Students Enrollment(person)	32248	54424	14573	47999	82651	9946
招生数	New Student Enrollment	4638	9392	2079	8037	16480	18697
毕业生数	Graduates	6625	8307	2802	8170	12120	15057
专任教师数	Full－time Teachers	1577	1601	566	1987	2363	2939

19－15 续表(continued)

指 标 名 称	Item	关岭县 Guanling	镇宁县 Zhenning	紫云县 Ziyun	威宁县 Weining	三都县 Sandu
人口	**Population**					
年末人口(万人)	Number of Population at the Year－end(10000 persons)	31.98	34.10	33.25	107.29	31.88
#少数民族人口	Minority Population	18.60	19.07	22.00	26.06	29.89
按农业非农业分	Grouped by Agricultural and Non－agricultural Population					
农业人口	Agricultural Population	29.35	31.09	31.44	102.89	30.20
非农业人口	Non－agricultural Population	2.63	3.01	1.81	4.40	1.68
人口密度(人/平方公里)	Population Density(person/sq. km)	218.14	198.49	145.83	170.44	133.95
运输条件	**Traffic Condition**					
民用汽车拥有量(辆)	Number of Civil Motor Vehicles Owned(unit)	597	768	329	6692	292
公路线路里程(公里)	Length of Highways(km)	547	868	399	1501	571
内河航道里程	Length of Navigable Inland Waterways	70				45
邮电、通讯	**Post and Telecommunications**					
邮电所总数(处)	Number of Post and Telecommunications Offices(unit)	9	33	27	16	35
#农村局所	Postal Offices of Rural Areas	8	31	24	14	32
邮路总长度(公里)	Length of Postal Routes(km)	79	160	40	397	105
农村投递线路总长度	Length of Rural Delivery Routes	257	274	366	3655	1458
本地电话年末用户(万户)	Number of Telephone Sets of Urban Areas(10000 units)	…	1.00	0.83	1.57	0.91
#城市电话用户	Number of Telephone Sets of Rural Areas	…	1.00	0.56	1.27	0.54
邮电业务总量(万元)	Business Volume of Post and Telecommunications Service(10000 yuan)	1210	1330	698	1913	550
教育	**Education**					
普通中学	Regular Secondary Schools					
学校数(所)	Number of Schools(unit)	8	12	19	41	16
在校学生数(人)	Students Enrollment(person)	12383	10204	8968	22671	11113
招生数	New Student Enrollment	5095	4284	3863	10108	4424
毕业生数	Graduates	3445	2644	1965	4606	2181
专任教师数	Full－time Teachers	566	499	542	1247	477
小学校	Primary Schools					
学校数(所)	Number of Schools(unit)	119	149	119	286	141
在校学生数(人)	Students Enrollment(person)	49416	44421	46452	193400	44395
招生数	New Student Enrollment	8086	8282	10154	32500	8727
毕业生数	Graduates	7084	6775	4798	19200	6030
专任教师数	Full－time Teachers	1550	1587	1472	3700	1514

20

Twenty

城市建设与发展

General Survey of Cities

20-1 城市公用事业基本情况
Basic Statistics on Urban Public Utilities

指　　标	Item	2000	2001	2001年比2000年增长(%) Increase Rate in 2001 over 2000(%)
城市规模	**Scale of Cities**			
城市总户数(万户)	Number of Total Urban Households(10000 households)		220.4	
城市人口(万人)	Population of Cities(10000 persons)		864.4	
#非农业人口	Non-agricultural Population		309.3	
城市面积(平方公里)	Cities Areas (sq.m)		22864	
#建成区面积	Developed Area	291.65	304.08	4.3
城市人口密度(人/平方公里)	Population Density of Urban Districts(persons/sq.km)	334	378	13.2
城市供水及供气	**Water Supply and Gas Supply**			
供水管道长度(公里)	Length of Water Supply Pipelines(km)	2904	3143	8.2
自来水年供水量(亿吨)	Annual Supply of Tap Water(100 million tons)	4.59	4.64	1.1
#生活用水量	Water Consumption for Residential Use	1.87	2.19	17.1
人均生活用水(升)	Per Capita Water Consumption for Residential Use(liter)	137.55	179.84	30.7
用水普及率(%)	Percentage of Population with Access to Tap Water(%)	94.17	38.54	
煤气供气量(万立方米)	Coal Gas Supply(10000 cu.m)	8727	9143	4.8
#家庭用量	Consumption of Coal Gas for Residential Use	5098	5360	5.1
液化石油气供气量(万吨)	Liquefied Petroleum Gas Supply(10000 tons)	2.89	3.09	6.9
#家庭用量	Consumption of Liquefied Gas for Residential Use	2.75	2.94	6.9
煤气管道长度(公里)	Length of Gas Pipelines(km)	1121	1275	13.7
用气普及率(%)	Percentage of Population with Access to Gas(%)	54.42	23.53	
市政工程	**Municipal Engineering**			
城市道路长度(公里)	Length of Paved Roads(km)	1682	1743	3.6
平均每万人拥有	Length of Paved Roads Per 10000 Population	5.50	2.02	
城市道路面积(万平方米)	Area of Paved Roads(10000 sq.m)	1584	1843	16.4
人均拥有道路面积(平方米)	Area of Paved Roads Per Capita(sq.m)	5.21	2.13	-59.1

20-1 续表(continued)

指　　标	Item	2000	2001	20I01 年比 2000 年增长(%) Increase Rate in 2001 over 2000(%)
城市桥梁(座)	Number of Bridges(unit)	310	307	-1.0
排水管道长度(公里)	Length of Drainpipe(km)	1665	1755	5.4
污水处理能力(万吨/日)	Disposal Capacity of Sewage(10000 tons/day)	4.3	8.0	86.0
路灯盏数(盏)	Number of Street Lamp(unit)	43863	57023	30.0
公共交通	**Public Traffic**			
公共汽车总数(标台)	Number of Public Transportation Vehicles(unit)	4144	4263	2.9
平均每万人拥有公交车(标台)	Number of Public Transportation Vehicles Per 10000 Population(unit)	13.62	4.93	
客运总量(万人次)	Number of Passengers Carried(10000 person-times)	68629	77475	12.9
出租汽车(万辆)	Taxi(10000 units)	0.74	0.76	2.7
城市绿化	**Afforestation in Cities**			
绿化面积(公顷)	Public Green Areas(hectare)	11660	12220	4.8
园林绿地面积	Areas of Green Land	9940	10372	4.3
#公共绿地面积	Public Green Areas	2507	2829	12.8
人均公共绿地面积(平方米)	Per Capita Public Green Areas(sq.m)	8.20	3.27	
公园数(个)	Number of Parks(unit)	41	45	9.8
公园游人数(万人次)	Number of Visitors to Parks(10000 person-times)	2892	3169	9.6
建城区绿化覆盖率(%)	Coverage Rate of Urban Green Areas(%)	24.70	25.45	3.0
环境卫生	**Environmental Sanitation**			
清运垃圾(万吨)	Volume of Garbage Disposal(10000 tons)	248.35	164.00	-34.0
清运粪便	Volume of Excrement and Urine Disposal	14.62	5.50	-62.4
每万人有公厕(座)	Number of Public Lavatories Per 10000 Population(unit)	5.58	2.07	

20－2 城市主要经济社会指标占全省比重(2001)
Major Social and Economic Indicators of Cities as Percentage to Provincial Total

指　　标	Item	全　省 Provincial Total	全部城市 Total Cities	占全省比重(%) As Percentage to Provincial Total(%)	地级市 City at Prefectural Level	占全省比重(%) As Percentage to Provincial Total(%)
年末总人口(万人)	Total Population at The Year－end(10000 persons)	3777.12	1965.38	52.0	1609.65	42.6
国内生产总值(亿元)	Gross Domestic Product(100 million yuan)	1084.90	844.90	77.9	709.88	65.4
地方财政收入	Local Financial Revenue	99.75	57.75	57.9	49.99	50.1
财政支出	Financial Expenditure	275.20	102.26	37.2	87.75	31.9
农林牧渔业总产值	Gross Output Value of Farming, Forestry, Animal Husbandry and Fishery	418.61	265.19	63.4	214.08	51.1
规模以上工业总产值	Total Gross Industrial Output Value above Designated Size	696.63	596.03	85.6	497.62	71.4
旅客运量(万人)	Passenger Traffic(10000 persons)	5.56	5.52	99.2	4.48	80.6
货物运量(万吨)	Freight Traffic(10000 tons)	1.99	1.54	77.6	1.31	65.7
邮电业务总量(亿元)	Business Volume of Post and Telecommunications Service(100 million yuan)	47.57	34.88	73.3	28.08	59.0
社会消费品零售总额	Total Retail Sales of Consumer Goods	378.01	302.74	80.1	224.24	59.3

注:表中地级市即指贵阳、六盘水、遵义、安顺等四个城市。

Note:The cities at prefectural level in this table are Guiyang,Liupanshui,Zunyi ,Anshun.

20－3 各地级市主要经济社会指标(2001)
Major Social and Economic Indicators by Cities at Prefectural Level

指标	Item	贵阳市 Guiyang	六盘水市 Liupanshui	遵义市 Zunyi	安顺市 Anshun
人口、劳动力及土地面积	**Population, Labor and Land Area**				
行政区域土地面积(平方公里)	Land Area of Administrative District(sq.km)	8034	9914	30762	9264
#建成区面积	Developed Areas	107	28	48	18
年末总人口(万人)	Total Population at The Year－end(10000 persons)	341.29	291.11	722.08	255.17
年末总户数(万户)	Total Households at The Year－end(10000 households)	97.18	79.83	188.28	67.16
年末单位从业人员数(万人)	Number of Employed Persons at The Year－end(10000 persons)	53.80	18.87	27.41	10.63
第一产业	Primary Industry	0.61	1.11	0.65	0.54
第二产业	Secondary Industry	26.80	10.63	9.44	3.40
第三产业	Tertiary Industry	26.39	7.13	17.32	6.69
城镇个体从业人员(人)	Urban Self－employed Individuals(person)	104696	42495	178700	33007
综合经济	**General Economy**				
国内生产总值(万元)	Gross Domestic Product(10000 yuan)	3027470	908799	2527461	635033
第一产业	Primary Industry	250919	139517	826653	189223
第二产业	Secondary Industry	1526873	491289	916475	230440
#工业	Industry	1228304	402000	752530	178020
第三产业	Tertiary Industry	1249678	277993	784333	215370
财政、金融、保险	Government Finance, Banking and Insurance				
地方财政收入(万元)	Local Financial Revenue(10000 yuan)	279687	54114	124652	41453
地方财政支出	Financial Expenditure	361699	120669	281214	113890
年末金融机构存款余额	Total Savings Deposit Balancs(year－end)	6452190	863751	2062409	687158
#城乡镇居民储蓄	Urban and Rural Resident Savings Deposits	2401281	389997	1170426	394305
年末金融机构贷款余额	Total Loan Balance(year－end)	4863088	746562	1560012	690570
承保额	Amount Insured	10795300	795600	2660312	273055
保　费	Premium	95221	13100	24412	10355
农业	**Agriculture**				
农林牧渔业总产值(万元)	Gross Output Value of Farming, Forestry, Animal Husbandry and Fishery(10000 yuan)	389659	207819	1277528	265804

20－3 续表 1(continued)

指　　标	Item	贵阳市 Guiyang	六盘水市 Liupanshui	遵义市 Zunyi	安顺市 Anshun
年末实有耕地面积(万亩)	Cultivated Area(year－end)(10000 mu)	160.24	158.77	592.42	174.19
蔬菜产量(吨)	Output of Vegetable(ton)	704129	273902	1665106	243217
水果产量	Output of Fruit	37962	11204	69761	14347
肉类总产量	Output of Meat	126966	59241	401499	74129
奶类产量	Output of Milk	15932	317	4519	520
水产品产量(万吨)	Output of Aquatic Products(10000 tons)	0.86	0.08	1.32	0.33
工业(规模以上)	**Industry(above designated size)**				
工业企业数(个)	Number of Industrial Enterprises(unit)	587	93	245	128
内资企业(个)	Domestic－funded Enterprises(unit)	546	90	236	125
港、澳、台商投资企业(个)	Enterprises Funded by Hongkong, Macao and Taiwan(unit)	24	3	4	
外商投资企业(个)	Foreign Funded Enterprises(unit)	17		5	3
规模以上工业总产值(万元)	Total Gross Industrial Output Value above Designated Size(10000 yuan)	2588494	654406	1218984	514363
#内资企业	Domestic Funded Enterprise	2494669	652624	1190960	491390
港澳台商投资企业	Funded by Entrepreneurs from Hong Kong, Macao and Taiwan	41319	1782	7599	
外商投资企业	Foreign Funded Enterprises	52506		20425	22973
交通运输、邮电通信、能源电力	**Transportation, Postal and Telecommunications Service, Energy and Electricity**				
铁路客运量(万人)	Passenger Traffic of Railways(10000 persons)	641.54	399.85	300.58	96.49
铁路货运量(万吨)	Freight Traffic of Railways(10000 tons)	902	1620	246	287
境内铁路里程(公里)	Length of Railways in Churchyard(km)	299	333	194	101
民用汽车拥有量(辆)	Number of Civil Motor Vehicles Owned(unit)	64552	21075	63652	15294
#私人汽车拥有量	Number of Motor Vehicles Owned by Individuals	20260	7110	45021	8251
公路客运量(万人)	Passenger Traffic of Highways(10000 persons)	16555	9444	12316	4905
公路货运量(万吨)	Freight Traffic of Highways(10000 tons)	3978	3202	1968	745
境内公路里程(公里)	Length of Highways in Churchyard(km)	2203	2495	14700	1610
水运客运量(万人)	Passenger Traffic of Waterways(10000 persons)	62.2		70	34
水运货运量(万吨)	Freight Traffic of Waterways(10000 tons)	4		94	27

20－3 续表 2(continued)

指　　标	Item	贵阳市 Guiyang	六盘水市 Liupanshui	遵义市 Zunyi	安顺市 Anshun
民用航空货邮运量(吨)	Freignt Traffic of Civil Aviation(ton)	8625			
民用航空客运量(人)	Passenger Traffic of Civil Aviation(person)	754725			
年末邮电局(所)数(处)	Number of Post & Telecommunications Offices at The Year－end(unit)	386	188	287	83
邮政业务总量(万元)	Business Volume of Post Service(10000 yuan)	15015	3089	11151	2738
电信业务总量(万元)	Business Volume of Telecommunications Service(10000 yuan)	154562	14007	58400	21796
本地电话用户数(万户)	Local Telephone Subscribers(10000 subscribers)	61.11	12.57	41	12.73
年末移动电话用户数	Number of Mobile Telephone Subscribers at The Year－end	676707	89620	192961	104692
国际互联网用户数	Number of Subscribers of Internet Service	89599	1924	15600	3360
全年用电量(万千瓦时)	Electricity Consumption of The Whole Year(10000 kwh)	1166478	186778	458929	158426
#工业用电	Electricity Consumption for Industry	980747	157093	441086	100148
城乡居民生活用电	Electricity Consumption for Urban and Rural Households	86193	29685	17843	17707
贸易、外经、旅游	**Tourism, Foreign Trade and Economic Cooperation**				
社会消费品零售总额(万元)	Total Retail Sales of Consumer Goods(10000 yuan)	1216556	199189	595140	231547
进口额(万美元)	Total Imports(USD 10000)	16313	2807	8	
出口额(万美元)	Total Exports(USD 10000)	33114	316	8	14
当年新签项目(合同)数(个)	Number of Contracts Newly Signed in 2001(unit)	37	7	11	7
当年合同外资金额(万美元)	Value of Foreign Capital Through Signed Contracts in 2001(USD 10000)	4203	3126	2407	1785
当年实际使用外资金额	Value of Foreign Capital Actually Utilized in 2001	5941	3026	2407	220
国际旅游者人数(人)	Number of International Tourists(person)	59501	1101	650	45700
外国人	Foreigners	20825	649	150	17400
港、澳、台同胞	Compatriots from Hong Kong, Macao and Taiwan	38676	452	500	28300

20-3 续表 3(continued)

指　　标	Item	贵阳市 Guiyang	六盘水市 Liupanshui	遵义市 Zunyi	安顺市 Anshun
国际旅游收入(万美元)	Earnings from International Tourism(USD 10000)	1633	44	22	1363
固定资产投资	**Investment in Fixed Assets**				
固定资产投资(万元)	Investment in Fixed Assets	1467685	316016	606755	154085
#住宅	Residential Buildings	292016	29483	219651	3525
本年施工住宅面积(万平方米)	Floor Space of Residential Buildings under Construction(10000 sq.m)	659.44	58.59	248.52	15.34
本年竣工住宅面积(万平方米)	Floor Space of Residential Buildings Completed(10000 sq.m)	255.19	25.57	223.65	8.58
人民生活	**People's Livelihood**				
住宅建筑面积(万平方米)	Floor Space of Residence(10000 sq.m)	2825	324	666	329
住宅使用面积(万平方米)	Living Space of Residence(10000 sq.m)	2119	240	360	247
在岗职工平均人数(万人)	Average Number of Staff and Workers on Their Posts(10000 persons)	49.49	16.3	25.52	10.48
在岗职工工资总额(万元)	Total Wages of Staff and Workers on Their Posts(10000 yuan)	525095	148606	250720	90057
城镇居民人均可支配收入(元)	Per Capita Annual Disposable Income of Households(yuan)	6909	5146	5540	4839
城镇居民人均消费支出	Per Capita Annual Living Expenditures for Consumption of Households	5776	3558	4383	3562
居民消费价格指数(上年为100)	General Consumer Price Index(preceding year = 100)	103.2	100.9	100.3	101.6
年末离休、退休、退职人员数(万人)	Number of Persons Retired and Resigned(10000 persons)	19.92	6.20	3.18	3.45
基本养老保险参保职工(人)	Staffs and Workers Accepted Basic Endowment Insurance(person)	249600	22314	88423	59245
基本医疗保险参保人数	Number of Persons Accepted Basic Medical Insurance	58508	37047	150000	
失业保险参保人数	Number of Persons Accepted Unemployment Insurance	287809	77883	145222	56011
社会福利院数(个)	Number of Beds of Welfare Home(unit)	68	50	251	4
社会福利院床位数(张)	Number of Welfare Home(unit)	1820	960	3679	94
社区服务设施数(个)	Number of Urban Welfare Facilities(unit)	1206	87	1766	183
居民最低生活保障人数(人)	Number of Persons Receiving Lowest Cost of Life(person)	66052	45323	37907	15977

20－4 各县级市主要经济社会指标(2001)
Major Social and Economic Indicators by Cities at County Level

指　标	Item	铜仁市 Tongren	兴义市 Xingyi	毕节市 Bijie	凯里市 Kaili
土地面积	**Total Land Area**				
行政区域土地面积(平方公里)	Land Area of Administrative District(sq.km)	1514	2911	3412	1306
人口	**Population**				
年末总人口(万人)	Total Population at the Year－end(10000 persons)	33.49	72.91	125.85	44.79
#非农业人口	Non－agricultural Population	8.86	11.50	11.66	16.12
人口密度(人/平方公里)	Population Density(person/sq.km)	221	250	369	343
国民核算	**National Accounting**				
国内生产总值(万元)	Gross Domestic Product(10000 yuan)	113500	314685	356259	234649
第一产业	Primary Industry	27601	65488	111219	39651
第二产业	Secondary Industry	43842	152574	123510	104443
第三产业	Tertiary Industry	42057	96623	121530	90555
固定资产投资	**Investment in Fixed Assets**				
固定资产投资(万元)	Investment in Fixed Assets(10000 yuan)	52405	75685	98743	143286
#房地产开发投资	Investment of Real Estate Development	14025	7011	8617	25654
财政	**Government Finance**				
地方财政收入(万元)	Local Financial Revenue(10000 yuan)	7068	18398	18049	12460
财政支出	Financial Expenditure	15718	28671	32801	20321
农业	**Agriculture**				
农林牧渔业总产值(万元)	Gross Output Value of Farming, Forestry, Animal Husbandry and Fishery(10000 yuan)	45580	110343	184296	61030
主要农产品产量	Output of Major Farm Products				
粮食(万吨)	Grain(10000 tons)	13.34	24.55	38.09	10.64
水果(吨)	Fruit(ton)	3948	12850	10967	3745
肉类总产量	Total Output of Meat	14408	52276	50859	16958
水产品	Aquatic Products	1276	2416	370	1519
工业	**Industry**				
规模以上工业总产值(万元)	Total Gross Industrial Output Value above Designated Size(10000 yuan)	63354	379233	173289	139116

20-4 续表 1(continued)

指标	Item	铜仁市 Tongren	兴义市 Xingyi	毕节市 Bijie	凯里市 Kaili
轻工业	Light Industry	40016	46077	135186	34856
重工业	Heavy Industry	23338	333156	38103	104260
主要工业产品产量	**Output of Major Industrial Products**				
原煤(万吨)	Coal(10000 tons)		20.60	44.70	153.40
发电量(万千瓦小时)	Electricity(10000 kwh)	10649	1248199	24556	374867
化肥(万吨)	Chemical Fertilizer(10000 tons)	0.33	7.69	6.58	0.04
交通运输、邮电	**Transportation and Post**				
旅客发送量(万人)	Passenger Traffic(10000 persons)	1424	1144	1002	5339
货物运输量(万吨)	Freight Traffic(10000 tons)	78	790	186	874
邮电业务总量(万元)	Business Volume of Post and Telecommunications Service(10000 yuan)	1753	11728	9129	14554
国内商业	**Domestic Trade**				
社会消费品零售总额(万元)	Total Retail Sales of Consumer Goods(10000 yuan)	50821	97501	46895	72324
教育	**Education**				
普通中学	Secondary Schools				
学校数(所)	Number of Schools(unit)	23	54	34	31
在校生数(人)	Students Enrollment(person)	20051	46394	55146	27995
专任教师数	Full-time Teachers	1054	2074	2417	1554
小学	Primary Schools				
学校数(所)	Number of Schools(unit)	54	250	416	152
在校生数(人)	Students Enrollment(person)	38254	102037	167794	48218
专任教师数	Full-time Teachers	1710	3682	4835	2411
人均生活水平	**Standard of Living Per Capita**				
人均国内生产总值(元)	Per Capita GDP(yuan)	3408	4340	2847	5268
人均地方财政收入	Per Capita Local Financial Revenue	212	254	144	280
职工平均货币工资	Per Capita Annual Disposable Income of Urban Households	9229	8468	8640	8064
城镇居民人均储蓄	Per Capita Urban and Rural Resident Savings Deposits	2861	2288	1067	4212

20 - 4 续表 2(continued)

指　　标	Item	都匀市 Duyun	福泉市 Fuquan	清镇市 Qingzhen	赤水市 Chishui	仁怀市 Renhuai
土地面积	**Total Land Area**					
行政区域土地面积(平方公里)	Land Area of Administrative District(sq. km)	2274	1688	1492	1801	1788
人口	**Population**					
年末总人口(万人)	Total Population at the Year - end(10000 persons)	48.15	30.54	50.53	30.80	59.20
# 非农业人口	Non - agricultural Population	16.61	4.96	10.85	6.94	5.47
人口密度(人/平方公里)	Population Density(person/sq. km)	212	181	339	171	331
国民核算	**National Accounting**					
国内生产总值(万元)	Gross Domestic Product(10000 yuan)	186106	144997	286478	112181	238680
第一产业	Primary Industry	33438	45873	41496	41300	66719
第二产业	Secondary Industry	61709	52836	172755	51516	135230
第三产业	Tertiary Industry	90959	46288	72227	19365	36731
固定资产投资	**Investment in Fixed Assets**					
固定资产投资(万元)	Investment in Fixed Assets(10000 yuan)	75163	16547	41066	45100	33671
# 房地产开发投资	Investment of Real Estate Development	28434	1092	4831	6726	
财政	**Government Finance**					
地方财政收入(万元)	Local Financial Revenue(10000 yuan)	12075	6896	12727	6968	15973
财政支出	Financial Expenditure	21017	11209	20327	14450	27824
农业	**Agriculture**					
农林牧渔业总产值(万元)	Gross Output Value of Farming, Forestry, Animal Husbandry and Fishery(10000 yuan)	52247	57654	63971	62528	101163
主要农产品产量	Output of Major Farm Products					
粮食(万吨)	Grain(10000 tons)	9.13	10.71	12.88	13.36	24.61
水果(吨)	Fruit(ton)	3889	6664	4701	4772	14224
肉类总产量	Total Output of Meat	14571	10326	18986	19310	37532
水产品	Aquatic Products	673	344	4244	651	524
工业	**Industry**					
规模以上工业总产值(万元)	Total Gross Industrial Output Value above Designated Size(10000 yuan)	113526	115608	278109	99066	184339

20－4 续表 3(continued)

指　　标	Item	都匀市 Duyun	福泉市 Fuquan	清镇市 Qingzhen	赤水市 Chishui	仁怀市 Renhuai
轻工业	Light Industry	21073	1719	8608	10765	181827
重工业	Heavy Industry	92453	113889	269500	88301	2512
主要工业产品产量	Output of Major Industrial Products					
原煤(万吨)	Coal(10000 tons)	7.28	43.10	38.94	3.41	26.00
发电量(万千瓦小时)	Electricity(10000 kwh)		3803	757176	14169	6589
化肥(万吨)	Chemical Fertilizer(10000 tons)	0.42	5.51	3.04	27.16	0.43
交通运输、邮电	**Transportation and Post**					
旅客发送量(万人)	Passenger Traffic(10000 persons)	1080	337	569.26	343	447
货物运输量(万吨)	Freight Traffic(10000 tons)	178	228	1014	220	120
邮电业务总量(万元)	Business Volume of Post and Telecommunications Service(10000 yuan)	18020	2377	2950	2980	4568
国内商业	**Domestic Trade**					
社会消费品零售总额(万元)	Total Retail Sales of Consumer Goods(10000 yuan)	71100	36135	40902	20489	23558
教育	**Education**					
普通中学	Secondary Schools					
学校数(所)	Number of Schools(unit)	28	18	29	14	26
在校生数(人)	Students Enrollment(person)	27808	19273	24920	13404	33597
专任教师数	Full－time Teachers	1306	991	1254	766	1305
小学	Primary Schools					
学校数(所)	Number of Schools(unit)	247	144	271	101	241
在校生数(人)	Students Enrollment(person)	47548	36662	62118	24917	81213
专任教师数	Full－time Teachers	2388	1833	2631	1340	2856
人均生活水平	**Standard of Living Per Capita**					
人均国内生产总值(元)	Per Capita GDP(yuan)	3887	4774	5702	3663	4055
人均地方财政收入	Per Capita Local Financial Revenue	252	227	253	228	271
职工平均货币工资	Per Capita Annual Disposable Income of Urban Households	8269	9129	10988	10506	11979
城镇居民人均储蓄	Per Capita Urban and Rural Resident Savings Deposits	4241	1437	1699	2814	996

20－5 各地级城市市政公用事业(2001)
Municipal Public Utility by Cities at Prefectural Level

指　标	Item	贵阳市 Guiyang	六盘水市 Liupanshui	遵义市 Zunyi	安顺市 Anshun
年末实有铺装道路面积(万平方米)	Area of Paved Road at The Year－end(10000 sq.m)	632	82	320	108
排水管道总长度(公里)	Length of Drainpipe(km)	913	90	210	61
供水综合生产能力(包括自备水源)(万吨/日)	Production Capacity of Tap Water (10000 tons/day)	122	4	12	9
全年供水总量(万吨)	Annual Supply of Tap Water(10000 tons)	26043	901	3407	1869
生活用水量(万吨)	Water Consumption for Residential Use	11257	620	2441	846
用水人口(万人)	Number of Residents with Access to Tap Water(10000 persons)	198.7	17	43	21.8
#非农业用水人口(万人)	Consumption of Tap Water by Non－agriculture Population (10000 persons)	130.76	14	30.42	21.8
煤气(人工、天然气)供气总量(万立方米)	Total Gas Supply(10000 cu.m)	8321	595	78	
用煤气人口(人)	Population with Access to Gas(person)	695600	86000	5220	
液化石油气供气总量(吨)	Total LPG Supply(ton)	21000		2100	1200
家庭用量(吨)	Consumption of Liquefied Gas for Residential Use(ton)	20950		2100	1200
用液化气人口(人)	Number of Person Used Liquefied Gas(person)	595000		180000	35000
年末实有公共汽(电)车营运车辆数(辆)	Number of Public Transportation Vehicles(year－end)(unit)	1921	69	242	161
全年公共汽(电)车客运总量(万人次)	Number of Passengers Carried of Public Transportation Vehicles(10000 person－times)	43136	270	4000	2357
年末实有出租汽车数(辆)	Number of Taxis(year－end)(unit)	2199	868	922	291
园林绿地面积(公顷)	Total Area of Parks, Gardens and Green Areas(hectare)	4279	71	995	122
#公共绿地面积(公顷)	Public Green Areas	1665	35	110	3
建成区绿化覆盖面积(公顷)	Coveraged Areas by Afforestation in Developed Area(hectare)	3540	56	1720	140
生活垃圾粪便清运量(万吨)	Volume of Garbage, Excrement and Urine Disposal(10000 tons)	55	12	12	13
生活垃圾粪便无害化处理量(万吨)	Volume of Garbage, Excrement and Urine Innocuous Treatment(10000 tons)	34	7		

20－6 各地级城市教育、科技、文化、出版、卫生情况(2001)
Statistics on Education, Science and Technology, Culture, Publishing and Health Care by Cities at Prefectural Level

指标	Item	贵阳市 Guiyang	六盘水 Liupanshui	遵义市 Zunyi	安顺市 Anshun
学校数(所)	Number of Schools(unit)				
高等学校	Institutions of Higher Education	13	1	2	2
中等专业学校	Specialized Secondary Schools	41	6	11	3
普通中学	Regular Secondary Schools	274	195	439	126
小学	Primary Schools	1187	1095	3425	1043
专任教师数(人)	Full－time Teachers(person)				
高等学校	Institutions of Higher Education	5586	127	672	375
中等专业学校	Specialized Secondary Schools	2410	380	751	179
普通中学	Regular Secondary Schools	11614	6251	18318	5616
小学	Primary Schools	18082	11846	30546	12057
在校学生数(人)	Students Enrollment(person)				
高等学校	Institutions of Higher Education	76514	1965	9113	2054
中等专业学校	Specialized Secondary Schools	51313	4853	12876	4263
普通中学(万人)	Regular Secondary Schools(10000 persons)	19.15	14.12	39	10.59
小学(万人)	Primary Schools(10000 persons)	36.78	40.42	88.98	34.05
成人高等教育学校在校学生数(人)	Students Enrollment of Adult Higher Education(person)	26352	2008	6882	4592
各类专业技术人员数(万人)	Number of Specialized Technical Personnels(10000 persons)	14.47	2.67	8.19	2.88
#中级技术职称以上人员数(万人)	Number of Personnels at and above Medium Titles(10000 persons)	3.78	0.47	2.68	0.52
从事科技活动人员数(人)	Number of Persons Engaged in S&T Activities(person)	13102	19909	10561	94
剧场、影剧院数(个)	Number of Theatres and Cinemas(unit)	14	1	3	1
公共图书馆图书藏量(千册、件)	Total Book Collections of Public Libraries(1000 volumes)	3053	216	859	287
医院、卫生院数(个)	Number of Hospitals(unit)	177	169	297	120
医院、卫生院床位数(张)	Number of Hospital Beds(bed)	12710	5387	9668	4414
医生数(人)	Doctor(person)	5571	3953	3806	2719
交通事故件数(件)	Number of Traffic Accidents(case)	1138	587	640	468
交通事故死亡人数(人)	Number of Deaths in Traffic Accidents(person)	313	112	186	68
刑事案件立案数(件)	Number of Registered Criminal Cases(case)	28164	2165	11394	5628
犯罪人数(人)	Offenders(person)	7672	2325	4119	2087

21

Twenty-One

经济强县建设

Strongly Economic County

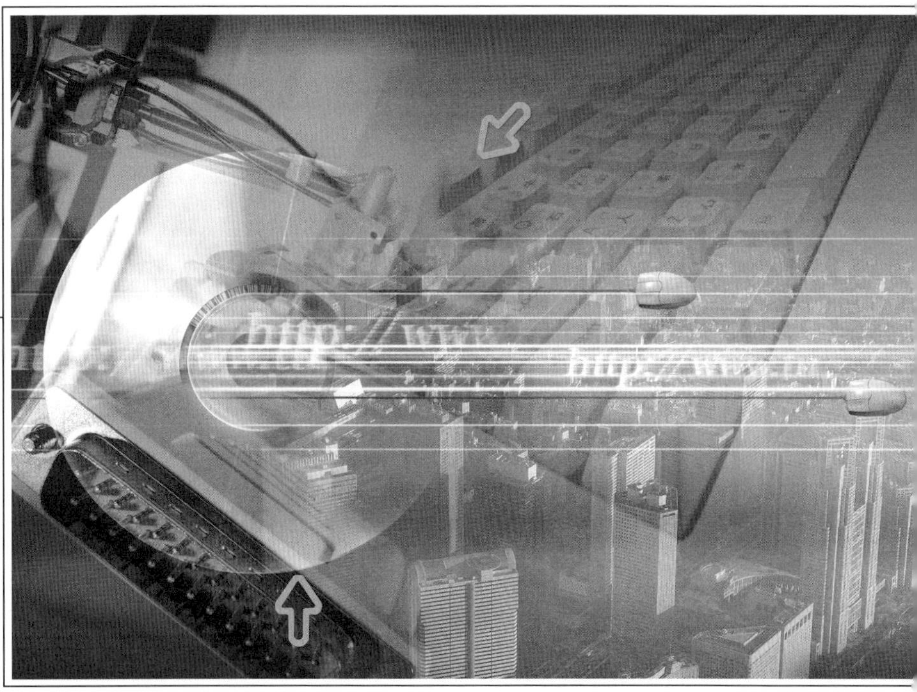

21－1 经济强县主要指标(一)(2001)
Major Indicators of Strongly Economic County(1)

县(市、区)名称 County(City,Section)		年末常住人口(万人) Number of Permanent Total Population (year－end) (10000 persons)	2001年比2000年增长(%) Increase Rate in 2001 over 2000(%)	计划生育率(%) Family Planning Rate(%)	固定资产投资(万元) Investment in Fixed Assets (10000 yuan)	2001年比2000年增长(%) Increase Rate in 2001 over 2000(%)
云岩区	Yunyan	53.07	1.2	98.53	133467	409.3
南明区	Nanming	49.20	1.1	98.46	113725	342.3
乌当区	Wudang	30.04	1.1	96.43	33950	93.0
白云区	Baiyun	16.69	1.2	98.19	45979	121.2
花溪区	Huaxi	31.43	1.1	91.00	19900	105.4
红花岗区	Honghuagang	62.34	1.1	96.92	136734	149.7
钟山区	Zhongshan	41.80	1.1	90.63	26146	62.2
兴义市	Xingyi	72.91	1.1	90.69	32045	39.4
都匀市	Duyun	48.15	1.1	91.79	33842	108.2
铜仁市	Tongren	33.49	1.1	90.79	29676	44.6
凯里市	Kaili	44.79	1.1	90.54	51497	124.5
清镇市	Qingzhen	50.53	1.1	85.72	14668	114.5
开阳县	Kaiyang	43.07	1.1	86.00	12825	70.6
西秀区	Xixiu	81.03	1.1	90.30	30871	32.9
仁怀市	Renhuai	59.20	1.1	88.71	16321	22.2
赤水市	Chishui	30.80	1.1	90.22	31836	37.9
金沙县	Jinsha	58.26	1.1	97.19	13690	25.6
遵义县	Zunyi	136.35	1.1	88.93	41857	113.6
盘　县	Pan	114.30	1.1	85.71	17022	－26.9
毕节市	Bijie	125.85	1.1	81.05	11986	－10.2

注:固定资产投资额统计口径为县及县以下。

Note: Statistical coverage of investment in fixed assets refer to the investment at and below county level.

21－2 经济强县主要指标(二)(2001)
Major Indicators of Strongly Economic County(2)

单位:万元
(10000 yuan)

县(市、区)名称	County(City,Section)	国内生产总值 Gross Domestic Product	第一产业 Primary Industry	第二产业 Secondary Industry	第三产业 Tertiary Industry	2001年比2000年增长(%) Increase Rate in 2001 over 2000(%)
云岩区	Yunyan	697555	4035	283964	409556	11.3
南明区	Nanming	565875	4640	281174	280061	11.9
乌当区	Wudang	286981	42122	142448	102411	12.1
白云区	Baiyun	359395	12558	203407	143430	11.7
花溪区	Guiding	246124	41068	90330	114726	11.7
红花岗区	Honghuagang	790798	38984	318735	433079	11.3
钟山区	Zhongshan	328706	8284	199226	121196	10.6
兴义市	Xingyi	314685	65488	152574	96623	12.1
都匀市	Duyun	186106	33438	61709	90959	11.0
铜仁市	Tongren	113500	27601	43842	42057	13.8
凯里市	Kaili	234649	39651	104443	90555	11.0
清镇市	Qingzhen	286478	41496	172755	72227	10.8
开阳县	Kaiyang	161798	44215	73819	43764	11.0
西秀区	Xixiu	282756	52527	82732	147497	10.1
仁怀市	Renhuai	238680	66719	135230	36731	15.0
赤水市	Tongzi	112181	41300	51516	19365	7.8
金沙县	Jinsha	160811	53104	61459	46248	11.8
遵义县	Zunyi	600271	199955	192814	207502	9.6
盘　县	Pan	323686	60761	167885	95040	10.3
毕节市	Bijie	356259	111219	123510	121530	11.4

注:云岩区国内生产总值未含卷烟。

Note:The GDP of Yunyan excluded cigarette figure.

21－3 经济强县主要指标(三)(2001)
Major Indicators of Strongly Economic County(3)

单位:万元
(10000 yuan)

县(市、区)名称 County(City,Section)		财政总收入 Total Financial Revenue	2001年比2000年增长(%) Increase Rate in 2001 over 2000(%)	地方财政收入 Local Financial Revenue	2001年比2000年增长(%) Increase Rate in 2001 over 2000(%)	财政支出 Financial Expenditure	2001年比2000年增长(%) Increase Rate in 2001 over 2000(%)
云岩区	Yunyan	40702	22.5	24330	33.4	26626	34.3
南明区	Nanming	37328	30.2	23463	41.9	22543	45.1
乌当区	Wudang	23219	27.8	13139	39.3	20131	49.5
白云区	Baiyun	52282	44.0	18588	50.7	19412	42.2
花溪区	Huaxi	16750	23.7	9651	31.7	16813	38.5
红花岗区	Honghuagang	28390	27.1	19523	26.1	33514	13.7
钟山区	Zhongshan	10007	18.6	7100	18.4	10519	21.9
兴义市	Xingyi	32172	14.3	18398	12.1	28671	24.0
都匀市	Duyun	18505	14.0	12075	13.8	21017	30.4
铜仁市	Tongren	8093	16.4	7068	16.1	15718	50.2
凯里市	Kaili	20146	9.4	12460	10.3	20321	22.2
清镇市	Qingzhen	24361	18.3	12727	16.4	20327	32.2
开阳县	Kaiyang	18378	23.7	11392	15.8	19172	29.3
西秀区	Xixiu	28108	29.7	15601	17.0	26657	29.3
仁怀市	Renhuai	56609	37.3	15973	21.6	27824	29.3
赤水市	Chishui	10291	－0.8	6968	7.7	14450	36.4
金沙县	Jinsha	17499	19.3	11307	15.2	21602	31.5
遵义县	Zunyi	25712	－1.2	17046	6.8	37603	38.3
盘　县	Pan	29755	9.5	16552	7.3	30188	24.5
毕节市	Bijie	22168	11.3	18049	12.3	32801	24.9

21－4 经济强县主要指标(四)(2001)
Major Indicators of Strongly Economic County(4)

单位:万元
(10000 yuan)

县(市、区)名称 County(City, Section)		规模以上工业总产值 Total Gross Industrial Output Value above Designated Size	2001年比2000年增长(%) Increase Rate in 2001 over 2000(%)	乡镇企业营业收入 Total Business Income of Township and Village Enterprise	2001年比2000年增长(%) Increase Rate in 2001 over 2000(%)
云岩区	Yunyan	741141		838155	25.7
南明区	Nanming	373719		804676	33.8
乌当区	Wudang	339243		776064	25.9
白云区	Baiyun	451374	5.0	449784	29.8
花溪区	Huaxi	154292		457840	25.9
红花岗区	Honghuagang	579642	11.4	591297	26.7
钟山区	Zhongshan	408660	19.0	310389	27.3
兴义市	Xingyi	379233	24.6	276941	25.2
都匀市	Duyun	113526	7.8	182958	26.2
铜仁市	Tongren	63354	－4.1	325431	37.8
凯里市	Kaili	139116	11.0	288511	25.0
清镇市	Qingzhen	278109	4.4	393085	25.1
开阳县	Kaiyang	121942	18.0	406210	25.7
西秀区	Xixiu	222957	9.7	541197	25.8
仁怀市	Renhuai	184339	42.7	507983	25.4
赤水市	Chishui	99066	－0.1	194376	27.9
金沙县	Jinsha	107381	23.1	429842	19.9
遵义县	Zunyi	196934	13.0	753699	25.2
盘　县	Pan	156266	26.0	407026	25.1
毕节市	Bijie	173289	31.0	439594	25.3

21－5 经济强县主要指标(五)(2001)
Major Indicators of Strongly Economic County(5)

单位:万元
(10000 yuan)

县(市、区)名称 County(City, Section)		农林牧渔业总产值 Gross Output Value of Farming, Forestry, Animal Husbandry and Fishery	2001年比2000年增长(%) Increase Rate in 2001 over 2000(%)	社会消费品零售总额 Tota l Retail Sales of Consumer Goods	2001年比2000年增长(%) Increase Rate in 2001 over 2000(%)	城乡居民储蓄余额 Urban and Rural Resident Savings Deposit Balance	2001年比2000年增长(%) Increase Rate in 2001 over 2000(%)
云岩区	Yunyan	6408	4.9	582275	11.4		
南明区	Nanming	6642	4.9	326023	13.0		
乌当区	Wudang	68840	5.3	20355	15.2		
白云区	Baiyun	21563	4.6	40510	12.0		
花溪区	Huaxi	61893	5.1	39157	12.9		
红花岗区	Honghuagang	59296	1.8	217744	14.5	501108	10.1
钟山区	Zhongshan	15451	2.1	109987	11.2	207682	12.0
兴义市	Xingyi	110343	5.7	97501	11.0	165923	18.7
都匀市	Duyun	52247	4.1	71100	7.7	203080	17.2
铜仁市	Tongren	45580	5.2	50821	10.3	95269	18.0
凯里市	Kaili	61030	4.2	72324	12.2	187583	19.9
清镇市	Qingzhen	63971	4.9	40902	11.0	85363	16.5
开阳县	Kaiyang	68554	4.3	41380	11.9	51395	11.2
西秀区	Xixiu	76716	2.2	138847	8.1	233536	19.8
仁怀市	Renhuai	101163	2.3	23558	14.9	58625	24.1
赤水市	Chishui	62528	5.3	20489	15.0	86166	14.8
金沙县	Jinsha	85661	－1.0	24886	8.8	43896	32.8
遵义县	Zunyi	300373	3.2	118028	12.1	140100	27.2
盘　县	Pan	86912	4.0	51793	10.6	101691	27.2
毕节市	Bijie	184296	4.9	46895	8.0	133555	16.4

21－6 经济强县主要指标(六)(2001)
Major Indicators of Strongly Economic County(6)

单位:元
(yuan)

县(市、区)名称 County(City, Section)		人均国内生产总值 Per Capita Gross Domestic Product	人均地方财政收入 Per Capita Local Financial Revenue	人均财政支出 Per Capita Financial Expenditure	人均固定资产投资 Per Capita Investment in Fixed Assets
云岩区	Yunyan	17136	461	505	2529
南明区	Nanming	11565	480	461	1211
乌当区	Wudang	9608	440	674	2634
白云区	Baiyun	21657	1120	1170	2771
花溪区	Huaxi	7875	309	538	605
红花岗区	Honghuagang	12757	315	541	3932
钟山区	Zhongshan	7908	171	253	4876
兴义市	Xingyi	4340	254	395	1044
都匀市	Duyun	3887	252	439	1570
铜仁市	Tongren	3408	212	472	1574
凯里市	Kaili	5268	280	456	3217
清镇市	Qingzhen	5702	253	405	817
开阳县	Kaiyang	3778	266	448	334
西秀区	Xixiu	3509	194	331	1128
仁怀市	Renhuai	4055	271	473	572
赤水市	Chishui	3663	228	472	1473
金沙县	Jinsha	2776	195	373	1528
遵义县	Zunyi	4427	126	277	575
盘　县	Pan	2848	146	266	702
毕节市	Bijie	2847	144	262	789

21－7 经济强县主要指标(七)(2001)
Major Indicators of Strongly Economic County(7)

单位:元
(yuan)

县(市、区)名称 County(City,Section)		人均农林牧渔业产值 Per Capita Gross Output Value of Farming, Forestry, Animal Husbandry and Fishery	人均社会消费品零售总额 Per Capita Total Retail Sales of Consumer Goods	农民人均纯收入 Per Capita Annual Net Income of Rural Households	城乡居民人均储蓄 Per Capita Urban and Rural Resident Savings Deposits
云岩区	Yunyan	121	11035	3402	
南明区	Nanming	136	6663	3378	
乌当区	Wudang	2305	681	2491	
白云区	Baiyun	1299	2441	2789	
花溪区	Huaxi	1980	1253	2245	
红花岗区	Honghuagang	957	3513	2414	8084
钟山区	Zhongshan	372	2646	1582	4997
兴义市	Xingyi	1522	1345	1992	2288
都匀市	Duyun	1091	1485	1834	4241
铜仁市	Tongren	1369	1526	1704	2861
凯里市	Kaili	1370	1624	1617	4212
清镇市	Qingzhen	1273	814	2027	1699
开阳县	Kaiyang	1601	966	2118	1200
西秀区	Xixiu	952	1723	1843	2899
仁怀市	Renhuai	1719	400	1862	996
赤水市	Chishui	2042	669	1884	2814
金沙县	Jinsha	1479	430	1706	758
遵义县	Zunyi	2215	870	2138	1033
盘　县	Pan	765	456	1419	895
毕节市	Bijie	1473	375	1580	1067

22

Twenty-Two

扶贫与开发

Anti-poverty and Development

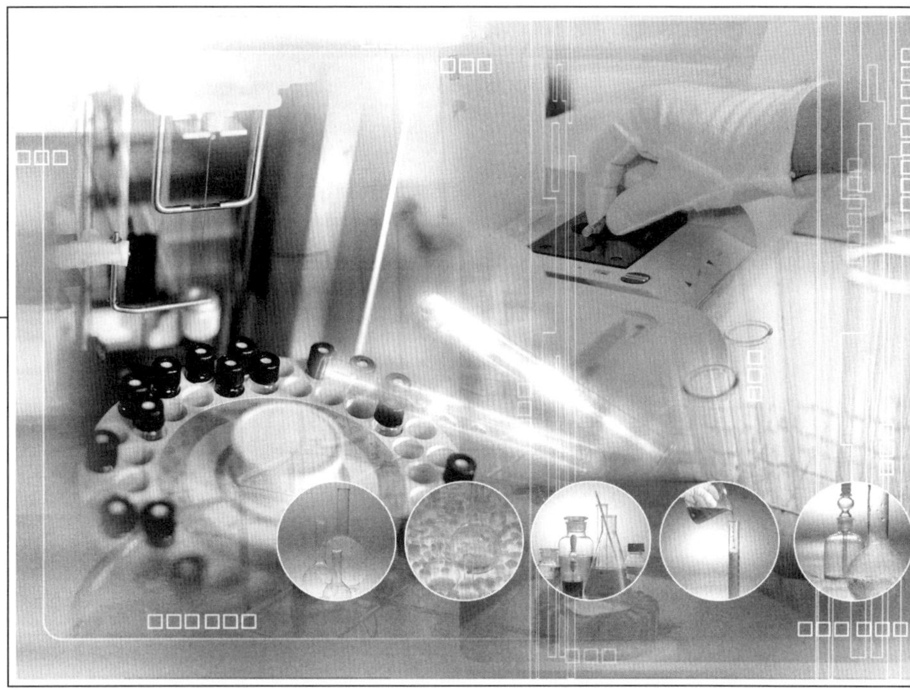

22 - 1 贫困县主要经济指标(2001)
Major Economic Indicators on Poverty Counties

单位:万元
(10000 yuan)

贫困县名称	County	国内生产总值 Gross Domestic Product	地方财政收入 Local Financial Revenue	财政支出 Financial Expenditure	农林牧渔业总产值 Gross Output Value of Farming, Forestry, Animal Husbandry and Fishery	粮食产量(万吨) Output of Grain (10000 ton)	规模以上工业总产值 Total Gross Industrial Output Value above Designated Size
贫困县合计	**Total**	**3448397**	**190309**	**638452**	**2495506**	**647.95**	**851861**
贵阳市	Guiyang						
息烽县	Xifeng	90661	4763	12761	35576	5.67	78586
六盘水市	Liupanshui						
水城县	Shuicheng	97454	5769	20180	63786	22.45	50957
盘　县	Pan	323686	16552	30188	86912	30.46	156266
六枝特区	Liuzhi	116394	5757	17719	41670	17.10	38523
遵义市	Zunyi						
正安县	Zhengan	110199	4229	14998	101908	24.72	5779
※务川县	Wuchuan	60039	3688	12788	51347	14.61	3736
凤冈县	Fenggang	77638	3152	11426	70795	15.72	7278
习水县	Xishui	124849	4920	18609	79249	23.75	27028
安顺市	Anshun						
普定县	Puding	81923	5496	15641	39822	11.53	73378
※关岭县	Guanling	50088	2841	11499	43101	10.43	13359
※镇宁县	Zhenning	70238	5708	14485	33515	11.44	30951
※紫云县	Ziyun	40290	2243	10260	37892	11.46	2171
铜仁地区	Tongren						
石阡县	Shiqian	45110	3405	13353	47549	12.22	6529
※印江县	Yinjiang	63783	2931	13315	70802	12.93	4411
德江县	Dejiang	89407	3863	13046	94878	14.46	6011
※沿河县	Yanhe	70660	3608	15947	72726	14.67	4871
※松桃县	Songtao	92843	3603	15441	94742	25.77	12432
黔西南州	Qianxinan						
兴仁县	Xingren	70085	5730	13865	55232	16.26	19536
普安县	Puan	37689	3851	11825	27946	8.50	7130
晴隆县	Qinglong	37710	3599	10592	26108	7.90	7641
贞丰县	Zhenfeng	45974	2395	10004	45151	10.32	4579
望谟县	Wangmo	48485	1658	10611	39373	9.13	2604

22－1 续表 1(continued)

单位:万元
(10000 yuan)

贫困县名称	County	国内生产总值 Gross Domestic Product	地方财政收入 Local Financial Revenue	财政支出 Financial Expenditure	农林牧渔业总产值 Gross Output Value of Farming, Forestry, Animal Husbandry and Fishery	粮食产量(万吨) Output of Grain (10000 ton)	规模以上工业总产值 Total Gross Industrial Output Value above Designated Size
册亨县	Ceheng	28875	1366	7229	32228	6.61	3418
安龙县	Anlong	94086	6262	13675	57553	16.93	11499
毕节地区	Bijie						
大方县	Dafang	145385	9530	22142	101941	28.71	20511
织金县	Zhijin	146017	8385	21417	92085	26.18	17085
纳雍县	Nayong	116207	7903	22429	81188	23.98	11309
※威宁县	Weining	175629	7123	20370	130298	33.96	27687
赫章县	Hezhang	93718	3644	15074	70414	19.20	23493
黔东南州	Qiandongnan						
黄平县	Huangping	43614	2392	11624	42812	10.91	1334
施秉县	Shibing	34503	3081	8468	19373	5.99	34567
三穗县	Sansui	37173	1820	8870	35709	6.07	4714
岑巩县	Cengong	31355	1821	8813	26215	7.58	9276
天柱县	Tianzhu	53515	3681	12885	49157	12.86	5328
剑河县	Jianhe	32010	1313	8940	32873	7.09	962
台江县	Taijiang	25446	1412	8757	26586	5.15	2872
黎平县	Liping	60471	3010	15396	58407	16.07	9288
榕江县	Rongjiang	52053	2131	11848	44837	9.68	10371
从江县	Congjiang	40554	2363	11062	40345	10.40	4526
雷山县	Leishan	18413	1292	7443	16711	4.65	1360
麻江县	Majiang	39583	2348	7836	24346	7.00	9121
丹寨县	Danzai	23290	1517	7465	18248	5.26	2588
黔南州	Qiannan						
荔波县	Libo	49185	3990	10270	30710	5.31	3278
独山县	Dushan	65800	3344	13099	53659	10.98	11326
平塘县	Pingtang	39401	2226	11220	32854	9.56	7852
罗甸县	Luodian	71990	3438	11350	51763	8.51	31164
长顺县	Changshun	41534	3434	9808	25555	9.28	18949
※三都县	Sandu	43385	1722	12409	39559	8.53	4227

22 - 1 续表 2(continued)

单位:万元
(10000 yuan)

贫困县名称	County	金融机构存款余额 Total Savings Deposit Balance	金融机构贷款余额 Total Loan Balance	城乡居民储蓄额 Urban and Rural Resident Savings Deposit Balance	固定资产投资 Investment in Fixed Assets	社会消费品零售总额 Total Retail Sales of Consumer Goods
贫困县合计	**Total**	**2000019**	**2401897**	**1272347**	**691834**	**743378**
贵阳市	Guiyang					
息烽县	Xifeng	58238	50009	32847	41883	21710
六盘水市	Liupanshui					
水城县	Shuicheng	45569	13171	17678	20122	14530
盘　县	Pan	221922	102840	101691	79770	51793
六枝特区	Liuzhi	86440	424248	62946	13443	22879
遵义市	Zunyi					
正安县	Zhengan	56291	49109	41290	15660	24463
※务川县	Wuchuan	33921	40580	23767	4751	18543
凤冈县	Fenggang	37435	43929	25262	10580	18185
习水县	Xishui	72158	151754	47354	87370	20364
安顺市	Anshun					
普定县	Puding	41199	132617	18690	12010	15045
※关岭县	Guanling	33806	29695	21575	7406	15653
※镇宁县	Zhenning	42910	47242	25552	14559	17106
※紫云县	Ziyun	23590	32253	12507	5471	14965
铜仁地区	Tongren					
石阡县	Shiqian	31570	34288	22094	4886	11898
※印江县	Yinjiang	41981	45629	33148	8979	13164
德江县	Dejiang	24210	45628	19395	6912	15079
※沿河县	Yanhe	43471	44416	30180	8889	15711
※松桃县	Songtao	45422	50047	33088	18255	24267
黔西南州	Qianxinan					
兴仁县	Xingren	38288	44783	25680	20467	23622
普安县	Puan	29130	36448	17800	13465	7050
晴隆县	Qinglong	22775	23913	15177	5325	8769
贞丰县	Zhenfeng	30697	22136	20181	7208	11662
望谟县	Wangmo	21437	27703	11309	4429	11788

22－1 续表 3(continued)

单位:万元
(10000 yuan)

贫困县名称	County	金融机构存款余额 Total Savings Deposit Balance	金融机构贷款余额 Total Loan Balance	城乡居民储蓄额 Urban and Rural Resident Savings Deposit Balance	固定资产投资 Investment in Fixed Assets	社会消费品零售总额 Total Retail Sales of Consumer Goods
册亨县	Ceheng	18701	20018	11141	4972	5996
安龙县	Anlong	54263	33403	34890	10042	22493
毕节地区	Bijie					
大方县	Dafang	69711	56097	46827	3245	23944
织金县	Zhijin	59614	54769	39049	7198	26397
纳雍县	Nayong	47149	65172	20690	79526	18751
※威宁县	Weining	49935	52372	31645	1858	22502
赫章县	Hezhang	46102	58426	30887	2429	15179
黔东南州	Qiandongnan					
黄平县	Huangping	40362	29661	27983	6075	9893
施秉县	Shibing	25820	22731	17648	15015	7980
三穗县	Sansui	25633	19817	19072	7768	8478
岑巩县	Cengong	22901	27742	15054	3173	8749
天柱县	Tianzhu	52948	33724	44454	4118	19636
剑河县	Jianhe	26938	21869	18127	2612	6399
台江县	Taijiang	20484	19325	15982	2824	4476
黎平县	Liping	46937	39903	36744	11324	21815
榕江县	Rongjiang	33445	34030	22351	4809	9508
从江县	Congjiang	20765	26591	12967	8341	10395
雷山县	Leishan	15794	18349	9282	4131	4931
麻江县	Majiang	27920	30201	19438	41932	8432
丹寨县	Danzai	19261	20849	15113	5149	3790
黔南州	Qiannan					
荔波县	Libo	32780	40465	20966	9049	13602
独山县	Dushan	59754	41349	41209	13011	18877
平塘县	Pingtang	27580	31914	17955	5655	9314
罗甸县	Luodian	26157	49157	14310	14373	11982
长顺县	Changshun	20371	36055	11854	6833	16624
※三都县	Sandu	26234	25470	17498	4532	14989

22 – 2 贫困县主要经济指标占全省比重(2001)

Major Economic Indicators of Poverty Counties and Its Percentage to Provincial Total

指 标	Item	全省合计 Provincial Total	贫困县合计 Poverty Counties Total	贫困县占全省的比重(%) As Percentage to Provincial Total(%)
国土面积(万平方公里)	Area of Territory(10000 sq.km)	17.61	11.14	63.3
耕地面积(万亩)	Area of Cultivated Land(10000 mu)	2748.42	1576.32	57.4
年末总人口(万人)	Total Population at the Year – end(10000 persons)	3777.12	2028.25	53.7
国内生产总值(亿元)	Gross Domestic Product(100 million yuan)	1084.90	344.84	31.8
固定资产投资(亿元)	Investment in Fixed Assets(100 million yuan)	534.00	69.18	13.0
地方财政收入(亿元)	Local Financial Revenue(100 million yuan)	99.75	19.03	19.1
财政支出(亿元)	Financial Expenditure(100 million yuan)	275.20	63.85	23.2
农林牧渔业总产值(亿元)	Gross Output Value of Farming, Forestry, Animal Husbandry and Fishery(100 million yuan)	418.61	249.55	59.6
粮食产量(万吨)	Output of Grain(10000 tons)	1100.30	647.95	58.9
规模以上工业总产值(亿元)	Total Gross Industrial Output Value above Designated Size(100 million yuan)	696.63	85.19	12.2
社会消费品零售总额(亿元)	Total Retail Sales of Consumer Goods(100 million yuan)	378.01	74.34	19.7
金融机构存款余额(亿元)	Total Savings Deposit Balance(100 million yuan)	1341.11	200.00	14.9
金融机构贷款余额(亿元)	Total Loan Balance(100 million yuan)	1212.23	240.19	19.8
城乡居民储蓄余额(亿元)	Urban and Rural Resident Savings Deposit Balance(100 million yuan)	641.67	127.23	19.8

22－3 贫困县主要经济指标人均水平及位次(一)(2001)
Major Per Capita Economic Indicators and Their Orders on Poverty Counties(1)

贫困县名称	County	人均耕地面积(亩) Per Capita Area of Cultivated Land(mu)	位次 Order	人均国内生产总值(元) Per Capita Gross Domestic Product(yuan)	位次 Order	人均地方财政收入(元) Per Capita Local Financial Revenue(yuan)	位次 Order
贫困县合计	Total	0.78	–	1710	–	94.36	–
贵阳市	Guiyang						
息烽县	Xifeng	0.97	6	3566	1	187.34	3
六盘水市	Liupanshui						
水城县	Shuicheng	0.69	35	1345	37	79.62	29
盘　县	Pan	0.58	47	2848	3	145.63	6
六枝特区	Liuzhi	0.60	44	1884	12	93.17	18
遵义市	Zunyi						
正安县	Zhengan	0.79	21	1865	13	71.56	35
※务川县	Wuchuan	1.03	4	1458	31	89.55	23
凤冈县	Fenggang	0.99	5	1926	10	78.19	30
习水县	Xishui	0.92	8	1848	14	72.82	33
安顺市	Anshun						
普定县	Puding	0.63	41	2041	8	136.90	9
※关岭县	Guanling	0.71	30	1575	22	89.34	24
※镇宁县	Zhenning	0.70	31	2071	7	168.33	4
※紫云县	Ziyun	0.91	10	1219	47	67.84	38
铜仁地区	Tongren						
石阡县	Shiqian	0.82	16	1206	48	91.04	21
※印江县	Yinjiang	0.68	37	1574	23	72.33	34
德江县	Dejiang	0.82	17	2030	9	87.72	26
※沿河县	Yanhe	0.73	28	1295	43	66.10	41
※松桃县	Songtao	0.65	39	1484	30	57.59	47
黔西南州	Qianxinan						
兴仁县	Xingren	0.75	24	1566	24	128.03	11
普安县	Puan	0.87	11	1348	36	137.73	8
晴隆县	Qinglong	0.80	19	1344	38	128.26	10
贞丰县	Zhenfeng	0.81	18	1372	34	71.45	36
望谟县	Wangmo	1.70	1	1760	17	60.17	45

22 - 3 续表 1(continued)

贫困县名称	County	人均耕地面积(亩) Per Capita Area of Cultivated Land(mu)	位次 Order	人均国内生产总值(元) Per Capita Gross Domestic Product(yuan)	位次 Order	人均地方财政收入(元) Per Capita Local Financial Revenue(yuan)	位次 Order
册亨县	Ceheng	1.11	2	1329	41	62.88	42
安龙县	Anlong	0.73	27	2233	6	148.60	5
毕节地区	Bijie						
大方县	Dafang	0.82	14	1523	27	99.86	15
织金县	Zhijin	0.74	25	1622	21	93.13	19
纳雍县	Nayong	0.69	36	1554	25	105.69	14
※威宁县	Weining	1.04	3	1646	19	66.77	39
赫章县	Hezhang	0.93	7	1485	29	57.75	46
黔东南州	Qiandongnan						
黄平县	Huangping	0.70	32	1275	44	69.91	37
施秉县	Shibing	0.79	20	2269	4	202.63	2
三穗县	Sansui	0.57	48	1833	16	89.72	22
岑巩县	Cengong	0.83	13	1458	31	84.66	28
天柱县	Tianzhu	0.61	43	1331	39	91.54	20
剑河县	Jianhe	0.59	45	1513	28	62.05	43
台江县	Taijiang	0.64	40	1545	26	85.76	27
黎平县	Liping	0.65	38	1228	46	61.12	44
榕江县	Rongjiang	0.63	42	1625	20	66.53	40
从江县	Congjiang	0.70	34	1306	42	76.09	31
雷山县	Leishan	0.74	26	1264	45	88.68	25
麻江县	Majiang	0.78	22	1839	15	109.11	12
丹寨县	Danzai	0.70	33	1455	33	94.75	17
黔南州	Qiannan						
荔波县	Libo	0.77	23	2991	2	242.63	1
独山县	Dushan	0.72	29	1921	11	97.65	16
平塘县	Pingtang	0.84	12	1331	39	75.20	32
罗甸县	Luodian	0.91	9	2252	5	107.54	13
长顺县	Changshun	0.82	15	1722	18	142.34	7
※三都县	Sandu	0.58	46	1369	35	54.32	48

22-3 续表 2(continued)

单位:元 (yuan)

贫困县名称	County	人均财政支出 Per Capita Financial Expenditure	位次 Order	农民人均纯收入 Per Capita Annual Net Income of Rural Households	位次 Order
贫困县合计	**Total**	**316.56**	-	-	-
贵阳市	Guiyang				
息烽县	Xifeng	501.91	5	1662	1
六盘水市	Liupanshui				
水城县	Shuicheng	278.50	40	1272	24
盘　县	Pan	265.61	42	1419	4
六枝特区	Liuzhi	286.76	38	1270	26
遵义市	Zunyi				
正安县	Zhengan	253.79	43	1306	14
※务川县	Wuchuan	310.50	31	1288	19
凤冈县	Fenggang	283.45	39	1604	2
习水县	Xishui	275.42	41	1235	33
安顺市	Anshun				
普定县	Puding	389.61	14	1304	15
※关岭县	Guanling	361.60	21	1244	30
※镇宁县	Zhenning	427.16	8	1271	25
※紫云县	Ziyun	310.30	32	1180	44
铜仁地区	Tongren				
石阡县	Shiqian	357.03	22	1227	35
※印江县	Yinjiang	328.60	27	1312	13
德江县	Dejiang	296.23	36	1216	38
※沿河县	Yanhe	292.18	37	1162	45
※松桃县	Songtao	246.80	44	1242	32
黔西南州	Qianxinan				
兴仁县	Xingren	309.80	33	1360	9
普安县	Puan	422.93	9	1244	30
晴隆县	Qinglong	377.48	18	1182	42
贞丰县	Zhenfeng	298.45	35	1361	8
望谟县	Wangmo	385.08	15	1250	29

22 – 3 续表 3(continued)

单位:元 (yuan)

贫困县名称	County	人均财政支出 Per Capita Financial Expenditure	位次 Order	农民人均纯收入 Per Capita Annual Net Income of Rural Households	位次 Order
册亨县	Ceheng	332.75	26	1206	39
安龙县	Anlong	324.51	28	1505	3
毕节地区	Bijie				
大方县	Dafang	232.02	47	1076	48
织金县	Zhijin	237.86	46	1274	22
纳雍县	Nayong	299.95	34	1205	40
※威宁县	Weining	190.94	48	1269	28
赫章县	Hezhang	238.91	45	1225	36
黔东南州	Qiandongnan				
黄平县	Huangping	339.73	25	1291	18
施秉县	Shibing	556.92	2	1402	5
三穗县	Sansui	437.27	7	1397	6
岑巩县	Cengong	409.72	11	1346	11
天柱县	Tianzhu	320.44	29	1343	12
剑河县	Jianhe	422.50	10	1347	10
台江县	Taijiang	531.86	3	1294	17
黎平县	Liping	312.64	30	1274	22
榕江县	Rongjiang	369.90	19	1270	26
从江县	Congjiang	356.21	23	1296	16
雷山县	Leishan	510.84	4	1231	34
麻江县	Majiang	364.13	20	1282	21
丹寨县	Danzai	466.27	6	1283	20
黔南州	Qiannan				
荔波县	Libo	624.51	1	1200	41
独山县	Dushan	382.51	16	1222	37
平塘县	Pingtang	379.05	17	1161	46
罗甸县	Luodian	355.02	24	1182	42
长顺县	Changshun	406.55	12	1370	7
※三都县	Sandu	391.45	13	1096	47

22-4 贫困县主要经济指标人均水平及位次(二)(2001)
Major Per Capita Economic Indicators and Their Orders on Poverty Counties(2)

贫困县名称	County	人均粮食(公斤) Per Capita Output of Grain(kg)	位次 Order	人均农业产值(元) Per Capita Gross Agricultural Output Value (yuan)	位次 Order
贫困县合计	**Total**	**321**	**–**	**1237**	**–**
贵阳市	Guiyang				
息烽县	Xifeng	276	48	1399	15
六盘水市	Liupanshui				
水城县	Shuicheng	330	35	880	46
盘　县	Pan	322	40	765	47
六枝特区	Liuzhi	343	30	674	48
遵义市	Zunyi				
正安县	Zhengan	448	1	1724	6
※务川县	Wuchuan	383	10	1247	25
凤冈县	Fenggang	414	5	1756	4
习水县	Xishui	399	7	1173	31
安顺市	Anshun				
普定县	Puding	312	42	992	43
※关岭县	Guanling	344	27	1355	17
※镇宁县	Zhenning	366	13	988	44
※紫云县	Ziyun	366	13	1146	33
铜仁地区	Tongren				
石阡县	Shiqian	335	32	1271	22
※印江县	Yinjiang	344	27	1747	5
德江县	Dejiang	358	18	2154	1
※沿河县	Yanhe	284	47	1332	19
※松桃县	Songtao	431	4	1514	11
黔西南州	Qianxinan				
兴仁县	Xingren	398	8	1234	26
普安县	Puan	320	41	999	42
晴隆县	Qinglong	312	42	930	45
贞丰县	Zhenfeng	323	39	1347	18
望谟县	Wangmo	356	20	1429	13

22 - 4 续表 1(continued)

贫困县名称	County	人均粮食(公斤) Per Capita Output of Grain(kg)	位次 Order	人均农业产值(元) Per Capita Gross Agricultural Output Value (yuan)	位次 Order
册亨县	Ceheng	330	35	1483	12
安龙县	Anlong	440	2	1366	16
毕节地区	Bijie				
大方县	Dafang	326	38	1068	39
织金县	Zhijin	311	44	1023	41
纳雍县	Nayong	343	30	1086	38
※威宁县	Weining	351	22	1221	28
赫章县	Hezhang	332	34	1116	36
黔东南州	Qiandongnan				
黄平县	Huangping	352	21	1251	23
施秉县	Shibing	439	3	1274	21
三穗县	Sansui	329	37	1760	3
岑巩县	Cengong	391	9	1219	29
天柱县	Tianzhu	358	18	1223	27
剑河县	Jianhe	374	11	1554	10
台江县	Taijiang	346	25	1615	8
黎平县	Liping	351	22	1186	30
榕江县	Rongjiang	333	33	1400	14
从江县	Congjiang	351	22	1299	20
雷山县	Leishan	346	25	1147	32
麻江县	Majiang	360	17	1131	35
丹寨县	Danzai	374	11	1140	34
黔南州	Qiannan				
荔波县	Libo	362	16	1867	2
独山县	Dushan	365	15	1567	9
平塘县	Pingtang	344	27	1110	37
罗甸县	Luodian	292	45	1619	7
长顺县	Changshun	405	6	1059	40
※三都县	Sandu	291	46	1248	24

注:表中人均粮食产量按乡村人口计算。

Note: Per Capita Output of Grain in this table were calculated by rural population.

22－4 续表 2(continued)

单位:元 (yuan)

贫困县名称	County	人均工业产值(规模以上) Per Capita Total Gross Industrial Output Value above Designated Size	位次 Order	城乡居民人均储蓄 Per Capita Urban and Rural Resident Savings Deposit	位次 Order
贫困县合计	**Total**	**422**	–	**631**	–
贵阳市	Guiyang				
息烽县	Xifeng	3091	1	1292	1
六盘水市	Liupanshui				
水城县	Shuicheng	703	8	244	48
盘　县	Pan	1375	4	895	11
六枝特区	Liuzhi	623	9	1019	6
遵义市	Zunyi				
正安县	Zhengan	98	41	699	20
※务川县	Wuchuan	91	44	577	29
凤冈县	Fenggang	181	29	627	25
习水县	Xishui	400	14	701	18
安顺市	Anshun				
普定县	Puding	1828	3	466	39
※关岭县	Guanling	420	13	678	22
※镇宁县	Zhenning	913	6	754	16
※紫云县	Ziyun	66	46	378	45
铜仁地区	Tongren				
石阡县	Shiqian	175	30	591	28
※印江县	Yinjiang	109	40	818	14
德江县	Dejiang	136	37	440	41
※沿河县	Yanhe	89	45	553	31
※松桃县	Songtao	199	26	529	34
黔西南州	Qianxinan				
兴仁县	Xingren	437	10	574	30
普安县	Puan	255	22	637	24
晴隆县	Qinglong	272	19	541	33
贞丰县	Zhenfeng	137	36	602	27
望谟县	Wangmo	95	42	410	44

22－4 续表 3(continued)

单位:元
(yuan)

贫困县名称	County	人均工业产值(规模以上) Per Capita Total Gross Industrial Output Value above Designated Size	位次 Order	城乡居民人均储蓄 Per Capita Urban and Rural Resident Savings Deposit	位次 Order
册亨县	Ceheng	157	33	513	35
安龙县	Anlong	273	18	828	13
毕节地区	Bijie				
大方县	Dafang	215	24	491	37
织金县	Zhijin	190	27	434	42
纳雍县	Nayong	151	34	277	47
※威宁县	Weining	260	21	297	46
赫章县	Hezhang	372	15	490	38
黔东南州	Qiandongnan				
黄平县	Huangping	39	48	818	15
施秉县	Shibing	2273	2	1161	4
三穗县	Sansui	232	23	940	9
岑巩县	Cengong	431	11	700	19
天柱县	Tianzhu	133	39	1106	5
剑河县	Jianhe	45	47	857	12
台江县	Taijiang	174	31	971	7
黎平县	Liping	189	28	746	17
榕江县	Rongjiang	324	17	698	21
从江县	Congjiang	146	35	418	43
雷山县	Leishan	93	43	637	23
麻江县	Majiang	424	12	903	10
丹寨县	Danzai	162	32	944	8
黔南州	Qiannan				
荔波县	Libo	199	25	1275	2
独山县	Dushan	331	16	1203	3
平塘县	Pingtang	265	20	607	26
罗甸县	Luodian	975	5	448	40
长顺县	Changshun	785	7	491	36
※三都县	Sandu	133	38	552	32

22－5 贫困县主要经济指标人均水平占全省平均水平的比重(2001)

Major Per Capita Economic Indicators of Poverty Counties as Percentage to Provincial Average

单位：%
(%)

贫困县名称	County	人均耕地面积 Per Capita Area of Cultivated Land	人均国内生产总值 Per Capita Gross Domestic Product	人均地方财政收入 Per Capita Local Financial Revenue	人均财政支出 Per Capita Financial Expenditure	农民人均纯收入 Annual Per Capita Net Income of Rural Households	人均农业产值 Per Capita Gross Agricultural Output Value	人均工业产值 Per Capita Gross Industrial Output Value
贫困县合计	**Total**	**107.2**	**59.1**	**35.7**	**43.5**	**–**	**111.6**	**22.9**
贵阳市	Guiyang							
息烽县	Xifeng	132.9	123.2	70.9	68.9	117.7	126.3	167.6
六盘水市	Liupanshui							
水城县	Shuicheng	94.8	46.5	30.1	38.2	90.0	79.4	38.1
盘　县	Pan	79.6	98.4	55.1	36.5	90.1	69.0	74.5
六枝特区	Liuzhi	82.2	65.1	35.3	39.4	100.5	60.8	33.8
遵义市	Zunyi							
正安县	Zhengan	108.1	64.4	27.1	34.8	92.5	155.6	5.3
※务川县	Wuchuan	142.2	50.4	33.9	42.6	91.2	112.5	4.9
凤冈县	Fenggang	135.8	66.5	29.6	38.9	113.6	158.5	9.8
习水县	Xishui	126.7	63.8	27.6	37.8	87.5	105.8	21.7
安顺市	Anshun							
普定县	Puding	86.6	70.5	51.8	53.5	92.4	89.5	99.1
※关岭县	Guanling	98.0	54.4	33.8	49.6	88.1	122.3	22.8
※镇宁县	Zhenning	96.5	71.5	63.7	58.6	90.0	89.2	49.5
※紫云县	Ziyun	124.5	42.1	25.7	42.6	83.6	103.4	3.6
铜仁地区	Tongren							
石阡县	Shiqian	112.6	41.7	34.5	49.0	86.9	114.7	9.5
※印江县	Yinjiang	93.7	54.4	27.4	45.1	92.9	157.7	5.9
德江县	Dejiang	112.6	70.1	33.2	40.7	86.1	194.4	7.4
※沿河县	Yanhe	100.6	44.7	25.0	40.1	82.3	120.2	4.8
※松桃县	Songtao	89.1	51.3	21.8	33.9	88.0	136.6	10.8
黔西南州	Qianxinan							
兴仁县	Xingren	102.8	54.1	48.5	42.5	96.3	111.4	23.7
普安县	Puan	119.9	46.6	52.2	58.0	88.1	90.2	13.8
晴隆县	Qinglong	109.5	46.4	48.6	51.8	83.7	84.0	14.8
贞丰县	Zhenfeng	111.4	47.4	27.1	41.0	96.4	121.5	7.4
望谟县	Wangmo	234.3	60.8	22.8	52.9	88.5	128.9	5.1

22-5 续表(continued)

单位:%
(%)

贫困县名称	County	人均耕地面积 Per Capita Area of Cultivated Land	人均国内生产总值 Per Capita Gross Domestic Product	人均地方财政收入 Per Capita Local Financial Revenue	人均财政支出 Per Capita Financial Expenditure	农民人均纯收入 Annual Per Capita Net Income of Rural Households	人均农业产值 Per Capita Gross Agricultural Output Value	人均工业产值 Per Capita Gross Industrial Output Value
册亨县	Ceheng	152.6	45.9	23.8	45.7	85.4	133.9	8.5
安龙县	Anlong	101.0	77.1	56.3	44.5	106.6	123.2	14.8
毕节地区	Bijie							
大方县	Dafang	113.3	52.6	37.8	31.8	76.2	96.4	11.7
织金县	Zhijin	102.3	56.0	35.3	32.6	90.2	92.3	10.3
纳雍县	Nayong	94.8	53.7	40.0	41.2	85.4	98.0	8.2
※威宁县	Weining	142.5	56.9	25.3	26.2	89.9	110.2	14.1
赫章县	Hezhang	127.6	51.3	21.9	32.8	86.8	100.7	20.2
黔东南州	Qiandongnan							
黄平县	Huangping	96.5	44.0	26.5	46.6	91.4	112.9	2.1
施秉县	Shibing	108.9	78.4	76.7	76.4	99.3	115.0	123.3
三穗县	Sansui	78.4	63.3	34.0	60.0	99.0	158.8	12.6
岑巩县	Cengong	114.0	50.4	32.1	56.2	95.3	110.0	23.4
天柱县	Tianzhu	83.6	46.0	34.7	44.0	95.1	110.3	7.2
剑河县	Jianhe	80.4	52.3	23.5	58.0	95.4	140.2	2.5
台江县	Taijiang	88.1	53.4	32.5	73.0	91.7	145.7	9.5
黎平县	Liping	89.4	42.4	23.1	42.9	90.2	107.0	10.2
榕江县	Rongjiang	86.4	56.1	25.2	50.8	90.0	126.3	17.6
从江县	Congjiang	95.5	45.1	28.8	48.9	91.8	117.2	7.9
雷山县	Leishan	101.0	43.7	33.6	70.1	87.2	103.5	5.1
麻江县	Majiang	107.4	63.5	41.3	50.0	90.8	102.1	23.0
丹寨县	Danzai	96.2	50.3	35.9	64.0	90.9	102.8	8.8
黔南州	Qiannan							
荔波县	Libo	106.0	103.3	91.9	85.7	85.0	168.5	10.8
独山县	Dushan	99.6	66.4	37.0	52.5	86.6	141.4	17.9
平塘县	Pingtang	115.2	46.0	28.5	52.0	82.2	100.1	14.4
罗甸县	Luodian	125.2	77.8	40.7	48.7	83.7	146.1	52.9
长顺县	Changshun	113.2	59.5	53.9	55.8	97.0	95.6	42.6
※三都县	Sandu	79.6	47.3	20.6	53.7	77.6	112.6	7.2

22-6 扶贫开发效益及成果(2001)
Benefits and Achievements of Anti-poverty

贫困县名称	County	当年新增基本农田(亩) Farmland Newly Increased in 2001(mu)	当年新增公路里程(公里) Length of Highways Newly Increased in 2001(km)	当年新增经济林和茶桑果园面积(亩) Area of Cash Forest, Tea Plantations, Mulberry Plantations and Orchards Newly Increased in 2001(mu)	当年向外省输出劳动力(人) Loborers Transferred to Other Provinces in 2001(person)	当年解决温饱的贫困人口(万人) Number of People Met the Basic Requirements for Food and Clothing in 2001(10000 persons)
贫困县合计	**Total**	**218934**	**3708**	**371307**	**1128308**	**45.73**
贵阳市	Guiyang					
息烽县	Xifeng	420	37.30	3544.5	3216	0.25
六盘水市	Liupanshiu					
水城县	Shuicheng	14805	210.00	3000	40000	1.89
盘　县	Pan					3.69
六枝特区	Liuzhi	12675	125.00	4965	264	0.77
遵义市	Zunyi					
正安县	Zhengan	4995	120.00	1995	7860	6.45
※务川县	Wuchuan	3000	78.80		50000	0.62
凤冈县	Fenggang	5505	53.00	86880	65000	0.30
习水县	Xishui	1440	54.00		54300	0.80
安顺市	Anshun					
普定县	Puding		181.20		7280	0.70
※关岭县	Guanling	7901	70.00		5000	0.82
※镇宁县	Zhenning	4995	127.00	6750	20000	1.00
※紫云县	Ziyun	3240	191.00	7500	6100	1.13
铜仁地区	Tongren					
石阡县	Shiqian	1650	155.40		40000	0.50
※印江县	Yinjiang	7500	75.00	7500	58000	0.72
德江县	Dejiang	255	54.00	120	95000	0.69
※沿河县	Yanhe	7005	38.63		70000	0.30
※松桃县	Songtao	6645	31.00	14500.5	52160	1.20
黔西南州	Qianxinan					
兴仁县	Xingren				6500	0.69
普安县	Puan	1530	178.25		26000	0.60
晴隆县	Qinglong	945	6.70		273	0.70
贞丰县	Zhenfeng	130.5	50.00		22000	0.41
望谟县	Wangmo	774	158.00	21360	21000	0.80
册亨县	Ceheng	2130	70.40	18120	5520	0.60

22 - 6 续表(continued)

贫困县名称	County	当年新增基本农田(亩) Farmland Newly Increased in 2000(mu)	当年新增公路里程(公里) Length of Highways Newly Increased in 2001(km)	当年新增经济林和茶桑果园面积(亩) Area of Cash Forest, Tea Plantations, Mulberry Plantations and Orchards Newly Increased in 2001(mu)	当年向外省输出劳动力(人) Loborers Transferred to Other Provinces in 2001(person)	当年解决温饱的贫困人口(万人) Number of People Met the Basic Requirements for Food and Clothing in 2001(10000 persons)
安龙县	Anlong		59.00	15885	2450	0.55
毕节地区	Bijie					
大方县	Dafang	3270	126.30	4890	21580	0.30
织金县	Zhijin	70.95	49.00	8070	55382	3.50
纳雍县	Nayong	7500	66.50	1200	97506	0.14
※威宁县	Weining	9000	67.70	8700	250	3.00
赫章县	Hezhang	27000	56.00	13650	12710	1.00
黔东南州	Qiandongnan					
黄平县	Huangping	14700	245.00		25430	1.40
施秉县	Shibing		33.00	450	5000	0.50
三穗县	Sansui	90	20.00	990	35890	0.10
岑巩县	Cengong	4500	78.00	2400	26000	0.51
天柱县	Tianzhu		60.00		28019	0.63
剑河县	Jianhe	83.4	31.30		15000	0.25
台江县	Taijiang	192	12.00	345	9300	0.15
黎平县	Liping	12.75	47.00	55215	57800	1.65
榕江县	Rongjiang	135	81.00		14130	0.22
从江县	Congjiang	315	20.00	11805	7524	1.20
雷山县	Leishan	30	10.50		16800	0.13
麻江县	Majiang		10.00		8500	0.32
丹寨县	Danzai	325.05	23.00	6630	1073	0.11
黔南州	Qiannan					
荔波县	Libo	120	169.78	6195	3268	0.59
独山县	Dushan	381	38.50		3450	
平塘县	Pingtang	16005	65.00	3432	1400	1.50
罗甸县	Luodian	4449	53.00	3000	19786	0.63
长顺县	Changshun	28125	129.00	32970	680	0.70
※三都县	Sandu	15090	93.00	19245	3907	1.02

注:本表资源来源于省扶贫办。

Note: Datas in this table are obtained from anti - poverty office.

23

Twenty-Three

地县社会经济发展概况

Prefecture (County) Social and Economic Summary

23-1 各地区国内生产总值及构成(2001)
Gross Domestic Product and Its Composition by Region

州(市、地)名称 State(City, Prefecture)	国内生产总值 Gross Domestic Product	第一产业 Primary Industry	第二产业 Secondary Industry	第三产业 Tertiary Industry	2001年比2000年增长(%) Increase Rate in 2001 over 2000(%)	人均国内生产总值(元) Per Capita Gross Domestic Product(yuan)	位次 Order
绝对数(万元) Absolute figure(10000 yuan)							
贵阳市 Guiyang	3027470	250919	1526873	1249678	11.2	8921	1
六盘水市 Liupanshui	908799	139517	491289	277993	9.1	3122	3
遵义市 Zunyi	2527461	826653	916475	784333	8.6	3520	2
安顺市 Anshun	635033	189223	230440	215370	9.4	2503	5
铜仁地区 Tongren	673021	384642	133546	154833	8.1	1786	9
黔西南州 Qianxinan	672053	228981	228436	214636	9.4	2254	6
毕节地区 Bijie	1271620	542246	363800	365574	9.9	1831	8
黔东南州 Qiandongnan	859138	356926	249542	252670	9.3	2022	7
黔南州 Qiannan	1062412	357364	400172	304876	8.0	2782	4
构成(%) Composition(%)							
贵阳市 Guiyang	100.0	8.3	50.4	41.3			
六盘水市 Liupanshui	100.0	15.4	54.1	30.6			
遵义市 Zunyi	100.0	32.7	36.3	31.0			
安顺市 Anshun	100.0	29.8	36.3	33.9			
铜仁地区 Tongren	100.0	57.2	19.8	23.0			
黔西南州 Qianxinan	100.0	34.1	34.0	31.9			
毕节地区 Bijie	100.0	42.6	28.6	28.7			
黔东南州 Qiandongnan	100.0	41.5	29.0	29.4			
黔南州 Qiannan	100.0	33.6	37.7	28.7			

注:本表绝对数按当年价格计算,增长速度按可比价格计算。

Note: Absolute figures in this table are current prices while increase rate are calculated at comparable prices.

23-2 各地区常住人口
Permanent Residents by Region

州(市、地)名称	State(City, Prefecture)	总户数(万户) Total Number of Household (10000 households)		平均每户人数(人) Population of Per Household(person)		年末人口数(万人) Total Population at The Year-end(10000 persons)	
		2000	2001	2000	2001	2000	2001
贵 阳 市	Guiyang	111.7	97.18	3.02	3.51	337.45	341.29
六盘水市	Liupanshui	72.5	79.83	3.97	3.65	287.83	291.11
遵 义 市	Zunyi	178.87	188.28	3.99	3.84	713.94	722.08
安 顺 市	Anshun	60.72	67.16	4.16	3.80	252.3	255.17
铜仁地区	Tongren	92.88	104.20	4.03	3.64	374.77	379.04
黔西南州	Qianxinan	71.64	79.32	4.14	3.78	296.53	299.91
毕节地区	Bijie	160.67	186.94	4.30	3.74	690.63	698.50
黔东南州	Qiandongnan	100.01	111.67	4.22	3.83	422.49	427.30
黔 南 州	Qiannan	92.44	103.80	4.11	3.70	379.78	384.11

23-2 续表(continued)

州(市、地)名称	State(City, Prefecture)	按农业与非农业分(万人) By Agricultural and Non-Agricultural(10000 persons)			
		农 业 Agricultural		非 农 业 Non-Agricultural	
		2000	2001	2000	2001
贵 阳 市	Guiyang	182.34	184.71	155.11	156.58
六盘水市	Liupanshui	232.32	234.97	55.51	56.14
遵 义 市	Zunyi	613.07	620.06	100.87	102.02
安 顺 市	Anshun	213.53	215.96	38.77	39.21
铜仁地区	Tongren	341.86	345.76	32.91	33.28
黔西南州	Qianxinan	269.80	272.88	26.73	27.03
毕节地区	Bijie	648.41	655.80	42.22	42.70
黔东南州	Qiandongnan	378.48	382.79	44.01	44.51
黔 南 州	Qiannan	332.51	336.31	47.27	47.80

23－3 各地区职工人数、年平均工资(2001)
Number of Staff and Workers and Their Annual Average Wages by Region

州(市、地)名称	State(City, Prefecture)	合计 Total	国有经济 State－owned units	城镇集体经济 Urban Collective－owned Units	其他经济类型 Units of Other Types of Ownership	2001年比2000年增长(%) Increase Rate in 2001 over 2000(%)
职工人数(万人)	**Number of Staff and Workers(10000 persons)**	**189.17**	**148.87**	**15.73**	**24.58**	**－2.5**
贵阳市	Guiyang	50.05	36.06	5.54	8.45	－6.6
六盘水市	Liupanshui	16.59	9.45	0.62	6.52	－3.5
遵义市	Zunyi	25.71	20.25	1.95	3.51	－14.5
安顺市	Anshun	10.48	8.48	1.17	0.83	－8.6
铜仁地区	Tongren	12.56	11.19	1.06	0.31	－0.5
黔西南州	Qianxinan	10.36	8.77	1.01	0.58	4.3
毕节地区	Bijie	16.49	14.62	1.41	0.46	－1.6
黔东南州	Qiandongnan	14.81	12.43	1.43	0.95	－13.0
黔南州	Qiannan	15.20	12.62	1.56	1.02	－3.2
平均工资(元)	**Annual Average Wages(yuan)**	**8991**	**9308**	**6218**	**8831**	**20.4**
贵阳市	Guiyang	10969	11808	7275	9755	24.9
六盘水市	Liupanshui	9028	8843	6612	9536	15.3
遵义市	Zunyi	8750	9253	5551	7780	24.6
安顺市	Anshun	9000	9528	6021	7308	39.3
铜仁地区	Tongren	8226	8522	5653	6718	32.0
黔西南州	Qianxinan	8047	8302	6098	7517	26.2
毕节地区	Bijie	7872	8180	4944	6904	27.8
黔东南州	Qiandongnan	8373	8848	5881	5934	42.0
黔南州	Qiannan	8077	8542	5370	6445	25.8

23－4 各地区固定资产投资(一)(2001)
Investment in Fixed Assets by Region(1)

州(市、地)名称 State(City,Prefecture)		固定资产投资总额 Total Investment in Fixed Assets	基本建设 Capital Construction	更新改造 Investment in Innovation	其他投资 Other Investment	房地产开发 Real Estate Development	2001年比2000年增长(%) Increase Rate in 2001 over 2000(%)
绝对数(万元)	**Absolute Figure(10000 yuan)**						
贵阳市	Guiyang	1467685	555418	394201	84739	433327	37.4
六盘水市	Liupanshui	316016	139434	148452	12231	15899	-0.1
遵义市	Zunyi	606755	236448	250477	13659	106171	43.1
安顺市	Anshun	154085	75760	50959	1549	25817	18.8
铜仁地区	Tongren	228524	155282	30614	21774	20854	48.5
黔西南州	Qianxinan	141593	62318	62667	9597	7011	17.0
毕节地区	Bijie	284987	226409	43212	2528	12838	71.5
黔东南州	Qiandongnan	337314	178398	98673	31974	28269	54.1
黔南州	Qiannan	188529	72369	74022	11689	30449	26.5
构成(%)	**Composition(%)**						
贵阳市	Guiyang	100.0	37.8	26.9	5.8	29.5	
六盘水市	Liupanshui	100.0	44.1	47.0	3.9	5.0	
遵义市	Zunyi	100.0	39.0	41.3	2.3	17.5	
安顺市	Anshun	100.0	49.2	33.1	1.0	16.8	
铜仁地区	Tongren	100.0	67.9	13.4	9.5	9.1	
黔西南州	Qianxinan	100.0	44.0	44.3	6.8	5.0	
毕节地区	Bijie	100.0	79.4	15.2	0.9	4.5	
黔东南州	Qiandongnan	100.0	52.9	29.3	9.5	8.4	
黔南州	Qiannan	100.0	38.4	39.3	6.2	16.2	

注:1.本表投资总额不包括国有单位零星固定资产投资和城乡私人投资。(下表同)

2.本表投资总额除贵阳市、六盘水市外其余地区均未含省直统单位(铁路、国防系统等)资料 。(下表同)

Note:1. Total investment of this table exclude urban and rural individual,and the scattered investment of state－owned unit.(Same to next.)

2. Total investment of this table exclude the unit that straight calculated by province(railway and national defence system).(except Guiyang and Liupanshui.)(Same to next.)

23－5 各地区固定资产投资(二)(2001)
Investment in Fixed Assets by Region(2)

州(市、地)名称	State(City, Prefecture)	固定资产投资总额 Total Investment in Fixed Assets	按国有非国有分 Grouped by State－owned and Non－state－owned	
			国有经济 State－owned	非国有经济 Non－state－owned
绝对数(万元)	Absolute Figure (10000 yuan)			
贵阳市	Guiyang	1467685	873567	594118
六盘水市	Liupanshui	316016	290856	25160
遵义市	Zunyi	606755	450531	156224
安顺市	Anshun	154085	86660	67425
铜仁地区	Tongren	228524	183031	45493
黔西南州	Qianxinan	141593	122848	18745
毕节地区	Bijie	284987	270867	14120
黔东南州	Qiandongnan	337314	265833	71481
黔南州	Qiannan	188529	128866	59663
构成(%)	Composition(%)			
贵阳市	Guiyang	100.0	59.5	40.5
六盘水市	Liupanshui	100.0	92.0	8.0
遵义市	Zunyi	100.0	74.3	25.7
安顺市	Anshun	100.0	56.2	43.8
铜仁地区	Tongren	100.0	80.1	19.9
黔西南州	Qianxinan	100.0	86.8	13.2
毕节地区	Bijie	100.0	95.0	5.0
黔东南州	Qiandongnan	100.0	78.8	21.2
黔南州	Qiannan	100.0	68.4	31.6

23－6 各地区农业耕地面积(2001)
Cultivated Area by Region

单位:万亩
(10000 mu)

州(市、地)名称	State(City、Prefecture)	耕地面积 Cultivated Area	水田 Paddy Fields	旱地 Dry Fields	年内减少耕地面积 Decrease in Cultivated Area in The Year	#国家基建占地 Capital Construction
贵阳市	Guiyang	160.24	61.41	98.83	1.33	0.61
六盘水市	Liupanshui	158.77	33.01	125.76	0.78	0.37
遵义市	Zunyi	592.42	286.52	305.90	6.46	2.23
安顺市	Anshun	174.19	84.79	89.40	0.54	0.16
铜仁地区	Tongren	265.92	156.93	108.99	1.41	0.89
黔西南州	Qianxinan	253.98	79.97	174.00	2.35	0.84
毕节地区	Bijie	586.06	74.70	511.35	6.10	1.35
黔东南州	Qiandongnan	277.27	205.62	71.63	1.48	0.59
黔南州	Qiannan	279.58	161.95	117.63	2.92	0.33

23－7 各地区乡村从业人员数(2001)
Rural Employment by Region

州(市、地)名称	State(City、Prefecture)	合计 Total	农林牧渔业 Farming, Forestry, Animal Husbandary, Fishery	工业 Industry	建筑业 Construction	运输邮电业 Transportation and Post	批发零售贸易业、餐饮及服务业 Wholesale, Retail Sale and Catering Trades	其他劳动力 Others
绝对数(万人)	**Absolute Figure(10000 Persons)**							
贵阳市	Guiyang	105.70	78.57	5.21	3.13	1.98	2.99	13.82
六盘水市	Liupanshui	117.77	93.21	6.70	2.01	1.91	1.89	12.05
遵义市	Zunyi	352.99	257.28	9.64	7.91	3.17	6.92	68.07
安顺市	Anshun	121.51	96.72	3.93	3.42	1.43	3.34	12.67
铜仁地区	Tongren	209.26	146.42	5.69	4.29	1.88	4.16	46.82
黔西南州	Qianxinan	153.73	122.23	3.16	3.16	1.88	3.26	20.04
毕节地区	Bijie	361.37	264.12	24.39	6.15	3.55	6.29	56.87
黔东南州	Qiandongnan	209.73	161.10	4.32	2.86	1.76	3.63	36.06
黔南州	Qiannan	189.45	148.63	5.60	4.57	2.00	3.65	25.00
构成(%)	**Composition(%)**							
贵阳市	Guiyang	100.00	74.33	4.93	2.96	1.87	2.83	13.07
六盘水市	Liupanshui	100.00	79.15	5.69	1.71	1.62	1.60	10.23
遵义市	Zunyi	100.00	72.89	2.73	2.24	0.90	1.96	19.28
安顺市	Anshun	100.00	79.60	3.23	2.81	1.18	2.75	10.43
铜仁地区	Tongren	100.00	69.97	2.72	2.05	0.90	1.99	22.37
黔西南州	Qianxinan	100.00	79.51	2.06	2.06	1.22	2.12	13.04
毕节地区	Bijie	100.00	73.09	6.75	1.70	0.98	1.74	15.74
黔东南州	Qiandongnan	100.00	76.81	2.06	1.36	0.84	1.73	17.19
黔南州	Qiannan	100.00	78.45	2.96	2.41	1.06	1.93	13.20

23－8 各地区农、林、牧、渔业总产值及构成(2001)
Gross Output Value and Its Composition of Farming, Forestry, Animal Husbandary, Fishery by Region

州(市、地)名称	State(City、Prefecture)	农林牧渔业总产值 Gross Output Value of Farming, Forestry, Animal Husbandary, Fishery	农业 Farming	林业 Forestry	牧业 Animal Husbandary	渔业 Fishery	2001年比2000年增长(%) Increase Rate in 2001 over 2000(%)
绝对数(万元)	Absolute Figure(10000 Persons)						
贵阳市	Guiyang	389659	237175	6769	137845	7870	4.1
六盘水市	Liupanshui	207819	144329	4882	58396	212	2.5
遵义市	Zunyi	1277528	805502	41670	418512	11844	-0.7
安顺市	Anshun	265804	168792	10009	84519	2484	1.2
铜仁地区	Tongren	600652	392976	16259	181735	9682	0.2
黔西南州	Qianxinan	393934	233639	19061	137913	3321	3.4
毕节地区	Bijie	839316	573633	11970	251750	1803	1.6
黔东南州	Qiandongnan	560466	364865	25753	153247	16601	3.1
黔南州	Qiannan	545443	345875	34590	161282	3696	-0.3
构成(%)	Composition(%)						
贵阳市	Guiyang	100.00	60.87	1.74	35.38	2.02	
六盘水市	Liupanshui	100.00	69.45	2.35	28.10	0.10	
遵义市	Zunyi	100.00	63.05	3.26	32.76	0.93	
安顺市	Anshun	100.00	63.50	3.77	31.80	0.93	
铜仁地区	Tongren	100.00	65.42	2.71	30.26	1.61	
黔西南州	Qianxinan	100.00	59.31	4.84	35.01	0.84	
毕节地区	Bijie	100.00	68.35	1.43	29.99	0.23	
黔东南州	Qiandongnan	100.00	65.10	4.59	27.34	2.96	
黔南州	Qiannan	100.00	63.41	6.34	29.57	0.68	

注：本表绝对数按当年价格计算，增长速度按可比价格计算。

Note: Data in absolute figure in this table are calculated at current prices, while the increase rate are calculated at comparable prices.

23－9 各地区农民人均纯收入(2001)
Per Capita Net Income of Rural Households by Region

单位：元
(yuan)

州(市、地)名称	State(City、Prefecture)	农村居民人均纯收入 Per Capita Net Income of Rural Households	位次 Order	农村居民人均年现金收入 Annual Per Capita Cash Income of Rural Households	位次 Order	农村居民人均年消费性支出 Annual Per Capita Living Expenditures of Rural Households	位次 Order
贵阳市	Guiyang	2229	1	2015	1	1014	1
六盘水市	Liupanshui	1361	6	1123	5	473	9
遵义市	Zunyi	1744	2	1359	2	683	3
安顺市	Anshun	1382	4	1151	4	597	5
铜仁地区	Tongren	1306	8	1070	6	628	4
黔西南州	Qianxinan	1406	3	1262	3	717	2
毕节地区	Bijie	1292	9	1009	8	545	8
黔东南州	Qiandongnan	1326	7	999	9	580	6
黔南州	Qiannan	1366	5	1056	7	565	7

23－10 各地区农业机械总动力及拥有量(2001)

Total Power and Possession of Agricultural Machinery by Region

单位:台
(set)

州(市、地)名称	State(City、Profecture)	农业机械总动力(千瓦) Total Power of Agricultural Machinery(kw)	大中型农用拖拉机 Large and Medium Agricultural Tractors	小型拖拉机 Mini Agricultural Tractors	农用运输车 Transpotr Trucks for Agricultural Use	农用水泵 Agricultural Water Pump
贵阳市	Guiyang	535200	1200	1900	8000	11000
六盘水市	Liupanshui	7000	1000	6000	3000	4000
遵义市	Zunyi	1401600	3900	6800	7400	24500
安顺市	Anshun	458400	1700	2800	3700	10100
铜仁地区	Tongren	4000	1600	2400	3800	8000
黔西南州	Qianxinan	8600	2700	5900	2200	6900
毕节地区	Bijie	18000	3400	14600	3600	3800
黔东南州	Qiandongnan	6800	900	5900	3700	12900
黔南州	Qiannan	8900	1600	7300	3700	15500

注:本表资料由省农机部门提供。

Note: Data in this table are obtained from the agricultural machinery department.

23－11 各地区农用化肥施用量(2001)

Consumption of Chemical Fertilizers for Agricultural Use by Region

单位:吨
(ton)

州(市、地)名称	State(City、Profecture)	合计 Total	氮肥 Nitrogenous Fertilizer	磷肥 Phosphate Fertilizer	钾肥 Potash Fertilizer	复合肥 Compound Fertilizer	2001年比2000年增长(%) Increase Rate in 2001 over 2000(%)
贵阳市	Guiyang	66321	36234	11461	6513	12113	2.2
六盘水市	Liupanshui	48222	33392	7113	2784	4933	4.0
遵义市	Zunyi	144790	91936	20542	16376	15936	－2.8
安顺市	Anshun	51952	28301	12703	2056	8892	2.3
铜仁地区	Tongren	66503	34899	10581	5323	15701	－0.3
黔西南州	Qianxinan	57691	40051	8816	5519	3305	5.8
毕节地区	Bijie	160260	100363	19279	7203	33415	－2.1
黔东南州	Qiandongnan	49273	20883	9054	3555	15781	－11.4
黔南州	Qiannan	54467	35047	9307	2787	7326	－11.1

注:本表按折纯法计算。

Note: Consumption of chemical fertilizers is required in calculation to convert the gross weight into weight containing 100% effective component.

23－12 各地区主要农作物播种面积(2001)
Sown Areas of Major Farm Crops by Region

单位:万亩
(10000 mu)

州(市、地)名称	State(City、Profecture)	总计 Total	粮食作物 Sown Areas of Grain Arops	#夏粮 Summer Grain Crops	按品种分 #稻谷 Rice	#小麦 Wheat	#玉米 Corn	#大豆 Soybeans	油菜籽 Rapeseed	烤烟 Fluecured Tobacco
贵阳市	Guiyang	342.50	206.64	65.09	60.23	20.54	60.00	19.11	55.13	12.52
六盘水市	Liupanshui	357.49	284.60	124.60	31.02	61.15	101.55	18.49	7.18	6.95
遵义市	Zunyi	1676.83	1163.41	415.56	269.61	179.70	219.91	90.23	190.30	87.37
安顺市	Anshun	376.44	256.87	83.85	84.72	53.66	68.14	15.70	72.20	6.08
铜仁地区	Tongren	756.95	528.23	163.92	157.49	83.67	93.39	36.68	73.35	30.61
黔西南州	Qianxinan	570.28	388.96	127.29	81.93	96.21	136.84	24.80	32.62	16.68
毕节地区	Bijie	1503.56	960.42	410.48	74.00	183.57	249.28	111.27	74.45	75.22
黔东南州	Qiandongnan	755.29	458.11	110.93	206.02	22.09	56.51	21.15	75.84	12.32
黔南州	Qiannan	635.76	434.04	125.62	159.94	80.14	97.07	27.26	87.17	25.82

23－13 各地区主要农产品产量(2001)
Output of Major Farm Crops by Region

单位:万吨
(10000 tons)

州(市、地)名称	State(City、Profecture)	粮食 Grain	#夏粮 Summer Grain Crops	2001年比2000年增长(%) Increase Rate in 2001 over 2000(%)	油菜籽 Rapeseeds	烤烟 Fluecured Tobacco	茶叶 Tea	水果 Fruits
贵阳市	Guiyang	58.56	10.01	-7.7	5.22	1.37	0.14	5.53
六盘水市	Liupanshui	72.57	15.32	2.7	0.55	0.82	0.03	1.57
遵义市	Zunyi	284.3	68.48	-14.0	22.68	7.25	0.72	12.02
安顺市	Anshun	77.54	10.53	1.6	7.07	0.60	0.13	3.26
铜仁地区	Tongren	129.91	26.31	-10.8	6.78	2.92	0.18	6.00
黔西南州	Qianxinan	100.21	13.82	0.5	1.85	1.79	0.20	7.55
毕节地区	Bijie	217.67	51.95	-6.1	6.59	8.37	0.07	4.80
黔东南州	Qiandongnan	134.24	15.79	1.3	5.87	0.99	0.19	16.20
黔南州	Qiannan	118.55	14.38	0.8	6.86	2.27	0.19	6.00

注:水果产量包括原属于蔬菜类的果用瓜。

Note: Output of fruits include the melon that belonged to vegetable.

23－14 各地区牲畜出存栏量(2001)

Amount of Livestocks in Hand and Slaughtered by Region

单位:万头
(10000 heads)

州(市、地)名称	State(City、Profecture)	出栏 Amount of Slaughtered Livestocks			存栏 Amount of Livestock in Hand		
		猪 Hogs	牛 Cattle and Buffalo	羊 Sheep and Goats	猪 Hogs	牛 Cattle and Buffalo	羊 Sheep and Goats
贵阳市	Guiyang	118.18	4.42	5.41	119.15	37.19	7.06
六盘水市	Liupanshui	53.64	3.91	7.01	92.86	36.12	21.30
遵义市	Zunyi	399.17	19.63	61.94	470.51	126.15	102.99
安顺市	Anshun	66.41	5.69	2.23	91.84	56.60	6.01
铜仁地区	Tongren	181.46	12.91	75.24	232.03	77.60	92.61
黔西南州	Qianxinan	139.72	12.62	12.10	158.00	87.96	22.88
毕节地区	Bijie	235.50	15.17	32.31	336.40	114.32	70.82
黔东南州	Qiandongnan	169.88	20.37	27.56	239.87	121.11	54.24
黔南州	Qiannan	143.99	11.55	11.48	187.72	100.63	19.50

23－15 各地区主要畜产品及水产品产量(2001)

Output of Major Livestock Products and Aquatic Products by Region

单位:万吨
(10000 tons)

州(市、地)名称	State(City、Profecture)	肉类总产量 Total Output of Meat	#猪肉 Pork	#牛肉 Beef	2001年比2000年增长(%) Increase Rate in 2001 over 2000(%)	禽蛋 Poulty and Eggs	水产品 Aquatic Products
贵阳市	Guiyang	12.7	10.87	0.52	9.9	1.05	0.86
六盘水市	Liupanshui	5.92	5.24	0.29	5.7	0.29	0.08
遵义市	Zunyi	40.15	34.96	2.15	6.0	2.31	1.32
安顺市	Anshun	7.41	6.13	0.55	3.5	0.58	0.33
铜仁地区	Tongren	19.14	16.09	1.32	11.6	1.19	0.89
黔西南州	Qianxinan	14.59	11.92	1.27	6.9	1.24	0.77
毕节地区	Bijie	26.83	23.43	1.28	3.8	1.73	0.35
黔东南州	Qiandongnan	15.83	12.59	1.74	5.9	0.49	1.72
黔南州	Qiannan	14.22	12.3	1.04	1.8	0.52	0.55

注:其中水产品产量为部门数。

Note: Output of aquatic products in this table are obtained from the fishery department.

23－16 各地区主要林产品产量(2001)
Output of Major Forestry Products by Region

单位:吨
(ton)

州(市、地)名称	State(City、Prefecture)	生漆 Lacquer	油桐籽 Tung－Oil Seed	油茶籽 Tea－Oil Seed	乌桕籽 Tallow－seeds	五倍籽 Nutgall	棕片 Palm－flake	核桃 Walnuts	板栗 Chestnut
贵阳市	Guiyang	26	343	132	79	42	100	151	134
六盘水市	Liupanshui	77	137	33			52	966	242
遵义市	Zunyi	301	7889	173	1623	656	1580	578	638
安顺市	Anshun	25	9083	322	89	15	180	183	179
铜仁地区	Tongren	69	12322	1881	1720	215	638	232	699
黔西南州	Qianxinan	58	48982	2199	58	111	1343	942	2961
毕节地区	Bijie	382	198	9	36	28	290	3408	434
黔东南州	Qiandongnan	50	10054	4885	367	198	276	203	1498
黔南州	Qiannan	59	14689	322	92	204	328	347	1025

23－17 各地区规模以上轻重工业总产值(2001)
Total Gross Industrial Output Value above Designated Size of Light Industry and Heavy Industry by Region

单位:万元
(10000 yuan)

州(市、地)名称	State(City, Prefecture)	合计 Total	轻工业 Light Industry	重工业 Heavy Industry	2001年比2000年增长(%) Increase Rate in 2001 over 2000(%)
贵阳市	Guiyang	2588494	902276	1686218	4.3
六盘水市	Liupanshui	654406	26362	628044	5.0
遵义市	Zunyi	1218984	558450	660534	12.2
安顺市	Anshun	514363	106380	407983	14.3
铜仁地区	Tongren	155345	74686	80659	11.3
黔西南州	Qianxinan	435640	64816	370824	6.1
毕节地区	Bijie	392120	206966	185154	24.8
黔东南州	Qiandongnan	275044	52372	222672	26.7
黔南州	Qiannan	503441	146836	356605	9.7

注:1.表中绝对数按当年价计算,增长速度按可比价格计算。
2.表中除贵阳市、安顺市外其余均未含省直统单位(国防系统等)资料。

Note:1. Absolute figures in this table are current prices while increase rate are calculated at comparable prices.
2. The data of this table exclude the unit that straight calculated by province(national defence system etc).(except Guiyang and Anshun.)

23－18 各地区规模以上工业企业主要工业产品产量(2001)
Ouput of Major Industrial Products above Designated Size by Region

州(市、地)名称 State(City, Prefecture)		原煤(万吨) Coal (10000 tons)	发电量(万千瓦小时) Electricity (10000 kwh)	化肥(万吨) Chemical Fertilizer (10000 tons)	饮料酒(万吨) Alcoholic Beverages (10000 tons)	水泥(万吨) Cement (10000 tons)
贵阳市	Guiyang	390.52	914116	20.79	2.82	222.10
六盘水市	Liupanshui	1533.47	603624	1.39	3.92	135.86
遵义市	Zunyi	363.02	546700	35.12	8.35	168.11
安顺市	Anshun	213.80	514191	4.29	2.90	43.00
铜仁地区	Tongren	76.20	54550	0.36	4.30	64.30
黔西南州	Qianxinan	381.10	1286435	7.76	2.35	75.06
毕节地区	Bijie	524.68	441849	10.56	0.47	57.08
黔东南州	Qiandongnan	173.74	401985	0.04	0.49	46.74
黔南州	Qiannan	294.44	47077	8.98	0.03	108.39

23－19 各地区社会消费品零售总额(2001)
Total Retail Sales of Consumer Goods by Region

单位:万元
(10000 yuan)

州(市、地)名称 State(City, Prefecture)		社会消费品零售总额 Total Retail Sales of Consumer Goods	按销售地区分 Grouped by Distribution Area		
			市 City	县 County	县以下 Below County Level
贵阳市	Guiyang	1216556	1114138	48845	53573
六盘水市	Liupanshui	199189	160137		39052
遵义市	Zunyi	595140	244221	139993	210926
安顺市	Anshun	231547	128520	46951	56076
铜仁地区	Tongren	187839	36785	71206	79848
黔西南州	Qianxinan	188881	70011	53273	65597
毕节地区	Bijie	207465	31093	72849	103523
黔东南州	Qiandongnan	225069	58020	81934	85115
黔南州	Qiannan	289618	75050	98004	116564

23-20 各地区地方财政收入(2001)
Local Financial Revenue by Region

州(市、地)名称	State(City, Prefecture)	合计(万元) Total (10000 yuan)	#增值税 Value-added Tax	#营业税 Operation Tax	#农业五税 Agricultural and Related	#企业收入 Revenue from Enterprises	2001年比2000年增长(%) Increase Rate in 2001 over 2000(%)	人均地方财政收入(元) Per Capita Local Financial Revenue(yuan)	位次 Order
贵阳市	Guiyang	279687	35932	80926	10365	46105	15.8	824.14	1
六盘水市	Lupanshui	54114	7140	12481	4704	5111	14.3	186.94	2
遵义市	Zhunyi	124652	14879	24173	22504	10990	7.5	173.61	3
安顺市	Anshui	41453	5107	9898	4240	6032	16.4	163.37	4
铜仁地区	Tongren	40395	1859	9040	9257	2722	11.0	107.18	9
黔西南州	Qianxinan	45903	4599	8701	7401	8071	10.1	153.92	6
毕节地区	Bijie	83258	6456	10860	16902	2921	16.2	119.87	8
黔东南州	Qiandongnan	51659	3647	13026	8757	3057	7.2	121.58	7
黔南州	Qiannan	60304	5954	12651	9210	6393	8.9	157.89	5

23-21 各地区财政支出(2001)
Financial Expenditure by Region

州(市、地)名称	State(City, Prefecture)	合计(万元) Total (10000 yuan)	#基本建设支出 Expenditure for Capital Construction	#支援农村生产支出 Expenditure for Supporting Agricultural Production	#教育事业费 Operating Expenses for Education	#农林水气事业费 Agricultural Operating Expenses	2001年比2000年增长(%) Increase Rate in 2001 over 2000(%)	人均财政支出(元) Per Capita Financial Expenditure (yuan)	位次 Order
贵阳市	Guiyang	361699	26675	9889	47303	10813	16.5	1065.80	1
六盘水市	Lupanshui	120669	1839	3722	24455	6798	19.5	416.86	5
遵义市	Zhunyi	281214	5264	7875	70129	18245	26.4	391.65	7
安顺市	Anshui	113890	2803	1575	26299	7271	31.4	448.85	4
铜仁地区	TongRen	147196	5	2831	40217	13805	37.1	390.54	8
黔西南州	Qianxinan	122484	1958	3048	29179	8927	32.6	410.72	6
毕节地区	Bijie	209239	1718	4794	55491	16483	32.3	301.25	9
黔东南州	Qiandongnan	194754	169	4415	51716	18231	40.7	458.36	3
黔南州	Qiannan	180056	1456	5122	46919	11080	34.2	471.42	2

23-22 各地区所在地城市居民消费价格指数(2001)
Residents Consumer Price Indices of Major Cities by Region

城市名称 City		居民消费价格指数 Residents Consumer Price Index		商品零售价格指数 Retail Price Index of Commodities	
		2000	2001	2000	2001
贵阳市	Guiyang	98.7	103.2	95.8	96.3
六盘水市	Liupanshui	99.3	100.9	98.4	100.6
遵义市	Zunyi	99.6	100.3	97.7	101.1
安顺市	Anshun	99.5	101.6	98.9	100.7
铜仁市	Tongren	103.8	99.6	95.9	99.2
兴义市	Xingyi	98.4	100.7	99.0	97.0
毕节市	Bijie	98.3	101.9	97.8	101.6
凯里市	Kaili	100.0	97.9	97.9	96.3
都匀市	Duyun	99.1	99.9	97.9	99.4

23-23 各地区城市居民家庭人均收支(2001)
Per Capital Annual Income and Expenditure of Urban Residents by Region

单位:元
(yuan)

各调查市名称 City	城市居民家庭人均可支配收入 Per Capita Annual Disposal Income of Urban Household	位次 Order	2001年比2000年增长(%) Increase Rate in 2001 over 2000(%)	城市居民家庭人均消费性支出 Per Capita Annual Consumer Expenditnres of Urban Household	位次 Order	2001年比2000年增长(%) Increase Rate in 2001 over 2000(%)
贵阳市 Guiyang	6908.50	1	7.1	5775.59	1	4.1
六盘水市 Liupanshui	5145.95	7	7.0	3558.09	9	8.7
遵义市 Zunyi	5539.89	5	6.2	4382.96	5	11.0
安顺市 Anshun	4838.75	9	4.4	3562.41	8	-0.9
铜仁市 Tongren	5737.39	3	11.5	4678.66	2	3.2
兴义市 Xingyi	5785.45	2	22.4	4431.82	4	-3.1
毕节市 Bijie	4845.16	8	12.4	3577.03	7	7.2
凯里市 Kaili	5240.27	6	5.0	4272.90	6	4.0
都匀市 Duyun	5588.99	4	13.5	4556.76	3	16.2

23-24 各地区教育事业主要指标(2001)
Major Indicators of Education by Region

州(市、地)名称 State(City, Prefecture)		高等学校(所) Institutions of Higher Education (unit)	在校学生(人) Students Enrollment (person)	普通中学(所) Secondary Schools (unit)	在校学生(人) Students Enrollment (person)	小学(所) Primary Schools (unit)	在校学生(万人) Students Enrollment (10000 persons)
贵阳市	Guiyang	13	76514	274	191463	1187	36.78
六盘水市	Liupanshui	1	1965	195	141220	1095	40.42
遵义市	Zunyi	2	9113	439	390891	2702	88.98
安顺市	Anshun	2	2054	126	105892	1043	34.05
铜仁地区	Tongren	1	2771	228	179932	1661	50.49
黔西南州	Qianxinan	1	3094	202	160498	1132	44.36
毕节地区	Bijie	2	4307	262	276803	2709	99.04
黔东南州	Qiandongnan	3	3463	254	214228	2102	50.88
黔南州	Qiannan	3	3970	209	185088	1708	45.17

23-25 各地区城乡居民年末储蓄余额(2001)
Urban and Rural Resident Savings Deposit Balance at The Year-end by Region

单位:万元
(10000 yuan)

州(市、地)名称 State(City, Prefecture)		金融机构存款余额 Total Savings Deposit Balance	#城乡居民储蓄余额 Urban and Rural Resident Savings Deposit Balance	2001年比2000增长(%) Increase Rate in 2001 over 2000(%)	金融机构贷款余额 Total Loans Balance	2001年比2000增长(%) Increase Rate in 2001 over 2000(%)
贵阳市	Guiyang	6452190	2401281	21.7	4863088	20.2
六盘水市	Liupanshui	863751	389997	12.8	746562	19.6
遵义市	Zunyi	2062409	1170426	23.7	1560012	7.9
安顺市	Anshun	687158	394305	14.8	690570	30.4
铜仁地区	Tongren	491852	326875	20.9	547839	6.5
黔西南州	Qianxinan	602395	307194	28.4	478609	7.3
毕节地区	Bijie	667779	397231	30.5	807058	5.6
黔东南州	Qiandongnan	789755	517651	18.7	785643	9.1
黔南州	Qiannan	783453	512702	18.5	754037	3.3

23-26 各县(市、区)国内生产总值(2001)
Gross Domestic Product by County(City,Section)

单位:万元
(10000 yuan)

县(市、区)名称 County(City,Section)		国内生产总值 Gross Domestic Product	第一产业 Primary Industry	第二产业 Secondary Industry	第三产业 Tertiary Industry	位次 Order	2001年比2000年增长(%) Increase Rate in 2001 over 2000(%)
南明区	Nanming	565875	4640	281174	280061	4	11.9
云岩区	Yunyan	904177	4035	490586	409556	1	10.0
花溪区	Huaxi	246124	41068	90330	114726	13	11.7
乌当区	Wudang	286981	42122	142448	102411	10	12.1
白云区	Baiyun	359395	12558	203407	143430	5	11.7
小河区	Xiaohe	127475	3921	70512	53042	27	14.0
开阳县	Kaiyang	161798	44215	73819	43764	19	11.0
息烽县	Xifeng	90661	23300	43976	23385	43	17.9
修文县	Xiuwen	109575	36404	43443	29728	36	13.0
清镇市	Qingzhen	286478	41496	172755	72227	11	10.8
钟山区	Zhongshan	328706	8284	199226	121196	7	10.6
六枝特区	Liuzhi	116394	26856	49715	39823	31	6.0
水城县	Shuicheng	97454	43541	34290	19623	39	10.1
盘　县	Pan	323686	60761	167885	95040	8	10.3
红花岗区	Honghuagang	790798	38984	318735	433079	2	11.3
遵义县	Zunyi	600271	199955	192814	207502	3	9.6
桐梓县	Tongzi	151523	74822	35132	41569	22	5.8
绥阳县	Suiyang	128791	67052	38549	23190	26	4.3
正安县	Zhengan	110199	62344	20560	27295	35	5.3
※道真县	Daozhen	63638	37495	11170	14973	57	7.0
※务川县	Wuchuan	60039	32451	14275	13313	59	3.7
凤冈县	Fenggang	77638	42837	20529	14272	49	-2.0
湄潭县	Meitan	171171	73110	39051	59010	18	8.1
余庆县	Yuqing	87064	55284	16465	15315	45	8.4
习水县	Xishui	124849	47628	50725	26496	28	6.3
赤水市	Chishui	112181	41300	51516	19365	34	7.8
仁怀市	Renhuai	238680	66719	135230	36731	14	15.0
西秀区	Xixiu	282756	52527	82732	147497	12	10.1
平坝县	Pingba	123634	21266	75173	27195	30	9.6

23－26 续表 1(continued)

单位:万元
(10000 yuan)

县(市、区)名称	County(City, Section)	国内生产总值 Gross Domestic Product	第一产业 Primary Industry	第二产业 Secondary Industry	第三产业 Tertiary Industry	位次 Order	2001年比2000年增长(%) Increase Rate in 2001 over 2000(%)
普定县	Puding	81923	26500	34193	21230	47	12.9
※镇宁县	Zhenning	70238	24478	31100	14660	53	8.8
※关岭县	Guanling	50088	27140	11656	11292	63	7.8
※紫云县	Ziyun	40290	27623	5144	7523	72	4.1
铜仁市	Tongren	113500	27601	43842	42057	33	13.8
江口县	Jiangkou	36950	19104	7304	10542	78	17.5
※玉屏县	Yuping	57463	20076	18260	19127	60	17.4
石阡县	Shiqian	45110	29005	6818	9287	67	3.0
思南县	Sinan	109316	71280	19753	18283	37	5.2
※印江县	Yinjiang	63783	43817	8818	11148	56	4.7
德江县	Dejiang	89407	64773	8449	16185	44	1.9
※沿河县	Yanhe	70660	46413	7670	16577	52	2.2
※松桃县	Songtao	92843	58764	14523	19556	42	12.5
万山特区	Wanshan	12007	5288	2879	3840	87	10.8
兴义市	Xingyi	314685	65488	152574	96623	9	12.1
兴仁县	Xingren	70085	33934	19680	16471	54	9.6
普安县	Puan	37689	17286	10306	10097	76	11.1
晴隆县	Qinglong	37710	16187	10495	11028	75	7.3
贞丰县	Zhenfeng	45974	28039	8760	9175	66	9.8
望谟县	Wangmo	48485	24322	12158	12005	65	7.2
册亨县	Ceheng	28875	19434	3443	5998	83	7.9
安龙县	Anlong	94086	35371	35459	23256	40	11.4
毕节市	Bijie	356259	111219	123510	121530	6	11.4
大方县	Dafang	145385	68377	40534	36474	24	7.5
黔西县	Qianxi	152432	56376	48333	47723	21	11.2
金沙县	Jinsha	160811	53104	61459	46248	20	11.8
织金县	Zhijin	146017	62233	39666	44118	23	9.7
纳雍县	Nayong	116207	54913	40069	21225	32	21.7
※威宁县	Weining	175629	88861	38115	48653	17	－1.1

23－26 续表 2(continued)

单位:万元
(10000 yuan)

县(市、区)名称 County(City,Section)		国内生产总值 Gross Domestic Product	第一产业 Primary Industry	第二产业 Secondary Industry	第三产业 Tertiary Industry	位次 Order	2001 年比 2000 年增长(%) Increase Rate in 2001 over 2000(%)
赫章县	Hezhang	93718	46750	24264	22704	41	7.0
凯里市	Kaili	234649	39651	104443	90555	15	11.0
黄平县	Huangping	43614	25593	6381	11640	68	5.3
施秉县	Shibing	34503	12366	15382	6755	79	20.5
三穗县	Sansui	37173	20488	5521	11164	77	7.0
镇远县	Zhenyuan	72135	25685	27619	18831	50	10.7
岑巩县	Cengong	31355	17923	4513	8919	81	7.3
天柱县	Tianzhu	53515	34005	6648	12862	61	6.8
锦屏县	Jinping	30552	14120	4936	11496	82	2.3
剑河县	Jianhe	32010	20748	2790	8472	80	5.9
台江县	Taijiang	25446	17079	3186	5181	84	6.6
黎平县	Liping	60471	31998	10651	17822	58	9.3
榕江县	Rongjiang	52053	31381	6485	14187	62	9.0
从江县	Congjiang	40554	25642	4680	10232	71	9.2
雷山县	Leishan	18413	10805	2170	5438	86	8.8
麻江县	Majiang	39583	15697	13501	10385	73	8.1
丹寨县	Danzhai	23290	10892	3405	8993	85	8.0
都匀市	Duyun	186106	33438	61709	90959	16	11.0
福泉市	Fuquan	144997	45873	52836	46288	25	6.7
荔波县	Libo	49185	16135	14824	18226	64	8.2
贵定县	Guiding	124510	27742	50124	46644	29	－8.3
瓮安县	Wengan	101510	45243	25606	30661	38	3.6
独山县	Dushan	65800	33805	14007	17988	55	7.5
平塘县	Pingtang	39401	20315	6505	12581	74	5.1
罗甸县	Luodian	71990	29974	27285	14731	51	－3.3
长顺县	Changshun	41534	17358	10834	13342	70	8.6
龙里县	Longli	82816	16075	52629	14112	46	10.1
惠水县	Huishui	78517	41160	20155	17202	48	8.1
※三都县	Sandu	43385	25323	4421	13641	69	6.8

注:1.带※符号者为少数民族自治县。(以下各表同) 2.表中绝对数按当年价格计算,增长速度按可比价格计算。

Note:1.The countys with "※"are autonomeus county.(Same to next.) 2.Absolute figures in this table are current prices while increase rate are calculated at comparable prices.

23－27 各县(市、区)人均国内生产总值及位次(2001)

Per Capita Gross Domestic Product and Its Order by County(City, Section)

单位:元
(yuan)

县(市、区)名称 County(City、Section)		人均国内生产总值 Per Capita Gross Domestic Product(yuan)	位次 Order	县(市、区)名称 County(City、Section)		人均国内生产总值 Per Capita Gross Domestic Product(yuan)	位次 Order
南明区	Nanming	11565	4	湄潭县	Meitan	3685	20
云岩区	Yunyan	17136	2	余庆县	Yuqing	3030	27
花溪区	Huaxi	7875	8	习水县	Xishui	1848	49
乌当区	Wudang	9608	6	赤水市	Chishui	3663	21
白云区	Baiyun	21657	1	仁怀市	Renhuai	4055	17
小河区	Xiaohe	11226	5	西秀区	Xixiu	3509	25
开阳县	Kaiyang	3778	19	平坝县	Pingba	3610	23
息烽县	Xifeng	3566	24	普定县	Puding	2041	40
修文县	Xiuwen	3640	22	※镇宁县	Zhenning	2071	39
清镇市	Qingzhen	5702	9	※关岭县	Guanling	1575	60
钟山区	Zhongshan	7908	7	※紫云县	Ziyun	1219	86
六枝特区	Liuzhi	1884	45	铜仁市	Tongren	3408	26
水城县	Shuicheng	1345	76	江口县	Jiangkou	1682	56
盘　县	Pan	2848	30	※玉屏县	Yuping	4146	15
红花岗区	Honghuagang	12757	3	石阡县	Shiqian	1206	87
遵义县	Zunyi	4427	12	思南县	Sinan	1758	54
桐梓县	Tongzi	2348	34	※印江县	Yinjiang	1574	61
绥阳县	Suiyang	2577	33	德江县	Dejiang	2030	41
正安县	Zhengan	1865	47	※沿河县	Yanhe	1295	82
※道真县	Daozhen	1923	43	※松桃县	Songtao	1484	68
※务川县	Wuchuan	1458	69	万山特区	Wanshan	1846	50
凤冈县	Fenggang	1926	42	兴义市	Xingyi	4340	14

23－27 续表(continued)

单位:元 (yuan)

县(市、区)名称 County(City、Section)		人均国内生产总值 Per Capita Gross Domestic Product(yuan)	位次 Order	县(市、区)名称 County(City、Section)		人均国内生产总值 Per Capita Gross Domestic Product(yuan)	位次 Order
兴仁县	Xingren	1566	62	锦屏县	Jinping	1398	72
普安县	Puan	1348	75	剑河县	Jianhe	1513	66
晴隆县	Qinglong	1344	77	台江县	Taijiang	1545	64
贞丰县	Zhenfeng	1372	73	黎平县	Liping	1228	85
望谟县	Wangmo	1760	53	榕江县	Rongjiang	1625	58
册亨县	Ceheng	1329	80	从江县	Congjiang	1306	81
安龙县	Anlong	2233	38	雷山县	Leishan	1264	84
毕节市	Bijie	2847	31	麻江县	Majiang	1839	51
大方县	Dafang	1523	65	丹寨县	Danzai	1455	71
黔西县	Qianxi	1871	46	都匀市	Duyun	3887	18
金沙县	Jinsha	2776	32	福泉市	Fuquan	4774	11
织金县	Zhijin	1622	59	荔波县	Libo	2991	28
纳雍县	Nayong	1554	63	贵定县	Guiding	4418	13
※威宁县	Weining	1646	57	瓮安县	Wengan	2252	36
赫章县	Hezhang	1485	67	独山县	Dushan	1921	44
凯里市	Kaili	5268	10	平塘县	Pingtang	1331	78
黄平县	Huangping	1275	83	罗甸县	Luodian	2252	37
施秉县	Shibing	2269	35	长顺县	Changshun	1722	55
三穗县	Sansui	1833	52	龙里县	Longli	4123	16
镇远县	Zhengyuan	2883	29	惠水县	Huishui	1858	48
岑巩县	Cengong	1458	70	※三都县	Sandu	1369	74
天柱县	Tianzhu	1331	79				

23-28 各县(市、区)年末常住人口主要指标(2001)
Major Indicators of Permanent Residents at The Year-end by County(City, Section)

单位:万人
(10000 persons)

县(市、区)名称	County(City, Section)	总人口 Total Population	按农业非农业分 By Agricultural and Non-agricultural 农业人口 Agricultural	 非农业人口 Non-agricultural
南明区	Nanming	49.20	2.37	46.83
云岩区	Yunyan	53.07	2.26	50.81
小河区	Xiaohe	11.42	2.19	9.23
花溪区	Huaxi	31.43	23.17	8.26
乌当区	Wudang	30.04	21.16	8.88
白云区	Baiyun	16.69	6.67	10.02
开阳县	Kaiyang	43.07	37.94	5.13
息烽县	Xifeng	25.57	22.79	2.78
修文县	Xiuwen	30.27	26.49	3.78
清镇市	Qingzhen	50.53	39.68	10.85
钟山区	Zhongshan	41.80	17.13	24.67
六枝特区	Liuzhi	62.14	49.50	12.64
水城县	Shuicheng	72.87	71.58	1.29
盘　县	Pan	114.30	96.76	17.54
红花岗区	Honghuagang	62.34	26.24	36.10
遵义县	Zunyi	136.35	123.54	12.81
桐梓县	Tongzi	64.89	52.83	12.06
绥阳县	Suiyang	50.27	46.62	3.65
正安县	Zhengan	59.43	55.96	3.47
※道真县	Daozhen	33.27	30.61	2.66
※务川县	Wuchuan	41.42	38.52	2.90
凤冈县	Fenggang	40.54	37.77	2.77
湄潭县	Meitan	46.72	41.78	4.94
余庆县	Yuqing	28.90	26.15	2.75
习水县	Xishui	67.95	62.45	5.50
赤水市	Chishui	30.80	23.86	6.94
仁怀市	Renhuai	59.20	53.73	5.47
西秀区	Xixiu	81.03	58.80	22.23
平坝县	Pingba	34.44	27.17	7.27

23－28 续表 1(continued)

单位:万人
(10000 persons)

县(市、区)名称	County(City,Section)	总人口 Total Population	按农业非农业分 By Agricultural and Non－agricultural	
			农业人口 Agricultural	非农业人口 Non－agricultural
普定县	Puding	40.37	38.11	2.26
※镇宁县	Zhenning	34.10	31.09	3.01
※关岭县	Guanling	31.98	29.35	2.63
※紫云县	Ziyun	33.25	31.44	1.81
铜仁市	Tongren	33.49	24.63	8.86
江口县	Jiangkou	22.09	20.09	2.00
※玉屏县	Yuping	13.94	11.48	2.46
石阡县	Shiqian	37.61	35.29	2.32
思南县	Sinan	62.52	58.64	3.88
※印江县	Yinjiang	40.75	38.28	2.47
德江县	Dejiang	44.29	41.11	3.18
※沿河县	Yanhe	54.89	51.64	3.25
※松桃县	Songtao	62.92	59.72	3.20
万山特区	Wanshan	6.54	4.88	1.66
兴义市	Xingyi	72.91	61.41	11.50
兴仁县	Xingren	45.01	41.74	3.27
普安县	Puan	28.12	26.24	1.88
晴隆县	Qinglong	28.22	25.86	2.36
贞丰县	Zhenfeng	33.71	31.38	2.33
望谟县	Wangmo	27.71	26.39	1.32
册亨县	Ceheng	21.85	20.70	1.15
安龙县	Anlong	42.38	39.16	3.22
毕节市	Bijie	125.85	114.19	11.66
大方县	Dafang	95.97	91.82	4.15
黔西县	Qianxi	81.93	76.18	5.75
金沙县	Jinsha	58.26	53.16	5.10
织金县	Zhijin	90.55	86.18	4.37
纳雍县	Nayong	75.20	71.53	3.67
※威宁县	Weining	107.29	102.89	4.40

23-28 续表 2(continued)

单位:万人
(10000 persons)

县(市、区)名称	County(City, Section)	总人口 Total Population	按农业非农业分 By Agricultural and Non-agricultural	
			农业人口 Agricultural	非农业人口 Non-agricultural
赫章县	Hezhang	63.45	59.85	3.60
凯里市	Kaili	44.79	28.67	16.12
黄平县	Huangping	34.41	32.13	2.28
施秉县	Shibing	15.29	14.03	1.26
三穗县	Sansui	20.40	18.84	1.56
镇远县	Zhenyuan	25.16	22.22	2.94
岑巩县	Cengong	21.63	20.09	1.54
天柱县	Tianzhu	40.44	37.63	2.81
锦屏县	Jinping	21.98	19.91	2.07
剑河县	Jianhe	21.28	19.70	1.58
台江县	Taijiang	16.56	15.03	1.53
黎平县	Liping	49.53	46.51	3.02
榕江县	Rongjiang	32.21	29.84	2.37
从江县	Congjiang	31.23	29.56	1.67
雷山县	Leishan	14.65	13.61	1.04
麻江县	Majiang	21.64	20.22	1.42
丹寨县	Danzhai	16.10	14.80	1.30
都匀市	Duyun	48.15	31.54	16.61
福泉市	Fuquan	30.54	25.58	4.96
荔波县	Libo	16.54	15.20	1.34
贵定县	Guiding	28.34	23.90	4.44
瓮安县	Wengan	45.33	40.83	4.50
独山县	Dushan	34.44	30.76	3.68
平塘县	Pingtang	29.77	28.44	1.33
罗甸县	Luodian	32.15	30.06	2.09
长顺县	Changshun	24.26	22.41	1.85
龙里县	Longli	20.20	18.40	1.80
惠水县	Huishui	42.51	38.99	3.52
※三都县	Sandu	31.88	30.20	1.68

23－29 各县(市、区)固定资产投资(2001)
Investment in Fixed Assets by County(City, Section)

单位:万元
(10000 yuan)

县(市、区)名称	County(City, Section)	固定资产投资 Total Investment in Fixed Assets	基本建设 Capital Construction	更新改造 Innovation	其他投资 Other Investment	房地产投资 Real Estate
南明区	Nanming	59259	17457	410	12505	28887
云岩区	Yunyan	133467	40584		7316	85567
花溪区	Huaxi	18920	7082	841	4962	6035
乌当区	Wudang	78680	37685	14382	17689	8924
白云区	Baiyun	45979	15030	4993	8234	17722
小河区	Xiaohe	81205	25188	3132		52885
开阳县	Kaiyang	14311	10755	1838	320	1398
息烽县	Xifeng	41883	7629	32925	649	680
修文县	Xiuwen	18220	9355	3074	4762	1029
清镇市	Qingzhen	41066	24914	4376	6945	4831
钟山区	Zhongshan	202681	97433	83679	5943	15626
六枝特区	Liuzhi	13443	6604	5905	771	163
水城县	Shuicheng	20122	18713		1299	110
盘　县	Pan	79770	16684	58868	4218	
红花岗区	Honghuagang	243747	70957	79118	1930	91742
遵义县	Zunyi	77941	57107	19025	429	1380
桐梓县	Tongzi	34262	14331	13627	6304	
绥阳县	Suiyang	8899	6531	2368		
正安县	Zhengan	15660	11450	4060	150	
※道真县	Daozhen	11594	8859	2400	335	
※务川县	Wuchuan	4751	4214	500	37	
凤冈县	Fenggang	10580	7290	1609	891	790
湄潭县	Meitan	16286	5169	5640	765	4712
余庆县	Yuqing	16894	5551	10522		821
习水县	Xishui	87370	4386	82394	590	
赤水市	Chishui	45100	26943	9203	2228	6726
仁怀市	Renhuai	33671	13660	20011		
西秀区	Xixiu	90922	25163	41137	344	24278
平坝县	Pingba	5101	2182	2245	104	570

23－29 续表 1(continued)

单位:万元
(10000 yuan)

县(市、区)名称 County(City,Section)		固定资产投资 Total Investment in Fixed Assets	基本建设 Capital Construction	更新改造 Innovation	其他投资 Other Investment	房地产投资 Real Estate
普定县	Puding	12010	9725	1356	220	709
※镇宁县	Zhenning	18858	10450	4109	4299	
※关岭县	Guanling	7406	4922	2100	144	240
※紫云县	Ziyun	3670	2921	12	737	
铜仁市	Tongren	52405	26690	5941	5749	14025
江口县	Jiangkou	10084	9325	725	34	
※玉屏县	Yuping	27263	16213	580	9950	520
石阡县	Shiqian	4886	4388	212	12	274
思南县	Sinan	10877	7805	96	951	2025
※印江县	Yinjiang	8979	5568	1170	2241	
德江县	Dejiang	6912	6912			
※沿河县	Yanhe	8889	5767	74	538	2510
※松桃县	Songtao	18255	13868	1353	1534	1500
万山特区	Wanshan	3482	2717		765	
兴义市	Xingyi	75685	37552	24759	6363	7011
兴仁县	Xingren	20467	4934	15207	326	
普安县	Puan	13465	6042	7308	115	
晴隆县	Qinglong	5325	4947	378		
贞丰县	Zhenfeng	7208	2613	4330	265	
望谟县	Wangmo	4429	1521	2795	113	
册亨县	Ceheng	4972	2187	2785		
安龙县	Anlong	10042	2522	5105	2415	
毕节市	Bijie	98743	54056	34935	1135	8617
大方县	Dafang	3245	1426	570	223	1026
黔西县	Qianxi	3480	1659	895	263	663
金沙县	Jinsha	88508	83945	3756	807	
织金县	Zhijin	7198	3883	1090		2225
纳雍县	Nayong	79526	77956	1510		60
※威宁县	Weining	1858	1155	456		247

23－29 续表 2(continued)

单位：万元
(10000 yuan)

县(市、区)名称 County(City, Section)		固定资产投资 Total Investment in Fixed Assets	基本建设 Capital Construction	更新改造 Innovation	其他投资 Other Investment	房地产投资 Real Estate
赫章县	Hezhang	2429	2329		100	
凯里市	Kaili	143286	73328	28316	15988	25654
黄平县	Huangping	6075	4365	1070	640	
施秉县	Shibing	15015	14487		178	350
三穗县	Sansui	7768	4717	2344	575	132
镇远县	Zhenyuan	17356	5522	4680	6854	300
岑巩县	Cengong	3173	2552		410	211
天柱县	Tianzhu	4118	4118			
锦屏县	Jinping	3589	2640	576	373	
剑河县	Jianhe	2612	2612			
台江县	Taijiang	2824	1541	1188	95	
黎平县	Liping	11324	10007	452	58	807
榕江县	Rongjiang	4809	2253	466	2090	
从江县	Congjiang	8341	2796	5367	178	
雷山县	Leishan	4131	2264	344	1523	
麻江县	Majiang	41932	38959	568	2225	180
丹寨县	Danzhai	5149	3130	597	787	635
都匀市	Duyun	75163	16225	30444	60	28434
福泉市	Fuquan	16547	7256	7917	282	1092
荔波县	Libo	9049	7864	1185		
贵定县	Guiding	6992	6657	335		
瓮安县	Wengan	7406	5299	1451	656	
独山县	Dushan	13011	3927	1573	7488	23
平塘县	Pingtang	5655	2399	3242	14	
罗甸县	Luodian	14373	4591	6671	3111	
长顺县	Changshun	6833	5783	1050		
龙里县	Longli	18642	4747	13895		
惠水县	Huishui	5817	2789	2050	78	900
※三都县	Sandu	4532	4532			

23-30 各县(市、区)乡村从业人员(2001)
Number of Rural Employment by County(City, Section)

单位:人
(person)

县(市、区)名称	County(City, Section)	乡村从业人员 Rural Employment	第一产业 Primary Industry	第二产业 Secondary Industry	第三产业 Tertiary Industry	2001年比2000年增长(%) Increase Rate in 2001 over 2000(%)
南明区	Nanming	17447	7021	5069	5357	5.6
云岩区	Yunyan	13127	7403	2846	2878	-3.1
花溪区	Huaxi	134868	107438	14244	13186	1.2
乌当区	Wudang	126724	78998	22433	25293	4.5
白云区	Baiyun	40897	26520	9086	5291	4.3
小河区	Xiaohe	20180	12370	3517	4293	4.3
开阳县	Kaiyang	211206	170987	9069	31150	-2.6
息烽县	Xifeng	115133	87237	7391	20505	-0.7
修文县	Xiuwen	147636	116148	9457	22031	1.3
清镇市	Qingzhen	229745	171564	20082	38099	0.7
钟山区	Zhongshan	84509	62247	15405	6857	-2.9
六枝特区	Liuzhi	264962	184640	31808	48514	5.9
水城县	Shuicheng	344030	290946	15300	37784	0.4
盘　县	Pan	484233	394271	43684	46278	2.1
红花岗区	Honghuagang	141971	95364	22401	24206	3.0
遵义县	Zunyi	695534	525892	42401	127241	1.8
桐梓县	Tongzi	312259	211364	12817	88078	-0.2
绥阳县	Suiyang	275093	202473	11177	61443	0.2
正安县	Zhengan	333695	249071	11796	72828	-0.1
※道真县	Daozhen	151657	101148	4926	45583	1.2
※务川县	Wuchuan	225154	180258	5051	39845	3.5
凤冈县	Fenggang	222388	155991	11200	55197	1.9
湄潭县	Meitan	265494	196920	11993	56581	7.9
余庆县	Yuqing	169747	120788	8798	40161	1.9
习水县	Xishui	297538	217507	11634	68397	2.3
赤水市	Chishui	123175	88423	32120	2632	0.1
仁怀市	Renhuai	316193	227584	20909	67700	1.3
西秀区	Xixiu	319757	233171	40646	45940	1.5
平坝县	Pingba	161547	132211	11367	17969	1.9

23－30 续表 1(continued)

单位：人
(person)

县(市、区)名称	County(City, Section)	乡村从业人员 Rural Employment	第一产业 Primary Industry	第二产业 Secondary Industry	第三产业 Tertiary Industry	2001 年比 2000 年增长(%) Increase Rate in 2001 over 2000(%)
普定县	Puding	201401	156161	10941	34299	3.8
※镇宁县	Zhenning	178538	151877	10838	15823	0.5
※关岭县	Guanling	170239	140945	8729	20565	1.4
※紫云县	Ziyun	183650	152866	5333	25451	2.0
铜仁市	Tongren	147323	93022	16047	38254	－2.1
江口县	Jiangkou	124460	84720	6727	33013	0.5
※玉屏县	Yuping	68890	45457	10563	12870	0.8
石阡县	Shiqian	214755	166104	9326	39325	0.9
思南县	Sinan	362594	266269	17820	78505	2.0
※印江县	Yinjiang	225147	136283	16206	72658	0.4
德江县	Dejiang	256188	201326	10583	44279	4.5
※沿河县	Yanhe	296393	208001	10228	78164	1.3
※松桃县	Songtao	369166	247036	19596	102534	4.3
万山特区	Wanshan	27670	15946	1436	10288	－0.1
兴义市	Xingyi	344007	277004	25083	41920	－0.1
兴仁县	Xingren	241974	186080	14159	41735	3.1
普安县	Puan	139345	98398	9363	31584	1.5
晴隆县	Qinglong	141233	110414	4248	26571	2.5
贞丰县	Zhenfeng	183669	136425	10846	36398	3.4
望谟县	Wangmo	143584	129773	3096	10715	0.6
册亨县	Ceheng	113023	99277	1727	12019	－0.8
安龙县	Anlong	230437	184962	13514	31961	2.1
毕节市	Bijie	602772	407490	51552	143730	0.7
大方县	Dafang	530831	390864	40660	99307	2.9
黔西县	Qianxi	407188	288415	40885	77888	1.3
金沙县	Jinsha	306821	213592	42786	50443	4.1
织金县	Zhijin	472456	331734	63778	76944	0.6
纳雍县	Nayong	405964	257975	37538	110451	2.7
※威宁县	Weining	586504	501470	37658	47376	2.2

23－30 续表 2(continued)

单位:人 (person)

县(市、区)名称 County(City, Section)		乡村从业人员 Rural Employment	第一产业 Primary Industry	第二产业 Secondary Industry	第三产业 Tertiary Industry	2001 年比 2000 年增长(%) Increase Rate in 2001 over 2000(%)
赫章县	Hezhang	301145	249615	26019	25511	2.5
凯里市	Kaili	151350	117540	11338	22472	－1.5
黄平县	Huangping	149243	113839	4346	31058	1.1
施秉县	Shibing	79885	69846	2306	7733	0.3
三穗县	Sansui	109268	72935	6390	29943	4.9
镇远县	Zhenyuan	119412	81457	7796	30159	1.8
岑巩县	Cengong	107654	77234	4070	26350	0.8
天柱县	Tianzhu	224450	177812	15631	31007	0.2
锦屏县	Jinping	110858	77816	2721	30321	0.9
剑河县	Jianhe	107176	84935	2637	19604	2.5
台江县	Taijiang	82648	51620	5361	25667	3.0
黎平县	Liping	250704	190396	6736	53572	2.0
榕江县	Rongjiang	158891	129458	5746	23687	6.4
从江县	Congjiang	176586	157264	3404	15918	2.1
雷山县	Leishan	79971	60465	1740	17766	－2.7
麻江县	Majiang	111416	95400	4457	11559	0.7
丹寨县	Danzhai	77746	53016	4654	20076	0.8
都匀市	Duyun	172273	138790	10370	23113	0.9
福泉市	Fuquan	157456	119855	14832	22769	1.3
荔波县	Libo	93494	82785	2515	8194	2.0
贵定县	Guiding	128420	97201	8695	22524	0.9
瓮安县	Wengan	206510	180800	12390	13320	0.0
独山县	Dushan	182771	139495	11937	31339	2.8
平塘县	Pingtang	175304	121696	10894	42714	2.1
罗甸县	Luodian	159518	130555	4534	24429	－2.6
长顺县	Changshun	132219	105444	5539	21236	4.2
龙里县	Longli	108388	92916	4240	11232	2.4
惠水县	Huishui	223185	152878	29445	40862	2.8
※三都县	Sandu	154969	123859	6397	24713	3.0

23－31 各县(市、区)耕地面积(2001)
Cultivated Areas by County(City, Section)

单位:万亩
(10000 mu)

县(市、区)名称	County(City, Section)	耕地面积 Cultivated Area	水田 Paddy Fields	旱地 Dry Fields
南明区	Nanming	0.37	0.01	0.36
云岩区	Yunyan	0.49		0.49
花溪区	Huaxi	18.88	10.04	8.84
乌当区	Wudang	16.05	8.05	8.01
白云区	Baiyun	4.40	2.37	2.03
小河区	Xiaohe	0.85	0.45	0.41
开阳县	Kaiyang	39.36	13.85	25.50
息烽县	Xifeng	24.58	7.67	16.91
修文县	Xiuwen	26.28	9.43	16.85
清镇市	Qingzhen	28.98	9.54	19.44
钟山区	Zhongshan	5.99	0.31	5.68
六枝特区	Liuzhi	36.96	15.01	21.95
水城县	Shuicheng	50.00	6.92	43.08
盘　县	Pan	65.82	10.76	55.06
红花岗区	Honghuagang	17.50	10.39	7.10
遵义县	Zunyi	113.93	57.33	56.6
桐梓县	Tongzi	55.68	19.10	36.57
绥阳县	Suiyang	41.23	21.23	20.01
正安县	Zhengan	46.50	23.69	22.80
※道真县	Daozhen	35.21	15.02	20.19
※务川县	Wuchuan	42.62	16.92	25.70
凤冈县	Fenggang	39.84	22.81	17.03
湄潭县	Meitan	46.52	28.79	17.73
余庆县	Yuqing	28.77	17.14	11.64
习水县	Xishui	62.29	22.89	39.40
赤水市	Chishui	20.44	16.31	4.13
仁怀市	Renhuai	41.88	14.88	27.00
西秀区	Xixiu	44.59	28.53	16.07
平坝县	Pingba	27.85	14.50	13.35

23 - 31 续表 1(continued)

单位:万亩
(10000 mu)

县(市、区)名称	County(City, Section)	耕地面积 Cultivated Area	水 田 Paddy Fields	旱 地 Dry Fields
普定县	Puding	25.30	10.75	14.56
※镇宁县	Zhenning	23.82	12.50	11.32
※关岭县	Guanling	22.68	8.35	14.33
※紫云县	Ziyun	29.95	10.17	19.77
铜仁市	Tongren	18.74	11.73	7.01
江口县	Jiangkou	16.71	11.30	5.41
※玉屏县	Yuping	8.51	5.91	2.61
石阡县	Shiqian	30.65	18.56	12.09
思南县	Sinan	43.38	26.61	16.77
※印江县	Yinjiang	27.64	17.81	9.83
德江县	Dejiang	36.08	20.16	15.92
※沿河县	Yanhe	39.97	16.73	23.24
※松桃县	Songtao	40.57	25.80	14.76
万山特区	Wanshan	3.66	2.31	1.35
兴义市	Xingyi	44.48	13.60	30.88
兴仁县	Xingren	33.48	12.19	21.29
普安县	Puan	24.39	7.54	16.86
晴隆县	Qinglong	22.35	7.08	15.27
贞丰县	Zhenfeng	27.18	10.01	17.17
望谟县	Wangmo	46.98	8.41	38.58
册亨县	Ceheng	24.13	6.39	17.74
安龙县	Anlong	30.97	14.76	16.21
毕节市	Bijie	95.37	10.01	85.36
大方县	Dafang	78.68	8.54	70.14
黔西县	Qianxi	70.30	14.01	56.29
金沙县	Jinsha	53.85	16.40	37.46
织金县	Zhijin	67.05	16.10	50.95
纳雍县	Nayong	51.57	6.45	45.12
※威宁县	Weining	110.63	1.20	109.43

23－31 续表 2(continued)

单位:万亩
(10000 mu)

县(市、区)名称	County(City,Section)	耕地面积 Cultivated Area	水 田 Paddy Fields	旱 地 Dry Fields
赫章县	Hezhang	58.60	2.00	56.60
凯里市	Kaili	20.24	14.00	6.25
黄平县	Huangping	24.02	16.54	7.48
施秉县	Shibing	12.05	7.05	5.00
三穗县	Sansui	11.57	8.16	3.41
镇远县	Zhenyuan	18.53	11.16	7.37
岑巩县	Cengong	17.84	11.18	6.66
天柱县	Tianzhu	24.46	17.58	6.87
锦屏县	Jinping	13.04	10.19	2.85
剑河县	Jianhe	12.38	10.55	1.83
台江县	Taijiang	10.56	8.66	1.90
黎平县	Liping	32.02	28.42	3.60
榕江县	Rongjiang	20.14	15.84	4.30
从江县	Congjiang	21.59	18.24	3.35
雷山县	Leishan	10.71	8.44	2.27
麻江县	Majiang	16.81	10.62	6.19
丹寨县	Danzhai	11.21	9.00	2.21
都匀市	Duyun	20.60	15.78	4.82
福泉市	Fuquan	24.55	11.90	12.65
荔波县	Libo	12.69	9.73	2.96
贵定县	Guiding	18.68	10.59	8.09
瓮安县	Wengan	40.51	18.26	22.26
独山县	Dushan	24.82	19.61	5.21
平塘县	Pingtang	24.82	13.42	11.40
罗甸县	Luodian	29.12	10.83	18.29
长顺县	Changshun	19.87	8.11	11.76
龙里县	Longli	16.29	9.78	6.51
惠水县	Huishui	29.29	18.59	10.70
※三都县	Sandu	18.36	15.38	2.98

23－32 各县(市、区)农林牧渔业总产值及位次(2001)

Gross Output Value of Farming, Forestry, Animal Husbandry and Fishery and Its Order by County(City, Section)

单位:万元
(10000 yuan)

县(市、区)名称 County(City, Section)		农林牧渔业总产值 Gross Output Value of Farming, Forestry, Animal Husbandry and Fishery	农业 Farming	林业 Forestry	牧业 Animal Husbandry	渔业 Fishery	位次 Order	2001年比2000年增长(%) Increase Rate in 2001 over 2000(%)
南明区	Nanming	6642	3817	3	2670	152	85	4.9
云岩区	Yunyan	6408	4848	13	1437	110	86	4.9
花溪区	Huaxi	61893	40290	546	20739	318	33	5.1
乌当区	Wudang	68840	44720	1493	21733	894	26	5.3
白云区	Baiyun	21563	14237	445	6578	303	79	4.6
小河区	Xiaohe	5869	3994	20	1594	261	87	4.3
开阳县	Kaiyang	68554	37975	807	29441	331	27	4.3
息烽县	Xifeng	35576	23418	708	10584	866	62	－7.5
修文县	Xiuwen	50343	27952	1077	20737	577	45	9.0
清镇市	Qingzhen	63971	35924	1657	22332	4058	30	4.9
钟山区	Zhongshan	15451	8658	375	6345	73	83	2.1
六枝特区	Liuzhi	41670	30939	592	10069	70	53	1.1
水城县	Shuicheng	63786	44231	2348	17190	17	31	1.7
盘　县	Pan	86912	60501	1567	24792	52	16	4.0
红花岗区	Honghuagang	59296	35236	601	23103	356	35	1.8
遵义县	Zunyi	300373	196726	6331	90649	6667	1	3.2
桐梓县	Tongzi	108808	72392	5193	30668	555	5	－3.7
绥阳县	Suiyang	101628	68250	2395	30448	535	9	－6.3
正安县	Zhengan	101908	60832	3906	36668	502	8	－0.9
※道真县	Daozhen	57897	34072	2281	21331	213	37	1.1
※务川县	Wuchuan	51347	34094	1686	15460	107	44	－0.8
凤冈县	Fenggang	70795	47265	1138	22223	169	24	－10.8
湄潭县	Meitan	101541	68060	2011	30595	875	10	1.9
余庆县	Yuqing	80995	50891	1891	27837	376	19	5.0
习水县	Xishui	79249	45025	2680	31295	249	20	－9.4
赤水市	Chishui	62528	33329	8055	20428	716	32	5.3
仁怀市	Renhuai	101163	59330	3502	37807	524	11	2.3
西秀区	Xixiu	76716	50440	840	25034	402	21	2.2
平坝县	Pingba	34758	22117	770	11259	612	63	2.0

23－32 续表 1(continued)

单位:万元
(10000 yuan)

县(市、区)名称 County(City,Section)		农林牧渔业总产值 Gross Output Value of Farming, Forestry, Animal Husbandry and Fishery	农 业 Farming	林 业 Forestry	牧 业 Animal Husbandry	渔 业 Fishery	位次 Order	2001 年比 2000 年增长(%) Increase Rate in 2001 over 2000(%)
普定县	Puding	39822	25829	788	12566	639	55	0.7
※镇宁县	Zhenning	33515	22247	1766	9011	491	64	－0.4
※关岭县	Guanling	43101	26983	2248	13643	227	51	1.6
※紫云县	Ziyun	37892	21176	3597	13006	113	60	持平
铜仁市	Tongren	45580	31849	928	11704	1099	48	5.2
江口县	Jiangkou	29717	17377	1363	9486	1491	70	4.6
※玉屏县	Yuping	31130	20751	1771	7929	679	68	4.1
石阡县	Shiqian	47549	31043	1045	14971	490	47	－2.5
思南县	Sinan	104786	65664	1163	36247	1712	6	－2.7
※印江县	Yinjiang	70802	44354	2126	23311	1011	23	1.9
德江县	Dejiang	94878	65381	2987	25782	728	12	－2.4
※沿河县	Yanhe	72726	44523	2457	24666	1080	22	－4.3
※松桃县	Songtao	94742	66410	2093	24993	1246	13	4.9
万山特区	Wanshan	8742	5624	326	2646	146	84	－3.6
兴义市	Xingyi	110343	55751	4796	47902	1894	4	5.7
兴仁县	Xingren	55232	32586	1676	20875	95	40	4.8
普安县	Puan	27946	17654	1083	9162	47	72	6.0
晴隆县	Qinglong	26108	16912	839	8332	25	75	0.3
贞丰县	Zhenfeng	45151	31312	2001	11748	90	49	4.8
望谟县	Wangmo	39373	25112	4198	10008	55	57	－3.3
册亨县	Ceheng	32228	18662	2681	10828	57	67	－0.8
安龙县	Anlong	57553	35650	1787	19058	1058	39	4.9
毕节市	Bijie	184296	133963	1735	48192	407	2	4.9
大方县	Dafang	101941	71591	1550	28619	180	7	1.0
黔西县	Qianxi	93433	59104	1496	32624	207	14	－1.5
金沙县	Jinsha	85661	53523	728	31029	380	17	－1.0
织金县	Zhijin	92085	57186	1625	33012	261	15	－1.6
纳雍县	Nayong	81188	54738	1082	25258	109	18	6.0
※威宁县	Weining	130298	93307	1842	35090	59	3	－0.1

23 - 32 续表 2(continued)

单位:万元
(10000 yuan)

县(市、区)名称	County(City, Section)	农林牧渔业总产值 Gross Output Value of Farming, Forestry, Animal Husbandry and Fishery	农业 Farming	林业 Forestry	牧业 Animal Husbandry	渔业 Fishery	位次 Order	2001年比2000年增长(%) Increase Rate in 2001 over 2000(%)
赫章县	Hezhang	70414	50219	1911	18084	200	25	2.8
凯里市	Kaili	61030	41984	725	16832	1489	34	4.2
黄平县	Huangping	42812	29168	2786	10432	426	52	3.5
施秉县	Shibing	19373	14237	408	4131	597	80	1.6
三穗县	Sansui	35709	21470	801	13252	186	61	0.6
镇远县	Zhenyuan	39233	26137	2198	10621	277	58	3.0
岑巩县	Cengong	26215	17001	458	8552	204	74	-0.2
天柱县	Tianzhu	49157	34152	759	14111	135	46	1.8
锦屏县	Jinping	24584	16735	1006	5785	1058	77	-1.7
剑河县	Jianhe	32873	18587	2422	10617	1247	65	4.7
台江县	Taijiang	26586	19412	1157	4818	1199	73	6.3
黎平县	Liping	58407	35983	4666	14603	3155	36	3.0
榕江县	Rongjiang	44837	28307	2823	10888	2819	50	3.6
从江县	Congjiang	40345	24735	1792	11740	2078	54	5.1
雷山县	Leishan	16711	10891	1298	3766	756	82	2.8
麻江县	Majiang	24346	15423	1708	7047	168	78	5.1
丹寨县	Danzhai	18248	10643	746	6052	807	81	7.0
都匀市	Duyun	52247	27709	3427	20543	568	42	4.1
福泉市	Fuquan	57654	40115	853	16425	261	38	3.2
荔波县	Libo	30710	17597	4633	7911	569	69	3.0
贵定县	Guiding	39017	29310	1850	7704	153	59	-2.4
瓮安县	Wengan	65244	42709	3187	19044	304	29	-4.5
独山县	Dushan	53659	36881	3375	13045	358	41	5.7
平塘县	Pingtang	32854	21201	1727	9823	103	66	3.0
罗甸县	Luodian	51763	28231	5462	17831	239	43	-21.0
长顺县	Changshun	25555	16400	612	8473	70	76	1.9
龙里县	Longli	28733	20217	1151	7255	110	71	3.8
惠水县	Huishui	68448	40429	6574	21140	305	28	3.6
※三都县	Sandu	39559	25076	1739	12088	656	56	3.1

23－33 各县(市、区)农民人均纯收入及位次(2001)
Per Capita Net Income of Rural Households and Its Order by County(City, Section)

县(市、区)名称	County(City, Section)	纯收入(元) Net Income(yuan)	位次 Order	县(市、区)名称	County(City, Section)	纯收入(元) Net Income(yuan)	位次 Order
南明区	Nanming	3378	2	湄潭县	Meitan	2128	9
云岩区	Yunyan	3402	1	余庆县	Yuqing	2142	7
花溪区	Huaxi	2245	6	习水县	Xishui	1235	68
乌当区	Wudang	2491	4	赤水市	Chishui	1884	15
白云区	Baiyun	2789	3	仁怀市	Renhuai	1862	16
小河区	Xiaohe			西秀区	Xixiu	1843	17
开阳县	Kaiyang	2118	10	平坝县	Pingba	1583	26
息烽县	Xifeng	1662	23	普定县	Puding	1304	48
修文县	Xiuwen	1906	14	※镇宁县	Zhenning	1271	59
清镇市	Qingzhen	2027	11	※关岭县	Guanling	1244	65
钟山区	Zhongshan	1582	27	※紫云县	Ziyun	1180	80
六枝特区	Liuzhi	1270	60	铜仁市	Tongren	1704	21
水城县	Shuicheng	1272	58	江口县	Jiangkou	1260	63
盘　县	Pan	1419	35	※玉屏县	Yuping	1716	19
红花岗区	Honghuagang	2414	5	石阡县	Shiqian	1227	70
遵义县	Zunyi	2138	8	思南县	Sinan	1177	81
桐梓县	Tongzi	1669	22	※印江县	Yinjiang	1312	46
绥阳县	Suiyang	1983	13	德江县	Dejiang	1216	74
正安县	Zhengan	1306	47	※沿河县	Yanhe	1162	83
※道真县	Daozhen	1319	45	※松桃县	Songtao	1242	67
※务川县	Wuchuan	1288	52	万山特区	Wanshan	1173	82
凤冈县	Fenggang	1604	25	兴义市	Xingyi	1992	12

23－33 续表(continued)

县(市、区)名称 County(City, Section)		纯收入(元) Net Income(yuan)	位次 Order	县(市、区)名称 County(City, Section)		纯收入(元) Net Income(yuan)	位次 Order
兴仁县	Xingren	1360	40	锦屏县	Jinping	1226	71
普安县	Puan	1244	65	剑河县	Jianhe	1347	41
晴隆县	Qinglong	1182	78	台江县	Taijiang	1294	50
贞丰县	Zhenfeng	1361	39	黎平县	Liping	1274	55
望谟县	Wangmo	1250	64	榕江县	Rongjiang	1270	60
册亨县	Ceheng	1206	75	从江县	Congjiang	1296	49
安龙县	Anlong	1505	29	雷山县	Leishan	1231	69
毕节市	Bijie	1580	28	麻江县	Majiang	1282	54
大方县	Dafang	1076	86	丹寨县	Danzhai	1283	53
黔西县	Qianxi	1274	55	都匀市	Duyun	1834	18
金沙县	Jinsha	1706	20	福泉市	Fuquan	1498	30
织金县	Zhijin	1274	55	荔波县	Libo	1200	77
纳雍县	Nayong	1205	76	贵定县	Guiding	1472	32
※威宁县	Weining	1269	62	瓮安县	Wengan	1484	31
赫章县	Hezhang	1225	72	独山县	Dushan	1222	73
凯里市	Kaili	1617	24	平塘县	Pingtang	1161	84
黄平县	Huangping	1291	51	罗甸县	Luodian	1182	78
施秉县	Shibing	1402	36	长顺县	Changshun	1370	38
三穗县	Sansui	1397	37	龙里县	Longli	1427	34
镇远县	Zhenyuan	1345	43	惠水县	Huishui	1432	33
岑巩县	Cengong	1346	42	※三都县	Sandu	1096	85
天柱县	Tianzhu	1343	44				

23－34 各县(市、区)粮食、肉类产量及位次(2001)
Output of Grain, Meat and Its Order by County(City, Section)

县(市、区)名称	County(City, Section)	粮食产量(万吨) Output of Grain (10000 tons)	位次 Order	2001年比2000年增长(%) Increase Rate in 2001 over 2000(%)	人均粮食产量(公斤) Per Capita Output of Grain(kg)	位次 Order	肉类产量(吨) Output of Meat(ton)	位次 Order	2001年比2000年增长(%) Increase Rate in 2001 over 2000(%)
南明区	Nanming						2943	84	7.2
云岩区	Yunyan						1627	86	13.6
花溪区	Huaxi	8.73	59	－4.8	392	24	18222	36	1.3
乌当区	Wudang	7.35	69	－5.8	365	39	16079	42	3.9
白云区	Baiyun	2.24	83	－3.6	351	50	7346	75	5.3
小河区	Xiaohe	0.20	85	－4.9	74	85	1389	87	1.9
开阳县	Kaiyang	13.14	35	－9.2	353	48	27682	15	12.4
息烽县	Xifeng	5.67	76	－25.5	276	83	11171	54	6.2
修文县	Xiuwen	8.36	63	－6.0	333	64	21521	27	26.3
清镇市	Qingzhen	12.88	38	－0.7	331	67	18986	33	8.8
钟山区	Zhongshan	2.56	82	0.5	172	84	7345	76	6.4
六枝特区	Liuzhi	17.10	22	2.1	343	61	10810	58	0.0
水城县	Shuicheng	22.45	17	2.6	330	69	15873	43	1.5
盘　县	Pan	30.46	4	3.4	322	74	25213	20	11.4
红花岗区	Honghuagang	9.08	57	－9.9	379	31	17242	38	0.3
遵义县	Zunyi	57.02	1	－7.1	463	8	82681	1	7.2
桐梓县	Tongzi	21.96	19	－24.6	386	28	29699	13	0.6
绥阳县	Suiyang	23.16	16	－22.1	506	5	31159	10	0.3
正安县	Zhengan	24.72	9	－16.3	448	10	33544	8	12.4
※道真县	Daozhen	13.06	36	－12.6	438	15	24336	24	11.0
※务川县	Wuchuan	14.61	30	－15.7	383	30	19270	32	5.8
凤冈县	Fenggang	15.72	28	－27.7	414	18	24696	23	9.7
湄潭县	Meitan	26.77	6	－1.2	650	2	26407	18	3.0
余庆县	Yuqing	16.48	25	持平	653	1	24727	22	7.2
习水县	Xishui	23.75	14	－25.6	399	22	30896	12	3.8
赤水市	Chishui	13.36	33	2.6	582	3	19310	31	10.5
仁怀市	Renhuai	24.61	10	－12.3	478	6	37532	5	5.7
西秀区	Xixiu	22.36	18	2.6	389	26	23391	25	5.8
平坝县	Pingba	10.32	50	0.6	377	32	9635	63	2.7

注：表中人均粮食产量按乡村人口计算。

Note: Per Capita Output of Grain in this table are calculated by rural population.

23－34 续表 1(continued)

县(市、区)名称	County(City, Section)	粮食产量(万吨) Output of Grain (10000 tons)	位次 Order	2001年比2000年增长(%) Increase Rate in 2001 over 2000(%)	人均粮食产量(公斤) Per Capita Output of Grain(kg)	位次 Order	肉类产量(吨) Output of Meat(ton)	位次 Order	2001年比2000年增长(%) Increase Rate in 2001 over 2000(%)
普定县	Puding	11.53	41	2.1	312	76	10949	57	2.6
※镇宁县	Zhenning	11.44	43	0.3	366	37	8464	70	2.6
※关岭县	Guanling	10.43	48	2.5	344	58	9200	67	3.4
※紫云县	Ziyun	11.46	42	0.6	366	38	12490	49	1.4
铜仁市	Tongren	13.34	34	2.4	582	4	14408	45	5.4
江口县	Jiangkou	8.74	58	0.0	440	12	11312	53	5.4
※玉屏县	Yuping	5.13	80	1.3	457	9	8268	71	13.1
石阡县	Shiqian	12.22	40	－22.4	335	63	23134	26	15.6
思南县	Sinan	20.89	20	－16.6	364	41	31957	9	9.1
※印江县	Yinjiang	12.93	37	－11.0	344	59	25726	19	8.8
德江县	Dejiang	14.46	31	－17.6	358	45	21188	29	1.8
※沿河县	Yanhe	14.67	29	－20.1	284	82	24775	21	5.1
※松桃县	Songtao	25.77	8	－0.5	431	16	26537	17	32.3
万山特区	Wanshan	1.76	84	1.2	363	42	2528	85	5.4
兴义市	Xingyi	24.55	11	1.6	405	19	52276	2	7.0
兴仁县	Xingren	16.26	26	2.0	398	23	21059	30	11.9
普安县	Puan	8.50	62	1.6	320	75	7808	74	5.5
晴隆县	Qinglong	7.90	66	－5.8	312	77	9337	65	10.4
贞丰县	Zhenfeng	10.32	51	－4.3	323	73	12348	50	14.2
望谟县	Wangmo	9.13	55	3.8	356	47	9774	62	－9.0
册亨县	Ceheng	6.61	73	1.0	330	70	12037	51	8.7
安龙县	Anlong	16.93	23	1.1	440	13	21301	28	5.1
毕节市	Bijie	38.09	2	－6.3	389	27	50859	3	3.0
大方县	Dafang	28.71	5	－7.5	326	72	27479	16	6.8
黔西县	Qianxi	23.96	13	－17.0	331	68	30946	11	5.7
金沙县	Jinsha	23.58	15	－6.9	469	7	36988	6	2.8
织金县	Zhijin	26.18	7	－10.5	311	78	35497	7	4.9
纳雍县	Nayong	23.98	12	－0.3	343	62	29226	14	4.5
※威宁县	Weining	33.96	3	1.4	351	51	39194	4	2.3

23－34 续表 2(continued)

县(市、区)名称	County(City, Section)	粮食产量(万吨) Output of Grain (10000 tons)	位次 Order	2001年比2000年增长(%) Increase Rate in 2001 over 2000(%)	人均粮食产量(公斤) Per Capita Output of Grain(kg)	位次 Order	肉类产量(吨) Output of Meat(ton)	位次 Order	2001年比2000年增长(%) Increase Rate in 2001 over 2000(%)
赫章县	Hezhang	19.20	21	0.6	332	66	18075	37	持平
凯里市	Kaili	10.64	47	持平	385	29	16958	40	8.4
黄平县	Huangping	10.91	45	3.3	352	49	10470	59	2.5
施秉县	Shibing	5.99	75	0.6	439	14	5827	80	4.7
三穗县	Sansui	6.07	74	－2.3	329	71	10238	61	4.4
镇远县	Zhenyuan	8.17	64	1.1	374	33	11011	56	6.2
岑巩县	Cengong	7.58	67	3.0	391	25	8720	69	1.3
天柱县	Tianzhu	12.86	39	0.6	358	46	13950	47	5.9
锦屏县	Jinping	6.71	72	0.9	345	57	9235	66	10.6
剑河县	Jianhe	7.09	70	2.8	374	34	11017	55	7.7
台江县	Taijiang	5.15	79	3.1	346	55	4900	83	5.4
黎平县	Liping	16.07	27	0.5	351	52	17053	39	5.8
榕江县	Rongjiang	9.68	52	3.7	333	65	9125	68	6.4
从江县	Congjiang	10.40	49	0.4	351	53	13154	48	6.7
雷山县	Leishan	4.65	81	3.5	346	56	5203	81	0.4
麻江县	Majiang	7.00	71	0.2	360	44	5065	82	0.5
丹寨县	Danzhai	5.26	78	0.1	374	35	6329	77	12.6
都匀市	Duyun	9.13	56	1.8	303	79	14571	44	0.2
福泉市	Fuquan	10.71	46	4.5	404	21	10326	60	0.5
荔波县	Libo	5.31	77	3.1	362	43	6086	79	1.3
贵定县	Guiding	8.12	65	3.8	348	54	7917	73	2.3
瓮安县	Wengan	16.89	24	－2.0	441	11	18668	34	0.3
独山县	Dushan	10.98	44	0.5	365	40	14098	46	7.0
平塘县	Pingtang	9.56	53	5.5	344	60	11792	52	2.2
罗甸县	Luodian	8.51	61	－12.0	292	80	16417	41	0.8
长顺县	Changshun	9.28	54	2.3	405	20	8148	72	1.5
龙里县	Longli	7.53	68	1.1	422	17	6160	78	0.1
惠水县	Huishui	13.99	32	1.2	371	36	18579	35	1.3
※三都县	Sandu	8.53	60	4.3	291	81	9415	64	5.1

23－35 各县(市、区)油菜籽、烤烟产量及位次(2001)
Output of Rapeseed and Flue－cured Tobacco and Its Order by County(City, Section)

县(市、区)名称	County(City, Section)	油菜籽产量(吨) Output of Rapeseed(ton)	位次 Order	2001 年比 2000 年增长(%) Increase Rate in 2001 over 2000(%)	烤烟产量(吨) Output of Fluecured Tobacco(ton)	位次 Order	2001 年比 2000 年增长(%) Increase Rate in 2001 over 2000(%)
南明区	Nanming						
云岩区	Yunyan						
花溪区	Huaxi	2343	64	－30.2			
乌当区	Wudang	3420	59	－20.4			
白云区	Baiyun	1109	72	－14.0			
小河区	Xiaohe	3	84	－94.7			
开阳县	Kaiyang	21990	7	－0.3	8693	9	－2.0
息烽县	Xifeng	8196	24	－3.0	1192	43	－60.9
修文县	Xiuwen	6772	32	－25.1	1667	40	－40.8
清镇市	Qingzhen	8414	22	－8.4	2054	36	－19.2
钟山区	Zhongshan						
六枝特区	Liuzhi	5168	39	1.4			
水城县	Shuicheng	45	82	2.3	6063	18	－1.7
盘　县	Pan	277	79	－28.2	2141	35	－0.1
红花岗区	Honghuagang	9036	17	－1.6	42	63	－92.0
遵义县	Zunyi	66644	1	1.6	11850	4	－25.0
桐梓县	Tongzi	14085	12	－3.9	5143	23	－43.4
绥阳县	Suiyang	28017	3	－4.4	5215	22	－22.2
正安县	Zhengan	16153	10	3.1	8000	11	－11.1
※道真县	Daozhen	9023	18	0.2	10500	7	16.7
※务川县	Wuchuan	8569	21	－2.0	10516	6	22.7
凤冈县	Fenggang	18118	8	－6.2	4272	26	－33.3
湄潭县	Meitan	24691	5	0.6	6397	17	－26.7
余庆县	Yuqing	18071	9	2.2	8104	10	－13.5
习水县	Xishui	4855	43	－14.4			
赤水市	Chishui	788	76	0.5			
仁怀市	Renhuai	8764	19	0.9	2472	33	－28.9
西秀区	Xixiu	34724	2	5.8	3462	29	－30.2
平坝县	Pingba	11155	15	－11.3	415	55	－23.9

23 - 35 续表 1(continued)

县(市、区)名称	County(City, Section)	油菜籽产量(吨) Output of Rapeseed(ton)	位次 Order	2001 年比 2000 年增长(%) Increase Rate in 2001 over 2000(%)	烤烟产量(吨) Output of Fluecured Tobacco(ton)	位次 Order	2001 年比 2000 年增长(%) Increase Rate in 2001 over 2000(%)
普定县	Puding	9418	16	-20.7	195	58	-22.3
※镇宁县	Zhenning	7586	27	-2.8			
※关岭县	Guanling	3566	54	-1.8	965	45	-33.2
※紫云县	Ziyun	4226	48	-16.9	1013	44	-22.6
铜仁市	Tongren	6278	34	-8.7	43	62	-12.2
江口县	Jiangkou	3513	55	持平	576	51	-16.3
※玉屏县	Yuping	4044	50	15.6			
石阡县	Shiqian	7378	29	-16.1	5080	24	-2.4
思南县	Sinan	12080	13	-7.7	6431	16	-18.1
※印江县	Yinjiang	8714	20	-7.7	4165	28	14.8
德江县	Dejiang	8339	23	-1.1	7990	12	-7.6
※沿河县	Yanhe	5355	36	5.6	4422	25	-20.6
※松桃县	Songtao	11431	14	0.9	495	52	-52.9
万山特区	Wanshan	622	77	-22.9			
兴义市	Xingyi	5210	38	5.2	7890	13	6.6
兴仁县	Xingren	3379	60	-1.5	2850	32	2.2
普安县	Puan	857	74	-6.2	4178	27	18.9
晴隆县	Qinglong	556	78	-6.9	758	48	-33.9
贞丰县	Zhenfeng	3488	57	2.2	804	47	-18.7
望谟县	Wangmo	2052	65	-23.6	7	65	-22.2
册亨县	Ceheng	965	73	-6.9			
安龙县	Anlong	2030	66	-5.0	1446	42	35.0
毕节市	Bijie	4050	49	-20.6	13990	3	-11.4
大方县	Dafang	6891	31	-13.5	16864	1	-3.8
黔西县	Qianxi	22121	6	-10.8	10556	5	-10.4
金沙县	Jinsha	25157	4	0.7	8804	8	-17.8
织金县	Zhijin	7286	30	-1.2	5601	20	-39.4
纳雍县	Nayong	235	80	-63.8	6456	15	-13.7
※威宁县	Weining	127	81	-34.5	15544	2	-2.6

23－35 续表 2(continued)

县(市、区)名称	County(City,Section)	油菜籽产量(吨) Output of Rapeseed(ton)	位次 Order	2001年比2000年增长(%) Increase Rate in 2001 over 2000(%)	烤烟产量(吨) Output of Fluecured Tobacco(ton)	位次 Order	2001年比2000年增长(%) Increase Rate in 2001 over 2000(%)
赫章县	Hezhang	15	83	－91.5	5911	19	－28.4
凯里市	Kaili	3109	62	－28.7	495	53	－49.1
黄平县	Huangping	6608	33	0.5	1500	41	－28.6
施秉县	Shibing	3834	52	－13.7	3419	30	－17.5
三穗县	Sansui	1914	69	－11.2	86	59	258.3
镇远县	Zhenyuan	5850	35	－2.0	1793	39	17.9
岑巩县	Cengong	4244	47	－3.2	329	57	2.2
天柱县	Tianzhu	3352	61	－15.0	77	60	－42.1
锦屏县	Jinping	3454	58	－5.6			
剑河县	Jianhe	1967	68	3.3			
台江县	Taijiang	2028	67	－13.4	4	66	－55.6
黎平县	Liping	7518	28	1.9			
榕江县	Rongjiang	5332	37	－2.0			
从江县	Congjiang	3949	51	－1.0			
雷山县	Leishan	790	75	－19.6			
麻江县	Majiang	3503	56	－9.9	1796	38	－1.2
丹寨县	Danzhai	1275	71	－17.3	370	56	34.1
都匀市	Duyun	4972	41	－1.3	661	49	8.7
福泉市	Fuquan	7844	26	1.7	3336	31	－8.6
荔波县	Libo	3629	53	－31.0	10	64	－87.5
贵定县	Guiding	5151	40	－20.9	461	54	－63.4
瓮安县	Wengan	15873	11	5.6	6934	14	－34.6
独山县	Dushan	4496	44	－2.5	840	46	1.4
平塘县	Pingtang	8170	25	5.0	2010	37	0.5
罗甸县	Luodian	1808	70	－24.1			
长顺县	Changshun	4887	42	－1.7	5543	21	－1.4
龙里县	Longli	4371	46	－16.8	2200	34	持平
惠水县	Huishui	3001	63	10.2	612	50	13.5
※三都县	Sandu	4442	45	－4.8	60	61	－31.8

23-36 各县(市、区)乡镇企业主要指标(2001)

Major Indicators of Township and Village Enterprises by County(City, Section)

县(市、区)名称 County(City, Section)		企业单位数(个) Number of Enterprises (unit)	年末职工人数(人) Staff and Workers (year-end) (person)	固定资产原值(万元) Original Value of Fixed Assets (10000 yuan)	营业收入(万元) Operating Revenue (10000 yuan)	实交国家税金(万元) Taxes Paid (10000 yuan)	纯利润(万元) Net Profits (10000 yuan)
南明区	Nanming	6908	31761	113744	711771	8213	6965
云岩区	Yunyan	3614	24135	105757	741384	11886	14889
花溪区	Huaxi	10208	45629	94992	404979	5944	20950
乌当区	Wudang	13631	74612	316522	686462	6971	49159
白云区	Baiyun	5788	22965	101558	397853	6391	23975
开阳县	Kaiyang	8248	28902	105941	359310	5957	10460
息烽县	Xifeng	4044	19894	119185	177749	1672	9689
修文县	Xiuwen	6263	22610	79718	237838	2656	16616
清镇市	Qingzhen	9422	47690	65862	347701	5446	24315
小河区	Xiaohe	3799	22303	21945	299294	4465	10464
钟山区	Zhongshan	7873	43897	52129	274552	5547	24846
六枝特区	Liuzhi	16124	63253	36584	238024	4551	12022
水城县	Shuicheng	7032	28924	43040	106996	1988	4381
盘　县	Pan	17203	85770	132911	360032	6539	14141
红花岗区	Honghuagang	9763	39412	70028	523028	11513	25162
遵义县	Zunyi	20922	97023	145824	666679	7621	31396
桐梓县	Tongzi	12679	52591	76358	329566	2317	24928
绥阳县	Suiyang	9964	36908	47846	161809	1862	13493
正安县	Zhengan	7548	35864	20231	126210	1868	5152
※道真县	Daozhen	5166	20460	24000	51277	1327	2686
※务川县	Wuchuan	7968	23586	33546	70725	424	5886
凤冈县	Fenggang	7548	21957	22985	78760	1255	4854
湄潭县	Meitan	12314	32693	54530	224049	2717	17018
余庆县	Yuqing	5040	16128	46566	73148	1176	4818
赤水市	Chishui	8520	32940	43768	171934	2832	5048
习水县	Xishui	13087	39450	95350	223636	2359	9252
仁怀市	Renhuai	15812	73269	203137	449333	7588	45885
西秀区	Xixiu	17040	54572	78278	541197	4409	35698
平坝县	Pingba	6208	30113	41853	241282	1465	15291

23－36 续表 1(continued)

县(市、区)名称 County(City, Section)		企业单位数(个) Number of Enterprises (unit)	年末职工人数(人) Staff and Workers (year－end) (person)	固定资产原值(万元) Original Value of Fixed Assets (10000 yuan)	营业收入(万元) Operating Revenue (10000 yuan)	实交国家税金(万元) Taxes Paid (10000 yuan)	纯利润(万元) Net Profits (10000 yuan)
※关岭县	Guanling	6940	25199	30706	65525	1776	4510
普定县	Puding	8696	29673	49992	240986	3051	18023
※镇宁县	Zhenning	9030	23030	61721	128143	5747	13494
※紫云县	Ziyun	5992	21599	8397	35110	1010	1916
铜仁市	Tongren	9836	27011	17091	237304	1791	8459
江口县	Jiangkou	2017	5168	12024	13147	164	482
※玉屏县	Yuping	4567	12864	8495	68490	1084	3376
石阡县	Shiqian	2587	9606	7530	35393	674	590
思南县	Sinan	9124	31323	38616	89839	3020	4314
※印江县	Yinjiang	3201	8484	7374	20538	442	989
德江县	Dejiang	9096	27515	8198	50942	1478	2446
※沿河县	Yanhe	8523	24172	18946	64872	529	5066
※松桃县	Songtao	13052	29940	9440	54838	916	2761
万山特区	Wanshan	1167	3357	3350	10397	259	675
兴义市	Xingyi	24333	73675	123132	260184	7129	23402
兴仁县	Xingren	2883	16309	16321	43915	1657	1881
普安县	Puan	2110	11018	16767	22613	1346	3192
晴隆县	Qinglong	3755	9764	7800	21759	776	1500
贞丰县	Zhenfeng	2835	16000	8569	42848	1793	2917
望谟县	Wangmo	3515	6318	3224	15260	680	1127
册亨县	Ceheng	5404	8217	8845	13408	402	658
安龙县	Anlong	7340	21325	24318	52931	1895	4031
毕节市	Bijie	21416	70124	93126	388840	3669	33466
大方县	Dafang	15759	63014	28123	167928	1696	15973
黔西县	Qianxi	17016	47180	43510	178758	1715	15630
金沙县	Jinsha	13301	53604	91984	380214	3873	26233
织金县	Zhijin	12069	60727	30209	189007	3295	24156
纳雍县	Nayong	8987	57572	76388	216746	3994	21739
※威宁县	Weining	16141	57127	30195	215186	3839	18301

23-36 续表 2(continued)

县(市、区)名称 County(City, Section)		企业单位数(个) Number of Enterprises (unit)	年末职工人数(人) Staff and Workers (year-end) (person)	固定资产原值(万元) Original Value of Fixed Assets (10000 yuan)	营业收入(万元) Operating Revenue (10000 yuan)	实交国家税金(万元) Taxes Paid (10000 yuan)	纯利润(万元) Net Profits (10000 yuan)
赫章县	Hezhang	9223	36882	34210	175054	2690	8793
凯里市	Kaili	13510	49012	66944	255200	4318	5468
黄平县	Huangping	8114	17216	14232	35674	527	1948
施秉县	Shibing	2626	8112	10208	35251	1450	1164
三穗县	Sansui	4183	11354	7201	24524	377	654
镇远县	Zhenyuan	3401	10907	16057	52031	1088	1080
岑巩县	Cengong	2880	6692	4040	20040	541	569
天柱县	Tianzhu	8033	23424	12558	61364	824	2533
锦屏县	Jinping	4996	13486	17736	31116	754	1031
剑河县	Jianhe	4106	8700	6492	32732	578	1259
台江县	Taijiang	4340	10346	3474	22007	559	1340
黎平县	Liping	7002	17902	24146	47277	1099	1642
榕江县	Rongjiang	6589	14293	13129	52356	672	766
从江县	Congjiang	3574	7850	4949	31957	405	784
雷山县	Leishan	2772	7008	4355	19946	610	1343
麻江县	Majiang	5111	11932	17193	29328	719	1054
丹寨县	Danzhai	3686	7516	10693	25741	727	583
都匀市	Duyun	5756	33437	32111	161834	1913	7885
福泉市	Fuquan	8574	30747	31966	230901	4632	14433
荔波县	Libo	2258	9561	11428	69067	3119	4494
贵定县	Guiding	4888	19118	15655	93707	1987	6400
瓮安县	Wengan	4484	18231	55230	155540	2543	10026
独山县	Dushan	6774	20836	24466	112454	1287	9564
平塘县	Pingtang	3490	12165	13095	51388	602	1319
罗甸县	Luodian	3140	20402	25411	76172	1649	6880
长顺县	Changshun	3315	13028	16598	48940	1063	3460
龙里县	Longli	2258	11241	83427	133574	3024	9282
惠水县	Huishui	3708	27434	22882	108547	1249	9574
※三都县	Sandu	1585	18298	9247	27228	558	1398

说明:本表资料由省乡镇企业局提供,表中数据均含有一部分暂不符合四个条件的企业 。

Note: Data in this table are obtained from Township and Village Enterprise Bureau and some parts of Enterprises in this table are not conform with four conditions.

23－37 各县(市、区)规模以上工业总产值及位次(2001)

Total Gross Industrial Output Value and Its Order above Designated Size by County (City, Section)

单位:万元
(10000 yuan)

县(市、区)名称 County(City, Section)		工业总产值 Total Gross Industrial Output Value	2001年比2000年增长(%) Increase Rate in 2001 over 2000(%)	位次 Order
南明区	Nanming	373719		6
云岩区	Yunyan	741141		1
花溪区	Huaxi	154292		16
乌当区	Wudang	339243		7
白云区	Baiyun	451374	5.0	3
小河区	Xiaohe	160481	8.4	13
开阳县	Kaiyang	121942	18.0	18
息烽县	Xifeng	78586	101.6	23
修文县	Xiuwen	30365	191.5	36
清镇市	Qingzhen	278109	4.4	8
钟山区	Zhongshan	408660	19.0	4
六枝特区	Liuzhi	38523	21.0	30
水城县	Shuicheng	50957	34.5	29
盘　县	Pan	156266	26.0	15
红花岗区	Honghuagang	579642	11.4	2
遵义县	Zunyi	196934	13.0	10
桐梓县	Tongzi	26160	8.4	41
绥阳县	Suiyang	8638	9.9	58
正安县	Zhengan	5779	24.9	66
※道真县	Daozhen	5458	22.1	67
※务川县	Wuchuan	3736	19.9	76
凤冈县	Fenggang	7278	0.9	62
湄潭县	Meitan	67105	22.2	26
余庆县	Yuqing	7821	－7.2	60
习水县	Xishui	27028	60.9	40
赤水市	Chishui	99066	－0.1	22
仁怀市	Renhuai	184339	42.7	11
西秀区	Xixiu	222957	9.7	9
平坝县	Pingba	158659	24.2	14

23－37 续表 1(continued)

单位:万元
(10000 yuan)

县(市、区)名称 County(City,Section)		工业总产值 Total Gross Industrial Output Value	2001 年比 2000 年增长(%) Increase Rate in 2001 over 2000(%)	位次 Order
普定县	Puding	73378	45.4	25
※镇宁县	Zhenning	30951	16.8	35
※关岭县	Guanling	13359	17.5	48
※紫云县	Ziyun	2171	－34.5	84
铜仁市	Tongren	63354	－4.1	27
江口县	Jiangkou	3597	0.1	77
※玉屏县	Yuping	20335	38.5	44
石阡县	Shiqian	6529	－19.1	64
思南县	Sinan	29631	95.6	37
※印江县	Yinjiang	4411	17.6	73
德江县	Dejiang	6011	－53.0	65
※沿河县	Yanhe	4871	11.6	69
※松桃县	Songtao	12432	35.8	49
万山特区	Wanshan	4174	15.8	75
兴义市	Xingyi	379233	24.6	5
兴仁县	Xingren	19536	－1.2	45
普安县	Puan	7130	8.0	63
晴隆县	Qinglong	7641	18.9	61
贞丰县	Zhenfeng	4579	42.4	71
望谟县	Wangmo	2604	25.2	82
册亨县	Ceheng	3418	18.4	78
安龙县	Anlong	11499	82.6	50
毕节市	Bijie	173289	31.0	12
大方县	Dafang	20511	64.4	43
黔西县	Qianxi	11365	－31.3	51
金沙县	Jinsha	107381	23.1	21
织金县	Zhijin	17085	86.2	47
纳雍县	Nayong	11309	－12.1	53
※威宁县	Weining	27687	－0.9	39

23－37 续表 2(continued)

单位:万元
(10000 yuan)

县(市、区)名称 County(City,Section)		工业总产值 Total Gross Industrial Output Value	2001 年比 2000 年增长(%) Increase Rate in 2001 over 2000(%)	位次 Order
赫章县	Hezhang	23493	－19.7	42
凯里市	Kaili	139116	11.0	17
黄平县	Huangping	1334	29.1	86
施秉县	Shibing	34567	142.7	32
三穗县	Sansui	4714	54.3	70
镇远县	Zhenyuan	36943	32.5	31
岑巩县	Cengong	9276	13.9	56
天柱县	Tianzhu	5328	24.5	68
锦屏县	Jinping	2678	－54.5	81
剑河县	Jianhe	962	－75.1	87
台江县	Taijiang	2872	49.3	80
黎平县	Liping	9288	13.3	55
榕江县	Rongjiang	10371	100.1	54
从江县	Congjiang	4526	54.0	72
雷山县	Leishan	1360	66.9	85
麻江县	Majiang	9121	239.5	57
丹寨县	Danzhai	2588	14.8	83
都匀市	Duyun	113526	7.8	20
福泉市	Fuquan	115608	27.1	19
荔波县	Libo	3278	－5.7	79
贵定县	Guiding	59914	－1.0	28
瓮安县	Wengan	33217	－3.3	33
独山县	Dushan	11326	27.9	52
平塘县	Pingtang	7852	10.1	59
罗甸县	Luodian	31164	－13.0	34
长顺县	Changshun	18949	14.3	46
龙里县	Longli	74824	18.3	24
惠水县	Huishui	29556	2.9	38
※三都县	Sandu	4227	－6.4	74

23-38 各县(市、区)规模以上轻重工业总产值及位次(2001)

Total Gross Industrial Output Value and Its Order above Designated Size of Light Industry and Heavy Industry by County(City, Section)

单位:万元
(10000 yuan)

县(市、区)名称 County(City, Section)		轻工业产值 Output Value of Light Industry	位次 Order	重工业产值 Output Value of Heavy Industry	位次 Order
南明区	Nanming	167689	4	206030	8
云岩区	Yunyan	504715	1	236426	7
花溪区	Huaxi	44213	12	110079	16
乌当区	Wudang	93888	6	245355	6
白云区	Baiyun	34068	16	417306	1
小河区	Xiaohe	17582	23	142899	11
开阳县	Kaiyang	3499	46	118443	14
息烽县	Xifeng	28185	17	50401	22
修文县	Xiuwen	14893	25	15472	37
清镇市	Qingzhen	8608	34	269500	5
钟山区	Zhongshan	10867	32	397793	2
六枝特区	Liuzhi	294	70	38229	25
水城县	Shuicheng	11685	30	39272	23
盘　县	Pan	3516	45	152750	9
红花岗区	Honghuagang	202251	2	377391	3
遵义县	Zunyi	57170	9	139764	12
桐梓县	Tongzi	17746	22	8414	48
绥阳县	Suiyang	4590	41	4048	62
正安县	Zhengan	3222	48	2557	75
※道真县	Daozhen	549	66	4909	59
※务川县	Wuchuan	1496	57	2240	79
凤冈县	Fenggang	4054	42	3224	70
湄潭县	Meitan	58653	8	8452	47
余庆县	Yuqing	3960	43	3861	65
习水县	Xishui	12167	29	14861	38
赤水市	Chishui	10765	33	88301	19
仁怀市	Renhuai	181827	3	2512	76
西秀区	Xixiu	91441	7	131516	13
平坝县	Pingba	11140	31	147519	10

23－38 续表 1(continued)

单位:万元
(10000 yuan)

县(市、区)名称 County(City, Section)		轻工业产值 Output Value of Light Industry	位次 Order	重工业产值 Output Value of Heavy Industry	位次 Order
普定县	Puding	1252	58	72126	21
※镇宁县	Zhenning	5200	38	25751	29
※关岭县	Guanling	55	86	13305	39
※紫云县	Ziyun	158	78	2013	80
铜仁市	Tongren	40016	13	23338	32
江口县	Jiangkou	271	73	3326	68
※玉屏县	Yuping	691	64	19644	35
石阡县	Shiqian	4946	39	1583	81
思南县	Sinan	21969	19	7662	50
※印江县	Yinjiang	1767	54	2644	74
德江县	Dejiang	1563	56	4448	60
※沿河县	Yanhe	2103	52	2768	73
※松桃县	Songtao	1153	60	11279	41
万山特区	Wanshan	207	76	3967	63
兴义市	Xingyi	46077	11	333156	4
兴仁县	Xingren	12246	28	7290	53
普安县	Puan	276	72	6854	55
晴隆县	Qinglong	149	79	7492	52
贞丰县	Zhenfeng	3254	47	1325	82
望谟县	Wangmo	2231	51	373	87
册亨县	Ceheng	70	85	3348	67
安龙县	Anlong	513	67	10986	42
毕节市	Bijie	135186	5	38103	26
大方县	Dafang	16572	24	3939	64
黔西县	Qianxi	5323	37	6042	57
金沙县	Jinsha	22350	18	85031	20
织金县	Zhijin	13815	26	3270	69
纳雍县	Nayong	3704	44	7605	51
※威宁县	Weining	7034	36	20653	33

23-38 续表 2(continued)

单位:万元
(10000 yuan)

县(市、区)名称 County(City,Section)		轻工业产值 Output Value of Light Industry	位次 Order	重工业产值 Output Value of Heavy Industry	位次 Order
赫章县	Hezhang	2982	50	20511	34
凯里市	Kaili	34856	15	104260	17
黄平县	Huangping	829	62	505	86
施秉县	Shibing	114	80	34453	27
三穗县	Sansui	1203	59	3511	66
镇远县	Zhenyuan	12330	27	24613	31
岑巩县	Cengong	913	61	8363	49
天柱县	Tianzhu	98	82	5230	58
锦屏县	Jinping	217	75	2461	77
剑河县	Jianhe	343	69	619	85
台江县	Taijiang	71	84	2801	72
黎平县	Liping	612	65	8676	46
榕江县	Rongjiang			10371	43
从江县	Congjiang	85	83	4441	61
雷山县	Leishan	244	74	1116	84
麻江县	Majiang	172	77	8949	45
丹寨县	Danzhai	285	71	2303	78
都匀市	Duyun	21073	20	92453	18
福泉市	Fuquan	1719	55	113889	15
荔波县	Libo	113	81	3165	71
贵定县	Guiding	49653	10	10261	44
瓮安县	Wengan	7980	35	25237	30
独山县	Dushan	4688	40	6638	56
平塘县	Pingtang	718	63	7134	54
罗甸县	Luodian	19493	21	11671	40
长顺县	Changshun	386	68	18563	36
龙里县	Longli	36055	14	38769	24
惠水县	Huishui	1947	53	27609	28
※三都县	Sandu	3011	49	1216	83

23－39 各县(市、区)规模以上工业主要产品产量(2001)
Ouput of Major Industrial Products above Designated Size by County (City, Section)

州(市、地)名称	County(City, Section)	原煤(万吨) Coal (10000 tons)	发电量(万千瓦小时) Electricity (10000 kwh)	化肥(万吨) Chemical Fertilizer (10000 tons)	饮料酒(万吨) Alcoholic Beverages (10000 tons)	水泥(万吨) Cement (10000 tons)
南明区	Nanming		127982		2.79	80.16
云岩区	Yunyan					
花溪区	Huaxi	68.53			0.02	24.25
乌当区	Wudang	63.00	4056			16.90
白云区	Baiyun	16.80	24902	3.05	0.01	36.20
小河区	Xiaohe					4.51
开阳县	Kaiyang	30.95		4.99		13.08
息烽县	Xifeng	28.53		9.71		3.72
修文县	Xiuwen	25.00				20.51
清镇市	Qingzhen	38.94	757176	3.04		22.77
钟山区	Zhongshan	485.40	105561		1.98	84.31
六枝特区	Liuzhi	197.82	11695		0.90	38.88
水城县	Shuicheng	81.31	4929		0.54	
盘　县	Pan	768.94	481439	1.39	0.50	12.67
红花岗区	Honghuagang	37.84	165960	0.54	0.19	36.32
遵义县	Zunyi	69.51	288899	0.98	0.26	48.37
桐梓县	Tongzi	68.00	4567	0.501		28.84
绥阳县	Suiyang	17.74	1471	1.11		3.83
正安县	Zhengan	12.00	6599	1.05		7.37
※道真县	Daozhen	7.40	5441	1.52		8.10
※务川县	Wuchuan	12.00	2423			0.21
凤冈县	Fenggang		3802	0.19		3.42
湄潭县	Meitan	5.90	8850	0.66	0.27	11.40
余庆县	Yuqing	0.72	5070	0.89		2.61
习水县	Xishui	102.50	32860	0.08	2.88	9.53
赤水市	Chishui	3.41	14169	27.16		3.00
仁怀市	Renhuai	26.00	6589	0.43	4.75	5.11
西秀区	Xixiu	101.99	489	1.11	3.37	4.57
平坝县	Pingba	72.00		3.19	0.41	20.23

23－39 续表 1(continued)

州(市、地)名称 County(City, Section)		原煤(万吨) Coal (10000 tons)	发电量(万千瓦小时) Electricity (10000 kwh)	化肥(万吨) Chemical Fertilizer (10000 tons)	饮料酒(万吨) Alcoholic Beverages (10000 tons)	水泥(万吨) Cement (10000 tons)
普定县	Puding	52.00	469545	16.80	0.70	16.80
※镇宁县	Zhenning	0.16	12230		1.03	0.71
※关岭县	Guanling	1.30	20727			2.70
※紫云县	Ziyun	1.00	5247			2.40
铜仁市	Tongren		10649	0.33	0.30	13.80
江口县	Jiangkou		1690		0.10	7.70
※玉屏县	Yuping		25987		0.20	3.70
石阡县	Shiqian	8.40	1902		0.30	2.10
思南县	Sinan	31.90	5480		0.40	7.30
※印江县	Yinjiang	6.10	2769		0.70	3.80
德江县	Dejiang	7.40	1670		0.40	12.80
※沿河县	Yanhe	22.40	1543		0.50	9.10
※松桃县	Songtao		2860	0.03	1.30	4.00
万山特区	Wanshan				0.10	
兴义市	Xingyi	20.60	1248199	7.69	2.11	40.87
兴仁县	Xingren	167.70	3499			8.16
普安县	Puan	76.00	5404	0.07	0.16	4.74
晴隆县	Qinglong	12.00	3210			6.40
贞丰县	Zhenfeng	30.40	1396		0.08	2.53
望谟县	Wangmo		349			
册亨县	Ceheng		2095			6.67
安龙县	Anlong	74.40	22283			5.69
毕节市	Bijie	44.70	24556	6.58	0.42	15.05
大方县	Dafang	81.08	685	1.82		9.27
黔西县	Qianxi	69.14	2329	0.36		8.00
金沙县	Jinsha	100.56	400980		0.04	7.20
织金县	Zhijin	72.00	1921	0.17		8.51
纳雍县	Nayong	65.18	5067		0.01	3.50
※威宁县	Weining	62.22	3131	0.25		4.21

23－39 续表 2(continued)

州(市、地)名称	County(City,Section)	原煤(万吨) Coal (10000 tons)	发电量(万千瓦小时) Electricity (10000 kwh)	化肥(万吨) Chemical Fertilizer (10000 tons)	饮料酒(万吨) Alcoholic Beverages (10000 tons)	水泥(万吨) Cement (10000 tons)
赫章县	Hezhang	29.80	3180	1.38		1.34
凯里市	Kaili	153.40	374867	0.04		18.32
黄平县	Huangping		496			
施秉县	Shibing		1491			2.80
三穗县	Sansui		228			5.16
镇远县	Zhenyuan		5956		0.47	3.21
岑巩县	Cengong		3300		0.01	3.08
天柱县	Tianzhu	18.95	2418			0.51
锦屏县	Jinping		3581			1.30
剑河县	Jianhe		927			
台江县	Taijiang		884			1.25
黎平县	Liping		3088		0.01	3.84
榕江县	Rongjiang		2626			
从江县	Congjiang	0.14				2.52
雷山县	Leishan		920			
麻江县	Majiang		1203			4.75
丹寨县	Danzhai	1.25				
都匀市	Duyun	7.28		0.42		48.84
福泉市	Fuquan	43.10	3803	5.51		4.76
荔波县	Libo	69.25	2411			2.16
贵定县	Guiding	10.01		0.55	0.03	7.10
瓮安县	Wengan	122.77	9339	1.59		11.30
独山县	Dushan	3.90	1035			3.36
平塘县	Pingtang	4.80	3184			5.73
罗甸县	Luodian	0.25	15086			4.12
长顺县	Changshun	10.20	5780	0.22		8.42
龙里县	Longli	18.47		0.69		8.68
惠水县	Huishui	4.40	6439			3.92
※三都县	Sandu	0.01				

23-40 各县(市、区)社会消费品零售总额(2001)
Total Retail Sales of Consumer Goods by County (City, Section)

单位:万元
(10000 yuan)

县(市、区)名称 County(City,Section)		社会消费品零售总额 Total Retail Sales of Consumer Goods	市、县 City and County	县以下 Below County Level	位次 Order	2001年比2000年增长(%) Increase Rate in 2001 over 2000(%)
南明区	Nanming	326023	158600		3	13.0
云岩区	Yunyan	582275	281852		1	11.4
花溪区	Huaxi	39157	39157		17	12.9
乌当区	Wudang	20355	20355		43	15.2
白云区	Baiyun	40510	40510		16	12.0
小河区	Xiaohe	81000	81000		8	12.5
开阳县	Kaiyang	41380	23897	17483	14	11.9
息烽县	Xifeng	21710	14957	6753	40	11.8
修文县	Xiuwen	23227	9760	13467	34	13.0
清镇市	Qingzhen	40902	25825	15077	15	11.0
钟山区	Zhongshan	109987	109987		6	11.2
六枝特区	Liuzhi	22879	17671	5208	35	-13.7
水城县	Shuicheng	14530	5960	8570	60	12.6
盘　县	Pan	51793	26519	25274	11	10.6
红花岗区	Honghuagang	217744	217744		2	14.5
遵义县	Zunyi	118028	36450	81578	5	12.1
桐梓县	Tongzi	30560	12310	18250	22	8.1
绥阳县	Suiyang	33904	14415	19489	20	11.7
正安县	Zhengan	24463	10771	13692	29	9.7
※道真县	Daozhen	13973	5870	8103	61	11.9
※务川县	Wuchuan	18543	8561	9982	47	7.9
凤冈县	Fenggang	18185	8111	10074	48	11.1
湄潭县	Meitan	37729	22423	15306	18	10.2
余庆县	Yuqing	17600	11204	6396	49	13.3
习水县	Xishui	20364	11393	8971	42	12.4
赤水市	Chishui	20489	14881	5608	41	15.0
仁怀市	Renhuai	23558	10081	13477	33	14.9
西秀区	Xixiu	138847	128520	10327	4	8.1
平坝县	Pingba	29931	13849	16082	24	10.2

23－40 续表 1(continued)

单位:万元
(10000 yuan)

县(市、区)名称 County(City,Section)		社会消费品零售总额 Total Retail Sales of Consumer Goods	市、县 City and County	县以下 Below County Level	位次 Order	2001 年比 2000 年增长(%) Increase Rate in 2001 over 2000(%)
普定县	Puding	15045	8791	6254	57	12.6
※镇宁县	Zhenning	17106	8693	8413	50	9.9
※关岭县	Guanling	15653	8242	7411	54	12.6
※紫云县	Ziyun	14965	7376	7589	59	8.9
铜仁市	Tongren	50821	36785	14036	12	10.3
江口县	Jiangkou	12012	7148	4864	65	5.2
※玉屏县	Yuping	11886	6666	5220	68	7.1
石阡县	Shiqian	11898	5481	6417	67	7.4
思南县	Sinan	28987	12464	16523	25	11.5
※印江县	Yinjiang	13164	7891	5273	63	4.3
德江县	Dejiang	15079	8959	6120	56	7.8
※沿河县	Yanhe	15711	7494	8217	53	9.2
※松桃县	Songtao	24267	12592	11675	30	5.5
万山特区	Wanshan	4014	2511	1503	86	4.6
兴义市	Xingyi	97501	70011	27490	7	11.0
兴仁县	Xingren	23622	12366	11256	32	3.3
普安县	Puan	7050	4442	2608	81	9.9
晴隆县	Qinglong	8769	6071	2698	76	2.8
贞丰县	Zhenfeng	11662	8117	3545	70	－3.0
望谟县	Wangmo	11788	6153	5635	69	1.3
册亨县	Ceheng	5996	3956	2040	83	1.4
安龙县	Anlong	22493	12168	10325	38	11.7
毕节市	Bijie	46895	31093	15802	13	8.0
大方县	Dafang	23944	11772	12172	31	7.8
黔西县	Qianxi	28911	13325	15586	26	9.6
金沙县	Jinsha	24886	12532	12354	28	8.8
织金县	Zhijin	26397	10092	16305	27	8.2
纳雍县	Nayong	18751	8511	10240	46	9.7
※威宁县	Weining	22502	9227	13275	37	10.2

23－40 续表 2(continued)

单位:万元
(10000 yuan)

县(市、区)名称 County(City, Section)		社会消费品零售总额 Total Retail Sales of Consumer Goods	市、县 City and County	县以下 Below County Level	位次 Order	2001 年比 2000 年增长(%) Increase Rate in 2001 over 2000(%)
赫章县	Hezhang	15179	7390	7789	55	8.3
凯里市	Kaili	72324	58020	14304	9	12.2
黄平县	Huangping	9893	4542	5351	73	8.2
施秉县	Shibing	7980	4526	3454	80	7.5
三穗县	Sansui	8478	5618	2860	78	5.1
镇远县	Zhenyuan	16663	8702	7961	51	10.2
岑巩县	Cengong	8749	4048	4701	77	13.4
天柱县	Tianzhu	19636	10038	9598	44	2.9
锦屏县	Jinping	11600	6610	4990	71	5.1
剑河县	Jianhe	6399	4046	2353	82	8.3
台江县	Taijiang	4476	3034	1442	85	8.8
黎平县	Liping	21815	9741	12074	39	11.5
榕江县	Rongjiang	9508	5717	3791	74	12.8
从江县	Congjiang	10395	4822	5573	72	15.4
雷山县	Leishan	4931	2732	2199	84	7.2
麻江县	Majiang	8432	4583	3849	79	11.0
丹寨县	Danzhai	3790	3175	615	87	10.1
都匀市	Duyun	71100	59298	11802	10	7.7
福泉市	Fuquan	36135	15752	20383	19	6.5
荔波县	Libo	13602	7978	5624	62	9.7
贵定县	Guiding	31177	18704	12473	21	6.5
瓮安县	Wengan	30227	14883	15344	23	4.5
独山县	Dushan	18877	8962	9915	45	7.4
平塘县	Pingtang	9314	5314	4000	75	5.7
罗甸县	Luodian	11982	6680	5302	66	7.1
长顺县	Changshun	16624	8503	8121	52	8.5
龙里县	Longli	12859	5915	6944	64	7.5
惠水县	Huishui	22732	15228	7504	36	7.1
※三都县	Sandu	14989	5837	9152	58	7.1

23－41 各县(市、区)地方财政收支及位次(2001)
Revenne and Expenditures of Local Government and Its Order by County(City, Section)

县(市、区)名称	County(City, Section)	地方财政收入(万元) Revenue of Local Governments(10000 yuan)	位次 Order	2001年比2000年增长(%) Increase Rate in 2001 over 2000(%)	人均地方财政收入(元) Per Capita Revenue of Local Governments(yuan)	位次 Order
南明区	Nanming	23463	2	41.9	479.52	3
云岩区	Yunyan	24330	1	33.4	461.10	4
花溪区	Huaxi	9651	18	31.7	308.78	7
乌当区	Wudang	13139	11	39.3	439.87	5
白云区	Baiyun	18588	4	50.7	1120.10	1
小河区	Xiaohe	12528	13	92.3	1103.30	2
开阳县	Kaiyang	11392	16	15.8	265.98	10
息烽县	Xifeng	4763	42	23.5	187.34	24
修文县	Xiuwen	5555	34	16.2	184.55	25
清镇市	Qingzhen	12727	12	16.4	253.30	12
钟山区	Zhongshan	7100	24	18.4	170.82	26
六枝特区	Liuzhi	5757	31	19.7	93.17	54
水城县	Shuicheng	5769	30	12.7	79.62	66
盘　县	Pan	16552	8	7.3	145.63	31
红花岗区	Honghuagang	19523	3	26.1	314.94	6
遵义县	Zunyi	17046	7	6.8	125.71	40
桐梓县	Tongzi	4934	38	－16.6	76.47	69
绥阳县	Suiyang	5222	37	3.4	104.47	48
正安县	Zhengan	4229	46	－10.3	71.56	74
※道真县	Daozhen	4278	45	0.7	129.30	36
※务川县	Wuchuan	3688	53	－3.4	89.55	59
凤冈县	Fenggang	3152	64	－21.8	78.19	67
湄潭县	Meitan	5385	36	－15.7	115.92	41
余庆县	Yuqing	4228	47	4.1	147.14	30
习水县	Xishui	4920	39	－3.3	72.82	72
赤水市	Chishui	6968	26	7.7	227.53	17
仁怀市	Renhuai	15973	9	21.6	271.35	9
西秀区	Xixiu	15601	10	17.0	193.63	23
平坝县	Pingba	4340	43	15.3	126.73	39

23－41 续表 1(continued)

县(市、区)名称	County(City, Section)	地方财政收入(万元) Revenue of Local Governments(10000 yuan)	位次 Order	2001年比2000年增长(%) Increase Rate in 2001 over 2000(%)	人均地方财政收入(元) Per Capita Revenue of Local Governments(yuan)	位次 Order
普定县	Puding	5496	35	13.8	136.90	35
※镇宁县	Zhenning	5708	33	12.6	168.33	27
※关岭县	Guanling	2841	68	13.1	89.34	60
※紫云县	Ziyun	2243	74	0.1	67.84	77
铜仁市	Tongren	7068	25	16.1	212.25	19
江口县	Jiangkou	1906	77	10.7	86.77	63
※玉屏县	Yuping	3408	61	24.4	245.89	14
石阡县	Shiqian	3405	62	10.1	91.04	57
思南县	Sinan	4848	41	2.8	77.98	68
※印江县	Yinjiang	2931	67	－2.5	72.33	73
德江县	Dejiang	3863	51	3.9	87.72	62
※沿河县	Yanhe	3608	56	9.0	66.10	80
※松桃县	Songtao	3603	57	16.2	57.59	86
万山特区	Wanshan	742	87	11.2	114.07	42
兴义市	Xingyi	18398	5	12.1	253.75	11
兴仁县	Xingren	5730	32	17.2	128.03	38
普安县	Puan	3851	52	17.9	137.73	34
晴隆县	Qinglong	3599	58	7.3	128.26	37
贞丰县	Zhenfeng	2395	69	10.2	71.45	75
望谟县	Wangmo	1658	81	13.5	60.17	84
册亨县	Ceheng	1366	84	－14.1	62.88	81
安龙县	Anlong	6262	29	9.0	148.60	29
毕节市	Bijie	18049	6	12.3	144.23	32
大方县	Dafang	9530	19	11.9	99.86	51
黔西县	Qianxi	8387	20	29.3	102.95	49
金沙县	Jinsha	11307	17	15.2	195.18	22
织金县	Zhijin	8385	21	21.6	93.13	55
纳雍县	Nayong	7903	22	38.5	105.69	47
※威宁县	Weining	7123	23	－3.7	66.77	78

23－41 续表 2(continued)

县(市、区)名称 County(City, Section)		地方财政收入(万元) Revenue of Local Governments(10000 yuan)	位次 Order	2001 年比 2000 年增长(%) Increase Rate in 2001 over 2000(%)	人均地方财政收入(元) Per Capita Revenue of Local Governments(yuan)	位次 Order
赫章县	Hezhang	3644	55	9.4	57.75	85
凯里市	Kaili	12460	14	10.3	279.75	8
黄平县	Huangping	2392	70	9.1	69.91	76
施秉县	Shibing	3081	65	9.3	202.63	20
三穗县	Sansui	1820	79	9.0	89.72	58
镇远县	Zhenyuan	3907	50	9.9	156.16	28
岑巩县	Cengong	1821	78	9.1	84.66	65
天柱县	Tianzhu	3681	54	6.1	91.54	56
锦屏县	Jinping	2311	73	6.6	105.74	46
剑河县	Jianhe	1313	85	－22.9	62.05	82
台江县	Taijiang	1412	83	11.6	85.76	64
黎平县	Liping	3010	66	9.4	61.12	83
榕江县	Rongjiang	2131	76	5.4	66.53	79
从江县	Congjiang	2363	71	4.1	76.09	70
雷山县	Leishan	1292	86	9.8	88.68	61
麻江县	Majiang	2348	72	9.3	109.11	43
丹寨县	Danzhai	1517	82	8.0	94.75	53
都匀市	Duyun	12075	15	13.8	252.19	13
福泉市	Fuquan	6896	28	1.2	227.07	18
荔波县	Libo	3990	49	4.0	242.63	16
贵定县	Guiding	6906	27	－2.8	245.07	15
瓮安县	Wengan	4895	40	－2.5	108.60	44
独山县	Dushan	3344	63	12.9	97.65	52
平塘县	Pingtang	2226	75	－7.5	75.20	71
罗甸县	Luodian	3438	59	5.0	107.54	45
长顺县	Changshun	3434	60	2.1	142.34	33
龙里县	Longli	4006	48	18.7	199.45	21
惠水县	Huishui	4292	44	7.7	101.54	50
※三都县	Sandu	1722	80	12.3	54.32	87

23-41 续表 3(continued)

县(市、区)名称 County(City, Section)		财政支出(万元) Expenditures of Governments (10000 yuan)	位次 Order	2001 年比 2000 年增长(%) Increase Rate in 2001 over 2000(%)	人均财政支出(元) Per Capita Expenditures of Governments(yuan)	位次 Order
南明区	Nanming	22543	9	45.1	460.72	22
云岩区	Yunyan	26626	8	34.3	504.61	14
花溪区	Huaxi	16813	26	38.5	537.93	10
乌当区	Wudang	20131	19	49.5	673.95	4
白云区	Baiyun	19412	20	42.2	1169.75	1
小河区	Xiaohe	12062	53	122.1	1062.26	2
开阳县	Kaiyang	19172	21	29.3	447.63	24
息烽县	Xifeng	12761	49	37.4	501.91	16
修文县	Xiuwen	13288	44	46.7	441.46	25
清镇市	Qingzhen	20327	16	32.2	404.56	33
钟山区	Zhongshan	10519	70	21.9	253.07	79
六枝特区	Liuzhi	17719	25	59.0	286.76	71
水城县	Shuicheng	20180	18	40.8	278.50	73
盘　县	Pan	30188	4	24.5	265.61	76
红花岗区	Honghuagang	33514	2	13.7	540.64	9
遵义县	Zunyi	37603	1	38.3	277.32	74
桐梓县	Tongzi	14956	37	26.6	231.79	85
绥阳县	Suiyang	15982	27	49.3	319.74	60
正安县	Zhengan	14998	36	24.5	253.79	78
※道真县	Daozhen	11552	58	28.7	349.16	52
※务川县	Wuchuan	12788	48	34.2	310.50	62
凤冈县	Fenggang	11426	60	13.9	283.45	72
湄潭县	Meitan	15382	34	37.6	331.12	55
余庆县	Yuqing	10956	67	31.4	381.28	40
习水县	Xishui	18609	23	32.8	275.42	75
赤水市	Chishui	14450	39	36.4	471.84	19
仁怀市	Renhuai	27824	6	29.3	472.67	17
西秀区	Xixiu	26657	7	29.3	330.86	56
平坝县	Pingba	12373	52	44.3	361.31	48

23－41 续表 4(continued)

县(市、区)名称	County(City, Section)	财政支出(万元) Expenditures of Governments (10000 yuan)	位次 Order	2001 年比 2000 年增长(%) Increase Rate in 2001 over 2000(%)	人均财政支出(元) Per Capita Expenditures of Governments(yuan)	位次 Order
普定县	Puding	15641	31	46.4	389.61	37
※镇宁县	Zhenning	14485	38	26.5	427.16	28
※关岭县	Guanling	11499	59	44.8	361.60	47
※紫云县	Ziyun	10260	72	28.5	310.30	63
铜仁市	Tongren	15718	30	50.2	472.01	18
江口县	Jiangkou	8781	79	50.5	399.77	34
※玉屏县	Yuping	8177	82	50.8	589.97	6
石阡县	Shiqian	13353	42	53.6	357.03	49
思南县	Sinan	17975	24	52.8	289.13	70
※印江县	Yinjiang	13315	43	43.6	328.60	57
德江县	Dejiang	13046	46	31.9	296.23	68
※沿河县	Yanhe	15947	28	42.3	292.18	69
※松桃县	Songtao	15441	32	29.3	246.80	81
万山特区	Wanshan	4496	87	45.2	691.16	3
兴义市	Xingyi	28671	5	24.0	395.43	35
兴仁县	Xingren	13865	40	32.3	309.80	64
普安县	Puan	11825	55	60.0	422.93	29
晴隆县	Qinglong	10592	69	28.7	377.48	42
贞丰县	Zhenfeng	10004	74	39.7	298.45	67
望谟县	Wangmo	10611	68	52.4	385.08	38
册亨县	Ceheng	7229	86	30.2	332.75	54
安龙县	Anlong	13675	41	33.1	324.51	58
毕节市	Bijie	32801	3	24.9	262.11	77
大方县	Dafang	22142	11	39.3	232.02	84
黔西县	Qianxi	18645	22	52.4	228.86	86
金沙县	Jinsha	21602	12	31.5	372.90	43
织金县	Zhijin	21417	13	32.5	237.86	83
纳雍县	Nayong	22429	10	45.6	299.95	66
※威宁县	Weining	20370	15	27.1	190.94	87

23－41 续表 5(continued)

县(市、区)名称	County(City，Section)	财政支出(万元) Expenditures of Governments (10000 yuan)	位次 Order	2001 年比 2000 年增长(%) Increase Rate in 2001 over 2000(%)	人均财政支出(元) Per Capita Expenditures of Governments(yuan)	位次 Order
赫章县	Hezhang	15074	35	29.3	238.91	82
凯里市	Kaili	20321	17	22.2	456.24	23
黄平县	Huangping	11624	57	62.9	339.73	53
施秉县	Shibing	8468	81	30.8	556.92	8
三穗县	Sansui	8870	77	53.2	437.27	27
镇远县	Zhenyuan	11767	56	57.5	470.30	20
岑巩县	Cengong	8813	78	47.7	409.72	31
天柱县	Tianzhu	12885	47	41.5	320.44	59
锦屏县	Jinping	11082	65	61.5	507.07	13
剑河县	Jianhe	8940	76	42.4	422.50	30
台江县	Taijiang	8757	80	65.6	531.86	11
黎平县	Liping	15396	33	52.0	312.64	61
榕江县	Rongjiang	11848	54	49.9	369.90	44
从江县	Congjiang	11062	66	57.8	356.21	50
雷山县	Leishan	7443	85	47.1	510.84	12
麻江县	Majiang	7836	83	40.7	364.13	46
丹寨县	Danzhai	7465	84	40.7	466.27	21
都匀市	Duyun	21017	14	30.4	438.95	26
福泉市	Fuquan	11209	63	28.3	369.08	45
荔波县	Libo	10270	71	54.9	624.51	5
贵定县	Guiding	15844	29	22.6	562.24	7
瓮安县	Wengan	11184	64	29.7	248.12	80
独山县	Dushan	13099	45	68.7	382.51	39
平塘县	Pingtang	11220	62	58.8	379.05	41
罗甸县	Luodian	11350	61	29.5	355.02	51
长顺县	Changshun	9808	75	26.9	406.55	32
龙里县	Longli	10091	73	46.2	502.41	15
惠水县	Huishui	12725	50	44.4	301.04	65
※三都县	Sandu	12409	51	66.8	391.45	36

23－42 各县(市、区)城乡居民储蓄存款余额及位次(2001)
Urban and Rural Resident Savings Deposit Balance and Its Order by County(City, Section)

县(市、区)名称 County(City,Section)		城乡居民储蓄存款(万元) Urban and Rural Resident Savings Deposit(10000 yuan)	位次 Order	人均储蓄(元) Per Capita Savings Deposit(yuan)	位次 Order
南明区	Nanming				
云岩区	Yunyan				
花溪区	Huaxi				
乌当区	Wudang	89969	12	3012	7
白云区	Baiyun				
小河区	Xiaohe	126386	9	11130	2
开阳县	Kaiyang	51395	20	1200	21
息烽县	Xifeng	32847	40	1292	17
修文县	Xiuwen	38384	33	1275	18
清镇市	Qingzhen	85363	14	1699	13
钟山区	Zhongshan	207682	3	4997	3
六枝特区	Liuzhi	62946	18	1019	33
水城县	Shuicheng	17678	69	244	82
盘　县	Pan	101691	10	895	41
红花岗区	Honghuagang	501108	1	8084	1
遵义县	Zunyi	140100	7	1033	30
桐梓县	Tongzi	62955	17	976	35
绥阳县	Suiyang	51290	21	1026	31
正安县	Zhengan	41290	29	699	51
※道真县	Daozhen	34892	36	1055	29
※务川县	Wuchuan	23767	52	577	60
凤冈县	Fenggang	25262	51	627	56
湄潭县	Meitan	64897	16	1397	16
余庆县	Yuqing	32720	41	1139	24
习水县	Xishui	47354	23	701	49
赤水市	Chishui	86166	13	2814	9
仁怀市	Renhuai	58625	19	996	34
西秀区	Xixiu	233536	2	2899	6
平坝县	Pingba	82445	15	2408	10

23－42 续表 1(continued)

县(市、区)名称 County(City,Section)		城乡居民储蓄存款(万元) Urban and Rural Resident Savings Deposit(10000 yuan)	位次 Order	人均储蓄(元) Per Capita Savings Deposit(yuan)	位次 Order
普定县	Puding	18690	65	466	73
※镇宁县	Zhenning	25552	50	754	47
※关岭县	Guanling	21575	56	678	53
※紫云县	Ziyun	12507	78	378	79
铜仁市	Tongren	95269	11	2861	8
江口县	Jiangkou	21207	57	965	37
※玉屏县	Yuping	26920	47	1942	12
石阡县	Shiqian	22094	55	591	59
思南县	Sinan	35445	35	570	62
※印江县	Yinjiang	33148	38	818	44
德江县	Dejiang	19395	63	440	75
※沿河县	Yanhe	30180	44	553	63
※松桃县	Songtao	33088	39	529	67
万山特区	Wanshan				
兴义市	Xingyi	165923	6	2288	11
兴仁县	Xingren	25680	49	574	61
普安县	Puan	17800	68	637	55
晴隆县	Qinglong	15177	73	541	66
贞丰县	Zhenfeng	20181	61	602	58
望谟县	Wangmo	11309	80	410	78
册亨县	Ceheng	11141	81	513	68
安龙县	Anlong	34890	37	828	43
毕节市	Bijie	133555	8	1067	28
大方县	Dafang	46827	24	491	71
黔西县	Qianxi	40612	31	498	69
金沙县	Jinsha	43896	26	758	46
织金县	Zhijin	39049	32	434	76
纳雍县	Nayong	20690	59	277	81
※威宁县	Weining	31645	42	297	80

23－42 续表 2(continued)

县(市、区)名称 County(City, Section)		城乡居民储蓄存款(万元) Urban and Rural Resident Savings Deposit(10000 yuan)	位次 Order	人均储蓄(元) Per Capita Savings Deposit(yuan)	位次 Order
赫章县	Hezhang	30887	43	490	72
凯里市	Kaili	187583	5	4212	5
黄平县	Huangping	27983	45	818	45
施秉县	Shibing	17648	70	1161	23
三穗县	Sansui	19072	64	940	39
镇远县	Zhenyuan	27212	46	1088	27
岑巩县	Cengong	15054	75	700	50
天柱县	Tianzhu	44454	25	1106	26
锦屏县	Jinping	26101	48	1194	22
剑河县	Jianhe	18127	66	857	42
台江县	Taijiang	15982	72	971	36
黎平县	Liping	36744	34	746	48
榕江县	Rongjiang	22351	54	698	52
从江县	Congjiang	12967	77	418	77
雷山县	Leishan	9282	82	637	54
麻江县	Majiang	19438	62	903	40
丹寨县	Danzhai	15113	74	944	38
都匀市	Duyun	203080	4	4241	4
福泉市	Fuquan	43656	27	1437	15
荔波县	Libo	20966	58	1275	19
贵定县	Guiding	43411	28	1540	14
瓮安县	Wengan	50412	22	1118	25
独山县	Dushan	41209	30	1203	20
平塘县	Pingtang	17955	67	607	57
罗甸县	Luodian	14310	76	448	74
长顺县	Changshun	11854	79	491	70
龙里县	Longli	20535	60	1022	32
惠水县	Huishui	23247	53	550	65
※三都县	Sandu	17498	71	552	64

23-43 各县(市、区)教育事业基本情况(2001)
Basic Conditions of Education by County(City, Section)

县(市、区)名称 County(City, Section)		普通中学 Secondary Schools 学校数(所) Number of School (unit)	在校生数(人) Students Enrollment(person)	专任教师数(人) Full-time Teachers(person)	小学 Primary Schools 学校数(所) Number of School (unit)	在校生数(人) Students Enrollment(person)	专任教师数(人) Full-time Teachers(person)
南明区	Nanming				35	24851	1873
云岩区	Yunyan	1	932	93	44	31558	1906
花溪区	Huaxi	30	16252	1093	120	32554	1809
乌当区	Wudang	30	13362	962	120	28772	1802
白云区	Baiyun	17	9898	875	59	18258	1179
小河区	Xiaohe	10	5942	445	25	9514	568
开阳县	Kaiyang	29	26111	1370	199	52139	2166
息烽县	Xifeng	18	14781	734	95	27430	1336
修文县	Xiuwen	23	18389	842	115	33612	1507
清镇市	Qingzhen	29	24920	1254	271	62118	2631
钟山区	Zhongshan	49	26977	1443	132	54886	2547
六枝特区	Liuzhi	46	23889	1282	218	83048	2294
水城县	Shuicheng	35	24087	880	258	96315	2538
盘　县	Pan	65	66266	2646	487	169945	4467
红花岗区	Honghuagang	43	41316	2154	135	66154	2728
遵义县	Zunyi	121	93269	3487	491	164216	6092
桐梓县	Tongzi	36	30093	1297	249	92118	2236
绥阳县	Suiyang	36	30252	1508	246	61835	2232
正安县	Zhengan	24	27540	1184	176	71177	2212
※道真县	Daozhen	24	16952	934	158	32248	1577
※务川县	Wuchuan	20	16238	820	170	54424	1601
凤冈县	Fenggang	21	17472	845	187	56001	1756
湄潭县	Meitan	25	23733	1285	162	52416	1983
余庆县	Yuqing	16	14921	743	48	24921	1167
习水县	Xishui	33	32104	1612	338	108110	2766
赤水市	Chishui	14	13404	766	101	24917	1340
仁怀市	Renhuai	26	33597	1305	241	81213	2856
西秀区	Xixiu	48	38778	2140	307	101161	3748
平坝县	Pingba	24	17824	1024	151	42139	1762

23-43 续表 1(continued)

县(市、区)名称 County(City, Section)		普通中学 Secondary Schools			小学 Primary Schools		
		学校数(所) Number of School (unit)	在校生数(人) Students Enrollment(person)	专任教师数(人) Full-time Teachers(person)	学校数(所) Number of School (unit)	在校生数(人) Students Enrollment(person)	专任教师数(人) Full-time Teachers(person)
普定县	Puding	15	17735	845	191	56959	1938
※镇宁县	Zhenning	12	10204	499	149	44421	1587
※关岭县	Guanling	8	12383	566	126	49416	1550
※紫云县	Ziyun	19	8968	542	119	46452	1472
铜仁市	Tongren	23	20051	1054	54	38254	1710
江口县	Jiangkou	15	11528	562	133	29012	922
※玉屏县	Yuping	12	7873	414	81	14573	566
石阡县	Shiqian	23	17336	846	164	47689	1971
思南县	Sinan	39	30514	1490	294	75371	2815
※印江县	Yinjiang	21	20275	976	142	47999	1983
德江县	Dejiang	29	22586	1096	230	63858	1963
※沿河县	Yanhe	26	21057	1029	216	82651	2363
※松桃县	Songtao	34	25720	1221	308	99467	2939
万山特区	Wanshan	6	2992	214	39	5992	399
兴义市	Xingyi	54	46394	2074	250	102037	3682
兴仁县	Xingren	30	22799	984	167	67081	2142
普安县	Puan	23	16454	632	102	44587	1325
晴隆县	Qinglong	19	14098	546	89	42312	1391
贞丰县	Zhenfeng	18	17395	532	160	52714	1632
望谟县	Wangmo	12	7852	350	95	37212	1416
册亨县	Ceheng	21	10542	409	82	34267	970
安龙县	Anlong	25	24964	1064	187	63414	2210
毕节市	Bijie	34	55146	2417	416	167794	4835
大方县	Dafang	63	58474	2054	381	137152	3506
黔西县	Qianxi	21	29547	1439	321	109398	3138
金沙县	Jinsha	39	36446	1390	301	66413	2983
织金县	Zhijin	16	31031	1290	368	127356	3360
纳雍县	Nayong	17	28409	1020	266	115643	3067
※威宁县	Weining	41	22671	1247	286	169896	3726

23－43 续表 2(continued)

县(市、区)名称 County(City, Section)		普通中学 Secondary Schools			小学 Primary Schools		
		学校数(所) Number of School (unit)	在校生数(人) Students Enrollment(person)	专任教师数(人) Full－time Teachers(person)	学校数(所) Number of School (unit)	在校生数(人) Students Enrollment(person)	专任教师数(人) Full－time Teachers(person)
赫章县	Hezhang	31	15079	917	370	96748	2714
凯里市	Kaili	31	27995	1554	152	48218	2411
黄平县	Huangping	18	15950	699	133	38479	1513
施秉县	Shibing	10	7019	371	81	19007	786
三穗县	Sansui	15	11068	461	90	23273	1072
镇远县	Zhenyuan	21	16878	631	44	28287	1339
岑巩县	Cengong	15	11492	400	114	27704	1041
天柱县	Tianzhu	27	25521	1076	162	48251	1879
锦屏县	Jinping	15	15475	621	170	27099	1223
剑河县	Jianhe	12	9546	450	188	26146	1193
台江县	Taijiang	11	6192	327	70	18332	804
黎平县	Liping	18	21060	825	290	64595	2049
榕江县	Rongjiang	27	14821	646	158	38415	1661
从江县	Congjiang	7	7539	451	223	39743	1401
雷山县	Leishan	7	6680	309	81	16471	862
麻江县	Majiang	10	10036	513	106	25791	1071
丹寨县	Danzhai	10	6956	438	40	18970	1008
都匀市	Duyun	28	27808	1306	247	47548	2388
福泉市	Fuquan	18	19273	991	144	36662	1833
荔波县	Libo	13	10180	545	99	19746	1163
贵定县	Guiding	13	13776	697	121	35399	1443
瓮安县	Wengan	27	30904	1327	185	52584	2157
独山县	Dushan	24	17234	859	145	43722	1621
平塘县	Pingtang	17	9794	627	125	33544	1450
罗甸县	Luodian	7	10325	589	131	39121	1517
长顺县	Changshun	15	9066	544	104	28513	1455
龙里县	Longli	15	9982	555	108	24727	1190
惠水县	Huishui	16	15747	708	157	45765	1935
※三都县	Sandu	16	10999	493	142	44395	1514

24

全国各省资料

Information of Each Province of National Total

Twenty-Four

24－1 全国各省(市、区)主要经济指标排序(2001)(一)
The Orders of Major Economic Indicators by Province(City, Region) in China(1)

单位:亿元
(100 million yuan)

地区	Region	总人口(万人) Total Population (10000 persons)	位次 Order	国内生产总值 Gross Domestic Product	位次 Order	第一产业 Primary Industry	位次 Order
全国总计	National Total	127627		95933.3		14609.9	
北京	Beijing	1383	26	2817.6	15	93.0	26
天津	Tianjin	1004	27	1826.7	21	78.6	28
河北	Hebei	6699	6	5577.7	6	914.1	6
山西	Shanxi	3272	19	1774.6	22	160.4	25
内蒙古	Inner Mongolia	2377	23	1545.5	24	361.3	18
辽宁	Liaoning	4194	13	5033.1	7	545.0	13
吉林	Jilin	2691	21	2032.5	19	409.6	16
黑龙江	Heilongjiang	3811	15	3561.0	13	408.9	17
上海	Shanghai	1614	25	4950.8	8	85.5	27
江苏	Jiangsu	7355	5	9514.6	2	1088.4	3
浙江	Zhejiang	4613	11	6700.0	4	690.0	10
安徽	Anhui	6328	8	3290.1	14	754.2	8
福建	Fujian	3440	18	4258.4	11	652.4	11
江西	Jiangxi	4186	14	2173.8	17	506.0	14
山东	Shandong	9041	2	9438.3	3	1359.5	1
河南	Henan	9555	1	5645.0	5	1234.0	2
湖北	Hubei	5975	9	4662.3	9	692.2	9
湖南	Hunan	6596	7	3983.0	12	826.0	7
广东	Guangdong	7783	4	10556.5	1	1008.5	4
广西	Guangxi	4788	10	2231.2	16	556.2	12
海南	Hainan	796	28	545.3	28	200.3	24
重庆	Chongqing	3097	20	1749.8	23	293.0	19
四川	Sichuan	8640	3	4421.8	10	981.7	5
贵州	Guizhou	3799	16	1084.9	26	274.2	22
云南	Yunnan	4287	12	2077.5	18	450.5	15
西藏	Tibet	263	31				
陕西	Shanxi	3659	17	1841.2	20	280.5	21
甘肃	Gansu	2575	22	1074.9	27	207.0	23
青海	Qinghai	523	30	300.8	29	41.1	30
宁夏	Ningxia	563	29	298.1	30	49.5	29
新疆	Xinjiang	1876	24	1483.5	25	287.4	20

24－2 全国各省(市、区)主要经济指标排序(2001)(二)

The Orders of Major Economic Indicators by Province(City, Region) in China(2)

单位:亿元
(100 million yuan)

地 区	Region	第二产业 Secondary Industry	位次 Order	第三产业 Tertiary Industry	位次 Order	国内生产总值比上年增长(%) Increase Rate of GDP in 2001 over 2000(%)	位次 Order
全国总计	National Total	49069.1		32254.3		7.3	
北 京	Beijing	1063.7	15	1660.9	11	11.0	3
天 津	Tianjin	891.5	17	856.6	18	12.0	1
河 北	Hebei	2744.3	5	1919.3	7	8.7	25
山 西	Shanxi	917.2	16	697.0	23	8.3	27
内蒙古	Inner Mongolia	624.4	25	559.7	24	9.6	9
辽 宁	Liaoning	2444.2	7	2043.8	6	9.0	18
吉 林	Jilin	880.8	18	742.0	21	9.3	12
黑龙江	Heilongjiang	1998.7	10	1153.4	14	9.3	13
上 海	Shanghai	2355.5	8	2509.8	5	10.2	5
江 苏	Jiangsu	4913.7	2	3512.6	2	10.2	6
浙 江	Zhejiang	3440.0	4	2570.0	4	10.5	4
安 徽	Anhui	1415.2	14	1120.7	15	8.6	26
福 建	Fujian	1904.2	11	1701.8	9	9.0	20
江 西	Jiangxi	784.8	22	883.0	16	8.8	24
山 东	Shandong	4654.5	3	3424.3	3	10.1	8
河 南	Henan	2662.3	6	1748.7	8	9.1	17
湖 北	Hubei	2313.7	9	1656.5	12	9.1	16
湖 南	Hunan	1570.0	13	1587.0	13	9.0	21
广 东	Guangdong	5301.9	1	4246.1	1	9.5	10
广 西	Guangxi	816.9	20	858.1	17	8.2	28
海 南	Hainan	110.4	30	234.6	28	8.9	22
重 庆	Chongqing	726.6	23	730.1	22	9.0	19
四 川	Sichuan	1756.9	12	1683.2	10	9.2	14
贵 州	Guizhou	419.7	27	391.0	26	8.8	23
云 南	Yunnan	880.5	19	746.4	19	6.5	30
西 藏	Tibet						
陕 西	Shanxi	815.7	21	745.0	20	9.1	15
甘 肃	Gansu	482.5	26	385.3	27	9.4	11
青 海	Qinghai	132.6	29	127.1	29	12.0	2
宁 夏	Ningxia	134.8	28	113.8	30	10.1	7
新 疆	Xinjiang	638.8	24	557.4	25	8.0	29

24-3 全国各省(市、区)主要经济指标排序(2001)(三)
The Orders of Major Economic Indicators by Province(City, Region) in China(3)

单位:亿元
(100 million yuan)

地 区	Region	地方财政收入 Local Financial Revenue	位次 Order	地方财政收入比上年增长(%) Increase Rate of Local Financial Revenue in 2001 over 2000(%)	位次 Order	# 增值税 Value - added Tax	位次 Order
地方合计	National Total	7803.30		21.8		1341.66	
北 京	Beijing	454.17	6	31.6	3	59.00	7
天 津	Tianjin	163.64	18	22.5	9	34.87	14
河 北	Hebei	283.50	8	14.0	24	48.85	9
山 西	Shanxi	132.76	20	16.0	20	30.87	16
内蒙古	Inner Mongolia	99.43	25	4.6	31	14.84	25
辽 宁	Liaoning	370.44	7	25.3	7	66.51	6
吉 林	Jilin	121.10	22	16.6	18	24.20	19
黑龙江	Heilongjiang	213.64	13	15.3	22	52.56	8
上 海	Shanghai	609.47	2	25.6	6	111.95	3
江 苏	Jiangsu	572.15	4	27.6	4	131.99	2
浙 江	Zhejiang	500.69	5	46.1	1	102.41	4
安 徽	Anhui	192.18	15	7.5	29	28.28	18
福 建	Fujian	274.28	9	17.2	16	40.78	11
江 西	Jiangxi	131.98	21	18.3	14	17.23	24
山 东	Shandong	573.18	3	23.6	8	100.29	5
河 南	Henan	267.75	11	8.6	27	44.35	10
湖 北	Hubei	231.94	12	8.2	28	37.13	13
湖 南	Hunan	205.41	14	16.0	19	29.38	17
广 东	Guangdong	1160.51	1	27.5	5	172.48	1
广 西	Guangxi	178.67	17	21.5	11	23.87	20
海 南	Hainan	43.77	28	11.6	26	3.52	30
重 庆	Chongqing	106.12	23	21.6	10	17.76	22
四 川	Sichuan	271.12	10	15.9	21	38.01	12
贵 州	Guizhou	99.75	24	17.0	17	14.26	26
云 南	Yunnan	191.28	16	5.8	30	33.62	15
西 藏	Tibet	6.11	31	13.5	25		
陕 西	Shanxi	135.81	19	18.1	15	23.33	21
甘 肃	Gansu	69.95	27	14.1	23	13.38	27
青 海	Qinghai	19.82	30	19.5	13	3.85	29
宁 夏	Ningxia	27.57	29	32.4	2	3.85	28
新 疆	Xinjiang	95.09	26	20.3	12	17.39	23

24－4 全国各省(市、区)主要经济指标排序(2001)(四)

The Orders of Major Economic Indicators by Province(City, Region) in China(4)

单位：亿元

(100 million yuan)

地　区	Region	#营业税 Operation Tax	位次 Order	财政支出 Financial Expenditure	位次 Order	财政支出比上年增长(%) Increase Rate of Financial Expenditure in 2001 Over 2000(%)	位次 Order
地方合计	**National Total**	**1849.10**		**13134.57**		**25.9**	
北　京	Beijing	181.35	3	559.11	8	26.2	15
天　津	Tianjin	42.99	13	234.67	27	25.5	17
河　北	Hebei	50.02	11	514.63	9	24.2	21
山　西	Shanxi	26.11	23	289.50	21	28.7	12
内蒙古	Inner Mongolia	19.61	26	319.26	20	29.2	10
辽　宁	Liaoning	87.85	7	634.40	5	22.7	26
吉　林	Jilin	28.03	20	326.43	19	25.2	19
黑龙江	Heilongjiang	36.31	16	478.27	13	25.2	18
上　海	Shanghai	191.12	2	708.14	4	16.4	29
江　苏	Jiangsu	109.49	5	729.64	3	23.4	24
浙　江	Zhejiang	124.89	4	597.30	6	38.5	4
安　徽	Anhui	32.65	19	403.80	15	25.2	20
福　建	Fujian	61.42	9	374.31	16	15.5	30
江　西	Jiangxi	26.62	22	283.71	22	27.1	13
山　东	Shandong	92.69	6	753.78	2	23.0	25
河　南	Henan	52.89	10	508.58	10	14.5	31
湖　北	Hubei	44.68	12	484.40	12	31.0	9
湖　南	Hunan	36.44	15	431.70	14	24.1	22
广　东	Guangdong	318.16	1	1321.33	1	23.5	23
广　西	Guangxi	32.87	18	351.65	17	36.0	7
海　南	Hainan	12.74	28	78.00	31	21.9	27
重　庆	Chongqing	27.84	21	237.55	25	26.6	14
四　川	Sichuan	62.81	8	594.10	7	31.5	8
贵　州	**Guizhou**	**22.08**	**25**	**275.19**	**23**	**37.5**	**6**
云　南	Yunnan	36.68	14	496.43	11	19.9	28
西　藏	Tibet	0.00	31	104.57	28	74.4	1
陕　西	Shanxi	33.50	17	350.05	18	28.9	11
甘　肃	Gansu	17.35	27	235.87	26	25.9	16
青　海	Qinghai	4.87	30	101.30	29	48.4	3
宁　夏	Ningxia	7.52	29	93.58	30	54.0	2
新　疆	Xinjiang	25.25	24	263.32	24	37.9	5

24-5 全国各省(市、区)主要经济指标排序(2001)(五)
The Orders of Major Economic Indicators by Province(City, Region) in China(5)

单位:亿元
(100 million yuan)

地 区	Region	#挖潜改造支出 Innovation Funds	位次 Order	#科技三项费用 Science and Technology Promotion Funds	位次 Order	#支援农村生产支出 Expenditure for Supporting Agricultural Production	位次 Order
地方合计	**National Total**	**602.12**		**142.49**		**246.66**	
北 京	Beijing	35.47	5	4.87	10	11.73	7
天 津	Tianjin	28.25	7	6.06	6	2.37	27
河 北	Hebei	19.39	12	5.62	7	7.25	15
山 西	Shanxi	2.29	28	2.36	18	6.35	19
内蒙古	Inner Mongolia	9.76	21	2.36	19	6.08	20
辽 宁	Liaoning	26.35	8	11.76	3	14.00	5
吉 林	Jilin	11.57	18	3.06	16	2.58	25
黑龙江	Heilongjiang	17.58	13	5.32	8	7.80	13
上 海	Shanghai	95.27	1	1.29	24	10.14	8
江 苏	Jiangsu	60.54	2	9.39	5	21.26	2
浙 江	Zhejiang	43.43	4	12.40	2	13.08	6
安 徽	Anhui	23.35	9	2.08	21	6.44	18
福 建	Fujian	12.57	15	4.83	11	9.11	9
江 西	Jiangxi	11.66	17	1.21	25	4.84	22
山 东	Shandong	52.39	3	11.53	4	14.60	4
河 南	Henan	20.11	11	4.14	14	8.65	10
湖 北	Hubei	10.11	19	4.62	13	7.42	14
湖 南	Hunan	9.77	20	5.15	9	6.55	17
广 东	Guangdong	20.97	10	23.61	1	28.20	1
广 西	Guangxi	13.55	14	1.91	22	8.48	11
海 南	Hainan	0.14	31	0.20	31	1.90	28
重 庆	Chongqing	4.85	24	2.42	17	3.02	24
四 川	Sichuan	30.33	6	4.63	12	8.17	12
贵 州	**Guizhou**	**4.45**	**26**	**1.49**	**23**	**4.96**	**21**
云 南	Yunnan	12.35	16	4.05	15	16.53	3
西 藏	Tibet	0.33	30	0.26	30	1.27	31
陕 西	Shanxi	8.22	23	2.28	20	6.94	16
甘 肃	Gansu	8.62	22	1.20	27	3.88	23
青 海	Qinghai	1.13	29	0.50	29	1.66	29
宁 夏	Ningxia	4.53	25	0.71	28	1.42	30
新 疆	Xinjiang	2.80	27	1.20	26	2.46	26

24－6　全国各省(市、区)主要经济指标排序(2001)(六)

The Orders of Major Economic Indicators by Province(City,Region)in China(6)

单位:亿元
(100 million yuan)

地　区	Region	固定资产投资额 Investment in Fixed Assets	位次 Order	#基建投资 Capital Construction	位次 Order	#更新改造 Innovation	位次 Order
全国总计	National Total	36898.4		14567.0		5889.2	
北　京	Beijing	1410.3	6	387.3	14	186.5	14
天　津	Tianjin	612.5	17	309.4	21	141.9	17
河　北	Hebei	1085.4	10	591.8	9	339.6	5
山　西	Shanxi	549.8	21	325.9	18	145.2	16
内蒙古	Inner Mongolia	418.3	24	268.8	23	69.6	27
辽　宁	Liaoning	1166.6	8	490.8	10	329.9	6
吉　林	Jilin	580.2	19	317.8	20	127.4	19
黑龙江	Heilongjiang	845.5	13	481.7	11	201.9	9
上　海	Shanghai	1793.6	5	710.5	5	432.0	3
江　苏	Jiangsu	1837.0	3	838.0	4	402.2	4
浙　江	Zhejiang	1879.1	2	979.4	2	319.1	7
安　徽	Anhui	659.4	15	347.8	16	185.3	15
福　建	Fujian	881.7	12	341.7	17	201.7	10
江　西	Jiangxi	415.4	25	235.0	25	103.1	23
山　东	Shandong	1801.0	4	848.9	3	517.7	1
河　南	Henan	977.3	11	633.4	8	198.5	11
湖　北	Hubei	1108.4	9	657.2	7	282.7	8
湖　南	Hunan	762.1	14	440.4	12	198.3	12
广　东	Guangdong	2786.0	1	1201.4	1	480.8	2
广　西	Guangxi	458.4	23	307.6	22	86.6	26
海　南	Hainan	171.9	29	137.0	28	14.0	30
重　庆	Chongqing	568.5	20	258.5	24	105.6	22
四　川	Sichuan	1169.4	7	696.1	6	196.4	13
贵　州	Guizhou	413.4	26	230.9	27	102.7	24
云　南	Yunnan	513.6	22	321.0	19	97.0	25
西　藏	Tibet	85.0	31	75.3	31	5.5	31
陕　西	Shanxi	632.3	16	372.7	15	133.1	18
甘　肃	Gansu	383.6	27	232.1	26	112.1	20
青　海	Qinghai	178.0	28	133.8	29	20.7	29
宁　夏	Ningxia	151.9	30	102.1	30	25.3	28
新　疆	Xinjiang	608.6	18	389.0	13	108.6	21

24-7 全国各省(市、区)主要经济指标排序(2001)(七)
The Orders of Major Economic Indicators by Province(City, Region) in China(7)

地区	Region	农林牧渔业总产值(亿元) Gross Output Value of Farming, Forestry, Animal Husbandry and Fishery(100 million yuan)	位次 Order	农林牧渔业总产值比上年增长(%) Increase Rate of Gross Agriculture Output Value in 2001 over 2000(%)	位次 Order	粮食产量(万吨) Output of Grain (10000 tons)	位次 Order
全国总计	National Total	26179.6		4.2		45263.7	
北京	Beijing	214.1	27	7.5	6	104.9	29
天津	Tianjin	169.5	28	8.0	3	143.3	28
河北	Hebei	1680.5	5	5.3	12	2491.8	8
山西	Shanxi	301.5	25	-7.0	31	692.1	24
内蒙古	Inner Mongolia	555.9	18	2.0	29	1239.1	16
辽宁	Liaoning	1045.7	12	6.6	8	1394.4	15
吉林	Jilin	659.3	17	6.9	7	1953.4	10
黑龙江	Heilongjiang	711.0	15	6.4	9	2651.7	6
上海	Shanghai	227.6	26	7.5	5	151.4	27
江苏	Jiangsu	1956.1	3	4.5	15	2942.1	3
浙江	Zhejiang	1108.0	10	3.2	22	1072.7	18
安徽	Anhui	1258.1	8	2.8	25	2500.3	7
福建	Fujian	1061.6	11	3.9	20	817.3	21
江西	Jiangxi	790.3	14	3.0	24	1600.0	12
山东	Shandong	2454.0	1	4.0	19	3720.6	2
河南	Henan	2102.8	2	5.6	10	4119.9	1
湖北	Hubei	1172.8	9	3.0	23	2138.5	9
湖南	Hunan	1283.1	7	4.0	18	2700.3	5
广东	Guangdong	1688.0	4	4.3	17	1600.1	11
广西	Guangxi	872.9	13	4.9	14	1511.4	13
海南	Hainan	325.1	24	13.5	1	195.8	26
重庆	Chongqing	431.2	21	2.1	28	1023.5	19
四川	Sichuan	1466.8	6	2.6	26	2926.5	4
贵州	Guizhou	418.6	22	1.2	30	1100.3	17
云南	Yunnan	703.5	16	3.6	21	1486.3	14
西藏	Tibet	52.8	31	5.4	11	98.3	31
陕西	Shanxi	478.8	20	2.5	27	976.6	20
甘肃	Gansu	344.6	23	7.8	4	753.2	23
青海	Qinghai	63.3	30	5.2	13	103.2	30
宁夏	Ningxia	85.3	29	8.0	2	274.8	25
新疆	Xinjiang	496.8	19	4.5	16	780.0	22

24-8 全国各省(市、区)主要经济指标排序(2001)(八)

The Orders of Major Economic Indicators by Province(City, Region) in China(8)

单位:万吨
(10000 tons)

地　　区	Region	油料产量 Oil-bearing Crops	位次 Order	肉类产量 Output of Pork, Beef and Mutton	位次 Order	水产品产量 Aquatic Products	位次 Order
全国总计	National Total	2864.8		6333.9		4381.3	
北　京	Beijing	4.3	30	69.1	23	7.4	23
天　津	Tianjin	3.9	31	36.4	28	26.5	18
河　北	Hebei	153.8	7	445.7	5	84.9	13
山　西	Shanxi	18.1	25	63.5	25	2.8	28
内蒙古	Inner Mongolia	80.6	11	149.6	15	7.6	22
辽　宁	Liaoning	46.3	15	234.7	11	350.8	5
吉　林	Jilin	34.3	20	192.9	14	11.0	21
黑龙江	Heilongjiang	36.3	19	137.5	18	40.2	15
上　海	Shanghai	12.8	26	56.1	26	29.8	17
江　苏	Jiangsu	232.5	5	343.1	6	320.9	6
浙　江	Zhejiang	58.2	13	136.1	19	472.9	4
安　徽	Anhui	298.8	3	306.7	8	159.9	9
福　建	Fujian	26.1	23	140.0	17	542.5	3
江　西	Jiangxi	90.5	9	193.8	13	132.3	11
山　东	Shandong	377.3	1	595.4	1	686.1	1
河　南	Henan	362.5	2	537.9	3	31.5	16
湖　北	Hubei	279.4	4	264.3	10	242.2	8
湖　南	Hunan	137.4	8	456.8	4	141.0	10
广　东	Guangdong	80.9	10	333.3	7	609.7	2
广　西	Guangxi	57.2	14	266.1	9	247.8	7
海　南	Hainan	10.3	27	39.7	27	95.6	12
重　庆	Chongqing	30.0	21	146.3	16	19.7	19
四　川	Sichuan	181.0	6	541.3	2	57.1	14
贵　州	Guizhou	71.3	12	131.7	20	6.9	24
云　南	Yunnan	27.7	22	219.5	12	18.0	20
西　藏	Tibet	4.4	29	16.0	31		
陕　西	Shanxi	37.5	18	85.5	22	6.3	25
甘　肃	Gansu	38.4	17	65.1	24	1.5	29
青　海	Qinghai	23.0	24	22.2	29	0.2	30
宁　夏	Ningxia	7.3	28	16.3	30	4.1	27
新　疆	Xinjiang	42.6	16	90.8	21	6.1	26

24－9 全国各省(市、区)主要经济指标排序(2001)(九)
The Orders of Major Economic Indicators by Province(City, Region) in China(9)

地 区	Region	规模以上工业增加值(亿元) Gross Industrial Added Value(100 million yuan)	位次 Order	工业增加值比上年增长(%) Increase Rate of Gross Industrial Added Value in 2001 over 2000(%)	位次 Order	发电量(亿千瓦时) Electricity (100 million kwh)	位次 Order
全国总计	**National Total**	**26950.0**		**9.9**		**14780.0**	
北 京	Beijing	817.2	11	13.8	4	132.7	29
天 津	Tianjin	689.6	14	13.0	6	217.4	23
河 北	Hebei	1215.9	9	10.6	21	901.6	4
山 西	Shanxi	490.2	19	10.8	20	707.4	7
内蒙古	Inner Mongolia	307.2	24	12.9	8	463.7	13
辽 宁	Liaoning	1236.7	8	10.6	22	662.1	8
吉 林	Jilin	557.3	16	15.1	1	329.0	19
黑龙江	Heilongjiang	1253.5	7	10.6	23	438.1	15
上 海	Shanghai	1924.3	4	14.9	2	572.9	11
江 苏	Jiangsu	2920.7	2	12.0	12	986.6	3
浙 江	Zhejiang	1781.2	5	12.5	11	713.5	6
安 徽	Anhui	550.1	18	11.6	15	387.5	16
福 建	Fujian	813.6	12	11.8	13	446.3	14
江 西	Jiangxi	286.0	26	10.9	19	216.2	24
山 东	Shandong	2908.4	3	14.8	3	1069.1	2
河 南	Henan	1270.0	6	10.0	24	791.1	5
湖 北	Hubei	1096.8	10	12.8	9	587.3	9
湖 南	Hunan	617.9	15	13.8	5	384.4	17
广 东	Guangdong	3553.8	1	12.8	10	1351.7	1
广 西	Guangxi	339.1	22	8.6	28	292.3	21
海 南	Hainan	55.1	30	11.5	16	42.6	30
重 庆	Chongqing	333.0	23	11.7	14	170.4	26
四 川	Sichuan	776.1	13	13.0	7	583.6	10
贵 州	**Guizhou**	**235.9**	**27**	**9.8**	**25**	**480.3**	**12**
云 南	Yunnan	553.3	17	3.9	31	340.4	18
西 藏	Tibet	9.5	31	5.8	30	7.0	31
陕 西	Shanxi	455.0	20	9.7	26	303.5	20
甘 肃	Gansu	296.5	25	11.5	17	285.7	22
青 海	Qinghai	71.6	29	11.2	18	137.8	28
宁 夏	Ningxia	82.6	28	9.2	27	150.3	27
新 疆	Xinjiang	358.3	21	7.4	29	180.4	25

24－10 全国各省(市、区)主要经济指标排序(2001)(十)
The Orders of Major Economic Indicators by Province(City,Region)in China(10)

单位:万吨
(10000 tons)

地　区	Region	钢 Steel	位次 Order	原煤 Coal	位次 Order	水泥 Cement	位次 Order
全国总计	National Total	15266.1		110700.0		64000.0	
北　京	Beijing	824.9	6	690.2	21	809.0	24
天　津	Tianjin	395.3	15			339.0	26
河　北	Hebei	1759.5	2	5865.7	5	4878.0	4
山　西	Shanxi	603.8	9	21897.6	1	1309.3	17
内蒙古	Inner Mongolia	453.6	12	7422.2	4	636.2	25
辽　宁	Liaoning	1660.7	3	4468.2	9	2100.5	12
吉　林	Jilin	200.6	19	1632.1	14	895.5	22
黑龙江	Heilongjiang	92.1	26	5120.7	7	910.0	21
上　海	Shanghai	1874.7	1			334.8	27
江　苏	Jiangsu	836.1	5	2451.1	11	5135.7	3
浙　江	Zhejiang	182.5	21	72.0	27	4762.8	5
安　徽	Anhui	553.6	10	5347.5	6	2133.3	11
福　建	Fujian	155.3	22	512.3	23	1525.5	15
江　西	Jiangxi	399.4	14	1517.5	17	1606.7	13
山　东	Shandong	722.6	7	10687.8	2	6924.8	1
河　南	Henan	531.0	11	8448.4	3	4200.8	6
湖　北	Hubei	1003.9	4	333.9	24	2603.7	8
湖　南	Hunan	441.9	13	1546.1	16	2496.0	9
广　东	Guangdong	352.5	16	123.6	26	5804.7	2
广　西	Guangxi	128.5	24	613.5	22	2140.5	10
海　南	Hainan	0.2	29	2.0	29	312.6	28
重　庆	Chongqing	185.0	20	1154.7	19	1511.2	16
四　川	Sichuan	690.8	8	2159.8	12	2816.6	7
贵　州	Guizhou	147.0	23	3731.4	10	920.0	20
云　南	Yunnan	219.6	18	1111.8	20	1534.0	14
西　藏	Tibet			2.5	28	49.6	31
陕　西	Shanxi	69.4	27	4531.9	8	1110.2	18
甘　肃	Gansu	236.6	17	1795.4	13	885.1	23
青　海	Qinghai	44.3	28	169.0	25	166.0	30
宁　夏	Ningxia			1551.1	15	311.2	29
新　疆	Xinjiang	127.5	25	1458.2	18	930.6	19

24－11 全国各省(市、区)主要经济指标排序(2001)(十一)
The Orders of Major Economic Indicators by Province(City, Region) in China(11)

地　区	Region	农用化肥(万吨) Chemical Fertilizers (10000 tons)	位次 Order	卷烟(万箱) Cigarettes (10000 cases)	位次 Order	白酒(万吨) Liguor (10000 tons)	位次 Order
全国总计	National Total	3396.5		3402.1		420.2	
北　京	Beijing	3.8	29	20.1	25	10	12
天　津	Tianjin	14.9	27	16	26	4.4	19
河　北	Hebei	183.1	7	117.1	12	19.6	7
山　西	Shanxi	159.9	9	24.5	24	6	17
内蒙古	Inner Mongolia	35.0	24	28	23	8.5	15
辽　宁	Liaoning	159.6	10	31	22	18.2	8
吉　林	Jilin	3.1	30	58.6	19	6.2	16
黑龙江	Heilongjiang	44.8	23	64.1	18	9.4	13
上　海	Shanghai	13.1	28	130.8	10	0.7	29
江　苏	Jiangsu	187.6	6	117.5	11	29.9	5
浙　江	Zhejiang	62.5	19	105.2	13	1.5	25
安　徽	Anhui	167.1	8	172.6	8	35.7	3
福　建	Fujian	57.4	20	101.3	15	1.3	26
江　西	Jiangxi	48.1	21	54.6	20	8.9	14
山　东	Shandong	423.9	1	222.1	4	78.2	1
河　南	Henan	280.1	4	291.6	2	23.9	6
湖　北	Hubei	283.4	2	189	5	16.3	10
湖　南	Hunan	146.1	11	244.2	3	2.7	20
广　东	Guangdong	21.3	26	185	6	16.6	9
广　西	Guangxi	73.8	16	81.9	16	35.4	4
海　南	Hainan	24.9	25	11.2	27	0.3	30
重　庆	Chongqing	77.6	15	67.7	17	2.5	22
四　川	Sichuan	282.8	3	132.9	9	58.2	2
贵　州	Guizhou	86.8	13	180.8	7	12.1	11
云　南	Yunnan	194.8	5	599.5	1	1.1	27
西　藏	Tibet					2	31
陕　西	Shanxi	97.3	12	104.3	14	2.5	22
甘　肃	Gansu	45.0	22	36.9	21	2.6	21
青　海	Qinghai	79.4	14			1.6	24
宁　夏	Ningxia	69.2	18	2.6	29	1	28
新　疆	Xinjiang	70.2	17	11	28	4.9	18

24－12 全国各省(市、区)主要经济指标排序(2001)(十二)

The Orders of Major Economic Indicators by Province(City, Region) in China(12)

单位:亿元
(100 million yuan)

地　区	Region	工业企业产品销售收入 Sales Revenue of Industrial Enterprises	位次 Order	工业企业利润总额 Total Profits of Industrial Enterprises	位次 Order	工业企业亏损企业亏损额 Loss of Loss－making Enterprises	位次 Order
全国总计	National Total	92278.0		4657.2		1112.4	
北　京	Beijing	2762.9	11	127.0	11	44.9	7
天　津	Tianjin	2826.2	10	184.1	8	50.1	5
河　北	Hebei	3709.3	7	194.3	7	43.0	8
山　西	Shanxi	1275.2	18	39.1	21	22.0	20
内蒙古	Inner Mongolia	797.5	26	20.4	24	15.1	26
辽　宁	Liaoning	4425.6	6	133.2	10	69.5	4
吉　林	Jilin	1790.1	16	85.6	15	38.5	11
黑龙江	Heilongjiang	2406.3	13	493.5	3	34.5	14
上　海	Shanghai	7191.5	5	447.3	5	96.1	2
江　苏	Jiangsu	11269.5	2	420.8	6	82.1	3
浙　江	Zhejiang	7472.2	4	451.8	4	27.8	17
安　徽	Anhui	1798.5	15	52.6	19	22.3	19
福　建	Fujian	2730.0	12	113.7	13	36.4	13
江　西	Jiangxi	958.1	23	14.2	26	17.6	24
山　东	Shandong	9146.0	3	571.5	2	46.1	6
河　南	Henan	3620.6	8	138.5	9	41.4	9
湖　北	Hubei	3198.9	9	119.3	12	40.5	10
湖　南	Hunan	1778.8	17	51.7	20	30.1	16
广　东	Guangdong	13462.0	1	583.5	1	152.0	1
广　西	Guangxi	1016.7	22	37.3	22	21.5	21
海　南	Hainan	164.8	30	6.4	28	4.4	30
重　庆	Chongqing	1057.9	21	21.8	23	22.4	18
四　川	Sichuan	2274.0	14	84.6	16	36.5	12
贵　州	Guizhou	630.4	27	16.9	25	13.5	27
云　南	Yunnan	1123.2	20	81.1	17	20.6	23
西　藏	Tibet	11.7	31	0.9	31	0.6	31
陕　西	Shanxi	1256.1	19	60.4	18	30.6	15
甘　肃	Gansu	818.8	25	7.1	27	17.1	25
青　海	Qinghai	189.8	29	4.8	29	7.9	28
宁　夏	Ningxia	266.8	28	3.8	30	6.3	29
新　疆	Xinjiang	848.8	24	90.3	14	21.2	22

24－13 全国各省(市、区)主要经济指标排序(2001)(十三)
The Orders of Major Economic Indicators by Province(City, Region) in China(13)

地 区 Region	工业企业税金总额(亿元) Total Taxes of Industrial Enterprises (100 million yuan)	位次 Order	工业企业综合效益指数(%) Efficiency Indices of Industrial Enterprises(%)	位次 Order	社会消费品零售总额(亿元) Total Retail Sales of Consumer Goods (100 million yuan)	位次 Order
全国总计 National Total	5429.0		122.1		37595.2	
北 京 Beijing	120.6	18	131.6	9	1593.5	11
天 津 Tianjin	134.4	16	134.2	7	832.7	18
河 北 Hebei	211.9	11	117.5	12	1778.3	9
山 西 Shanxi	105.8	19	84.8	27	679.9	21
内蒙古 Inner Mongolia	58.8	27	90.6	26	537.3	24
辽 宁 Liaoning	247.4	8	100.6	21	2034.9	5
吉 林 Jilin	132.2	17	111.1	16	909.1	17
黑龙江 Heilongjiang	258.2	7	213.1	1	1198.9	14
上 海 Shanghai	380.7	4	157.2	2	1861.3	8
江 苏 Jiangsu	523.2	1	122.3	11	2869.0	2
浙 江 Zhejiang	364.0	5	143.6	4	2555.5	4
安 徽 Anhui	141.0	14	98.6	23	1142.8	15
福 建 Fujian	138.4	15	124.8	10	1499.5	13
江 西 Jiangxi	76.0	22	82.4	28	763.3	19
山 东 Shandong	487.9	3	134.5	6	2834.9	3
河 南 Henan	217.9	9	101.4	20	1979.8	6
湖 北 Hubei	214.0	10	112.2	15	1975.2	7
湖 南 Hunan	182.4	12	102.3	17	1511.1	12
广 东 Guangdong	493.6	2	133.2	8	4515.3	1
广 西 Guangxi	84.5	21	102.2	19	935.9	16
海 南 Hainan	12.2	30	113.9	13	187.5	28
重 庆 Chongqing	75.3	23	94.6	24	699.3	20
四 川 Sichuan	166.7	13	99.5	22	1680.4	10
贵 州 Guizhou	72.9	24	92.4	25	378.0	27
云 南 Yunnan	263.0	6	150.1	3	655.4	23
西 藏 Tibet	1.3	31	113.4	14	49.0	31
陕 西 Shanxi	98.9	20	102.2	18	665.1	22
甘 肃 Gansu	64.4	26	75.4	31	395.4	26
青 海 Qinghai	15.6	28	80.7	30	90.4	30
宁 夏 Ningxia	15.5	29	81.8	29	98.9	29
新 疆 Xinjiang	70.9	25	143.3	5	406.3	25

24-14 全国各省(市、区)主要经济指标排序(2001)(十四)

The Orders of Major Economic Indicators by Province(City, Region) in China(14)

单位:亿美元
(USD 100 million)

地　　区	Region	海关进出口额 Total Exports and Imports	位次 Order	# 出口额 Exports	位次 Order	# 进口额 Imports	位次 Order
全国总计	National Total	5097.7		2661.6		2436.1	
北　京	Beijing	276.4	6	79.1	9	197.2	4
天　津	Tianjin	182.7	9	88.7	8	94.0	9
河　北	Hebei	58.2	10	34.7	10	23.5	11
山　西	Shanxi	32.7	17	25.9	11	6.8	26
内蒙古	Inner Mongolia	21.9	21	9.0	24	12.9	18
辽　宁	Liaoning	210.4	8	107.5	7	102.9	7
吉　林	Jilin	35.0	14	15.3	18	19.7	12
黑龙江	Heilongjiang	41.0	12	21.8	12	19.3	13
上　海	Shanghai	607.1	2	268.6	3	338.4	2
江　苏	Jiangsu	544.8	3	293.9	2	250.9	3
浙　江	Zhejiang	369.1	4	242.6	4	126.5	6
安　徽	Anhui	36.5	13	21.7	13	14.8	17
福　建	Fujian	243.9	7	147.9	6	96.0	8
江　西	Jiangxi	18.0	25	10.9	23	7.1	25
山　东	Shandong	323.3	5	184.8	5	138.5	5
河　南	Henan	34.2	15	18.4	14	15.8	16
湖　北	Hubei	41.6	11	18.0	15	23.7	10
湖　南	Hunan	29.2	18	17.4	16	11.8	20
广　东	Guangdong	1800.1	1	958.3	1	841.8	1
广　西	Guangxi	20.8	24	13.5	20	7.3	24
海　南	Hainan	16.3	26	6.4	26	9.9	22
重　庆	Chongqing	21.4	23	11.7	21	9.7	23
四　川	Sichuan	33.6	16	16.8	17	16.8	15
贵　州	Guizhou	8.7	28	5.1	27	3.5	28
云　南	Yunnan	21.5	22	11.5	22	10.0	21
西　藏	Tibet	1.1	31	0.8	31	0.2	31
陕　西	Shanxi	26.5	19	14.2	19	12.3	19
甘　肃	Gansu	9.1	27	4.8	28	4.4	27
青　海	Qinghai	2.5	30	1.7	30	0.9	30
宁　夏	Ningxia	6.3	29	3.9	29	2.4	29
新　疆	Xinjiang	23.7	20	6.7	25	17.0	14

注:按境内目的地、货源地分。

Note: Data in this table are grouped by places of destination or origin in China.

24－15 全国各省(市、区)主要经济指标排序(2001)(十五)
The Orders of Major Economic Indicators by Province(City, Region) in China(15)

地 区	Region	外商实际直接投资额(万美元) Foreign Direct Investments (USD 10000)	位次 Order	国际旅游接待人数(万人次) Number of International Tourists Received (10000 person－times)	位次 Order	# 外国人 Foreigners	位次 Order
全国总计	National Total	4687759		8901.0		1122.4	
北 京	Beijing	176818	9	285.8	2	239.9	2
天 津	Tianjin	213348	8	42.1	18	37.5	16
河 北	Hebei	66989	12	44.5	17	39.1	15
山 西	Shanxi	23393	23	19.8	27	12.9	26
内蒙古	Inner Mongolia	10703	24	40.0	19	39.6	14
辽 宁	Liaoning	251612	6	72.4	11	60.7	8
吉 林	Jilin	33766	20	27.2	24	23.7	19
黑龙江	Heilongjiang	34114	19	61.2	13	56.5	10
上 海	Shanghai	429159	3	204.3	3	151.6	3
江 苏	Jiangsu	691482	2	183.7	4	108.6	4
浙 江	Zhejiang	221162	7	147.0	6	82.0	5
安 徽	Anhui	33672	21	38.1	20	18.6	23
福 建	Fujian	391804	4	163.5	5	46.5	13
江 西	Jiangxi	39575	16	19.6	28	5.5	29
山 东	Shandong	352093	5	82.9	9	59.2	9
河 南	Henan	45729	15	36.6	21	24.9	18
湖 北	Hubei	118860	10	66.8	12	54.3	12
湖 南	Hunan	81011	11	50.5	15	18.8	22
广 东	Guangdong	1193203	1	1292.4	1	240.4	1
广 西	Guangxi	38416	17	126.7	7	55.0	11
海 南	Hainan	46691	14	45.7	16	13.0	25
重 庆	Chongqing	25649	22	31.3	22	21.9	20
四 川	Sichuan	58188	13	57.5	14	28.1	17
贵 州	Guizhou	2829	28	20.5	26	7.9	28
云 南	Yunnan	6457	26	113.1	8	69.6	6
西 藏	Tibet			12.7	29	11.6	27
陕 西	Shanxi	35174	18	75.9	10	63.8	7
甘 肃	Gansu	7439	25	22.3	25	14.6	24
青 海	Qinghai	3649	27	4.0	30	1.8	30
宁 夏	Ningxia	1680	30	0.9	31	0.6	31
新 疆	Xinjiang	2035	29	27.3	23	21.9	21

24－16 全国各省(市、区)主要经济指标排序(2001)(十六)

The Orders of Major Economic Indicators by Province(City, Region) in China(16)

单位:元

(yuan)

地 区	Region	职工平均工资 Average Wage of Staff and Workers	位次 Order	城镇居民人均可支配收入 Per Capita Annual Disposable Income of Urban Households	位次 Order	农民人均纯收入 Per Capita Annual Net Income of Rural Residents	位次 Order
全国总计	National Total	10870		6859.6		2366.40	
北 京	Beijing	19155	2	11577.8	2	5025.50	2
天 津	Tianjin	14308	6	8958.7	5	3947.72	4
河 北	Hebei	8730	24	5984.8	16	2603.60	9
山 西	Shanxi	8122	28	5391.1	28	1956.05	22
内蒙古	Inner Mongolia	8250	27	5535.9	23	1973.37	20
辽 宁	Liaoning	10145	13	5797.0	20	2557.93	10
吉 林	Jilin	8771	23	5340.5	30	2182.22	16
黑龙江	Heilongjiang	8910	22	5425.9	27	2280.28	13
上 海	Shanghai	21781	1	12883.5	1	5870.87	1
江 苏	Jiangsu	11842	9	7375.1	8	3784.71	5
浙 江	Zhejiang	16385	4	10464.7	3	4582.34	3
安 徽	Anhui	7908	31	5668.8	21	2020.04	18
福 建	Fujian	12013	8	8313.1	6	3380.72	7
江 西	Jiangxi	8026	29	5506.0	24	2231.60	14
山 东	Shandong	10008	14	7101.1	9	2804.51	8
河 南	Henan	7916	30	5267.4	31	2097.86	17
湖 北	Hubei	8619	25	5856.0	17	2352.16	11
湖 南	Hunan	9623	17	6780.6	11	2299.46	12
广 东	Guangdong	15682	5	10415.2	4	3769.79	6
广 西	Guangxi	9075	20	6665.7	13	1944.33	23
海 南	Hainan	8321	26	5838.8	19	2226.47	15
重 庆	Chongqing	9523	18	6721.1	12	1971.18	21
四 川	Sichuan	9934	16	6360.5	15	1986.99	19
贵 州	Guizhou	8991	21	5451.9	26	1411.73	30
云 南	Yunnan	10537	10	6797.7	10	1533.74	27
西 藏	Tibet	19144	3	7869.2	7	1404.01	31
陕 西	Shanxi	9120	19	5483.7	25	1490.80	29
甘 肃	Gansu	9949	15	5382.9	29	1508.61	28
青 海	Qinghai	12906	7	5853.7	18	1557.32	26
宁 夏	Ningxia	10442	11	5544.2	22	1823.05	24
新 疆	Xinjiang	10278	12	6395.0	14	1710.44	25

25

Twenty-Five

西部资料

Western Provinces

25－1 行政区划(一)(2001年底)
Divisions of Administrative Areas(1)

单位:个
(unit)

地区	Region	地级区划数 Unit at Prefectural Level	# 地级市 City at Prefectural Level	县级区划数 Unit at County Level	# 县级市 City at County Level	地县级市个数 Number of Cities at Prefectural and County Level	市辖区数 District under the Jurisdiction of City
全　国	**National Total**	**332**	**265**	**2053**	**393**	**658**	**808**
内蒙古	Inner Mongolia	12	7	82	13	20	19
广　西	Guangxi	14	9	81	10	19	28
重　庆	Chongqing			25	4	4	15
四　川	Sichuan	21	18	139	14	32	41
贵　州	**Guizhou**	**9**	**4**	**78**	**9**	**13**	**9**
云　南	Yunnan	16	5	119	10	15	9
西　藏	Tibet	7	1	72	1	2	1
陕　西	Shanxi	10	10	86	3	13	21
甘　肃	Gansu	14	6	75	8	14	11
青　海	Qinghai	8	1	39	2	3	4
宁　夏	Ningxia	4	4	16	2	6	8
新　疆	Xinjiang	14	2	85	17	19	11

25－2 行政区划(二)(2001年底) Divisions of Administrative Areas(2)

单位:个 (unit)

地区	Region	镇数 Town	乡数 Township	#民族乡 Ethnic Community Township	街道办事处 Urban Sub－district Office
全国	**National Total**	**20358**	**20012**	**1165**	**5972**
内蒙古	Inner Mongolia	496	731	17	178
广西	Guangxi	749	598	61	63
重庆	Chongqing	680	668	4	98
四川	Sichuan	1888	3165	107	197
贵州	**Guizhou**	**696**	**764**	**253**	**77**
云南	Yunnan	540	1006	183	39
西藏	Tibet	136	549	8	8
陕西	Shanxi	930	684	3	125
甘肃	Gansu	328	1216	40	108
青海	Qinghai	114	285	30	26
宁夏	Ningxia	79	234	1	31
新疆	Xinjiang	218	639	43	125

25－3 年底总人口
Total Population at The Year－end

单位：万人
(10000 persons)

地　区	Region	2000	2001
全国总计	**National Total**	**126583**	**127627**
内蒙古	Inner Mongolia	2376	2377
广　西	Guangxi	4489	4788
重　庆	Chongqing	3090	3097
四　川	Sichuan	8329	8640
贵　州	**Guizhou**	**3525**	**3799**
云　南	Yunnan	4288	4287
西　藏	Tibet	262	263
陕　西	Shanxi	3605	3659
甘　肃	Gansu	2562	2575
青　海	Qinghai	518	523
宁　夏	Ningxia	562	563
新　疆	Xinjiang	1925	1876

25－4 国内生产总值、增长速度和人均国内生产总值(2001)
GDP and It's Increase Rate and Per Capita GDP

单位:亿元
(100 million yuan)

地 区	Region	国内生产总值 GDP	第一产业 Primary Industry	第二产业 Secondary Industry	工 业 Industry	建筑业 Construction
全国总计	National Total	95933.3	14609.9	49069.1	42607.1	6462.0
内蒙古	Inner Mongolia	1545.5	361.3	624.4	507.0	117.4
广 西	Guangxi	2231.2	556.2	816.9	671.2	145.7
重 庆	Chongqing	1749.8	293.0	726.6	576.6	150.1
四 川	Sichuan	4421.8	981.7	1756.9	1407.8	349.0
贵 州	Guizhou	1084.9	274.2	419.7	335.0	86.6
云 南	Yunnan	2077.5	450.5	880.5	722.1	158.4
西 藏	Tibet					
陕 西	Shanxi	1841.2	280.5	815.7	604.9	210.8
甘 肃	Gansu	1074.9	207.0	482.5	356.3	126.2
青 海	Qinghai	300.8	41.1	132.6	89.2	43.4
宁 夏	Ningxia	298.1	49.5	134.8	102.0	32.8
新 疆	Xinjiang	1483.5	287.4	638.8	450.0	188.8

注：本表绝对数按当年价格计算,增长速度按可比价格计算。

Note: Absolute figures in this table are calculated at current prices, while indices are calculated at comparable prices.

25－4 续表(continued)

单位:亿元
(100 million yuan)

地　区	Region	第三产业 Tertiary Industry	#交通运输仓储邮电通信业 Transportation, Storage, Post and Telecommunications	#批发和零售贸易餐饮业 Wholesale Retail & Catering Trade	国内生产总值比上年增长(%) Increase Rate of GDP(%)	人均国内生产总值(元/人) Per Capita GDP (yuan/persor)
全国总计	**National Total**	**32254.3**	**5222.1**	**7823.5**	**7.3**	**7543**
内蒙古	Inner Mongolia	559.7	163.7	148.3	9.6	6458
广　西	Guangxi	858.1	178.0	301.3	8.2	4697
重　庆	Chongqing	730.1	109.7	168.1	9.0	5655
四　川	Sichuan	1683.2	313.8	474.8	9.2	5250
贵　州	**Guizhou**	**391.0**	**70.1**	**82.0**	**8.8**	**2865**
云　南	Yunnan	746.4	136.8	214.3	6.5	4872
西　藏	Tibet					
陕　西	Shanxi	745.0	183.5	124.9	9.1	5015
甘　肃	Gansu	385.3	56.6	123.0	9.4	4173
青　海	Qinghai	127.1	22.8	23.1	12.0	5732
宁　夏	Ningxia	113.8	21.0	23.6	10.1	5338
新　疆	Xinjiang	557.4	131.3	128.2	8.0	7898

25－5 国内生产总值构成(2001)

Composition of Gross Domestic Product

单位:%
(%)

地 区	Region	国内生产总值 GDP	第一产业 Primary Industry	第二产业 Secondary Industry	工 业 Industry	建筑业 Construction	第三产业 Tertiary Industry	#交通运输仓储邮电通信业 Transportation, Storage, Post and Telecommunications	#批发和零售贸易餐饮业 Wholesale Retail & Catering Trade
全国总计	**National Total**	**100.0**	**15.2**	**51.1**	**44.4**	**6.7**	**33.6**	**5.4**	**8.2**
内蒙古	Inner Mongolia	100.0	23.4	40.4	32.8	7.6	36.2	10.6	9.6
广 西	Guangxi	100.0	24.9	36.6	30.1	6.5	38.5	8.0	13.5
重 庆	Chongqing	100.0	16.7	41.5	33.0	8.6	41.7	6.3	9.6
四 川	Sichuan	100.0	22.2	39.7	31.8	7.9	38.1	7.1	10.7
贵 州	**Guizhou**	**100.0**	**25.3**	**39.0**	**31.0**	**8.0**	**35.7**	**6.5**	**7.6**
云 南	Yunnan	100.0	21.7	42.4	34.8	7.6	35.9	6.6	10.3
西 藏	Tibet	100.0							
陕 西	Shanxi	100.0	15.2	44.3	32.9	11.4	40.5	10.0	6.8
甘 肃	Gansu	100.0	19.3	44.9	33.2	11.7	35.8	5.3	11.4
青 海	Qinghai	100.0	13.7	44.1	29.7	14.4	42.3	7.6	7.7
宁 夏	Ningxia	100.0	16.6	45.2	34.2	11.0	38.2	7.0	7.9
新 疆	Xinjiang	100.0	19.4	43.1	30.3	12.7	37.6	8.9	8.6

注:本表按当年价格计算。

Note: Figures in this table are calculated at current prices.

25－6 就业人员（2001）
Employed Personnels

单位：万人
（10000 Persons）

地　区	Region	2000	2001
全国总计	**National Total**	**72085**	**73025**
内蒙古	Inner Mongolia	1017	1013
广　西	Guangxi	2530	2543
重　庆	Chongqing	1636	1624
四　川	Sichuan	4436	4415
贵　州	**Guizhou**	**2046**	**2068**
云　南	Yunnan	2295	2323
西　藏	Tibet	123	125
陕　西	Shanxi	1813	1785
甘　肃	Gansu	1182	1187
青　海	Qinghai	239	240
宁　夏	Ningxia	274	278
新　疆	Xinjiang	672	685

25-7 职 工 人 数(2001)
Number of Staff and Workers

单位:万人
(10000 persons)

地 区	Region	年末人数 Number of Staff and Workers at the Year-end	#国有单位 State-owned Unit	#集体单位 Collective-owned Unit	#股份合作单位 Share Holding Unit	#联营单位 Joint-owned Unit
全国总计	National Total	10792	7409	1241	147.3	43
内蒙古	Inner Mongolia	251	186	20	2.2	0.5
广 西	Guangxi	274	219	24	1.2	0.3
重 庆	Chongqing	201	135	24	3.6	3.9
四 川	Sichuan	487	351	58	5.6	1.1
贵 州	Guizhou	189	149	16	1.4	0.5
云 南	Yunnan	262	207	20	4.4	0.3
西 藏	Tibet	16	15	1	0.02	0.01
陕 西	Shanxi	324	258	27	3.1	0.3
甘 肃	Gansu	193	159	20	2.9	1.7
青 海	Qinghai	44	36	4	0.4	0.02
宁 夏	Ningxia	60	48	4	1	0.1
新 疆	Xinjiang	247	198	12	0.9	0.4

25－7 续表(continued)

单位:万人
(10000 persons)

地　区	Region	# 有限责任公司 Limited Liability Corporation	# 股份有限公司 Share Holding Corporations Ltd.	# 港澳台商投资单位 Economic Unit Funded by Entrepreneurs from Hongkong, Macao and Taiwan	# 外商投资单位 Foreign Funded Economic Unit
全国总计	**National Total**	**809.6**	**461.7**	**315.3**	**328.2**
内蒙古	Inner Mongolia	29	9.3	1.6	1.7
广　西	Guangxi	15.7	8.2	2.8	3.7
重　庆	Chongqing	20.3	9.9	2.1	2.6
四　川	Sichuan	35.2	29.1	2.3	3
贵　州	**Guizhou**	**16.8**	**4.1**	**0.7**	**1**
云　南	Yunnan	16.2	10.2	1.6	1.3
西　藏	Tibet	0.3	0.3		0.02
陕　西	Shanxi	21.8	10.4	1.5	2.2
甘　肃	Gansu	4.3	3.2	0.6	1.4
青　海	Qinghai	2	1.1	0.03	
宁　夏	Ningxia	4.5	1.9	0.3	0.8
新　疆	Xinjiang	26.1	8.8	0.9	0.5

25-8 国有及国有控股企业就业人员和劳动报酬(2001)

Number of Employed Personnels and Wages of State-owned or Controlling Share Hold Enterprises

单位:万人

(10000 persons)

地区	Region	就业人员 Employed Persons	#女性 Female	在岗职工 Staff and Workers on Their Posts
全国总计	National Total	5332.9	1893.3	5141.4
内蒙古	Inner Mongolia	122.2	42.7	120.4
广西	Guangxi	117.2	18.8	44.0
重庆	Chongqing	148.2	51.7	146.3
四川	Sichuan	220.6	77.8	212.1
贵州	Guizhou	94.4	30.3	87.9
云南	Yunnan	108	39.7	105.7
西藏	Tibet	16.8	5.8	15.5
陕西	Shanxi	164.5	57.6	160.3
甘肃	Gansu	117.8	42	114.8
青海	Qinghai	19.9	7	19.3
宁夏	Ningxia	30.9	11.2	30.2
新疆	Xinjiang	151.1	61.6	147.6

25－8 续表(continued)

单位:万元
(10000 yuan)

地 区	Region	就业人员劳动报酬 Wages of Employed Persons	在岗职工工资总额 Total Wages of Staff and Workers on Their Posts	在岗职工平均工资(元) Average Wages of Staff and Workers on Their Posts(yuan)
全国总计	**National Total**	**59368597**	**57663579**	**11014**
内蒙古	Inner Mongolia	1004843	992137	8112
广 西	Guangxi	310479	305429	6879
重 庆	Chongqing	1520420	1505392	10073
四 川	Sichuan	2308981	2226439	10237
贵 州	**Guizhou**	**865726**	**821348**	**9226**
云 南	Yunnan	1163563	1152700	10751
西 藏	Tibet	301075	291116	19453
陕 西	Shanxi	1530962	1501032	9286
甘 肃	Gansu	1205488	1189970	10251
青 海	Qinghai	275423	271716	13506
宁 夏	Ningxia	330862	324154	10615
新 疆	Xinjiang	1545058	1510457	9589

25－9 职工平均工资(2001)
Average Wages of Staff and Workers

单位:元
(yuan)

地 区	Region	平均工资 Average Wages	# 国有单位 State－owned Unit	# 集体单位 Collective－owned Unit	# 股份合作单位 Share Holding Unit	# 联营单位 Joint－owned Unit
全国总计	National Total	10870	11178	6867	8398	11887
内蒙古	Inner Mongolia	8250	8737	5525	4900	6353
广 西	Guangxi	9075	9209	6388	6926	7093
重 庆	Chongqing	9523	10035	6614	7572	9247
四 川	Sichuan	9934	10783	6575	7862	7568
贵 州	Guizhou	8991	9308	6218	7231	7059
云 南	Yunnan	10537	10880	7203	7927	10960
西 藏	Tibet	19144	20112	6236	12833	7868
陕 西	Shanxi	9120	9440	5293	5582	8015
甘 肃	Gansu	9949	10442	6728	5762	14133
青 海	Qinghai	12906	14028	6101	6257	3203
宁 夏	Ningxia	10442	11112	7166	7922	8807
新 疆	Xinjiang	10278	10145	8197	8335	9132

25－9 续表(continued)

单位:元
(yuan)

地 区	Region	#有限责任公司 Limited Liability Corporation	#股份有限公司 Share Holding corporations Ltd.	#港澳台商投资单位 Economic Unit Funded by Entrepreneurs from Hongkong, Macao and Taiwan	#外商投资单位 Foreign Funded Economic Unit
全国总计	**National Total**	**10993**	**12385**	**12544**	**16101**
内蒙古	Inner Mongolia	7896	7706	5396	6882
广 西	Guangxi	10763	10759	6637	10309
重 庆	Chongqing	8581	11033	10694	12903
四 川	Sichuan	8172	9124	10167	10408
贵 州	**Guizhou**	**8777**	**9631**	**9695**	**8871**
云 南	Yunnan	10016	11700	10965	13611
西 藏	Tibet	13546	12564		17877
陕 西	Shanxi	9450	10479	9788	13524
甘 肃	Gansu	7038	10647	9822	11911
青 海	Qinghai	9662	8490	5727	
宁 夏	Ningxia	8260	8449	6469	10797
新 疆	Xinjiang	10569	15617	10873	10153

25－10 财政收入情况
Statistics of Financial Revenue

单位:亿元
(100 million yuan)

地 区	Region	2000	2001
全国地方总计	National Total	6406.1	7803.3
内蒙古	Inner Mongolia	95.0	99.4
广 西	Guangxi	147.1	178.7
四 川	Chongqing	233.9	271.1
重 庆	Sichuan	87.2	106.1
贵 州	Guizhou	85.2	99.8
云 南	Yunnan	180.7	191.3
西 藏	Tibet	5.4	6.1
陕 西	Shanxi	115.0	135.8
甘 肃	Gansu	61.3	70.0
青 海	Qinghai	16.6	19.8
宁 夏	Ningxia	20.8	27.6
新 疆	Xinjiang	79.1	95.1

25－11 财政支出情况
Statistics of Financial Expenditure

单位:亿元
(100 million yuan)

地　区	Region	2000	2001
全国地方总计	National Total	10436.6	13134.6
内蒙古	Inner Mongolia	247.1	319.3
广　西	Guangxi	258.5	351.6
四　川	Chongqing	451.9	237.6
重　庆	Sichuan	187.6	594.1
贵　州	Guizhou	200.1	275.2
云　南	Yunnan	414.0	496.4
西　藏	Tibet	60.0	104.6
陕　西	Shanxi	271.6	350.1
甘　肃	Gansu	187.3	235.9
青　海	Qinghai	68.3	101.3
宁　夏	Ningxia	60.8	93.6
新　疆	Xinjiang	191.0	263.3

25－12 固定资产投资
Total Investment in Fixed Assets

单位:亿元
(100 million yuan)

地　区	Region	2000	2001
全国总计	**National Total**	**32917.7**	**36898.4**
内蒙古	Inner Mongolia	423.6	418.3
广　西	Guangxi	583.3	458.4
重　庆	Chongqing	572.6	568.5
四　川	Sichuan	1418.0	1169.4
贵　州	**Guizhou**	**397.0**	**413.4**
云　南	Yunnan	684.0	513.6
西　藏	Tibet	64.1	85.0
陕　西	Shanxi	653.7	632.3
甘　肃	Gansu	395.4	383.6
青　海	Qinghai	151.1	178.0
宁　夏	Ningxia	157.5	151.9
新　疆	Xinjiang	610.4	608.6

注:1.由于有不分地区项目,因此分地区相加不等于总计(以下分地区表同)。
2. 2000年数据不含城乡集体与个体。

Note:1. The numbers of the whole nation is not equal to the sum of each region.(same to next.)
2.The data in 2000 exclude urban and rural collective unit and individual person.

25－13 基本建设投资
Total Investment in Capital Construction

单位：亿元
(100 million yuan)

地　区	Region	2000	2001
全国总计	**National Total**	**13427.3**	**14567.0**
内蒙古	Inner Mongolia	229.4	268.8
广　西	Guangxi	267.5	307.6
重　庆	Chongqing	215.6	258.5
四　川	Sichuan	636.9	696.1
贵　州	**Guizhou**	**148.0**	**230.9**
云　南	Yunnan	341.9	321.0
西　藏	Tibet	54.7	75.3
陕　西	Shanxi	303.6	372.7
甘　肃	Gansu	208.3	232.1
青　海	Qinghai	99.0	133.8
宁　夏	Ningxia	86.2	102.1
新　疆	Xinjiang	392.8	389.0

25－14 更新改造投资
Total Investment in Innovation

单位:亿元
(100 million yuan)

地　区	Region	2000	2001
全国总计	**National Total**	**5107.6**	**5889.2**
内蒙古	Inner Mongolia	58.6	69.6
广　西	Guangxi	80.2	86.6
重　庆	Chongqing	89.9	105.6
四　川	Sichuan	173.9	196.4
贵　州	**Guizhou**	**93.3**	**102.7**
云　南	Yunnan	81.1	97.0
西　藏	Tibet	4.5	5.5
陕　西	Shanxi	135.2	133.1
甘　肃	Gansu	89.0	112.1
青　海	Qinghai	17.1	20.7
宁　夏	Ningxia	22.7	25.3
新　疆	Xinjiang	77.5	108.6

25 – 15 房地产开发企业(单位)完成投资额
Total Investment Completed of Real Estate Development Enterprises

单位:亿元
(100 million yuan)

地 区	Region	2000	2001
全国总计	National Total	4984.1	6245.5
内蒙古	Inner Mongolia	45.2	65.8
广 西	Guangxi	38.7	55.6
重 庆	Chongqing	139.6	196.7
四 川	Sichuan	196.0	266.2
贵 州	Guizhou	46.6	60.9
云 南	Yunnan	83.2	80.6
西 藏	Tibet	1.0	1.6
陕 西	Shanxi	78.9	99.2
甘 肃	Gansu	27.7	31.4
青 海	Qinghai	13.5	15.2
宁 夏	Ningxia	15.6	22.2
新 疆	Xinjiang	57.4	97.3

25－16 房地产开发企业(单位)住宅竣工面积
Completed Space of Tenement of Real Estate Development Enterprises

单位：万平方米
(10000 sq.m)

地　区	Region	2000	2001
全国总计	National Total	25104.9	27303.2
内蒙古	Inner Mongolia	412.9	448.7
广　西	Guangxi	226.7	330.7
重　庆	Chongqing	849.4	1020.6
四　川	Sichuan	1285.3	1713.2
贵　州	Guizhou	349.2	310.0
云　南	Yunnan	426.0	337.9
西　藏	Tibet	6.7	
陕　西	Shanxi	585.3	578.8
甘　肃	Gansu	187.1	188.9
青　海	Qinghai	74.3	87.9
宁　夏	Ningxia	155.5	150.5
新　疆	Xinjiang	330.1	567.7

25－17 房地产开发企业(单位)住宅销售面积
Sold Space of Tenement of Real Estate Development Enterprises

单位:万平方米
(10000 sq.m)

地　区	Region	2000	2001
全国总计	**National Total**	**18637.1**	**20779.2**
内蒙古	Inner Mongolia	293.8	309.8
广　西	Guangxi	191.4	296.7
重　庆	Chongqing	580.0	746.1
四　川	Sichuan	945.6	1307.1
贵　州	**Guizhou**	**251.7**	**257.4**
云　南	Yunnan	343.2	287.6
西　藏	Tibet	4.8	
陕　西	Shanxi	396.4	390.7
甘　肃	Gansu	123.0	110.5
青　海	Qinghai	39.9	23.6
宁　夏	Ningxia	104.5	113.5
新　疆	Xinjiang	262.5	364.3

25-18 建筑业主要效益指标(2001)
Main Benefit Indicators on Construction

地区	Region	企业个数(个) Number of Construction Enterprises (unit)	计算劳动生产率的平均人数(万人) Average Number of Person Used by Calculating Labor Productivity (10000 persons)	按建筑业总产值计算的劳动生产率(元/人) Labor Productivity Calculated at Gross Output Value of Construction (yuan/person)	人均竣工产值(元/人) Average Per Capita Output Value Completed (yuan/person)	人均施工面积(平方米) Average Per Capita Floor Space of Buildings under Construction (sq.m)	人均竣工面积(平方米) Average Per Capita Floor Space of Buildings Completed (sq.m)
全国总计	**National Total**	**48639**	**2001.9**	**69934**	**43809**	**83.4**	**39.1**
内蒙古	Inner Mongolia	955	28	58357	26306	40.2	22.3
广西	Guangxi	1179	7.30	39560	22560	53.7	18.3
重庆	Chongqing	1767	78.5	52148	32448	96.4	43
四川	Sichuan	3122	157.3	4938.3	36273	73.8	39.3
贵州	**Guizhou**	**684**	**24.4**	**52016**	**27627**	**79.4**	**30.6**
云南	Yunnan	1487	53	59241	48168	70.2	40.7
西藏	Tibet						
陕西	Shanxi	829	37.2	74265	39540	59.8	23.5
甘肃	Gansu	550	31.5	50800	34393	55.3	29.7
青海	Qinghai	248	8.3	54520	18829	37.9	14
宁夏	Ningxia	501	8.1	79680	46917	56.7	33.9
新疆	Xinjiang	677	25.1	101167	64285	93.0	43.2

25－19 居民消费价格分类指数(上年＝100)(2001)
Residents Consumer Price Indices(Preceding Year＝100)

地 区	Region	居民消费价格指数 Residents Consumer Price Index	食 品 Food	烟酒及用品 Tobacco and Liguor	衣 着 Clothing	家庭设备用品及服务 Household Appliances and Services
全 国	**National Total**	**100.7**	**100.0**	**99.7**	**98.1**	**97.7**
内蒙古	Inner Mongolia	100.6	101.8	99.2	97.7	99.0
广 西	Guangxi	100.6	98.5	99.2	96.3	97.0
重 庆	Chongqing	101.7	99.2	96.8	97.4	95.7
四 川	Sichuan	102.1	101.3	99.3	97.9	99.2
贵 州	**Guizhou**	**101.8**	**98.5**	**100.2**	**97.8**	**94.6**
云 南	Yunnan	99.1	98.3	98.9	96.3	98.5
西 藏	Tibet	100.1	99.3	99.6	101.1	99.4
陕 西	Shanxi	101.0	99.2	100.0	97.3	96.2
甘 肃	Gansu	104.0	100.0	100.0	99.9	98.2
青 海	Qinghai	102.6	102.2	98.6	99.4	96.2
宁 夏	Ningxia	101.6	100.1	97.9	99.4	97.4
新 疆	Xinjiang	104.0	104.3	98.8	98.7	100.2

25－19 续表(continued)

地 区	Region	医疗保健和个人用品 Health Care & Individual Goods	交通和通信 Transportation and Communication	娱乐教育文化 Recreational, Educational & Cultural	居 住 Housing
全 国	**National Total**	**100.0**	**99.0**	**106.6**	**101.2**
内蒙古	Inner Mongolia	98.1	98.4	102.0	103.7
广 西	Guangxi	97.7	98.7	112.6	100.4
重 庆	Chongqing	98.9	102.4	114.8	102.6
四 川	Sichuan	98.8	105.4	111.9	99.9
贵 州	**Guizhou**	**102.4**	**107.0**	**115.0**	**99.5**
云 南	Yunnan	106.2	92.5	98.6	101.6
西 藏	Tibet	100.1	103.6	98.7	101.3
陕 西	Shanxi	99.7	98.2	112.6	100.5
甘 肃	Gansu	98.3	103.6	123.2	102.8
青 海	Qinghai	98.6	102.4	115.3	101.2
宁 夏	Ningxia	99.8	100.6	112.4	102.5
新 疆	Xinjiang	116.1	105.2	101.6	102.6

25－20 城镇居民人均可支配收入
Urban Household Per Capita Disposable Income

单位:元
(yuan)

地　区	Region	2000	2001
全国总计	**National Total**	**6280.0**	**6859.6**
内蒙古	Inner Mongolia	5129.1	5535.9
广　西	Guangxi	5834.4	6665.7
重　庆	Chongqing	6276.0	6721.1
四　川	Sichuan	5894.3	6360.5
贵　州	**Guizhou**	**5122.2**	**5451.9**
云　南	Yunnan	6324.6	6797.7
西　藏	Tibet	7426.3	7869.2
陕　西	Shanxi	5124.2	5483.7
甘　肃	Gansu	4916.3	5382.9
青　海	Qinghai	5170.0	5853.7
宁　夏	Ningxia	4912.4	5544.2
新　疆	Xinjiang	5644.9	6395.0

25－21 农村居民人均纯收入
Per Capita Annual Average Net Income of Rural Households

单位:元
(yuan)

地 区	Region	2000	2001
全国总计	**National Total**	**2253.39**	**2366.40**
内蒙古	Inner Mongolia	2038.21	1973.37
广 西	Guangxi	1864.51	1944.33
重 庆	Chongqing	1892.44	1971.18
四 川	Sichuan	1903.60	1986.99
贵 州	**Guizhou**	**1374.16**	**1411.73**
云 南	Yunnan	1478.60	1533.74
西 藏	Tibet	1330.81	1404.01
陕 西	Shanxi	1443.86	1490.80
甘 肃	Gansu	1428.68	1508.61
青 海	Qinghai	1490.49	1557.32
宁 夏	Ningxia	1724.30	1823.05
新 疆	Xinjiang	1618.08	1710.44

25 – 22 农林牧渔业总产值和指数(2001)
Gross Output Value and Indices of Farming, Forestry, Animal Husbandry and Fishery

单位:亿元
(100 million yuan)

地区	Region	农林牧渔业总产值 Gross Output Value of Farming, Forestry, Animal Husbandry and Fishery	农业 Farming	林业 Forestry	牧业 Animal Husbandry	渔业 Fishery	农林牧渔业总产值指数(上年=100) Indices of Farming, Forestry, Animal Husbandry and Fishery (preceding year = 100)
全国总计	**National Total**	**26179.6**	**14462.8**	**938.8**	**7963.1**	**2815.0**	**104.2**
内蒙古	Inner Mongolia	555.9	307.6	26.1	216.2	6.0	102.0
广西	Guangxi	872.9	439.9	39.4	292.3	101.2	104.9
重庆	Chongqing	431.2	250.4	11.2	154.4	15.2	102.1
四川	Sichuan	1466.8	769.9	50.9	605.0	41.0	102.6
贵州	**Guizhou**	**418.6**	**279.9**	**15.1**	**118.5**	**5.1**	**101.2**
云南	Yunnan	703.5	431.3	47.2	210.6	14.4	103.6
西藏	Tibet	52.8	27.6	1.3	23.9	0.0	105.4
陕西	Shanxi	478.8	337.4	23.6	114.1	3.8	102.5
甘肃	Gansu	344.6	254.0	8.6	80.9	1.1	107.8
青海	Qinghai	63.3	28.9	1.8	32.5	0.1	105.2
宁夏	Ningxia	85.3	49.4	3.5	30.3	2.1	108.0
新疆	Xinjiang	496.8	348.8	10.1	134.0	3.9	104.5

25－23 主要农产品产量(2001)
Output of Major Farm Products

单位:万吨
(10000 tons)

地 区	Region	粮食 Grain	油料 Oil	糖料 Sugars	水果 Fruits
全国总计	National Total	45263.7	2864.8	7635.3	6225.1
内蒙古	Inner Mongolia	1239.1	80.6	141.3	21.4
广 西	Guangxi	1511.4	57.2	2937.9	360.1
重 庆	Chongqing	1023.5	30.0	9.1	81.7
四 川	Sichuan	2926.5	181.0	166.8	252.6
贵 州	Guizhou	1100.3	71.3	66.7	31.1
云 南	Yunnan	1486.3	27.7	1420.6	77.0
西 藏	Tibet	98.3	4.4		0.7
陕 西	Shanxi	976.6	37.5	1.8	493.8
甘 肃	Gansu	753.2	38.4	37.9	121.6
青 海	Qinghai	103.2	23.0	0.1	2.2
宁 夏	Ningxia	274.8	7.3	0.3	19.3
新 疆	Xinjiang	780.0	42.6	265.0	151.9

25 - 23 续表(continued)

单位:万吨
(10000 tons)

地 区	Region	猪肉 Pork	牛肉 Beef	羊肉 Mutton	奶类 Milk	水产品 Aquatic Products
全国总计	**National Total**	**4031.4**	**532.8**	**274.0**	**919.1**	**4381.3**
内蒙古	Inner Mongolia	76.6	21.8	31.8	83.0	7.6
广 西	Guangxi	206.8	9.8	2.5	1.7	247.8
重 庆	Chongqing	132.1	4.4	1.9	5.6	19.7
四 川	Sichuan	419.1	23.8	16.2	28.9	57.1
贵 州	**Guizhou**	**104.8**	**7.0**	**4.2**	**1.7**	**6.9**
云 南	Yunnan	172.6	12.8	5.8	14.7	18.0
西 藏	Tibet	0.8	8.5	5.7	20.4	
陕 西	Shanxi	60.9	7.9	5.4	63.9	6.3
甘 肃	Gansu	38.9	7.9	7.5	13.7	1.5
青 海	Qinghai	7.0	6.4	7.0	21.3	0.2
宁 夏	Ningxia	8.8	3.3	3.3	23.6	4.1
新 疆	Xinjiang	10.8	22.2	37.5	78.2	6.1

注:水产品总数包括水产品总公司 17.58 万吨。
Note: Amount of aquatic products include 175,800 tons obtained from aquatic products company.

25－24 全部国有及规模以上非国有工业企业工业增加值和增长速度

Gross Output Value and Its Increase Rate of All State－owned and Non－State－owned above Designated Size Industrial Enterprises

单位:亿元
(100 million yuan)

地　区	Region	工业增加值 Added Value of Industry		比上年增长(%) Increase Rate(%)
		2000	2001	
全国总计	**National Total**	**25394.8**	**26950.0**	**9.9**
内蒙古	Inner Mongolia	279.5	307.2	12.9
广　西	Guangxi	323.9	339.1	8.6
重　庆	Chongqing	283.7	333.0	11.7
四　川	Sichuan	662.4	776.1	13.0
贵　州	**Guizhou**	**217.0**	**235.9**	**9.8**
云　南	Yunnan	531.5	553.3	3.9
西　藏	Tibet	9.3	9.5	5.8
陕　西	Shanxi	411.2	455.0	9.7
甘　肃	Gansu	244.7	296.5	11.5
青　海	Qinghai	65.3	71.6	11.2
宁　夏	Ningxia	73.7	82.6	9.2
新　疆	Xinjiang	356.6	358.3	7.4

注:1.本表绝对数按当年价格计算,增长速度按可比价格计算。

2.规模以上非国有企业为年产品销售收入500万元以上的企业。

Note:1.Absolute figures in this table are calculated at current prices,while indices are calculated at comparable prices.

2.Non－state－owned above designated size industrial enterprises refere to the enterprises that revenue of products sales above 5000000 yuan.

25－25 全部国有及规模以上非国有工业企业主要经济指标(2001)

Major Economic Indicators of All State－owned and Non－State－owned above Designated Size Industrial Enterprises

单位:亿元
(100 million yuan)

地　区	Region	产品销售收入 Sales Revenue	#产品销售成本 Sales Cost	#产品销售费用 Sales Expense	#产品销售税金及附加 Taxes and Sales Extra Changes	税金总额 Total Taxes	利润总额 Total Profits
全国总计	**National Total**	**92278.0**	**75690.0**	**3401.8**	**1554.5**	**5429.0**	**4657.2**
内蒙古	Inner Mongolia	797.5	644.7	39.5	12.7	58.8	20.4
广　西	Guangxi	1016.7	808.8	40.9	19.4	84.5	37.3
重　庆	Chongqing	1057.9	859.2	53.1	23.1	75.3	21.8
四　川	Sichuan	2274.0	1775.0	121.7	52.1	166.7	84.6
贵　州	**Guizhou**	**630.4**	**475.6**	**29.1**	**33.3**	**72.9**	**16.9**
云　南	Yunnan	1123.2	722.8	35.4	172.2	263.0	81.1
西　藏	Tibet	11.7	8.1	1.1	0.3	1.3	0.9
陕　西	Shanxi	1256.1	957.5	52.2	33.3	98.9	60.4
甘　肃	Gansu	818.8	674.8	21.4	23.2	64.4	7.1
青　海	Qinghai	189.8	146.3	5.2	2.8	15.6	4.8
宁　夏	Ningxia	266.8	227.5	7.7	3.3	15.5	3.8
新　疆	Xinjiang	848.8	624.5	20.6	22.7	70.9	90.3

25－26 全部国有及规模以上非国有工业企业主要经济效益指标(2001)
Major Economic Benefit Indicators of State－owned and Non－State－owned above Designated Size Industrial Enterprises

地 区	Region	综合指数(%) Synthetical Index(%)	总资产贡献率(%) Ratio of Total Assets to Industrial Output Value(%)	资本保值增值率(%) Ratio of Capital Hold and Rise(%)	资产负债率(%) Assets－debt Ratio(%)
全国总计	National Total	122.1	9.3	113.0	59.4
内蒙古	Inner Mongolia	90.6	6.0	113.6	58.6
广 西	Guangxi	102.2	7.9	111.4	66.1
重 庆	Chongqing	94.6	6.7	115.1	64.2
四 川	Sichuan	99.5	7.2	111.9	62.6
贵 州	Guizhou	92.4	7.1	131.9	64.4
云 南	Yunnan	150.1	16.2	115.4	53.7
西 藏	Tibet	113.4	6.7	163.0	23.5
陕 西	Shanxi	102.2	7.5	116.1	65.4
甘 肃	Gansu	75.4	5.3	110.7	65.3
青 海	Qinghai	80.7	4.9	107.0	71.0
宁 夏	Ningxia	81.8	5.2	110.3	59.4
新 疆	Xinjiang	143.3	10.4	105.7	63.4

25－26 续表(continued)

地 区	Region	流动资产周转次数(次) Turnover of Total Circulating Funds(time)	成本费用利润率(%) After－tax Profits/Cost(%)	全员劳动生产率(元/人) Total Labor Productivity (yuan/person)	产品销售率(%) Sales Rate of Industrial Products(%)
全国总计	**National Total**	**1.6**	**5.4**	**46315**	**97.7**
内蒙古	Inner Mongolia	1.3	2.6	27296	97.9
广 西	Guangxi	1.4	3.9	34016	96.9
重 庆	Chongqing	1.2	2.1	37905	99.2
四 川	Sichuan	1.2	3.9	33755	98.0
贵 州	**Guizhou**	**0.9**	**2.9**	**30060**	**95.1**
云 南	Yunnan	1.2	9.2	53332	99.7
西 藏	Tibet	0.7	8.2	28994	88.3
陕 西	Shanxi	1.1	5.2	31193	97.0
甘 肃	Gansu	1.1	0.9	20703	97.0
青 海	Qinghai	0.8	2.7	28766	96.1
宁 夏	Ningxia	1.2	1.5	24869	97.0
新 疆	Xinjiang	1.4	12.4	41041	99.0

25－27 主要工业产品产量(2001)
Output of Major Industrial Products

单位:万吨
(10000 tons)

地 区	Region	原煤 Coal	水泥 Cement	农用化肥 Chemical Fertilizer
全国总计	**National Total**	**110700.0**	**64000.0**	**3396.5**
内蒙古	Inner Mongolia	7422.2	636.2	35.0
广 西	Guangxi	613.5	2140.5	73.8
重 庆	Chongqing	1154.7	1511.2	77.6
四 川	Sichuan	2159.8	2816.6	282.8
贵 州	**Guizhou**	**3731.4**	**920.0**	**86.8**
云 南	Yunnan	1111.8	1534.0	194.8
西 藏	Tibet	2.5	49.6	
陕 西	Shanxi	4531.9	1110.2	97.3
甘 肃	Gansu	1795.4	885.1	45.0
青 海	Qinghai	169.0	166.0	79.4
宁 夏	Ningxia	1551.1	311.2	69.2
新 疆	Xinjiang	1458.2	930.6	70.2

25－27 续表(continued)

单位:万吨
(10000 tons)

地　区	Region	发电量(亿千瓦小时) Electricity (100 million kwh)	钢 Steel	生铁 Pig Iron	成品钢材 Steel Products
全国总计	**National Total**	**14780.0**	**15266.1**	**14541.0**	**15745.4**
内蒙古	Inner Mongolia	463.7	453.6	474.6	381.7
广　西	Guangxi	292.3	128.5	152.1	140.4
重　庆	Chongqing	170.4	185.0	174.7	161.4
四　川	Sichuan	583.6	690.8	601.0	629.0
贵　州	**Guizhou**	**480.3**	**147.0**	**149.5**	**138.6**
云　南	Yunnan	340.4	219.6	318.6	181.0
西　藏	Tibet	7.0			
陕　西	Shanxi	303.5	69.4	71.6	64.2
甘　肃	Gansu	285.7	236.6	220.7	225.6
青　海	Qinghai	137.8	44.3		36.3
宁　夏	Ningxia	150.3		5.4	0.4
新　疆	Xinjiang	180.4	127.5	111.4	127.8

25－28　全社会旅客周转量
Total Passenger－Kilometers

单位:亿人公里
(100 million passenger－km)

地　区	Region	2000	2001	#铁 路 Railways	#公 路 Highways	#水 运 Waterways
全国总计	**National Total**	**12261.0**	**13155.2**	**4766.8**	**7207.1**	**89.9**
内蒙古	Inner Mongolia	200.1	209.3	87.4	121.9	…
广　西	Guangxi	451.5	475.2	100.5	372.1	2.6
重　庆	Chongqing	242.7	250.0	40.5	183.7	25.8
四　川	Sichuan	496.8	530.5	143.2	383.5	3.8
贵　州	Guizhou	238.4	251.1	124.2	125.8	1.1
云　南	Yunnan	205.5	269.2	35.6	232.8	0.8
西　藏	Tibet	4.1	5.3		5.3	
陕　西	Shanxi	331.1	358.6	192.6	165.6	0.4
甘　肃	Gansu	226.0	249.5	171.6	77.8	0.2
青　海	Qinghai	29.7	33.0	13.4	19.6	
宁　夏	Ningxia	52.1	51.4	18.0	33.4	
新　疆	Xinjiang	186.8	215.0	85.0	130.0	

25 – 29 全社会货物周转量
Total Ton – kilometers

单位:亿吨公里
(100 million ton – km)

地 区	Region	2000	2001	#铁 路 Railways	#公 路 Highways	#水 运 Waterways
全国总计	**National Total**	**44452.3**	**47590.0**	**14575.0**	**6330.0**	**25989.0**
内蒙古	Inner Mongolia	943.2	985.0	765.0	220.0	
广 西	Guangxi	707.0	736.0	441.0	212.0	83.0
重 庆	Chongqing	289.0	322.0	111.0	76.0	135.0
四 川	Sichuan	622.9	675.0	472.0	191.0	12.0
贵 州	**Guizhou**	**404.1**	**439.0**	**365.0**	**70.0**	**4.0**
云 南	Yunnan	481.9	516.0	196.0	318.0	1.0
西 藏	Tibet	13.5	17.0		17.0	
陕 西	Shanxi	573.0	676.0	516.0	160.0	…
甘 肃	Gansu	639.5	679.0	565.0	114.0	…
青 海	Qinghai	86.6	97.0	59.0	38.0	
宁 夏	Ningxia	205.2	223.0	165.0	58.0	
新 疆	Xinjiang	457.3	495.0	319.0	177.0	

25－30 社会消费品零售总额(2001)
Total Retail Sales of Consumer Goods

单位:亿元
(100 million yuan)

地区	Region	按销售单位所在地分			按行业分
		市 City	县 County	县以下 Below County Level	批发零售贸易业 Wholesales and Retail Sales Trade
全国总计	National Total	21110.3	4217.2	8825.1	23042.3
内蒙古	Inner Mongolia	288.4	117.1	78.5	314.5
广西	Guangxi	416.4	176.4	266.4	590.9
重庆	Chongqing	361.6	88.9	192.9	383.2
四川	Sichuan	713.1	271.2	539.4	885.3
贵州	Guizhou	197.4	66.8	79.5	232.4
云南	Yunnan	309.3	139.1	134.8	376.5
西藏	Tibet	16.3	18.5	8.1	33.9
陕西	Shanxi	400.7	103.1	103.8	380.7
甘肃	Gansu	234.0	57.5	71.2	235.2
青海	Qinghai	50.7	19.8	11.6	56.9
宁夏	Ningxia	58.9	16.6	14.7	54.0
新疆	Xinjiang	233.7	65.1	75.7	242.3

25－30 续表(continued)

单位:亿元
(100 million yuan)

地区	Region	按行业分			
		餐饮业 Catering Trade	其他行业 Others	# 制造业 Manufacturing	# 农业生产者 Farm Producers
全国总计	**National Total**	**3752.6**	**7357.7**	**2191.8**	**4035.8**
内蒙古	Inner Mongolia	48.1	121.4	34.7	66.1
广西	Guangxi	96.3	172.0	44.1	109.0
重庆	Chongqing	54.6	205.6	38.3	15.5
四川	Sichuan	222.4	416.0	89.9	275.8
贵州	**Guizhou**	**42.3**	**69.0**	**18.0**	**43.1**
云南	Yunnan	74.9	131.8	27.0	90.0
西藏	Tibet	4.2	4.8	1.8	2.1
陕西	Shanxi	63.1	163.8	52.5	97.9
甘肃	Gansu	46.6	80.9	16.7	46.4
青海	Qinghai	11.3	13.9	3.6	8.1
宁夏	Ningxia	10.9	25.3	3.7	19.9
新疆	Xinjiang	38.2	94.0	22.0	51.2

25－31 外商投资企业进出口商品总值
Total Imports and Exports of Foreign－funded Enterprises

单位：万美元
（USD 10000）

地 区	Region	2000	出口额 Exports	进口额 Imports	2001	出口额 Exports	进口额 Imports
全国总计	**National Total**	**23671390**	**11944121**	**11727269**	**25909797**	**13323506**	**12586290**
内蒙古	Inner Mongolia	18156	13798	4358	17852	12894	4958
广 西	Guangxi	55340	34112	21228	46242	24353	21889
重 庆	Chongqing	32389	9666	22723	31346	9228	22118
四 川	Sichuan	61524	24517	37007	66734	23997	42737
贵 州	**Guizhou**	**5690**	**4012**	**1678**	**6325**	**4423**	**1902**
云 南	Yunnan	19658	8113	11545	21190	10952	10238
西 藏	Tibet	634	389	245	236	217	19
陕 西	Shanxi	35435	11612	23823	36600	10808	25792
甘 肃	Gansu	5657	3833	1824	8910	5294	3616
青 海	Qinghai	925	202	723	2328	154	2174
宁 夏	Ningxia	6125	4294	1831	7443	5904	1539
新 疆	Xinjiang	11559	9120	2439	9579	5877	3702

25－32 外商实际直接投资额
Total Directly Actual Investment of Foreigner

单位：万美元
(USD 10000)

地　区	Region	2000	2001
全国总计	**National Total**	**4071481**	**4687759**
内蒙古	Inner Mongolia	10568	10703
广　西	Guangxi	52466	38416
重　庆	Chongqing	24436	25649
四　川	Sichuan	43694	58188
贵　州	**Guizhou**	**2501**	**2829**
云　南	Yunnan	12812	6457
陕　西	Shanxi	28842	35174
甘　肃	Gansu	6235	7439
青　海	Qinghai		3649
宁　夏	Ningxia	1741	1680
新　疆	Xinjiang	1911	2035

注：全国总计中包括部门统计数据，故各地区相加不等于全国总计。

Note: The numbers of the whole nation were not equal to the sum of each region, because numbers of the whole nation included the statistics of department.

25-33 国际旅游接待情况
Operating Status of International Tourism

地 区	Region	2001 旅游人数（万人次）Number of Tourists (10000 person-times)	2001 #外国人 Foreigners	2001 旅游创汇总额（亿美元）Total Amount of Foreign Exchange Earnings (USD 100 million)	2000 旅游人数（万人次）Number of Tourists (10000 person-times)	2000 #外国人 Foreigners	2000 旅游创汇总额（亿美元）Total Amount of Foreign Exchange Earnings (USD 100 million)
全国总计	National Total	8901.0	1122.4	177.90	8344.4	1016.0	162.2
内蒙古	Inner Mongolia	40.00	39.60	1.40	39.19	38.74	1.26
广 西	Guangxi	126.70	55.00	3.00	122.91	50.80	3.07
重 庆	Chongqing	31.30	21.90	1.60	26.61	19.29	1.38
四 川	Sichuan	57.50	28.10	1.70	46.20	19.97	1.22
贵 州	Guizhou	20.50	7.90	0.70	18.39	7.12	0.61
云 南	Yunnan	113.10	69.60	3.70	100.11	66.59	3.39
西 藏	Tibet	12.70	11.60	0.50	15.00	13.58	0.52
陕 西	Shanxi	75.90	63.80	3.10	71.28	58.48	2.80
甘 肃	Gansu	22.30	14.60	0.40	21.31	14.34	0.55
青 海	Qinghai	4.00	1.80	0.10	3.26	1.46	0.07
宁 夏	Ningxia	0.90	0.60	0.03	0.78	0.58	0.03
新 疆	Xinjiang	27.3	21.90	1.00	25.61	20.84	0.95

25－34 各类学校基本情况(2001)
Basic Statistics in Various Schools

单位:万人
(10000 persons)

地 区 Region	招收研究生(人) Postgraduates (person)	普通高校招收本专科生 Undergraduate Entering Regular Institutions of Higher Education	普通高校在校本专科生 Undergraduate Enrollment in Regular Institutions of Higher Education	普通中学在校生 Students Enrollment in Regular Secondary Schools	小学在校生 Students Enrollment in Primary Schools	小学学龄儿童入学率(%) School－Age Children Enrollment Rate(%)
全国总计 National Total	170000	268	719	7919	12543.5	95.5
内蒙古 Inner Mongolia	904	4.05	9.96	150.72	189.35	98.36
广 西 Guangxi	1547	5.85	15.16	292.96	525.29	98.4
重 庆 Chongqing	3400	6.10	16.16	154.03	277.78	99.8
四 川 Sichuan	7617	12.00	31.70	428.30	794.90	99.1
贵 州 Guizhou	659	4.46	10.82	184.60	490.17	98.2
云 南 Yunnan		4.25	11.90	200.46	465.50	
西 藏 Tibet		0.24	0.68	7.17	31.20	87.2
陕 西 Shanxi	11000	11.60	31.70	254.7	461.60	98.4
甘 肃 Gansu			11.09	146.00	318.98	98.0
青 海 Qinghai	74	0.70	1.79	24.46	50.17	95.4
宁 夏 Ningxia	122	0.85	2.28	33.48	65.11	96.8
新 疆 Xinjiang	827	4.14	10.81	122.86	243.57	97.4

25－35 文化艺术事业基本情况(2001)
Basic Statistics of Culture and Art

单位:个
(unit)

地　区 Region	各种艺术表演团体 Various Art Troupes	文化馆 Culture Centers	公共图书馆 Public Libraries	博物馆 Museums	广播人口覆盖率(%) Listener Rating(%)	电视人口覆盖率(%) Viewer Rating(%)
全国总计 National Total	2621	2899	2689	1394	92.9	94.1
内蒙古 Inner Mongolia	116	104	108	25	88.1	83.5
广　西 Guangxi	118	98	94	40	86.2	91.00
重　庆 Chongqing						
四　川 Sichuan	90	172	131	52	93.7	94.5
贵　州 Guizhou	28	85	90	9	78.3	87.2
云　南 Yunnan	129	128	148	30	89.00	90.0
西　藏 Tibet	25	51			81.7	80.1
陕　西 Shanxi	118	111		98	90.6	92.5
甘　肃 Gansu	77	83	91	64	88.5	88.2
青　海 Qinghai	14	43	38	12	80.5	87.8
宁　夏 Ningxia	14	25	21	5	85.6	87.4
新　疆 Xinjiang	88	92	81	24	91.27	90.93

25－36 出版、卫生事业基本情况(2001)
Basic Statistics of Publishing and Health Care

地区 Region	出版图书(万册) Publishing Books (10000 copies)	杂志(万册) Magazines (10000 copies)	报纸(亿份) Newspapers (100 million copies)	卫生机构床位(万张) Number of Beds of Health Institution (10000 beds)	各类卫生技术人员(万人) Medical Technical Personnels (10000 persons)	# 医生(万人) Doctors (10000 persons)
全国总计 National Total	**630000**	**290000**	**216**	**319**	**449**	**209**
内蒙古 Inner Mongolia	6844	1567	1.76	6.67	12.46	4.95
广西 Guangxi	22200	5500	5.97	8.56	12.79	6.13
重庆 Chongqing	11300	3300	5.48	6.50	8.64	4.47
四川 Sichuan	25500	5947	14.3	19.00	24.90	13.10
贵州 Guizhou	12696	1210	3.17	5.91	7.36	3.84
云南 Yunnan				9.98	12.3	6.23
西藏 Tibet	461	77	0.37	0.64	0.88	0.51
陕西 Shanxi	17500	5175	6.90	9.90	13.50	6.60
甘肃 Gansu	7000		1.37	6.03	8.00	3.80
青海 Qinghai	587.52	110.33	0.75	1.65	1.83	0.85
宁夏 Ningxia	2520	172	0.68	1.44	2.24	1.05
新疆 Xinjiang	7550	1100	2.95	7.09	9.75	4.54

25－37 全部金融机构存贷款(2001)

Saving Deposits and Loans of Financial Institutions

单位:亿元
(100 million yuan)

地 区 Region	存款余额 Saving Deposits	比上年增减(%) Increase(Decrease) Rate in 2001 over 2000	城乡居民储蓄余额 Saving Deposits of Urban and Rural Household	比上年增减(%) Increase(Decrease) Rate in 2001 over 2000	贷款余额 Loan	比上年增减(%) Increase(Decrease) Rate in 2001 over 2000
全国总计 National Total	143167	14.4	73762	14.7	112314	11.6
内蒙古 Inner Mongolia	1498.79	18.2	986.73	12.7	1470.75	9.7
广 西 Guangxi	2518.94	11	1538.95	12.0	1764.05	9.1
重 庆 Chongqing	2294.05	20.4	1317.17	21.3	1871.98	15.6
四 川 Sichuan	5256.00	16.5	3123.40	16.0	4498.60	11.0
贵 州 Guizhou	1341.11	21.2	641.67	18.9	1212.23	13.8
云 南 Yunnan	2779.71	12.7	1295.53	13.8	2173.45	9.3
西 藏 Tibet	212.90	46.8	50.18	24.0	96.62	19.8
陕 西 Shanxi	3205.00	20.4	1768.00	16.2	2538.0	13.8
甘 肃 Gansu	1615.73	15.4	920.71	12.8	1268.39	8.3
青 海 Qinghai	391.06	26.8	188.53	18.5	422.03	15.3
宁 夏 Ningxia	468.57	18.2	257.97		441.39	15.2
新 疆 Xinjiang	1972.55	5.8	994.0	9.4	1584.73	12.9

中国统计出版社最新资料书简目

中国统计年鉴–2002
中国统计摘要–2002
2002 中国发展报告
中国城市统计年鉴–2001
中国农村统计年鉴–2002
中国劳动统计年鉴–2002
中国人口统计年鉴–2002
中国社会统计资料–2001
中国工业经济统计年鉴–2001
中国市场统计年鉴–2002
2001 中国城市发展报告
中国建筑业统计年鉴–2001
中国价格及城镇居民家庭收支调查统计年鉴–2002
国际统计年鉴–2002
中国西部统计年鉴–2001
中国对外经济贸易统计年鉴–2001
中国商品交易市场统计年鉴–2001
中国基本单位统计年鉴–2001
中国食品工业年鉴–2001
中国民政统计年鉴–2002
如何使用统计年鉴
中国市民的经济观
北京统计年鉴–2002
天津统计年鉴–2002
河北经济年鉴–2002
山西统计年鉴–2002
内蒙古统计年鉴–2002
辽宁统计年鉴–2002
吉林统计年鉴–2002
黑龙江统计年鉴–2002
上海统计年鉴–2002
江苏统计年鉴–2002
浙江统计年鉴–2002
安徽统计年鉴–2002
福建统计年鉴–2002
江西统计年鉴–2002
山东统计年鉴–2002
河南统计年鉴–2002
湖北统计年鉴–2002
湖南统计年鉴–2002
广东统计年鉴–2002
广西统计年鉴–2002
贵州统计年鉴–2002
云南统计年鉴–2002

海南统计年鉴–2002
四川统计年鉴–2002
重庆统计年鉴–2002
西藏统计年鉴–2002
陕西统计年鉴–2002
甘肃年鉴–2002
青海统计年鉴–2002
宁夏统计年鉴–2002
新疆统计年鉴–2002
新疆生产建设兵团统计年鉴–2002
石家庄统计年鉴–2002
唐山统计年鉴–2002
保定统计年鉴–2002
邯郸统计年鉴–2002
张家口统计年鉴–2002
伊克昭盟统计年鉴–2002
太原统计年鉴–2002
临汾年鉴–2002
呼和浩特经济统计年鉴–2002
沈阳年鉴–2002
大连统计年鉴–2002
吉林市社会经济统计年鉴–2002
四平统计年鉴–2002
延吉统计年鉴–2002
哈尔滨统计年鉴–2002
齐齐哈尔经济统计年鉴–2002
黑龙江垦区统计年鉴–2002
牡丹江统计年鉴–2002
上海浦东新区统计年鉴–2002
连云港统计年鉴–2002
南京统计年鉴–2002
苏州统计年鉴–2002
无锡统计年鉴–2002
常州统计年鉴–2002
徐州统计年鉴–2002
南通统计年鉴–2002
盐城统计年鉴–2002
杭州统计年鉴–2002
宁波统计年鉴–2002
绍兴统计年鉴–2002
台州统计年鉴–2002
舟山统计年鉴–2002
温州统计年鉴–2002
福州年鉴–2002

厦门经济特区年鉴–2002
福州经济技术开发区年鉴–2002
南昌统计年鉴–2002
九江统计年鉴–2002
河池地区年鉴–2002
青岛统计年鉴–2002
天水统计年鉴–2002
泰安统计年鉴–2002
昆明统计年鉴–2002
济南统计年鉴–2002
郑州统计年鉴–2002
洛阳统计年鉴–2002
十堰统计年鉴–2002
三门峡统计年鉴–2002
平顶山统计年鉴–2002
南阳经济统计年鉴–2002
武汉统计年鉴–2002
宜昌统计年鉴–2002
广州统计年鉴–2002
深圳统计信息年鉴–2002
惠州统计年鉴–2002
珠海统计年鉴–2002
东莞统计年鉴–2002
南宁统计年鉴–2002
南宁地区统计年鉴–2002
桂林经济社会统计年鉴–2002
柳州经济统计年鉴–2002
柳州地区统计年鉴–2002
贵阳统计年鉴–2002
海口统计年鉴–2002
成都统计年鉴–2002
广安统计年鉴–2002
攀枝花统计年鉴–2002
西安统计年鉴–2002
兰州年鉴–2001
西宁统计年鉴–2002
乌鲁木齐统计年鉴–2002
巴音郭楞统计年鉴–2002
吐鲁番统计年鉴–2002
石河子统计年鉴–2002
庆阳年鉴–2002
银川统计年鉴–2002

编辑部电话：(010) 63262276 63266600–30607
欲购以上图书请与中国统计出版社发行部联系。电话(010) 63459084 同楫行书店电话：68585978
通讯地址：北京市西城区三里河月坛南街 75 号。邮政编码：100826

开拓进取中的省公安厅出入境管理局

Creative and advancing Exit and Entry Administration of Public Security Bureau of Guizhou Province

省公安厅出入境管理局与贵州神奇集团开展警民共建活动
The Administration held cooperating construction of police and citizen with Guizhou Shenqi Group

贵州省公安厅出入境管理局，下设秘书科、公民出国出境科、境外人员管理科、案件查处科、制证科，在编民警17人。主要负责中国公民因私出国事务管理，外国人入出境、居留事务管理，内地居民因私往来港澳地区和港澳居民来往内地事务管理，大陆居民往来台湾地区和台湾居民来往大陆事务管理，入籍、退籍、复籍等国籍事务管理，打击非法移民活动，查处违反出入境管理法律、法规的违法犯罪活动，承担制作签发出国境证件，因私出入境中介机构审批和管理、公安外事工作等任务。

随着我国加入世界贸易组织和全省西部大开发的纵深发展，贵州省出入境管理工作大幅度增长，2001年全省公民因私出国（境）量达21700余人次，比上一年增长23%，为1992年成立出入境管理处之初2018人次的11倍；2001年来黔境外人员为81700余人次，比上一年增长48%，为1992年5600余人次的15倍。

该局在简化手续、警务公开、为民服务等方面走在全国先进行列，成为贵州省公安机关为人民群众服务的重要窗口。

The Exit and Entry Administration of Public Security Bureau of Guizhou Province has set Secretary Department, Exit and Entry Department, Administrative Department of Emigrant, Investigation Department, License Department. The Administration has registered staff of 17 policemen. The Administration mainly deals with exit affairs of Chinese citizens for private reasons, entry affairs of foreigners, Management of residence, intercoursebetween HongKong Macao areas and mainland, intercourse between Taiwan and mainland, nationality affairs of naturalization, with draw and restitution, striking illegal immigration, investigation of activities contrary to exit and entry laws, signing and issuing of political view for exit, examination and management of private exit and entry agents, foreign affairs of public security, Etc.

With further development of China's Joining in WTO and the West Developing, works of the Administration has been increased greatly. The total amount of exit of the province in 2001 was 21700, 23% more than last year and 11 times of that of 1992 when the Administration was founded, which was 2018. The total amount of entry of the province in 2001 was over 81700, 48% more than last year and 15 times of that of 1992, which was 5600.

The Administration steps in the front of the country in the field of simplifying process, publicizing police work, serving the people. It is an important window of public security organizations of the province to serve the people.

不断提高科技管理水平，认真制作出国（境）证照
Keep raising the standard of technology and management, make exit license carefully

出入境管理局民警热情接待申请群众
Policemen of the Administration were receiving applicants warmly

——全面推动消防工作跨越式发展的

Fire controlling work is fully developed at leaping speed by

贵州省公安消防总队

General Public Security & Fire Brigade of Guizhou Province

省委书记钱运录(中)率四大班子领导到消防总队慰问时与省消防总队政委江建民（右一）、总队长张高潮（左一）合影

The Secretary of the Provincial Party Committee,Qian Yunlu (the middle) expressed regards to the General Fire Brigade. Jiang Jianmin, the chief of political affaires of the General Fire Brigade (the first from right). Zhang Gaochao, the head of the General Fire Brigade(the first from left).

省委常委、副省长王正福深入公众聚集场所检查消防工作

Wang Zhengfu, the member of the standing committee of the provincial Party Committee & Vice-governor of the province, was inspecting fire works in public places.

2001年，全省公安消防部队在省委、省政府的领导下，紧紧围绕贵州西部大开发和富民兴黔战略，按照总队制定的“一二三四”的基本思路，依靠党委政府对消防工作的关心重视，消防安全责任制全面落实，城市公共消防设施建设进展较快，农村火灾得到明显控制，社会消防安全意识普遍提高，灭火救援能力和教育管理能力得到了明显的提高，部队正规化建设取得了新成效，保持了火灾稳定和部队稳定，受到省政府的通令嘉奖。

2001年，全省共发生火灾719起，每万人火灾发生率仅为0.19起，直接经济损失1945万元，人均火灾损失仅0.52元，远远低于全国平均水平。全年抢救财产价值2750.2万元，保护财产价值上亿元，为贵州经济发展和社会稳定作出了突出贡献。

苦练精兵，严阵以待，随时做好灭大火打恶仗的战斗准备

Makes preparation for fire prevention and hard battles.

消防部队为提高抢险救援能力，利用现代化消防装备开展实战演练

In order to improve rescue ability, fire departments were holding fire drills with modern fire equipment.

In 2001, led by the Provincial Party Committee and Government, the Public Security & Fire Brigades of the province work closely around the strategy of the West Developing and building the Province. According to the proceeding route of “one two three four”, the Brigade conducted the system of security responsibility thoroughly with the attention and concern of the Party Committee and Government. The public fire equipment construction has been improved fast. Fires in rural area have been tangibly controlled. Fire and Security consciousness of the society has been improved a lot. Capabilities of rescue and management have been obviously improved. The Brigade has made new achievement in standard construction of the troops. The Brigade has kept stability in fire disaster and the troops, which was praised by the provincial government.

There are 719 fires happened in 2001 of the Province. The occurrence rate of fires per 10 thousand people is 0.19. The directly financial loss is 19.45 million yuan. The financial loss per person is just 0.52 yuan, which is much less than the average level of the nation. The property that was rescued of the year is worth of 27.502 million yuan. And the property that was protected is worth of more than 100 million yuan. The Brigade has made great contributions to economy development and society’s steadiness of Guizhou Province.

贵州省公安厅交通警察总队

General Traffic Police Troop of Public Security Bureau of Guizhou Province

省委常委、副省长王正福，省政法委书记、省公安厅厅长姜延虎在贵阳客车站参加春运交通安全宣传活动并发表电视讲话

Wang Zhengfu, the member of the Standing Committee of the provincial Party Committee and the vice-governor of the province, and Jiang Yanhu, the Secretary of the provincial Political and Law Committee and the header of provincial Public Security Bureau, attended the promotion of traffic security during spring festival at Guiyang railway station and made TV speech.

贵州省公安厅交通警察总队是统领全省10个交警支队、上百个交警大队、四千交警队伍的指挥机关。这支队伍肩负着全省40000公里道路的安全与畅通，13个大中城市的交通秩序，50余万辆机动车的安全管理和交通参与者的法制宣传教育，同时，作为公路治安巡警还担负着交通治安和打击车匪路霸的重任，他们恪守着“严格执法、热情服务”的宗旨，涌现出了像冯毓青、姚世凤这样的全国英模，以及无数个不知姓名的典范。

进入新世纪，贵阳市被评为全国畅通工程三等管理水平城市；省交警总队直属支队贵遵一大队从北京捧回创建平安大道模范集体奖牌。

2002年省公安厅交警总队要办的8件实事：

1、在高速公路上建成三个道路监控点；

2、建设16个中队；

3、建设5个大队；

4、建设总队、支队办公自动化系统；

5、建设省交警制证中心；

6、建设全省道路交通管理信息系统三期工程；

7、建设黔东南车管中心，开工建设六盘水车管中心；

8、按照平安大道实施方案要求，建成贵毕、大纳、玉铜三条平安大道。

毕节公安交警支队赫章大队民警姚世凤以坚强的毅力与癌症抗争，并先后收养了6个孤儿，荣获全国“十行百佳”妇女、全国“三八”红旗手、国家级“人民满意的公务员”等荣誉称号。她载誉归来，省交警总队领导、毕节地区公安处领导到机场迎接

Yao Shifeng, a policewoman of Hezhang unite of Bijie Public Security Traffic Branch, resisted cancer with strong will and successively adopted 6 orphans. She was awarded national “100 excellent woman of 10 fields”, national “8th March” red flag standard-bearer, national “satisfying public servant”. She came back with honors. Leaders of the general troop and public security board of Bijie area were receiving her at the airport.

飒爽英姿

Valiant and heroic policewomen

General Traffic Police Troop of Public Security Bureau of Guizhou Province is the command organization that governs 10 traffic police branches, over 100 traffic police units, and over 4000 traffic police teams of the province. The Troop is responsible for the safety and smooth running of 40 thousand km road of the province, traffic order of 13 large and middle cities, safe management of 500 thousand vehicles and publicizing and education of traffic participators. Meanwhile, as patrol police for road security, they are responsible for traffic security and striking traffic bandit and despot. They stick to the aim of “enforce law strictly and serve warmly”. National heroes like Feng Yuqing and Yao Shifeng, and a lot of unknown models sprang up.

Stepping into a new century, Guiyang City has been awarded the city of third level management in the project of National Smooth Traffic. Guizhun branch directly under the general traffic police troop has got an example unit medal for constructing Safe Avenue in Beijing.

The general troop will finish 8 main tasks in 2002 as:

1. construct 3 supervision points in freeway

2. found 16 traffic police teams

3. found 5 traffic police units

4. construct office automation system of the general troop and branch

5. construct provincial traffic license center

6. construct the third period of the information system project of provincial traffic management

7. construct vehicle management center of Southeast Qian prefecture and Liupanshui city

8. construct 3 Safe Avenues of Guibi, Dana and Yutong according to the requirement of Safe Avenue

路查

Road inspection

稽查

Inspection

贵州水利辉煌五十年

The marvelous 50 years of Guizhou water conservancy

贵州省水利厅

The Water Conservancy Bureau of Guizhou Province

水城县双嘎水保综合治理小流域
Shuangga river in general water-protection government at Shuicheng County

独山县人饮工程--山村提灌站
Artificial drinking water project of dushan County --irrigation station in village

关岭新断桥电站发电机组
Generating set of Guanling Xinduanqiao Power Station

建国五十年来，特别是改革开放以来，贵州省水利事业取得了长足进展，水利基础设施得到加强，对国民经济和社会发展的支撑作用日益显著。

截止1998年底，全省有效灌溉面积达到63.86万公顷，约占全省总耕地面积的三分之一，水利工程年农灌供水量47亿方，为全省农业的可持续发展提供了有力的保证；截止1998年底，全省地方电力装机容量达到90万千瓦，年发电量达到29亿千瓦时，全省已先后建成13个农村初级电气化县。90%的乡镇、70%的村、60%的农户结束了无电的历史；截止1998年底，全省已解决853.24万人/549.2万头大牲畜饮水困难，目前全省年供水量达到22621万立方米；全省累计完成水土流失防治面积1.64万平方公里，起到了显著的社会、经济和生态效益；全省建立了200多个抗旱排涝服务组织，水利设施每年的减灾效益达到150亿元；同时加强了水资源管理和水政执法工作。

今后5年贵州水利总的发展思路是以依法治水，推进水利产业化为重点，以深化两项水利改革为突破口，带动政府职能的全面履行和水利产业化发展，争取5年内实现以下5大目标：

1、有效灌溉面积净增100万亩，提高农田水利化程度；

2、解决300万人饮水困难，基本解决全省农村饮水困难问题；

3、水土保持面积净增6000平方公里；

4、地方电力装机净增30万千瓦；

5、水利产业进一步壮大，水利经济总产值达到50亿元。

In the 50 years after China was founded, especially after Opening and Reform, The Water Conservancy Industry of Guizhou Province has been fully developed. The fundamental installations of water conservancy have been enforced. And the important effect of water conservancy on national economy and social progress becomes obvious.

Up to the end of 1998, the effective irrigated land of the province is 638.6 thousand hectare, holding 1/3 of the general cultivated land of The province. The annual water supply for agricultural irrigation is 4.7 billion m^3, which is a powerful insurance of continuos agricultural development of the province. Up to the end of 1998, the installed capacity of local electricity of the province is up to 900 thousand KW. The annual generated energy is 2.9 billion KWh. 13 primarily electrified counties were successively constructed. 90% of all the towns and townships, 70% of all the villages and 60% of all the peasants have ended the history without electricity. Up to the end of 1998, the province has solved the drinking water problem for 8.5324 million people and 5.492 million big livestock. At present, the annual water supply of the province is up to 226.21 million m^3. The province has governed land of 16.4 thousand km^2 to protect soil erosion, which plays obvious role in social, economic and ecological benefit. The province has founded over 200 drought-relief and flood-drained organizations. The water conservancy installation has gained annual profit of 15 billion yuan for the province. Meanwhile, the Bureau has strengthened the management of water resource and law enforcement.

In the future 5 years, the developing route of Guizhou water conservancy is to take legal water government and industrialization of water conservancy as key point, to take deepening two water conservancy reforms as breakthrough, to drive the fulfillment of government's functions and the industrialization of water conservancy, and to try to realize 5 aims in 5 years as:

1. The net increase of effective irrigated land will be 1 million mu and to improve the water conservancy of farmland.

2. Solve the drinking problem for 3 million people, and primarily solve the drinking problem for countryside of the province.

3. The net increase of soil will be kept at 6000 km^2.

4. The net increase of local electric installed capacity will be 300 thousand KW.

5. Further develop water conservancy industry to realize the gross water conservancy value of 5 billion yuan.

省人大副主任龚贤永视察贵州省（贵阳市）文化市场

Gong Xianyong, the vice-director of the provincial People's Congress, was inspecting Guizhou Province (Guiyang City) Cultural Market.

贵州省文化厅主要职责简介

Responsibilities of the Culture Bureau of Guizhou Province

1、贯彻执行党和国家关于文化艺术工作的方针、政策和法律、法规，研究拟定全省文化艺术工作的政策、法规及实施办法并组织实施；参与制定文化事业劳动人事政策。

2、研究全省文化事业发展战略，编制并监督实施文化事业中长期发展规划和年度计划；指导文化体制改革。

3、管理全省文学、艺术事业、指导艺术创作与生产，扶持代表性、示范性、实验性文化艺术品种，推动各门类艺术的发展；归口管理全省性重大文化活动。

4、拟定全省文化产业发展规划和政策措施，指导、协调文化产业发展；统筹安排国家划拨的文化事业经费，贯彻落实文化经济政策，调控投资方向；规划、指导重点文化设施建设。

5、拟定文化市场的发展规划；归口管理全省文化市场；归口管理进口音像制品；指导、监督全省文化市场的稽查工作，参与"扫黄打非"工作。

6、管理社会文化事业，拟定社会文化事业的发展规划并组织实施，指导各类社会文化事业的建设，协调、指导民族民间文化艺术和少儿文化艺术事业的发展。

7、管理图书馆事业，指导图书文献资源的建设和开发利用，组织推动图书馆标准化、现代化建设。

8、归口管理全省对外和对香港、澳门特别行政区及台湾地区文化交流联络工作。

9、承办省人民政府和文化部交办的其他事项。

10、管理贵州省文物局。

1. To implement literature and art guiding principles, policies, laws and regulations of the Party and state. To research and draw up policies, laws, regulations and implementation program for literature and art of the province and organize to implement. To attend the formulation of personal policies for cultural undertaking.

2. To research development strategy of the provincial cultural undertaking. To draw up and supervise the implementation of middle and long term plan and yearly plan of cultural undertaking. To guide the structural reform of culture.

3. To manage literature and art undertakings of the province. To guide the creation and production of art. To assistant example, demonstrative and testing cultural sort. To improve art development of all kinds. To manage large provincial cultural program.

4. To draw up development plan and policies of cultural industry of the province. To guide and regulate the development of cultural industry. To unitarily distribute cultural funds appropriated by the state. To implement economic policies of culture. To guide the investment. To plan and guide key constructions of cultural institutions.

5. To draw up development plan of cultural market. To manage cultural markets of the province. To manage imported video products. To guide and supervise examination of cultural markets of the province. To attend the work of "striking obscene and illegal activities".

6. To manage social cultural undertaking. To draw up development plan for social cultural undertaking and organize to implement. To guide the construction of all kinds of social cultural undertakings. To regulate and guide the development of nationality folk cultural undertaking and child cultural undertaking.

7. To manage library undertaking. To guide the construction and development of book resource. To organize to improve the standard and modern construction of library.

8. To manage the cultural communication work of the province with HongKong, Macao and Taiwan.

9. To undertake other tasks assigned by the provincial government and the Ministry of Culture.

10. To manage the Cultural Relic Bureau of Guizhou Province.

出土文物--东汉铜车马

An unearthed relic--copper carriage and horses of East Han Dynasty

全国重点文物保护单位--镇远青龙洞

A national key protecting site--Zhenyuan Black Dragon Carve

侗歌小合唱《蝉之歌》获全国第二届蒲公英奖金奖

The chorus of "song of cicada" by Dongzu was awarded golden prize of the second dandelion match.

贵州省林业厅

The Forestry Department of Guizhou Province

省林业厅厅长：张锦林
The Director of the Forestry Department: Zhang Jinlin

贵州林业建设在省委、省政府的高度重视和有力领导下，在国家林业局的大力支持下，在全社会广泛参与及全省广大林业职工的努力下，取得了较好成绩。森林面积达到8143万亩，森林覆盖率达30.83%。

从2001年至2010年，贵州林业厅按照江总书记“三个代表”重要思想的要求，进一步解放思想，转变观念，改进作风，遵循现代林业思想，以建立两大林业体系为目标，以恢复和扩大森林植被为中心，以实施六大林业工程为重点，保障全省森林覆盖率每年增长一个百分点，森林面积年均净增300万亩。到2010年，全省水土流失和石漠化基本得到控制，林业生态环境明显改善。

Led by provincial Party Committee and government, encouraged by national Forestry Bureau, helped by society and forestry workers, the forestry construction of Guizhou Province has made good achievements. Forest area is 81.43 million mu and percentage of forest cover is 30.83%.

From 2001 to 2010, according to the General Party Secretary Jiang's "three represents", Guizhou Forestry Department will further emancipate minds, change ideals, improve conduct, obey modern forestry theory, set its aim as to build two major forestry systems, and set its central work as to recover and enlarge forest areas. Thus to ensure the forest-cover rate increase 1% and Forest area increase 3 million mu annually. In 2010, soil erosion and desertisation of the province will be mainly controlled and the forestry ecological environment will be obviously improved.

天然林保护（喀斯特森林）
Natural forest protection (Karst Forest)

长坡岭森林公园
Changpoling forest park

对外交流与合作
Exchange and cooperation

贵州省国
National Tax Bureau

贵州省国家税务局党委书记、局长：刘毓文
The Secretary of the Bureau Party Committee and the head of the Bureau, Liu Yuwen

贵州省国家税务局公开选拔副处级领导干部笔试考场
Testing room for vice-director electing of the Bureau

贵州省国家税务局公开选拔副处级领导干部面试考场
Interview room for vice-director electing of the Bureau

2001年，在省委、省政府和国家税务总局的正确领导下，贵州省国家税务局按照“依法治税，从严治队，强基固本，稳中求进”的基本工作思路，着力“抓改革，实管理，建基层，保收入”，各项税收工作取得较大成绩。全年共完成税收收入94.99亿元，比上年增长13.96%，增收11.63亿元；地方级收入完成15亿元，比上年增长12.58%，增收1.59亿元，均超额完成上级下达任务，为全省经济与社会的发展提供了有力的财力保障。

同时，贵州省国家税务局以依法治税为“立身之本，执法之基，工作之魂”，按照“内外并举，重在治内，以内促外”的指导方针和“治税先治队，治外先治内，治标又治本”的思路，着力整顿基层执法队伍、规范税收执法行为、健全税收执法监督制约机制，依法治税水平进一步提高。2001年，贵州省国家税务局将查处大案要案、打击以骗取进出口退税和虚开增值税专用发票为重点的涉税犯罪行为、开展对重点行业和区域的专项检查整治作为整顿和规范税收秩序工作的重点，集中全省稽查骨干力量分别对商贸企业、部分重点企业实施了重点检查，全省国税税收秩序明显好转。

Developing town and township enterprises of Guizhou Province

黄瑶副书记在全省乡镇企业改革发展研讨会议上讲话
Huang Yao, the vice-Secretary was speaking at the Reform and Development Seminar for Town and Township Enterprises of the Province

In 2001, town and township enterprises of Guizhou Province have kept a good development. According to statistics, general output value of town and township enterprises of Guizhou Province is 113.68 billion yuan, increasing by 14.4% and 31.02 billion yuan, accounting for 28.7% of GDP of the province. Town and township industrial output value increased by 15.5 billion yuan, which is 8.5%, accounting for 46.3% of the industrial output increase of the province. With the increase of general economic quantity, economic indexes are kept corresponding increasing.

In 2001, Attention of leaders of all levels provided powerful insurance for the development of town and township enterprises. In the reform of prefectural and county government, Town and Township Enterprise Administration of Guizhou province was designated to be a governmental organization, which provided organ insurance and reassured team and individuals. Greater assistance was carried out. The provincial Party Committee and government reemphasized to continue to provide 20 million yuan development fund from finance for 5 years.

Change work style, improve functions of service. Organizations of all levels have strengthened basic research, service and solution, and made full use of development fund for town and township enterprises. Town and Township Enterprise Administration of the province has assisted some key projects, key industries, key enterprises and provided 37.54 million yuan in the year for loan interests, subsidy of technique progress and expending of beginning period.

Pay greater emphasis in structure regulation, rectify industrial structure. Structure regulation was set to be the key point of the year's work. The Administration has organized the research for the structure of town and township enterprises and drawn up " opinions about strengthening the structure regulation of town and township enterprises" and " plan of town and township enterprises of Guizhou Province during the Tenth Five-year Plan". In the new developed projects, food and medical projects held about 15%. Fundamental equipment and real estate project held about 25%. Tourist projects held about 5%. The old structure dominated by developing underground resources has been primarily changed. The industrial structure regulation of town and township enterprises has got obvious progress.

Improve technical progress vigorosly, strengthen competitive capability of enterprises. Encouraging mechanism for technical progress was set up to improve technical reform. 88 key technical projects were supported. The Administration has solved the problem of 10.05 million yuan for technical development and carried out comprehensive certification work of quality management and quality certification in enterprises with sales above 5 million yuan. The Administration has carried out evaluation of professional titles with personal departments in the town and township enterprise system of the province. The area network of the Administration and office software of CTEOA have been constructed and put into use. At present, there are over 1000 enterprises publishing commercial information on the network, which creates good conditions for technical progress of enterprises.

团结如一的领导班子
United leader group

Create environment, the situation of inviting investment is pleasant. Every local place has improved the hard and soft environment of investment to strengthen the work of inviting capitals. According to statistics, town and township enterprises of the province have finished 2259 construction projects in 2001 and finished the investment of 5.84 billion yuan, 40.99% more than last year. The invited capital is 4.242 billion yuan, holding 72.63% of the total investment. The structure that takes inviting investment to develop town and township enterprises as main channel is in construction.

不断发展壮大的贵州乡镇企业

钱运禄书记视察久美企业发展公司
Qian Yunlu, the Secretary was inspecting Jiumei Enterprise Development Company

莫时仁副省长视察普定县耐火材料厂
Mo Shiren, the vice-governor of the province was inspecting Puding Refractory Factory

原乡企局局长：赵友良（现任贵州省纪委副书记）
The former director of the Administration, Zhao Youliang (present the vice-secretary of Provincial Discipline Inspection Committee)

2001年，贵州省乡镇企业保持了较好的发展势头，据统计，全省完成乡镇企业总产值（90价）1136.8亿元，增长14.4%；增加值310.2亿元，增长10.1%，占全省国内生产总值的28.7%，其中，乡镇工业增加值155亿元，增长8.5%，占全省工业增加值的46.3%。在经济总量增大的同时，各项经济指标保持同步增长。

2001年，各级领导的重视，为乡镇企业发展提供了有力的保证。在地、县机构改革中，明确把乡镇企业局列为政府组成部门，稳定了机构、队伍、人心，提供了组织保证；加大扶持力度，省委、省政府再次明确，每年继续从财政解决2000万元发展基金，保持5年不变。

转变工作作风，增强服务职能。各级主管部门加大了下基层调研、服务和解决实际问题的力度。积极发挥乡镇企业发展基金的作用，省局对部分重点项目、重点产业、重点企业进行了扶持，全年共解决贷款贴息、科技进步补贴和项目前期费用补贴资金3754万元。

加大调整力度，优化产业产品结构。把结构调整作为全年工作的重点，组织力量对乡镇企业结构状况进行调研，草拟了《关于加强乡镇企业结构调整的意见》；制订了《贵州省乡镇企业“十五”规划》。在新上项目中，食品、医药行业约占15%，基础设施及房地产开发类约占25%，旅游类约占5%，初步改变了以地下资源开发利用为主的模式，乡镇企业产业结构调整取得了明显进展。

积极推进科技进步，增强企业竞争力。建立了技术进步激励机制，推进技术改造，重点扶持了88个科技项目，解决科技开发基金1005万元。对销售额在500万元以上的企业开展了全面质量管理和质量认证工作。会同人事部门在全省乡镇企业系统内部开展了职称评审工作。省局局域网和办公自动化CTEOA软件已建成并投入使用，目前已有1000多家企业在网上发布商业信息，为企业科技进步创造了条件。

大力营造环境，招商引资形势喜人。各地改善投资软硬环境，加强招商引资。据统计，2001年全省乡镇企业完成建设项目2259个，实际完成投资额58.40亿元，比上年增长40.99%，其中引进资金42.42亿元，占总投资额的72.63%。把引资发展乡镇企业作为主渠道的格局正在形成。

贵州省工商行政管理局
Industrial and Commercial Administration of Guizhou Province

工商执法人员深入商店认真检查假冒伪劣产品
Industrial and commercial law enforcement officials were carefully examining fakes in shops.

工商执法人员在整顿和规范市场经济工作中对文化市场进行专项治理
Industrial and commercial law enforcement officials have conducted specialized regulations on cultural market

2001年贵州省各级工商行政管理机关扎扎实实开展了整顿和规范市场经济秩序工作，为促进全省经济发展和西部大开发作出了积极的贡献。

1、整顿和规范市场经济秩序取得明显成效

（1）紧紧围绕整顿和规范市场经济秩序这一中心工作，加大监管力度。2001年全省工商行政管理系统查处经济违法违章案件60373件，案值17692.86万元，罚款2623.10万元。

（2）认真履行职责，积极开展市场专项整治。

2、依法做好注册登记工作，促进各类市场主体健康发展。2001年，全省共有内资企业66491户，外资企业714户，私营企业22248户，个体工商户394124户。

In 2001, industrial and commercial administrations of all levels of Guizhou Province have regulated and standardized the order of market economy to contribute to the development of provincial economy and the West Developing.

1. Obvious progress was made in regulation and standardization of the order of market economy

(1) The Administration has strengthened supervision of the market with the aim of regulating and standardizing the order of market economy. In 2001, industrial and commercial administrative system of the Province has checked and dealt with 60,373 illegal cases or cases contrary to regulations, whose total value is 176.9286 million yuan, and has fined 26.231 million yuan.

(2) Fulfill duty carefully and carry out special government on market.

2. Do well in registration work according to laws to improve the health development of the main market of all kinds. In 2001, there are 66491 enterprises with domestic investment, 714 enterprises with foreign investment, 22248 enterprises with private investment and 394124 individual industrial and commercial enterprises.

工商部门在整顿和规范市场经济秩序专项整治行动中将查获的假冒伪劣商品付之一炬
Industrial and commercial organizations were burning fake commodities during the program of specialized regulation on the order of market economy.

贵州省卫生厅

Health Department of Gui zhou Province

贵州省卫生厅是省人民政府管理卫生事业的行政机构，是省人民政府的组成部门，主要职责是：贯彻执行党和国家关于卫生工作的方针、政策和法律、法规，研究提供卫生事业发展规划和战略目标；拟定全省卫生工作规章、技术标准和实施办法并组织实施；研究提供卫生规划、统筹规划与协调卫生资源配置；拟定社区卫生服务发展规划和服务标准，指导卫生规划的实施。研究拟定农村卫生、妇幼卫生工作规划和政策措施。贯彻预防为主的方针，组织对重大疾病的综合防治；负责向卫生部和省人民政府报告传染病的监测情况；指导医疗机构的改革；依法监督和管理采供血机构及临床用血质量；负责医疗卫生系统信息网络的规范化建设和管理；负责对传染病防治及食品、职业、环境、放射、学校卫生实施监督管理；负责食品化妆品质量的规范化管理和认证工作；负责卫生医疗事业对外合作交流；贯彻中西医并重的方针，促进中西医共同发展；承担省爱国卫生运动委员会的日常工作；负责省委保健委员会的日常工作；组织调度卫生技术力量，配合有关部门对重大突发疫情、病情实施应急处置、防止发生和蔓延。省卫生厅内设医政、疾病控制、基层与妇幼保健、卫生法制与监督、科技教育、中医药管理、保健及爱国卫生运动委员会办公室等12个职能处（室、局）以及直辖9所省级医院，10个防保、科研等事业单位。各地（州、市）、县都分别设有卫生局分级负责全省卫生行政管理工作。

Health Department of Guizhou Province is the administrative organization for health of Guizhou Provincal Government. Its main responsibilities are as follows: to implement health policies, laws and rules of the Party and Nation. Provide developing plan and strategic objects for health industry. Draw up rules, technique standards and implement methods for provincial health work and carry out. Discuss and provide health planning, unified planning and assistance to resources distribution. Draw up developing planning and service standard of residential district health. Guide the implementation of health planning. Research and draw up work planning, policy and measures of rural health, and women & children's health. Implement the prevention-led policy. Organize comprehensive prevention and treatment of great dangerous diseases. Report to the Health Ministry and Provincial government about the monitoring results of infectious diseases. Guide the reforms of medical organizations. Supervise and govern blood taking and providing organizations and clinical blood. Construct and govern the information network of medical system. Prevent infectious diseases and supervise food, profession, environment, radioactivity and schoolyard health. Be responsible for the standardized management and confirmation on the quality of food and cosmetics. Be responsible for exchange and cooperation of medical industry. Implement the policy with two stresses of Chinese and west medicine. Improve the development of Chinese and west medicine. Undertake everyday work of patriotic health campaign committee and the health care department of the Provincial Party Committee. Organize and coordinate health technique resources. Assistant relating departments to give emergent treatment and prevention on unexpected dangerous epidemic situation and diseases. There are 12 functional departments (or offices, bureaus) subordinate to Health Department of Guizhou Province, which are: health policy, disease controlling, grass-root & women and children's health care, health legal system & supervision, science & technology education, Chinese medicine administration, health care, patriotic health campaign committee, etc. Also there are 9 provincial hospitals and 10 prevention & health care institutions directly under the Health Department of Guizhou Province. There are health offices in every city or county engaged in health administration work of its level.

以发展为主题，以创新为动力，推动农垦经济持续快速健康发展

Take development as the subject, take creation as the motive power, develop reclamation economy continuously, fast and healthily

贵州省农业厅农垦局

The Reclamation Board of Agriculture Bureau of Guizhou Province

局长赵宣富到省山京畜牧场检查工作

Zhao Xuanfu, the head of the board was inspecting Shanjing livestock farm

There are 48 reclamation enterprises in Guizhou, among which 44 are national farms, 4 are commercial enterprises. The managing system of 3 levels of province, city (prefecture) and county was conducted. Of all the reclamation enterprises, 5 are under provincial government, 15 are under city' s (prefecture) government, and 28 are under county's government. The general population at the end of 2001 is 30.4 thousand. The average number of workers in this field is 11.3 thousand. Guizhou has rich resources of land. The general area of land is 503.7 thousand mu. Existing cultivated land is 51 thousand mu. Lands of tea, fruit and mulberry are 66.5 thousand mu. Land of trees is 59.4 thousand mu. There are 54.3 thousand mu land can be reclaimed, 77.7 thousand mu can be planted with trees and 123.2 thousand mu herbage land to be developed.

The GNP of reclamation enterprises of Guizhou Province of 2001 is 98.47 million yuan, 7.2% more than last year. Business incomes are 162.98 million yuan, 3.95% more than last year. The profit of business is 33.72 million yuan. The average net income of per person is 1546 yuan per year. Main agricultural products: the output of grains and beans is 6,070 tons, the output of tea is 3,135 tons, the output of fruits is 4,683 tons, the reserve of big livestock is 7,200, among which 4800 are milk cow. The output of milk is 19,162 tons, the output of meat is 710 tons.

In 2002, the Bureau will improve quality and benefit of reclamation economy, and protect developing reclamation economy continuously, fast and healthily.

贵州省农垦企业48户，其中：国有农场44户，商业企业4户，实行条块结合，以块为主，省、地（市）、州、县三级管理体制。其中：省管5户，地（市）、州管15户，县管28户。2001年末总人口3.04万人，平均从业人员1.13万人。土地资源丰富，总面积50.37万亩，现有耕地5.1万亩，茶果桑园6.65万亩，林地5.94万亩，还有5.43万亩可垦荒地，7.77万亩宜林地，12.32万亩牧草地等待开发利用。

2001年贵州省农垦企业国民生产总值达到9847万元（90可比价），比上年增长7.2%；营业收入达到16298万元，比上年增长3.95%，营业利润3372万元，人均纯收入1546元/年。主要农产品：粮豆产量6070吨；茶叶产量3135吨；各类水果产量4683吨；大牲畜存栏7200头；其中奶牛存栏4800头；牛奶产量19162吨；肉类产量710吨。

2002年，贵州农垦局着力提高农垦经济的质量和效益，保障农垦经济持续、快速、健康发展。

乌当奶牛场牛群

Herds of cows in Wudang milk cow farm

遵义页岩砖厂

Zunyi Yeyan brick field

腈隆柑桔场果园

The orchard of Qinglong orange yard

家税务局

of Guizhou Province

In 2001, under the scientific leading of provincial Party Committee and Government, the Bureau kept its working route as "basing on the laws, administering teams strictly, strengthening foundation, proceeding steadily", emphasized "strengthening reform, stressing management, building foundation, insuring income". Works of all sides were improved. The total tax revenue of 2001 was 9.499 billion yuan, 13.96% higher than last year and increased by 1.163 billion yuan. Local tax revenue was 1.5 billion yuan, 12.58% higher than last year and increased by 159 million yuan. Both total tax revenue and local tax revenue were more than planned, which provided a powerful financial support for the development of the provincial economy and society.

Meanwhile, the Bureau took legal taxation as the base of work. Guided by the working route of "governing the working teams as well as the payers" and "building a good taxation system through administering a good taxation team", the Bureau strengthened grass-root construction, standardized taxation action, built a comprehensive supervision system, and thus improved taxation. In 2001, the Bureau set its working emphasis as conducting big and important cases, punishing actions of cheating returned import or export tax and illegal writing value added tax invoice. The Bureau also conducted inspection on major fields and major districts and gathered key members to supervise commercial and trading companies and some key enterprises. The order of the provincial taxation got better obviously.

贵州省"诚信纳税企业"授牌大会
The ceremony for "honest and credit unit" of Guizhou Province.

在全省第十一个税收宣传月活动上，获得"诚信纳税企业"称号的100家企业在百米长卷上庄重地签上自己的名字
In the activity of 11st month of tax popularization, the 100 awarded enterprises were signing in the 100-meter-long paper.

整顿税收秩序，治理纳税环境，保障国家税收
Governing taxation order, managing taxation condition, insuring national tax revenue.

贵州省

Local Taxation Administr-

全省地方税收连续第7年实现快速增长

Annual local taxes got 7th continuous fast increase

全省地方税务工作会议
Local taxes conference of the province

2001年全省地税系统坚决贯彻省委、省政府和国家税务总局的各项重大决策，按照年初全省地方税务工作会议明确的各项工作部署，以江总书记"三个代表"重要思想总揽全局，深入落实"加强征管，堵塞漏洞，惩治腐败，清缴欠税"的工作方针，切实加强作风建设，地方税收工作开局良好，为全省国民经济和社会发展作出了新的贡献。

2001年全省地税系统收入为52亿元，比上年实际完成数增长11%，增加5亿元。经过全体地税干部职工的共同努力，地方税收连续第7年快速增长，收入突破55亿元。据统计，2001年税收和教育附加费两项收入共计入库55.89亿元，为年计划的107.5%，超额完成了年初计划任务，比去年同期增收9亿元，增长19.34%。营业税、企业所得税、个人所得税、城建税和房产税等主体税种完成计划情况较好，实现了大幅度的增长增收。

地税局

ation of Guizhou Province

地方税收收入突破55亿元

local taxes are over 5.5 billion yuan

In 2001, local taxes systems of the province firmly carry out major policies of provincial Party Committee and government. Based on the assignment of provincial local taxes conference, held at the beginning of the year, led by General Party Secretary Jiang's "three represents", Guizhou local taxes department conducted "strengthen tax-collecting, stop up loopholes, punish corruption, make up due tax". On the other hand, the department strengthened Pary conduct construction, so the local taxes work began well and made contributions for provincial economic and society development.

Expected Local tax collection of the province for 2001 is 5.2 billion yuan, 11% higher than last year. With all the leaders and workers' efforts of the local tax system, the annual local tax got 7th continuous fast increase, which is over 5.5 billion yuan. According to statistics, local tax and education surcharge are up to 5.589 billion yuan, which is 1.075 times of annual plan and is 0.9 billion yuan more than the same period of last year. Growth rate is 19.34%. Major taxes as business tax, enterprise income tax, individual income tax, city construction tax and real estate tax, were finished well and increased quite a lot.

税法宣传

Tax law promotion

发展中的贵
Developing Sports

近几年来，贵州省体育局在认真实施国家《全民健身计划纲要》和《奥运争光计划纲要》的同时，大力发展体育产业，所建成的鸳鸯岛水上健身中心和玉田体育运动村既是家庭娱乐休闲的好去处，更是单位集体活动的好地方。

In recent years, Guizhou Sports Bureau has carefully implemented Essentials of the Nation Health Plan and Essentials of the Plan for Honors in the Olympics. Meanwhile, the Bureau has founded Mandarin Duck Island Gymnastic Center and Yu Tian Sports Village which are good places for family entertainment and group activities.

鸳鸯岛水上健身中心 该中心为贵州省体育局水上运动管理中心的一部分，座落于国家级风景名胜区红枫湖，占地面积80余亩，宜人的气候条件和优美的自然风光，成为理想的训练、比赛、健身和休闲娱乐的场所。2001年4月被国家体育总局命名为“国家体育总局水上运动管理中心贵州红枫湖亚高原水上训练基地”。（图1）

联系电话：0851-2152083 2152056/57/58

Mandarin Duck Island Gymnastic Center It is a part of the Aquatic Sports Administrative Center of Guizhou Sports Bureau, located in the National scenic area of Hongfeng Lake. It covers over 80 mu. The pleasant weather and beautiful natural scenes made it an ideal training, match and entertainment place. It was awarded “Guizhou Hongfeng Lake sub-plateau climate Aquatic Training Base of General State Sports Bureau Aquatic Sports Administrative Center” by General State Sports Bureau in April 2001. (picture 1)

Tel: 0851-2152083 2152056-8

贵州玉田体育运动村 该村位于贵阳市南部朝阳洞路（玉田坝），隶属于贵州省体育局射击射箭运动管理中心（原省军体校）。此处地理位置好，三面环山，绿树四季常青，空气清新，环境幽静，既有市区交通之方便，又无闹市之嘈杂。提供目前国内最大的人工攀岩场，六片标准网球场（其中四片在室内），省内独一无二有惊无险的军事体能竞技场，贵阳市内最大的乒乓球练习馆，以及射击场、游泳池等体育设施和完备的后勤保障服务。（图2-6）

联系电话：0851-5753503

Guizhou Yutian Sports Village The Village lies in Chaoyangdong Road, south of Guiyang City and is subordinate to Shooting & Archery Administrative Center of the Provincial Sports Bureau. It is in a good geographic situation with three faces surrounded by mountains. Trees are green most of a year with fresh airflow. You can enjoy convenient communication as in urban area but no noisy as in market. It provides the largest artificial climb space of China, 6 standard tennis spaces(4 of them are inside), the only military physics area of the Province, the largest table tennis center of Guiyang City, shooting site, swimming pool, and comprehensive logistic services. (picture2-6)

Tel: 0851-5753503

贵州省招商引资局（外协办）

Introduction of Merchants Bureau (External Communication Office) of Guizhou Province

省委书记钱运录、省长石秀诗、副省长陈大卫出席贵州振华公司与日本京瓷公司合资开发CDMA手机项目签字仪式，标志着国际大型跨国公司入黔

Qian Yunlu, the secretary of the provincial Party Committee, Shi Xiushi, the governor of the province, Chen Dawei, the vice governor of the province, were attending the signature ceremony of the cooperation in developing CDMA mobile phone between Guizhou Zhenhua Company and Japanese Jingci Company, which stands for large international company entering the province

党组书记、局长（主任）：石 超

The Secretary of the leading Party group and the Dirctor of the Bureau: Shi Chao

贵州省招商引资局（外协办）局长（主任）石超与法国洛泽尔省企业发展局局长Pierre PAGES在发展省际友好关系备忘录仪式上签字

Shi Chao, the Director of the Merchant Bureau of Guizhou Province and Pierre PAGES, the Director of the Enterprise Development Bureau of Lozere Province, France, were signing on the memorandum ceremony of developing provincial friendship.

贵州省招商引资局（外协办）履行省政府赋予的招商引资及对外经济协作行政管理职能。主要负责贯彻执行国家和省有关招商引资和经济协作的法律、法规及方针政策，研究拟订全省相关政策、措施及建议的组织实施。开展与国（境）外、省外的经济合作交流，组织协调全省参与国际国内重大招商引资活动和对口帮扶、东西部合作以及六省区市七方区域经济协作等重大项目的洽谈及跟踪落实。负责全省招商引资和经济协作的数据统计，全省招商引资网站、项目库建设和对外统一发布信息。督促检查全省各地各部门改善投资环境。组织指导全省建立外商投资“一站式”工作机制，协调处理外商投诉案件，维护外商合法利益。

近年来，在省委、省政府的领导下，省招商引资局（外协办）与有关单位共同组织开展了全省投资软环境综合整治工作，按照《贵州省投资软环境综合整治实施方案》，建立和实施科学的投资环境评价考核公示制度，建成符合国际标准的招商引资网站及项目数据库，启动运行省外商投资服务中心和外商投诉中心，全方位为外来投资者提供优质、高效、便捷的服务。

去年，全省引进国（境）外资金19545万美元，较上年增长8.2%；实施经济协作项目1698个，引进省外到位资金48.53亿元，较上年增长43%；实施省内协作资金32亿元，比上年增长63.4%。实现了招商引资到位资金总额保持两位数增长的目标，全省招商引资工作呈现良好势头。

Merchants Bureau (External Communication Office) of Guizhou Province undertakes functions of inviting investment and managing external communication assigned by provincial government. Its main responsibility is to implement relating inviting investment and economic cooperation laws, regulations and policies of the state and the province, to research and draw up relating policy, measure and proposal of the province and organize to implement, to carry out international (or area) economic cooperation and exchange, to organize the province to join international and domestic important program for inviting investment and conference and follow-up work of projects as Partner Assistance, cooperation between east and west, area economic cooperation of 6 provinces and 7 areas, to be responsible for the data statistics of inviting investment and economic cooperation of the province, to construct inviting investment web site and project base of the province and publish information, to supervise departments of every area of the province to improve investment environment, to organize and guide to construct “one-stop” work mechanism for foreign investor, to deal with opinions of foreign investors to ensure legal benefit of foreign merchants.

In recent years, under the leadership of the provincial Party Committee and government, the Merchants Bureau (External Communication Office) has carried out general government on soft environment of investment with relating enterprises, set and carried out scientific examination and publicizing system on investment environment according to “ implementation program of general government on soft environment of investment of the province”, constructed inviting investment web site and project base of international standard, run the service center of foreign merchant of the province, and provided quality, efficient and convenient service for investor.

Last year, the province has invited 195.45 million US$ foreign (external) capital, 8.2% higher than the year before. The province has carried out 1698 economic cooperation projects, and invited 4.853 billion yuan from areas out of the province, 43% higher than last year. The province has realized cooperation of 3.2 billion yuan, 63.4% higher than last year. The province has realized the aim of keeping the increase of invited investment by two-figure number. The work of inviting investment of the province takes a good trend.

贵州省药品监督管理局
The Medicine Administrative Bureau of Guizhou Province

贵州省药品监督管理局局长：黄穗生
The head of the Bureau: Huang Suisheng

贵州省药品监督管理局为省人民政府直属机构，是省人民政府主管全省药品监督管理的职能部门（正厅级）。其主要职责是负责对全省药品（包括中药材、化学原料药及其制剂、麻醉药品、医疗器械、卫生材料等）的研究、生产、流通、使用进行依法行政监督和技术监督。

贵州省药品监督管理局内设办公室、政策法规处、计划财务处、药品注册处、医疗器械处、安全监管处、市场监督处、人事教育处、机关党委处、纪检监察室、离退休干部处等11个处室，还设有贵州省药品稽查总队、机关服务中心及培训中心等机构。贵州省药品监督管理局直属单位设有省药品检验所、省新药评审中心、省医疗器械检测中心等机构。

贵州省药品监督管理体制实行垂直管理。目前，全省9个市（州、地）、76个县药品监督管理局或分局已建立，省以下药品监督管理新体制已基本建立。

The Medicine Administrative Bureau of Guizhou Province is directly under the provincial government. It is the department of the provincial government in charge of medicine administration of the province. Its main responsibility is to undertake administrative and technical supervision to the research, production, circulation and usage of the medicine (including drugs, chemical raw materials and preparation, anaesthetic, medical equipment, health materials, etc) in the province.

The Medicine Administrative Bureau of Guizhou Province has set 11 departments as: office, policy and law department, planning and financial department, medicine registration department, medical equipment department, security supervision department, market supervision department, personnel and education department, the Party Committee office, discipline inspection office, retired cadres office. In addition, there are institutions as General Medicine Inspection Brigade of Guizhou Province, Organ Service Center and Training Center, etc. Institutions directly under the Medicine Administrative Bureau of Guizhou Province includes Provincial Medicine Exam Institute, Provincial Assessing Center for New Medicines, Exam Center for Medical Equipment of the Province.

A vertical management system has been conducted in the Medicine Administration of Guizhou Province. At present, the system has been carried out in 76 medicine administrative bureaus of 9 cities (prefectures). A new medicine supervision system has been set under provincial level.

贵州省药品监督管理局执法人员上街向群众宣传《药品管理法》及有关法规，接受群众现场咨询。
Law enforcement officials of the medicine administrative Bureau of Guizhou Province were popularizing "medicine administration law" and relating regulations to people and receiving consultation on the street.

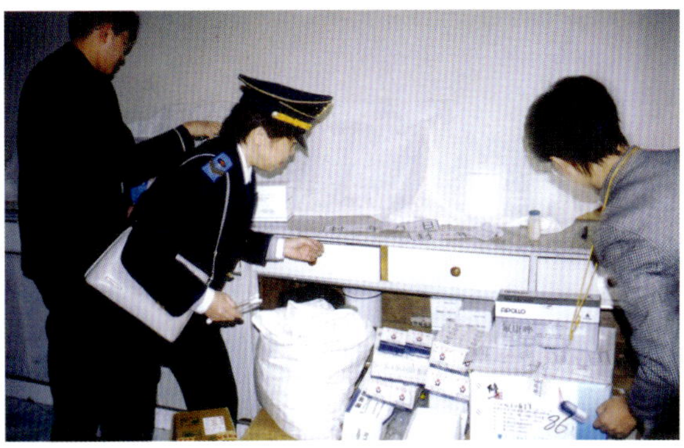

药监执法人员正在查处伪劣药品
Law enforcement officials were examining forged medicine

贵阳铁路分局
Guiyang Railway Bureau

贵阳铁路分局领导班子
The leading group of the Guiyang Railway Bureau

“九五”期间建成的贵阳火车站新站房，2000年12月30日正式投入使用
The new railway station room built in “Ninth Five-year Plan”, put into use on 30th Dec 2000

贵阳铁路分局管辖川黔、黔桂、贵昆（复线）、湘黔（复线）四条铁路干线和开阳、湖林、水大三条铁路支线，随着株六复线11月20日全线开通，铁路正线延展里程1946.3公里，营业里程1401.8公里，运营车站168个（其中有10个线路所）。有184条专用线（开通使用）。

随着西部大开发的呼唤，贵阳铁路分局充分发挥铁路运输优势，加强客货营销力度，形成了夕发朝至、城际旅游、假日列车、学生专列、民工专列、球迷专列等产品。货物运输确保国家重点物资和国有大中型企业生产需要，近年来不断挖潜扩能，在未增加新线的情况下年递增运100万吨以上，运输业全员劳动生产率一直处全路领先水平，为地方经济发展做出了积极贡献。2001年工作更是展现了三个亮点：一是货物发送量同比增运203万吨，再创历史新高；二是株六复线提前一年零50天开通运营，创造了既有线改造施工“安全、高速、高效”的成功经验；三是集中整治基础设备，投入5000万元70天内更换水泥枕31万根，增强了保证安全运输的能力。全年货物发送2950万吨，旅客发送1857.2万人，换算周转量完成461亿吨公里，运输收入212059万元。各项工作再迈新台阶。

分局长：兰开锋
The head of the Bureau: Lan Kaifeng
地　址：贵阳市双峰路16号　邮　编（Post Code）：550003
Address: Shuangfeng road No.16, Guiyang City

Guiyang Raiway Bureau has governed 4 mainlines of Chuanqian, Qiangui, Guikun (double-tracking) and Xiangqian (double-tracking) and 3 branch lines of Kaiyang, Hulin and Shuida. With the opening of Zhuliu Double-tracking railway on 20th Nov, the Bureau has governed main lines of 1,946.3 km, working lines of 1,401.8 km, working stations of 168 (including 10 route bureaus), and 184 special railway lines (in working).

With the West Developing, Guiyang Railway Bureau takes full advantages of railway transportation, stresses the sales of passenger train and goods train, develops business of trains leaving in evening and arriving in morning, city-to-city tourist train, holiday train, student train, farmer worker train, soccer fans train, etc. In the field of goods transportation, the Bureau ensures transportation of national key commodities and the production of large and middle level national enterprises. The Bureau keeps developing potential in recent years. In the condition of no increased lines, the Bureau has increased annual transportation by more than 1 million tons. The transportation productivity of the Bureau keeps in the front of the national railway transportation, contributing for the local economic development. The work of 2001 shows 3 bright points. Firstly, that the transportation of goods has increased by 2.03 million tons morethan last year, setting a new record. Secondly, Zhuliu Double-Tracking railway has been put into use 1 year and 50 days before, providing experience for “safe, fast, efficient” rebuilding on existing lines. Thirdly, the Bureau has concentrated in fundamental equipment and invested 50 million yuan to change 310 thousand of cement sleepers in 70 days, ensuring the safety of transportation. The Bureau has transported 29.5 million tons of goods and 18.572 million passengers in 2001. The conversion turnover of the year is 46.1 billion ton km. Incomes from transportation are 2120.59 million yuan. Works of all sides were put on a new stage.

贵阳南站编组场，日编解能力为7866辆
The switchyard of Guiyang South Railway Station with daily capacity of 7,866 trains.

成都铁路局株六复线建设指挥部

The Command Post for Zhuliu Double-tracking Railway of Chengdu Railway Administration

株六复线东起湖南重镇株州，西至贵州“煤都”六盘水市，是国家西部大开发战略实施项目，“九五”重点建设工程，铁道部“决战西南”的主战场。由成都铁路局担当建设任务的株六复线贵州段东起湘黔铁路大龙站，西至贵昆铁路六盘水枢纽，全长594.11公里，总投资136.3亿元，总工期4.5年，建设标准为国家一级电气化铁路干线。2002年底全线建成投入运营。

株六复线建设，充分体现了党中央、国务院对西南少数民族地区的关怀。它的建成将形成我国长江以南铁路网中重要的东西通道的主干部分，加强了西南与华东、华南地区的联系，对促进南方能源基地和原材料基地建设，巩固国防、改善西南路网结构，促进西南地区特别是贵州的经济大发展，帮助沿线人民尽快脱贫致富都具有十分重要的意义。

1998年4月，成都铁路局成立株六复线建设指挥部，6月份正式开工，截止2001年底，累计完成投资101.5亿元，除贵阳枢纽外，湘黔、贵昆正线全部开通投入运营，提前一年实现了国家下达的建设目标，多次受到铁道部、贵州省和路局领导的表扬。2001年5月，指挥部被授予贵州省2000年度“五一劳动奖状”和铁道部“火车头奖杯”。

株六复线（贵州段）正线开通庆功表彰大会
The commending meeting for the opening of main lines of Zhuliu double-tracking railway (Guizhou part)

Zhuliu double-tracking railway begins at Zhuzhou in the east, an important city of Hunan Province, and ends at Liupanshui in the west, the “Coal City” of Guizhou Province. It is a strategic project of the West Developing and key project of “Ninth Five-year Plan”. It is also the main spot for “southwest battle” of the Ministry of Railways. The part of Zhuliu double-tracking railway that is built by Chengdu Railway Administration begins at Dalong station of Xiangqian railway in the east and ends at Liupanshui station of Guikun railway in the west. The total length is 594.11 km. The total investment is 13.63 billion yuan. The total construction period is 4.5 years. The construction standard is first level national electrified trunk railway. The whole railway will be finished and put into use by the end of 2002.

The construction of Zhuliu double-tracking railway proved the concern of the Central Party Committee and the State Council to minority nationality areas in southwest. It is the main part of east to west trunk railway in the railway network of south to Changjiang River. It stressed the communication of southwest to east and south China. It is of great value in improving the construction of power resource base and raw material base in the south, strengthening national defense, changing railway network in southwest, improving economic development of southwest areas, especially Guizhou, and helping the poor people along the railway to make fortune.

Chengdu Railway Administration has founded the Command Post for Zhuliu Double-tracking Railway in April 1998 and begun to construct in June. Up to 2001, the Command Post has finished investment of 10.15 billion yuan. Except Guiyang pivot, main lines of Xiangqian and Guikun were all put into use, finishing national construction plan one year before. The Command Post has been praised by the Ministry of Railways, Provincial government and Provincial Railway Administration for several times. In May 2001, the Command Post was awarded “5.1 Labor testimonial” of 2000 by Provincial government and “locomotive cup” by the Ministry of Railways.

快速建成的南山河特大桥
Fast-built extra large Nanshan river bridge

背景图为：热烈庆祝株六复线全线开通
The background is : celebrate the opening of the whole Zhuliu double-tracking railway

加大货币信贷投入 支持贵州经济较快发展

Enlarge money investment of loans support Guizhou economy to be developed fast

中国人民银行

The People's Bank of China

2002年1月16日，贵州银行业协会成立，图为会员单位《公约》签字仪式（人行一分行行长当监证人）

Guizhou Bank Association was founded on 16th Jan 2002. Here in the picture is the signing ceremony of the Convention attended by member banks (a president of a branch People's Bank was the supervisor)

2001年，人行贵阳中支认真贯彻执行稳健的货币政策，优化信贷结构，强化金融监管，既支持了贵州经济较快增长，又防范了金融风险，确保金融安全稳健运行，维护一方金融平安。年末，全省广义货币M_2余额1598.5亿元，狭义货币M_1余额850.6亿元，分别比上年增长18.2%和16.9%，高于全国平均增幅的3.8和4.2个百分点；各项存款余额1341.1亿元，增长21.2%，同比提高了4.8个百分点，扩大了支持经济发展的信贷资金来源；各项贷款余额1212.2亿元，增长13.7%，其中，中长期贷款和农业贷款分别增长26.6%和23.7%。广义货币供应量M_2增长幅度高于当年全省经济增长和物价上涨之和的7.6个百分点，适应了贵州经济进入快速发展的需要，有力地支持全省经济增长连续5年高于全国平均水平。

中国人民银行贵阳中支营业部营业大厅

Business hall of the People's Bank of China, Guiyang Central Branch

贵阳中心支行

Guiyang Central Branch

In 2001, the People's Bank of China, Guiyang Central Branch has carefully implemented steady and healthy currency policy, regulated credit structure, stressed financial supervision, supported Guizhou economy to be developed fast and prevented financial risk to ensure a safe and steady circulation of financial. At the end of the year, the sum total of generalized currency M_2 of the province is 159.85 billion yuan. The sum total of currency of narrow sense M_1 is 85.06 billion yuan, respectively increasing by 18.2% and 16.9%, 3.8% and 4.2% higher than average national increase respectively. The sum total of all kinds of savings is 134.11 billion yuan, increasing by 21.2% and 4.8% higher than last year. Thus the Branch has enlarged the capital source of loans for supporting economic development. The total amount of loans is 121.22 billion yuan, increasing by 13.7%. Loans of middle and long term have increased by 26.6%. Agricultural loan has increased by 23.7%. The increase of the supply of generalized currency M_2 is 7.6% more than the sum of the provincial economic increase and price increase. The currency supply has fitted for the fast development of the provincial economy and supported provincial economy to increase larger than average national level for continuos 5 years.

2001年11月22日召开创建贵阳金融安全区工作会议，确保一方金融平安。
Guiyang Financial Safety Conference was held on 22nd Nov 2001, to ensure financial safety of the place

2001年全省人民银行系统电子联行到县，图为工作人员办理电子联行业务
Electric business network of the provincial People's Bank system was constructed in counties in 2001. Here in the picture is a clerk dealing with electric business

中国工商银行 贵州省分行

INDUSTRIAL AND COMMERCIAL BANK OF CHINA GUIZHOU BRANCH

中国工商银行贵州省分行是省内最大的一家国有商业银行，实力雄厚，服务优良，信誉良好，电子化程度一流。截止2001年12月底，人民币各项存款余额377亿元，人民币各项贷款余额308亿元，拥有员工8000余人，营业网点700余个，城市电子化营业网点覆盖率达到100%，柜台业务上机率达到99%，实现活期储蓄、牡丹灵通卡、信用卡全国及全省异地通兑。

工商银行贵州省分行面向企业及社会公众办理本、外币存款、贷款、结算、融资、中间业务代理等多元化金融服务，坚持"信誉第一、服务第一、客户第一"的经营方针，以市场为导向，以客户为中心，以发展为目标，抢抓机遇，深化改革，与时俱进，加快发展，积极支持西部大开发中省内重点项目建设，支持电力、交通、通讯、供水等基础设施建设，支持教育、文化、新闻、体育、医疗等非生产流通领域的发展，支持有效益、有市场、有信誉的产品和企业的生产与流通，支持城市住房改革，满足广大群众日益增长的各类消费性需求，拉动经济增长，为促进贵州经济发展和兴黔富民作出积极贡献。

Industrial and Commercial Bank of China, Guizhou Branch is the largest national commercial bank in Guizhou Province. The Branch has strong capability, quality services, good reputation and credit and first-class electrician. Up to the end of Dec 2001, general savings of RMB are 37.7 billion yuan. General loans of RMB are 30.8 billion yuan. The Branch has over 8,000 employees and over 700 business spots. Electrical business spots cover every urban area. 99% of the businesses on counters are via computer. The Branch has developed businesses of current deposit, peony card and credit card in different places of the province and China.

机关竞聘上岗动员大会
Mobilization meeting for competitive mechanism

工行贵州省分行行长陈焕祥同志给中央金融工委领导介绍该行业务发展状况
Chen Huanxiang, the president of the Branch, was introducing business development of the Branch to leaders of Financial Worker Committee of the Party Central Committee.

与贵州省电力公司合作协议签字仪式
The signing ceremony for cooperation with Provincial Electricity Company

The Branch provides services of saving, loan, check-up, raising fund and agent services of domestic and foreign currency to enterprises and society. The Branch sticks to the policy of "credit is first, service is first, client is first", takes market as its guidance, takes clients as its center, takes development as its aim, grasps chance, deepens reforms and is developed with times. The Branch supports key projects of the West Developing in the province, supports fundamental constructions of electricity, traffic, communication and water supply, supports the development of non-production industries as education, culture, news, sports and medicine, supports the production and circulation of profitable, promising and credit enterprises and products, supports urban housing reform, meets people's increasing consuming requirements of all sides, drives economic development and makes active contributions for economic development and people's life of Guizhou.

中国建设银行贵州省分行 China Construction Bank Guizhou Branch

行长：龚蜀雄
The president of the Branch Bank: Gong Shuxiong

Since it was founded in 1954, China Construction Bank, Guizhou Branch has worked tightly around the economic development of Guizhou Province and is also developed with the provincial economy, especially after the Open and Reform policy. In recent years, the Branch took headquarter's strategy and the West Developing strategy of Provincial Party Committee and Government as its guidance, supported for fundamental construction actively. The loans for industries of electricity, traffic, communication, petroleum account for more than 80% of the recent two years' total loans. Up to 2001, the total savings are 28.4 billion yuan, 5.2 billion more than those of the beginning of the year. The total loans are 15.758 billion yuan, 2.684 billion more than those at the beginning of the year. The rate of improper loans is 14.49%, 6.51% or 0.612 billion yuan less than that at the beginning of the year. It has made the profit of 0.16 billion yuan, standing at the front of the local 5 commercial banks. The Branch achieved both in supporting local economic construction and in making Profit.

At present, the Branch Bank takes full advantages of its own network and technology, develops services actively, provides comprehensive and personalized quality financial services by all means.

中国建设银行贵州省分行自1954年成立以来，紧紧围绕贵州省经济的发展开展工作，随着贵州经济的发展而发展，改革开放以来各项业务更是蓬勃发展。特别是近几年来，建行贵州分行紧紧围绕总行发展战略和贵州省委省政府西部大开发的战略目标，积极向支持基础设施建设倾斜，向电力、交通、通讯、石油等行业投放力度占该行近两年贷款的80%以上。到2001年底止，该行各项存款达284亿元，比年初增加52亿元；贷款157.58亿元，比年初增加26.84亿元；不良贷款余额比年初下降6.12亿元，不良率14.49%，比年初下降6.51个百分点；实现利润达1.6亿元，名列当地五大商业银行榜首，实现了支持地方经济建设和自身效益的双丰收。

目前，该行利用自身网络优势和科技支撑，积极开发服务品种，采取不同的服务手段，为客户提供综合化、个性化的优质的金融服务。

省建行大楼
Buildling of China Construction Bank, Guizhou Branch

贵阳市商业银行
GUIYANG COMMERCIAL BANK

贵阳市商业银行是经中国人民银行总行批准成立，贵州省第一家具有独立法人资格的地方性股份制商业银行。1997年4月18日正式开业，现有职工2000余人，营业机构91个，遍布贵阳市10个区、市、县。

贵阳市商业银行以做“市民自己的银行”为己任，“立足中小，服务市民，回报社会”为宗旨，推出了“365天天天营业，24小时时时服务”的独家品牌，开通了储蓄、对公业务通存通兑，资金异地汇划24小时可抵达全国各地8000多个网点；在全省首家推出DPI指纹密码保管箱及多功能、智能化的“甲秀卡”，在全省首家推出“储户免填单”服务，在全国城市商行首家代理国家开发银行贷款；还推出了“市民小额融资贷款”、“住房按揭贷款”、“住房装修贷款”、“汽车消费贷款”、“个人耐用消费品贷款”；开发了“保得利保险”、“代理资产评估”、“贷款承诺”、“企业信用等级评估”、“企业财务顾问”、“代理工程监理”等中间业务，以及各种代收代付业务；作为国债、金融债承销团成员，进一步拓展了投资业务。

贵阳市商业银行综合营业大厦
The office plaza of Guiyang Commercial Bank

贵阳市商业银行致力于建立具有行业特色的企业文化和良好的企业风貌。通过开展“三优两满意”活动，按照“优质服务”、“优良作风”、“优美环境”的要求，积极提升员工和企业的素质，培养“市民满意的银行员工”，建设“市民满意的银行”。有2个支行荣获国家级“青年文明号”及国家级“青年文明号信用建设示范单位”称号，近30个支行荣获省、市、区级“文明单位”、“青年文明”称号。

经过4年多的发展，截止2001年12月末，全行总资产达129亿元，是建行之初的4.3倍；各项存款余额109亿元，是建行之初的4倍；各项贷款余额75亿元，是建行之初的5.3倍。累计实现利润3.21亿元，上缴税金1.9亿元，股东回报1.2亿元，为贵阳地方经济发展和社会进步做出了积极的贡献。

Guiyang Commercial Bank was founded with the approval of the headquarter of the People's Bank of China. It is the first local stock commercial bank with independent corporate organization. The Bank was opened on 18th April 1997 and now has over 2,000 staff members, 91 sales centers all through the districts, cities and counties of Guiyang.

Guiyang Commercial Bank takes "being citizens' bank" as its responsibility, and "stand on middle and small accounts, server citizens, reciprocate the society" as its aim. The Bank has provided "365 days' business, 24 hours' service" and services of saving and acceptance of public business. Remitted money can reaches over 8000 sales centers through the country in 24 hours. It is the first bank to promote DPI coffer, multi-functional intellectual "Jiaxiu Card" and "exempt from filling" service in the province. It is the first bank of the city commercial banks to be the agent of loan of the State Development Bank. In addition, the Bank has provided "small loan for citizens' investment", "house loan", "loan for house decoration", "loan for auto", loan for personal consumer goods" and "profitable insurance", capital assessment", "commitment for loan", "registration and evaluation of enterprise's credit", "financial consultant for enterprise", "agent of project supervision" and agent of other acceptance and payment. As a member of sales group of national and other financial debt, the Bank has further developed its investment business.

丰富多彩的“商行之夜”文娱演出
Colorful programs of "night of Commercial Bank"

Guiyang Commercial Bank is devoted to building enterprise culture with trade features and good style and features of the enterprise. With the program of "three excellences and two satisfies", the Bank has vigorously improved the quality of staff members and enterprise, cultivated "satisfying bank employees" and built "satisfying bank" according to the requirement of "quality service", "fine style of work" and "beautiful working conditions". Two branch banks have been awarded national "youth civilized unite" and "youth civilized demonstrative unit of credit construction". Nearly 30 branch banks have been awarded provincial, city or district "civilized unit" and "youth civilization".

With the 4 years' development, the general assets of the Bank are 12.9 billion yuan at the end of Dec 2001, 4.3 times of those at the foundation of the bank. The general savings of all sorts are 10.9billion yuan, 4 times of those at the foundation of the bank. The total amount of loans is 7.5billion yuan, 5.3 times of those at the foundation of the bank. The total profits are 321 million yuan. Handed taxes are 190 million yuan. 120 million yuan has been reciprocated to shareholders. The bank has made great contributions to local economic development and progress of the society.

向郊县扩张——新组建的小河支行
Extend to suburbs--newly built Xiaohe Branch Bank

国家开发银行

China Development Bank

办好银行与信用建设并举

To commit to not only a good bank, but also a healthy credit environment

贵州省委书记钱运录和国家开发银行行长陈元共同为贵阳分行揭牌

Qian Yunlu, the Secretary of the Provincial Party Committee and Chen Yuan, the Governor of China Development Bank, were unveiling for Guiyang Branch.

贵州省省长石秀诗和国家开发银行行长陈元代表双方签定新一轮金融合作协议

Shi Xiushi, the Governor of Guizhou Province, and Chen Yuan, the Governor of China Development Bank, signed a new turn financial cooperation Agreement.

国家开发银行贵阳分行，是国家开发银行为支持西部大开发、支持贵州省经济发展，在西部地区设立的又一家分行，也是国家开发银行成立的第30家分行。国家开发银行贵阳分行成立后，将继续贯彻“既要防范金融风险，又要支持经济建设”的方针，立足于发展贵州省经济，充分发挥国家开发银行债券银行、批发银行的优势，与金融同业优势互补，为客户提供优质高效的金融服务。同时以提高信贷资产质量为重点，防范和化解信贷风险，并与地方政府密切配合，共同推进信用建设，以金融的高效率支持贵州经济发展，为贵州实施西部大开发战略增添动力。

国家开发银行自1994年成立以来，已累计向贵州发放贷款224.8亿元，贷款涉及电力、煤炭、公路、铁路、城建、通信、民航、化工等15个行业的98个建设项目，为贵州省经济发展做出了突出贡献。在“十五”期间，国家开发银行贵阳分行将继续加大对贵州省的贷款力度，预计承诺贷款超过300亿元，投放贷款超过200亿元，在基础设施等长期融资领域充分发挥主力银行作用。

国家开发银行支持的重点项目--贵阳市中心环线（图为大营坡立交桥）

The key project supported by China Development Bank--the Center Loop line of Guiyang City(the picture is Dayingpo cloverleaf junction)

国家开发银行支持的重点项目--安顺电厂二期工程

The key project supported by China Development Bank--Anshun Power Plant project(Phase II)

贵阳分行

Guiyang Branch

以金融的高效率支持贵州经济发展

To support the economic development of Guizhou Province by providing efficient financial services

In order to support developing the west and promoting the economic development in Guizhou, China Development Bank(CDB) set up its 30th branch - Guiyang Branch in Guiyang, Guizhou Province. Guiyang Branch will continue to follow out the policy of "preventing risk as well as promoting economic development", promote the economic development of Guizhou by taking the strength of CDB as a debenture and wholesale bank, enhance the cooperation with the other financial institutions and provide high quality financial services to its clients. Meanwhile, Guiyang Branch will focus on improving its asset quality and controlling credit risks, perfecting the credit environment together with the local government, and supporting the economic development of Guizhou Province by providing efficient financial services.

CDB has made great contributions to the economic development of Guizhou Province. Since it was founded in 1994, CDB has granted loan 22.48 billion yuan to 98 projects in Guizhou Province which covered 15 fields, e.g. power, highway, coal, railway, urban infrastructure, communication, civil aviation and etc. During the Tenth Five-Year Plan Period, CDB will further enlarge the loan support to Guizhou Province and play an important role as the main force in the long-term financing field such as infrastructure. It is expected that the admitted loan will be more than 30 billion yuan and the loan disbursement will be more than 20 billion yuan.

国家开发银行支持的重点项目--贵阳市龙洞堡机场
The key project supported by China Development Bank--Guiyang Longdongbao Airport

国家开发银行支持的重点项目--贵阳至毕节高等级公路
The key project supported by China Development Bank--Guiyang--Bijie high-level way

国家开发银行支持的重点项目--水柏铁路（图为北盘江大桥）
The key project supported by China Development Bank--Shuicheng--Baiguo Railway(the picture is Beipan River Bridge)

党委书记、行长：陆辉君
The Secretary of the Party Committee & President: Lu Huijun

加强收购
Strengthen the ma-

为贵州农业和农
Make contributions for the development

中国农业发展
The Agriculture Development

中国农业发展银行贵州省分行成立于1995年1月5日，是贵州省首家政策性银行。目前主要办理由国务院确定的粮食、油料、棉花收购、调销、储备贷款等业务，肉类、烟叶等国家专项储备贷款；中央财政对主要农产品补贴资金的拨付，为中央和省级政府建立的粮食风险基金开户及拨付；粮食企业简易建仓贷款；开户单位的存款和结算等等。当前最主要的任务是，对收购资金实行封闭管理，确保实现封闭运行。

--严格执行信贷政策，保证了收购资金供应。1999年至2001年，累计发放粮油收购、调销贷款35.7亿元，支持收购、调入粮食43.13亿斤，油菜籽6.2亿斤，保护了农民利益，促进了粮食生产。

--从严加强信贷监管，当期收购资金贷款实现了封闭运行。业务经营指标完成情况良好，经营亏损逐年减少，国有粮食购销企业亏损挂帐势头得到有效遏制，其中2001年比上年减亏1.4亿元。

--加强内部管理，构建了较为完备的内部管理考核体系。创造性地实施了对省分行机关和地县行的三级考核，初步建立了任务明确、责任到岗、考核到人、绩效挂钩的内部管理考核体系。

--系统党建和精神文明建设取得丰富成果。立足“干好工作，带好队伍”目标，全面加强系统党的思想、组织、作风建设，深入开展“比勤奋、比负责、比奉献”活动和形式多样的精神文明创建活动。

地　址：贵阳市神奇路32号
Address: Shenqi Road No. 32, Guiyang City.
邮　编（Post Code）：550002
电　话（Tel）：0851-5874965

The Agriculture Development Bank of China, Guizhou Branch was founded on 5th Jan 1995. It is the first policy bank of the province. Its current businesses are purchasing, regulating and providing loans to crops, oil plants, and cotton, which are designated by the State Council, providing special saving loans to meat, tobacco leaf, etc, providing subsidy from the central financial to main agricultural products, open the account for central and provincial grain risk fund and appropriating to it, providing loans to grain trading enterprises' simple store house, saving and checking up for enterprises' accounts. The most important task at present is to manage the purchasing fund to insure its circulation.

--Implemented credit policy strictly, insured purchasing fund. from 1999 to 2001, the branch bank has lent purchasing fund and loans of 3.57 billion yuan for crops and oil and has purchased crops of 4.313 billion jin, rapeseeds of 0.62 billion jin, thus protect farmers' benefit and improve crop production.

--Strengthened supervision on credit, the purchasing fund of current period has been circulated with no diversion. Business objects have been well achieved. Business loss has been reduced year by year. The arrears of public crops trading enterprises have been effectively controlled. The loss of 2001 is 140 million yuan less than that of last year.

--Strengthened internal management, built a comprehensive managing & exam system. The branch bank creatively conducted three-level check-up to provincial, prefectural and county organs and built a primary internal exam System.

--Made great achievements in Party construction and cultural & ideological progress of the system. Taking the aim as "do well in work and leading the team", the branch bank strengthened Party thought, organs and style construction, and held activities of "hardworking, responsibility and contribution" and all kinds of programs for cultural & ideological Progress.

资金封闭管理

–nagement of purchasing fund

村经济发展作贡献

of agriculture and rural economy of Guizhou

银行贵州省分行

Bank of China, Guizhou Branch

中国农业发展银行贵州省分行领导成员：党委书记、行长陆辉君（中）、党委副书记、副行长樊荣（右二）、党委委员、副行长刘定华（左二）、党委委员、行长助理：胡世才（左一）、巡视员汤学成（右一）

The Members of the leading group of the Agriculture Development Bank of China, Guizhou Branch: the Secretary of the Party Committee & President: Lu Huijun(the middle), the vice-secretary of the Party Committee & vice-president: Pang Rong(the second from right), the Member of the Party Committee & vice-president: Liu Dinghua(the second from left), the Member of the Party Committee & President Assistant: Hu Shicai(the first from left), the Inspector: Tang Xuecheng(the first from right)

中国农业发展银行贵州省分行办公大楼外景

Office building of the Agriculture Development Bank of China, Guizhou Branch

中国人寿保
China Life Insurance

中国人寿保险公司贵州省分公司副总经理（主持工作）：唐 群
The vice-General Manager of China Life Insurance Guizhou Branch(presides works): Tang Qun

一、贵州中国人寿保费跃上8亿。2001年，中国人寿贵州省分公司坚持“发展才是硬道理”的方针，总保费自分业经营以来，首次突破8亿，达到81059万元，完成自订年计划的101.3%，与去年同期比增长10.7%，占全省寿险市场的68.38%，继续保持国有商业寿险公司的龙头地位。

二、红红火火推出系列分红险种。到年底，省、地7个分公司获准开办10个分红产品，两个分公司获准开办其中2个分红险种，迅速掀起了推广销售分红保险的热潮。全省系统全年实现分红保险费12648万元，占首年保费的42%，成为新的业务增长点。

三、“95519”客服专线顺利开通。2001年9月20日，中国人寿贵州省分公司在全省各地同时开通“95519”客服专线，实现了与全国系统专线电话网的衔接。

四、寿险重大赔案：

1. 水城县双戛乡发生特大瓦斯爆炸。该矿于2001年10月投保井下作业人员20人，每人死亡保险金额2万元，按照保险条款规定，中国人寿六盘水分公司于10月14日下午14：10分现场预付赔款20万元。

2. 册亨县境内发生一起特大交通事故。中国人寿贞丰县支公司预付16万元，赔付总额19.7万元，作为伤者的抢救费和死者的善后费用。

3. 中国人寿兑现一笔29万余元理赔案。杨某生前已在中国人寿贵州省分公司投保了《养老金还本保险（97版）》等四个险种，总保额达29.6万元。经核准，中国人寿保险公司同意给付杨某死亡保险金29.6万元。

中国人寿保险公司贵州省分公司办公大楼
Office building of China Life Insurance Guizhou Branch

险公司 贵州省分公司
Company, Guizhou Branch

1. The insurance premium of Guizhou China Life Insurance has broken 800 million yuan. In 2001, China Life Insurance Guizhou Branch stuck to the policy of "development is key point". Since independent business management, the general premium has broken 800 million yuan for the first time, which is 810.59 million yuan. The premium of 2001 is 1.013 times of what is expected and 10.7% more than last year, holding 68.38% of the provincial premium and standing at the front of the field in the province.

2. Start bonus-sharing insurance. By the end of the year, 7 provincial or prefectural branch companies were approved to begin 10 kinds of bonus-sharing product. 2 branch companies were approved to begin two of the bonus-sharing insurance. The company brought the fad of bonus-sharing insurance. The insurance system of the province has got 126.48 million yuan premium for bonus-sharing insurance, holding 42% of the premium of the year. The bonus-sharing insurance becomes a new growing point of business.

3. "95519" service line. China Life Insurance Guizhou Branch has opened service line of "95519" simultaneously in every area of the province on 20th Sep 2001, connected with the national system telephone network.

4. Major indemnity cases:

(1) Big gas explosion happened in Shuangjia Township Shuicheng County. The mining company has paid for life insurance of 20 thousand yuan for 20 underground miners. According to insurance regulations, China Life Insurance Liupanshui Branch has paid 200 thousand yuan at 14:10 on 14th Oct.

公司员工在街头开展宣传咨询活动
Employees were conducting popularizing and consulting activity on street.

(2) A big traffic accident happened in Ceheng County. China Life Insurance Zhenfeng County Branch paid deposit premium of 160 thousand yuan and the total indemnity of 197 thousand yuan for clinic and funeral use.

(3) China Life Insurance has paid over 290 thousand yuan as promised. Yang had bought 4 kinds of insurance whose total indemnities are 296 thousand yuan. After confirmation, China Life Insurance agreed to pay 296 thousand yuan to Yang.

地　址：贵阳市遵义路45号保险大厦
Address : Zunyi Road 45#, Guiyang City
电　话（Tel）: 0851-5849250
传　真（Fax）: 0851-5815110
邮　编（Post Site）: 550002

森林之城
City of forest

市委书记：王晓东
The Secretary of the City Party Committee: Wang Xiaodong

市长：孙国强
The Mayor: Sun Guoqiang

“贵阳”由来，中国古代以山北为阴，山南为阳。“贵阳”因城区位于境内贵山以南而得名，古代贵阳盛产竹子，以制作乐器築而闻名，古简称“築”，后简化为筑。

贵阳市位于中国西南云贵高原东部。是贵州省省会，全省政治、经济和文化中心。2002年，全市国内生产总值302.75亿元，全市地方财政收入27.97亿元。贵阳市现辖云岩区、南明区、花溪区、乌当区、白云区、小河区、清镇市、开阳县、修文县、息烽县。2002年，全市总人口335.81万人，其中非农业人口156.56万人，占总人口的46.6%。贵阳是一个以汉族为主的多民族聚居的城市。据第五次人口普查资料统计，汉族人口占总人口的84.6%。少数民族人口占15.4%，贵阳民族共有50个，其中以布依族、苗族的人口为多，二者合计占少数民族人口总数的70%。

贵阳市人民政府新闻办供稿
Writen by News Office of Guiyang Government

——贵阳

——Guiyang

The north to a mountain is called Yin and the south to a mountain is called Yang in ancient times of China. The name of "Guiyang" is called because that the city lies in the south to Gui Mountain. Guiyang is famous for growing bamboo and making an instrument "zhu" with bamboo in ancient times.

Guiyang situates in the east of Yungui plateau of southwest China. It is the capital and political, economic, cultural center of Guizhou Province. The GDP of the city of 2002 is 30.275 billion yuan. The local revenue is 2.797 billion yuan. Guiyang city governs Yunyan District, Nanming District, Huaxi District, Wudang District, Baiyun District, Xiaohe District, Qingzhen City, Kaiyang County, Xiuwen County and Xifeng County. The general population of 2002 is 3.3581 million. 1.5656 million people are not agricultural people, holding 46.6% of the general population. Guiyang is a city of muti-nationality people, of which most are Hanzu. According to the 5th census, Hanzu holds 84.6% and minority nationality holds 15.4%. There are 50 nationalities in Guiyang. Most of minority nationality people are Buyi and Miaozu, holding 70%.

贵阳火车站
Guiyang Railway Station

全国乡镇企业东西合作经贸洽谈会
An Economic and Trade Fair of East-West Cooperation of National Township Enterprise

贵阳市甲秀楼夜景
A night view of Jiaxiu Pavilion, Guiyang

森林之城

City of forest

贵阳市人民政府新闻办供稿
Writen by News Office of Guiyang Government

贵阳属亚热带湿润温和型气候，夏无酷暑，冬无严寒，阳光充足，雨水充沛。空气不干燥，四季无风沙，年平均气温在15.3℃左右。其中，最热的七月下旬平均气温为24℃，最冷的一月上旬，平均气温是4.6℃，宜人的气候是贵阳的骄傲，搏得了“上有天堂下有苏杭，气候宜人数贵阳”之誉。

1987年贵阳市确定的市花为：兰花、紫薇。市树为樟树、竹子。贵阳市被称为“森林之城”，贵阳市行政区域内现有林地面积275万亩，森林覆盖率为34.8%，此外，市区四周群山环抱，林木苍翠，宽1至7公里，长逾70公里的环城林带，为贵阳市提供了绿色生态屏障。目前，投资1.1亿元人民币，总长223公里，面积43万亩的新环城林带正在建设中。2010年前人均环城林带面积将达到207平方米。

贵阳拥有全国科教兴市先进城市，全国“双拥”模范城市，全国卫生城市，全国园林绿化先进城市，中日环境合作示范城市，中国优秀旅游城市等称号。

2001年首届中国贵阳国际围棋文化节
The 1st China Guiyang International Go Culture Festival '2001

——贵阳

——Guiyang

Guiyang belongs to humid warm subtropical climate. There is no intense heat in summer or bitter coldness in winter. There are enough sunshine and rainfall. There is no dry air or sandstorm. The average annual temperature is about 15.3℃. The average temperature of the third 10 days of July, which is the hottest of a year, is 24℃. The average temperature of the first 10 days of Jan, which is the coldest of a year, is 4.6℃. The pleasant climate is the pride of Guiyang, bringing the praise of "Suhang is the paradise of the world, but the most pleasant climate is in Guiyang".

In 1987, Guiyang has set Orchid and crape myrtle as the flower of the city, and camphor tree and bamboo as the tree of the city. Guiyang is called "city of forest". 2.75 million mu of the total administrative areas are forest, which is 34.8%. The urban district is held around by mountains and trees. The round-the-city forest band of 1 to 7 km's wide and over 70 km's long provides a green ecological barrier for Guiyang. Now, a new round-the-city forest band, invested by 110 million yuan, which is 223 km long and 430 thousand mu, is under construction. The average forest area per person will arrive at 207 m^2 before 2010.

Guiyang owns tittles of National advanced city in building by the science and education, National example city in "Two supports" program, National health city, National advanced afforested city, demonstrative city of the cooperation between China and Japan, National advanced tourist city, etc.

贵阳西部大开发高层研讨会
The high-level seminar held in Guiyang on development of West China

贵阳金阳新区观山东路奠基
The construction ceremony of East Guanshan Road at Jinyang New Area of Guiyang

贵阳龙洞堡机场
Guiyang Longdongbao Airport

遵义市 Zunyi City

中共遵义市委书记傅传耀（中）、副书记卢守祥（右二）、刘文献（左二）、陈平安（右一）、张志年（左一）

Fu Chuanyao, the secretary of Zunyi Party Committee (middle), Lu Shouxiang, the vice-secretary (the second from right) Liu Wenxian, the vice-secretary (the second from left), Chen Ping'an, the vice-secretary (the first from right), Zhang Zhinian, the vice-secretary (the first from left).

遵义市位于贵州省北部，总面积30762平方公里，总人口722.08万人。遵义市是国务院首批公布的历史文化名城之一，因1935年中国共产党在遵义举行了政治局扩大会议，实现了革命历史大转折而闻名于世。因出产国酒“茅台酒”和众多名优酒而被誉为名酒之乡。

解放50多年，特别是改革开放以来，遵义人民在党和政府的领导下，团结奋斗、艰苦创业，使黔北大地发生了翻天覆地的变化，国民经济建设取得巨大发展，各项社会事业全面进步。遵义已成为贵州省重要的农产品生产基地和新兴工业城市。形成了能源、化工、机电、烟酒、建材、冶金、军工等支柱产业。2001年全市国内生产总值达252.57亿元，地方财政收入12.47亿元。遵义市已被列为国家西电东送的能源基地。

跨进新世纪，遵义人民正满怀信心地投入到西部大开发和全面建设小康社会的伟大事业中，遵义人民将不断开拓、努力进取，为实现富民兴遵，把遵义早日建设成现代化文明城市而继续努力。

Zunyi City lies in the north of Guizhou Province with general area of 30,762 km^2 and general population of 7.2208 million. Zunyi is one of the first group of historical cultural cities approved by the State Council. It is famous for the enlarged meeting of the Political Bureau of the Communist Party in 1935, which brought a big historic turn. It is called hometown of famous wines for manufacturing National Wine of “Maotai” and other famous wines.

In the 50 years after liberation, especially after Open and Reform, led by the Party and government, Zunyi people have united and made efforts to change North Guizhou quite a lot. Great achievements were made in national economy construction. Great progress was made in all kinds of social trades. Zunyi has become an important agricultural product base and new industrial city of Guizhou. Industries of resource, chemistry, machine & electricity, tobacco & wine, building materials, metallurgy, war industry, etc, have become the pivot industries. The GDP of 2001 is 25.257 billion yuan. The local revenue is 1.247 billion yuan. Zunyi has been designated the resource base for transmitting electricity from west to east.

In the new century, Zunyi people are confidently joining the West Developing and the construction of well-off society. Zunyi people will keep developing and advancing to build Zunyi as a modern civilized city.

1935年1月，红军长征到遵义，党中央在这里召开了政治局扩大会议，图为革命纪念地--遵义会议会址

In Jan 1935, the Red Army arrived in Zunyi in the Long March, the Central Party Committee held enlarged meeting of Political Bureau there. Here in the picture is the location of Zunyi meeting.

桫椤--国家级“赤水桫椤自然保护区”
Spinulose tree fern--National “Chishui natural protective area of spinulose tree fern”

赤水十丈洞瀑布
Shizhang Waterfall in Chishui

茅台酒厂（集团）有限责任公司茅台酒系列产品
Series products of Maotai Wine Factory (group) CO., Ltd

赤水亚热带沟谷风光
View of subtropical valley in Chishui

安顺市--黔中大地展新颜

Anshun City--taking on a new look in the middle of Guizhou

安顺市位于贵州省中西部，是世界上典型的喀斯特地貌集中地区。大部分地区属亚热带季风湿润气候，冬无严寒，夏无酷暑，雨量充沛，气候宜人。

全市国土面积9264平方公里，2001年末总人口255.17万人，有苗、布依、回、仡佬等39个少数民族，少数民族人口占总人口的38.4%，是一个多民族聚居的地区。境内旅游、能源、矿产、生物资源极为丰富。

境内有气势磅礴的黄果树瀑布和以她为中心的“十八飞瀑”瀑布群，“天然大盆景”之称的天星桥风景区以及有“地下岩溶博物馆”之称的龙宫，是国家著名风景名胜区。境内文物古迹遍布，有被世界考古学界称为“亚洲文明之灯”的普定穿洞古人类遗址、中国八大神秘文字之一的“千古之迷”红崖天书、石雕艺术建筑群安顺府文庙等众多的人文景观。古朴粗犷的屯堡地戏、原始的石头村落与优美田园风光相交辉映。安顺还是著名的无产阶级革命家王若飞，著名教育家黄齐生的故乡。丰富的旅游资源带动以旅游为龙头的第三产业较快发展。2001年全年共接待旅游总人数126万人次，其中海外游客50万人次，实现营业收入达3亿元，利润总额为2250万元。

2001年全市国内生产总值达到63.50亿元，是1978年的5.7倍。农村经济向高效、生态农业迈出坚定步伐，结构调整朝优质化和多元化发展。2001年全市农业生产总值达26.58亿元，粮食总产量达77.54万吨，油菜籽为7.07万吨，肉类总产量达7.41万吨，水产品产量达3310吨。工业在保持五金、酿酒、制革、染织等传统工业的基础上，形成了以飞机、微型轿车、机械、食品等为主的新的工业体系。2001年全市工业总产值达38.83亿元。2001年全市实现社会消费品零售额23.15亿元，是1978年的13.5倍，年均递增12.3%。投资环境日益改善，交通、通讯设施不断巩固和完善。基础设施建设增强，2001年全社会固定资产投资规模近19个亿。全市科技、教育、文化以及对外开放等各项社会事业发展迅速，人民综合素质普遍得到提高，生活水平日益改善。

展望未来，安顺市将成为在全省率先实现现代化的地区之一。

世界名瀑--黄果树

An international famous waterfall--Huangguoshu

Anshun City lies in the middle and west area of Guizhou province. It is a typical centralized place of Karst topography. Most area of the City belongs to wet subtropical monsoon climate. There is no intense heat in summer or bitter coldness in winter. There is enough rainfall. The climate there is very pleasant.

安顺机场
Anshun Airport

西秀区街景
Street scene of Xixiu district

老一辈无产阶级革命家王若飞故居
The former residence of Wang Ruofei, a proletarian revolutionary of the older generation

The territory of the City is 9264 k㎡. The general population at the end of 2001 is 2.5517 million. There are 39 minority nationalities living in the City as Miao, Buyi, Hui, Gelao, etc. the population of minority nationality accounts for 38.4% of the general population. It is a place where a lot of nationality people live in compact communities. There are rich resources of tourist, energy, mine and biology in the City.

There are the majestic Huangguoshu Waterfall and the surrounding waterfall group of "18 Flying Waterfall", Tianxingqiao scenic spot which is called "Big Natural Potted Landscape" and the Dragon Palace which is called "Underground Karst Museum" are all famous national scenic spots. There are lots of cultural relics and historic sites through the City as the ruins of paleozoic human in Puding Chuandong which is called "the Lamp of Asian Civilization", Hongya Heaven Script which is one of the 8 mistrial scripts of China and is considered to be a mystery of thousands of years, the carved stone group of Anshunfu Culture Temple. There are unsophisticated and straightforward local opera of Tunbao, primeval stone village and beautiful countryside scenery. In addition, Anshun is the hometown of Wang Ruofei, who is famous proletarian revolutionary, and Huang Qisheng, who is famous educationist. The rich tourist resource has driven the development of the third industry. In 2001, the city has received 1.26 million tourists, 500 thousand are overseas tourists. The City has realized sales income of 300 million yuan and profit of 22.5 million yuan.

The GDP of the City of 2001 is up to 6.35 billion yuan, which is 5.7 times of that of 1978. The rural economy is developed to be efficient, and ecological. The structure regulation is developed to be quality and diversified. In 2001, the gross agricultural output value of the City is 2.658 billion yuan. The general output of grain is 775.4 thousand tons. The general output of rapeseed is 70.7 thousand tons. The general output of meat is 74.1 thousand tons. The general output of aquatic product is 3310 tons. In the field of industry, on the base of keeping traditional industries of hardware, wine-making, tannery, dying and textile, the City has cultivated new industrial system dominated by flight, micro-car, engineering and food industry. The gross industrial output value of 2001 is 3.883 billion yuan. The City has realized its social retail incomes of consumer goods of 2.315 billion yuan, which is 13.5 times of that of 1978. The average annual growth rate is 12.3%. The environment of investment has been improved gradually. Equipment of traffic and communication has been consolidated and improved. Fundamental construction has been strengthened. The investment for fixed assets of 2001 is almost 1.9 billion yuan. All kinds of social trades as technology, education, culture and opening have been developed fast. The general quality of people has been raised. Living standard has been improved.

Looking forward, Anshun City will become one of the areas realizing moderation in the front of the province.

安顺发电厂是贵州省目前单机容量最大、投资最多、自动化程度最高的大型火力发电厂
Anshun Power Plant is a thermal power plant with the largest per unit installed capacity, largest investment and highest automation of the province.

黔西南布依族

Southwest Qian Buyizu Miaozu

认真实践“三个代表”重要思想

Practice the theory of “three representatives” carefully,

黔西南州州长：黄康生

The Governor of the Prefecture: Huang Kangsheng

黔西南布依族苗族自治州地处黔、滇、桂三省区结合部，全州行政区域面积16.9万公顷，辖8县市129个乡镇。

2001年，黔西南州认真实践江总书记“三个代表”重要思想，全州国内生产总值67.2亿元，比上年增长9.4%；财政总收入7.73亿元，比上年增长11.97%；固定资产投资完成18亿元，比上年增长20%；粮食实现连续9年丰收，总产量100.14万吨。经济结构调整取得进展，综合经济实力明显增强，在全省的位次向前移。

“十五”期间全州国内生产总值年均增长11%以上，财政收入年均增长11%以上，人口自然增长率控制在11%以内，农村居民人均收入和城镇居民人均可支配收入年均增长5%以上。实现上述目标，将抓好以下工作：一是主攻水火电。形成电力基地，西电东送的枢纽，争取“十五”到“十一五”期间装机容量在现有350万千瓦基础上增加300万千瓦，实现能源兴州。二是主攻煤炭和黄金。“十五”期末实现年产1000万吨原煤（可实现税费2.5亿元）、20万两黄金，使全州煤炭和黄金真正形成规模，形成产业。三是主攻以中草药为主的医药工业，把医药工业培育成新的支柱产业。在天地、云峰、华圣通过GMP认证基础上，继续抓好贵州苗药药业、心意药业、圣都药业的GMP认证工作，积极提高产品在市场上的知名度及占有率。四是主攻以南北盘江流域为主的绿色产业带。在低热地带发展亚热带水果、早熟蔬菜；温带发展优质水稻、玉米；高寒地带发展茶叶。落实退耕还林还草，形成以南北盘江流域为主的绿色产业带。五是主攻旅游业。

兴义市街心花园

A central garden of the street in Xingyi

兴义布依族查白歌节

The Cha Bai Singing Festival of Buyi minority nationality in Xingyi

苗族自治州
Autonomous Prefecture

推进黔西南经济社会跨越式发展
promote the social development of Southwest Qian at leap speed

Southwest Qian Buyizu Miaozu Autonomous Prefecture is located in the joint of three provinces as Qian, Dian and Gui. The general administrative area is 169 thousand hectare, with 8 counties and 129 towns and townships.

In 2001, the Prefecture has summarized the important theory of "three representatives" of General Secretary Jiang. The GDP of the Prefecture is 6.72 billion yuan, 9.4% more than last year. The general revenue is 773 million yuan, 11.97% more than last year. Investment on fixed assets is 1.8 billion yuan, 20% more than last year. The Prefecture has got grain harvest for continuos 9 years. The general grain output is 1.0014 million tons. Economic structure has been obviously regulated. General economic capacity has been obviously strengthened, holding higher position in the Province.

贵州醇酒厂园区景观
The garden area in the Guizhou Mellow Wine Brewery

During "Tenth Five-year Plan", the average annual increase of GDP of the Prefecture will be more than 11%. The revenue will be increased by over 11%. The natural population growth rate will be controlled within 11%. The average annual income increase of peasants and residents will be over 5%. In order to achieve the above aims, the Prefecture will stress the following works: first is water, fire and electricity. The Prefecture will found electricity base to be the pivot of transmitting electricity from west to east. The Prefecture will try to increase its installed capacity of 3.5 millioan KW during "Tenth Five-year Plan" by 3 million KW in "Eleventh Five-year Plan". Second is coal and gold. The Prefecture will achieve annual capacity of 10 million tons of raw coal (with tax fee of 250 million yuan) and 200 thousand of gold at the end of "Tenth Five-year Plan", cultivating the industries of coal and gold. Third is the medicine industry, dominated by Chinese drugs. The Prefecture will cultivate medicine industry to be a new main industry. On the base of the GMP certification of Tiandi, Yunfeng and Huasheng, the Prefecture will continue to strengthen the certification of Miaoyao, Xinyi and Shengdu to improve the holding rate and reputation of medicines. Fourth is the green industrial band of South and North Panjiang valley. The Prefecture will grow subtropical fruits and early-maturing vegetables in low heat areas, grow quality rice and corns in warm areas, and grow tea in extra cold areas. The Prefecture will change cultivated land to forest and grass, forming a green industrial band of South and North Panjiang valley. Fifth is tourist.

马岭河峡谷
The Maling River Gorge

Developing Bijie 发展中

毕节市区新貌
New look of the urban area of Bijie

贵毕高等级公路落脚河大桥雄姿
Majestic appearance of Luojiao River Bridge of Guibi high-standard way

的毕节

毕节市10万吨自来水厂
100-thousand-ton waterworks of Bijie

宽阔笔直的贵毕路缩短了毕节与世界的距离
Broad and Straight Guibi Road which shortens the distance between Biejie and the world

内昆铁路的开通结束了毕节地区无铁路的历史
The opening of Neikun railway ends the history of Bijie's lacking railway

毕节市倒天河改造初见成效--清澈河水穿城而过
Primary progress of the rebuilding of Pouring Heaven River--limpid river goes through the city

Developing Bijie 发展中

蓄水50亿立方米，装机60万千瓦的洪家渡水电站工地夜景
Night scene of the construction site of Hongjiadu Hydroelectric Station with water reserve of 5 billion m³ and installed capacity of 600 thousand KW

待运的原煤
Raw coal to be transported

纳雍阳长煤炭收费站
Toll station for coal of Nayong Yangchang

的毕节

金沙火电厂一期工程（50万千瓦）已投产运行
The first period of Jinsha Thermal Power Plant project (500 thousand KW) has been finished and put into use

装机120万千瓦的纳雍火电一厂建设工地
The construction site of Nayong No.1 Thermal Power Plant with installed capacity of 1.2 million KW

装机60万千瓦的索风营水电站工地
The construction site of Suofengying hydroelectric Station with installed capacity of 600 thousand KW.

强大的电流正源源不断输往沿海工业城市
Strong electric current is transported to coastal industrial cities

毕节化肥厂12万吨尿素生产线
The 120 thousand tons urea production line of Bijie Fertilizer Factory

Developing Bijie 发展中

威宁高原牧场牛羊成群
Herds of cattle and flock of sheep on the grazing land of Weining plateau

"中日3356工程"、"长治"、"长防"等工程项目的实施使
"China-Japan 3356 project", "long-governing pro-
ecological environment of Bijie

大方安洛万亩草场
10 thousand-mu grassland of Dafang Anluo

毕节松林烤烟基地
Songlin flue-cured tobacco base of BijIe

绿树成林梯田环绕
Green forest surrounded by terraced fields

的毕节

全区生态环境明显改善
ject" and "long-prevention project" have improved the

全国重点风景名胜区--织金洞
National key scenic area--Zhijin Cave

毕节卷烟厂咀烟车间
The grinding workshop of Bijie cigarette factory

国家森林公园--百里杜鹃林带
National forest park--100-Li Cuckoo Forest Band

国家自然保护区--草海晨曦
First ray of the morning sun in Sea of Grass--National natural protection area

国家重点文物保护单位--大方奢香墓
National key cultural protection site--Dafang Shexiang Tomb

中国唯一的综合电信运营商

The only comprehensive telecom managing corporation in China

中国联合通信有限公司

China United Communication Co., Ltd

CDMA开通仪式

The opening ceremony for CDMA

中国联合通信有限公司（简称中国联通）是经国务院批准成立的我国第二家经营电信基本业务和增值业务的全国性国有企业，是国务院直接管理的44家大型国有骨干企业之一，也是我国目前唯一经营电信综合业务的电信运营企业。去年，中国联通圆满完成在美国、香港的首次股票公开发行，成为国际性电信运营商。2000年，被中国企业联合会等团体评为当年最具影响力企业。

贵州分公司是中国联通在贵州的分支机构，下设8个地市分公司。在中共贵州各级党委、政府的支持和社会各界的帮助下，在整整3年的艰苦奋斗历程中，贵州联通人通过自身的努力，使贵州分公司取得了长足的发展。目前除130GSM网络已实现全省覆盖外，已开通了“如意通”智能网、193长途网、ATM数据骨干网、165互联网、IP电话网、IP宽带城域网、1001客户服务等业务。还开通了130移动网业务，使130手机短讯和联通寻呼机可互相传送信息。2002年元月，在全省开通了新一代移动通信网---联通新时空CDMA133移动通信网。事实证明，中国联通为贵州人民提供了更多的通信选择和更全面的通信服务。

China United Communication Co., Ltd (called China Unicom) is the second nationwide public enterprise approved by the State Council, dealing with basic telecom business and business for increasing value. It is one of the 44 large pivot enterprises directly under the State Council, and also at present, the only telecom managing enterprise dealing with comprehensive telecom business in China. Last year, China Unicom has successively finished its first stock issue on American and Hong Kong market and becomes an international telecom managing enterprise. In 2000, it was awarded the most impressive enterprise of the year by Chinese Enterprise Association and other group.

Guizhou Branch is the branch of China Unicom in Guizhou, with 8 prefectural or city branches. With support of the Party Committee and Government of its level in Guizhou and helps of all the fields of the society, after 3 years' hard working, people of Guizhou Unicom has made efforts for the fast development of Guizhou Unicom. Besides that the GSM network of 130 is available through the province, the Company has opened the network of “Ru Yi Tong”, long-distance network of 193, ATM data network, 165 Internet, IP telephone network, IP broad band network, 1001 client service. In addition, the Company has opened the mobile business for 130 to connect sms of 130 with BP of Unicom. In Jan 2002, Guizhou Branch has opened the CDMA network of 133 in the province. It is proved that China Unicom has provided more communication choices and more comprehensive services for Guizhou people.

中国联通贵州分公司

The China Unicom, Guizhou Branch

贵州省数据通信局

Guizhou Data Communication Bureau

贵州省数据通信局是中国电信集团贵州省分公司下属的专业局，是贵州电信公用数据通信网的专业管理和运营部门，担负着全省数据通信各项业务的网络建设、运行维护、业务经营和技术服务，并向用户提供业务咨询、组网方案设计、系统集成及协调全省集团用户进网的一条龙服务等服务。贵州电信公用数据通信网经过多年建设，目前已建设成为一个设备、技术先进、管理完善、优质畅通、覆盖全省各地、州、市、县、通达全国的数据通信网，向社会开放分组交换、数字数据网（DDN）、帧中继网、计算机互联网（163/169）、ISDN、中国电信宽带网、域名注册、网站建设、虚拟主机、服务器托管等各项业务，热忱向全省用户提供优质、高速、安全、经济、便捷的服务。

Guizhou Data Communication Bureau is a specialized bureau under China Telecom Group, Guizhou Branch. Also, it is the managing department of Guizhou telecom public data communication network. It is responsible for the net construction , management, maintenance, business and technique service of the data communication of the province. Also, the Bureau provides users with business consultant, network program design, system integration and assistance for group users of the province to join in the network. After several years' construction, Guizhou telecom public data communication network has become a quality and smooth data communication network with advanced equipment and technique, complete management, covering all the areas, prefectures, cities and counties of the province. The Bureau opens group exchange, DDN, relay net, net of 163/169, ISDN China Telecom wide band, domain rgister, Website design, virtual hosting, hosting service to the society. The Bureau provides quality, speedy, safe, economic and convenient service for users of the province warmly and sincerely.

地　址：贵阳市延安东路3号智诚大厦15层
Address: Zhicheng Building 15F, No. 3 East Yan'an Road, Guiyang City
业务咨询电话（Business consultant）**：0851-6858288**
故障申告电话（Consumer service）**：0851-6616800**
http://www.gzinfo.net
E-mail:wabwaster@public.gz.cn

贵州省粮食局
Guizhou Grain Bureau

省委常委、副省长王正福（左三）、省粮食局局长刘启云（左二）在粮改试点调研动员会上
Wang Zhengfu, the member of the standing committee of the provincial Party Committee and the vice-Governor of the Province(the third from left), Liu Qiyun, the head of the Provincial Grain Bureau (the second from left) were at the promotion meeting for grain reform.

刘启云局长在豫贵粮食经贸合作洽谈会上讲话
Liu Qiyun, the head of the Bureau, was speaking at the conference of He'nan and Guizhou Grain Trading Meeting.

贵州省粮食局是省政府直属机构，负责贯彻落实国家有关粮食政策，研究和实施全省粮食宏观调控、总量平衡，制定中长期和年度计划，负责全社会粮食流通的管理和行业指导，保证军需民食和粮食安全。

几年来，在省委、省政府的领导下，省粮食局认真贯彻落实粮改"三项政策"，加快粮食购销企业改革，取得了初步成效。1997-2001年5年间，共收购粮食279.5万吨，销售263.2万吨，省外粮食调入逐年减少，年末库存粮食保持稳定，保证了退耕还林粮食供应、军粮供应以及救灾救济等粮食供应。全省粮食购销企业减员分流达46.8%；扭亏增盈工作成效显著，2001年同比减亏35.6%。开展大规模的粮食清仓查库工作，进行了清资核货工作，促进了库存粮食的规范管理。抓好中央储备粮库和省级储备库建设，逐步实现储备粮垂直管理，为搞好粮食宏观调控、确保粮食安全奠定了基础。

省粮食局召开企业座谈会，对全国"放心粮油"我省产品进行授牌
The Provincial Grain Bureau held meeting to awarded "national safe products" of the province.

Guizhou Grain Bureau is a provincial government's organ in charge of implementing national grain policies, researching and carrying provincial grain distribution, drawing up middle or long term plan and yearly plan, governing and guide the circulation of grains, ensuring military and civil grain and the safety of the grains.

In recent years, under the leadership of Provincial Party Committee and Government, the Bureau has implemented "three reform policies" carefully and accelerated the reform of grain trading enterprises and made primary success. During the 5 years of 1997 to 2001, the Bureau has purchased 2.795 million tons of grain and sold 2.632 million tons. The allocation from other provinces gets less and less. The storage at the end of the year is kept steady to ensure the grain supply, military supply, and assistance to disaster area. The trading enterprises of the province have reduced 46.8% of their staff to reduce loss and increase profit. The loss of 2001 has been reduced by 35.6%. The Bureau has conducted large scope exams to storage houses, assets and goods to improve the standard management of grains. Meanwhile, it stressed the construction of the Central Party reserve and provincial reserve, realized vertical management of reserve grains, laid foundation for macroscopic regulation and safety of grains.

贵州省农机局
Agricultural Machine Bureau of Guizhou Province

2002年6月9日，贵州省人民政府副省长刘长贵看望“全国安全生产活动月”贵州省农机局宣传点
On 9th June 2002, Liu Changgui, the vice-governor of Guizhou Province was inspecting the popularizing spot of Guizhou Agricultural Machine in the program of "the State Safe Production Month"

联合收割机进行机收水稻作业
Combine harvester is working on rice

农业机械化是用机器逐步代替人、畜力进行农业生产的技术改造和经济发展的过程。全省农机工作始终坚持因地制宜，分类指导，有选择地发展农机化的工作方针，实行国家、集体、合作和农户个人等多种形式并存的农业机械所有制和经营形式，以提高土地产出率和经济效益为中心，以田间作业为主，与农副产品加工、生态环境改善相结合，实现了农、林、牧、副、渔各业机械综合发展。

2001年全省农机总动力达到648万千瓦，农机经营总收入达23.64亿元。大中型拖拉机1.8万台，小型拖拉机5.36万台，农用运输车3.91万辆，农副产品加工机械30.23万台。全省已建立了比较完整的农机化管理和服务体系。从事农机工作的人员4043人。农业机械作业水平进一步提高。2001年全省机耕面积达到232万亩，机械植保面积244万亩，机械、半机械脱粒量193万吨，机电排灌面积333万亩，机械运输作业量131121.56万吨公里。

省农机局走上街头宣传农机安全生产知识
The Bureau went on the street to promote safe production knowledge of agricultural machine.

Mechanization of agriculture means the technical reform process and economic development of machine replacing manpower and livestock. The work of agricultural machine of the province has been carried around the policy of different ways in different conditions, guide in sorts, elective agricultural development. The Bureau has carried out all kinds of systems of agricultural machine ownership as national, collective, cooperative and private to improve land productivity and profit. The Bureau took field work as main task, cooperated agricultural by-products processing and improvement of ecological environment, and realized integrated mechanical development of farming, forestry, animal husbandry, side-line production and fishery.

The agricultural mechanical capacity of the province of 2001 is 6.48 million KW. The general sales of agricultural machine are 2.364 billion yuan. The Bureau has 18 thousand of large or middle level tractors, 53.6 thousand of small tractors, 39.1 thousand of agricultural transport vehicles, and 302.3 thousand of processing machines for agricultural by-products. A complete managing and service system of agricultural machine has been built in the province. 4043 persons are engaged in agricultural machine work. Mechanization of agriculture has been improved. In 2001, mechanically cultivated land is 2.32 million mu. Mechanically planted forest is 2.44 million mu. Mechanical or semi-mechanical threshed capacity is 1.93 million tons. Mechanically irrigated and drained area is 3.33 million mu. Mechanical transport capacity is 1.3112156 billion tons km.

贵州高速公

Guizhou Freeway Devel-

贵州高速公路开发总公司是专门从事高速公路和高等级公路建设的大型国有企业，其主要职责是负责省内高速公路和高等级公路建设项目的融资、建设、养护、经营管理及项目开发，按照中央和地方政府下达的公路建设计划，遵循市场规律并参照国际惯例组织实施。

贵州高速公路开发总公司先后修建了贵阳至黄果树公路、贵阳至遵义公路、贵阳东北绕城公路、贵阳东出口公路等高速公路和高等级公路；即将建成通车的有贵阳至新寨公路、贵阳至毕节公路；目前正在建设的项目主要有遵义至崇溪河公路、凯里至麻江公路、玉屏至铜仁公路、水城至黄果树公路、关岭至兴仁公路等。

在贵州高速公路开发总公司承建的项目中，贵黄公路荣获“改革开放十五年来全国十大公路工程”称号并获第六届全国优秀设计银质奖、交通部优质工程一等奖、贵州省科技进步一等奖；江界河大桥荣获全国科技进步二等奖、首届全国土木工程（詹天佑）大奖、贵州省科技进步一等奖；乌江大桥荣获贵州省科技进步一等奖。

党委书记：彭伯元
The Secretary of the Party Committee: Peng Boyuan
总 经 理：许德友
The General Manager: Xu Deyou
电 话（Tel）：**0851-6509635**
传 真（Fax）：**0851-6509635**
地 址：贵州省贵阳市北京路266号
Address: Beijing Road 266#, Guiyang City, Guizhou Province
邮 编（Post Code）：**550004**
背 景：贵阳至毕节公路
Highway of Guiyang to Bijie

Guizhou Freeway Development General Company is a large public enterprise specialized in constructions of freeway and high quality way. Its main responsibilities are: to raise money, construct, maintain and manage freeway and high quality way projects of the province, to implement Central Party and local governments' high-way construction plan according to market laws and international practices.

Guizhou Freeway Development General Company successively built highways as: Guiyang to Huangguoshu, Guiyang to Zunyi, northeast part of round the city highway in Guiyang, east exit highway of Guiyang. Projects that are about to be finished are Guiyang to Xinzhai, Guiyang to Bijie. Major projects that are under construction are Zunyi to Chongxihe, Kaili to Majiang, Yuping to Tongren, Shuicheng to Huangguoshu, Guanling to Xingren, etc.

Among all the projects constructed by Guizhou Freeway Development General Company, the project of Guiyang to huangguoshu highway was awarded "National 10 Major Highway Projects during the 15 years after Reforms", silver award of the 6th national excellent designing, first grade award of high-quality project awarded by the ministry of Communication, first grade award of science and technology progress of Guizhou Province. The project of Jiangjiehe Bridge was awarded second grade award of national science and technology progress, 1st Zhan Tianyou Award and first grade award of science and technology progress of Guizhou Province. The project of Wujiang Bridge was awarded first grade award of science and technology progress of Guizhou Province.

贵阳至遵义公路
Highway of Guiyang to Zunyi

六广河大桥
Bridge on Liuguang river

贵阳至新寨公路贵定互通式立交工程
Guiding Interactive Intersection project on the highway of Guiyang to Xinzhai

贵州省土地开发中心
Guizhou Land Development Center

该中心是贵州省国土资源厅直属事业机构，下设办公室（综合事务部），土地开发整理事务部、征地事务部、土地储备交易部。

该中心的宗旨是：为保护和合理利用土地提供土地开发整理技术服务。其业务范围是：承担征地的事务性、技术性工作；承担耕地补充工作，负责土地开发整理项目的实施；承担土地交易、土地收购储备的事务性、技术性工作；面向社会开展征地、土地交易、土地收购储备、土地开发整理等有关法律、法规、技术咨询等服务工作。

该中心自成立以来，以振兴贵州经济为目的，全方位开展土地开发整理、统一征地、土地收购储备等事务性、技术性工作，并取得较好成绩。

土地开发整理方面：已完成台江、惠水、锦屏、麻江、荔波、龙里等6个项目，新增耕地面积4000余亩（其中惠水项目在国土资源报和贵州日报上都作了专题报道），在实施土地开发整理项目过程中，该中心把土地开发整理同移民搬迁、扶贫结合起来一起抓，帮助项目区群众脱贫致富，取得了较好的社会效益，真正达到"开发一片，带动一方"的目的。

统一征地方面：配合厅相关处室，开展西电东送、龙滩电站、公路、铁路基础设施等省或国家重点项目的统一征地工作。

团结进取的领导班子,开发中心主任祝存伟(中),副主任黎将(左),副主任陈林(右)

The united and advancing leading group. Zhu Cunwei, the director of the Center (middle), Li Jiang, the vice-director (left), Chen Lin, the vice-director (right)

土地收购储备方面：积极开展土地收购储备，建立土地使用权有形市场的工作；中心已在部分市、县开展试点工作，力争早日把用市场方式配置土地资源、深化土地管理改革这项新工作推向全省。

该中心将以团结、进取、求实、创新的精神，本着热情、周到的服务宗旨，以活地兴黔为目标，为创美好的未来努力奋斗。

地　址：贵州省贵阳市中华北路191号
Address: North Zhonghua Road No.191, Guiyang City, Guizhou Province
邮　编(Code)：**550004**
电　话(Tel)：**0851-6827722　6815564**
传　真(Fax)：**0851-6827722**

新开发土地上农作物
Crops in newly developed land

(贵州省土地储备交易中心)

(Guizhou Land Reserve Transaction Center)

The Center is an institute directly under the Land Resource Bureau of Guizhou Province. It has four organs as office, land development and regulation, requisition of land and land reserve transaction.

The object of the Center is to provide technical services of land developing and regulating for protection and legitimate usage of land. Businesses of the Center include: undertaking routine and technical work for requisition of land, undertaking subsidiary work for cultivated land, implementing program of land developing and regulating, undertaking routine and technical work of land transaction and purchase for reserve, providing consultation of laws, regulations and technique about land requisition, transaction and purchase for reserve.

Since foundation, with the aim of building economy of Guizhou, the Center has conducted routine and technical work of land developing regulation, unitary requisition and purchase and has got good achievement.

开发中心工作人员共同研究工作
Workers of the center were discussing works

土地开发机械化施工
Mechanical construction in land developing

土地开发前土地现状.
Situations of the land before development

In the field of land developing regulation, 6 projects as Taijiang, Huishui, Jinping, Majiang, Libo and Longli, were finished. Increased cultivated land is over 4,000 mu (the project of Huishui has been monographically reported in Land Resource Paper and Guizhou Daily). During the implementation of land developing regulation, the Center connected developing regulation with the settlement of migrants and assistance to the poor, and got good social effects, realizing the aim of "develop a place and drive the place".

In the field of unitary requisition, the Center has conducted unitary requisition for national key programs of transferring electricity from west to east, Longtan power station, fundamental construction of highway and railway to assistant relating departments of Guizhou Land Resource Bureau.

In the field of land purchase, the Center has undertaken reserve work of collected land and built a tangible market for the right of land usage. The Center has begun test work in some cities and counties to promote market-led land distribution and the reform of land management to the province early.

The Center will make efforts for beautiful future with the spirit of united, progress, practical and creative, with warm and comprehensive services and with the aim of making land active and making Guizhou flourishing.

中储粮总公司 SINOGRAIN

中央储备粮贵阳直属库

STATE GRAIN RESERVES GUIYANG DEPOT

法人代表：王华贵
Representative of the corporation: Wang Huagui

中央储备粮贵阳直属库大门
The gate of Depot

中央储备粮贵阳直属库位于贵阳市南面贵阳市规划的仓储区内，距市中心14公里，与西南最大的铁路编组站--贵阳南站相邻，粮库占地26.4万平方米，共有房式仓51栋，电气化铁路专用线两条，长2.433公里，站台3座，1500吨地面消防池1口，库内消防管网及灭火器械规范。有变压器2台，515千伏安，日产100吨大米生产线一条，微机10台，并国家粮油信息中心联网。现有职工235人，固定资产达1.2亿元，属国家大型一级仓储企业。

中央储备粮贵阳直属库自1992年被命名为国家粮食储备库以来，连续8年被省、市粮食局鉴定为“四无”粮库，多次受到上级部门表彰。1992年被中商部、国家粮食储备局和全国财贸工会授予“全国粮油保管先进单位”。1995年被国内贸易部、国家粮食储备局授予“全国‘一符四无’活动先进单位”。粮库主任王华贵同志1997年被授予贵阳市“新时期先进劳动者”光荣称号。1999年粮库二期扩建工程在全国44个线上项目中第一个完成建仓任务，受到中央、省、市领导的表扬，中央建库办、国家粮食储备局李俊玲副局长等领导亲自参加竣工典礼。原国内贸易部陈邦柱部长，国家粮食局局长聂振邦、副局长郄建伟都曾到粮库视察工作，对粮库各项工作都给予了充分肯定。

2001年11月，粮库上划为中国储备粮管理总公司直管。

State Grain Reserves Guiyang Depot lies in the storage area of south Guiyang city, 14 km far away from city center and near Guiyang south railway station, which is the largest railway switchyard of southwest China. The Depot covers 264 thousand m^2, with 51 storehouses, 2 electric railways for special use that are 2.433 km long, 3 railway platforms, 1 1500-ton fire-control pool, and standard fire-control pipes and network and hydrants. The Depot has 2 transformers, 515 kvolt-ampere rice production line with daily capacity of 100 tons and 10 computers. The Depot is connected with the network of national grain and oil information center. The Depot now has staff of 235 persons and fixed assets of 120 million yuan. It is a first-level large national storage enterprise.

Since it was named National Grain Reserves in 1992, the Depot has been awarded depot without 4 sorts of pollution" by provincial and city grain bureau for continuos 8 years and was commended by higher organizations for several times. In 1992, the Depot was awarded "national advanced unite for grain and oil storage" by the Chinesse Commercial Ministry, the State Grain Storage Bureau and National Financial and Trade Union. In 1995, the Depot was awarded "national advanced unit in the program of '1 standard and 4 cleanings'" by the Domestic Commercial Ministry and the State Grain Storage Bureau. The director of the Depot, comrade Wang Huagui, was awarded "advanced worker of new times" of Guiyang in 1997. In 1999, the second period of the extending project of the Depot was first finished among the 44 construction project of the country, which was praised by leaders of the Central Party Committee, provincial and city government. Li Junling, the vice-director of Central Storehouse Construction Office and the State Grain Storage Bureau, and other leaders were attending the complement ceremony.Chen Bangzhu, former Minster of the Ministry of Domestic Trades, Nie Zhenbang, the Director of the State Grain Bureau, and Qie Jianwei, the vice-Director of the State Grain Bureau, have all come to inspect the Depot and commended all the work for the Depot.

In Nov 2001, the Depot was upgraded to be directly under the government of China Storage Grain Management Company.

中央储备粮贵阳直属库全貌
The overall picture of Depot

贵州省卫生防疫站
Guizhou Epidemic Prevention Station

贵州省卫生防疫站建于1953年6月4日，位于贵阳市云岩区八鸽岩路73号，占地4.71万平方米，内设38个职能科室，在职职工336人，其中专业人员269人。

防疫站拥有各类色谱仪、酶免疫测定仪、哺乳动物细胞中空纤维培养仪、CT检测仪等现代化设备以及大小汽车14辆，中外文书刊8万余册。

省防疫站先后获得科技成果奖189项，在国内外公开发表论文及学术交流文章1139篇，有9名科技人员享受国家或省政府特殊津贴。在省卫生厅领导下，防疫站承担了全省的急性传染病、寄生虫病等疾病的预防与控制，并承担食品卫生、环境卫生、学校卫生、放射卫生的检测，以及全省上述业务的科研培训和健康教育的技术指导。

省防疫站档案室
Archives of the Station

省防疫站毒理检测用二级医学动物实验室
Second-class animal laboary

Guizhou Epidemic Prevention Station was founded on 4th June 1953. It is located at Bageyan Road No.73, Yunyan District of Guiyang City. The Station covers 47.1 thousand m² and has 38 executive departments. It has 336 workers among which, 269 are professionals.

The Station has modern appliances as: chromatograph of all kinds, ferment immunization indicator, culture instrument for hollow fiber in mammal cells and CT. Also, it has 14 cars and over 80 thousand Chinese and foreign books.

The Station has been successively awarded 189 prizes for technique achievements and has published 1139 research papers in domestic and overseas media. 9 professionals got national or provincial government's special allowance. Under the leading of Health Department of Guizhou Province, the Station undertakes prevention and controlling works of acute infectious disease, parasitic disease of the Province. Meanwhile, it is responsible for food hygiene, environment hygiene, school hygiene, radiation hygiene, and research training and health education about the above works of the Province.

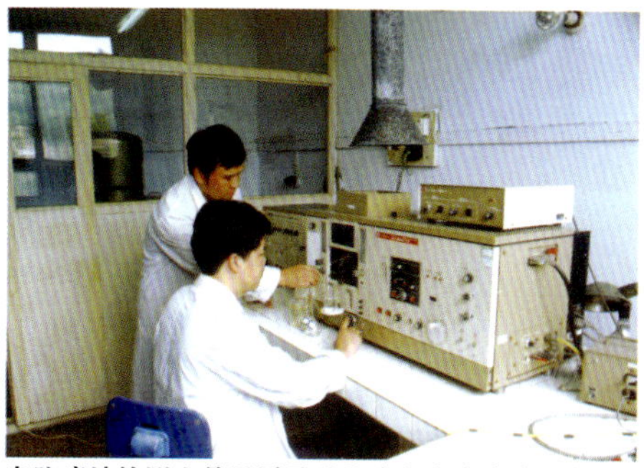
省防疫站检测人员用原子吸收分光光度计分析食品
Workers of the Station were analyzing foods with photometer.

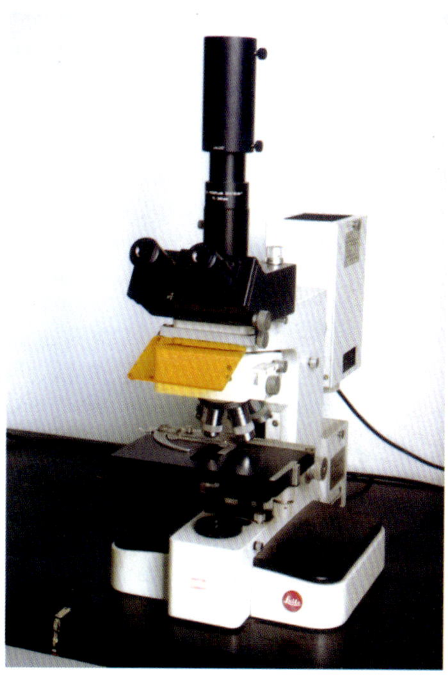

贵州省机械工业学校

Guizhou Engineering Industry School

校长：倪茂林
The Schoolmaster: Ni Maolin

校园春色
Spring scenery of the schoolyard

贵州省机械工业学校是一所以机电工程专业类为主的省级公办普通中专学校，地处贵阳市富源南路186号，毗邻贵阳南站，龙洞堡飞机场，交通十分方便。

该校有一支高素质、教学水平和管理水平过硬的教职工队伍。学校占地面积24735平方米，各类教学班31个，在校学生1524人。专兼职教师53人，其中，高级讲师13人，讲师36人。教学条件完善，校内实习实验场所齐全。具有计算机（3个计算机房共150余台）、大型的实习工厂（有车、钳、刨、铣、钻、焊、磨等几十台设备）、液压、力学、金相、电工电子电力拖动、多媒体教学、PLC（可编程序控制器）、汽车修理等实验室。学校还建有多个校外实习基地。

该校特别重视学生毕业后的就业工作，设有专门的招生就业办公室，积极联系用人单位，每年学校联系的用人单位指标数都超过当年的毕业生人数。毕业生的就业率一直名列全省前茅。

为解决学生的经济困难，学校专门实行“奖学金”、“贷学金”、“困难补助金”、“勤工俭学金”等制度，多方面帮助学生完成学业。

学校先后被省政府、省经委、市政府授予“先进教学单位”、“职工教育先进集体”、“精神文明建设先进单位”等荣誉称号。1986年至今，学校连续13年被上级主管部门评为“先进单位”。

校微机室
Computer room

实习工厂的指导老师在认真指导学生实习
Tutors of the practice factory were directing students carefully

Guizhou Engineering Industry School is a provincial public secondary school majoring in mechanical and electrical projects. It lies in south Fuyuan Road 186# of Guiyang City, near South Railway Station of Guiyang and Longdongbao Airport. It has very convenient traffic.

The School has a staff team of high quality and teaching & managing standard. It covers 24,735 ㎡ with 31 classes and 1,524 students. There are 53 full or part time teachers, among which 13 are senior lectures, 36 are lectures. The School has comprehensive teaching conditions and places for practice and experiment. The School has computers (3 computer rooms with over 150 computers), big attached factory (with instruments of lathe, pincers, digging, casting, drill, welding, grinding, etc), imitators of hydraulic pressure, mechanics, metallography and electrical traction, labs of multimedia education, PLC, and auto repairing. In addition, the School has built several practice bases outside school.

The School pays special attention to students' works after graduation. Employment office was founded to contact enterprises actively. The number of positions got by the office per year is always more than that of graduates of the year. Graduates with job keep a highest proportion in graduates in the Province.

In order to solve the economic problem for students, the School has set “scholarship”, “loan for education”, “subsidy”, “work-study fund” to assist students to finish their study in all ways.

The School has successively been awarded “advanced school”, “advanced group in staff education”, “advanced unit in cultural and ideological civilization” by provincial government, provincial economic committee and city government. From 1986 to now, the school has continuously been awarded “advanced unit” by superior department for 13 years.

国家级重点中等专业学校
The nation-level key secondary school

贵州省林业学校
Guizhou Forestry School

贵州省林业学校创建于1956年，经过40多年的发展，现已形成集农林类、资源与环境类、信息技术类、商贸与旅游类为一体的综合性国家级重点中等专业学校。

学校座落于贵阳市北郊，占地361亩，校舍建筑面积4.8万平方米，校内现代化教学设施完备，有先进的电子阅览室，近200台电脑连接校园网，400米标准田径运动场，28个专业实验室，各类生物标本7万余件，藏书11.5万册。

学校师资力量雄厚，有高级讲师20人，讲师40人，中高级职称占教师总数的68%，教师中有28人正在攻读硕士研究生。近10年来，学校教学、科研成果显著。

学校建校40多年来，已为国家输送了8000多名大、中专毕业生，为林业生态环境建设作出了重要贡献。

地　址：贵阳市修文县扎佐镇
Address: Zhazuo Town, Xiuwen County, Guiyang City
邮　编(Post code)**：550201**
电　话(Tel)**：0851-2354027**
传　真(Fax)**：0851-2354027**

实验图书大楼
Test library

学校计算机教室
Computer classroom

前排左一为书记兼校长：吴传远
The first one from left of the first row: Wu Chuanyuan, the Party Secretary & Principal.

Guizhou Forestry School, founded in 1956, is one of the nation-level key secondary schools integrating agriculture and forestry, resource and environment, IT, commercial trade and tourism, after its development for more than 40 years.

The School is situated in the north suburbs of Guiyang. The campus covers an area of 240,643㎡. The floor space of the various buildings on the campus totals 48,000㎡. The School has advanced facilities as: a reading room equipped with computers, vcd or cd players, a campus network with 200 terminal computers, a standard track and field ground with eight 400m-long circle tracks. There are 28 labs and more than 70 thousand plant and animal specimens. The school library has a book collection of over 115 thousand volumes.

The School attached great importance to its faculty development. Among the faculty, there are 20 senior lectures and 40 lectures, accounting for 68% of the entire faculty. And now, 28 teachers are taking classes for master degree. In the recent 10 years, the School has made a lot of great achievements in educational and scientific research Fields.

During over 40 years after its founding, the School has made great contributions to the country's ecological and environmental construction by its cultivation of more than 8000 college and secondary graduates.

建于80年代的贵州省新华书店办公大楼
Office building of Guizhou Province Xinghua Bookstore built in 80's.

贵州新華書店
Guizhou Province Xinhua Bookstore

——创新求变，与时俱进，再现辉煌

Be creative to seek change, developed with times, recreate wonders

贵州省新华书店是一个拥有87个地、州、市、县支店，由省级店统管全省新华书店的国有发行企业群体，由于点多面广，从而在全省范围内形成了强力、有效的发行网络。

贵州省新华书店是社会主义精神文明建设的窗口。她继承和发扬新华书店光荣的革命传统，把“为人民服务，为社会主义服务”作为发行工作的根本方针；把宣传马列主义、毛泽东思想、邓小平理论，传播科学文化知识，丰富广大人民群众的精神文化生活作为自己的基本任务。

跨入新世纪，新华书店将二次创业提上了议事日程。新世纪第二年，批销大楼、物流中心相继打下了第一根桩基。

Guizhou Province Xinhua Bookstore is a national publishing enterprise group with 87 prefectural, city and county branches. Xinhua Bookstores of the province are unitarily governed by provincial Xinhua Bookstore. As its broad publishing network, it has powerful and effective publishing channels in the province.

苗族姑娘在新华书店购书
Miaozu girl bought books in Xinhua Bookstore

新装修的贵阳市新华书店瑞北门市吸引了广大读者
The renovated Xinhua Bookstore at Ruibei attracted a lot of readers

Guizhou Province Xinhua is the window of the construction of socialist spiritual civilization. She carries on the glorious revolutionary traditions of Xinhua Bookstore, takes “serving people, serving socialism” as its essential aim, takes promoting Marxism-Leninism, Mao Zedong thought, Deng Xiaoping Theory, spreading knowledge, and making people's life colorful as its essential task.

In the new century, Xinhua Bookstore has proposed second creation. In the second year of new century, the Wholesale Building and Circulation Center were in construction.

新颖别致的花溪新华书店休闲书吧
Novel and special casual Book Bar of Huaxi Xinghua Bookstore

地址：贵阳市延安中路13号
Address: Middle Yan'an Road No. 13, Guiyang City

在建的贵州省新华书店图书批发中心综合大楼
Wholesale Building of Guizhou Province Xinghua Bookstore under construction

即将建成的贵州省新华书店物流中心
Circulation Center of Guizhou Province Xinghua Bookstore which is about to be finished

新世纪第一年的贵阳公交

Guiyang Public Transit in the first Year of the New Century

党委书记、总经理：李涌泉
The Secretary of the Party Committee & GM: Li Yongquan

贵阳市公共交通总公司属国有大二型企业。在新世纪的第一年，该公司取得了两个文明建设双丰收。公司拥有营运车辆1300多辆，营运线路73条，线路长度1165公里，客运人次3.4亿，票款收入近2亿元。全员劳动生产率37620元/人，利润316万元。四项安全指数全面下降。

公司新开辟线路9条，延伸线路11条，并对部分线路行驶段面进行了调整。9月11日起顺利实施启用新的IC卡电子收费系统，取代TM卡电子收费系统。总计发行15万张IC卡。公司投资500万元，一批现代式、仿古式的候车廊遍布贵阳市。

为提高该公司管理水平，聘请贵州省9000质量体系技术咨询中心开始对公司贯标认证。全公司各条线路开展“创品牌线路”活动；公司党委被中共中央组织部评为“全国先进基层党组织”；公司荣获贵州省委、省政府授予“贵州省有突出贡献的国有企业”称号。

2001年是公司50周年，全公司上下在欢庆的同时表示，要发扬公交艰苦创业的精神，以积极姿态投入二次创业，为公交明天的辉煌而努力。

Guiyang Public Transit General Company is a second grade largest public company. In the first year of the new century, the Company made achievements in the two civilizations construction. It has over 1,300 buses, 73 routes and 340 million passengers. The length of its bus lines is 1,165 km. Its ticket income is almost 200 million yuan and profit is 3.16 million yuan. Productivity of the whole Company is 37,620 yuan per person. The four security indexes have been lowered.

The Company opened 9 new routes, extended 11 routes and regulated some routes. From 11st Sep, the Company used IC ticket system to replace TM ticket system. There were total 150 thousand IC cards issued. The Company has invested 5 million yuan to build modern and classic bus stations all through Guiyang City.

In order to improve its management, the Company invited ISO-9000 consulting center to do the certification. Every route of the Company has conducted “ build brand” program. The Party Committee of the Company has been awarded “ Advanced National Basic Party Group” by the Organization Department of the Centre Party Committee. The Company has been awarded “ public enterprise with great contributions of Guizhou Province” by the provincial Party Committee and Government.

2001 is the 50th anniversary of the Company. As the whole staff celebrating the anniversary, they expressed that they must develop hardworking sprite of the public transit and actively join in the second creation, make efforts for public transit's good future.

1路“黄海”牌公交车投入营运
Renewal bus of “yellow sea” brand in 2001

地处花溪的仿古式候车廊。
Bus stop of classic style located in Huaxi

贵阳市
Guiyang Public

贵阳市公安局局长林连华（左二）在布置工作
Lin Lianhua, the director of Guiyang Public Security Bureau (the second from left) was assigning work.

贵阳市公安局

人民公安坚持以马列主义、毛泽东思想和邓小平理论为指针，忠于党，忠于祖国，忠于人民，忠于法律，为保卫国家安全，为社会创造良好的治安环境，作出了重要贡献。在改革开放的新形势下，全面提高了民警队伍素质，严格执法，热情服务，深入开展严打、扫除黄、赌、毒、打击拐卖人口，加强治安、交通、消防管理，全面实施社会治安综合治理，为维护政治社会稳定，保障改革开放和经济发展又创建了不朽的功勋。

江泽民总书记指出："实践证明，公安队伍是一支党和人民完全可以信赖的、有坚强战斗力的队伍，不愧为坚强的共和国后盾。"

在新世纪，贵阳市公安局将不断激励自己，继往开来，勇往直前，为人民公安工作创造更加辉煌的业绩。

为壮烈牺牲的英雄送行
See off heroes

公安局

Security Bureau

People's public security officers stick to be guided by Marxism-Leninism, Mao Zedong Thought and Deng Xiaoping Theory. They are loyal to the Party, their country, their people and the law. They have made important contributions in protecting national security and creating good social environment. In the new situation of opening and reform, the Bureau has improved the integrated quality of police group. The Bureau has strictly enforced the law and served warmly. The Bureau has deeply stricken activities of obscene, gamble, drugs and kidnapping, and strengthened government of security, traffic and fire controlling. The Bureau has conducted integrated government in social security and has made immortal contributions for the steady political society and ensuring opening & reform and the economic Development.

The General Secretary Jiang has proposed, "It is proved by practice that public security group is a reliable and powerful team. It deserve to be called strong backing of the republic country."

In the new century, Guiyang Public Security Bureau will keep encouraging themselves, carry on the past and be brave in the future to create more outstanding achievements for people's public security Work.

销毁收缴的赌博工具淫秽物品现场会

The meeting of destroying gamble tools and obscene goods.

销毁收缴的赌博工具淫秽物品现场

The site of destroying gamble tools and obscene goods.

被销毁的非法枪支管制刀具

Destroyed illegal firearms and cutting tools

贵阳市旅游局
GUI YANG TOURIST BUREAU

2001年是新世纪的第一年，也是“十五”计划的开局之年，按照贵阳市委、市政府关于大力发展旅游业、把贵阳市建设成为以生态旅游和民族旅游为主体的旅游城市的指示，围绕全年的工作重点--继续深入开展创建“中国优秀旅游城市”活动；大力宣传促销，拓展旅游客源市场；多渠道筹集资金加大旅游景区开发建设和管理力度；加强行业管理，开展旅游行业行风整治工作等任务，全市旅游行业齐心协力、真抓实干，取得了可喜的成绩。2001年全市共接待海内外旅游者1005万人次，较上年增长1.1%；其中海外旅游者5.95万人，较上年增长19.8%；旅游创汇1632万美元，较上年增长10%；全市旅游业总收入34亿元，较上年增长18%。

天河潭
Tianhe Pond

2001年元月中旬，全国旅游工作会在北京举行。会上宣布我市荣获第二批“中国优秀旅游城市”称号，我市红枫湖、黔灵公园两景区荣获全国第一批4A级（最高级）旅游区（点）称号。

开阳香火岩峡谷
Xianghuoyan Ravine in Kaiyang

花溪黄金大道
Huaxi Golden Road

2001 is the first year of “Tenth Five-year Plan” as well as the first year of the new century. According to the instruction of Guiyang City Party Committee and Government to develop tourism and to build Guiyang as a tourist city of biological tour and nationality tour, the tourist system of Guizhou worked around the key point of the year--to conduct the program of building “Chinese excellent Tourist city”, popularized and promoted hard, explored tourist market, raised funds in all ways for the development and management of scenery areas, strengthened trade management, held activities to build the trade conduct. With efforts of all the people of tourist trade, great achievements were made. In 2001, Guiyang has received 10.05 million and overseas tourists are from overseas, 19.8% more than last year. Foreign exchange from tourism is 16.32 million US dollars, 10% more than last year. The total tourist income of the city is 3.4 billion yuan, 18% more than last year.

In the second ten days of Jan 2001, the National Tourist Meeting was held in Beijing. Guiyang was awarded the second group of “Chinese Excellent Tourist City” at the meeting. Two scenic spots, Hongfeng lake and Qiangling Park, were awarded the first group of national 4A scenic spots.

宏福寺--深山藏古寺
Hongfu Temple--deep in the mountain with ancient deposit

与时俱进，扎实推进贵阳特色蔬菜产业发展
Developed with times, improve the development of special vegetables industry of Guiyang

贵阳市蔬菜工作办公室
Guiyang Vegetable Office

无公害棚内的水培生菜
Lettuce in shed with no environmental pollution

2001年贵阳市蔬菜总产量70.4万吨，产值实现92707万元（现价）。

1、初步构建了以五里冲蔬菜中心批发市场为龙头，产地批发市场（72个）为骨架，农贸市场（64个）为基础的市场体系。

2、培育了以贵阳蔬菜科技示范中心为龙头，各层次示范（育苗）基地（园）为辐射，农民科技示范户和龙头企业科技队伍为基础的蔬菜科技创新体系。

3、建设了一批各具特色的专业化商品蔬菜基地，推进了布局区域化、生产专业化、产品优质化。全市建商品蔬菜基地10万余亩，2001年全市蔬菜外销2.6万吨，销售额达到2868万元。1998年启动了无公害蔬菜工作，2001年示范面积2万余亩，播面4万余亩。

科技示范园节水喷灌
Economizing water irrigation in technical demonstrative park

General vegetable output of Guiyang of 2001 is 704 thousand ton. The general output value is 927.07 million yuan. (current price)

1. The city has primarily built a market system dominated by Wulichong vegetable wholesale market, with the framework of 72 wholesale markets of producing areas, based on 64 agricultural trade markets.

高山秋淡菜基地
Alpine off-season vegetable base for autumn

2. The city has created a new vegetable technical creation system led by Guiyang Vegetable Technical Demonstrative Center, extended by demonstrative bases (parks) of all levels, based on example peasant households and leading technical teams.

3. The city has built commercial vegetable bases of features to improve area distribution, specialized production and quality of products. There are over 100 thousand mu commercial vegetable base built in the city. 26 thousand tons of vegetables were sold out of the city in 2001, whose value is 28.68 million yuan. Vegetables with no environmental pollution were grown in 1998. The demonstrative areas of 2001 are over 20 thousand mu. Over 40 thousand mu of land were seeded.

贵阳市河
Guiyang River

处长：冉贞敏
The director: Ran Zhenmin

领导班子成员
The leading group

贵阳市河道管理处是在原贵阳市河道治理指挥部的基础上，于1986年成立的全额拨款城建公益事业单位，隶属于市政府城市管理局。

其主要职责包括：对流经贵阳市南明区、云岩区、小河区等城区内的南明河及其市西河、小车河、贯城河等几条支流总计20公里和两岸5-25米的环境进行治理（污水、清淤）、建设（堡坎、截污沟、坝、水体景观、河边广场）、保洁（滨河道清扫、漂浮物打捞、垃圾清运）、管理（摊点、堆占、圈占、挖掘、建筑）、维养（绿化、河道设施日常维修、养护）等工作。

在各级党政领导的高度重视下，城区河道设施日益完善，水质不断改善，环境大为改观。尤其是市委市政府提出的南明河三年变清，大大激励了河道建设热情，加大了治理力度，强化了管理措施。迄今，城区河道已相继建成自控翻板坝10座，1999年开展全市10万军民义务清淤和大规模机械清淤，2002年进入河道治理攻坚年，河道两岸大规模美化、绿化（植树种草10万平方米）、亮化工程全面展开，使青山林城绕以绿水彩带，为贵阳城市建设增色添彩。

现借国家西部大开发和加入WTO这一大好时机，河道管理法规将进一步健全，管理进一步规范，服务进一步到位，建设步伐进一步加快，热忱欢迎海内外有识之士前来投资、创业，共建文明、秀美、亮丽的新贵阳。

Guiyang River Course Administration was founded in 1986 on the base of former Guiyang River Course Governing Command. It is a public welfare institute with full appropriated investment, subordinate to city administration of the government.

Its main responsibilities are to govern, construct, clean, administrate and take after Nanming river, Shixi river, Xiaoche river and Guancheng river that go through Nanming district, Yunyan district and Xiaohe district, and the areas of 5 to 25 m of both banks.

With great attention of Party and government leaders, equipment of river course becomes gradually comprehensive. The quality of water becomes better and better. The environment has been changed a lot. The aim of taking 3 years to make Nanming river cleaning, made by the city Party Committee and government encourages river course construction and insures administration. Up to present, 10 automatic turning dams were built up. In 1999, 100 thousand people of the city attended the mechanical cleaning project. 2002 is the break-through year of river course administration. Large scope programs of decoration and afforest (building 100 thousand m^2 trees and plants) on banks were warmly held. The light up program made the city more colorful.

With the good chance of the West Developing and China's joining in WTO, the Administration will makes river course governing regulations more sound, provides administration more standard, provides more satisfying service, constructs faster. The Administration sincerely welcomes people of the world to invest, create business there to build a civilized and beautiful new Guiyang.

治理后的甲秀楼滨河广场
Jiaxiu Pavilion Binghe Square after governing

1999年4月1日南明河全市10万全民义务清淤场景之一
A view of voluntary cleaning program attended by 100 thousand citizens in Nanming river on 1st April 1999

1999年南明河机械清淤场景一
A view of mechanical cleaning in Nanming river in 1999

治理后的南明河青元路口广场
Qingyuan road square by Nanming river after governing

贵阳甲秀楼景区夜景
Night View of the Jiaxiu Pavilion, Guiyang

南明区——向经济强县迈进

Nanming District——stepping to strong economic county

中共南明区委书记：蒋星恒
The Secretary of the district Party Committee: Jiang Xingheng

南明区人民政府区长：陈广宇
The governor of Nanming District: Chen Guangyu

通过3年来的建强工作，南明区区域经济布局、生产力布局发生了深刻的变化，经济结构向更加合理的方向发展。招商引资工作迈出了较大步伐，从1999年到2001年共引进资金40.84亿元，实际到位资金34.36亿元，培育了一批效益高、竞争力强的支撑项目，使全区经济保持持续、快速、健康发展的势头；地方财政收入在1999年基础上接近翻了一番，极大地鼓舞和激励了全区上下团结一心、实现“跨越式发展”和“强区升位”目标的信心和决心。

在招商引资方面，政府各部门树立“服务出效益”观念，一是切实转变工作作风，简化办事程序，提高服务质量和办事效率；二是对招商引资实行“全程化”服务，切实抓好项目的跟踪服务，为企业解决落户、生产经营过程中遇到的困难和问题，提高招商引资的到位率；三是坚持“谁投资、谁受益；谁引进、谁受益”的原则，充分调动有关部门、乡（办）和个人的积极性，使招商引资工作取得突破性进展。全年共引进项目650个，投资规模在1000万元以上的项目有22个，500万元以上的项目有32个，合同引进资金14.29亿元，实际到位资金12.96亿元，资金到位率为91%。

今年，区政府配合市政府重点抓好南明河及沿岸环境治理，继续加快城区的环境建设及整治，按照“优环境、创特色、上品位”的要求，全面推进城市形象工程建设，以龙洞堡片区整体开发为中心，抓好产业结构、城乡结构、财源结构战略性调整，促进工业化、城市化、信息化进程，推动经济社会各项事业向前发展。

人民广场
The People's Square

甲秀广场一角
A corner of Jiaxiu Square

大昌隆超市
Dachanglong Supermarket

贵阳东方金属材料交易中心
Guiyang Orient Metal Material Exchange Center

After 3 years' construction of strong economic county, the economic structure and productive force structure have been changed deeply. The economic structure becomes more justified. The work of inviting capitals has been developed a lot. Invited capitals from 1999 to 2001 are 4.084 billion yuan. 3.436 billion yuan has been actually invested to cultivate a group of profitable and competitive projects and to keep a continuos, fast and healthy development of economy. The local revenue has doubled that of 1999, which has encouraged the people to unite and realize "developed with leap speed" and "upgrading the district".

In the field of inviting capitals, departments of the government have built up the ideal of "profit comes from service". Firstly, they have transformed work style and simplified working process to raise the quality and efficiency of service. Secondly, they have provided "generalized service" for inviting capitals. They stressed follow-up service to solve the problems of settlement and business for enterprises, thus increasing more capitals invested to projects. Thirdly, they stick to the principle of "inventor gets the profit, inviter gets the profit", to encourage relating departments, townships and individuals to invite investment. The work of inviting investment has made a breakthrough. There are 650 projects invited to the district of the year. There are 22 projects whose investment is more than 10 million yuan and 32 projects whose investment is more than 5 million yuan. Contracted invited capital is 1.429 billion yuan. The actual investment is 1.296 billion yuan, holding 91%.

This year, in order to coordinate with city government to stress the governing of Nanming River and the environment of the banks, the government of the District will accelerate the environmental construction of urban area and improve the project of building city image according to the requirements of "good environment, being special, high grade". Taking integrated development of Longdongbao area as central work, the District will stress on the strategic regulation of industrial structure, urban and rural structure and financial resource structure, to improve the process of industrialization, urbanization, information and the development of all trades of the economic society.

"巧姑"辣椒系列产品
Chili products of "Qiaogu" brand

全省唯一的清真辣椒食品（山里红）
The only Muslims chili food (Shanlihong) in the province

来自山野的"山珍棒棒菇"
"Shanzhen Bangbanggu" from mountains

畅销全国的"老干妈"辣椒产品
Chili products of "Laoganma" brand, selling well all over the country

区委书记王明铮（左二）在友谊文化市场调研
Wang Mingzheng, the Secretary of the district Party Committee (the second from left), was inspecting Friendship Cultural Market

区长翟彦（中）在小关花鸟市场调研
Zhai Yan, the governor of the district (middle) was inspecting Xiaoguan Flower& Bird Market

云岩区 Yunyan District

云岩区是贵阳市中心城区之一，位于市区北半部，总面积67.5平方公里，辖15个街道办事处、1个镇，总人口51万，是全省政治、经济、科技、文化、教育、信息中心，环境优美、交通便利、通讯发达、商贸繁荣。辖区内气候宜人，夏无酷暑，冬无严寒，雨量充沛，属北亚热带湿润温和型气候，自然环境优美，人文景观丰富，是旅游度假的好地方。

2002年，全区坚持以邓小平理论和江泽民“三个代表”重要思想为指导，着眼于营造全区大环境、总形象，以实施城市形象建设工程为突破口，结合经济发展、结构调整、市场布局、社区建设、城市改造和环境整治，统筹安排、相互渗透、协调推进，着力提高城市品位，增强城市集聚、辐射能力，优环境、建精品，建设整洁、文明、亮丽、开放、有序的现代化城区。云岩区是中共贵州省委、省人民政府确定全省首批建设的二十个经济强县（区）之一，被国家计生委授予“全国县级计划生育‘三为主’先进集体”光荣称号，2000年被省委、省政府评为“发展非公有制经济先进单位”。

Yunyan District is one of the central districts of Guiyang City. It lies in the north of the city. The general area is 67.5km^2. Yunyan District governs 15 administrative offices and 1 town. The general population is 510 thousand. It is the political, economic, technical, cultural, educational and information center of the province. The District has beautiful environment, convenient traffic, advanced communication and flourishing trades. Climate in the District is pleasant. There is no intense heat in summer or bitter coldness in winter.

正在建设中的云岩区行政综合大楼效果图
General administrative building of Yunyan district under construction

There is enough rainfall. It belongs to north subtropical wet and warm climate. Natural environment is beautiful. Artificial scenery is rich. It is an ideal place to spend holiday.

In 2002, the District sticks to Deng Xiaoping Theory and Jiang Zemin's Thought of “three representatives”, stresses on general environment and reputation of the district, takes the project of building city image as breakthrough point, connects with economic development, structure regulation, market layout, community construction, city rebuilding and environment government to build an orderly, civilized, beautiful and open modern district. Yunyan District is one of the 20 counties (districts) in the first group of the province which are designated to be built strong economic county (district) approved by Guizhou provincial Party Committee and government. The District has been awarded “advanced community in county family planning ‘three points’ project” by the State Family Planning Commission. In 2000, the District was awarded “advanced unit to develop non-public economy” by provincial Party Committee and government.

高原社区之星
A Star Community at Plateau

贵阳市云岩区环城北路街道办事处
North Around-city Road Subdistrict Office of Yunyan District, Guiyang City

贵阳市云岩区环城北路街道办事处，是贵阳市城区最小的街道办事处，所辖面积仅0.7平方公里。常住人口不足2万人，辖区内既无成型市场，又无繁华街道，更无可供开发利用的土地，而这样的劣势办事处却在办事处书记余正才及其张保兰主任的领导下，2001年创造财政收入3360余万元，地方财政收入1700余万元的佳绩，成为全省财政收入最高的街道办事处。

环北办事处现有益佰制药、大成贸易、雅温食坊、海蓝云天等大中型企业及三产企业百余户。办事处领导班子对社区内各企业给予了大力扶持和帮助。

2002年，环北办事处将在云岩区委、区政府的领导下，团结带领办事处广大党员、干部、群众身体力行"三个代表"重要思想，把环北办事处建设成为经济繁荣，科教发达、功能齐全、环境优美的现代化社区。

North Around-city Road Subdistrict Office of Yunyan District is the smallest subdistrict office of Guiyang urban area. The governed area is only 0.7 km^2. Inhabitants of the Subdistrict are less than 20 thousand. There is no mature market, or flourishing street or land to be developed. But under the leadership of the secretary of Yu Zhengcai, the Subdistrict Party Committee, and Zhang Baolan, the director of the Subdistrict Office, the poorSubdistrict has created revenue of 33.6 million yuan in 2001, and local revenue of 17 million yuan. It becomes the subdistrict with most revenue in the province.

The Subdistrict has large and middle enterprises as Yibai Pharmacy, Dacheng Trade, Yawen Restaurant, Hailan Yuntian, and over 100 third industry enterprises. Leaders of the Subdistrict Office has provided great assistance and help to the enterprises in the Subdistrict.

In 2002, under the leadership of Yunyan District Party Committee and government, the Subdistrict Office will unite and lead all the Party members, cadres and mass people of the Subdistrict Office to practice the important thought of " three representatives" to build the subdistrict to be a modern community with flourishing economy, advanced technology and education , complete functions and beautiful environment.

参加贵阳市奔向新世纪环城赛跑活动
Attending the program of Heading for New Century Round-city Race of Guiyang City

办事处参加魅力飞扬时装表演
The Subdistrict attended the program of Flying Charm Fashion Show

贵州益佰制药
Guizhou Yibai Pharmacy

花溪区委区政府
The District Party Committee and Government of Huaxi District

花溪区
Huaxi District

花溪区是贵州省著名的风景区、文化区、生态区和省会贵阳市的城市片区。全区辖3镇11乡（其中7个民族乡）；土地面积957.6平方公里；总人口31.43万人，城镇化水平达32%；少数民族占总人口的34.74%。这里风景秀丽、气候宜人、物产丰富、人杰地灵、自然资源（特别是旅游资源）较为丰富，区位条件、生态环境较为优越，基础设施较为完善，智力资源可为经济社会发展提供良好的支撑。

2001年，该区积极实施“城市带动、旅游带动、科技带动、文化带动、开放带动和可持续发展”六大战略，进一步加强农业、拓展城市、壮大工业、发展旅游，经济结构战略性调整明显加快，全区实现国内生产总值246124万元，比上年增长11.7%。其中：第一产业增加值41068万元，比上年增长4.1%；第二产业增加值90330万元，比上年增长15%；第三产业增加值114726万元，比上年增长12.1%。实现财政总收入17211万元，比上年增长24.28%；地方财政收入10156.9万元，比上年增长31.55%；城镇居民人均可支配收入5951.4元，增长8.6%；农民人均纯收入2244.84元，增长5.95%；全年完成农林牧渔业总产值61893万元，同比增长5.06%；完成规模以上工业总产值154292万元，增长12.2%；招商引资到位资金37245万元，比上年增长69.58%；完成固定资产投资24821万元，比上年增长54.48%；全年共接待中外游客271万余人次，旅游总收入1.49亿元，同比增长13.74%；社会消费品零售总额39156.7万元，增长12.9%。

花溪区在实施西部大开发战略的进程中，将立足新的起点，加快经济强区建设步伐，按照“三个代表”的要求，与时俱进，开拓创新，努力把花溪建设成为经济繁荣、旅游兴旺、商贸发达、人民富裕、民族团结、社会安定、文明民主的现代化、开放型、花园式经济强区。

花溪鸟瞰
Bird's view of Huaxi

花溪区城市主干道南大街
South avenue, the main street of Huaxi District

Huaxi District is famous scenic, cultural, ecological district of Guizhou Province, and the down town area of the Guiyang, the capital city. The District includes 3 towns and 11 townships (including 7 nationality townships). The general area is 957.6 km^2. The general population is 314.3 thousand. 32% of the District are towns. 34.74% people are minority nationalities. There are beautiful scenery, pleasant climate, rich products, famous people, rich natural resources (especially tourist resource), superior geological and ecological conditions and comprehensive fundamental equipment in the District. Intellect resource of the District is enough to support the social economic development.

In 2001, the District has actively carried out 6 strategies of "driven by urbanization, driven by tourist, driven by science and technique, driven by culture, driven by opening and continuos development" and stressed agriculture, extending the city, industry and tourist. The strategic regulation of economic structure has been obviously accelerated. The GDP of the District is 2461.24 million yuan, 11.7% more than last year. Of the GDP, the first industry has been increased by 410.68 million yuan, 4.1% more than last year. The second industry has been increased by 903.3 million yuan, 15% more than last year. The third industry has been increased by 1147.26 million yuan, 12.1% more than last year. The general revenue is 172.11 million yuan, 24.28% more than last year. The local area revenue is 101.569 million yuan, 31.55% more than last year. The average income of urban people is 5951.4 yuan, 8.6% more than last year. The average net income per peasant is 2244.84 yuan, 5.95% more than last year. The general output of agriculture, forestry, husbandry and fishery is 618.93 million yuan, 5.06% more than last year. The total industrial output of large scope is 1542.92 million yuan, 12.2% more than last year. 372.45 million yuan was invited to invest in the District, 69.58% more than last year. The District has finished fixed asset investment of 248.21 million yuan, 54.48% more than last year. The District has received over 2.71 million domestic and overseas tourists. The general tourist income is 149 million yuan, 13.74% more than last year. The total retail sales of social consumer goods are 391.567 million yuan, 12.9% more than last year.

通往市中心区的贵溪大道
Guixi avenue leading to the center of the city

风景优美的花溪河畔
Beautiful bank of Huaxi river

In the implementation of the West Developing, Huaxi District will stand on a new beginning, accelerate the construction of economic district, and make efforts to build a modern, open and garden district flourishing in economy, tourist, trade with rich people, united nationality, stable society and civilized democracy, according to three representatives.

位于花溪河畔内的花蓓山庄
Huabei mountain villa located in bank of Huaxi river

白云区--抢抓机遇，再现辉煌

Baiyun District--grasp chance to create wonders

副省长莫时仁在区领导的陪同下检查农业开发项目
Mo Shiren, the vice-governor of the province was examining the agricultural project accompanied by leaders of the distric

区委书记秦如培（右）、区长马长青在研究城市建设
Qin Rupei, the secretary of the District Party Committee (right) and Ma Changqing, the head of the district were discussing city construction

白云区是贵阳市的次中心城区，是省级经济技术开发区。全区总面积259.6平方公里，辖5个乡、4个街道办事处，总人口17.2万人。

2001年，全区按照“工业强区、城市建区、会展活区、科教兴区”的思路，深化改革，扩大开放。国内生产总值完成35.42亿元，比上年增长12.2%；财政总收入完成5.22亿元，比上年增长43.44%；乡镇企业营业收入完成44.95亿元，比上年增长29.75%；固定资产投资完成15.82亿元，比上年增长51.24%；城镇居民可支配收入达6072元，比上年增长13.19%，计划生育率达98.9%，社会治安综合治理保持了模范县标准。

一、加大工业结构调整力度，不断壮大区域经济总量。着力于企业技术改造和科技创先，增强企业的市场竞争能力。全年对不符合国家产业政策和环保政策的“十五小”企业，关、停、转9家，各级财政投入技改贴息、科技三项费等资金423万元，带动金融资金注入7200万元，实施技改项目6个，开发新产品6个，培育形成了贵阳纤具厂、云峰酒业等一批年产值5000万元以上的骨干企业。

二、加大基础设施建设投入，加快城市化建设步伐。2001年共投入建设资金5.1亿元，其中贷款贴息640万元，对15个项目2.98亿元贷款进行了贴息，拉动GDP增长2.5个百分点。

三、创新市场运作机制，大力发展会展经济。围绕打造白云品牌，提升白云知名度，充分利用“风筝节”、“兰花博览会”两大品牌发展会展经济。“两会”期间，举办了白云区首届房地产投资贸易洽谈会、花鸟奇石交易会等，游园门票创收140多万元，各类商品交易额上千万元，签定贸易合同12.9亿元。

四、面向市场，大力发展都市农业。该区以发展都市农业为目标，以结构调整促进农业和农村经济的发展，在结构调整方面，区委、区政府提出作好“菜、花、禽、加、游”五篇文章，大力发展农业产业龙头企业，今年共安排支农资金2600万元；引进了利丰、东森等37家花卉企业，引进了原野野生养殖基地，原野野生资源公司等10多家农业产业化龙头企业，辐射带动全区3000多户农户；创新土地流转机制，实现土地流转5100亩，发展订单农业3000多亩，农民收入稳步增长，农民人均纯收入达2789元，比上年增长5.2%。

五、贯彻科教兴区战略，推动科技事业不断发展。“科教兴区”战略深入实施，各乡科技示范村工作全面展开，开展了全区第二届科技进步奖评比，通过了国家首批科技进步先进县考核，取得了全省综合考核第一名的好成绩；全面实施了教师“双聘制”，教育教学水平全面提高，被评为全国“两基”工作先进县。

正在建设中的白云行政中心大楼正面图
The front of Baiyun administrative center under construction

Baiyun District is the sub center of Guiyang city. It is the economic and technical development area of the province. The district covers 259.6 km² with 5 townships, 4 administrative offices. The District has a total population of 172 thousand.

In 2001, the District deepened reform and enlarged opening according to the thought of "industrial district, city construction, conference & exhibition district, developed by science and technique". The District has finished GDP of 3.542 billion yuan, 12.2% more than last year. General revenue is 522 million yuan, 43.44% more than last year. Incomes of towns and townships are 4.495 billion yuan, 29.75% more than last year. Investments on fixed assets are 1.582 billion yuan, 51.24% more than last year. Incomes that can be budgeted by citizens are 6,072 yuan, 13.19% more than last year. 98.9% of the households have conducted family planning. The social security situation has arrived the level of exemplary county.

1. Accelerate the regulation of industrial structure, keep developing area economy. Concentrating on technical reform and creation, concerning organizations have closed, stopped and transferred 9 enterprises that were variant with policies of industry and environment protection. Finances of all levels have paid 4.23 million yuan for interests for technical reform, three technical fees, etc. 72 million yuan was invested in technology field. 6 projects of technical reform were carried out. 6 new products were developed. Large enterprises with annual output of over 50 million yuan as: Guiyang Fiber Instrument Plant, Yunfeng Wine Industry, were cultivated.

2. Invest more in fundamental construction, accelerate urbanization. In 2001, the District has invested 510 million yuan in construction, among which 6.4 million was paid for the interests for loans of 298 million yuan for 15 projects to increase GDP by 2.5%.

3. Create mechanism of market, develop economy of conference and exhibition. In order to build the brand of Baiyun, improve the reputation of Baiyun, the District made full use of "Kite Festival" and "Orchid Fair" to develop economy of conference and exhibition. During the two festivals, the first Conference of Real Estate Investment and Trade of Baiyun District, Trading Meeting for Flowers, Birds and magical stones, were held. Incomes from tickets were more than 1.4 million yuan. Transactions were over 10 million yuan. Contracts of 1.29 billion yuan were signed.

4. Develop urban agriculture facing to market. The District set its object as developing urban agriculture and has regulated structure to improve the development of agriculture and rural economy. In the field of structure regulation, the District Party Committee and government proposed 5 articles of "vegetables, flowers, poultry, processing and tourism" to develop leading agricultural enterprises. 26 million yuan was supported to agriculture. 37 enterprises of flowers and plants as Lifeng, Dongsen, were situated in the district. Open wild raising base and over 10 leading agricultural enterprises in industrialization as Open Wild Resource Company, were led in the District, encouraging over 3,000 households farmers of the district. New mechanism of land circulation was created to make 5,100 mu land circulated. The District has developed order agriculture of more than 3,000 mu. Farmers' incomes have been increased steadily. The average net income per farmer was up to 2,789 yuan, 5.2% more than last year.

5. Implement the policy of "science and education builds the district", keep promoting the development of science and technology industry. The strategy of science and technology builds the District" has been deeply carried out. Every township has conducted the program of technical demonstrative village. The second technical progress prize was held. The District has passed national exam for the first group of advanced counties with technical progress and got the champion in the general exam of the province. The system of "double employ" " was carried in teachers to improve the teaching level. The District has got the award of "advanced county" in national "two basic" works".

基础设施完善的景宏工业园区
Jinghong Industrial Park with comprehensive fundamental equipment

云峰酒业白酒灌装线
The wine pouring line of Yunfeng Wine Industry

以科技为依托，大力发展有特色、有市场的都市农业。图为白云万亩花卉基地一角
Develop special and promising urban agriculture by science and technique. Here in the picture is a corner of the 10 thousand-mu flowers & plants base

开放的乌当

Opening Wudang

市委书记王晓东视察高新园区
Wang Xiaodong, the Secretary of the city Party Committee was inspecting high-tech Park.

乌当区举行新行政中心奠基仪式
The foundation ceremony of new administration center of Wudang

At the first year of "Tenth Five-year Plan", with the great support of the provincial and city leaders, and relating departments, the whole district of Wudang liberated minds, developed and created, united and worked hard according to the general objective of "Tenth Five-year Plan" and the aim of building a wealthy county (district). They practiced "three represents" carefully and grasped the historical chance of the West Developing. They carried out high-tech-guided and urbanization strategy. They finished all the aims of the year to give a good beginning to "Tenth Five-year Plan" and to lay a solid foundation for the future's work. In 2001, they have achieved 4 breakthroughs in economic structure, city construction, inviting tenders and financial resource. Today's Wudang has become a good place for investment. The strong developing motive and hardworking spirit contribute a lot for district construction.

“十五”开局之年，在省、市领导及相关部门的大力支持下，乌当区全区上下解放思想，开拓创新，紧紧围绕“十五”计划总体目标及建设贵州省经济强县（区）的工作要求，团结一致，奋力拼搏，认真实践“三个代表”，抢抓西部大开发的历史机遇，积极实施高新技术带动和城镇化战略，狠抓各项工作落实，圆满完成了全年各项工作目标，为全面完成强区建设任务及“十五”计划开好局、起好步奠定了坚实的基础。2001年实现了在经济结构调整、城市建设、招商引资、财税建设、培育后续财源上的四大突破。今日的乌当，已成为一片投资的热土，全区上下强烈的发展意识及不甘落后的敬业热情为“强区升位”目标的实现积蓄了充足的发展启动。

杨梅压弯腰，果农喜眉梢。阿栗杨梅喜获丰收
Peasants were pleased to get a good harvest of red bayberry

贵阳经济技术开发区

Gui yang Economic & Technique Development Zone

贵阳经济技术开发区（以下简称开发区）始建于1993年3月，是经国务院批准成立的国家级开发区，位于贵阳市中心南隅，总人口14.9万，总面积63.13平方公里。2000年2月，国务院批准建立贵阳市小河区，与开发区实行“两块牌子，一套班子”的管理体制。建区9年来，开发区在经济发展、城市建设、社会进步等方面成就显著，地方财政收入突破亿元大关，为建区前的20倍。

立足于开发区、中心区和生态区三位一体的定位，开发区将努力构建充分体现开放意识、创新意识和率先意识，以西部大开发工业园区、外商投资工业园区、中小企业科技园区为载体，以经济实力强劲、投资环境优越，示范、凝聚、辐射、带动效应显著为特征的经济强区；努力构建充满浓郁的现代文化气息、具备优美人居环境、充分体现以人为本精神的现代化都市新区；努力构建以推广高新农业技术、发展生态农业为基础，充分体现有机、绿色、环保、可持续发展的生态农业示范区。

海信工业园举办奠基仪式
The foundation ceremony of Haisense Industry Park

Guiyang Economic & Technical Development Zone (here in after referred to as the Development Zone), located in the south downtown of Guiyang city, was established in March, 1993 and it has been approved to be the National-level Economic & Technical Development Zone by the State Council. It covers an area of 63.13km² whih the population of 149 thousand. Xiaohe District of Guiyang city was approved to be the city administrative district in February, 2000. The Development Zone has streamlined its administration and established a highly efficient, well-coordinated and standardized administrative system and operating mechanism through restructuring. Through nine-year development, the Development Zone has got great achievements in economic development, city construction and social progress; the revenue has amounted to RMB 100 million yuan, an increase of 2000 per cent over 1993.

Depending on the “3-1 combination” location (the national-level economic & technical development zone, the central zone of Guiyang city and the ecological zone), the development Zone will completely showed the open consciousness, creative consciousness and leading consciousness. Based on the Western Development Industrial Park, the Foreign-founded Industrial Pak and the Scientific & Technical Park for Large & Small Enterprises, the Development Zone will become the Special Economic Zone with the characteristics of great ecological potential, nice investment environment and the functions of demonstration, coherence, radiation and precedence; the Development Zone will construct the new modernized city district full of modernized culture and with the nice living environment which can completely show the spirit of persons; based on expanding the high and new agricultural technology and developing the ecological agriculture, the Development Zone will construct the ecological agricultural demonstration zone with biotic, green, environmental protection and sustainable development.

欧式建筑的住宅小区
Residential areas of European style

贵州省修文县 乘势争先强县升位

Xiuwen County of Guizhou Province take the chance to upgrade the county in front

县城中心龙岗广场
Longgang Square in the middle of the county

修文，因一代哲人王阳明谪居悟道而享誉中外的龙场古驿，地处黔中腹地，总面积1071平方公里，总人口30万人。修文交通畅达，贵遵、贵毕高等级公路纵贯全境，川黔铁路、210国道横穿县境；旅游资源丰富，贵阳高尔夫度假中心、阳明洞风景名胜区、六广河风景区等人文、自然景观融合一体，交相辉映，既有深厚的历史文化内蕴，又有极高的观赏价值；矿产资源丰富，铝矾土等矿产资源储量大、易于开采。

修文县依托丰富的自然资源和良好的投资环境，工业生产和乡镇企业快速发展。近年来，一大批制药、旅游开发等企业先后落户修文，为修文经济发展奠定了坚实基础。农业产业结构调整成效显著，2001年，农民人均纯收入达1906元。

城乡城镇化建设步伐加快，卫星城镇功能不断完善，文化、教育、卫生事业蓬勃发展，党的建设和民主法制建设不断深入，社会事业全面进步。2001年完成国内生产总值10.96亿元，比上年增长13%；完成乡镇企业增加值4.86亿元，增长23.17%；全县财政总收入10018.70万元，增长25.19%，其中县级财政收入5635.37万元，增长16.09%；社会消费品零售总额2.32亿元，增长13%，完成固定资产投资5.95亿元，增长88.8%。

阳明先生及其弟子铜群雕
Mr. Yangming and his pupils group of Flute Carve

农业产业结构调整硕果累累
Great achievements of Agricultural structure regulation

美丽的六广河峡谷风光
Beautiful canyon in Liuguang River

Xiuwen, where Wang Yangming, a philosopher of a generation, living alone to understand doctrines, is an international famous place. It lies in the middle of Guizhou Province. The general area is 1071 km². The general population is 300 thousand. Xiuwen has convenient traffic. Gui zun and Guibi high-standard way go through the County from north to South. Chuanqian railway and No.210 National Avenue go through the County from west to east. The County has rich tourist resources of natural and Artificial scenery as Guiyang Golf Holiday Village, Yangming Carve and Liuguang River. The scenery has long history and is of great value to be visited. Xiuwen has rich mineral resources. There is great reserve of bauxite that is easy to be explored.

Depending on rich natural resource and good investment environment, industry and town and township enterprises have been developed fast. In recent years, a lot of pharmacy and tourist companies have settled down in Xiuwen, which lays a solid foundation for economic development of Xiuwen. The regulation of agricultural structure has achieved a lot. The average net income per peasant of 2001 is 1906 yuan.

The urbanization of the county has been accelerated. Functions of a satellite county have been improved. Industries of culture, education and health have been developed vigorously. The construction of the Party and democratic legal system have been deepened. All the social trades are improved. The County has finished its GDP of 1.096 billion yuan in 2001, 13% more than last year. The County has increased the output of town and township enterprises by 486 million yuan, 23.17% higher than last year. The general revenue of the County is 100.187 million yuan, 25.19% higher than last year. Revenue of the County level is 56.3537 million yuan, 16.09% more than last year. The total retail income of social consumer goods is 232 million yuan, 13% higher than last year. The County has finished investment of 595 million yuan on fixed assets, 88.8% more than last year.

贵州唯一的高尔夫球场
The only golf field of Guizhou province

腾飞中的清镇

市委书记王学军在农村对农业产业结构调整进行调研
Wang Xuejun, the secretary of the city Party Committee, was researching on agricultural structure in countryside

清镇是贵州省中部重要的工业基地和电力基地，是贵阳市重要的卫星城市，也是贵州西线交通枢纽和旅游风景区第一站。距贵阳市中心区23公里，距贵阳国际机场30公里。全市行政区域面积1492平方公里，辖4个镇、6个乡（其中3个民族乡），总人口50万人。境内红枫湖、百花湖、东风湖水域面积91.4平方公里，被誉为"珠联璧合之地"。清镇市区位独特、交通便利、自然资源丰富、工农业基础较好，发展前景广阔。1998年被省委、省政府列为全省首批建设经济强县的县（市、区）之一。近年来，清镇市委、市政府紧密团结和依靠全市各族人民，进一步认清形势，抢抓机遇，真抓实干，推动全市经济持续、健康、快速发展，人民生活水平不断提高，取得了较为明显的工作成效。

Qingzhen is an important industrial and electrical base of central Guizhou, and an important satellite city of Guiyang City. Also, it is the first stop of west traffic and tour line of Guizhou. It is 23 km far away from Guiyang downtown and 30 km far away from Guiyang International Airport. The general administrative area of the city is 1492 km^2, with 4 towns, 6 townships (including 3 nationality townships). The general population is 500 thousand. The total water areas of Hongfeng Lake, Baihua Lake and Dongfeng Lake inside the city are 91.4 km^2. The City is called "city with strings of pearls and girdles of jad". Qingzhen has special geological situation with convenient traffic, rich natural resources, good agricultural and industrial bases and prosperous prospect. It was listed in the first group of counties to be built powerful economic counties of the province by provincial Party Committee and government in 1998. In recent years, the City Party Committee and government unite and depend on people of all the nationalities tightly to grasp chances and do practical works to promote the city economy developed continuously, healthily and fast. People's lives have been kept rising. The City has made obvious achievement.

市长夏钢到田间地头了解农业发展情况
Xia Gang, the mayor of the city, was consulting agricultural development in field

发展中的大棚示范园区
The developing demonstrative park of sheds

位于红枫湖畔的兴隆度假村
Xinlong Holiday Village located on of Hongfeng Lake

生态立市
Build the city on ecology

科教立市
Build the city on science & technique

开放强市
Build the city on opening

遵义路街道办事处
Subdistrict Office of Zunyi Road

遵义路：贵阳市最亮丽的迎宾大道，商贾云集，人潮涌动；
Zunyi Road,: the most beautiful welcome street of Guiyang City, where merchants gathered and people floated.

遵义路街道：民政部授予的“中国街道之星”，星光灿烂，十里繁华。
Zunyi Subdistrict: “Chinese star subdistrict” awarded by the Ministry of Civil Affairs, bright and flourishing.

团结奋进的遵义路街道领导班子
Courageous leading group

遵义路街道办事处地处贵州省省会城市旱码头——火车站的遵义路街道，面积1.83平方公里，人口5万余人，社区居委会8个，企事业单位74个。改革开放以来，辖区经济持续发展，社会稳定。成为全省街道建设的“领头雁”，曾先后被国家民政部、省委、省政府授予“中国街道之星”、“国家级文化站”、“省级文明单位”、“省全优街道办事处”、“省先进文化办事处”多种荣誉，是贵州省在全国城市社区工作委员会和常务委员会中的唯一代表。

蓬勃发展的社区经济、福泽万民的社区服务、丰富多彩的社区文化描绘出遵义路街道办事处更辉煌的明天。

Subdistrict office of Zunyi Road lies on Zunyi street which connects Han wharf with Railway station, in the capital of Guizhou Province. The Subdistrict covers 1.83km^2 with over 50 thousand people. There are 8 neighborhood committees and 74 enterprises and institutions. Since open and reform, the Subdistrict economy keeps developing and the society is stable. It is the model in subdistrict construction and was awarded “Chinese Star Subdistrict”, “National Culture Station”, “Provincial Civilized Unit”, “Advanced Subdistrict Office”, by the Ministry of Civil affaires, Provincial Party Committee and Provincial Government. It is the only representatives for Guizhou Province in the National Community Committee and Standing Committee.

The flourishing district economy, useful district services, colorful district culture make a wonderful future for the Subdistrict Office of Zunyi Road.

中国民政部授予的“街道之星”
“Star Subdistrict” awarded by the Ministry of Civil Affairs

丰富多彩的社区文化
Colorful community culture

抓住西部开发机遇 创“十五”乡企辉煌

Take Advantage of West Developing Create Wonders in "Tenth Five-year Plan"

六盘水市乡镇企业局“二次创业”促发展

Town and Township Enterprises Administration of Liupanshui promote Second Creation to improve development

六盘水市乡镇企业局局长：荣文财

The Director of Town and Township Enterprises Administration of Liupanshui : Rong Yicai

六盘水市乡镇企业面对“十五”计划新开局，在西部大开发和中国加入WTO的机遇与挑战中，围绕乡镇企业“二次创业”，努力推进结构调整，进一步解放思想，锐意改革，加快发展。

“十五”期间，该市乡镇企业的奋斗目标是：经过5年的努力，使全市乡镇企业实现快速、健康、稳定发展，为该市乡镇企业在西部大开发和国际市场竞争中打下坚实的基础。到2005年，亿元乡镇40个，亿元村20个，15个工业小区形成规模，营业收入上亿元的企业8个。上缴国家税全年均增长12%，达到3.2亿元；从业人员年均增长2%，达到27万人。

六盘水市乡镇企业局领导班子 从左到右：副局长：付召祥、局长：荣文财、副局长：易定芬

Leading group of Town and Township Enterprises Administration of Liupanshui, from the left to the right: the vice-Director : Fu Zhaoxiang, the Director : Rong Yicai,thevice-Director: Yi Dingfen

Facing a new beginning of "Tenth Five-year Plan", with the chance and challenge of the West Developing and China joining WTO, Town and Township Enterprises Administration of Liupanshui emphasized Second Creation of enterprises, tried to improve structure regulation, further emancipated minds, conducted reform with keen determination to improve development.

The developing objective of town and township enterprises in the city during "Tenth Five-year Plan" is to realize a fast, healthy and stable development after 5 years' efforts, to build 40 towns or townships and 20 villages of over 100 million yuan by 2005, to build 15 industrial districts and 8 enterprises with business income of more than 100 million yuan. The average annual increase of tax is up to 12%, which is 320 million yuan. The average annual increase rate of people with jobs is 2%, which is 270 thousand people.

钟山区——奋力抢抓机遇，

Zhongshan District--grasp chance, build

六盘水市委常委、钟山区委书记：张选进

Zhang Xuanjin, the member of the Standing Committee of liupanshui Party Committee and the vice-Secretary of Zhongshan District Party Committee

六盘水市钟山区人民政府区长：徐光毅

The governor of Zhongshan district: Xu Guangyi

钟山区办公大楼

Office building of Zhongshan district

凤凰新区--行政办公区

Phoenix new area--administrative area

钟山区位于贵州省西部的六盘水市中心区，是1988年经国务院批准建设的县级行政区，是六盘水市的政治、经济、文化、交通、金融中心。全区总人口42.13万人，总面积477.7平方公里，辖4镇1乡4个办事处。区内矿产资源贮量丰富，富有煤、铁、铅、锌、铜、石灰石等矿产资源，煤的贮量达20亿吨，煤质好、品种全，煤炭开采和铅锌冶炼具有较强的优势。交通便利，即将开通的株六复线、内昆、水柏铁路和已投入使用的西南最大的铁路货运编组站--六盘水编组站以及贯穿于钟山区东西南北的水（城）威（宁）、水（城）毕（节）、水（城）盘（县）、水（城）六（枝）公路和已开工建设的水（城）黄（黄果树）高等级公路，形成了北上四川、南下广西、东出湖南、西进云南的交通大“十”字，一跃成为西南最大的交通枢纽和物资集散地。区内邮电通讯设施一应俱全。

1999年，钟山区被列为全省首批20个建设的经济强县（区）之一。按照发展全区经济的指导思想，明确提出了“巩固煤炭、改造铅锌、调整结构、发展市场、开发凤凰”的二十字工作方针，动员全区上下努力抢抓机遇，奋力拼搏，加快了建设经济强区的工作步伐。

2000年、2001年连续两年各项建强考核指标均全面完成，2001年财政总收入完成10006万元，已成为六盘水市第二个财政总收入上亿元的县（区）。2002年，钟山区区委、区政府决心在邓小平理论伟大旗帜下，以江泽民总书记“三个代表”重要思想为指导，团结带领全区广大干部群众解放思想、实事求是，真抓实干，抢抓机遇，开拓创新，力争做好推动钟山区跨越式发展的新篇章。

建设经济强区

strong economic district

新世纪广场一角
A corner of the New Century Square

明湖高架桥
Minghu viaduct

西南最大的铁路货运编组站--六盘水编组站
The largest goods train switchyard in the southwest China --Liupanshui switchyard

Zhongshan District lies in the central area of Liupanshui City which is in the west of Guizhou Province. It is an administrative district of county level founded in 1988 with the approval of the State Council. It is the political, economic, cultural, traffic and financial center of Liupanshui City. The general population of the District is 421.3 thousand. The general area is 477.7 km². The District governs 4 towns, 1 township and 4 administrative offices. There are rich mineral resources in the District as coal, iron, lead, zinc, copper and limestone. The coal reserve is up to 2 billion tons. The coal is of high quality and of all sorts. The District has great advantage in coal mining and lead and zinc smelting. The traffic of the District is very convenient. Zhuliu double-tracking railway, Neikun railway and Shuibo railway that are to be opened, and Liupanshui switchyard, which is the largest good train switchyard in the southwest China, and highways of Shuiwei, Shuibi, Shuipan, Shuiliu which go through the District, and Shuihuang high-standard way have formed a large "Cross" of the traffic connecting Sichuan, Guangxi, Hunan and Yun nan province. It is the largest traffic pivot and commodity transfer station of southwest area. Post and telephone appliances of the District are Comprehensive.

Zhongshan District has been designated to be one of the 20 counties (districts) in the first group of the province which are to be built strong economic counties in 1999. According to the guidance of developing district economy, the District has clearly proposed work policy as "consolidate coal industry, transform lead and zinc industry, regulate structure, develop market, open Phoenix new area". The District has mobilized all the people to grasp chance and work hard to accelerate the construction of strong economic district.

Testing indexes for building strong economic district of 2000 and 2001 were all finished. General revenue of 2001 is 100.06 million yuan. It has already been the second county (district) whose revenue is up to 100 million yuan. In 2002, guided by Deng Xiaoping Theory and General Secretary Jiang's Thought of "three representatives", the District Party Committee and government of Zhongshan have decided to unite cadres and mass of the people to liberate minds, practice, grasp chance and create, to write a new chapter in the development of Zhongshan economy with leap speed.

崛起的盘县 Rising Pan County

县委书记：万晓流
The Secretary of the county Party Committee: Wan Xiaoliu

县长：杨兴光
The governor of the county: Yang Xingguang

贵州省的西大门--盘县，地处滇、桂、黔三省综合部，面积4056平方公里，人口113.01万，素有“江南煤海”之称。

盘县有丰富的矿产资源，境内有煤、铁、铜、铅、锌、黄金等23种具有较高开发价值的矿产，其中煤已探明储量105亿吨。在电力方面，继100万千瓦的盘县火力发电厂投产后，盘南360万千瓦的响水火力发电厂即将开工兴建。便捷的交通和通讯，320国道横贯东西，盘水、盘兴公路纵贯南北，程控和移动电话遍布城乡。

改革开放以来，县城经济有了长足发展，2000年国民生产总值为28.93亿元，财政总收入2.93亿元，乡镇企业营业收入为32.54亿元，农民人均纯收入达1363元。面临西部大开发和建设省经济强县的大好时机，随着红果新城城市功能的逐步完善，盘县的经济必将迎来一个腾飞。

Pan County, the west gate of Guizhou Province, is located in the joint of three provinces as Yunnan, Guangxi and Guizhou. It has a total area of 4,056 km^2 and a population of 1.1301 million. It is called “Coal Sea of the south to Changjiang River”.

There are 23 kinds of mineral resources in Pan County as coal, iron, copper, lead, zinc, gold, etc, which are of high developing values. Proved reserves of coal are 10.5 billion tons. Traffic and communication of the County are convenient. No.320 National Avenue goes from the east to the west. Panshui and Panxing road go from the north to the south. Program controlling phones and mobile phones are available all through the County.

Since Reform and Open policy was implemented, the economy of the County has been developed fast. GNP of year 2000 is 2.893 billion yuan. Financial revenue is 293 million yuan. Business income of town and township enterprises is 3.254 billion yuan. Average net income of peasants is 1,363 yuan. With the good chance of the West Developing and Building a well-off county, and with the completion of city's functions of Hongguo new city, economy of Pan County must be greatly improved.

红果新城
Hongguo new city

遵义市工商行政管理局

Zunyi Industrial and Commercial Administration

遵义市工商局副局长（主持工作）、党组成员：穆旭
The vice-director of Zunyi Industrial and Commercial Administration (presides works), member of leading Party Group: Mu Xu

遵义市工商局副局长、党组成员：任昌武
The vice-director of Zunyi Industrial and Commercial Administration, member of leading Party Group:Ren Changwu

遵义市工商局领导班子带领全市工商干部，认真贯彻落实“三个代表”的重要思想，深入开展“三讲”教育，深化工商行政管理体制改革，切实提高了干部队伍的综合素质。2001年，紧紧围绕当前工商系统的中心工作--整顿和规范市场经济秩序，截止10月12日，全市工商系统共查处各类违法违章案件15634件，查获了价值近300万元的假冒伪劣商品，在14个县级单位均开通了12315投诉电话，创建了“打假维权，消费者满意街（区）”。

通过全市工商干部职工不懈努力，遵义市工商行政管理局1988年至1999年，连续11年荣获贵州省工商系统年度工作一等奖；1997年至1999年，连续3年荣获全省“精神文明单位”；1997年至2000年连续4年荣获全省“发展非公有经济先进单位”；所辖红花岗区工商局曾两次荣获国家工商局表彰的“全国工商系统先进集体”。

遵义市工商局开展元旦、春节节日市场大检查，图为穆旭副局长陪同遵义市四大班子领导检查市场
Zunyi Industrial and Commercial Administration conducted examination for New Year's day and spring festival.

执法人员正在进行市场检查
Marketing examination

Leading group of Zunyi Industrial and Commercial Administration has led cadres of all the city's Industrial and Commercial departments to carefully carry out “three represents” thought, deeply conducted “three points” education, deepened structural reform of Industrial and Commercial Administration, thus to improve the integrated quality of the leader group. In 2001, the Administration has been working for its center aim: to rectify and govern the economic order of the market. Up to 12th Oct, the industrial and commercial administration departments of the city have dealt with 15634 cases and confiscated fakes and inferiors whose values are almost 3 million yuan. The Administration has opened telephone line of 12315 in 14 counties and founded “publish fakes and consumers satisfied streets (Districts)”.

With all the cadres and workers' efforts, Zunyi Industrial and Commercial Administration has been continuously awarded the first level prize for the work of the year of industrial and commercial administration system from 1988 to 1999, and “civilized unit” from 1997 to 1999, and “advanced unit to develop non-public economy” from 1997 to 2000. Honghuagang Industrial and Commercial Administration, subordinate to Zunyi Industrial and Commercial Administration, was awarded twice “ Advanced Unit of National Industrial and Commercial System ” by the Nation Industrial and Commercial Administration Bureau.

遵义市
Honghuagang

遵义市红花岗区区长：张明辉
The head of Honghuagang District: Zhang Minghui

遵义市红花岗区于1997年6月10日，经国务院批准设立,是一座具有光荣革命传统的城市，位于贵州省北部。全区总面积624.5平方公里，总人口50万，是黔北政治、经济、文化中心。

Honghuagang District of Zunyi City was founded in 10th June 1997 proved by the State Council. It is a district with glorious revolution traditions. It is located in the north of Guizhou Province. The District has an area of 624.5 km^2 and a population of 500 thousand. It is political, economic and cultural center of North Guizhou.

遵义市区夜景
Night scene of Zunyi City

遵义市红花岗区人民政府办公大楼
Government office building of the District

红花岗区

District of Zunyi City

遵义市红花岗区一角

A glimpse of Honghuagang District

遵义市红花岗区招商引资项目简介

遵义市红花岗区南部新城开发建设

项目单位：遵义市红花岗区南部新城开发建设指挥部

建设规模及内容：总规模18.5平方公里，建筑面积20万平方米的1号住宅小区，综合医院3所，学校21所，体育中心一座，市场4个，市政及文化娱乐设施开发。

遵义市坪桥冶金化工工业园区

项目单位：红花岗区坪桥工业园区办公室

建设规模及内容：规划用地1.84万平方公里，主要发展冶金、化工项目兼顾发展其他工业项目。

遵义市忠庄科技药业园区

项目单位：红花岗区忠庄药业有限责任公司

建设规模及内容：规划用地0.5平方公里，主要发展药业项目，兼顾发展食品加工项目。

遵义市农业科技示范园和种苗产业化基地

项目单位：遵义市农业科技发展有限公司

建设规模及内容：园区用地760公顷。含组培及生物技术、设施栽培等六个中心。

Introductions of the projects inviting tenders of Honghuagang District

Development and construction of south new city of Honghuagang District

Department in charge: Command center of Development and construction of south new city

Area and detailed: Total area is 18.5 km², including NO.1 residential area of 200 thousand m², 3 general hospitals, 21 schools, 1 sport center, 4 markets and development of municipal or cultural entertainment equipment.

Pingqiao Metallurgical Chemical Industry Park of Zunyi City

Department in charge: Pingqiao Industry Park Office

Area and detailed: planned area is 1.84km², mainly develop metallurgical and chemical projects, and other industry projects.

Zhongzhuang Science & Technology Pharmaceutical Industry Park of Zunyi City

Company in charge: Zhongzhuang Pharmaceutical Industry Co., Ltd of Hong huagang District

Area and detailed: planned area is 0.5km², mainly develop pharmaceutical projects, and food processing projects as well.

Zunyi Agricultural Science & Technology Demonstration Park and Base for Seedling Industrialization

Company in charge: Zunyi Agricultural Science & Technology Development Co., Ltd

Area and detailed: the Park covers 760 hectare, including 6 centers as: chemical technology, appliance cultivation, etc.

走发展之路 建美好桐梓

Walk on developing way, build beautiful Tongzi

桐梓县位于贵州省北部，地处川黔要道，区位优势明显，素有“黔北门户”、“川黔锁钥”之称。全县总人口64万人，面积3200平方公里，辖8乡16镇，498个行政村；境内资源十分丰富，其中已探明的矿藏29种，主要有煤、石灰岩矿、硫铁矿、钾矿等，具有很高的开发价值；全县水能蕴藏储量为20.33万千瓦；旅游资源独具特色，自然景观雄奇险峻；方竹笋等特色产品享誉省内外。

近年来，桐梓县切实加快所有制结构、产业产品结构、财政收支结构三大调整，大打基础设施、农业产业化建设和非公有制经济发展三大攻坚战，农业、教育、交通、通讯、电力、城镇等基础设施得到了长足的发展，保持了国民经济的平稳运行，推动了社会全面进步。

改造后的县城人民路路段
Rebuilt Renmin road of the county

Tongzi county lies in the north of Guizhou province and in the important location of Guizhou and Sichuan. It enjoys obvious geographical advantages and is called “the gate of north Guizhou” and “the key of Guizhou and Sichuan”. The general population of the county is 640 thousand. General area is 3200 km². The county governs 8 townships, 16 towns and 498 administrative villages. There are rich resources in the county. 29 mineral reserves have been approved. Main mines are coal, limestone, ferrisulphas, potassium, etc, which are of high developing value. The general water reserve of the county is 203.3 thousand KW. Tourist resource of the county is very special. Natural scenery is majestic and precipitous. Special products as square bamboo shoots are famous outside the province.

In recent years, the county has accelerated the regulation of ownership system, industrial and product structure and financial structure of expense and income. Meanwhile, the county stressed on three points as fundamental construction, industrialization of agriculture, and non-public economic development. Fundamental construction as agriculture, education, traffic, communication, electricity, town, etc, have been developed greatly to ensure the steady development of national economy and to promote the comprehensive progress of the society.

举行群众性文艺活动的--世纪广场
Century Square where mass theatrical activities are held

已改造的武胜路三叉路口段
Renovated fork of Wusheng road

特产--方竹笋
Special local product--square bamboo shoots

道真仡佬族苗族自治县 Daozhen Gelaozu Miaozu Autonomous County

省委书记钱运录视察猕猴桃基地
The Secretary of the Provincial Party Committee, Qian Yunlu was inspecting mihoutao base

道真仡佬族苗族自治县位于贵州省北部，行政区域总面积2156.2平方千米，驻地玉溪镇距省会贵阳360公里。全县总人口31.34万人，少数民族占64.3%。

“九五”以来，全县国民经济持续发展。2000年，全县国民生产总值完成37180万元，比“八五”期末增长59.4%。农业总产值完成33797万元，比“八五”期末增长46.5%，地方工业总产值完成18940万元，比“八五”期末增长35.5%。

“十五”期间，全县人民群众在各级领导的带领下，将继续以邓小平理论和江总书记“三个代表”的重要思想为指导，坚持以经济建设为中心，以改革开放和科技进步为动力，抢抓西部大开发机遇，努力把道真建设成为繁荣富裕的经济强县。

银杉之王
King of China fir

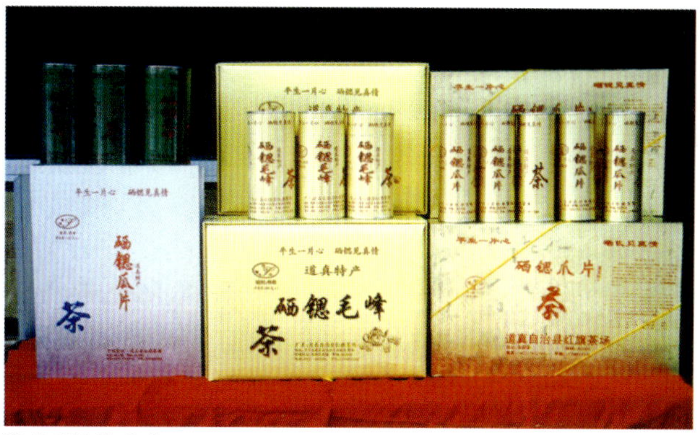

道真硒锶茶系列
Series Xisi tea in Daozhen

Daozhen Gelaozu Miaozu Autonomous County is located in the north of Guizhou Province, which covers 2,156.2km². Yuxi Town, where the county lies, is 360km far from Guiyang, the capital of the Province. The County has a population of 313.4 thousand, among which, minority nationality holds 64.3%.

Since "Ninth Five-year Plan", national economy has been continuously developed. GNP of the County for 2000 is 371.8 million yuan, 59.4% higher than that of the end of "Eighth Five-year Plan". Gross agriculture product is 337.97 million yuan, 46.5% higher than that of the end of "Eighth Five-year Plan". Gross local industry product is 189.4 million yuan, 35.5% higher than that of the end of "Eighth Five-year Plan".

In the period of "Tenth Five-year Plan", guided by leaders of every level, people of the County will continue to be guided by Deng Xiaoping's theory and General Secretary Jiang's important thought of "three represents", take economic construction as its center work, take open and reform as motive force, grasp the chance of the West Developing, make efforts to build the County to be a prosperous wealthy county.

长岩大桥及十里峡风光
Changyan Bridge and View of Shili Gorge

务川仡佬族苗族自治县

Wuchuan Gelaozu Miaozu Autonomous County

务川是镶嵌在黔北高原的丹砂古县，国土面积2777.59平方公里，平均海拔高度为1034米，人口41.04万，2001年GDP60039万元，地方财政收入3688万元，农林牧渔总产值51347万元，工业总产值39708万元。

务川是全国优质烤烟生产基地县，2001年烤烟产量为10516吨，品质在全省独占鳌头。务川资源丰富，拥有全省第二大集中连片草场--栗园草场（10736亩），汞矿、铝土矿等储量相当丰富，极具开发价值。务川是全国野银杏之乡，优质野银杏曾获国际金奖。基础设施建设日新月异，电力并入国网，全县通车里程达1338公里。

我们真诚希望，热烈欢迎各位有识之士投资务川、开发务川、建设务川。

Wuchuan is an old county in North Qian plateau. Its territory is 2,777.59 km^2 with an average elevation of 1,034 meter. It has 410.4 thousand people and the GDP of 2001 is 600.39 million yuan. The local revenue is 36.88 million yuan. The output value of agriculture, forestry, animal husbandry and fishery are 513.47 million yuan. The gross value of industrial output is 397.08 million Yuan.

Wuchuan is the producing base for quality flue-cured tobacco of China. The tobacco output of 2001 is 10,516 tons. The quality of the tobacco is on the front position of the province. Wuchuan has rich resources. Liyuan lawn (10,736 mu), the second largest of the province, is located here. The County has large reserve of mercury, bauxite, etc, which are of great developing value. Wuchuan is the hometown of wild ginkgo. The ginkgos here were awarded international golden prize. The fundamental construction of the County is developed fast. Electric power here is connected with national power network. The total bus route is 1,338 km.

We sincerely hope and welcome people to invest, develop and construct Wuchuan.

优质野银杏
Quality wild ginkgo

生命之水浇灌务川大地

青坪水库
Qingping Reservoir

百合基地
Lily base

栗园草场上牛羊成群
Flocks of cattle and sheep in Liyuan Lawn

赤水市简介

Introduction of Chishui

文化广场一角
A corner of the culture square

Chishui lies in the northwest of Guizhou and lower reaches of Chishui River. It is the joint area of Guizhou plateau and Sichuan basin. It is the trading bridge and economic and cultural place of Sichuan and Guizhou all the time. The City of Chishui covers 1,801.2 km^2 with 9 towns, 5 townships and 3 administrative offices. The total population is 300 thousand.

Chishui has typical subtropical monsoon climate. It is warm in winter and hot in summer. The annual average temperature is 18℃ It is one of the places with richest heat in the province. General sunshine time of a year is 1292.5 hours. The average annual rainfall is 1268.8 mm. Frost free period is 351 days. Southeast of the City is high and northwest of the City is low. The highest point is 1730 m above the sea. The lowest point is 221 m above the sea.

Chishui has a long history. It is famous for the battle of Chinese Red Army "Cross Chishui River for 4 times". It is the only national scenery place named by administrative name. It is awarded "city of thousands of waterfalls, hometown of bamboo, peak of red clouds topography, kingdom of spinulose tree fern, way of Long March". Chisshui is the green capital of Guizhou. It has rich forest resources. It is the biological demonstrative district of the country. Forest covers 62.18% of the city. Chishui is one of the 10 hometowns of bamboo in China. It has 35867 hectare of bamboo. It is the only place to grow phyllostachys pubescens in Guizhou. The bamboo products of the City have been sold to Southeast Asia and Japan.

赤水市位于贵州西北边陲，赤水河下游，地处贵州高原向四川盆地过渡地带，历为川黔边贸纽带和经济、文化重镇。全市总面积1801.2平方公里，辖9镇5乡和3个办事处，总人口30万人。

赤水属典型的中亚热带温暖湿润季风气候区，冬暖夏热，年平均气温18℃，是全省热量最丰富的地区之一。全年日照为1292.5小时，平均降雨量1268.8毫米，无霜期351天。境内地势呈东南部高，西北部低，海拔最高处1730米，最低处221米。

赤水历史悠久，人杰地灵，曾因当年红军“四渡赤水”而扬名中外，是国务院唯一以行政区划名称命名的国家级重点风景名胜区，被誉为“千瀑之市、竹子之乡、丹霞之冠、桫椤王国、长征之路”。赤水是黔北绿都，森林资源十分丰富，是全国的生态示范区，森林覆盖率达62.18%。赤水还是中国的十大“竹子之乡”，全市有竹面积35867公顷，是贵州唯一盛产楠竹的地方，生产的竹制品畅销东南亚及日本等国。

原生桫椤群落
Proto-spinulose tree community

十丈洞大瀑布（高76米宽80米）
Shizhangdong waterfall (76 meters' high and 80 meters' wide)

再创中国酒都新的辉煌

Recreate the wonder of city of wine in China

市委书记：何冀
The Secretary of the City Party Committee: He Ji

市委副书记、市长：曾永涛
The vice-Secretary of the City Party Committee and the Mayor: Zeng Yongtao

仁怀市位于黔北赤水河中游，背靠遵义，面向川南，是国酒茅台的故乡，是1935年红军长征四渡赤水第三次渡河的地方。全市面积1788平方公里，辖19个乡镇54个管理区，2001年末总人口57万。仁怀是全国文化先进市，省科技工作先进市、省治安模范市和省首批建设的20个经济强县（市）之一。

2001年，仁怀市委、市政府坚持以邓小平理论和党的十五大精神为指导，按照“三个代表”的要求，以市场为导向，以跨越式发展为主题，以农民增收、企业增效、财政增长、基础增强为工作主线，依靠体制创新和科技创新，加大改革开放力度，加快经济结构调整，大力培植特色产业，发展特色经济，建设特色城市，促进仁怀经济跨越式发展和社会全面进步。全年实现国内生产总值24亿元，同比增长15%，完成地方财政收入1.59亿元，同比增长21.64%，财政总收入5.66亿元，同比增长36.5%。科技教育、计划生育、文化卫生等各工作均取得新的成绩。

2002年是该市发展历史上不寻常的一年。在这一年里，仁怀将继续坚定不移地高举邓小平理论伟大旗帜，以强市升位为目标，加大产业和产品结构调整力度，发展特色经济；加快以路、水、电、讯为主的基础设施建设，完善城市功能，建设特色城市。推进工业化、城市化和农业产业化进程。提高经济增长的质量和效益。改进机关作风，提高工作效益。继往开来，抢抓机遇，开拓创新，团结拼搏，把富民兴市的宏伟事业不断推向前进。

酒都新城中心区详细规划鸟瞰图
A bird's view of the planning for central area of new City of Wine

——仁怀市

—— Renhuai City

仁怀市酒都新区会展中心透视图
The perspective drawing of Conference Center of new district of City of Wine of Renhuai

茅台河滨公园
The park of Maotai river

Renhuai City is located in the middle reaches of Chishui River in the north of Guizhou with its back to Zunyi and face to South Sichuan. It is the hometown of national wine, Maotai. It is where the Red Army passed Chishui River for the third times in 1935. The general area of the city is 1,788 km^2, with 19 towns and townships, and 54 administrative areas. The general population of 2001 is 570 thousand. Renhuai is a national advanced cultural city, provincial advanced city in technique work, provincial demonstrative city for public security and one of the first group of 20 economic counties (cities) of the province.

In 2001, the City Party Committee and government stuck to Deng Xiaoping Theory and the spirit of 15th meeting of the Party, based on "three representatives", took market as its guide, took development with leap speed as its subject, took its main work route as enlarging incomes for peasants, increasing efficiency for enterprises, increasing revenue and strengthening foundation. Depending on the creation of systems and technology, the city has enlarged Open and Reform, accelerated regulation of economic structure, cultivated special industries, developed special economy, built special city to improve the economic development of Renhuai at leap speed and the progress of the society. The GDP of the year is 2.4 billion yuan, 15.0% more than last year. The local revenue is 159 million yuan, 21.64% more than last year. The general revenue is 566 million yuan, 36.5% more than last year. New achievements were made in science education, family planning, culture & health, etc.

仁怀市酒都新区国酒大道开工典礼
The opening ceremony for the construction of National Wine Avenue in new district of City of Wine of Renhuai

The year of 2002 will be a special year in the history of the City. In the year, Renhuai will continue to stick to Deng Xiaoping Theory, take upgrading the city as its aim, accelerate the regulation of industrial and product structure, and develop special economy. The City will accelerate the fundamental construction of road, water, electricity and communication, complete the city's functions and build a special city. The City will improve industrialization, urbanization and agriculturization, improve the quality and efficiency of economic increase, and improve the style of institutions and efficiency. The City will grasp chance and be creative to improve the undertaking of making fortune for people and making the City flourishing.

仁怀市第一中学规划鸟瞰图
A bird's view of No.1 middle school of Renhuai City

二00一年，快速发展的普定县

2001, Fast Developing Puding County

2001年，全县人民认真实践江泽民总书记“三个代表”重要思想。经济建设取得较快增长，人民生活水平有了较大的转变，生活质量有所提高，综合实力进一步增强。

全县完成国内生产总值81923万元，增长12.89%。经济结构调整取得初步成效，农民收入有所增加。农业总产值为39822万元，增长0.67%，粮食总产量115260吨，增长2.1%，农民人均纯收入1304元，比上年增长20元，解决7010贫困人口的温饱问题。工业生产快速增长，工业总产值81687万元，增长38.9%。全社会固定资产投资16130万元，比上年增长5.1%。全年社会消费品零售总额15045万元，比上年增长12.6%。全年完成财政总收入10911万元，首次突破亿元大关，同比增长21.63%。严格控制人口增长，人口出生率控制在19.73‰以内。科教兴普战略进一步增强,各项社会事业得到全面发展。精神文明建设和民主法制建设进一步加强,社会稳定。

夜郎湖风景区
Scenic Area of Yelang Lake

四通八达的公路网
Convenient highway net

已建成的5000亩银杏基地
Constructed ginkgo base of 5,000 mu

丰富多彩的文化活动之一--地戏表演
Colorful cultural activities--local opera show

In 2001, the County has practiced the General Secretary Jiang's thought of "three representatives" carefully. Economic construction has been fast increased. Living standard has been greatly changed. Living quality has been improved. General capacity has been further strengthened.

The County has finished GDP of 819.23 million yuan, 12.89% more than last year. Primary achievement has been made in economic structure regulation. Peasants' incomes have been increased. General agricultural output is 398.22 million yuan, increasing by 0.67%. General output of grains is 115,260 tons, increasing by 2.1%. The net income of per peasant is 1,304 yuan, 20 yuan more than last year. 7010 poor people have solved the problem of food and clothes. Industrial production of the County has been fast improved. General industrial output is 816.87 million yuan, increasing by 38.9%. 161.3 million yuan has been invested on fixed assets, 5.1% more than last year. The total social retail sales are 150.45 million yuan, 12.6% more than last year. The general revenue of the year is 109.11 million yuan, breaking the point of 100 million yuan for the first time and 21.63% more than last year. The County has controlled population growth. The birth rate has been controlled within 19.73‰. The strategy of building Puding County by science has been further strengthened. All the social undertakings have been developed comprehensively. Constructions of spiritual civilization and democratic legal system have been further strengthened. The society is stable.

铜仁市　Tongren City

铜仁市是镶嵌于贵州省东北部武陵山主峰梵净山下的一颗璀璨明珠，是铜仁地区政治、经济、文化中心，是一座环境优美、资源丰富，基础日趋完善，开发前景广阔的内陆对外开放城市，素称“黔东门户”、“黔东重镇”。全市总面积1513.6平方公里。2000年末人口33.11万人，其中少数民族人口19.23万人。境内地形复杂多样，气候属亚热带季风湿润气候，冬无严寒，夏无酷暑，四季宜人。水能蕴藏量8.2万千瓦，森林面积5.3万公顷，森林覆盖率为37.99%，可开采矿种40多种，生物资源639种，野生动物26种。以省级风景名胜区十里锦江、九龙洞为代表的旅游景观多达200余处。

铜仁市今后一段时期经济社会发展的基本思路是根据建设商贸、轻工、旅游山水园林城市的功能定位，围绕建设经济强市目标，抓住西部大开发、加入WTO、建设经济强市、梵净山机场建设和渝怀铁路实施等机遇，推进体制和科技创新，实施经济结构调整、科教兴市、开放带动、可持续发展、城镇化战略，发展绿色、旅游、轻工、商贸等支柱产业，加快农业产业化、工业化、城市化进程，促进富民兴铜。

梵净山大道
Fanjing mountain Avenue

穿城而过的锦江
Jinjiang river going through the city

Tongren City is a bright pearl set at the foot of Fanjing mountain, the highest peak of Wuling range in the northeast of Guizhou province. It is the political, economic and cultural center of Tongren area. It is an open City with beautiful environment, rich resources, comprehensive foundation and prospecting further. It is called “the gate of east Guizhou” and “important city of east Guizhou”. The general area of the city is 1513.6 k㎡. The general population at the end of 2000 is 331.1 thousand. The population of minority nationality is 192.3 thousand. There are varies of topographies in the City. The climate there belongs to wet subtropical monsoon climate. There is no intense heat in summer or bitter coldness in winter. Climate around the year is always pleasant. The water reserve is 82 thousand KW. The forest area is 53 thousand hectare, covering 37.99% of the general area. There are over 40 sorts of mines to be explored, 639 sorts of biological resources and 26 sorts of wild animals. There are over 200 scenic spots represented by provincial scenic spot of 10-li Jinjiang river, 9-dragon carve.

The basic developing route of the economic society of Tongren is to grasp the chances of the West Developing, China's Joining in WTO, building strong economic city, the construction of Fanjing mountain airport and Yuhuai railway, to improve the creation of mechanism and technology, to carry out regulation of economic structure, building the city by science and education, driving the city by opening, continuos development and urbanization, to develop green industry, tourist, light industry and trade, and to accelerate agricultural industrialization, industrialization and urbanization, according to the city position of trade, light industry, tourist and countryside city and the aim of building a strong economic city.

东太大道
Dongtai Avenue

锦江一景--水晶阁风光
A scenery of Jinjiang river--Crystal Temple

西门大桥
The west gate bridge

乌江明珠--思南

A bright pearl of Wujiang River--Sihan

中共思南县委书记：晏世忠
The Secretary of the county Party Committee: Yan Shizhong

中共思南县委副书记、县长：代亮
The vice-Secretary of the county Party Committee and the governor of the county: Dai Liang

贵州楠木王
The King of nanmu in Guizhou

思南县位于黔东北铜仁地区西部，地处武陵山腹地乌江流域的中心地带，东与国家级自然保护区梵净山毗邻、南与泉都石阡县接壤，西与历史名称遵义交界，北经乌江至涪陵达重庆。全县地域面积2230平方公里，辖13个镇、14个民族乡，总人口62万，是一个汉、土家、苗、仡佬、蒙古等18个民族聚居的地方。

思南气候温和、土地肥沃，物产丰富，是全国优质烟基地、长防林工程和生态农业县，贵州著名的商品粮、商品猪、商品牛和蚕桑基地。矿产资源主要有煤、铁、雄雌黄、重晶石、冰洲石、大理石等，雄雌黄品位高，是国家中医药局的定点生产地。思南水能资源丰富，河流多、落差大、开发前景广阔，已列入“十五”计划，即将建设的装机容量120万千瓦的思林水电站，是国家西电东送的重点工程。思南交通方便，信息快捷。文化底蕴深厚，教育成绩显著。思南县城是一座美丽的文化古镇，依山傍水，错落有致，是旅游观光的好去处。

Si'nan county lies in the west of Tongren area that is in the northeast of Guizhou province. It is in the central area of Wujiang River that is in the middle of Wuling Mountain. It is in the west to Fanjing mountain, a national natural protection area, north to Shiqian county, the city of spring, east to famous historic city of Zunyi, and south to Fulin. The County covers 2230 km² with 13 towns and 14 nationality townships. The general population is 620 thousand. It is a place where Han, Tujia, Miao, Gelao, Mongol nationality living in compact communities.

Si'nan has temperate climate, rich land and products. It is the base of national quality tobacco, long protecting forest and ecological agricultural county. It is a famous base of commercial grain, commercial pig, commercial cattle and silkworm of the province. The main mineral resources are coal, iron, realgar, orpiment, barite, iceland spar and marble. The realgar and orpiment there are of high grade. It is the designated production base of the State Traditional Chinese Medicine Administration. Si'nan has rich water Resource and a lot of rivers with large drop, which are of great developing value and are planned in “Tenth Five-year Plan”. Silin hydroelectric station, whose installed capacity is 1.2 million KW and which is to be constructed is a key project of the national program of transporting electricity from west to east. Si'nan has convenient traffic, fast communication, rich cultural base and outstanding education achievement. Si'nan is a beautiful cultural town surrounded by river and hill. It is a good place to visit.

四野屯石人峰
The Stone Peak of Siye Tun

岑头盖仙壶石
The Stone of Gaixianhu In Centou

思南县城夜景
Night scene of Si'nan

与时俱进谋发展 开拓创新画德江

Developed with times Creative in building Dejiang

中共德江县委 德江县人民政府
Dejiang County Party Committee People's Government of Dejiang County

图为地区行署专员杨玉学（右）在县委书记陈达新（中）和代理县长杨频（左）的陪同下参观贵州酒圣酒业有限公司储酒车间。

Yang Yuxue, the commissioner of area administrative office (right), accompanied by Chen Daxin, the secretary of the county Party Committee (middle), and Yang Pin, the acting governor of the county (left), was inspecting storage workshop of Guizhou Jiusheng Wine Co., Ltd.

小城镇建设日新月异

Fast developing small city and town

德江县主要支柱产业之一的烤烟苗壮成长

Flue-cured tobacco, one of the main industries of Dejiang is flourishing

德江县主要支柱产业之一——畜牧产业蓬勃发展

Animal husbandry, one of Dejiang's main industries, is developed vigorously

德江县位于贵州省东北部、铜仁地区西部。全县总面积2071.9平方公里，辖20个乡镇355个行政村，聚居着汉、土家、苗、仡佬等28个民族，总人口44.29万人（2001年底止）。去年，全县国内生产总值在遭遇连续83天干旱情况下仍然比上年增长1.53%，财政总收入比上年增长6.30%，与此同时，其它各项事业都实现了较快发展。跨入新世纪，德江县委、县政府将在“三个代表”重要思想指导下，继续发扬“团结求实、拼搏争先”的德江精神，把富民兴德作为第一目标，抢抓西部大开发、新阶段扶贫开发和加入WTO三大机遇，紧紧围绕结构调整、招商引资、小城镇建设3个重点，积极培育烤烟生产、畜牧生产、以天麻为重点的中药材生产、以酿酒为重点的农产品加工生产、以水泥为重点的建材生产、以莹石为重点的矿业生产6大产业，全面提升县域经济发展水平，努力实现强县富民目标。

Dejiang County lies in the northeast of Guizhou province and the west to Tongren area. The general area of the County is 2071.9 km^2. The County governs 20 towns and townships, 355 administrative villages. There are 28 nationalities as Han, Tujia, Miao, Gelao, etc, living in compact communities. The general population is 442.9 thousand (by the end of 2001). Last year, with 83 days of drought, the GDP of the County still increased by 1.53% and the general revenue increased by 6.30%. Meanwhile, other undertakings have been developed fast. Stepping into a new century, guided by the important thought of “three representatives”, Dejiang Party Committee and government will continue to develop Dejiang spirit of “united and practical, making efforts to be the first”, take rejuvenating Dejiang and making fortune for people as the first aim, grasp 3 big chances of the West Developing, assist the poor in the new period and China's joining in WTO, work tightly around 3 construction key points as structure regulation, inviting investment and constructing small city and town, cultivate 6 main industries as flue-cured tobacco manufacture, animal husbandry, Chinese medicinal material manufacture, agricultural product processing dominated by wine-making, building material manufacture dominated by cement and mining industry dominated by fluorite, promote the economic developing standard of the County completely and make efforts to realize the aim of rejuvenating Dejiang and making fortune for people.

印江土家族苗族自治县

Yinjiang Tujiazu Miaozu Autonomous County

印江土家族苗族自治县位于贵州省东北部，全县土地总面积1969平方公里，下辖17个乡镇，2001年末总人口40.75万人，其中土家、苗等少数民族人口占总人口的70.5%。1992年被国务院列为国家内陆对外开放县，素有“书法之乡”的美称。

印江属中亚热带温暖润季风气候，年均气温16.8°C，日照时间长达1296小时，无霜期近300天，年降雨量1100mm左右。全县城乡用电与国家电网联网，基本实现村村通电；农户用电率达95%以上；程控电话、移动电话、无线寻呼在全县开通；城区6000吨自来水工程已投入使用；乡镇和农村集贸市场实现全部通公路，村通公路率达85%。

印江水资源较为丰富，有集雨面积20平方公里，水能蕴藏量极为丰富，达5.87万千瓦。凯望温泉水经国家检测属优质矿泉水。矿产中有大理石、玉带石产品蜚声全国。印江的生物资源丰富，梵净山就有生物种类2601种，其中有黔金丝猴、珙桐等国家一、二类保护动、植物。经济林木有茶叶、五倍子、吴茱萸、杜仲、黄柏等，其中梵净山贡茶在明朝万历年间就成了宫廷贡品。现已建成梵净山绿茶基地10000亩，开发了梵净山贡茶、梵净翠峰、雪峰等多种品牌的国家级名茶。

境内旅游资源丰富，佛教名山--梵净山气势磅礴，被专家誉为“中国第一佛山”。1986年被国务院确定为国家级自然保护区、被联合国科教文组织接纳为世界人与生物圈（NAB）保护区网成员。

梵净山万米睡佛
10-thousand-meter sleeping Buddha in Fanjing mountain

西环小区梵净山大道
Fanjing mountain avenue in west loop area

Yinjiang Tujiazu Miaozu Autonomous County lies in the northeast of Guizhou province. The general area is 1969 km^2 with 17 towns and townships. The general population at the end of 2001 is 407.5 thousand, among which, minority nationalities of Tujia, Miao, etc, holds 70.5%. In 1992, the County was designated national interior county for opening. The County has the honorable title of “hometown of handwriting”.

Yinjiang belongs to warm and wet subtropical monsoon climate. The average annual temperature is 16.8°C. The sunshine time is as long as 1296 hours. Frost-free period is about 300 days. Annual rainfall is about 1100 mm. The electrical net of the County is connected with national electrical net. Electricity primarily goes between villages. 95% of the farmers use electricity. Program-controlling telephone, mobile phone and wireless BP are available through the County. The 6000-ton urban water project has been put into use. Highways are available for collective trade markets in towns, townships and countryside. About 85% of the villages have highways.

Yinjiang has rich water resource. It has 20 km^2 land for collecting rainfall and 58.7 thousand KW water power reserve. Kaiwang hot spring water has been confirmed by the state to be quality mineral water. Mines of marble and jade belt stone are famous in the Country. Yinjiang has rich biological resource. There are 2601 sorts of livings in Fanjing mountain, including Qian golden monkey, dove tree, which are first and second level national protective animal and plant. There are economic forests of tea, gallnut, the bark of eucommia, etc. Fanjing mountain tribute tea has become palace tribute in Wanli period of Ming Dynasty. Now a 10-thousand -mu Fanjing mountain green tea base has been constructed. A lot of national famous teas as Fanjing mountain tribute tea, Fanjing jade tea, snow tea, have been developed.

The County has rich tourist resource. Fanjing mountain, a famous Buddhist mountain, is marvelous, which is called “the first Chinese Buddhist mountain” by experts. In 1986, it was confirmed to be a national natural protective area by the State Council, and was accepted by UNESCO as a member of NAB.

印江民族中学
Yinjiang Nationality middle school

印江县城全貌
A full view of Yinjiang

黔东北门户 乌江要律--沿河土家族自治县

The northeast gate of Guizhou An important point of Wujiang river--Yanhe Tujiazu Autonomous County

中共沿河土家族自治县委书记：龙长春
The secretary of the autonomous county Party Committee: Long Changchu

中共沿河土家族自治县人民政府代理县长：文玉强
The acting governor of the County: Wen Yuqiang

乌江上最大的港口码头--沿河港
The largest port of Wujiang river--Yanhe port

沿河土家族自治县位于贵州省东北角、乌江下游。扼黔渝要冲，近邻湘鄂，处在三省一市通衢地，是贵州走向重庆、江浙沪和沿海地区的重要通道，为黔东北门户、乌江要津。全县总面积2468.8平方公里，辖22个乡镇。总人口54万人，其中土家、苗等少数民族人口26.5万人。

县域地处亚热带岩溶山区，生物、水能、矿产、旅游等资源丰富。生物有1000多种。农作物以水稻、玉米、烤烟、花生等为主，树种以松、杉、油桐、乌桕、漆树等为主，畜禽以猪、牛、羊为大宗。属国家保护的珍稀动植物有黑叶猴、豹、黑熊、猕猴和银杏、黄杉等37种。山羊、油桐、乌桕、中蜂被誉为“沿河四宝”，名扬省内外，沙子空心李、武陵春富硒茶、中药材、黄豆等远近闻名，水能开发量104.1万千瓦，矿产有20多种，其中煤储量2亿吨、萤石保有储量150万吨、金属铅锌储量7.69万吨，开发价值大。旅游资源有著名的乌江山峡、省级麻阳河黑叶猴自然保护区、黔东特区革命委员会旧址等文物古迹和土家过“赶年”、傩堂戏等独具特色的民族风情。

全县基础设施日臻完善，建成水陆交通网络，实现县电网和国家电网联网运行；全县22个乡镇开通了程控电话和移动通讯，县城供水普及率达到95%以上。农林牧渔业稳步发展，已建成油桐、黄牛、山羊、中蜂、黄豆、茶叶、柑桔等农产品基地。地方工业初具规模，基本建成煤、萤石、铅锌等采矿业，水泥、砂砖等建材业，油脂加工、肉类加工、酿造等农产品加工及电力等工业体系。

国家实施西部大开发战略，为沿河提供了前所未有的机遇。沿河各族人民热忱欢迎中外朋友、有识之士前来考察、观光、旅游、投资开发。

沿河江黎之峡
Yanhe Jiangli valley

Yanhe Tujiazu Autonomous County lies in the northeast of Guizhou and the lower reaches of Wujiang river. It is an important joint of Guizhou and Chongqing. It is near Hu'nan and Hubei. The County lies in the joint of three provinces and one city. It is an important traffic place of Guizhou to Chongqing, Jiangsu, Zhejiang, Shanghai and coastal areas. It is the northeast gate of Guizhou and an important point of Wujiang river. The general area of the County is 2468.8 km^2. The County governs 22 towns and townships. The general population of the County is 540 thousand, among which 265 thousand are minority nationalities as Tujia, Miao, etc.

The County lies in subtropical karst mountain area with rich biological, water, mineral and tourist resources. There are over 1000 sorts of living things. Main crops are rice, corn, flue-cured tobacco and peanut. Main trees are pine, China fir, tung oil tree, etc. Main livestock are pig, cattle and sheep. There are 37 sorts of rare animals and plants as black-leaf monkey, leopard, black bear, macaque and ginkgo, yellow China fir, Chinese tallow tree, etc, which belong to national protective animal and plant. Sheep, tung oil tree, Chinese tallow tree and middle honeybee are called “four treasures of Yanhe”, which are famous out of the province. Shazi hollow plum, Wulingchun Fuxi tea, Chinese medicinal materials and soybean are famous far and wide. The developed waterpower is 1041 thousand KW. There are over 20 sorts of minerals. The coal reserve is 200 million tons. The fluorite reserve is kept at 1500 thousand tons. The mineral reserve of lead and zinc is 76.9 thousand tons, which is of great developing value. Tourist resources there include famous Wujiang gorge, provincial Mayang protective area of black-leaf monkey, former site of Qiandong special area revolutionary committee, and national customs as “ drive spring festival” of Tujiazu, Nuotang opera.

The fundamental construction of the County has been developed completely. Traffic net of water and land are constructed. The electrical network of the County has been connected to national electrical network. 22 towns and townships have opened business of program control telephone and mobile phone. The cover rate of water supply is above 95%. Industries of agriculture, forest, animal husbandry and fishery have been developed steadily. The County has constructed production bases of tung oil tree, ox, goat, middle honeybee, soybean, tea and orange. Local industry has primary scope. The County has primarily cultivated mining industries of coal, fluorite, lead and zinc, building material industries of cement and sand brick, agricultural product processing industries of oil processing, meat processing, wine-making, etc, and electrical industry.

The state has implemented the strategy of the West Developing, which provided unprecedented chance for Yanhe. All the nationalities people of Yanhe warmly welcome domestic and foreign friends, talents to come to research, visit, travel and invest in Yanhe.

Developing Pu'an 奋进中的普安

普安县位于黔西南州北部，全县国土面积1429平方公里，辖8镇6乡，2000年末总人口277182人。2000年，全县国民生产总值达到32372万元，“九五”期间年递增10.5%。农业产业化进程加快，茶叶、烤烟、苗山乌鸡等特色产业初具规模。五年累计投入扶贫资金19279万元，有17.2万人解决了温饱。农民人均纯收入1194元，适龄少年入学率98.37%，精神文明和民主法制建设进一步加强。

普安县充分利用资源优势培育支柱产业，形成以煤炭、电力为龙头，其他产业齐头并进的新格局。涌现出了武贵复合肥厂、冠合铁合金厂、金鑫煤矿等大批非公有制企业。县委、县政府进一步明确了“十五”期间的发展思路、重点和目标，决心带领全县各族人民，立足资源优势，抢抓机遇，艰苦奋斗，建设普安。

省委书记钱运录（左二）在黔西南州委书记许正维（左一）、常务副州长王胜业（右二）及普安县委书记龚修明（左三）、县长付贵林（右一）等陪同下，视察万亩茶园。
Qian Yunlu,the Secretary of the Provincial Party Committee (the second from left), accompanied by Xu Zhenwei, the Secretary of the Party Committee of Southwest Qian Prefecture(the first from left), Wang Shengye, the Chief Vice-Magistrate of Southwest Qian Prefecture(the second from right), Gong Xiuming,the Secretary of the County Party Committee of Pu'an(the third from left), and Fu Guilin, the head of Pu'an County(the first from right), was inspecting tea plantation of more than 10 thousand mu.

Pu'an County lies in the north to Southwest Qian Prefecture. It covers 1,429km² with 8 towns and 6 townships. Its population at the end of 2000 was 277,182. GNP of 2000 is up to 323.72 million yuan. Average annual increase rate during “Ninth Five-year Plan” is 10.5%. The speed of industrialization of agriculture was improved. Industries of tea, flue-cured tobacco and dark chick are of primary scope. The total cash for assisting the poor of the 5 years is 192.79 million yuan. There are 172 thousand people that have settled the problems of clothes and eating. The average net income of peasants is 1,194 yuan. 98.37% of the youth of school age have gone to school. The constructions of ideological civilization and democratic legal system have been Strengthened.

Pu'an County makes full use of resources advantages to cultivate major industries. Now it's led by coal and electricity industry with other industries proceeding together. Some non-public enterprises were founded as Wugui Compound fertilizer Plant, Guanhe Iron Alloy Plant, Jinxin Coal Mine, etc. The County Party Committee and Government makes clear developing thought, key points and objects of “Tenth Five-year Plan” and determined to lead all the people of the County to grasp chance and to work hard to build Pu'an.

黄皮塘电站机房
Machine room of Electric Station in Huangpitang

新建的龙吟黄猫坪特困苗移民新村
Newly built Immigrates Village in Longyin Huangmaoping

投资24万元新建的普安县一中电化教学室
Newly built Computer adaptive classroom invested with 240 thousand yuan in No.1 Middle School of Pu'an County

贞丰县简概

Introduction of Zhenfeng County

天下第一奇峰--双乳峰
The first marvelous spectacle--double breast peak

三岔河
Sancha River

三岔河
Sancha River

Zhenfeng County lies in the southwest of Guizhou province, at 105°25'-- 105°56' east longitude and 25°07'-- 25°44' north latitude. It belongs to the Southwest Qian autonomous prefecture of Buyizu Miaozu. The County has 6 towns and 7 townships. The County covers 1,511.9 km² and has 340 thousand people. There are 25 minority nationalities living in the county as Han, Miao, Buyi, Gelao, Hui, Yao, etc. 163 thousand people are minority nationalities that accounts for 48% of the population of the county. The County government situates in Mingu Town.

Zhenfeng has rich resources. Cultivated area is 18,121 hectare. Forest area is 364,888 mu. Forests covers 15.2% of the county. The County has pleasant climate and rich rains and sunshine, which are fit for lots of crops. The County has a large output of rice, corn, wheat, rape, tobacco leaf, Chinese prickly ash, honeysuckle, tung oil tree, tea, early-maturing vegetables and subtropical fruits like sugarcane. The County has a large reserve of water and minerals. It has been confirmed that the county has reserves of gold, antimony, coal, iron, aluminum, mercury, etc. The gold there is of great quantity and high standard. Large developed national gold mines of Lannigou and Shuiyindong were respectively confirmed to have gold reserve of 60 and 15 metal-ton. Their prospects are more considerable. With the development and mining of gold mines, Zhenfeng must be developed to be a real "city of gold".

Zhenfeng belongs to typical Karst topography with rich tourist resources. It has marvelous spectacle of "double breast peak" and provincial scenery spot of Sancha River.

Zhenfeng enjoys the advantage of geological situation. It is the golden waterway from Guizhou to the nearest sea. Zhenfeng is the necessary post from Xingyi, Xingren, Anlong, Ceheng to the capital of the province. The County has comprehensive communication equipment. Program-controlling phones were installed in villages and households. Mobile phones and wireless BP are available everywhere. By the end of 2001, the County has finished GDP of 459.74 million yuan and has general revenue of 31.4 million yuan. The developments of all kinds of social undertakings have laid certain foundation for economic development of Zhenfeng.

贞丰县位于贵州省西南部，东经105°25'--105°56'，北纬25°07'--25°44'，隶属黔西南布依族苗族自治州，全县辖6镇7乡，总面积1511.9平方公里。人口34万，居住着汉、苗、布依、仡佬、回、瑶等25个民族，少数民族人口16.3万，占全县总人口的48%。县人民政府驻在珉谷镇内。

贞丰县资源丰富，全县耕地面积为18121公顷，有林地364888亩，森林覆盖率15.2%。县内气候宜人，雨量丰富，光照充足，适应多种农作物生长，盛产水稻、玉米、小麦、油菜、烟叶、花椒、砂仁、金银花、油桐、茶叶、早熟蔬菜和甘蔗等亚热带水果。县境内水能蕴藏量高，地下矿产储量大，品种多，目前已探明的矿产有金、锑、煤、铁、铝、汞等。其中黄金的储量大，品位高，已经开发的全国特大型金矿--烂泥沟金矿和水银洞金矿，具探明储量分别为60个和15个金属吨，远景储量更为可观。随着金矿的开采和开发，贞丰县必将成为名副其实的“黄金之都”。

贞丰县属典型的喀斯特地貌，旅游资源丰富。有天下奇观“双乳峰”和省级风景名胜区三岔河。

贞丰县区位优越，是贵州出海最近的黄金水道。贞丰县是州内兴义、兴仁、安龙、册亨到省府的必经之地，通信设施齐全，程控电话进村入户，移动通信、无线寻呼四通八达。2001年底，全县完成国内生产总值45974万元，财政总收入达3140万元。各项社会事业的发展，为贞丰的经济腾飞奠定了一定的基础。

板澜群峰（喀斯特奇观）
Banlan peaks (wonders of Karst)

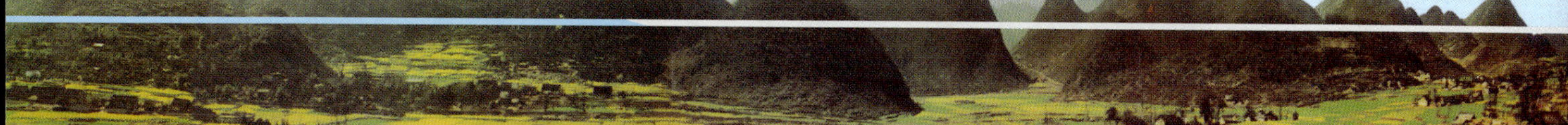

富饶的黔西北

A Treasured place in north-

中共毕节市市委书记：陈万桥
The secretary of Bijie City Party Committee: Chen Wanqiao

毕节市人民政府市长：沈先启
The mayor of Bijie City: Shen Xianqi

毕节市位于贵州西北部，川、滇、黔三省交界处，总面积3412平方公里，聚居着23个民族，总人口124万，少数民族占9.56%。毕节地形从西南向东北逐渐倾斜，境内属喀斯特岩溶地貌，山脉河流纵横交错，市区群山环抱，一水中流，天然景观与人文景观交相辉映，山城显得秀美多姿。

毕节资源丰富。地下资源主要有硫、铁、煤、锌等20余种矿藏，其中煤储量21.6亿吨，硫铁矿储量8.41亿吨。农作物资源包括粮食、蔬菜等455种之多，主要产玉米、小麦、稻谷等粮食作物，还盛产烤烟、油菜籽、柑桔等经济作物和天麻、杜仲等名贵药材。全市范围内拥有丰富的水资源，主要河流29条，河流总长约695公里。地下水储量4.33亿立方米，水能资源可开发量为115714千瓦，水电开发利用潜力很大。

毕节历史悠久，风景颇多，有“倒天河游览区”、“七星古关遗址”、“大屯土司庄园”等。毕节交通方便，过境主干线有321、326国道，贵阳--毕节高速公路，大方--纳溪高等级公路等。毕节又是一座具有光荣革命传统的城市，中共贵州省第一个党支部于1934年1月在毕节诞生。

毕节居住着汉、苗、布依等23个民族，独特的民族风情有彝族的“火把节”，苗族的“逛花坡”、“跳花节”、仡佬族的“打篾鸡蛋”等。

毕节市竭诚欢迎各路客商前来观光旅游，投资开发，共谋发展。

毕节市街景
View of the streets in Bijie City

治理后的倒天河一期工程
The 1st period of Daotian River project after governing

宝地--毕节市
-west Guizhou--- Bi jie City

Bijie City lies in the northwest of Guizhou where Sichuan, Yunnan and Guizhou Province joint. It has a total area of 3,412 km² and total population of 1.24 million with 23 nationalities. The minority nationalities account for 9.56%. The City goes from southeast down to northwest and belongs to Karst topography. Hills and rivers crisscross. The downtown area is surrounded by hills with a river goes through it. The hill City looks beautiful with natural scenes and artificial scenes.

日产10万吨的新水厂
The new water factory with daily capacity of 100 thousand tons

沿河住宅区
Residential areas along the river

Bijie has rich resources. There are 20 main resources under ground as sulphur, iron, coal, zinc, etc. The coal reserve is 2.16 billion tons. The vulcanized iron reserve is 841 million tons. There are 455 kinds of crops including grains and vegetables. Main grains are corn, wheat and rice. Meanwhile, it also produces commercial crops as flue-cured tobacco, rapeseed and orange and valuable crude drugs as the bark of eucommia. The City has rich water resource. It has 29 main rivers. The total river length is 695 km. There are 433 million m³ water reserves in the City and 115714 KW water energy can be developed. There is a large quantity of potential water and electric energy.

Bijie has a long history and lots of scenery as "spot of pouring heaven river", "the ruins of seven-star gateway", "Datun Tusi Garden", etc. Bijie has a convenient communication. Main roads through the City are No.321, No.326 National Avenue, the freeway of Guiyang to Bijie, the high-standard way of Dafang to Naxi. Also, Bijie is a city with glorious revolution traditions. The first Party Branch of Guizhou Party Committee was founded here in Jan 1934.

There are 23 nationalities living in Bijie as Hanzu, Miaozu, Buyi, etc. Special national festivals include " torch festival" of Yizu, " strolling on the flower slope festival" and "jumping off flowers festival" of Miaozu.

Biejie sincerely welcomes guests and merchants to travel, invest here and to develop together.

国家级文物保护单位--大屯土司庄园
Cultural relics under national protection--Datun Tusi Manor

"团结进步，繁荣发展"
"United, proceeding, flourishing and developing"

毕节地区民族宗教事务局

The Bureau of Nationality and Religious Affaires of Bijie Prefecture

毕节地区是多民族散杂居地区，全区有35个民族，2000年末总人口690.63万人，其中少数民族人口170多万，占28%；又是多宗教地区，宗教信徒占全省四分之一强。

在地委、行署领导下，全区民族宗教工作部门始终以经济建设为中心，稳定和发展为主题，扶贫攻坚和民族教育为重点，积极参与和配合民族地区的各项建设，为民族地区经济社会发展作出了贡献。

2000年，该局荣获省民委"民族经费管理使用和民族法律法规宣传贯彻大检查"评比一等奖。

千名信徒聚精会神聆听党的民族政策
Thousands of believers were listening to national policies of the Party

Bijie Prefecture is an area inhibited by several nationalities. There are 35 nationalities in the prefecture. The total population at the end of 2000 is 6.9063 million, among which minority nationalities held 28% that is 1.7 million. It is also a place with several religious. Religious believers held 1/4 of the province.

Under the leadership of the Prefecture committee and Administrative Office, all the departments of nationality & religious have been working around economy construction, set stable and developing as their objects, took helping the poor and national education as key points, actively joined in and assisted all kinds of construction in multi-nation areas. The Bureau has contributed a lot for the development of society and economy in multi-nation areas.

In 2000, the Bureau was awarded the first grade prize of the "inspection on uses of administrative fee and popularization of national law and regulations", by the Provincial Nationality Committee.

民族教育蓬勃发展
Developing National education

扶持农户大力发展畜牧养殖业
Supported agriculture and developed animal husbandry aquaculture

毕节地区煤炭工业局
Coal Industry Bureau of Bi jie Prefecture

丰富的资源 待开发的宝地
Rich resources A treasured area to be explored

地处黔西北的毕节地区，是我国煤炭资源最富集的地区之一，贵州省的重点产煤区。主要为无烟煤，煤炭储量大，煤质优，赋存条件好，资源遍布全区一市七县，有纳雍、织金、大方、金沙4个重点产煤县，75个重点产煤乡镇，是原全国产量越千万吨的10个地区和3大无烟煤基地之一，该地区交通运输方便，电力供应方便，地理位置优越，投资政策优惠，是一块待开发的宝地。

1998年，煤炭税费突破8000万元。1999年，达到12134万元。2000年，达到17200万元，超过了烤烟。煤炭工业已经发展成为全区继“两烟”之后的另一支柱产业。

毕节地区煤炭工业局局长：张天明
The head of the Bureau: Zhang Tianming

金沙腾龙煤矿
Tenglong Coal Mine in Jinsha

Bijie, located in northwest of Guizhou Province, is one of the richest resources places in China. It is an important coal area of Guizhou. Non-smoke coal is the main product. It has an enormous coal reserve. And the coal is of good quality. Coal is reserved all through the prefecture, including one city and seven counties. There are 4 major coal counties as Nayong, Zhijin, Dafang and Jinssha, and 75 major coal towns and townships. It is one of the original 10 major prefectures whose coal production are more than 10 million tons and one of the three bases producing non-smoke coal. It is a treasured place to be developed with convenience communication and transportation, convenience power supply, good geographic situation and privilege Policy.

The taxes of coal in 1998 were more than 80 million yuan and up to 121.34 million yuan in 1999. Taxes of 2000 were 172 million yuan, which are more than those of flue-cured tobacco. Coal industry has been developed to be a major industry in the prefecture.

金沙贵源1号煤矿
Guiyuan No.1 coal mine in Jinshan

凯里市　Kaili City

市委书记：曹云平
The Secretary of the city Party Committee: Cao Yunping

市长：吴荣阳
The governor of the city: Wu Rongyang

凯里市是黔东南州首府所在地和全州政治、经济、文化和交通中心，是以电子、轻纺、建材为主的新兴工业城市。位于贵州省东部、自治州西部，清水江上游，苗岭东北麓。全市总面积1306平方公里。2000年末全市在本地普查登记的人口为43.32万人（包括外来人口，不包括外出人口）。境内有苗、汉、侗、畲、仫佬族等38个民族；少数民族人口为32.81万人，占75.75%（其中，苗族占62.2%）；居住在城镇的人口21.34万人，占总人口的49.26%。

2001年，全市完成国内生产总值234649万元，比上年增长11%。以民族风情为依托，该市努力扩大对外开放，共完成招商引资项目41个，项目投资总额16.76亿元，实际到位资金2.83亿元，比上年增长2.14倍。以城市道路建设为重点，加快基础设施建设。拉开城市框架，扩大城市规模，道路骨架变为“三纵四横”，形成了开放状的道路网络。完善配套设施，推进旧城改造。加快新区开发，拓展城市空间。凯里新区建设主要是博南片区，全区规划面积10.68平方公里。

凯里街景
Street Scene of Kaili

凯里在城市定位发展思路上，强化一个意识（区域性中等城市的龙头意识），优化两大环境（生态环境和投资环境），实现三大目标（建成黔东的高新技术产业高地、建成全省对外开放的东向枢纽、建成支撑旅游大省的民族生态旅游强市）。促进四个升级（产业、产品结构升级、城市功能升级、综合实力升级），培育五大产业（旅游业、高新技术产业、新型建材工业、农副产品加工业、冶金工业）。在西部大开发中，将凯里建设成为经济繁荣、社会进步、政治稳定、民族团结、景色秀丽并具有浓郁民族风情的区域性现代化旅游中心城市。

凯里“8.18”国际芦笙节
“18th Aug” Kaili International Lusheng Festival

凯里大阁山隧道南出口
South Gate of Dage Mountain in Kaili

金泉湖公园
Jinquan Lake Park

Kaili City is the capital of South-east Qian Prefecture and the political, economic, cultural and traffic enter of the prefecture. It is a new industrial city dominated by electronics, light textile and building materials. It lies in the east of Guizhou province, the west of the prefecture, the upper reaches of Qingshui River and the northeast of Miaoling range. The general area is 1306 km². The general population according to local census at the end of 2000 is 433.2 thousand (including immigrant from outside and excluding local people going outside). There are over 38 nationalities in the city as Miao, Han, Dong, She, Mulao, etc. The population of minority nationality is 328.1 thousand, accounting for 75.75% (Miaozu holds 62.2%) . Urban residents are 213.4 thousand, holding 49.26% of the general population.

The City has finished its GDP of 2346.49 million yuan in 2001, 11% more than last year. Based on national customs, the City is making efforts to enlarge opening. The City has finished 41 projects of inviting capitals. The total investment of the projects is 1.676 billion yuan. 283 million yuan has been invested to projects, increasing by 2.14 times. The City takes road construction as key point to accelerate

株六复线凯里段竣工
Complement of Kaili part of Zhuliu double-tracking railway

迷人的南花苗寨风光
Attractive scene of Nan Huamiao Village

Fundamental construction. The City has extended urban area and forms an open road network of "three north-south four west-east" . The City has built necessary equipment, rebuilt old urban area and improved new area construction gradually to enlarge urban space. The new area construction of Kaili is mainly Bonan new area. The planned area of Bonan is 10.68 km².

In the side of city position, Kaili stresses one consciousness (leading city of area middle cities), improves two environments (ecological and investment environment), and realizes three aims (to build a high-tech industrial band of east Guizhou, to build an east pivot for the opening of the province, to build a strong nationality tourist city supporting the large tourist province). promote four upgradings (upgrade industrial structure, upgrade product structure, upgrade city functions, upgrade general strength), cultivate five industries (tourist, high-tech, new building material, agricultural by-product processing, metallurgy). In the West Developing, the City will build Kaili to be an area modern tourist city with flourishing economy, advancing society, steady politics, united nationality, beautiful scenery and heavy nationality Customs.

蓬勃发展中的凯里供电局
Developing Kaili Electricity Board

凯里供电局是隶属于贵州省电力公司的国家中一型供电企业，现有职工654人，管辖着黔东南14个县（市）和遵义市余庆县等15个县（市）的供电网络。是省文明单位、省电力系统双文明单位、国家电力公司安全文明双达标企业。

随着城乡电网的建设和改造工作的顺利进行。供电辖区内已拥有220千伏变电站3座，每县有一座110千伏变电站，构成了110千伏环网供电网络，并在2001年建成了220千伏三角电网构架。

为保证电网的安全可靠运行，该局不断加大电网的科技投入，在省电力公司率先使用了开放性调度自动化主站系统，注重提高优质服务，为市民提供小时供电抢修服务。

可靠的电能，优质的服务，吸引了许多商家来黔东南投资办厂，极大地带动了地方经济的发展。至目前止，该局年供电量已实现8年较大范围的增长，2001年供电量达到20亿千瓦时。为黔东南州经济和社会的发展做出了巨大贡献。

局长：李启楠
The Head of the Board: Li Qinan

Kaili Electricity Board is a national middle scope electricity enterprise subordinate to Guizhou Provincial Electricity Company. It has 654 workers and governs the electricity network of 14 counties (cities) of southeast Guizhou and 15 counties (cities) including Zunyi, Yuqing, etc. It is provincial civilized enterprise, unit with two civilization of the provincial electricity system, and standard security and civilization enterprise of National Electricity Company.

With the smooth development and rebuilding of urban and rural electricity network, there are three 220 KV substations built in its governed areas. Every county has a 110 KV substation thus to construct a 110 kv electricity network. In 2001, a triangle 220 KV electrified wire net frame was built.

In order to ensure safe working of the electrified wire net, the Board keeps extending technique investment to the net and adopted open automatic dispatch main-station system for the first time in the Provincial Electricity Company and attended to improve quality service, provided 24-hour repairing service for citizens.

Reliable electric power and quality service attract lots of merchants to invest in southeast Guizhou, thus improve the local economic development. Up to present, the Board has realized 8-years' continuous fast increase of electricity supply. The electricity supply of 2001 is 2 billion KWh. It has made great contributions to the economic and society development of Southeast Qian Prefecture.

凯里供电局办公大楼
Office building

绿色的锦屏欢迎您
Green Jinping Welcome You

锦屏县人民政府县长：王甲鸿
The governor of the county: Wang Jiahong

被誉为“绿色抒情诗”的锦屏县位于贵州省东缘，黔东南州东部，全县辖6镇9乡，总面积1596平方公里，耕地面积12.8万亩，总人口21万。锦屏是我国南方典型的集体林区县，盛产杉木和楠竹，素有“杉木之乡”的称誉，森林面积133万亩，森林覆盖率58%，木材蓄积量406万立方米。

锦屏河流多、水域面积大，贵州第二大江——清水江流经县境57公里。全县河流总长1011公里，可大力发展水产业和开发水能资源。即将开工建设的国家“十五”重点建设项目三板溪水电站位于锦屏县境内，将给锦屏带来千载难逢的发展机遇。

锦屏有优美的自然风光、淳朴的民族风情、丰富的历史文化遗产，尤以隆里古城、飞山阁、清水江等自然风光最著名。锦屏资源丰富，地方特色产品较多，野桂花蜜、山茶油、香桔享誉省内外。

勇敢的锦屏人民热忱欢迎国内人士前来观光旅游、投资兴业、共同发展。

Jin Ping County, honorably called “green lyrics”, lies in the east edge of Guizhou Province and in the east to Southeast Qian Prefecture. The county governs 6 towns and 9 townships. The general area is 1596 km^2. The area of cultivated land is 128 thousand mu. The general population is 210 thousand. Jinping is typical compact forest county in the south of our country. The County produces China fir and phyllostachys pubescens. It is called “hometown of China fir”. Forest area of the County is 1330 thousand mu, covering 58% of the County. Wood reserve of the County is 4060 thousand m^3.

There are lots of rivers in the County. Qingshui River, the second largest river of the province, goes through 57 km in the County. The total length of rivers in the County is 1011 km. Water industry and warter resource can be greatly developed in the county. Sanbanxi Hydroelectric Station, which is about to be constructed and a national key construction project of “Tenth Five-year Plan”, lies in the County. It will bring unprecedented developing chance to Jinping.

Jinping has beautiful natural scenery, simple national custom and rich historic cultural legacy as Longli ancient city, Feishan loft, Qingshui river, etc. Jinping has rich resources and special local products. Wild sweet-scented osmanthus honey, camellia oil and fragrant orange are all famous out of the province.

Brave Jinping people sincerely welcome domestic guests to visit, invest and develop Jinping.

飞山阁
Feishan loft

被中国农科院誉为“国粹”的蜜中精品--野桂花蜜
Wild osmanthus flower honey, which is considered to be “national quintessence” honey by Chinese Agriculture Science Institute

苗疆圣地

The Holy Land of Miaozu

雷山县委书记：刘太安
The secretary of the county Party Committee: Liu Tai'an

雷山县人民政府县长：吴育标
The governor of the county: Wu Yubiao

雷山县城一角
A corner of the county

雷山县位于黔东南苗族侗族自治州西南部，总面积1208平方公里，苗岭山脉主峰雷公山自西南向东北横亘全境。人口14.49万人，其中少数民族占90.1%，主要是苗族。

境内群山耸立，峰峦叠翠，至今尚有保存良好的原始森林和珍稀动物，是全省10个林业县之一。林木种类繁多，主要以杉、马尾松、华山松为主，还有秃杉（台湾杉）、三尖杉、楠木等珍贵树种；水资源丰富，特别是地下水矿藏水质未受污染，山泉清澈，沁人心脾，具有较高饮用开发前景。

苗岭主峰国家级自然保护区雷公山就在雷山县境内，海拔2178米。森林覆盖率达83%，在已知的1390种植物中，被列为国家濒危、珍稀植物有20种，其中国家一级保护植物被誉为“万木之王”的秃杉（台湾杉）在这里连片生长。药材有80多种，其中16种为原始珍稀名贵中草药，动物有132科、58种，其中23种为国家保护动物。雷公山作为中亚热带宝贵的物种基因库，堪称绿色“聚宝盆”。2000年6月2日，当时的贵州省省长钱运录同志登上雷公山山顶感慨万千地对雷山的同志叮嘱说：“要保护好、开发好雷公山，让它更多地造福人类，因为雷公山不仅是贵州的，也是世界的”。

雷山县是苗族聚居之地，苗族风情古朴典雅，人文景观十分典型。西江“千户苗寨”傍山而建的层层叠叠的吊脚楼，被誉为“天然民族博物馆”。雷山县是芦笙的发源地，“芦笙之乡”的岔河南猛芦笙队，曾到莫斯科世界青年联欢节登台献艺，把芦笙艺术推向世界舞台。

集生态风光、民族风情、人文景观为一体的雷山欢迎你来领略民族风情，感悟自然真谛。

千户苗寨西江
Miao stockaded villages of the ages: Xijiang

雷山

----Leishan

雷公山云海
The cloud sea in Leigong mountain

Leishan County lies in southwest in the autonomous prefecture of Southeast Qian Miaozu Dongzu. The general area is 1,208 km². Leigong mountain of Miaoling mountain range goes through the County from southwest to northeast. The general population is 144.9 thousand, among which 90.1% are minority nationalities, especially Miaozu.

Rows of mountains rise straight up in the County. Some primeval forest and rare animals are still kept well. It is one of the 10 forestry Counties of the province. The County has all sorts of forest. Most are china fir, long-leaf pine, Huashan pine and some precious sorts as Taiwan China fir, Nanmu, etc. The County has rich water resource, especially groundwater that has not been polluted and is of great value to be developed to drink.

秃杉
Taiwan pine

雷公山牌杨梅
Leigong brand red baberry

Leigong mountain, the highest peak of Miaoling range and a national natural protection area, lies in Leishan County. The mountain is 2,178 m above sea and 83% of the mountain are covered by forest. Among the known 1390 kinds of plants in the mountain, 20 kinds are national rare plants or in the imminent danger. Taiwan pine, under 1st level national protection and "king of forest", grows in large area of the mountain. There are 80 kinds of medicinal materials, among which 16 kinds are valuable primeval medicinal herbs. There are 132 animal families and 58 kinds of animals. 23 kinds of the animals are under national protection. Leigong mountain, as precious gene house of subtropical species, is called "treasure-house". On 2nd June 2000, Mr. Qian Yunlu, the governor of the province at that time, climbed on the mountain and said with deep feelings to the comrades, "Do protect and develop Leigong mountain well to let it bring fortune to people, because it is not only belong to Guizhou but also belong to the world."

Leishan County is a place where Miaozu people live in compact communities. Leishan has simple and elegant customs of Miaozu and unique artificial scenery. Rows of houses of Xijiang "thousands of Miao stockaded villages" along the mountain are titled "natural national museum". Leishan County is the source of reed-pipe. The reed-pipe team of Chahe Nanmeng from "hometown of reed-pipe" has been to Moscow World Youth Festival to put the art of reed-pipe to the world.

Leishan County, gathering ecological quintessence, nationality customs and artificial scenery, welcome you to come to experience the nationality customs and feel the nature.

中国民间艺术之乡--郎德上寨
The hometown of Chinese folk art--Langdeshang Zhai

国家级重点中专--黔东南州卫生学校

National Key College--Southeast Qian Prefecture Health School

省人大主任刘方仁、省委副书记黄瑶到学校视察

Liu Fangren, the director of the PPC, and HuangYao, the vice-secretary of the provincial Party Committee, were inspecting the school.

学校党委书记、校长：曾纪长

Zeng Jichang, the secretary of the school Party Committee and the headmaster

省卫生厅厅长何崇远（前右二）到学校视察办学情况

He Chongyuan, the head of the Provincial Health Bureau (the second from right at the front) was inspecting the school

黔东南州卫生学校座落在州府凯里市东南郊风景秀丽的金泉湖畔，320国道与市区红洲路交汇于校门口前，交通便利，环境幽雅，校园内规划布局合理，各项设备设施齐全，管理完善，师资雄厚，办学40多年来以良好的教学及管理质量享誉社会。

在长期的办学实践中，学校根据黔东南的实际和人才市场的需求，勇于开拓，探索出一条培养农村基层卫生人才的路子。40多年来，为黔东南和全省培养了8000多名高、中、初级卫生技术人才。

黔东南卫生学校的两个文明建设，2001年又结出新的硕果，今年，校团委被评为“省‘五四’红旗团委”，学校由省级重点中专步入国家级重点中专，州人民政府为学校荣记集体三等功一次；校党委书记、校长曾纪长同志被省委人民政府授予“先进工作者”称号。

Southeast Qian Prefecture Health School is located in the bank of Jinquan Lake at the southeast suburb of Kaili, the capital of the prefecture. No.320 National Avenue meet Hongzhou Road, leading to downtown area, at the front of the gate. The School has convenient traffic, beautiful environment, reasonably schoolyard planning, complete equipment, good management and teaching group. The School is famous for its quality education and management of 40 years.

In the long practice of education, the School was brave in exploring and has developed a method to cultivate rural grass-root health talent according to actual situation of Southeast Qian and the requirements of talent market. In the past 40 years, the School has cultivated over 8000 senior, middle-level or primary health technicians for Southeast Qian and the Province.

The School has made new achievements in constructions of two civilizations in 2001. This year, the League Committee of the School has been awarded “Provincial ‘4th May’ Red Flag Committee”. The School has been upgraded from provincial key school to national key school. The prefectural government has recorded a Group Merit Citation Class 3 for the School. Zeng Jichang, the secretary of the School Party Committee and the headmaster, has been awarded “advanced worker” by the provincial government.

学校大门

The gate of the school

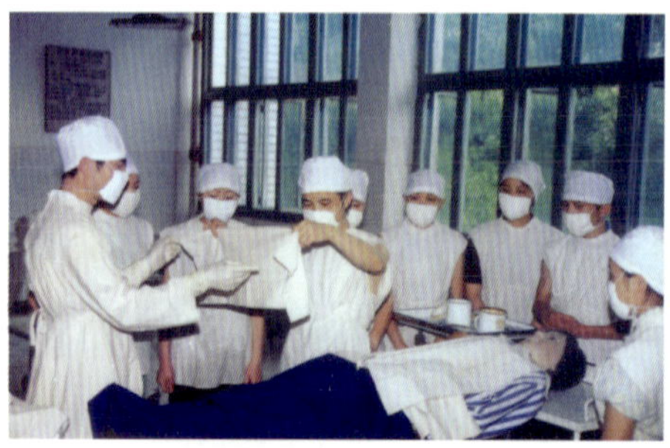

认真抓好实验课教学环节，注重学生动手能力的培养

Stress laboratory class and pay attention to the cultivation of students' practice capability

兴义市围山湖水库管理处

Administration of Weishan Lake Reservoir in Xingyi City

张崇光总经理（水电公司）（管理处主任）
The General Manager of the Water & Electricity Company: Zhang Chongguang (the Director of the Administration)

办公区一角
A corner of the working area

水厂一角
A corner of the water plant

围山湖水库属中型水库，位于兴义市东南面，距市区33公里。水库管理处设在顶效开发区城区，距围山湖水库19公里。该水库从原来单一的农业灌溉转向以供水、供发电与农业灌溉为一体的综合利用功能，推动水利产业发展。管理处现有小水力发电站5座，总装机2205千瓦；35千伏变电站2座，总容量20000千伏安；还有日供水规模达20000吨的城镇供水系统，围山湖管理处现有总资产8100多万元，在册职工236人，（包括离退休20人）。

管理处加强物质文明和精神文明建设管理，取得了较好的成绩：1996年获得水利部“先进单位”称号，1998年获得省委省政府、州委州政府“95 98年文明单位”称号，连续5年被省水利厅考核为“一等奖”，多次获“先进党支部”、“先进基层工会”、“水利建设先进单位”等称号。

Weishan Lake reservoir is a reservoir of middle scope, located in the southeast of Xingyi City, 33 km far away from downtown. The Administration situates in the development area of Dingxiao, 19 km far away from the reservoir. The reservoir was developed from simple irrigation to integrating water supply, generating electricity and agriculture irrigation. The Administration has 5 hydroelectric stations, general installed capacity of 2,205 KW, two 35 kv transformer substations with general capacity of 20,000 kvolt-ampere, and a 20,000 tons daily supply water supply system. The Administration now has general assets of over 81 million yuan and 236 registered workers (including 20 retired persons).

The Administration has stressed constructions of material civilization and spiritual civilization and made good achievements. In 1996, the Administration was awarded “advanced unit” by the Ministry of Water Resources. In 1998, it was awarded “civilized unit of 95---98” by provincial Party Committee and government and prefectural Party Committee and government. It was awarded the first prize for continuos 5 years in the exams by provincial water resources bureau. The Administration has been awarded “ advanced Party Branch”, “advanced basic trade union” and “ advanced unit in water conservancy construction” for several times.

围山湖水库
Weishan Lake Reservior

“资本置换”
谱写都匀发展壮丽诗篇

龙潭春涨
The Zhangchun Dragon's Pool

百子桥夜色
A Night View of Hundred-Son Bridge

1998年6月，县级市都匀创造性地提出“资本置换”思路并运用于实践。短短4年时间，调动各种形态的建设资本25亿元投入城市经营，使全市各条战线得到了高速发展，保持了全国卫生先进市、治安模范市称号，成功举办了“第十四次全国中小城市经济社会问题研讨会”，荣获第二批中国优秀旅游城市，并被省委、省政府明确为全省经济强市创建市和贵州南部中心大城市创建市，从而受到了各级领导和社会各界的广泛关注。

截止2001年，国内生产总值、工业总产值和全市乡镇企业营业收入均比1997年翻了一番；农业生产总值比1997年增长了12.44%；财政总收入比1997年增长53.27%；全社会固定资产投资比1997年翻了五番；商品零售总额比1997年增长了38.10%；农民人均纯收入比1997年增加了549元；招商引资比1997年增长了53.86%。

城市建设日新月异，先后完成了120个片区的开发改造，房屋开发面积40万平方米，相当于过去10年的总和；全市城镇国有土地收益相当于过去30年总和；城区面积已达21平方公里，比1997年扩大三分之一。以重庆源流集团、协和房地产公司、金榕房地产公司等为代表的60家房地产公司都为都匀作出了积极贡献。

引用“资本置换”进入企业，传统工业成功实施了改革改制，促进了工业经济持续发展。都匀袜厂、都匀内衣厂等一大批企业重现生机。

都匀城镇建设成效明显，政府每年投入400吨水泥和50万元的发展建设资金。农业基础设施建设力度加大，4年共争取项目资金1亿余元投入农业基础设施建设；农业产业化经营初见成效。随着“资本置换”的不断深入，资金流集聚效应愈加明显，涌现出金源超市、丽姿超市为代表的30多家超级市场，极大地带动全市商贸业的蓬勃发展。

今日裤裆街
The Crotch Street Today

"replacement of capital" wrote magnificent epic of Duyun's development

古色古香的石板街
Classic Stone Street

剑江长廊
The Long Corridor on Jianjiang River

In June 1998, Duyun City of county level has creatively proposed " replacement of capital" and practiced. During the short 4 years, the City has brought 2.5 billion yuan of construction capitals of all kinds to invest on city management. All trades of the city have been developed fast. The City has kept the tittle of national advanced cleaning city and demonstrative security city. The City has successively held " the 14th national seminar of economic and social problems in small and middle level cities" . The City has been awarded national excellent tourist city of the second group. The City is confirmed to be the city to be built a powerful economic city and to be built a large central city of south of Guizhou by provincial Party Committee and government. Thus it is widely concerned by cadres of all levels and the society.

Up to 2001, the GDP, General industrial output and enterprise sales incomes of town and township are all twice of those of 1997. The general agricultural output has increased by 12.44% compared with that of 1997. The general revenue has increased by 53.27% compared with that of 1997. Investment on fixed assets is 5 times of that of 1997. Retail sales are 38.10% more than those of 1997. The average net income of peasant is 549 yuan more than that of 1997. Invited investment is 53.86% more than that of 1997.

西苑大世界
Xiyuan Big World

剑江之夏
The Summer of Jianjiang River

Construction of the City has been developed very fast. Development and renovation for 120 areas were finished. The City has developed 400 thousand m^2 of houses, which is the total of the past 10 years. The profit from national urban land is the total of past 30 years. Urban area is 21 km^2, one-third more than that of 1997. 60 real estate companies as Chongqing Yuanliu Group, Xiehe Real Estate Company, Jinrong Real Estate Company, etc, have made contributions to Duyun.

" Replacement of capital" was introduced into enterprises. Traditional industries have successfully carried out reforms to improve the continuos development of industrial economy. A lot of enterprises as Duyun Sock Factory, Duyun Underwear Factory, etc, have taken on a vigorous look.

Duyun has made obvious achievement in urban construction. The government invests 400 tons cement and 500 thousand yuan per year as development fund. Agricultural fundamental construction has been enforced. Over 100 million yuan was invested in agricultural fundamental construction in 4 years. Primary success was made in the industrialization of agriculture. With further development of "replacement of capital", the collecting effect of cash flow will be stronger. Over 30 supermarkets as Jinyuan Supermarket, Lizi Supermarket appeared, which encouraged commercial development of the city greatly.

黔南州电信公司

The Telecom Company of South Qian Prefecture

黔南电信枢纽大楼
The South Qian Telecom Pivot Building

2001年，是我国实施“十五”计划的第一年，也是我国电信事业发展历程中不平凡的一年。黔南电信面对激烈的市场竞争，继续深化体制改革，实现了持续、稳定、健康发展。2001年黔南电信共完成业务收入1.609亿元，同比增长23.71%；完成固定资产投资1.23亿元，固定资产总值达到5.8亿元。截止2001年底，全州电话普及率达到5.68部/百人，主线普及率达到5.71线/百人，干线光缆达到1843.5公里，乡镇光缆达到1935公里。

结合电信市场的特点和企业自身状况，黔南电信努力培育业务增长点，一方面以“百万放号”工程的实施为契机，加大放号力度，另一方面积极推进卡式业务、IP电话、来电显示等业务的发展,同时积极开拓无线市话的市场空间。

在抓生产建设的同时，黔南电信一贯重视精神文明建设工作。全州12个电信企业均被评为各级“文明单位”。为做好服务，黔南电信在全州范围内推行了承诺服务制、首问负责制和值班长制度，并开通了投诉热线。

2001 is the first year of “Tenth Five-year Plan” and an unusual year of the development of our national telecom industry. Facing the intense competition of the market, the Telecom Company of South Qian Prefecture keeps deepening reform and realizes a continuous, stable, healthy development. The total business income of 2001 is 160.9 million yuan, 23.71% higher than last year. The Company finished fixed assets investment of 123 million yuan and now has fixed assets of 580 million yuan. Up to 2001, popularity rate of telephone in the prefecture is 5.68 per 100 persons. The popularity rate of main line is 5.71 per 100 persons. There are 1,843.5 km of main cable lines in the prefecture and 1,935 km cables in town and townships.

黔南电信中心营业厅
The South Qian Telecom Central Business Hall

Based on the features of telecom market and the Company's actual situations, the Company made efforts to cultivate business growth points. On one hand, it is used phone numbers largely with the project of “issuing 1 million numbers”, on the other hand, it improved Card business, IP phone and Caller Display business actively to explore the market of wireless phone.

While emphasizing production construction, South Qian Telecom keeps attention to cultural and ideological progress. The 12 telecom enterprises of the Prefecture were awarded “civilized unit” of their level. In order to provide good service, the Company conducted Commitment Service, First Receptionist Service and Director on Duty Service and built service hot line of 180.

西部大开发的桥头堡——都匀经济开发区

The important forward place for connecting the southwest with the developed areas of China——Duyun Economic Development Area

都匀具有“高原桥城”、“高原明珠”、“西部斗牛城”的美誉，地处贵州高原东南斜坡、苗岭山脉南侧，西北距贵阳140公里，东南距广西防城港直线距离不到400公里，贵（阳）新（寨）高等级公路、黔桂铁路和320、321国道贯通南北，丹桂、都惠公路横穿东西，是云、贵、川三省通往两广、两湖和华东地区的重要通道，是大西南南下出海的最近通道，都匀山川秀丽，自然旅游资源丰富，1994年剑江自然风景区被确定为省级风景名胜区，1999年都匀市被国家旅游局列为申报中国优秀旅游创建城市。

贵州省都匀经济开发区是由贵州省人民政府批准成立的省级经济开发区，位于都匀市区北郊，总体规划面积80.5平方公里，首期开发面积7.5平方公里，基础设施建设基本完成，开发区正逐步发展成为集工业、商住、贸易、金融、文化、体育为一体的综合现代化新区，更是理想的投资宝地。

Duyun, which also has the beautiful names as “plateau bridge city” “plateau bright pearl city” “west bull fight city”, is located on the southeast slope of Guizhou Plateau and on the south of Miaoling Mountains. It is about 140Km northwest of provincial capital of Guiyang and 400Km southeast of Fangchenggang city of Guangxi province. The Guixin High-grade road, the Guiyang-Guilin Railway, State road 320 and 321 cut the city from north to south, and the Dangui and Duhui roads traverse the city from east to west, making the city a hub of the traffic for traveling from Yunnan, Guizhou, and Sichuan to Guangdong, Guangxi, Hunan, Hubei and East China. It provides the shortest access to the sea for southwest areas. Duyun has plentiful natural scenic resources, which is suitable for tourist. Jianjiang Natural Scenic Spot was approved by the provincial government as the province-level scenic spot in 1994, and Duyun city was approved by the State Tourist Administration Bureau as the candidates city of China Excellent Tourist City in 1999.

Duyun Economic Development Area was established at the approval of provincial government as the province-level economic development area, which is located in the north suburbs of Duyun city. The long-term plan area of Duyun Economic Development Area is about 80.5 sq.km, the near-stage development area is about 7.5sq.km. Duyun Economic Development Area, whose infrastructure facilities construction have completed, is becoming a modern industry, commerce, culture, finance and resident area, and also is a most suitable place for business investment.

黔中重镇
An Important County in

红旗大道夜景
Night Scene of the Red Flag Street

贵定县位于贵州省中部，隶属黔南布依族苗族自治州。全县国土面积1630.8平方公里，辖8镇12乡，人口28.5万，其中少数民族人口约占51%左右。

贵定县是西南地区重要的交通口岸之一，黔桂、湘黔、株六铁路在县城交汇，贵新高等级公路，320、321国道和304省道纵横县境。县城距贵阳61公里，距都匀80公里。在定东乡集5条铁路和公路在一狭谷内并行排列，实为一大人文景观。该乡境内设置4个火车站，为全国之最。全县乡乡通公路、移动和程控电话，村村通广播电视。

县境内矿藏资源丰富，有煤、硫铁矿、铁矿等。其中高钙石灰石地质储量为全省储量的5%左右。旅游资源品位较高，定东高原苗寨古朴奇异的民俗民风，盘江音寨和云雾湖自然秀丽的风景，让游客留连忘返。贵定两烟生产历史悠久，享誉遐迩，“云雾雪芽”茶，野生百合粉为明清贡品。

贵定的城市建设，日新月异，基础设施得到加强，城市化功能日臻完善，红旗大道商贸新区，黄泥坝开发小区，老城区改造，教师新村，西门河治理，构成了县城亮丽的风景线。文化、教育、卫生、体育等事业全面进步。

烈士陵园银装素裹
The cemetery of revolutionary martyrs in silver dress

云雾茶基地
“Yunwu” tea base

县城全景
Full view of the County

——贵定县
Guizhou--Guiding County

定东乡“五路”景观
View of the 5 railways and roads in Dingdong township

苗族舞蹈“长衫龙”
“Long Clothing Dragon” Dance of Miaozu

Guiding County lies in the middle part of Guizhou Province and is directly under the Autonomous Prefecture of South Qian Buyi and Miaozu. The County has a total area of 1,630.8 km² with 8 towns and 12 townships. The total population is 285 thousand, among which 51% are minority nationalities.

Guiding County is one of the important communication centers in southwest China. There are 6 railways jointing here as Qiangui, Xiangqian, Zhuliu, etc. Guixin high-standard way, No.320, No.321 National Avenue and No.304 Provincial Avenue crisscross here. The County is 61km far away from Guiyang and 80 km far away from Duyun. 5 parallel railways and highways go through a narrow valley at Dingdong township, which is a great humane scene. There are 4 railway stations in the township, the only township in China with 4 stations. There are highways, mobile phones and program control phones between townships and every village has networks of broadcasts and TV program.

There are rich mineral resources in the County as coal, iron, etc. The limestone reserve holds about 5% of the provincial reserve. Tour resources are of high standard. Travelers can enjoy unsophisticated and fantastic folk customs and folkways of Miao village at Dingdong plateau, and beautiful natural scenes of Panjiangyin village and Yunwu lake. There's a long history in Guiding's tobacco manufacture. The tea of “Yunwu Snow Sprout” and wild lily powder are both tribute in Ming and Qing Dynasty.

The city construction of Guiding has been developed very fast. The fundamental construction has been strengthened. Functions of the city are gradually comprehensive. The commercial district of Red Flag Street, newly developed district of Huangniba, rebuilding of the old downtown area, the New Teacher's Village, regulation of Ximen river, all of the above make the County to take a beautiful new look. Industries of culture, education, health and sports have been developed fully.

云雾茶叶产品
Products of Yunwu tea

贵州水泥厂

Guizhou Cement Factory

法人代表：刘金华
Representative of the corporation: Liu Jinhua

贵州水泥厂是全国大中型水泥生产企业和贵州省目前最大的水泥生产企业。总厂位于贵阳市甘荫塘，东临花溪大道，西靠贵昆铁路，厂内有专用铁路直接贵阳西站；红枫水泥分厂位于贵阳市金华镇，毗邻贵黄高速公路，交通十分方便。全厂现有职工2700余人，各类工程技术人员及管理人员300余人。拥有ф4×150米、ф3×100.98米湿法回转窑生产线各一条，罗马尼亚引进ф3×88.68米湿法回转窑生产线四条，设计能力年产普通硅酸盐水泥81.3万吨。多次荣获“重合同、守信用”单位称号，先后被评为贵州省优秀企业、全国水泥产品质量百佳企业、全国环保先进企业。

Guizhou Cement Factory is the biggest cement enterprise in Guizhou province. The Factory lies in Gan Yingtang(in Guiyang city), east facing Huaxi Road, west facing Guikun railway. The special railway in the Factory can directly reach Guiyang western station; Hongfeng Cement Branch Factory lies in Jinhua town (in Guiyang city), nearby Guihuang highway, and has convenient transportation. Now the Factory has over 2700 staffs, with kinds of engineering technicians and managers over 300 persons. The Factory obtains each of 4x150 and 3x100.98 wet turning stove production lines, four Rumania imported 3x88.68 wet turning stove production lines, the production capacity is designed as 813,000 tons portland cement per year. The Factory has won many times “the reliable and believable company”, and continuously praised as the excellent enterprise of Guizhou province, one of the domestic 100 strong cement enterprises and environmental protection advanced enterprise.

贵阳市人民广场
People's square in Guiyang City

地　址：贵州省贵阳市南明区花溪大道中段
Address: Middle of Huaxi Avenue, Nanming District, Guiyang City, Guizhou province
电　话(Tel)：0851-3719094　3719061　3719086
传　真(Fax)：0851-3812760、3813549
邮　编(Code)：550006
电子信箱(E-mail)：cement@public.gz.cn
网　址：(http)：www.chinesecement.com　www.gzcement.com.cn

贵州省民族学院旅游系

Tourism Department of Gui Zhou Nation College

贵州省民族学院旅游系是贵州省创办最早，目前规模最大的旅游专业系科，招收“民族文化与旅游”专业专科生、“旅游管理”自学考试助读专科生及“旅游管理”专业四年制本科生，建系8年来已向社会输送毕业生2000余名。该系的培养目标是为旅游企业和旅游地区尤其是少数民族地区培养具有各类旅游专业知识的应用型人才。

该系在全省旅游界和教育界有良好声誉，并先后成立了“贵州省民族文化与旅游开发研究所”和“贵州省第四十八国家职业技能鉴定所”，同时开展了对旅游从业人员的等级鉴定工作。

党总支书记：周　俊(左)、系主任：杨昌儒(中)、党总支副书记：付光英(右)
The Party branch secretary: Zhou Jun (right), the Department head: Yang ChangRu(middle), the Party branch vice-secretary: Fu GuangYing(left)

旅游迎宾礼仪队
Honor team for reception

客房操作实践
Practice in guestroom

Tourism Department of Guizhou Nation College is the first and the largest tourism department in Guizhou province at present. It enrolls college students of Nationality Culture & Tourism, selfstudy college students and 4-year university students of Tourism Management. Since it was founded 8 years ago, it has trained over 2,000 graduates for the society. The aim of the Department is to cultivate professional tourism capable persons for tourism enterprises, tourism areas, especially minority areas.

The Department has a good reputation in tourism and education fields of the Province. “Guizhou Nationality Culture and Tourism Development Institute” and “Guizhou No. 48 Identification Institute of National Professional Skill” have been founded successively, and conducted standard identification on tourism workers.

招生、培训及旅游规划、开发咨询电话：0851-3610303　3610382
Tel for enrollment, training, tourism planning and developing: 0851-3610303　3610382

系主任：杨昌儒(教授)
The Department head: Yang ChangRu (professor)

贵州安易软件有限公司

Guizhou Anyi Software Co., Ltd

贵州安易软件有限公司于1999年5月18日正式宣布成立，是财政部北京安易软件有限责任公司在贵州的分公司，为安易财务及企业管理软件在贵州的唯一总代理。目前是贵州省最大的专门从事财务及企业管理软件的销售及服务机构之一。

借助新的会计制度，优质的服务质量，该公司先后为全省财政总预算、预算外两大系统、安顺市7个核算中心、88个零户统管、省财政厅、省工商系统、水钢（集团）、六枝工矿、贵州省桥梁工程公司、贵州省建工集团等500多家单位提供了财务及企业信息化建设服务。

随着我国信息化建设的不断深入，该公司将以“务实、合作、开拓、进取”的精神竭诚为政府企业在信息化系统方面提供实实在在的解决方案和全方位的服务，推动全省各行各业信息化建设事业的发展。

总经理：程建国

The General Manager: Cheng Jianguo

公司宗旨：致力于会计电算化　致力于管理现代化
致力于商务电子化　致力于软件产业化

The object of the Company: Devoting to computerized accounting　Devoting to modern management
Devoting to electrified business　Devoting to industrialization of software

Guizhou Anyi Software Co., Ltd was founded on 18th May 1999. It is the branch of Beijing Anyi Software Co., Ltd of the Ministry of Finance. It is the only agent of Anyi financial and enterprise management software in Guizhou. Now, it is one of the largest sales and service organizations specializing in financial and enterprise management software.

With the implementation of new accounting system and quality service, the Company has successively provided financial and information services for over 500 units as general budget and extra budget of the province, 7 accounting centers and unitary management of 88 accounts of Anshun City, provincial Financial Bureau, industrial and commercial system of the province, Shui Steel (group) Company, Liuzhi Ore, the Bridge Project Company of Guizhou Province, the Construction Group of Guizhou Province.

With the deepening of information construction, the Company will provide practical solutions and comprehensive services for governmental enterprises in information system with the spirit of practical, cooperative, creative and enterprising", and to promote the development of information in all fields of the province.

电　话（Tel）：0851-6508669 6505392
地　址：贵阳市枣山路9号
Address: No.9 Zaoshan Road, Guiyang City
技术支持热线（Tel for technical support）：0851-6508606
网　址（Web Site）：www.anyi.com.cn

市场部
Sales Dept.

客户服务部
Client Service Dept.

贵阳三联乳业有限公司

Guiyang Sanlian Dairy Industry Co., Ltd

省委副书记黄瑶视察三联公司人工草山
Huang Yao, the vice-Secretary of the Provincial Party Committee, were inspecting contrived grass hill of Sanlian Company

董事长：孙良缔
The Chairman of the Board: Sun Liangdi

集群饲养奶牛
Massively raise cows

贵阳三联乳业有限公司是目前贵州省规模最大、实力最强、效益最好的乳业企业。公司占地26平方公里，其中人工草场5000亩，饲料基地4670亩，森林4500亩，建筑占地2700亩，其余面积按草蓄配套原则继续开发建设。公司总资产8700万元，牛奶产量和市场分额均占全省的70%以上。贵阳三联乳业有限公司是全省第一个集牧草种植、饲料加工、奶牛养殖、乳品加工、销售为一体的专业化、多元化发展的乳业龙头企业。

公司目前有乌当、花溪、阳关三个奶牛饲养基地。现存栏5000余头优质高产奶牛，日产奶10万余斤。在饲料种植及加工方面，公司大力引进饲料新品种，推广饲料种植新技术，调整饲料品种结构，推行联产承包责任制，使种植业不仅为农户带来经济效益，还恢复了生态环境。在奶牛饲养方面，公司建立健全奶牛饲养的各种责任制，使饲养业发展壮大，形成了“牛—>粪—>草—>牛”的良性循环。同时促进了“种植、养殖、加工、销售”一体化发展，实现了整个乳业产业链的良性循环。公司于2001年10月把奶牛下放给职工自己饲养经营，自负盈亏，调动了职工的积极性，加强了职工的责任感，成功走上了“公司+农户”联合发展的道路。公司认真贯彻市委七届六次全会精神，将开发第三产业，加快发展。

为适应市场规则，公司已成立ISO国际质量体系推动工作领导小组，力争年内完成国际质量管理体系认证工作。

Guizhou Sanlian Dairy Industry Co., Ltd is currently the largest, most competitive and most profitable dairy company of Guizhou Province. The Company covers 26km^2, among which 5000 mu are artificial lawns, 4670 mu are raising base, 4500 mu are forest, 2700 mu are building areas. The rest are under development and construction according to grass storage principle. The general assets of the company are 87 million yuan. Both the milk output and market holding of the Company hold more than 70% of the Province. The Company is the first leading dairy enterprise integrating herbage planting, forage proceeding, cow raising, dairy proceeding and sales.

At present, the Company has three raising bases as Wudang, Huaxi and Yangguan. Now the Company has over 5000 quality high-production cows with daily production of 100 thousand jin. In the fields of fodder planting and processing, the Company imported fodder of new sorts, promoted new technique in cultivation, regulated the sort structure and promoted the contracted responsibility system with remuneration linked to output. Thus the Company has not only made profit for peasants but also make up for the biological environment. In the field of cow raising, the Company has built comprehensive responsibility systems of all kinds to improve raising. The company has built a good circulation of “cow—>dung—>grass—>cow”, Meanwhile, the Company has improved the integration development of “cultivation, raising, processing and selling” to realize the active circulation of dairy industry. The Company has lent cows to its workers to raise by themselves in Oct 2001, who would be responsible for the loss and profit. Thus the workers were largely encouraged and more responsible. The Company has succeeded in the development of “company + farmer”. The Company has implemented the spirit of 6th meeting of 7th session city Party Committee and will develop 3rd industry to accelerate development.

In order to adapt to market laws, the Company has set up a leading group for promoting the work of ISO International Quality System and tries to finish the certification of the system by the end of this Year.

华创证券经纪有限责任公司
Huachuang Securities Broking Co., Ltd

华创证券经纪有限责任公司是在整合贵州实联信托投资公司和贵州国际信托投资公司优质证券资产和业务的基础上，联合东西部地区大型企业和上市公司，经增资扩股，并按现代企业制度规范建立的一家股份制证券经营机构，是贵州省唯一的法人券商。注册资本金2亿元，现拥有4家证券交易营业部：

贵阳中华北路营业部 上海控江路营业部

贵阳中山东路营业部 上海淮安路营业部

长期以来，所属营业部以卓著的信誉、先进的交易设备，细致周到的服务和高水准的投资咨询服务赢得广大客户的信赖。继往开来，我们将以更高的服务质量、更好的服务设施、更新的服务理念、全面的业务领域、综合的服务品种，最快、最新、最丰富的权威咨询回报广大投资者。华创证券本着“广纳中华有才之士，为华创客户创造财富”的经营理念，为广大客户提供最专业的经纪服务。

Huachuang Securities Broking Co., Ltd was founded on the bases of integrating quality securities assets and businesses of Guizhou Shilian Trust Investment Company and Guizhou International Trust Investment Company. It is a stock securities broking organization founded according to modern enterprise system and with the expanded capital of large enterprises and some listed companies of east and west areas. It is the only corporation securities broker in Guizhou Province. It has a registered capital of 0.2 billion yuan and 4 security exchange departments As:

North Zhonghua Road Department in Gui yang
Kongjiang Road Department in Shanghai

East Zhongshan Road Department in Guiyang
Huai'an Road Department in Shanghai

For a long term, the subordinate departments were highly trusted by clients for its famous credit, advanced exchanging equipment, careful services and high standard investment consulting services. In the future, we will provide higher standard services, better equipment, new service ideal, comprehensive business, integrated services, the fastest, latest and richest consulting services. Sticking the business ideal of “employ the talents extensively and make fortune for clients”, Huachuang will provide the most professional broking services for its clients.

大户室
Large stock holders' room

中户区
Middle stock holders' room

证券交易大厅
Security exchange hall

云岩区农村信用联社
Rural Credit Cooperative of Yunyan District

在人行贵阳中支和当地政府的领导及大力支持下，在联社党委和理事会的正确领导下，联社完成了2001年度经营目标，年末各项存款余额51,239万元，较年初增加了9,382万元，各项贷款余额32,258万元，较年初增加4,784万元。不良贷款占比为20.8%，较年初下降了3.3个百分点。

为使职工更好地适应激烈的同业竞争，培育企业可持续发展的后劲，联社进行了职业道德和服务礼仪培训，组织会计人员进行再教育和财会电算化等培训。在强化素质教育培训中，联社开展了三次全员参加的学习和讨论。

2001年，联社在做好传统业务的基础上，拓展了保险代理、汽车消费贷款、住房按揭贷款等业务，并努力提高农贷比例和实施小额农贷，大力支持出租车行业。联社立足城郊，服务农村，面向城市，竭力服务“三农”，为中小型企业、个体工商业提供优质服务。

2001年，联社加强了会计核算管理，促进了经营目标逐步实现。针对西部大开发的实施、入世的影响，联社引入竞争机制，坚持可持续发展。联社在经营管理目标实行过程中，充分发挥各职能部门的作用，确保经营效益和目标的实现。

2001年，联社的长足发展为当地经济的发展、产业结构的调整、农业经济结构的调整和农民的勤劳致富作出了贡献。

With the leading and support of People's Bank of China Guiyang Branch and local government, with the scientific leading of the Party Committee and the board of directors, the Cooperative finished its business plan of 2001. Total savings are 512.39 million yuan at the end of 2001, which are 93.82 million yuan more than those of last year. Total loans are 322.58 million yuan, 47.84 million yuan more than those of last year. The rate of improper loans is 20.8%, 3.3% less than that at the beginning of the year.

In order to help workers applied for the keen competition inside the industry and to provide support for enterprise's continuous development, the Cooperative trained its staff on professional morals and service ceremony. Also, the Cooperative organized accountants to get re-educated and computer adaptive training. In the program of emphasizing quality education training, the Cooperative conducted three studies and discusses attended by all the staff.

In 2001, on the base of finishing traditional businesses, the Cooperative developed insurance agency, auto loan, house loan, etc. Also, it has made efforts to increase rural loans, undertakes small rural loans and encourages taxi industry. Based on the suburbs, facing to the city, The Cooperative provides quality services for middle and small enterprises and individual commercials.

In 2001, the Cooperative strengthened accounting management to improve the realization of business aims. Be aware of the West developing and China's joining WTO, the Cooperative adopted competition system and stick to continuous development. With the accomplishment of business aims, the Cooperative makes full uses of every department to ensure the profit and business aims.

In 2001, the fast development of the Cooperative makes great contributions for the local economic development, the regulation of industrial structure and rural economic structure, and peasants' Fortune.

贵阳市小河农村信用社
Xiaohe Rural Credit Cooperative of Guiyang City

贵阳市小河农村信用社是1954年成立的农村合作金融组织，经过40余年的耕耘，现已发展成多功能、全方位，集存款、贷款、结算等业务为一体的金融机构。目前下设1个营业部，7个分社，有员工59人。

近年来，贵阳市小河农村信用社内抓管理，外树形象，在致力于地方经济建设的同时，服务领域不断扩大，各项业务稳步上升。截止2001年末，各项存款余额为16,472万元，各项贷款达10,793万元，有力地支持了小河地区工业农业和农村商品经济的发展。

小河农村信用社业务范围：办理个人储蓄；集体、个体存款；国内结算业务；代发工资、代理收费款项及委托代办保险业务；代理发行、代理兑付承销政府债券；办理经中国人民银行批准的其他业务。

地址：贵阳市小河区黄河路433号
Address: Huanghe Road No. 433, Xiaohe district, Guiyang City.
邮编（Post Code）：550009
电话（Tel）：0851-3833147 3841396
传真（Fax）：0851-3803790

小河农村信用社贷款支持农民兴建的香江新村农贸市场
Xiangjiang New Village Rural Trading Market, supported by the loans of the Cooperative

小河农村信用社贷款支持发展起来的“黄河购物超市”
Huanghe Shopping Center, supported by the loan of the Cooperative

主任：雷成元
The Director of the Cooperative: Lei Chengyuan

Xiaohe Rural Credit Cooperative of Guiyang City is a rural cooperative organization founded in 1954. After 40 years' development, the Cooperative has become a muti-functional, integrated financial organization dealing with deposit, loan, check-up, etc. It has 59 workers and 1 business department, 7 Branches.

In recent years, the Cooperative strengthens both the internal management and building its image. While contributing to local economy construction, the Cooperative keeps extending business fields. Up to 2001, the total deposits are 164.72 million yuan. The total loans are 107.93 million yuan. Thus, the Cooperative provides powerful support to the development of local industry, agriculture and commercial economy of Xiaohe district.

The businesses of the Cooperative includes: individual saving, collective (or individual) deposit, domestic check-up, distributing salary, charge agency, insurance agency, issuing, cashing or selling governmental debenture, dealing with other businesses permitted by the People's Bank of China.

朝晖企业——白云民营企业中闪亮的新星

Zhaohui Enterprise--a new bright star of non-public enterprises of Baiyun District

朝晖花园大门
The gate of Zhaohui Garden

朝晖企业是一家集房地产开发、物业管理、环境绿化、文化娱乐、餐饮、民族文化及农业开发等于一体的多元化集团企业，拥有固定资产6000余万元，流动资产3000多万元、年上缴税金300多万元。

朝晖企业以房地产业为主，自成立以来，本着"提高居住品质，以人为本"的服务宗旨；以"秉承务实、高效实用"的企业精神；立足城郊、定位工薪、追求卓越品质，创建幸福家园的开发理念，首开白云花园式住宅小区的先河，先后成功开发了蔬办商住楼、科委商住楼、朝晖花园一期、二期、朝晖馨苑、朝晖景苑、铜仁"东方花园"、六盘水"交警支队商住楼"、朝晖麒麟苑等项目。目前开发总量已超过20万平方米，已于6月30日交付使用的"朝晖花园二期"，总建筑面积达8万余平方米，该小区的建成，将填补白云区无花园式住宅小区的空白。

企业所经营的项目均取得良好的社会声誉，多次受到上级领导及社会各界的好评。被白云区政府评为"纳税先进企业"，连续两年被白云区政府评为"重合同、守信用"单位，今年又被评为市级"重合同、守信用"单位。

朝晖企业积极参与社会公益活动。去年4月为白云首届房交会捐助30万元；8月，为区团委主办的朝晖红色之旅夏令营赞助5万元；9月，为牛场乡捐助教育奖学金3万元；今年，朝晖企业又投资近千万元修建白云民族民俗博物馆等建筑群体，为筑城民族教育、民族风情旅游事业作出重大贡献。

Zhaohui Enterprise is a group enterprise integrating real estate developing, apartment managing, cultural entertainment, restaurant, national culture and agricultural development, The company has over 60 million yuan fixed assets, over 30 million yuan current assets and pays over 3 million yuan taxes annually. Zhaohui Enterprise is mainly engaged in real estate. Since it was founded, the enterprise has stuck to its service policy as "improve the living quality, base on people", and the enterprise spirit of "be practical and efficient", stands on the suburb and wage earners, seeks outstanding quality, creates happy homeland. It built garden residential area for the first time in Baiyun District and successively developed Vegetable Business and Living Building, Science Committee Business and Living Building, the first and second period of Zhaohui Garden. Zhaohui Xinyuan, Zhaohui Jingyuan, "Orient Garden" of Tongren, "Traffic Police Business and Living Building" of Liupanshui, etc. The total developed area are over 200 thousand ㎡. The construction area of the second period of the project of "Zhaohui Garden", which was finished on 30th June, is over 80 thousand ㎡. The residential area of Zhaohui Garden has made up for the lack of garden residential area in Baiyun District.

Projects managed by the enterprise have got good social reputation and are highly praised by leaders and the society. It is awarded "advanced tax payer" by Baiyun District government, "credit unite" of continuos 2 years by Baiyun District government, and "credit unit" of the Guiyang City this year.

Zhaohui Enterprise attends social public welfare activity vigorously. Last April, Zhaohui enterprise has donated 300 thousand yuan for the first Real Estate Exchange of Baiyun District. Last August, Zhaohui supported 50 thousand yuan for Zhaohui Red Travel summer camp, organized by the League Committee of the district. Last September, the enterprise gave 30 thousand yuan scholarship to Niuchang township. This year, the enterprise has invested about 10 million yuan to build Baiyun District National and Folk Custom Museum, contributing a lot for national education and national custom tourist.

朝晖花园
Zhaohui Garden

《乌蒙山》牌水泥--与您共创辉煌

"Wumeng Mountain" Cement---- create brilliance with you

贵州水城水泥股份有限公司

Guizhou Shuicheng Cement Stock Co., Ltd

党委书记、董事长：闫世坤

The Party Committee Secretary、Board Chairman: Yan Shikun

党委副书记、总经理：金元新

The Party Committee Vice-Secretary、 General Manager: Jin Yuanxin

贵州水城水泥股份有限公司（原贵州水城水泥厂），位于中国西南重要原材料基地六盘水市，占地面积155公顷，现有职工近2000人。公司采用我国自行设计制造的水泥机械为主机设备，设计能力为年产普通硅酸盐水泥80万吨，是贵州省实际生产能力最大的水泥企业。公司于1999年12月通过了ISO9002质量体系认证，近30年出厂水泥合格率保持100%，产品除供应国家重点建设工程外，还曾出口到泰国、韩国、新加坡等国家和港澳地区。

《乌蒙山》牌525R型水泥曾获国家银质奖，并分别被中国建筑材料企业管理协会和中国建筑材料工业协会授予"2001年产品质量信得过单位"和"中国建材市场畅销品牌"称号。自1992年起，公司连续多年被国家统计局评为"行业百强企业"；1994年位列全国500家最佳经济效益工业企业非金属矿物制品业第55位；2001年底，获"98-2000年度贵州省有突出贡献的国有企业"称号。

公司的主要产品有：《乌蒙山》牌P.O42.5R、P.O42.5、P.O32.5R、 P.O32.5、P.C32.5(GB175-92: P.O525R、 P.O525、 P.O425R、 P.O425、P.C425)及中热525水泥。这些产品适应性强，广泛应用于工业、农业、水利、交通、军事及民用建筑。

此外，还可根据用户需要，生产其他品种、标号的水泥。

地 址：贵州省六盘水市钟山区响水河

Address: Xiangshuihe, Zhongshan District, Liupanshui City, Guizhou Province.

邮 编(Post Code)：**553027**

电 话(Tel)：**0858-8745225 8745226 8745202**

传 真(Fax)：**0858-8745231**

网 址(Web Site)：**http://www.gzscsn.gz.cn**

三台回转窑雄姿

Three Rotating Kilns

公司现代化办公大楼

Modernization Office Building

Guizhou Shuicheng Cement stock co., Ltd (originally was Guizhou Shuicheng Cement Plant), lies in Liupanshui, the important raw material base of southwest China. The Company covers 155 hectares and has about 2000 workers. The main engine of the Company is designed and manufactured by our country. Its annual capacity is 800 thousand tons of common portland cement. It has the largest cement capacity in Guizhou Province. The Company has got the certificate of ISO9002 quality system in Dec 1999. The Company has kept 100% qualified product rate for recent 30 years. Besides providing for national key projects, the Company sells its products to Thailand, Korea, Singapore and Hongkong, Macao, ect.

The 525R cement of "Wumeng Mountain" brand has been awarded national silver prize and "quality credit product of 2001" by Chinese Building Material Enterprise Administration Association and "Best Seller on Chinese building material market" by Chinese Building Material Industry Association. Since 1992, the Company has continuously been awarded " 100 most competitive enterprises of the Trade" by the State Statistic Bureau. In 1994, the Company held 55th of the 500 profitable mineral product enterprises of nonmetal industry. At the end of 2001, the Company was awarded "National enterprise of 1998-2000 in Guizhou with outstanding Contributions".

The main products are "Wumeng Mountain" cement of P.O42.5R, P.O42.5, P.O32.5R, P.O32.5(GB175-92: P.O525R、P.O525、P.O425R、P.O425、P.C425) and 525 cement. All these products have strong compatibility and can be adopted to industry, agriculture, water conservancy, communication, military and civil Buildings.

In addition, the Company can produce cement according to clients' requirements.

瑞雪丰年

A timely snow promises a good harvest

遵义瑞安房地

Rui'an Real Estate

董事长：李永强
The Chairman of the Board: Li Yongqiang

座落于遵义市碧云路的遵义瑞安房地产开发有限公司，是一家年轻而著名的民营企业；注册资本1080万元，目前拥有固定资产4000余万元，年纳税345万元；固定员工56人，其中，中、高级工程师人。

瑞安公司成立于1998年，董事长李永强凭借20多年从事建筑安装和房地产开发的丰富经验，将个人的理想和追求，高度融洽在公司的事业发展历程中。同时在各级党委、政府的正确领导下，以及有关职能部门的关心和支持下，通过瑞安公司全体员工努力开拓进取，截至2000年7月，策划承建了遵义瑞安花园商住楼、遵义纪念广场地下停车场和商场民居、市粮食局仓库开发等开发建设项目，总建筑面积近12万平方米，工程合格率100%，其中50%的建筑物被评为“优良工程”，为名城遵义的住宅文明和经济建设作出了积极的贡献。2000年被遵义市红花岗地方税务局授予“先进纳税户”称号，同年，公司迈进了遵义市房地产开发行业“排头”之列。2000年8月，瑞安公司又控股出资组建了4家下属企业，联营组建了2家公司，正在拟建1家公司和1家大酒店，为公司进一步迈向集团化发展奠定了基础。

在房地产开发市场竞争激烈的今天，2000年瑞安公司独立或联合开发了上海路建材市场、瑞安荷花池商住楼、火车站瑞鑫商住楼等项目，目前正在按原计划施工，预计2001年可全面投向市场。瑞安公司将争取做出更大的贡献，积极回报社会。（两年来，公司先后捐助30多万元支持地方经济建设，解决下岗职工、待业青年就业近人。）

中华路瑞安大厦
Rui'an Plaza at Zhonghua Road

该公司投资建造的“遵义纪念广场”地下停车场
Parking lot under Zunyi Commemorate Square

Rui'an Real Estate Developing Co., Ltd, located in Biyun Road of Zunyi City, is a young and famous non-public enterprise. Its registered capital is 10.8 million yuan. Now, the Company has a fixed capital of more than 40 million yuan and pays for 3.45 million yuan tax of a year. It has fixed staff of 56 persons, among which 22 are middle-level or senior engineers.

Rui'an Company was founded in 1998. With the help of 20-years' experience in construction and real estate developing, Li Yongqiang, the Chairman of the Board, combined his ideal and seeking with company's development tightly. Meanwhile, under the correct leading of the Party Committee and Government of local level, the whole staff made efforts to develop the Company with the concerning and support of relating departments. Till July 2000, the Company has planned developing and construction projects as Zunyi Rui'an Garden Commercial and Living Building, parking lot under Zunyi commemorate square, residential area, store areas of the grain bureau of the city, etc. The total construction areas are almost 120 thousand m². Qualified projects are 100%. 50% of the projects are awarded "excellent project". Thus the Company made active contributions to resident culture and economy construction of Zunyi. It was awarded "advanced tax payer" by Honghuagang Tax Bureau of Zunyi in 2000 and it stood at the front of real estate industry of Zunyi at the same year. On August 2000, Rui'an Company invested to found 4 holding joint ventures and cooperated in managing 2 companies. Now the Company is preparing to found a company and a large hotel to make good foundation for further development to be a group.

Today, as the competition of real estate market becomes so intense, Rui'an Company independently or cooperatively developed projects as building materials market at Shanghai Road, office and living building at Lotus Pool, Ruixin office and living building at the railway station, etc. Now all the projects are under construction as planned and are expected to be finished by 2001. Rui'an Company will try to make bigger contributions to reciprocate the society. (In recent two years, the Company has successively donated over 300 thousand yuan to support local areas' economic construction and to the solve job problems for about 1 thousand Persons.)

瑞安花园
Rui'an Garden

瑞安商城
Rui'an Shopping Center

上海路建材市场
Building Materials Market at Shanghai Road

发展中的
Developing Fuzhong

贵州富中地产是一家专业从事房地产开发经营、管理为一体的现代化民营企业。公司自1995年成立以来，累计实现经营额2亿余元，上缴税收2300多万元。多次获得贵阳市政府颁发的“百强纳税十佳企业”、贵阳市税务局颁发的“纳税大户”、中国农业银行颁发的“双A级信用企业”等多项荣誉。

公司现已独立投资完成了“市西鸿运商城”（17000平方米）、富中商务大厦（28000平方米）的房地产项目。其中位于黄金地段的富中商务大厦座落在风景秀丽的南明河畔，甲秀楼旁，是省内第一座智能化星级管理的高级写字楼。同时还经营全省唯一的三星级商务酒店--富中商务酒店。公司正进一步加大投资开发力度，倾力打造由国内著名设计师设计的“富中国际”（位于新华路，建筑面积65000平方米）及“西部创业大厦”（位于瑞金北路，建筑面积18000平方米）。

公司在房地产开发、经营管理等方面以开拓创新的思路与国内乃至国际知名的企业联手合作。公司是省内第一家引进上海锦江物业管理的公司，使富中商务酒店成为省内唯一的办公物业管理优秀示范单位，代表着贵州省物业管理的先进水平。

随着我国加入WTO及国家西部大开发政策的不断深入，富中人将以“团结、奉献、务实、创新”的企业精神，本着“优质信誉为本，特色互惠取胜”的企业方针，通过与国内外企业多种方式的合作，奋发图强，朝着高科技等多项领域探索发展。

整洁明亮的办公环境
Cleaning and bright working surrounding

富中商务大厦
Fuzhong Business Building

Fuzhong Real Estate Company

富中地产

Real Estate Company

Fuzhong Real Estate Company is a modern non-public enterprise engaged in real estate developing and managing. Since it was founded in 1995, the Company has got total business income of more than 200 million yuan, and handed in taxes of over 23 million yuan. It has been awarded "100 large excellent taxpayers" by Guiyang Government, "large taxpayer" by Gui Yang Tax Bureau, "Double A credit enterprise" by China Agriculture Bank for several times.

The Company has independently invested and finished "Hongyun Commercial City in the west of the city" (17 thousand m^2) and Fuzhong Business Building (28 thousand m^2). Fuzhong Business Building, located in the golden area of city by Nanming river and Jiaxiu pavilion, is the first intelligent office building with star-level management. Meanwhile, the Company runs the only 3-star business hotel of the province--Fuzhong Business Hotel. Now the Company is accelerating investment and development, and makes all of the efforts to construct "Fu zhong International" (located in Xinhua road, constructs 65 thousand m^2), designed by Chinese famous designer, and "the West Developing Building" (located in north Ruijin road, constructs 18 thousand m^2).

Guided by the policy of creation, the Company has cooperated with domestic and international famous enterprises. It is the Company which first adopted Shanghai Jinjiang building management in the province. Fuzhong Business Hotel is the only demonstrative building of office building management, standing for advanced building management in the province.

富中国际
Fuzhong International

With the deepening of China's joining in WTO and the West Developing, Fuzhong people will stick to the spirit of "United, Contribution, Practical and Creative", and the policy of "quality credit is the foundation, special and win-win business leads to success". The Company will cooperate with domestic and overseas enterprises in all ways to get developed in high-tech field.

Fuzhong Real Estate Company

中铁五局集团建筑工程有限责任公司
Construction Co., Ltd of No.5 China Railway Bureau Group

党委书记、董事长：尹书贵
The Secretary of the Party Committee & Chairman of the Board: Yin Shugui

总经理：聂旭
The General Manager: Nie Xu

中铁五局集团建筑工程有限责任公司是国家建筑施工一级企业，取得ISO9002质量体系双认证。

公司总部设在贵州省贵阳市八达巷15号。公司现有各类专业技术干部550人，下设9个工程公司及房地产开发公司、水电设备安装公司、装饰公司等。注册资金6060万元。拥有各种先进设备640台（套），具有年完成5亿元产值、40万平方米房屋、200公里高低压电力线路的施工能力。

公司自50年组建以来，先后承担了成渝、宝成、贵昆、成昆等18条铁路干线及武汉、衡阳、开封等8个铁路枢纽的各类生产、生活房屋和高低压电力线路、给排水、设备安装、各种配套设施的建设任务，并远援朝鲜、伊拉克等7个国家。

公司在省内外先后承建了200余项工程，质量合格率100%、优良率60%、合同履约率100%。公司承建的贵阳通源汽车有限公司综合楼为全国首家采用II型空腹夹层板施工，获贵州省科技进步一等奖；承建的遵义市红花岗区政府办公楼外墙工艺获国家级QC成果奖。公司先后获得了近百项荣誉称号。

上海金桥花园（优良工程）
Golden Bridge Park in Shanghai (quality project prize)

Construction Co., Ltd of No.5 China Railway Bureau Group is a national first-level construction enterprise, which has got the certificate of ISO9002 quality system.

The headquarter of the Company is located at Bada Alley No.15 of Guiyang City. At present, the Company has 550 professional cadres of all kinds with 9 subordinate construction companies and real-estate developing company, water and electricity equipment installation company, decoration company, etc. Its registered capital is 60.6 million yuan. The Company owns 640 (sets of) advanced equipment. It has the capability to make annual output value of 0.5 billion yuan and build 400,000m² buildings and 200km high-tension or low-tension lines.

Since the Company was founded in 1950's, it has successively built 18 main railways as Chengyu, Baocheng, Guikun, Chengkun, etc and manufacture, living rooms, high voltage lines, water pipes, equipment installation and necessary installation of 8 railway pivots as Wuhan, Hengyang, Kaifeng etc. The Company also assisted 7 countries as Korea, Iraq, etc.

The Company has successively constructed more than 200 projects and kept quality rate at 100%, excellent rate at 60% plus and obeyed 100% of the contracts. The General Building of Guiyang Tongyuan Auto Co., Ltd, constructed by the Company, is the first project to adopt II sandwich plank in China, which was awarded first prize of provincial technical progress. The office building of Honghuagang government of Zunyi, constructed by the Company, was awarded national QC prize for the craft of the outside wall. The Company has successively been awarded nearly 100 honorable titles.

长沙天龙大酒店（三星级酒店，该工程在湖南省首次采用高效预应力叠合结构新技术，获湖南省新技术推广奖）
Tianlong Hotel in Changsha (3-star level hotel. The project is the first project with laminated structure of concentrated prestressing force in Hunan Province. It was awarded provincial prize for technical promotion.)

贵州水柏铁路有限责任公司

Guizhou Shuibai Railway Co., Ltd

2001年元月20日，水柏铁路北盘江大桥主拱转体合拢。省委书记钱运录（右三）、在省人大副主任、水柏公司董事长杨谨华（右一）、副省长刘长贵（左一）的陪同下，亲临施工一线参加了大桥转体仪式，并同设计、施工单位负责人合影。

The main arch girder of Beipanjang bridge on Shuibai railway was turned and joined on 20th Jan 2001. Qian Yunlu, the Secretary of the provincial Party Committee (the third from right), accompanied by Yang Jinhua, the vice-director of the provincial People's Congress and the Chairman of Shuibai Company (the first from right) Liu Changgui, the vice-governor of the province (the first from left) was attending the turning ceremony and taking photos with designing and construction leaders.

贵州水柏铁路有限责任公司董事长：杨谨华

The Chairman of the Board of Guizhou Shuibai Railway Co., Ltd: Yang Jinhua

贵州省、铁道部合资兴建的六盘水至柏果铁路（简称水柏铁路），北起贵昆线六盘水站，南至盘西支线的柏果站，是我国西南铁路网中又一条南北线中重要的一段。本线为单线Ⅰ级电气化铁路，全线技术设计长度118.52公里，最小曲线半径450米，线路限坡12‰，加力坡23.5‰，年设计运输能力近期1000万吨，远期1800万吨。总投资32.47亿元。全线地质极其复杂，施工难度大，桥隧总长占线路总和的63.46%，为我国铁路之最。

项目自1997年12月1日开工建设以来到今年3月底，已累计完成投资24.13亿元，为项目总投资的74.32%。全线铺架工作现已全面展开。2002年3月完成运营配套及电气化工程，6月份达到运营条件，确保与内昆线同步建成。

在水柏铁路建设形势大好的情况下，该公司对长期以来关心、支持、帮助项目建设的社会各界表示最真挚的谢意。

The railway of Liupanshui to Baiguo (Shuibai railway), invested and constructed by Guizhou province and the Ministry of Railways, starts at Liupanshui station of Guikun railway in the north, and ends at Baiguo station of Panxi railway branch in the south. It is another important north-south part of the railway network in southwest China. Shuibai railway is a first-level single-tracking electric railway. The planed general length is 118.52 km. The minimum curve radius is 450 m. Limited slope is 12‰. The thrust slope is 23.5‰. The designed annual transportation capacity is 10 million tons of a short term and 18 million tons of a long term. The total investment is 3.247 billion yuan. The geology along the railway is very complicated that is hard to construct. Bridges and tunnels account for 63.46% of the total length, which is the unique in China.

Since it was constructed on 1st Dec 1997 to the end of March this year, 2.413 billion yuan has been invested, which is 74.32% of the general investment. The frame-laying project of the whole railway is carried out. Necessary equipment and electrification project will be finished by March 2002. The railway will ready to work by June, and be ensured to in simultaneous construction with Neikun railway.

In the great construction situation of Shuibai railway, the Company shows sincere thanks to all the social fields for their long term concerning, support and help.

水柏铁路全长6905米的松河隧道已施工完部分

Finished part of Songhe tunnel that is 6905 m long of Shuibai railway.

水柏铁路北盘江大桥，全长468.12米，主跨为236米的上承式钢管混凝土拱桥，其主跨度和单铰转体重量居世界同类型结构铁路大桥第一。图为大桥主拱转体情况

Beipanjiang Bridge, whose total length is 468.12 m, and whose main arch is 236 m, is a steel pipe and concrete arch bridge. Both the main span and the turning weight of single hinge of the bridge are unique among the railway bridges with the same structure of the world. Here in the picture is the situation of the turning the main arch.

水城钢铁（集团）有限责任公司

Shuicheng Iron and Steel (Group) Co., Ltd

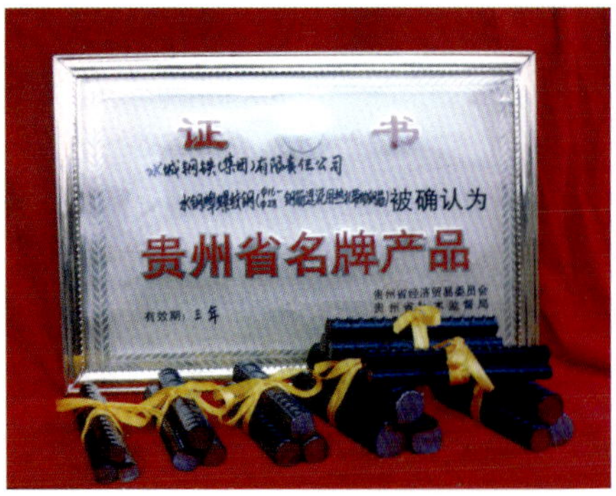

Shui Steel was founded in 1966, located in the "Golden Triangle" area in Southwest Coal Sea of China. It is one of the 49 national key iron and steel enterprises. After 30 years' construction and development, its total assets are up to 4.3 billion yuan and its annual capacity is 1.5 million tons iron, 1.6 million tons steel and 1.5 million tons steel products.

Main products are: small steel products, high-speed linear steel products, common linear steel products, base, cast iron, cement, coke, etc. Major products have got the certificate of International Production Standard. In 1999, the Company got internation the certificates of ISO-9002 Quality Standard and Good Measure & Examine System. In March 2001, series screw steel products of the Company got certificate of exempt from examination issued by National Technique Examination Bureau. The products are sold to countries and districts of Southeast Asia and are highly praised by users.

水钢始建于1966年，地处素有中国“西南煤海”之称的攀西--六盘水“金三角”地区，是全国49家重点钢铁企业之一。经过30多年的建设和发展，企业资产总额约43亿元，主体已具备年产铁150万吨、钢160万吨、钢材150万吨的综合配套生产能力。

水钢主要产品有小型材、高速线材、普通线材、连铸坯、铸造生铁、炼钢生铁、水泥、焦炭及焦化副产品等20余种。主要产品获得采用国际标准生产证书，1999年分别通过国家ISO-9002国际质量标准认证和完善计量检测体系认证，2001年3月，水钢螺纹钢系列产品获得国家质量技术监督局颁发的产品免检证书。产品远销东南亚国家和地区，深受用户的青睐。

董事长、总经理：王黎明
The Chairman of the Board & GM: Wang Liming
党委书记、副董事长：赵松桓
The Secretary of the Party Committee & Vice-Chairman of the Board: Zhao Songhuan
联系地址：贵州省六盘水市钟山区巴西中路
Address: Baxi Zhong Road, Zhongshan District, Liupanshui City, Guizhou Province
邮　编(Code)：**553028**
电　话(Tel)：**0858-8922071** **传　真**(Fax)：**0858-8950067**
网　址(Website)：www.shuigang.com.cn
销售热线(Sales line)：**0858-8922439**

贵州水城矿业（集团）有限责任公司

Guizhou Shuicheng Mining Industry (Group) Co., Ltd

贵州水城矿业（集团）有限责任公司，是原水城矿务局经贵州省人民政府于1999年9月批准整体公司制改制而成的国有独资大一型煤炭企业。矿区地理面积6800平方公里，包括水城煤田和纳雍煤田，地质储量138亿吨（现仅动用储量12.9亿吨），是江南重要的煤炭生产基地。截止2001年末，公司有生产矿井7个，选煤厂3座，原煤设计生产能力640万吨/年，核定生产能力618万吨/年，设计原煤入选能力500万吨/年。资产总额29亿多元，职工28498人，其中：各类中、高级专业技术人员1450人。

集团公司目前主要产品有冶炼精煤、洗精块煤、洗混煤和特殊加工煤等。自1999年以来，公司年销售量均在300万吨以上，销售收入始终保持在 万元以上。

法定代表人：魏永柱
Representative of the Corporation: Wei Yongzhu
企业地址：贵州省六盘水市钟山区开拓路16号
Address: Kaituo Road No. 16, Zhongshan District, Liupanshui City, Guizhou Province
邮　编（Post Code）：**553000**

Guizhou Shuicheng Mining Industry (Group) Co., Ltd is a large first-level national coal enterprise, founded on the base of the whole capital of Shuicheng Bureau of Mineral Affaires in Sep 1999 with Guizhou provincial government's permission. The mining area is 6,800 km², including Shuicheng coal field and Nayong coal field. The coal reserve is 13.8 billion tons (only 1.29 billion tons has been explored at present). It is an important coal base of south to Changjiang River. Up to 2001, the Company has 7 productive mines, 3 Coal-selecting Plants and its expected capacity of raw coal is 6.4 million tons per year, the confirmed capacity of raw coal is 6.18 million tons per year. The expected selected raw coal is 5 million tons per year. The general assets are over 2.9 billion yuan. It has a staff of 28,498 persons, among which 1450 are middle or senior Professional.

The main products are refined smelted coal, cleaned block coal, cleaned mixed coal, special processing coal, etc. Since 1999, the Company has kept its sales above 3 million tons, and sales income above 600 million yuan.

水城矿业总医院外景
The general hospital of Shuicheng Mining Industry

汪家寨选煤厂外景
Outside view of Wangjiazhai Coal-selecting Plant

汪家寨选煤厂公园
The park of Wangjiazhai Coal-slecting Plant

贵州黔能企业（集团）公司

Guizhou Qianneng Enterprise (group) Company

贵州黔能企业（集团）公司是隶属贵州省电力公司的多种经营企业，主要从事发电、铁合金、化工、制造、施工、贸易等多角产业。现拥有全资、控股、参股的黄磷、铁合金、磷酸盐、铝产品、黄磷包装桶制造、自营产品进出、物资经销、中小型水电站等企业20余家，同时，承接电力输配变工程项目的施工。

贵州黔能企业（集团）2001年黄磷产量达64000多吨，为国内最大的黄磷生产集团。同时，每年可产工业级及食品级磷酸30000吨、磷酸二氢铵万吨以上、六偏磷酸钠3000吨，以及硅钡、硅钙钡、硅铝钙钡等其他产品。产品销售全国各省（区），并直销到东南亚、北美、东欧、非洲等地区。

Guizhou Qianneng Enterprise (group) Company is a multi-business enterprise subordinate to Provincial Electricity Company. It is mainly engaged in industries of generating electricity, iron alloy, chemistry, manufacture, construction, trade, etc. Now the Company has over 20 full-invested, holding and stock-holding enterprises of yellow phosphorus, iron alloy, phosphate, aluminum product, package barrel of yellow phosphorus, import and export of own product, commodity agent and middle and small hydroelectric stations. Meanwhile, the Company undertakes construction of electrical transmission, distribution and transforming projects.

Guizhou Qianneng Enterprise (group) Company produced over 64 thousand tons of yellow phosphorus in 2001. It is the largest manufacture group of yellow phosphorus in China. Meanwhile, the Company can produce 30 thousand tons of industrial and food phosphoric acid annually. Products of the Company are sold all through the provinces (areas) of China and are sold directly to Southeast Asia, North America, East Europe and Africa.

待发运的黄磷产品

Yellow phosphorus products to be transported

法人代表、总经理：周继鹏
Representative of the Corporation & the General Manager: Zhou Jipeng
地　址：贵阳市市南路48号黔电发展楼
Address: Qian Electrical Development Building, Shinan Road 48#, Guiyang City
电　话(Tel)：0851-5524527 5592882　传　真(Fax)：0851-5524627
营销部电话(Tel of the Sales Department)：0851-5526241 5592986 5523544
营销部传真(Fax of Sales Department)：0851-5530184 5523529 5524867

李官水电站

Liguan hydroelectric station

深圳质量认证中心
质量体系认证证书
贵州黔能天和磷业有限公司
GB/T19002-1994 — ISO9002:1994
·黄磷产品的生产·

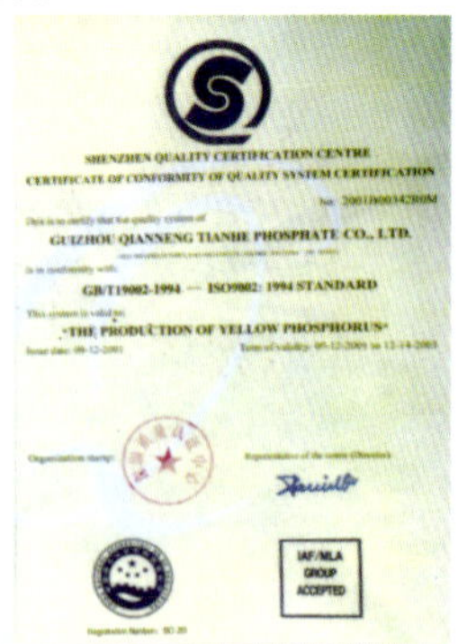
SHENZHEN QUALITY CERTIFICATION CENTRE
CERTIFICATE OF CONFORMITY OF QUALITY SYSTEM CERTIFICATION
GUIZHOU QIANNENG TIANHE PHOSPHATE CO., LTD.
GB/T19002-1994 — ISO9002: 1994 STANDARD
·THE PRODUCTION OF YELLOW PHOSPHORUS·
IAF/MLA GROUP ACCEPTED

赤天化股份有限公司

Chitian Chemical Fertilizer Stock Co., Ltd

销售公司电话（Tel of the sales Company）：0851-5284272
传真（Fax）：0851-5381501

贵州赤天化集团有限责任公司于1995年10月18日在贵阳市成立。集团公司基地——原贵州赤水天然气化肥厂，座落于中国工农红军谱写英雄篇章的赤水河畔，距赤水市3公里，占地面积83万平方米。1974年10月破土动工，1978年建成投产。拥有从美国、荷兰引进的成套先进大型化肥生产装置和相应的技术力量，经过“八五”节能增产技术大改造后，装置年生产能力已达36.6万吨合成氨、63万吨尿素，为国有大一型企业。

截止到2001年底，共生产合成氨651万吨、尿素1086万吨，累计实现利税17.7亿元，相当于国家当年投资总额的6.3倍。

1999年12月13日，赤天化股份公司A股在上交所发行成功，2000年2月21日又在上交所隆重上市。2001年生产尿素65.12万吨，销售尿素72.6万吨，累计实现主营业务收入6.31亿元，利税总额4213万元。“赤”牌尿素被评为国家免检产品和贵州省名牌产品。公司被授予“全国先进基层党组织”、“贵州省有突出贡献国有企业”荣誉称号。

生产厂区一角
A corner of the producing area

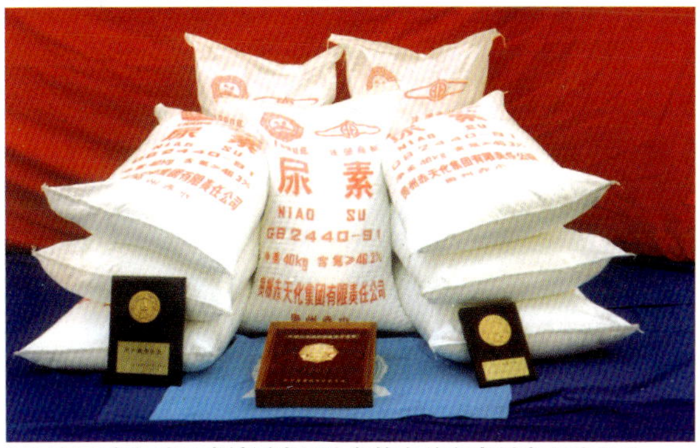

2001年“赤”牌尿素被国家评为免检产品和贵州省名牌产品
Urea of “Chi” brand was awarded product exempt from exam and provincial famous product at the end of 2001.

赤天化A股股票于2000年2月21日在上交所隆重上市，公司董事长李大学敲响了开市锣
Chitian Chemical Fertilizer Stock Co., Ltd was listed on the market in Shanghai Security Exchange on 21st Feb 2000, Li Daxue, the chairman of the Board of directors struck the gong for the company listed on the market

Chitian Chemical Fertilizer Stock Co., Ltd was founded in Guiyang City on 18th Oct 1995. The base of the group company, the former Guizhou Chishui Natural Gas Chemical Fertilizer Plant, lies in the bank of Chishui River, where Chinese army has written brilliant history. It is 3 km far from Chishui City and covers 830 thousand m². It was begun to build in Oct 1974 and was finished in 1978. The Company has sets of advanced large manufacturing devices imported from US and Holland and corresponding technology. After technique reform of “Eighth Five-year Plan”, it has the annual production capacity of 366 thousand tons of synthetic ammonia, 630 thousand tons of urea. It is a first-level large national enterprise.

Up to 2001, the Company has produced 6.51 million ton of synthetic ammonia and 10.86 million ton of urea. The total profit and tax is 1.77 billion yuan, which is 6.3 times of the total investment of the year by the nation.

On 13rd Dec 1999, A shares of Chitian Chemical Fertilizer Stock Co., Ltd were successfully issued in Shanghai Security Exchange. On 21st Feb 2000, Chitian Chemical Fertilizer Stock Co., Ltd was listed on the market in Shanghai Security Exchange. The Company produced 651.2 thousand ton of urea in 2001 and sold 726 thousand ton. The Company achieved its business income of 631 million yuan and the profit and tax is 42.13 million yuan. Urea of “Chi” brand was awarded national product exempt from exam and provincial famous product. The Company was awarded “national advanced basic Party unit” and “Guizhou national enterprise with outstanding Contributions”.

稳健运作，化解风险，构架银企合作桥梁

Stable running, lessening risks, building bridge between banks and enterprises

ZWD

总经理：王光琦

The General Manager of the Company: Wang Guangqi

本田雅阁倍受贵州人青睐

Honda Auto is deeply preferred by Guizhou people

贵州省众维中小企业信用担保公司创立于1999年10月18日，是省人民政府投资的国有独资公司，主管部门贵州省经贸委。公司实收资本6000万元，计划到2003年实收资本达到1亿元，担保贷款能力达到5亿元左右。

众维担保公司着力为具有成长性、前瞻的中小企业提供信用担保服务，促其顺利融资。众维实行市场化运作，企业化管理，构筑自我约束、自我发展的机制，努力实现战略与微观经济的统一。

公司承办对中小企业的银行贷款、承兑汇票、信用证、合同履约、资质证明等各种信用担保。

众维已与省内各专业银行建立了贷款与担保协作关系，分担贷款风险。

众维本着“社会责任第一”和“诚信、稳健、高效、创新”的宗旨审慎运作。截止2001年12月，已接待企业咨询和担保申请近500余家，累计担保50笔贷款，总金额近2亿元，创立以来担保代偿率为零。公司国有资产保值增值率106.49%。被担保企业新增销售收入5.7亿元，新增税收4000万元，扩大就业和减少下岗7100人。

众维担保公司将牢记肩负的社会责任，勇于探索，不断创新，为“富民兴黔”作出新的贡献。

公司地址：贵阳市中华北路18号银海大厦19层A、D座
Address: Yinhai Building 19 Floor, A D, North Zhonghua Road 18#, Guiyang City
电　话（Tel）：0851-6904284 6904009
网　址（Web Site）：http://www.ZWDanbao.com
电子信箱（E-mail）：ZWDanbao@ZWDdanbao.com

超豪华的大雅园酒楼

Luxurious Dayayuan Restaurant

贵州省众维中小企业信用担保公司

Guizhou Zhongwei Credit Guarantee Company for Middle and Small Enterprise

公司汇聚了各方人才

The company has gathered talents from every places

Guizhou Zhongwei Credit Guarantee Company for Middle and Small Enterprise was founded on 18th Oct 1999. It is a national company with only provincial government's investment. Its direct governing organization is Economic and Trade Committee of GuiZhou Province. The company has actually received capital of 60 million yuan. The company is expected to receive capital of 100 million yuan by 2003 and to guarantee for loans of about 500 million yuan.

Zhongwei Company concentrated in providing credit guarantee for promising middle and small enterprises to help enterprises to raise capital. Zhongwei promotes market-led running and enterprise management, builds self-restrict system and tries to realize the harmony of strategy and microcosmic economy.

The Company undertakes loans, cashing drafts, L/C, implementation of contracts, credentials for middle and small Enterprises.

Zhongwei has built cooperation in loan and guarantee with every special bank in the province to share the risk of loans.

Basing on the rules of "responsibility for the society is first" and "honesty, steady, efficient and creative", Zhongwei runs discreetly. Up to Dec 2001, it has received over 500 enterprises' consulting and loan application. Zhongwei has provided guarantee for 50 loans whose total amount is nearly 200 million yuan and never compensated for enterprises. The growth rate of national capital of the company is 106.49%. Enterprises guaranteed by Zhongwei have increased their income of 570 million yuan, tax of 40 million yuan and solved work problem for 7100 persons.

贵州联想总经理杨凯平酷爱攀登

Yang Kaiping, the General Manager of Guizhou Legend Company, loves climbing

威门药业靠质量和信用取胜

Weimen Medicine Industry achieved success by quality and credit

詹阳公司不断挖掘新的潜力

Zhanyang Company keeps developing new potential energy

Zhongwei will remember its responsibility for the society, be brave in exploring and creation, and make new contributions for people's benefit and Guizhou's development.

贵州省电信世纪鑫器材有限公司

Guizhou Telecom Century Xin Appliance Co., Ltd

贵州省电信世纪鑫器材有限公司经营业务：

通信设备及配套器材、无线电通讯设备、有色金属、黑色金属、建材、民用五金、摩托车、二、三类机电产品、办公自动化设备及机房配套设备的批零兼营，计算机信息网络、电信维护、设备安装。

Businesses of Guizhou Telecom Century Xin Appliance Co., Ltd:

Communication equipment & relating appliance, radio equipment, nonferrous metal, ferrous metal, building materials, hardware, motorbike, computer network, telecom maintenance, installation, etc.

贵州省邮电科研规划设计院

Guizhou Post and Telecommunication Scientific Research Planning and Designing Institute

Guizhou Post and Telecommunication Scientific Research Planning and Designing Institute is a corporation undertaking special and comprehensive scientific research, planning, designing, technology consulting and general-contracting projects in the fields of communication and construction. It has certifications as: second-rate project designing certification, project general-contracting certification, issued by the Ministry of Construction, secondary project consulting qualification, issued by the State Planning Commission, first-rate designing qualification for intellectualized system project of construction, issued by the Ministry of Construction. The Institute has got the certification of ISO9001:2000 on Sep, 2001.

As a highly technological enterprise in the field of communication, the Institute owns a strong managing and technical team, among which 40% have intermediate or senior professional tittles. There are 5 specialized design bureaus as: communication equipment, communication circuit, network planning, construction, integrated systems & software developing. Its designing capacities are 800 thousand program controlling designs, 1,000 km prospecting route, 150,000 m² construction designs, 10,000 communication lines and 500 wireless prospecting designs. All the process of production management, business management and designing are finished by computer. The popularity rate of computers is 1.5 unit per person. Also, the Institute has built a local network which uses FTTB + LAN to connect with Internet and enterprise management information system.

During the years, the Institute has advocated "scientific planning, careful designing" and tried to provide quality and well-served designing and technique consulting to its clients. In the period of "Ninth Five-year Plan", the Institute has finished 500 programs of communication projects designing, construction projects designing, technique consulting, etc. Qualified Productions held 100%. Excellent productions held over 90%. It was awarded 6 designing or consulting awards of ministry and province level. The Institute has been a strong support for the fast and healthy development of communication and IT construction in Guizhou province.

贵州省邮电科研规划设计院是在通信及建筑领域从事多专业、全方位的科研、规划、设计以及技术咨询和工程总承包的法人企业，具有国家建设部颁发的通信及建筑行业乙级《工程设计证书》、《工程总承包证书》，国家计划委员会颁发的乙级《工程咨询资质证书》，国家建设部颁发的甲级《建筑智能化系统工程设计资质证书》。该院已于2001年9月通过ISO9001：2000标准认证。

作为贵州省信息通信行业技术密集型企业，该院拥有一支较强的管理、技术专业队伍，具有高、中级职称的人员占40%。全院设有通信设备、通信线路、网络规划、建筑、系统集成及软件开发等5个专业设计所。年设计能力达到：各类程控交换设计80万门，光纤通信线路勘察设计1000公里，建筑设计15万平方米，移动通信信道1万个，无线基站勘察设计500个。全院生产管理、业务经营和设计生产各个流程已采用计算机信息化手段，计算机普及率达到1.5台/人，工程设计计算机出图率100%，建立了以FTTB+LAN方式宽带连入公用计算机互联网的计算机局域网和企业管理信息系统。

多年来，该院本着"科学规划、精心设计"的方针，努力为用户提供质量高、服务好的设计和技术咨询产品。"九五"期间，先后完成各类通信工程设计、建筑工程设计等项目500多个，质量合格率100%，优良品率90%以上，获部、省级优秀设计、咨询奖6项。为贵州通信事业的快速、健康发展和贵州信息化建设作出了有力的技术支撑。

本院信息（About the Institute）：

院　长：陈友清（法人代表、高级工程师）

The Director of the Institute: Chen Youqing (representative of the corporation & Senior engineer)

单位地址：贵州省贵阳市中华北路161号

Address: Zhonghua North Road 161#, Guiyang City, Guizhou Province

邮　编（Post Code）：**550004　电　话**（Tel）：**0851-6813167、6813036　传　真**（Fax）：**0851-6822843　网　址**（Web site）**http://www.gzpti.com.cn**

贵州黎阳航

Guizhou Liyang Air-

总经理：张大荣
The General Manager: Zhang Darong

办公大楼
Office building

贵州黎阳航空发动机公司是中国航空工业第一集团公司所属的国家大型企业，是目前国内生产航空涡轮喷气发动机的主要厂家。公司组建于1981年，下属3个专业厂，1个科研设计所和1个供应库，现有职工1.2万余人，其中专业技术人员4251人，具有雄厚的科研、生产、制造技术力量，拥有包括高精尖设备在内的各类设备6570台，固定资产原值8.2亿元，资产总额27亿元。2001年，完成工业总产值135463万元，实现销售收入126619万元，实现利税5611万元。

公司从1970年起生产航空涡轮喷气发动机，现已形成WP-7、WP-13两大系列十多种型号的发动机批生产和科研体系，并向多个国家出口，创汇4.11亿美元。其中两个机型囊括建国以来国家对航空发动机颁发的两个最高质量奖--银质奖；某新型发动机配装的出口型歼8IIM飞机被誉为“我国航空工业巨大成就的标志”。

1985年起，公司先后开发出汽车零部件、石材机械、燃气灶具、全自动燃烧机等数十种非航空产品，大都被评为国家级新产品或被定为国家级替代进口产品，部分产品开始向国外出口。其中轿车消声器排气管和汽车变速器已形成了年产40万套的规模。公司曾先后5次被部省评为“航空工业有重大贡献单位”，先后荣获“全国职业道德建设先进单位”、“全国思想政治工作优秀企业”等荣誉称号，公司总经理张大荣同志荣获全国劳动模范称号。公司各单位获得省部级以上科研成果奖200余项，其中国家级技术进步奖6项。1995年，公司整体通过ISO9001质量认证。

Guizhou Liyang Air-

空发动机公司

craft Engine Company

黎阳公司研制生产的WP-13B型航空发动机
WP-13B aircraft engine manufactured by Liyang Company

Guizhou Liyang Aircraft Engine Company is a large subordinate public enterprise of China Aviation Industry No. 1 Group Company. It is a major plant to manufacture turbojet in China. The Company was founded in 1981 and has 3 specialized plants, 1 research institute and 1 supply house. The Company has 12 thousand workers, among which 4,251 are specialized technique persons. The Company has strong research, producing and manufacture power and owns 6570 advanced appliances. Its original fixed assets are 0.82 billion yuan. The general assets are 2.7 billion yuan. Its gross value of industrial output of 2001 is 1354.63 million yuan. The total sales are 1266.19 million yuan. The profit and tax is 56.11 million yuan.

The Company began to manufacture turbojet in 1970. Now the Company has built a research and manufacture system for turbojet of more than 10 models of two series as WP-7 and WP-13, and has exported to several countries, which earned 411 million US dollars. Two of the 10 models were awarded the highest quality prizes for aircraft engine of the nation since the foundation of the country--silver prize. The flight of 8IIM with new engine is "the sign of great achievement of Chinese aviation industry".

Since 1985, the Company has successively developed 10 kinds of non-aerial products as auto components, gas stove, automatic burner, etc, most of which were awarded national new products or national substitutors for imported products. Some products have been exported. The Company has the annual capacity to manufacture 0.4 million exhaust pipes of silencer and gearboxes. The Company has successively been awarded national or provincial "great contributions to aviation industry" for 5 times and " advanced enterprise in profession morality construction", "national excellent enterprise in political work". Zhang Darong, the general manager of the Company, was awarded national labor model. Departments of the Company have been awarded over 200 science & technology prizes of ministry or above level. Among the prizes, there are 6 national technique prizes. The integration of the Company has been confirmed by ISO9001 in 1995.

craft Engine Company

中国贵州航空工业
CHINA NATIONAL GUIZHOU AV-

董事长：周万成
Mr. Zhou Wancheng, the Chairman of the Board

副董事长、总经理：张军
Mr. Zhang Jun, the Deputy Chairman of the Board and President

中国贵州航空工业集团是国家首批试点企业集团之一，也是国家重点扶持的512家大型企业之一，是以歼击教练机（含发动机）、微型轿车（含微轿发动机）为龙头产品，以资本和产品经营为联结纽带，跨地区、跨行业、跨部门，具有较强经济实力和技术实力的军民结合型大型企业集团。

集团母公司为中国贵州航空工业（集团）有限责任公司，有全资子公司62家，控股子公司6家、参股公司8家。职工7万人，总资产97亿元。

集团设有进出口公司、财务公司、供销公司、投资管理公司和国家认定的技术中心，具有国家授予的国有资产经营权、自营进出口权、简化外事审批权，对外开展承包工程和外派劳务人员等业务，具备强大的集团综合功能。

集团有飞机、发动机、机载设备、锻、铸、橡胶、标准件、工具、地面设备等专业化工厂、各厂均有自己的专业技术优势和科研生产能力。

集团依靠自身的优势和实力，研制生产了性能精良的航空和其它民用产品。歼教7系列高空高速高级歼击教练机曾在第37届法国巴黎航空航天博览会上被誉为“亚洲明星”，并参加过中国国际航空航天博览会。集团研制生产的涡喷系列航空发动机在国内居领先地位。云雀微型轿车是国家批准立项的8大轿车项目之一，已形成批量生产规模；汽车零部件生产企业已成为“小巨人”群体。另外在工程机械、电子元器件、轻工、环保等方面也具有较强的技术、生产优势。

贵航集团发展的宗旨：技术创新、产品创新、国内领先、扩大国际、国内两个市场。

歼教7飞机
FT-7 aircraft

（集团）有限责任公司

-IATION INDUSTRY (GROUP) CO,.LTD.

China National Guizhou Aviation Industry Group(GAIG) is one of the first reform experimental enterprise groups in China. As well as one of 512 large scaling experimental enterprise groups that Chinese government gives major support. It takes an advanced supersonic fighter trainer (including the aviation engine), mini car (including mini car motor) as the main products and takes the assets and products as ties. It is a large-scale enterprise group with scale management incorporating military with civil which owns the stronger economic and technological strength.

The core enterprise of the Group is China National Guizhou Aviation Industry(Group)co., Ltd(GAIC) owned 62 totally invested subsidiaries, 6 share holding corporations and 8 purchase of shares corporations. It has 70,000 employees, total assets 9.7 billion Yuan(RMB).

GAIG has established the Import and Export Company, the Financial Company, the Supply and Sales Company, the Investment and Management Company, and the Technical Center approved by the government. It has the powerfull multiple functions that are the state-own assets managing authority, the self-support import and export authority and the simplifing foreign affairs examining, contracting the engineering projects and the business to send the labours to the overseas and so on, authorized by the State.

GAIG has possessed the specialied factories of aircraft, engine, airborne equipment, forging, casting, rubber parts, standard parts, tools and ground support equipment. And every enterprise has its own advanced and special technology and the capability of research & manufacture.

GAIG has developed and manufactured the high quality aviation and other civil products with its own advance and strength. The advanced supersonic FT-7 series aircraft has named "Asia Star" in the 37th International Aviation and Space Fair in Paris, France and showed in China International Aviation and Space Exhibition. The turbojet series engines developed and manufactured by GAIG has taken up the advance position at home market. Yunque mini car is one of the 8-main cars approved by the government, and now is in batch production scale. The automobile parts and components enterprises have formed as "SmallGiant"group. In addition, the Group holds technique and manufacture advantages of mechanical engineering, electronic components, light industry and environmental protection, ect.

The principal aim of the Group is: new technology, new products, to be the front of the domestic market, extending domestic and international market.

灯光信号装置
Lighting signal device

发动机加力箱与起动箱
After burner and starter for engine

微动开关系列产品
Microswitch series

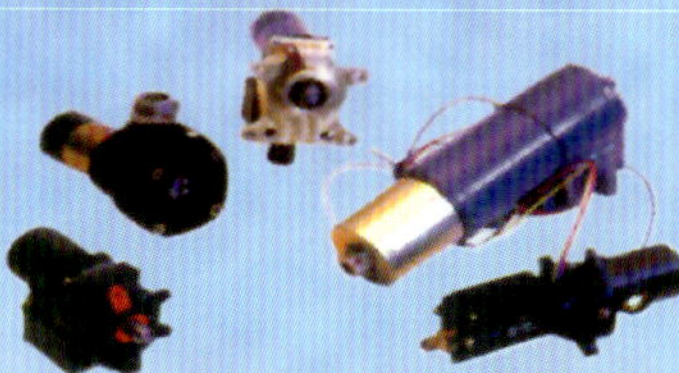

CM转角型电动机构系列产品
CM angled type motor series

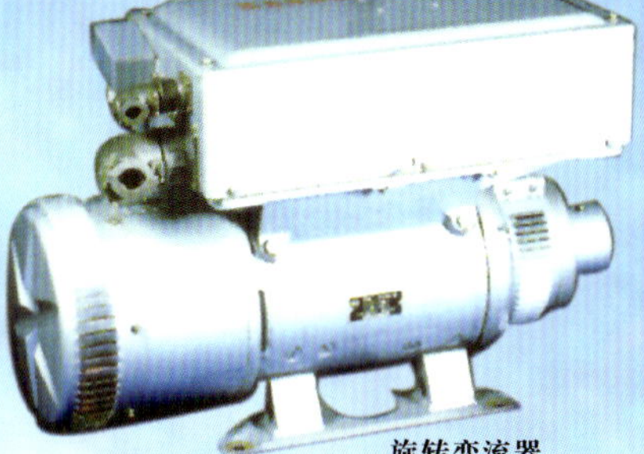

旋转变流器
Rotary inverter

航空继电器
Aerorelay

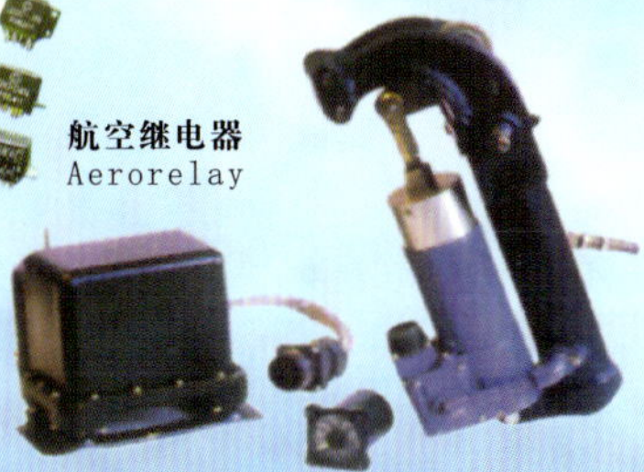

20-4000kg 电动推拉机构
20-4000kg electric push-pull mechanism

测速电机HZD-4（C），恒速直流电机
Speed-measuring motor HZD-4 (C).
Constant-speed DC motor

中国江南航天集团

China Jiangnan Space Group

总经理：谢柏堂
The President: Xie Baitang

党委书记：高德铭
The Secretary of the Party Committee: Gao Deming

中国江南航天集团是1964年经中央专委批准建立起来的配套完整、生产能力较强的航天产品科研生产基地。其核心企业中国江南航天工业集团公司是隶属于中国航天科工集团的国有独资公司。38年来，中国江南航天集团已发展成为军民结合、技工贸结合的综合性大型企业集团。

中国江南航天集团拥有23家专业生产厂（公司），8个研究所，1个技术中心，2个专业技术中心，3所院校及其它企事业单位。拥有固定资产原值12.2亿元，资产总值40.5亿元。还拥有中外合资、合作企业8家。在北京、天津、上海、深圳、广州、苏州等地设立分公司11家。现有员工18581人，其中各类专业技术人员5861人，高级工程师430人，各类专家70人。集团具有雄厚的经济、技术实力和强大的整体优势，可以承担航天产品的研制及批量生产，同时，还开发生产了航天牌轻型汽车、农用车、电冰箱、注塑机、微特电机、金属拉拔设备、液力变速器、卫星地面收发天线、油井测量仪器、铝工业技术装备、医疗设备、锂离子电池及家用电器等民用产品。以正负电子对撞机、重离子回旋加速器、同步辐射加速器关键部件等为代表的20多种高科技产品，在国内享有很高知名度及信誉，许多产品已达到九十年代世界同类产品的先进水平。有10项产品获国优称号，113项产品获省、部优质产品称号，471项科技成果获国家和省、部重大发明奖及科技进步奖。

改革开放以来，江南航天集团坚持“航天立业、团结拼搏、求实创新、追求卓越”的精神，科研生产长足发展，经济规模迅速增大。经贵州省政府批准，同意在贵阳、遵义两地建立江南航天高科技工业园区。“十五”期间，江南航天高科技工业园区将充分发挥高科技工业的优势，以西部大开发为契机，按照市场经济规律的要求，立足自己独特的技术优势，突出自身特点，促进高新技术的成果转化。通过“十五”发展，把江南航天集团建设成为具有一定研制能力和较强生产能力的航天产品批生产基地。使江南航天集团成为布局相对集中，队伍精干高效，产业结构和产品结构合理，专业化协作能力强，符合现代企业制度的适应市场经济需要的航天产品、民品、三产协调发展的知名企业集团。

地　址：贵州省遵义市北京路36号
Add: 36 Beijing Road, Zunyi City, Guizhou Province
电　话（Tel）：**0852-8611147**
传　真（Fax）：**0852-8611192**
邮　编（Post Code）：**563003**
网　址（Website）：**http://www.cjspace.cn**
电子信箱（E-mail）:cjsg@jspace.com.cn

江南航天高科技工业园（遵义园区）
Jiangnan Space High-tech Industrial Park (Zunyi Park)

China Jiangnan Space Group, founded in 1964 with the approval of specialized commission of the Party Central Committee, is an integrated space product research and manufacture base with powerful production capacity. Its key enterprise, China Jiangnan Space Industry Group Company, is a company exclusively with national capital subordinate to China Aerospace Science and Industry Corporation. Since it was founded 38 years ago, China Jiangnan Space Group has been developed into a large comprehensive enterprise group integrating army and civilian products, technology and trading.

China Jiangnan Space Group has 23 specialized plants (companies), 8 research institutes, 1 technology center, 2 special technology centers, 3 colleges and some institutes. The group owns fixed assets of 1.22 billion yuan original value. Total assets are 4.05 billion yuan. In addition, it also owns 8 joint or corporative ventures with domestic and foreign investment. The group has 11 branch companies located in Beijing, Tiajin, Shanghai, Shenzhen, Guangzhou and Suzhou. Now, the group has 18581 workers, among whom 5861 are professionals of all kinds, 430 are senior engineers, 70 are experts. The group enjoys strong financial capability, technique competition and high integration advantage. It can undertake research and mass-producing of space products. Meanwhile, it has developed light-duty auto, agricultural truck, fridge, plastics injector, micro electrical motor, metal drawing machine, hydraulic transmission, ground satellite T/R antenna, measuring instrument for oil well, technical equipment for aluminium indurstry, medical equipment, lithium ion battery, etc..20 high-tech products such as positive and negative electron collider, heavy ion cyclotron and key parts for synchronous radiation accelerator enjoy high popularity and credit in China. A lot of products have got advanced international

建国五十周年阅兵英姿
Military review on the 50 National Anniversary

level of the 1990s. There are 10 products awarded the title of national quality product. 113 products were awarded the title of provincial and ministerial quality product. 471 research products were awarded major invention and scientific progress prize of nation, province and ministry level.

Since reform & opening policy, Jiannan Space Group has stuck to the spirit of "Space is our career. Unite and work hard. Be practical and creative. Seek for perfection". Thus the research and production have been fully developed. The economic scope has been fast enlarged. With the approval of Guizhou Provincial Government, the group can build high-tech industrial park in Guiyang and Zunyi. During "Tenth Five-Year Plan", Jiangnan Space High-tech Industrial Park will make advantages of high-tech industry well, tack the chance of the West Developing, improve high and new research achievements' transform according to the laws of market economy and its unique technique advantage. With the development in the period of "Tenth Five-Year Plan", the group will build itself as a space product mass-producing base with certain research capability and strong capacity. Thus make Jiangnan Space Group a Famous enterprise group with centralized layout, efficient team, scientific industrial and product structure, strong specialized cooperation ability, modern enterprise system, and with space product, civil product and the 3rd industry developed harmoniously.

锂离子电池
Lithium ion battery

微特电机
Micro electrical motor

液力变速器
Hydraulic transmission

铝工业技术装备
Technical equipment for aluminium industry

红光车桥
Hong Guang axle

林城拓展 麒龙先行

Exploitation in Forest City, Qi Long goes first

秉承贵阳的规划理念
Guided by city layout idea of Guiyang
以提高居民生活品质为动力
To improve residents' life is our motive
我们愿意扮演先锋的角色
We wish to be the pioneer
美化林城
Beautify Forest City
建设家园
Build homeland

品质与管理是贵州麒龙房地产开发有限公司永恒的主题，公司在致力于房地产的开发、建设的同时，以培养高素质、规范化的员工队伍为核心，营造充满生机的新型企业环境，用特色的企业文化描绘灿烂的发展蓝图。

Quality and Management are eternal themes of Qi Long Real Estate development co., Ltd. The Company is mainly engaged in development and construction of real estate. Meanwhile, it set its key task as training a standardized team with high quality and building a new type enterprise full of vigor and vitality. Now, the Company is drawing its blueprint with characteristic enterprise culture.

公司成功开发的项目有
The Company has successfully developed

麒龙佳苑
Qilong Homeland
地址：贵州省贵阳市北新区路3号
Address: Beixinqu Road 3#, Guiyang City, Guizhou Province.
联系电话（Tel）：（0851）6502498

麒龙润园
Qilong Watery Garden
地址：贵州省贵阳市贵乌路幼育巷8号
Address: Guiwu Road Youyu Xiang 8#, Gui yang City, Guizhou Province.
联系电话（Tel）：（0851）6757723 6754781

麒龙城市花园
Qilong City Garden
地址：贵州省清镇市云岭大街中段
Address: Middle part of Yunling avenue, Qingzhen City, Guizhou Province.
联系电话（Tel）：（0851）2600278 2600588

麒龙城市花园

公司目前开发的项目有
The Company is developing

麒龙溪园

麒龙溪园
Qilong Dragon Garden
地址：贵州省贵阳市花溪区溪北路
Address: Huaxi District Xibei Road, Guiyang City, Guizhou Province
联系电话（Tel）：（0851）3625889 3625567

麒龙名苑

麒龙名苑
Qilong Elegant Garden
地址：贵州省贵阳市白云区白云南路20号
Address: Baiyun District South Baiyun Road 20#, Guiyang City, Guizhou Province.
联系电话（Tel）：（0851）4606835

麒龙快乐家园

麒龙快乐家园
Qilong Happy Home
地址：贵州省贵阳市望城路
Address: Wangcheng Road, Guiyang City, Guizhou Province.
联系电话（Tel）：（0851）5750108 5760108

麒龙地产
QILONG REAL ESTATE

公司总部地址：贵州省贵阳市贵乌路幼育巷8号
Headquarter address: Guiwu Road Youyu Xiang 8#, Guiyang City, Guizhou Province.
联系电话（Tel）：（0851）6757723 6754781
传 真（Fax）：(0851)6740082

麒龍名苑 麒龍城市花園 QILONG CITY GARDEN 快乐家园 Happy Home 麒龍溪園 DRAGON GARDEN